THOMAS

THOMAS

Sex and death are the only proper concerns for the serious mind

After W.B.Yeats

Barrie Allen

To order additional copies of this book, contact:
Xlibris
0-800-443-678
www.Xlibris.co.nz
Orders@Xlibris.co.nz
761545

Foreword

The story of Thomas Kendall is taken from research into the history of the period. This research varied between the correspondence of the settlers and other figures, Maori language, culture and history, general history and few bodice rippers – very useful for details of dress, manners etc. Unfortunately (and typically) I failed to keep a record of my sources. There was however one book that I particularly relied upon – Judith Binneys "Legacy of Guilt", an excellent and exhaustively researched biography of the life of Thomas Kendall.

So the events and actions of the major historical figures are based on fact. There are of course inventions (for example Kendall's fall from grace; he never spoke nor wrote of what had happened) and there are minor characters, provided for elaboration, contrast, etc.

My task, as I saw it, was to create an inner world that would make some kind of sense of the outer world.

Back to the question: what combination of character and circumstance could have made this possible?

My thanks go to my partner, Kim, for her encouragement and assistance with editing, without which this book would never have reached publication.

Barrie Allen
Matarau
April 2018

Aotearoa 1750

They trot through paradise, these warriors, through bush where the trees count their age in centuries and the streams are crystal clear. Through the clamour of birds, so loud that it can almost be felt, across shining white beaches, lapped by a sparkling sea.

Could there be a more united band? For all are kin; this man is brother to one, uncle to another, father to a third. And as they are united in blood, so are they held together in belief. None would doubt the righteousness of their cause, for all that it grew from an encounter a hundred years ago.

There is no fear upon them, no apprehension of injury or death. And if it comes later, it will only be a fleeting thing, found in the moment before a spear strikes home. And even then with the knowledge that death upon the battlefield is a fine and honourable end.

They are buoyed up on anticipation which, as the battle nears, will move into active hunger. When they will face their foe and dance their defiance. With wide, staring eyes, mouth agape, tongue protruding, stamping as one, palm slapping on chest, their roar will silence the birds and reach up to the sun and down to their tupuna, ancestors. And then they will explode into a world without limits.

But now, as they gather to make camp for the night, the mood is one of peace. They are together and will always be together. For those who leave the world of light, who are called to the darkness of Hine nui te po, they will not go away. They will be mourned in blood and perhaps more death, songs will be written and their story will be told down the ages. They will be tupuna, gathered amongst all the ancestors, not gone away.

They know who they are; they are where they are supposed to be, doing what they are supposed to be doing.

CHAPTER 1

North Thoresby, Lincolnshire, 1763

"Indeed, Edward, taking the entirety of your situation into account, it seems to me that this decision is not only pragmatic but right and proper." The Reverend James Truman adjusted his spectacles, laced his fingers over his portly belly and smiled benignly at his parishioner.

Edward Kendall shifted uncomfortably on the hard, oaken chair.

"Come, come Edward. Do I detect doubt? Consider your position, man. You are no longer young, fifty years if I mistake not." Edward nodded. "You have no heirs. Miss Surflit is a fine young woman, righteous and upstanding." The minister seemed not to notice the cloud that passed over the other's gaze. He continued, "She has many childbearing years ahead of her. I doubt not that she will be a worthy mother and," he raised an admonishing finger, "a source of much comfort to you in your declining years."

Edward remained silent and this time the minister waited with him. "You may be right," he finally mumbled, then, noticing the pursed lips, corrected himself. "I'm sure you're right. You're an educated man and I'm but a simple farmer. I know what it is to be responsible for my cattle and crops and I hope I am a moral man ..."

"Let none doubt it."

"... but I am become settled in my ways. What do I know of women and their ways?"

The reverend chuckled fatly. "Or any of us, my dear man. What do any of us understand about the ways of women? We can only do the best we can, Edward, guide them in their frailty and lend them our strength and understanding."

"Well," Edward shifted again, "I understand my cattle and my crops, but ..." He shrugged.

The cleric tapped a heavy leather-bound bible. "You have here all the guidance and understanding you will need. The Lord has written down His covenant and laws for the good governance of righteous wedlock."

"Aye, I'm sure He has. But, you see, I'm not a reading man. I work from early to late, there's no time for reading. And letters and me, you know, we never really got along."

"Yes, yes," the minister broke in, "but Miss Surflit now is well schooled in reading. Indeed, I do not recall a more apt pupil. And her bible is never far from her."

The Reverend Truman noticed that his words did not seem to be having much persuasive effect. He tried another tack. "She is also an industrious housekeeper and a fine cook."

"So's Mrs Fothergill. Best dumplings in all Thorseby, I reckon."

The minister's fingers drummed upon the oaken table and there was a sudden harshness in his tone. "Must you gainsay every opinion I proffer? We are speaking of matrimony, sir, of a wife for your ease and comfort and children for your posterity, heirs of your name and estate. And you talk to me of your housekeeper's dumplings?"

"I'm sorry, I'm sure," Edward mumbled, "if I have given offence."

"No, no," sighed the other, "forgive me my impatience, however provoked it may have been. But you see, Edward," he leaned across the table and rested his hand upon the farmer's arm, "this could be such a fine and worthy work, of such benefit to all it touches. Miss Surflit has need of a husband, she is twenty years old, of more than marriageable age and now, with the sad passing of her father, her circumstances are such that to do other than accept your kind offer could mean, nay, almost certainly would mean, a sad decline in the fortunes of the Surflit household. It would be an act of compassion, Edward, and all would love you for it."

The farmer tugged doubtfully at his earlobe. "Well, I suppose ... perhaps I might ...bairns would be good. Lots of noise and disturbance, though. I need a good rest for a good day's work."

"And you shall have it, Edward. Miss Surflit will know where her duty lies and will doubtlessly make it her place to secure for you untroubled rest." The minister pressed his advantage. "You have a spacious home which will cater well for your new domesticity. And heirs, Edward. You will have a son."

"Aye." The farmer looked up, a slow smile creasing his brown, lined face. "Aye. Bairns would be good."

Two women sat in a small, dark room. Dressed in mourning, they appeared almost as shadow and only their faces showed, pale and angular in the last light of an autumn day.

Birdsong and distant lowing did not intrude upon the silence of the room.

Finally the older woman spoke. "Susanna. This silence will not do."

"I am sorry, Mother. What would you have me say?"

"That you know your duty."

"My duty to give myself to this old man?" The daughter's face remained bowed but there was a tightness to her features and her tone.

It did not pass unremarked. "Your words and manner confirm the stubbornness of your silence. They tell of wilfulness, Susanna, of wilfulness and selfishness, unbecoming of a Christian woman."

Susanna's mouth tightened further. "Forgive me, Mother, but I do not see how weighing my choices in a decision that will shape my life might impugn my devotion to our Lord and His Son Jesus Christ."

"Your choices? Your decision? O see how pride informs your judgment. You have no choices, child, and there can be but one decision."

"That I should marry Edward Kendall?"

"Indeed. He is a well-established landholder. His farm thrives and he is the master of a fine house."

"And that is all I need to know before I give my life away?"

"If your dear father were still alive to provide for your needs or if you had a choice of suitors then you might look to further considerations. But as things stand, yes, that is all you need to know. And it is not so bad. Mr Kendall may be further advanced in years than you would wish but he is not decrepit. And he is known as a good man, well-regarded in the community."

"He is seldom seen in church. And I have heard that he absents himself to toil upon the Sabbath."

"Perhaps he does. There are greater faults."

"Than profaning a commandment?"

Mrs Surflit sighed. "His industry may lead to his neglecting other duties. Perhaps you could persuade him otherwise. But I doubt that his prosperity suffers."

"Always money. But my concern is with the welfare of my soul. Mammon has no call on me."

Mrs Surflit was exasperated now. "O but he does, my child and you are foolish to deny it. No." She held up her hand as her daughter made to speak. "Take heed of another commandment, honour thy mother and hear her out. Needs dictate to us. With no son to run it, we must sell the shop. I shall, as you know, go to my sister, Mary. With the proceeds from the shop and the house and her small allowance, we shall manage. Your uncle John has kindly agreed to take in your sister until she is of marriageable age. Where will you go, Susanna?"

The daughter made no answer and her mother continued. "Poverty is a terrible thing, my child and it has called more to sin than labouring upon the Sabbath ever did. What are your choices? The Work House?"

Again Susanna did not respond and a still, bitter silence descended.

At last she lifted her head and her gaze was steady, but her voice trembled as she spoke. "I am frightened, Mother. I feel no tenderness for Mr Kendall. How can I make him a wife?"

"I understand," her mother nodded. "You are thinking of love. It is not what you think it is. Romance, yes, don't frown and turn your head away, romance is not for us. It was not for me and it is not for you. God and duty are your loves, Susanna. And they are dependable and worthy loves. All others are uncertain. You may love your children, but do so wisely and in moderation, for children die sometimes and the grief is proportionate to the love. I know that and near all the women in Thorseby know it, too. You must hope that Mr Kendall will be kind and you must labour to make it so. And then you may find a comfortableness that sits well with the years. But that is all."

"But before that?" Susanna's face was very pale and her voice was hollow. "I do not think that I could bear to have him touch me."

"As to that," her mother answered, "you will learn. You must hope that Mr Kendall is kind, but even if he is it will be an unpleasant lesson to learn. But it is a brief thing that one," she shrugged, "simply becomes accustomed to. And after a time it is not so unpleasant. Then there is bearing and delivering of a child. That is not brief nor easy and women die, but it is your lot, Susanna. You will go to Mr Kendall as Sarah went to Abraham. And you will make him a good wife."

"This does not allay my fear."

"No. Only time will do that." Mrs Surflit smiled. "Perhaps time may serve as your ally. Mr Kendall, as you so often assert, is not young. He will not have the appetite nor the impetuousness of a younger man. Perhaps he will not prove overly bothersome."

Edward Kendall married Susanna Surflit one month later. As Mrs Surflt had predicted, he was not overly bothersome. But his restraint did not come so much from a lack of appetite than from a general diffidence which combined with a specific unease in the company of his young wife. For her part, Susanna had succeeded in transmuting her fear, with its attendant helplessness, into more comfortable, righteous resentment.

She had previously requested via her mother via the Reverend Truman that a separate bedroom be made available to her and on her wedding night she pre-empted her hesitant groom. "Mr Kendall," she said, "I hope I know my duty as a Christian wife. But within these strange surrounds I wonder if you might forebear your claim until I become more settled and release me to my room to pray for the soul of my father."

Edward stared at her vaguely. Who is this woman, he might have wondered, who looks at me with accusing eyes. He gestured meaninglessly and the back of his hand brushed against a glass of port; the contents ran off the solid table onto a greasy sheepskin rug. Man and wife stared at the dripping wine and neither moved.

When Edward raised his head he was caught by the hard gaze of his bride. He shrank before it and clumsily bent to dab ineffectually at the stain.

"You must do as you will," he said at last. "I will …" his voice trailed off and he looked away.

"Thank you, sir," replied his wife. "I see that your reputation as a compassionate man is not unearned. God grant you sound repose." And she walked from the room.

Edward gazed after her retreating back. Then he sighed, refilled his glass and left the house. The night was cold but he seemed not to notice as he leaned against a fence, staring sightlessly into a sea of stars.

Susanna found that the strangeness of her surrounds eased with time. She found that the house had much to commend it and was certainly an improvement on the one she had shared with her parents and sister.

Edward was absent from early morning to nightfall, indeed, his time in the fields had increased since his marriage, as had his custom at the local hostelry. This was also to Susanna's liking and she found her days moving comfortably along, industriously, purposefully, and her evenings restful. She read her bible and prayed and the winter passed.

It was in early spring, with even longer hours in the fields and inn, when Edward came to discover that he had become an intrusion in his home.

"She accuses me," he complained to his minister. "She says nothing but she accuses me. What have I done?"

"Truly, Edward, I do not know. From everything you have imparted, you have been a model husband. Unless," Truman rubbed his chin, "it's … this is difficult to say, how have you found, er, connubial arrangements?"

He received a blank stare.

"Was the wedding happily consummated? The …" he gestured vaguely, "…the marriage bed, Edward. Are you hopeful of an heir?"

"O I see. No, Reverend, my bed is as it was. Mrs Kendall was reluctant, you might say, as she was in mourning for her father."

"But that was three months ago. Has nothing occurred since?"

The farmer shook his head. "I was better off with Mrs Fothergill's dumplings. And she would laugh and sing about the house. Mrs Kendall is always gloomy. When I'm around, anyway. And she's always accusing me."

"Edward, listen to me. Mrs Kendall is not accusing you for having done something. Perhaps she is accusing you for having done nothing."

"No." Edward shook his head firmly. "She's very clear, though she says nothing. She hates the idea of me touching her."

"Then maybe she is accusing you for what you are going to do. Or perhaps she is accusing you for her failure as a spouse. Yes, Edward, there is your answer. Mrs Kendall is not fulfilling her duty as a Christian wife because you will not insist upon it. It is your duty to her and to yourself."

"But she hates the idea."

"And she will continue to hate it until it becomes reality. Then she will hate the reality. And then she will become used to it."

That night Edward came home early. The evening meal was served and consumed in silence. As Susanna began to clear the table, Edward leaned forward and poured a glass of port." He gestured towards her. "Would you like a sup before dishes?' he asked.

Susanna stopped but did not turn. Her body was tight. "No, thank you, Mr Kendall. The water from the well is good enough for me." She resumed her tidying.

For a time Edward busied himself with loading his pipe. Then, after a deep draught and inhalation of smoke, he addressed his wife. He remembered the minister's words, but his speech was still slow and hesitant. "This is a Christian marriage," he said, "and it needs be con, consummated in the eyes of the Lord."

Susanna became very still.

Edward studied her rigid form and wondered. It is such a natural thing, he thought. Why is she so, he reached for the word, opposed?

He continued. "I am decided, lass. I need heirs, the farm needs heirs and it is your duty to provide them."

At the last he saw her hands clench into fists against her side. When she spoke her voice was low and strained. "I do not think these are your words, sir. Have you perhaps taken up with others the matter of our," she paused, "condition?"

Edward remembered the minister's closing advice. "It would be better if Mrs Kendall were not to learn of this conversation. It might shame her to think that her situation had been made public."

"Even to you, her minister?"

"Even to me."

Now Edward stared at the unmoving figure and thought, this is all foolishness. And lying will make it more foolish. So he said, "Aye, I want to do the right thing, the responsible thing. So I spoke to Reverend Truman. And he advised me."

Susanna turned and her face was tight with anger. But Edward thought he could see fear there, too, and he said, placating, "Lass, lass, why do you take on so? It is not so dreadful a thing. Do you not wish to be a mother?" Susanna stared back at him and thought, I scarce know what I wish.

But aloud she said, "I know my duty as a Christian wife, sir. And I pray the Lord Jesus Christ will give me the strength to fulfil it." And she turned back to the dishes.

That night Edward and Susanna consummated their marriage. It was, of course, an utterly joyless affair. Edward was a healthy, vigorous man, fit and hard from years of industrious toil and he was quickly stirred by his wife's flesh, warm and naked beneath her flannel nightdress. But her response to his eager groping quite unnerved him. Turning her head to one side, eyes and mouth clenched shut, she pulled the dress up above her thighs, then hugged her shoulders. And lay there, like a beast to the slaughter, he thought. She was dry and tight and shuddered at the first touch of his questing penis. Insofar as he had given the matter much thought, Edward had meant to be kind ("you must be gentle," James Truman had said), but now he found himself, once again, repelled and shut out and his mood became one of resentment and determination. With no pleasure and some discomfort, he thrust doggedly and the consummation was effected. If he noted an absence of blood, he made no sign.

Susanna bore it all with the silence of a martyr. Afterwards, as her husband lay snoring she crept from the bed and shuffled painfully from the house to the well. She emptied the bucket and cleansed herself with icy water.

Both the Reverend Truman and Mrs Surflit proved to be wrong in their view that with time Susanna would adjust to the experience and that it would become less unpleasant. She did not and had it not been for Edward's now settled wish for heirs sexual relations might have ceased altogether. As it was he responded to her bitter compliance with resentment of his own.

"I will expect you in my bed tonight," he would grunt at the conclusion of a silent meal. And no more would be said.

He came to care little about his wife's sensibilities. He had never much concerned himself with personal hygiene and now he became quite indifferent. His non-observance of social niceties took on a perverse quality and he would belch or fart at will, grinning at Susanna's evident repulsion. "Better an empty house than a bad tenant."

Susanna retreated to her bible and her prayers and industry. The house was kept spotless, the table full and she would busy herself with a multitude of chores. She attended service each Sunday, invariably without her husband, but had few dealings with the minister.

By the end of the year she had conceived an heir. But it was a difficult pregnancy, exacerbated by Susanna's reluctance to accept any kind of assistance or advice. She opposed Edward's offer of a maid and was adamant that her mother should not come to stay. It seemed to Edward sometimes that she revelled in her pain and discomfort, turning her face away as he hovered helplessly. Eventually he learned, bitterly, to turn to his port. The child, a boy, was stillborn and Susanna, remembering her mother's advice, did not mourn him.

Edward was disappointed but philosophical and within six months Susanna was again pregnant. A miscarriage followed but this served only to fuel his determination. "I married for bairns and bairns I shall have."

Over the next eighteen years Susanna was to conceive on another nine occasions. She gave birth on six of them. The next child was born in March 1767 but lived only a few months. Edward was born in December 1768, Susanna in April 1773, Thomas in December 1778, Ellen in March 1780 and Mary in January 1781.

Mrs Surflit's remark that children sometimes die proved prophetic and by 1813 only Edward, Thomas and Ellen remained alive.

But in 1769 Edward was a proud father. Inverted nipples prevented Susanna from feeding the boy and a wet nurse from the village was engaged. Young Edward thrived and grew in the image of his father. He also developed in his ways and became loud and boisterous. Susanna watched him grow at a distance; she busied herself with her chores, read her bible and prayed.

Her next child was named for her and she felt some tenderness, but her ministrations were driven largely by duty. Besides, the girl was slow and like her father showed little interest in learning.

Thomas was different. From the beginning he was alert and curious and while Edward and Susanna had gazed vacantly at the books their mother showed them Thomas was more receptive. By the time he was five he had mastered his letters and was always willing to listen to the stories he was told. Inevitably they came from the bible and invariably the theme was sin and retribution. At an early age Thomas learned to judge. He learned of original sin, of disobedience to the word of God and of banishment from the source. And how punishment prevails through all the years of men. And how the sins of the father are visited upon the children and the children's children. And in sorrow are children brought forth. He may not have understood, but there was no doubting his mother's belief as her own experience daily reinforced her faith.

Sin was everywhere, striding through the halls of government as it permeated even the nursery.

"Are we all sinners, Mother?"

"None is without sin, Thomas. We must pray daily for forgiveness."

"I know Edward is a sinner. He often says rude things. And I have heard him say 'God' and 'Jesus' and not in prayer. That is a sin, isn't it?"

Susanna shook her head sorrowfully. "Thou shalt not take the name of the Lord thy God in vain," she murmured. "We must pray for him."

"And Father says so, too," continued the child. "And he and Edward work on Sundays while the rest of us are at church."

"Thou shalt keep the Sabbath holy."

"And he laughs at rude things, too. And makes disgusting noises. Even though he can see it upsets you." Thomas was building in intensity now. "I hate it when he upsets you. I hate him."

At some level Susanna must have thrilled at the loyalty of the child, but if she did she quelled it and fixed Thomas with a severe eye.

"And that, too, is sin, Thomas. Anger is one of the seven deadly sins. And remember too, 'judge not lest thou be judged.' You must pray for forgiveness for your anger and your evil thought."

The lessons continued as Susanna found her voice again. Even as she and Thomas jogged along in a small wagon, drawn by an old pony on their way to the village, she found occasion for continuous instruction.

"Look about you, my son," she advised, "and consider the wonders of God's creations."

Truly, it was a wondrous day. The spring air glowed under the bowl of a blue, transparent sky and the colours of the day pulsated in the bounty of new life. A lark soared in sudden flight and its cry rang wild and exultant. From the great oaks lining the country road to the puffs of dust beneath the pony's hooves the world shone, complete and perfect.

"It is all so pretty,' sighed the little boy. "O look!' as a pheasant, disturbed by their passage, burst from the undergrowth. "Perhaps her nest is there. Can we look?" He drummed his heels excitedly against the trap.

Susanna smiled as she settled the startled pony, but made no move to pull it up. "No, Thomas. We have our chores to see to and there is no time for idle play."

Thomas knew better than to argue. But his cheeks glowed darkly as he turned his head away. Susanna heard his breath come in short snorts and she sighed.

The pony trotted on, its unshod hooves soft in the dust. Thomas watched the fields and his mood settled. He became aware that his mother was continuing her lesson.

"… observe the oaks, Thomas. See how the great branches reach out and provide shade and shelter for the cattle. As they provide the wood for our house, our furniture and the fuel for our fires. And the cattle. How manifold are their uses …"

Thomas drifted off and his senses merged. He saw the humming of bees as golden motes and the lowing of the cattle moved as breath across the fields.

"… and you, too, must find your usefulness, the means of service that will justify your life …"

The useful oaks stood and awaited their service. Imbued with kindness and wisdom the boy felt them reach out to him, to tell him he belonged. He understood it far less than his mother's words but it made more sense and it was a greater comfort.

They were in the village now and the clopping of the pony's hooves on cobblestone brought him out of his reverie. Other sounds intruded, voices calling, iron wheels on stone. The houses and stores grew closer together and life contracted.

The monologue continued. "… to glorify His blessed name. Ah," the tone changed, "good morning, Mrs Appleby, a glorious day, praise the Lord." But their progress did not slow and Mrs Appleby's response was lost in the growing hubbub. Another tone, "good morning, Reverend Truman," and Susanna urged the pony on.

The street opened into a square where the villagers jostled among the open carts where barrow boys hawked their wares. Thomas stared open-eyed at the carnival of trade, but Susannah seemed less impressed. Then they were upon the hostelry where Edward had spent his honeymoon evenings. Susanna drew the pony up in the ostlers' yard. She passed it over to the charge of a grubby groom, advising they would soon return, and turned back to the main street. Thomas followed.

The streets were a rich, bustling chaos and Susanna took Thomas' hand as she hurried him along and the lessons continued. They passed an alleyway with its piles of rubbish and the reek of stale urine. An old man lay sprawled against the wall, close to the entrance, his clothes ragged and threadbare, smeared in vomit, staring dully at the passing life. ("Behold the degradation of God's work and see how the wages of sin is death.") A barefooted urchin scurried by, poking out his tongue at Thomas and Susanna tightened her grip. A polished carriage hurried by, dangerously close, leaving behind the laughter of a young fop, curled wig, tailored coat over tight-fitting trousers, shining, buckled shoes. ("'Vanity,' saith the Preacher.")

"Mrs Kendall, this is a surprise. We do not see you often about the village." Susanna halted at the greeting.

"Good morning, Mrs Cartwright. I trust I find you well."

"Passably, passably, Mrs Kendall. The gout continues to trouble me, but I try not to complain." Mrs Cartwright noted the small boy. "And how are you, young Thomas? Are you enjoying your visit to the village?"

"Thomas is very well, thank you, Mrs Cartwright," replied Susanna. "He has mastered his letters now."

"Indeed! And so young. You will be a great scholar, Thomas."

Susanna smiled proudly. "He will use his gifts to advance the Work of the Lord."

Mrs Cartwright nodded. "No doubt, no doubt. And Mr Kendall and the other children? I trust they fare well."

Susanna's smile faded. "Ellen and Mary are at home under the care of young Betsy. An industrious girl, although somewhat frivolous. Susanna is at her lessons at the village school, although I fear she is lacking in aptitude and application. Young Edward is with his father, about the work of the farm. He is not a scholar, neither, and Mr Kendall decided that it would be best for him to forego further learning and busy himself with the demands of the farm. It has been great pleasure conversing with you, Mrs Cartwright, but now we must be about our business. I trust I will see you at Church on Sunday."

She hurried Thomas off, leaving the other woman looking after them, leaning upon her cane.

"A good Christian woman, but given to excessive conversation, if allowed." She looked down at the boy. "Did you notice her face when I told her how you had mastered your lessons?"

Susanna led Thomas along the busy street, occasionally picking their way between horse and other manure. At length she turned into the grocery/drapery shop. A bell tinkled their entry into the dark interior. Shelved walls were packed with wares, ranging from sacks of sugar and flour to fowling pieces. Susanna summoned an earnest clerk to attend her as she circulated the store, marking off her provisions from a neat list and Thomas was left free to wander. There was much to interest a curious little boy as he walked about, contentedly gazing at the wealth of treasures, stroking, patting, occasionally sniffing and once or twice tasting. At length he found himself in the drapery section before a bolt of pale green shot silk. The colour and texture delighted him and he was holding a length against his cheek when he heard the door tinkle open. Turning, he watched a couple enter the room. The man was slim and elegantly dressed but Thomas' attention was seized by the woman. Her head was bare of the commonplace bonnet and a shining ebony mane fell past her shoulders. Emerald eyes were set in a dark, perfect face with an aquiline nose and full, coral lips, hoops of gold hung from her ears. She was dressed in pale green silk that drew in from bare shoulders to a tightfitting waist. The bodice was cut low across the swell of her full, uplifted breasts. Thomas thought he had never seen anyone so beautiful and wondered if she was a princess. His wide-eyed stare was noted by the man.

"It seems, Isabelle," he said, "that your beauty reaches even to the cradle. Observe," and he gestured towards the staring boy.

The young woman smiled and her teeth were white and perfect in the darkened room. "How charming," she murmured, and Thomas watched her glide towards him. A scent of musk, an inviting strangeness caught at him as she leaned forward with outstretched hand.

"Good morning, young sir," she smiled. "What is your name?"

Thomas was reaching out his hand when he felt it seized in an urgent grip. Looking up in shock, he saw the face of his mother, her cheeks mottled in anger. He thought she looked ugly next to the princess and felt a spasm of guilt at his wicked, disloyal thought.

Unprotesting, he let himself be led away.

Unusually, the trip home was conducted in complete silence.

Aotearoa 1787

Across the world the stars are fading, ancestral eyes blinking out over Rangihoua Pa. Its southern bony flank rises from the bay and drives up sharply to scrub, manuka, gnarled pohutukawa twisting out of the clay and rock in tangled root, spreading in green leaf and branch, offering its crimson flower to the first light to become the primary colour of the land. The vast, grey bay flows away to the south and to the east; its furthest shores are out of sight but for the greater dark here and there, on the horizon, in mountain and cloud and island. There are a great many islands here, some no more than rocky crags that lift their heads only at low tide; others are wooded with sandy beaches and sheer cliffs. The waters of this and many other bays run in from the ocean that lies beyond the furthest eastern headland.

And beyond that a silver glow reaches from behind the depths of Tangaroa and tells of the coming of Ra. Touches of pink whisper of his fires.

The first light touches on Rangihoua, massively crouching, domed head erect and gazing to the west, shoulders sloping to flanks that swell and fall away steeply to valley and the sea. The dome is scraped bare to earth and rock and is encircled by a palisade, edging the terracing like a crown of thorns. To the north, east and west the land rises in wider, gentler hills that fold back upon themselves in fern and manuka, a lone puriri.

Buildings make the dome a crest, but central and defining is the whare nui, the great house where people gather to talk of their lives, their tupuna, ancestors, lament their deaths and sleep together, secure in the ties of blood. The house lives. At the front, on the apex of the figure A the carven ancestor gazes down. His backbone is the ridge pole stretching out behind him; ribs angle away to low walls. These are supported by posts of totara, just a few feet above the ground. Ornate faces stare from the posts, defiant tongue and glittering eye. They bring their mauri to the spirit of this place and make it stronger.

Light fingers on the low door and solitary window reaching for the shadows of the sleepers, catching at the movement of drowsy awakenings. Normally there would not be many here; most people would be away at their summer encampments, closer to rocky bays and islands where the yield of kai moana, sea food, is greatest. Beaches where tuatua, shellfish, may be gathered in flax baskets, later to steam on hot stones, where kina, the spiny sea eggs lie still in kelp and crevice and pebbled beds where koura, crayfish, might also be taken. Closer to the richer inland soil, to the kumara and potato beds. But this morning the pa is full. Kin have come visiting to honour Te Whare whose remains have been taken from the earth. The remaining skin and sinew will be stripped away from his bones which will then be taken away to their final resting place. The families will gather to pray and talk and sing; tonight they will feast.

And now, in one of the many small whare, houses, that dot the crest Te Hine, the girl is waking to sound and movement. Drowsily she sees it is coming from a couple lying some feet away. She takes in taut, powerful buttocks rising and driving into the thud of flesh. She admires the precise blue spirals that curve across them; the tohunga, priest, she thinks, has done very fine work She leaves their sounds and creeps across the earthen floor, taking care not to step over a sleeper. Then she leaves the warmth and feels the morning air upon her skin, cool and silver, moist, sea salt on a dark green breath.

Her bladder is full and she must mimi. She crosses to the southern edge and clambers out along a branch that extends above the bay. At the end it has been cut into a fork and she squats there, relieving herself into the bay two hundred feet below. A piwaka darts out of the pohutukawa into the air she has disturbed, feeds then flicks to a branch to chirrup at her. She chirrups back, kia ora e manu iti, greeting the bird.

From the fork she watches the growing of light between the eastern headlands. She is very thankful that Maui has attended to Ra. In years past it had been his habit to shoot across the sky in a blaze of light. Doubtlessly that had been very fine to see but left the tangata whenua, people of the land, with little time in the light. With his brothers Maui had snared Ra in strong vines and then he had beaten him until the battered god had cried mercy and promised to slow his progress. Even today he still feels the blows and slowly, wearily he raises his great, golden head above the waters of Tangaroa. Hine watches as he bathes the sky in a pastel glow and she wriggles her toes in space.

The light is spreading now and the pa stirs into life in a growing clamour of voices, women's and girls' as they prepare the morning kai. Their rangatira, chief, sits apart from the throng, chatting with the tohunga. His food will be prepared and presented with special care for he is very tapu and that, combined with the power of kai, makes for an occasion that must be handled with due tika, correctly.

15

From her perch she looks over the palisade and into the sloping space between it and the next line. Two boys are practising with their taiaha, spears, while an older man stands to one side, taiaha in hand, watching intently. Hine scrambles back along the branch and hurries to the gate opening on to the next level. As she goes she looks to see if anyone is watching. Taiaha are not for girls and she would be in trouble if she were caught spying.

But she cannot help herself. She loves it, the play of muscle and sinew in their shoulders, the strain in their arms, their hard, flat stomachs and the curve of their bums still bare of moko. But mostly, though this is only practice she is excited by the intensity of the contest. She exults in their ferocity and pants with the blows, gasping at a powerful hit, hissing at a near miss, taking and delivering together. She thinks about a real battle where there is full force, where men fight in blood, their own and others' and step between broken bodies. Where a win means death. To feel the magic. She shivers.

Light but sturdy lengths of manuka twist and spin as the boys dance upon the sloping rock and grass. They move through the prelude and into free form but here too a pattern is apparent as one stalks the other. The aggressor's strikes are restrained but even so produce a grunt or a moan as they connect. Then there is a flurry of blows and a sweeping leg and the slower boy is on his back and the tip of a pole is resting at his throat. The man grunts in exasperation as he crosses to the combatants. He pats the victor on the shoulder and pulls the loser to his feet. Hine strains to hear his words. "You defend too much and for too long," he says. "You hold his blow after it is spent and then you wait for him to attack again. His attack ends at that moment and that is the time for yours to begin." The man pauses for thought, scratching an ornate cheek and when he speaks again his tone is harsher. "I think you may be afraid. Sometimes fear is useful but not here and never in battle. What are you afraid of? Pain?" As he speaks the taiaha in his hand flashes forward smacking the boy hard in the ribs. He falls back grunting and clutching his side and then the man is beside him, forcing him erect and pulling his hand away. "Kahore, no, you do not step back with pain. You step into it. You swallow it and you spit it back and you laugh at it. And then you become strong."

The lesson appears to be over and Hine slips back through the gate and makes her way to the little courtyard in front of her whare. Here her mother, aunt and two sisters are finishing their morning kai, fish and kina left over from the night before.

"Where've you been, eh?" her mother asks.

"Staring at the boys."

Her older sister walks up from behind. "I saw her watching Pere and a new boy." She mimics rapt attention. Hine drives an elbow into her ribs but she grins as she does so.

"He's alright, eh?"

"Which boy is this?" her mother asks. "Where is he from? Here," not waiting for an answer, "take the mokopuna. He's hungry but he won't eat."

Hine takes the fretful child with practised ease and soon he is lying quietly in her arms while she feeds him moistened pieces of fish. She massages his gums with a grubby finger and his attention moves away from his hunger and his teeth and he clutches at her hair and tries to taste it.

"He is from the Kerikeri hapu," says Hine's sister. "His father is Te Hotete and his mother is Tuhikura. Ko Hongi Hika te ingoa."

"Ae, I know who you mean." Her mother smiles at Hine. "He's alright, alright. A very handsome young man. And he will be a great warrior."

"I know, I saw him fi-, running with the others. He is very fast." "He will be a tohunga as well as a rangatira," adds her mother's sister.

"He knows heaps, all about the tupuna. He has learned much from Rakau."

Rakau is tohunga to the Rangihoua people. He is a learned man and a moving orator; he is clever and persuasive. He is also a warrior who has exulted in the glory of war and has fed upon its spoils.

"Rakau's going to be Hongi's father-in-law," says Hine's mother's sister importantly and swells in the attention they turn to her."

"Poor Hine," says her mother. "But cheer up, he's not married yet. There's still time."

Soon after Hine and her whanau are paddling to a bay on the northern coastline. The morning is clear and bright and the warm sun is carried on a cool breeze, delicious on the skin. Hine drives the paddle home, sweeping cleanly through the sea, in perfect time with her mothers and sisters and the waka slices across the surface. At the bay some will sit in the outgoing tide and feel for tuatua beneath the sand; young girls will play on the beach and watch the little ones. Others will swim out to the rocks in search of mussels or perhaps oysters. They will crouch upon the rocks like shags, squatting, standing, dropping into the clear channels searching the crevices for koura, scouring the sandy pebbly bottom for kina. And all the time when their heads are above the water they will talk to each other. Hine's being taken by the looks of Hongi Hika calls for much comment and ribald observation.

Tangaroa is kindly disposed towards Ngapuhi today and their flax bags lie full and heavy in the bottom of the waka. The trip back to Rangihoua is a slower one.

That night Hine sits with her people on the marae under the stars. The air is warm but the fire is good to look at, to watch the shadows of an old man's hands as he weaves his story. She has been watching for Hongi and now she sees him sitting a little aside, in the further shadows. But his head is lowered and she cannot catch his eye. She hears her mother laugh and voices breaking into a chant together. She joins them and her voice becomes a part of a vibrant, rhythmic whole; she is utterly at home, she is where she is supposed to be. The chant ends and she smiles into the fire. Her eyes are bright in the smoke and her cheeks and lips are greasy. A little further away the umu, oven, has been opened and the smell of cooked, human flesh hangs heavy in the air.

London 1800

Rough hands tied the rope about the child's body and then lowered it into hell. The rope slid up, settling around the armpits and the coarse fibres rubbed through a tattered, grubby shift, burning into old welts. The child hung in black, stony space. Above was a small square of night sky where a few stars glimmered dully through the fog.

"Work," commanded a gruff voice and the rope jerked. The child whimpered as it bit, then, raising a wire brush began to scrub. Now the last of the light dissolved in swirling soot and its breath came in wheeze and cough. It scrubbed with one hand, using the other to turn; but the rope did not turn, too and continued to burn. Deeper into the black, moving air, scrubbing, twisting, burning.

The lowering ceased at twelve feet and a diffused yellow light floated down into the pit. Had the child looked up and been able to see through the gloom it might have made out the face of its master, peering down. The man coughed as a little ash drifted into his face but seemed content with the child's work, for the lantern was withdrawn and a sack lowered in its place. The child, now standing freely in the settling ash, took the sack and swept the ash into it. The sack was then drawn up and the rope jerked about the scrawny little frame. "Work," commanded the master.

Now the child felt for the lateral length of pit and entered the blackness on callused knees and elbows, creeping along, scouring the ceiling, walls and floor. When it reached the end, it worked its way back, sweeping the ash before it. Then it brushed it into the sack and returned.

The master played out the rope as the child returned along the transverse. Despite his thick, greasy coat he shivered in the early autumn night. They were all the same, these rich bastards, he thought, no consideration, no planning, leave the chimneys all sooted up over summer, then as soon as the nights start cooling it's rush, rush, need it done yesterday. He felt the rope tighten slightly as it took the weight of the little body slipping into the next descent. He hoped the little fool had laid it over smooth stone. A bit of jagged stone would fray it and it was old enough as it was and it hadn't come cheap. That thieving whoreson chandler was making a pretty penny out of him. Still, you had to keep your rope in good nick. Otherwise, he sniggered, showing rotting teeth and empty gums behind a tangled, greasy beard, sniggered remembering Sanders and his monkey. Sanders so cheap he'd have sent them down on a shoe string. The rope had broken and the boy, or was it a girl, he couldn't remember, had plunged down into the grate. Scared shit out of the lady of the house. He wished he'd seen it. Blood and shit and ash and her Ladyship screaming like the devil himself had landed in the fireplace. No more work for Sanders in *that* house. More for him. And Nelson who was so stupid he couldn't see the monkey had grown past it. Sent it down anyway, he did, and it got stuck, of course. By the time Nelson had dragged it out he had busted its shoulder and an arm. *Then* he could see how useless it was. But this was a good one. Tiny little thing, cheap to keep, hardly ate anything and good for another two years. If its lungs held out. He'd bought it a couple of months ago and he'd paid a good price. A guinea which he'd bet had turned straight into gin. And it had learned the ropes fast. Odd that, seeing how it seemed, what was the word, retarded? Never said much, in fact he didn't even know if it could talk. But even if it could, what would it have to say?

The rope twitched in his hand. Was that a tug? He waited a moment and the rope twitched again. Good enough. He pulled steadily, not too swiftly, didn't want to damage the monkey, until the child was standing, passive, mute beside him. The last load of ash would be gathered from the grate by a maid in the morning. Lady of the house wouldn't want him or the monkey inside her fine establishment. Would lower the tone. He spat dourly, then the two carefully made their way across the great pitching roof to where the ladder stood.

They walked away into the cold foggy night. Behind them the lights of the great house glistened. Tomorrow the grates would be emptied, cleaned and polished and warmth would pervade the home of William Wilberforce, member of parliament, abolitionist and an outspoken voice for the Church Missionary Society.

CHAPTER 2

Somewhere between the worlds of the Lord and the Monkey Thomas Kendall sat at a desk, a small serviceable unit, ink stained and pitted where wax had dripped, burned and later been scraped away. A brace of candles cast a dull yellow pool over a writing pad; across the room a small fire burned in its iron grate. Dark, heavy drapes hung between dark panelling, holding out the cold night air. A small, solid night table bearing a heavy leather-bound bible stood beside a narrow cot and completed the garret's furnishings. Thomas sat bowed in shadow and considered the letter before him.

Dear Mother, he had written, *it is now two months since my Move to London and over a week since my last letter. I hope you can find it in your Heart to Forgive my Dilatoriness.* He paused, was that one l or two? *The Reverend and Mrs Kent have been the Kindest of Hosts and I have lacked for nothing. Mrs Kent provides a fine and ample Table and I am well Nourished. The weather has been Clement but now that the nights are drawing in earlier and colder I am grateful for the Small Size of my room, for it is that much easier to Warm.*

Here the writing ended and he tapped the quill against his nose, considering. He dipped the pen and wrote again.

I am enjoying good Health. As you know, I leave each morning for my Employment in Kirmington. If I walk briskly, as I usually do, I am there within the Hour. I am benefitting from the exercise. It will be less Pleasant, I know, when Winter sets in but Father has provided well for me with an excellent Coat and I am well prepared for the rain.

Father? He paused and his lips were drawn a little more tightly as he wrote, *please convey to Father my heartfelt Gratitude for the coat and all his*

21

other Kindnesses and assure him that he is daily in my Prayers. He scooped a little sand and sprinkled it over 'daily'. He would not lie.

I believe, Dearest Mother, he wrote, *that I have found Confirmation of my Vocation. I delight in teaching and hope that I may not be charged with Immodesty if I aver that my Industry has been attended by some small success. Already Amelia is reading simple sentences, slowly and not without error, but everyday a little more. John's writing is becoming clearer and Edward can almost* Thomas lowered his pen. His mother would not be interested in these small steps. But he was, intensely so, and he was disappointed that he appeared to be alone in that interest. Lady Worthing, the lady of the house and Amelia's mother, had been invited to attend a small recital of the children's skills. After barely ten minutes she had protested her delight in their prowess and had then hurried away to prepare for some pressing social event. Her husband had been more direct. "My dear young Kendall," he had sighed, "it is your function to instruct the children and mine to reimburse you for such instruction. If I were to seek performance I should find it at Covent Garden." He smiled. "Or elsewhere."

But this was little cause for complaint. Tutoring was, after all, not arduous work and the five children were obedient and attentive students. His employers were generous in his remuneration and Mr Worthing, at whose home the little group was based, seemed a kindly man. Twice he had insisted, as Thomas was making his way into a damp evening, that he accept the service of the Worthing coach and Thomas had leaned back against the rich upholstery as the cab had clattered over the cobblestones, feeling quite the gentleman.

He was startled from his reverie by a tap at the door and jumped up to answer it. The doorway was filled by the ample frame of the Reverend Joseph Kent, his host and mentor.

"Ah, young Thomas," beamed the minister, "I am pleased to see you still up, I was afraid I might have disturbed an early repose." He peered short-sightedly into the room and his gaze settled upon the quill and pad and an untidy assortment of papers and books littering the desk. "I hope I have not disturbed your marking or study."

"No, no, not at all," replied Thomas quickly. "I was writing to my mother, I have fallen behind in my correspondence and then I," he flapped his hands, "drifted off."

Best thing to do, thought Joseph, but he said, "well, now that you've drifted back, would you like to join me in a nightcap?"

Thomas smiled and nodded his agreement and the two made their way down the narrow stairs to the minister's study. There the Reverend Kent clapped Thomas on the shoulder and gently propelled him into one of the two sturdy armchairs, drawn at an angle to the fire. "That's it, that's it, make yourself comfortable." He poured two generous glasses of port, offered one to his guest and then sank with a grunt into the empty chair. For a time he busied himself preparing his pipe. Then he inhaled deeply and puffed the thick smoke contentedly.

They sat for a while in silence then and the Reverend watched the youth affectionately. "Your work is proceeding well?" he asked at last.

"O yes." Thomas was suddenly enthusiastic. "Amelia is beginning to read and Edward can almost recite the Twenty third Psalm without stumbling."

"The Twenty third Psalm, eh?" The Reverend was impressed. "That's a lot of learning for, how old is Edward now?"

"Nine." Thomas seemed as suddenly anxious. "Do you think it is too much?"

"No, no," replied the other reassuringly. "I'm sure he can manage. Tell me about the others."

With no more encouragement Thomas launched into a detailed account of his students' progress while the Reverend Kent sat silently, only half-listening, more intent on the play in the boy's features as he spoke. Animation filled his face now, even passion, but the Reverend knew the other shifts, the uncertainty that he feared might one day find despair and the certainty that could grow to denial or rage. An odd lad, he thought, quite plain to look at with that full nose over short, full lips and a small cleft chin. But the eyes, the eyes were bright and wide and full of longing. He became aware that the torrent of words was diminishing and brought his attention back. "You are doing good work," he said. "I hope the parents are appreciative."

"Well," Thomas paused, "they don't seem much interested. Any of them."

"Ah," Joseph puffed ruminatively, "perhaps that's just an indication of their confidence in you. There has been no complaint?"

"None. They don't care." A touch of bitterness now. "You're more interested."

"I'm your friend."

"And they're parents. Why don't they care? They're good people, are they not?"

"Ah," Joseph took refuge in his pipe again before answering. "As far as I know, Thomas. I would not have recommended you for service had I thought otherwise. But I do not really know them personally." He smiled. "Our paths are not inclined to cross. As you know, Mrs Farnwright made enquiry of the Reverend Thorley for a suitable tutor for Edward and John and for the Fortescue and Worthing children. John Thorley recalled my having spoken of your success as a monitor at Thorsby and asked if I thought you would be suitable. I assured him of it and matters went from there. I know the three young gentlemen are well regarded in the social circles of Kirmington. But little more." He paused, stroking his ample jowls, then continued, "But these are not Thoresby folk, Thomas. This is Regency London and what passes for sophistication here may well be regarded elsewhere as something less attractive."

He could see that he was not making himself clear to the young man. Indeed, he was not clear within his own mind. He recalled meeting James Worthing, the elegance and confidence of the man, his perfect manners and ready wit, and something within him had recoiled.

But now Thomas was rebuking himself for his complaint. "They are sophisticated people," he agreed, "and I am but the tutor of their children. They have their tasks to attend to and I have mine. It is not for me to judge them."

Thomas' life settled into a comfortable if rather monotonous routine. The latter quality was remarked upon by James Worthing. "My dear young Kendall," he asked, "what do you *do*?"

They were sitting in a spacious lounge on ornate if not particularly comfortable chairs, Thomas upright, holding a large snifter of fine French brandy. The unfamiliar liquor had gone quickly to his head and he felt a little dizzy. But it was not an unpleasant sensation and he smiled at the circulating warmth. Lord Worthing, he considered, was really quite a charming man. His kindnesses had continued: on further occasions he had solicitously ushered Thomas to the carriage protesting, "no, no, my dear young man, this drizzle, this fog, not at all the night for a Christian to be abroad." Yet at other times he had passed Thomas at the door without a word as the tutor had made his way into heavy rain. Thomas had registered his disappointment then in a touch of sullenness and had berated himself for his ingratitude and presumption.

But now he sat in this fine room, warm and relaxed, and considered his answer. "I try to keep myself productively occupied," he replied. "During the day, of course, there is my work with the children who, I am happy to report, continue to make progress."

"Yes, yes," Worthing waved the answer away, "but in the evenings, Kendall, the evenings. You are a healthy young man new to the delights of this great city. What do you do?"

Thomas pursed his lips. "I do not sit about in idleness, sir," he returned. "I mark the children's work and consider their academic needs and attempt to provide for these in my preparations for the next day's study."

Mr Worthing yawned.

"And there is my own study," the tutor continued. "The Reverend Kent, with whom I am lodged, has kindly brought to my attention texts for earnest study. I am presently reading Mr Burkitt's "New Testament" and Mr Doddridge's "Rise and Progress of Religion in the Soul". And Mr Kent is so kind as to share his wisdom and time and help my understanding. These are weighty matters," he said a little pompously, "and sometimes beyond my comprehension."

Worthing emptied his glass and refilled it and his guest's. "Anything else?" he asked.

Thomas sipped the brandy. The dizziness had passed and his confidence grew. "I am an earnest correspondent. I particularly feel it my duty to keep my mother acquainted with my work in London."

"Your mother, eh? You are a dutiful son."

"I try to be. My mother has made many sacrifices for me and it would be a serious failing to be unappreciative."

Mr Worthing smiled. "Ah, yes, where would we be without the sacrifices of our mothers?"

Thomas sipped from his glass again and the golden warmth slid down his throat and prompted him to boldness. "Your tone puzzles me, sir. Do you imply this is a matter for humour?"

Worthing smiled again. "Believe me, my young friend, I find little of humour in maternal sacrifice." He paused. "What, may I ask are the sacrifices she has made?"

"Why, a myriad, sir, too many to recount. But as simple examples ..." His voice trailed off.

Worthing leaned forward and but for a sardonic twitch at the corner of his mouth his demeanour was one of grave concern. "Yes?" he asked softly. "Well," Thomas hesitated, then spoke quickly, "well, for example, she had taught me my letters before I was five. And the beginnings of arithmetic. She has taught me my duties as a Christian. Of usefulness and industry. She has shown me the way to my salvation, sir."

Not much of sacrifice in any of that, thought Worthing, but he said,

"And, I warrant, the need for constant vigilance against the workings of sin and temptation?"

"Indeed!" Thomas began to grow excited and his voice rose. "The wickedness of the world is too much with us. The temptations of the Adversary are everywhere. We must always be on our guard."

"You are pious as well as dutiful, I think. But tell me," and now there was an edge to Worthing's voice, "what do you guard against, Thomas? What are your temptations?"

"Well." Thomas was drunk now and his natural candour greater than ever. "I know I have many faults. I am often intolerant and sometimes harbour resentments and self-pity as for example." He had nearly said, when I am cold and wet and there are miles to walk to my lodgings, but caught himself in time. He was not that drunk. "Sometimes I entertain unkind thoughts towards my fellows that can prompt me to anger. And I am a poor correspondent and do not always show the filial gratitude to which I am bound."

Worthing nodded. "Your mother's sacrifices again," he said. "Ah." He turned as his wife entered the room and rose, lithely, elegantly, Thomas also, but more clumsily, spilling a little of the brandy as he stumbled to his feet.

Mrs Worthing stood before them, poised, posed, and sketched a curtsey. "Mr Worthing, Mr Kendall." At twenty four Julia Worthing was as elegant as her husband, in a fine deep blue damask dress that slid over her full-bodied figure and drifted on the polished floor. Her gleaming jet hair was caught back in a jewelled coiffure and framed her pale, elaborately made up features, wide blue eyes and coral lips. A glittering filigree encircled her ivory throat, lying between bare shoulders, holding an amethyst pendant that hung between a deep, ivory cleavage. Lord Worthing followed the direction of Thomas' gaze and smiled. He nodded to his wife. "Good evening, my dear, he murmured, "Master Kendall and I were just discussing wickedness and temptation."

Mrs Worthing smiled at Thomas. "A provoking subject," she said, "I should have enjoyed to hear your thoughts."

Thomas stared mutely.

"Perhaps another time," said James Worthing. "Now I believe our society is required at Lady Siddely's." He took his wife's arm and led her from the room. Thomas was dismissed.

The long walk home through the cold night air took away the last of the brandy's effects. He dined in silence with the Kents and then excused himself, pleading a slight headache and a long day. Now, with the fire crackling in the grate and the rain against the window, he settled at his desk.

He wrote, *Dear Mother* and then stopped. Mentally he penned *what sacrifices have you made for me?* And his mind became as blank as the sheet before him.

What do you do, Thomas? Besides work and study and prayer and writing letters to your mother? There were readier answers here. On Sunday mornings he would take a small class of young students for bible study and afterwards he and they would attend the Reverend Kent's service. In the afternoon there might be a church-related function and at seven there would be evensong. On Saturdays he might assist the minister with a variety of tasks but more often he would just walk and lose himself in the worlds of London. Through the world of the nobility past the palace of the mad king, wondering at the splendour and the opulence, watching the great polished carriages roll by with their shining horses and immaculate drivers and attendants. Through the streets of Mayfair with its great houses, vast doors, vast wings and endless polished windows, watching the Lords in their gleaming coats and polished buckles and their Ladies, painted and bejewelled in their bonnets and capes, taking the air. He had sat and tried to pray in St Paul's but instead had stared at the heavenly vaults of ceiling and the arched stained windows that told of the passion of Christ and the devotion of the saints.

Through the markets where the vendors hawked their wares in constant clamour and where people thronged and laughed and pointed and fought. He had seen clowns and jugglers, a tormented dancing bear, an organ grinder with a performing monkey on a chain and he had tossed the man a coin and received a cursory nod. He had listened to a street prophet inveighing against the wickedness of man and the turning away from the Lord and had nodded his agreement while the noisy crowd had mocked and jeered.

And as his steps had sometimes taken him through the southern quarters he had walked past vomit and excrement on the streets with his hand in his coat pocket, tightly clutching his purse. There were beggars and street ruffians, criminals six years old who had taken refuge in squalid, abandoned shacks and tenement in hiding from their parents or the workhouse or their chimney sweep masters, invariably trading one master for another. Stepping over the occasional body in the street, drunk, wounded, ill or dead, he had not stopped to discover which. He had averted his eyes in fear from those who might threaten him and in shame and embarrassment from the disfigured and the crippled. And when he had come to the streets where the girls and women plied their wares he had frozen in fear and shame together. In shame as his eyes had locked upon the various shapes of female flesh, the scrawny, the voluptuous, held by the curve of buttock and thigh, the sweep of belly and the breast, full, boyish, pendulous or pert, the promise and threat of nipple. And in fear of that part of him that persisted with the shame. Then looking about, in fear of being caught looking, of being taken in his sin.

CHAPTER 3

James Worthing leaned upon the carved, polished balustrade and gazed down over the scene below. The tincture of laudanum he had taken half an hour before, carefully measured to ensure full and conscious participation, was taking delightful effect and he smiled at the play of light and shadow from the chandeliers on to the glitterati below. By the first step of the broad sweeping stairway a string quartet played Bach and Worthing's fingers tapped the shining oak in what he considered to be an elegant rhythmic counterpoint. Below London society swirled and posed, dipped and swooped in a fine ballet of elegance and affectation. Lords and ladies, assured of their lineage and breeding, graciously accepted the attention of successful merchants and factory owners, assured in their turn of their wealth and value in matrimonial alliance.

Worthing became absorbed in the charming play of tendons dancing beneath skin and was startled when a voice, caressing and tender, spoke in his ear. "My dear Worthing, pray you, join us. The pleasure of your hand is always available; the charms of this evening are not." Smiling, James turned his head slowly to take in the mocking gaze of his friend. Beneath the curls of his powdered periwig, Farnwright's eyes glittered above light mascara and beneath perfect arches of manicured eyebrow. Pale powdered cheeks and rosebud lips completed the picture. Farnwright continued, "I have not seen you on the floor. Could it be, could it possibly be that la danse does not attract you?"

"I have been there," answered James, "I have waltzed with Lady Worthing and gavotted with Lady Grimstead. And I have heard tell that George Byron is fucking his sister."

"A man of fine family feeling."

"But now I stand apace and muse. I prefer the company at a distance."
"Ah yes," sighed Farnwright, "a veritable young Werther, thou." He was
referring to the hero of the German, Goethe's novel, a young man so sunk
in boredom that he had foresaken his gifts and opportunities and ended
his life. A rash of fashionable suicides had followed.

"There is," Worthing agreed, "a certain tedious quality to repetition."

"So," suggested his friend, "look for something different. Perhaps you
might join the Church."

Worthing rolled his eyes. Then he said, "Odd that you should say that.
I was only this evening engaged in conversation with an earnest young
Churchman. You probably know of him. He is the tutor of your children."

"Indeed? They have a tutor now?"

"A pious young pudding. Thomas Kendall."

Farnwright shook his head. "No, I am afraid the name rings no bells.
But, damme, James, what strange pass has driven you to converse with
tutors?"

Worthing shrugged. "He amuses me, I suppose. He is so pious and
correct, such a piece of duty and devotion. And yet," he wagged a bejewelled
finger, "you should see how he stares at my wife's tits."

"He would be less than gallant if he did not."

"Pshaw. The boy gawps like a dolt. But that is not the point. He
professes purity and gawps, like a starving urchin at a Lord's banquet."
His lip curled.

Farnwright smiled. "Why, James," he said, "I do believe the boy has
made you angry."

Worthing turned away and tapped at the balustrade. "He's a fucking
hypocrite," he said. "A self-righteous, little creeping Jesus. And he's
ignorant. He declaims from a half-arsed jumble of nothing much," he
shook his head in exasperation, "you're right, he makes me angry. And that
makes me really angry: that an ignorant little twat has made me angry."

Farnwright was delighted.

"That little twat needs his come-uppance," he said.

"Yes." Worthing turned back and Farnsworth could see the anger fading
and a new excitement growing. "He needs to see himself for who he is."

"He does and we must assist him to this knowledge. But how?" "I don't
know. But we shall find a way." He raised his glass. To the education of
Thomas Kendall."

"To the punishment of Whatshisname."

They hurried outside, pausing only to replenish their glasses. Past lords and butlers and ladies, "how ravishing you look, dear Lady. Alas, I am caught in some urgent business but later, I beg …" Into the night air, oil drifting dark shadow over tired, grey lions.

Farnsworth raised his glass again. "He must be bedded," he said. "To the bedding of Whatshisname."

"His name's Kendall and, yes, I think a bedding is in order."

They drank.

"This is more than a bedding, you know. This is theatre –"

"It is. It is theatre and it need be about more than a bedding –"

"It is, it's about infinitely more, why, fuck, man, this is *fundamental.* This is the quest for knowledge, self-knowledge, as good as any other –"

"Better."

"And original sin! Who could ask for more?"

"Not me."

So, who would play Eve?

"She cannot be a common whore."

"Mmm, although there is something fine about a chance of the clap. By way of epilogue, you understand."

"Perhaps so, but the part calls for some subtlety. She must *tempt* him."

"Of course she must. So she must know how to play him."

"A player to play him."

"Precisely so. She must be an actress."

The quest began and immediately they were joined by their wives. Their advice proved invaluable.

"I think that one is too attractive, James," said his wife. "She has not needed to think as much as she might; we need greater talent."

"This one is too tall; he will need to stand above her."

"She must be able to read his mood."

"And then control it."

Farnwright clapped his hands. "This is so exciting," he said.

It was the ladies' team that found Mary Carpenter. "She will be perfect," sighed Julia Worthing. "Petite and buxom withal; no beauty but she's not plain, neither, in a knowing Irish way. She hates her life and would buy her way out of it. Her bitterness will help her remember her lines."

Mary was also very clear.

"You want me to whore myself," she said.

"Well," Worthing spread his hands, "think of it as ultimate theatre, art and life conjoin. Think of the greatness of the theme: The Fall."

"The first temptation had nothing to do with sex," said My Lady Farnwright.

"Well, it should have."

Mary said nothing during the happy banter. Think of bullshit, she thought. For her part she could not think past the money.

"What might I expect for my efforts?" she asked.

"We had thought," said Farnwright, "to enhance your appetite for success, you understand, to offer nothing for a failed attempt."

Mary nodded. "A failure is non-consummation," she said.

Worthing was on his feet.

"No, damme," he said. "this is more than a first fuck. This is looking to the soul of a man; this is about angels and demons. A failure would be his failing to confront his temptation. If he fought like Jacob and won, that would be a fine thing, a surprising outcome, I suppose, but a success, nonetheless."

"Yes." Lady Farnwright clapped her hands. "Well said, James. We will have great theatre here." She cocked her head. "I wonder, could we engage an orchestra, extempore, you know, perhaps not." She trailed off.

Mary's eyes widened. "You are planning to stage this?" she asked. "Do you not think an audience might inhibit his performance?" *Not to speak of my own.*

"Yes," said Lady Julia, "of course it would. O see how well she thinks, James. Isn't she perfect for the part?"

Worthing smiled and looked across at Mary.

"Well?" he asked.

They are really into this.

She looked levelly at him. "I will bring everything I can to the part," she promised. "But I must be well paid."

"Very well." He waved his purse. "Fifty guineas?"

She bowed then turned to Farnwright. "And for your part, sir? What might I hope for your part?"

Farnwright burst out laughing. "O," he said at last, "that was perfectly done. And you have doubled your taking. But," he pointed at her, "you have not earned your money yet, Mary Carpenter and with your doubling of the

---

32

fee my expectations shall be doubled. I want to see the woman for whom Christ himself might fall."

And so Mary was engaged.

"You will need a house," Worthing told her, "and it will be yours until your part is played."

"Rupert has rooms in Ransley," said Julia and giggled at her inadvertent fancy. "They will serve nicely."

The rooms were a continual reinforcement of her will to go through with this and to take away one hundred guineas. They were tasteful and Farnwright and Worthing were ready with their purses. The dresses were hers to keep.

"The props must be perfect," said Lady Farnwright

"How will I do this? Tell me about this man."

"His name is Thomas; he wants you but he will deny it. To you and to himself. But you will persuade him. He longs to be persuaded."

Mary did not ask why they were punishing this Thomas; she could afford no sympathy for him It might affect her performance and her purse. But she needed to know about him, she needed to be ready for whatever he might bring.

She set about her preparation.

Rangihoua

The eyes of the story teller, the tohunga of Rangihoua, are red from the smoke. It is less now, gathering thinly among the rafters as the last of the wood goes and embers twinkle on stone. They are very exposed here, on top of Rangihoua, and the thatched roof and walls shudder and twist under Tawhiri's blasts and the driving rain. But their home, their ancestor stands against Tawhiri as Tu once did and the people give little thought to the storm. Their eyes are fixed on the priest, following him as he moves about the whare. Even the children who have stayed awake are still and quiet and watch and listen. Who knows what they understand of his stories but they join the moment with their enchanted family.

Rakau finishes his story and the people smile and nod and shake their heads, the children, too and wait for more.

"Tell us of war," a man says.

"Talk of Tu, talk of death," says another.

"It is always war," says Rakau and the whare rumbles its assent. "And why not? It has been war since the beginning, since Tu spoke for the death of the parents. Even though they did not die they were wounded and bled and wept and still do. Listen," he whispers into the silence, "you can hear Tawhiri tell his father's grief and if you went outside you would see and feel and taste it, too.

"After the parting of the parents, Papa Tuanuku, our mother, lay alone and Rangi, our father, gazed down on her and Tawhiri roared in the spaces between. After the parting, I say," and he laces his fingers and slowly begins to draw them apart, "which came over many ages, many ages of pain ..." His voice trails away and the audience leans forward. They know what is coming but that makes it no less enthralling.

"After the parting was war as Tawhiri raged from the heavens, uprooting the children of Tane and driving Tangaroa from the shore to the ocean depths. He could not find Rongo or Haumia for they hid in their mother's bosom. And she protects them well to this day, the kumera and the fern root. And she was there for Tu; he stood safely upright on her breast and Tawhiri could not move him.

"Tu stands in the heart of the warrior and a warrior must have war. That is what his name means, that is what he is supposed to do.

"Tu found a take, a cause for war, for had not his brothers stood apart from him as he battled Tawhiri?"

"Ae," the people nod agreement.

"And for his mana did he take utu?"

"He did, he did."

"Tu went into the forests of Tane and from the ti whanake tree he took long, fibrous leaves and he fashioned them," the faint shadow of Rakau's hands moves across the whare wall, "into nooses. He set them here," bending, "and here," reaching, "and the children of Tane were caught and Tu made food of them.

"With harakeke, flax, he made nets. And mmm," Rakau wipes his hand across his mouth, "the children of Tangaroa were very good to eat.

"And with his ko, Tu dug into his mother's breast and drew out Rongo's and Haumia's children from their hiding place and he cooked them and made them common; then he ate them. And very good they were, too."

The people love to hear of kai, food and Rakau plays with them a little. "Koura and kumara with tuatua, mmm and mussels, steamed in the umu until they are just perfect, hot and juicy."

The audience smile and nod and close their eyes, ah, the succulence of flesh.

"And Tu consumes us, too. When the battle is upon us, he is there. He dances with us as we haka to our foe." His back fully erect, Rakau bends deeply, suddenly at his knees and his hands smack as a single sound against his thighs. His eyes protrude and his tongue reaches over a tattooed chin. There is a sudden, general shout of approval. "Ae! Kia ora, e Rakau!"

Rakau straightens and smiles. "Kia ora," he answers, then shifts into a quieter moment.

"Always war. And why not? It is all about us as we sit here. Down in the bay Tangaroa hurls his waves against Tane, ripping at the earth that holds his children's roots. Tawhiri fights them both, turning Tangaroa's waves to whirlpools and typhoons, tearing Tane's children from their home."

"War," the people whisper.

"Tell us how Tu became man," asks a woman.

"Very well," Rakau nods, "but this must be my last story for the night. I must return to my whare."

"But the weather …teeming …won't be able to see your way …slippery …stay with us."

"I know the gods are warring. But I have my warm cloak and I know the way and this is a fine time to walk among them.

"Now, Tane was the first father of the earth. There were no wahine yet, so he took from his mother's body and made a woman of it.

"He breathed life into her and she became Hine ahu one. By her he fathered the first child, Hine titama, Dawn, and by the child he fathered more children. So began the race of man. When Hine titama discovered her father, her shame was such that she could not abide the light. So she fled Tane and went to Rarohenga where she became Hine nui Te Po; she waits for her children there.

Rakau's eyes widen.

"And with Tu's aid, we'll send them to her."

CHAPTER 4

London 1802

Worthing had noted an edge to the tutor's manner and thought it wise to leave the subjects of sin and temptation alone. Instead, he inquired during their brief meetings in the hallway after the children's progress, expressed his satisfaction and every now and then, when the rain was heavy, directed the young man to his carriage.

A month after their last meeting they were again seated over brandy.

Worthing felt his way carefully. "You know, Thomas," he said. "I envy you."

Thomas looked back in astonishment. "You envy me?" he repeated. "Why?"

"I envy your faith. To believe that at the end of your life, however it may have turned out, an eternity of bliss awaits you. I cannot imagine the sense of comfort, of serenity, that must bring. And yet," Worthing paused, "you do not always seem so serene."

Thomas nodded. "Nor am I," he replied. "It is not just a matter of believing that ensures salvation, although I understand the Papists think so. One must earn it through a useful, virtuous life. It is a daily battle with the temptations of the Adversary and I am not always successful." He hesitated as past failures crowded in, then plunged on. "But I do believe that so long as I bow to the will of the Almighty and leave my fate in His hands I cannot fail." He looked curiously at Worthing. "You attend church. What do you believe?"

Worthing shrugged. "As to church-going, it is a convention my station demands. As to belief," he shrugged again, "nothing. I do not necessarily disbelieve. It is the height of arrogance, to which even I cannot aspire, to say that something is not because I cannot see it. But, and please do not take offence, I speak sincerely, it seems to me even more absurd to believe that something is because I wish it were. Does that make sense?"

Thomas was confused. "Not really," he said at last. "I believe because, because ... I *know* my Redeemer liveth." He looked down at his hands and said quietly, "It must be terrible to believe otherwise."

Worthing's smile did not reach his eyes. "I suppose it is," he murmured. "And perhaps that is why the mass of mankind seems to possess your kind of knowledge. The Musselman knows that Allah is great, the Jew knows Jehovah is almighty, the Hindu has his pantheon of gods, even the savages have their great spirits or await the embrace of their ancestors." He looked levelly at Thomas, noting a clouding in his eyes. "You cannot all be right, yet you all believe, or rather know, that you are."

Thomas shook his head unhappily. "I cannot debate these matters," he answered. "I will ask my mentor. Perhaps he can provide argument that will satisfy. All I know," steadfastly, "is that God sent His only begotten son Jesus Christ into the world for the salvation of sinners."

Worthing inclined his head and wondered if he should stop now, for he could see that the boy was becoming unsettled. Perhaps one more sortie. "Thank you," he said graciously, "I would appreciate the good Mr Kent's input. I wonder if I might put one further question that has troubled me. "Without waiting for an answer he continued. "You see, I have always wondered why the Lord's Prayer includes the line 'lead us not into temptation'. I would have thought that moral certainty can only be asserted where it has been tried in temptation."

"I do not understand."

"Very well. Let me state the problem by way of analogy." Worthing smiled. "Perhaps a parable. Imagine that you are sitting at my table with half a dozen others and I leave the room briefly with my purse on the table in full view. Could any of you assert that you leave it untouched solely through your adherence to the commandment that thou shalt not steal?"

"Well, no." Thomas was puzzled. "We may all be honest Christians, I would hope that we were, but to take it in full view would invite immediate apprehension. But I do not see what that has to do with –"

Worthing interrupted smoothly. "Precisely so. Self-preservation is clearly as much of a consideration as an ethic of honesty. Now, imagine that you are walking home, it is a dark night and the streets are empty. And here is my purse on the pavement, you recognise it and anyway it contains identification. Is this a matter for honesty?"

"Well, of course. There appears no chance of apprehension, one could steal it safely, so its return would be the act of an honest man. O I see. You are saying only when I could have stolen but chose not to can I assert honesty."

"Nicely put," smiled Worthing, and then put it more nicely. "With temptation sin may follow. Without it there is no opportunity for virtue." He rose to his feet. "Thank you for your kind attention, Thomas. I hope we may continue this conversation at some later date." Thomas was dismissed.

Joseph Kent puffed heavily on his pipe and his pink, fleshy features became lost in wreathes of acrid smoke. He was much concerned by Thomas' questions and concerns but could find no ready answers.

"I do not like this argument, Thomas," he said at last. "It sounds altogether like a call to meet with evil."

"But not to join with it, Reverend." Thomas was excited by this new train of thought and also by the uncertainty it had elicited in his mentor. It made him feel somehow more important, wiser perhaps, the pupil disputing with the teacher, the adolescent challenging the father. "If one avoids temptation, how can one be said to have overcome it? Where is the chance for virtue?"

"Ah, Thomas, this is the argument of the serpent in the Garden. And like that argument I do not like the source of this one." Since their last discussion, the Reverend Kent had made further inquiry about the character of James Worthing and was worried by what he had learned. "I must question your employer's motives," he continued. "Why is he taking the time, this wealthy and well-connected young man, to even debate these matters with you?" He regretted his words in the moment he spoke them as he saw injured pride flare in the face of his protégé.

"Do you mean, why should such an important, worthy man waste his time upon a creature such as I?"

Joseph held up his hands in futile protest as Thomas pressed on. "I think that for all his learning and standing Mr Worthing is an unhappy man. He said himself that he envies, yes, envies me my faith. I think he may be trying to find his way back to God."

"Ah, Thomas, please do not take offence. I am trying to help."

Thomas was instantly contrite. "Forgive me," he begged. "I am grateful, of course, for your kindness in hearing me. I get excited, probably too excited, by new ideas and I cannot put them to one side."

"I am not asking you to put them to one side. I am asking you to weigh them carefully."

"And that is what I am trying to do. There is something here that I feel is hugely important. And I must understand it. Do you know," flying off at a tangent, "I am put in mind of missionaries."

"Missionaries? Do you mean –"

"The missionary goes into the darkness, he seeks out the evil men do and he confronts it with the light of God."

"Thomas!" Joseph was becoming alarmed. "This is become entirely too fanciful."

"No, no," the young man broke in, his thoughts flying ahead of his words. "Don't you see? If the missionary were to avoid all temptation he would stay at home, hiding away from the world. He would be safer in bed! And how much virtue is there in that? Where is his usefulness?"

The minister tapped his now dead pipe into the ashtray, leaned across and took Thomas' hands in his. "Thomas. Listen to me. These are, as you say, weighty matters and containing not a little sophistry, I fear, but you are racing ahead of yourself. The missionaries you speak of are mature men, long trained in the service of our Lord. There may be little temptation for them, assured and strong in their faith and knowledgeable in the ways of the world."

Thomas jerked his hands away as he got to his feet and began to move agitatedly about the room. Words poured out as his tone rose. "While I am but a callow boy, you mean, weak and ignorant. No, no, you are right. But where am I to gain knowledge if I hide from the world? Where am I to gain strength? Perhaps this is my calling, yes, perhaps the Lord is speaking to me through this unhappy, lost man, reaching for salvation, maybe I can be its means, perhaps this should be the path of my industry, herein may lie my usefulness, no, no, please do not say anything, I cannot think, my mind is spinning, a million thoughts crowd upon me, o, there is so much energy here, my blood roars, I must lose it, I shall walk it off, yes, please excuse me, thank you for your kindness, forgive me, forgive me, I must go." And he stormed out of the room, out of the house, hatless, coatless, and plunged into the streets of London.

"Missionary, eh? Well." James Worthing shook his head in unfeigned astonishment. "And you came to that from my querying a line in a prayer? Truly, Thomas, I am at a loss for words."

"I know it seems impetuous, but I have thought about it deeply and have prayed for guidance."

"And guidance was forthcoming?"

"No, not really, but even that may be meaningful."

"An answer in no answer. The subtlety escapes me."

The two were seated in a paved courtyard on either side of an ornately carved coffee table on which sat a decanter of excellent cognac and two crystal balloon glasses. The day had been a fine one and was now sinking into evening. The conversation had, for the first time, been instigated by the tutor. Still excited by the new thoughts that continued to crowd his mind and dissatisfied with the reluctance of his mentor to embrace them he had turned to his employer. There was, he had sadly conceded to himself, no one else. For while he had met a number of fellow parishioners, including young men and women of his own age, he struggled with social intercourse. He found little of interest in their conversation, in the idle gossip and vague generalisations that their lives generated. More than once he had found himself yawning and had berated himself for his intolerance and lack of concern. For their part the congregationalists were unsettled by his intensity and a candour that seemed to hold no regard for the social niceties. James Worthing, of course, was charmed by both.

"I mean," Thomas continued, "that the Lord may be withholding judgement upon these thoughts. Perhaps He is saying I need further information."

"Further information about what?"

"I don't know. Obviously all answers to all questions are to be found in His Holy Scripture and I continue to study them industriously. But perhaps I should also look elsewhere."

"I see. Perhaps you are looking for the questions. That seems wise. People too often, it seems to me, are too ready with answers to indifferently constructed questions. The German poet Goethe wrote somewhere that the trouble with people who don't know is that they don't know that they don't know."

Thomas looked puzzled and made no response.

"Perhaps another quote. Pope, no, not the Roman one, the Englishman, Alexander, said, how did it go, o yes, 'presume not God to scan, the proper study of mankind is man'.

"Yes." Thomas nodded eagerly. "Perhaps that is it."

Worthing leaned forward and picked up his glass. He swirled the amber liquid and breathed the fumes. Then he raised the glass. "A toast," he proposed, "to the study of man." They drank. "And now," continued Worthing, "in return for your contributions to my understanding of God you must allow me to share some of my observations of man. Let me see. Today is Friday, tomorrow the last Saturday of the month. A very appropriate day for the study of man. You have engagements for tomorrow?"

Thomas shook his head.

"Excellent. Neither do I." This was not true. James Worthing's diary had the evening marked for dinner with the Buckinghams, but he was willing to let it pass. Julia would not complain; she would find this much more interesting. He could scarcely believe that Thomas had contrived to move himself into this position. Serendipitous? The hand of God? Another hand? Who cares? "So," he continued, "meet me here at eleven tomorrow morning and we shall commence your instruction."

Thomas arrived promptly at eleven in a state of anxiety and excitement. He had retired early the previous night, resisting Joseph's invitation to a nightcap, but had slept poorly. He had breakfasted in silence and departed without disclosing his destination to make his way to a common ground where he had sat and tried to assemble his thoughts. The more he thought the more he was obliged to concede to himself that he was in the grip of compelling unreason. Like James Worthing he was at a loss to fathom how questions of sin and virtue had led to thought of service in the mission, and how that had led to taking instruction in the study of man made no evident sense at all. He could hear the Reverend Kent – this is the argument of the serpent in the garden- and he feared that his secretiveness and the furtiveness of his departure suggested the presence of a lie. Yet throughout all the fear and doubt he could not quell an underlying excitement. Danger, he whispered to himself, there is danger here and I am courting it. And the thought thrilled him.

He was surprised by Worthing's appearance, a simple brown coat over breeches tucked into soft boots. He wore no wig, his brown hair pulled back into a short ponytail. He face was without makeup, his eyes bright pinpricks. He carried a narrow walking stick.

He greeted Thomas enthusiastically. "Excellent. You are here. Let us go." Thomas fell in mutely beside him, stretching his stride to keep up with Worthing's brisk pace. The accompanying monologue ran at a similar rate. "Now this is the home of my Lord Elgin." They were paused outside an imposing edifice. "They say the house was largely built upon the profits of the African slave trade. I understand his younger son, Edwin, Edwin Elgin, sounds like a character from a limerick, Edwin is presently fucking the queen. You look surprised Thomas, at the word or at the deed? Don't blame me, the expression comes from one of Her Majesty's attendants, 'Queen Caroline,' he said, 'is very fond of fucking.' Now that sounds like the punchline of a limerick, does it not? And there, along the road, you see that ridiculous building with its Corinthian columns and Doric arches, the owner maintains a factory in Pillsborough, I believe the yearly mortality rate of the labourers, is that the right word? rivals that of the latest campaign against Napoleon, perhaps I exaggerate, ludicrous man, no breeding but royal wealth, wanted something in the nature of an Athenian temple, absurd pretension, he wouldn't know the difference between Sisyphus and syphilis." The monologue continued, washing meaninglessly through Thomas' head. "Ah, we approach our destination. Your chance to observe the workings of London's soul. I pray we are not late."

They had reached the outskirts of Newgate and as they hurried along the narrow streets Thomas became conscious of a crowd building about them. Rich and poor, young and old, men and women crushed together as the crowd growled and rolled along the cobblestones, carrying Thomas and Worthing in the surge.

"See how some occasions bring us all together," Worthing shouted in Thomas' ear. "Behold the common denominator. My Lord," he gestured at a portly bewigged gentleman, "puffs alongside the common man and his brood." A roar arose behind them. "And here comes the cause." The crowd was split and Thomas found himself pressed against a shop window in a heated crush of bodies. Still he was driven forward with Worthing holding to his arm. "And here comes the common cause."

A clatter of hooves could be heard through the crowd and turning Thomas could make out a team of four horses moving down the centre of the roadway, drawing behind them an open carriage. Eleven figures stood within it unmoving, their wrists lashed to the rails. There were two women of indeterminate age, dressed in greasy rags, and nine men, although several could have been younger than Thomas. Seven of the men were also in filthy rags, the eighth was similarly attired but sported a seaman's jacket, a bright blue bandanna about his throat. The ninth was dressed as a gentleman. Beneath his periwig, somewhat askew, he gazed vaguely about as if searching for a familiar face or some meaning to his part in this carnival. "Henry Pettigrew," shouted Worthing, "he looks, does he not, as though some kindly hand has provided him with the wherewithal to make his journey somewhat easier."

As the carriage drew parallel Thomas could make out a twelfth figure, bound by the wrists to the back rail. His feet dragged along the ground and Thomas could see bone through the shreds of skin that lay ripped and open. Beside him strode a man behind a black leather mask; a squat, muscled man, his upper torso naked and dripping sweat. In one hand he carried a heavy, leather thong, matted in blood and skin. He raised it now and it cracked across the bleeding mess. The man screamed once, then his head fell forward in unconsciousness. The crowd roared its approval and Worthing roared with them. "Lay on," he bellowed, then to Thomas, "come, lad, young disciple, how can you hope to further your study if you do not enter into the spirit of the thing? Revel, I say, join in the glory of man and cry hallelujah to fucking British justice."

The procession surged on, carrying Thomas and Worthing with it and soon they were pressed towards the forefront of the crowd, gathered at the Newgate gallows. The eleven conscious condemned were untied and dragged up the short stairway that led to a long platform, crossed above by a single, heavy beam. A dozen nooses hung from the beam and were swiftly laid about the necks of the prisoners. The twelfth, still unconscious was propped up by a pair of guards.

A hush now settled upon the crowd. "We are approaching the moment," hissed Worthing, "hold fast to your purse. The money is always at the death."

Thomas stared vacantly back at him but obediently thrust his hand deep into his coat pocket and his fingers tightened about his wallet. He stared mesmerised at the faces on the gallows. He saw fear staring out of some, lips moving in desperate prayer. He saw rage on the face of one as he spat and cursed the bystanders. They cheered enthusiastically and cursed him back. The young seaman received a different kind of attention. He stared out boldly at the crowd, dear God, thought Thomas, he is smiling. "Huzzah, my lads, never fear, God bless the King," he roared. The crowd cheered him back and Thomas heard cries of "God bless you, John

Cashman." He turned enquiringly to Worthing, who had yelled out similar sentiments, but his response was lost in the general hubbub.

Then it ebbed again and his attention was taken by a scene closer at hand. A woman in a greasy shawl and tattered dress that stretched over her swollen belly stood nearby, gesticulating wildly at the gallows. Rage twisted her features and she could have been any age, seventeen, forty. Her attention was focused upon Number Five in the gallows line, a slight, foxy- faced man who stared wildly about, twisting his head against the chafing rope. His eyes were wide with fear and he babbled incoherently.

"John Smith!" screamed the woman from toothless gums, "John Smith, you miserable bastard!" The man looked down at her, his lips moving silently. "So you're going to leave me," she shrieked, "I always knew you would. And little Billy and Susan. And another on the way." She seized at her belly as if to thrust it at him.

The man managed to speak then, tears running unchecked over greasy cheeks and mucus over his lips and into his mouth. "Hey-oop, Nancy lass. This is a sorry pass."

"A sorry pass," howled the woman. "A sorry pass for you that will soon be over. A sorry pass for me and the little ones that sees no end. How will we manage?"

Her words brought an alternative to the man's terror and he roared back in sudden rage, "How should I know? They're going to fucking *hang* me." A new burst of terror opened with his words and a spasm shook his scrawny frame.

"Serves you right. If you hadn't been out drunk and thieving but had looked for honest work we'd all be at home right now."

"Honest work!' roared back the man. "And where is that for the likes of me?"

"It's there. A good father would have found it."

"Good father." This must have been an old argument. "How do I know if they're even mine?"

"Oooo," called the crowd in delight.

The woman shrieked then with incoherent fury. "O they're yours. And others too, I warrant. O, I hope the hell you're going to matches the hell here for us."

The word opened new floodgates for the man, the words a release for his terror, meaningless echoes of all the other fights. "Damn you, Nancy

Wharton. You've never been there for me. Never been grateful for what I've brung you, always complaints, always moaning, you fucking cunt –"

The last word was cut off as the hangman jerked the lever and the trapdoors opened. Their screams, cut short, lanced through the roar of the crowd which peaked and then trailed off into an orgasmic sigh. Five bodies, three corpulent, two lucky, hung motionless at the end of their ropes. Seven others jerked wildly, the foxy-faced man amongst them. A number of bystanders plunged forward to seize at their legs to add weight to hasten the end of suffering.

"Dance, you bastard," screeched Nancy Wharton. "Suffer." Then she too ran forward to swing from the legs of her hanging man. Her weight prevailed and soon he hung still. Then she collapsed beneath him, hunched and sobbing, her hair and shawl splattered and reeking with the contents of his now empty bowels.

Thomas allowed Worthing to steer him away from the gallows. His fingers remained locked about his wallet and his legs moved automatically. Indifferent to the bumps and jostling of the crowd he stared almost sightlessly ahead. The roar of the mob or perhaps it was the roar of his agitated blood continued to swell and echo within him.

The mass of bodies that had coalesced into one form, one voice, now dispersed, breaking into ever diminishing groups, disappearing down side roads, into carriages, the occasional laugh, farewells, best wishes.

Worthing guided Thomas into a dimly lit tavern and left him in a narrow cubicle, returning a short while later with two large brandies. As the liquor flowed in golden warmth through him Thomas felt his sense returning. He looked vaguely about the narrow rectangular room, candlelight flickering darkly on bottles and flagons, more lightly on glass. "What time is it?" he asked huskily. Worthing drew a silver timepiece from his fob pocket. "It is half after three," he answered, smiling.

Thomas continued to stare. There should be something he should say, he thought. "Who is John Cashman?" he heard himself ask.

"Ah, yes," said Worthing. "His is a celebrated although not uncommon story. He was a seaman, upon "The Invincible" I believe. He gave good service against the French in the Mediterranean and lost a leg somewhere. You would not have noticed at the scaffold but he walks, or walked rather, upon a wooden peg. Terrible business," he mused, "you know they cauterised the amputation with hot pitch. Can you imagine the agony? Anyway, he had to retire from active service and trotted or rather hobbled off to the Admiralty to secure his pension. He was a single man but supported his aged mother in Swansea. This was all reported in the gazette. You really should expand your reading. So our young tar finds himself at the Admiralty where some officious clerk tells him he does not exist. No records, you see. Try pensions he is told. And off he hobbles. To shorten the story Master Cashman receives no satisfaction anywhere, money is short, he is unfit to work and treacherously he decides to become angry about it. Gets drunk one night with some old mates and they break into a chandler's store, no doubt in search of further drinking funds. The next morning the owner finds young John asleep on a pile of canvas. He declines, under serious encouragement I might add, to give the names of his accomplices so the authorities wisely deduce that he is the ringleader. British justice accords him his day in court. You witnessed the result. But what I find the most astonishing aspect of all is that he goes down singing, 'God save the King.' What can he have been thinking?"

Thomas stared dumbly back, seeing again the bright eyes and the open cheerful smile.

Another question came from nowhere. "Why did you say the money is always at the death?"

Worthing nodded approvingly. "You were paying attention," he said. "Well, now. Besides visiting righteous retribution upon the heads of evil-doers our wise legislators have also decreed that public execution will have the further salubrious effect of deterring others in our midst from similar transgression. Unfortunately," he shook his head in mock sorrow, "the transgressors appear to have failed to grasp this. Indeed, the cutpurses seem to find the spectacle of their peers dancing upon the end of a rope the ideal place to practise their trade. I suppose they have a point. A crush of bodies, noise, jostling, everybody looking up. And there, at the death, you notice the cheer and the sigh as the trapdoors open, our attention is decidedly elsewhere. What better time to dip a hand into a pocket or cut a purse? This phenomenon has been brought to the attention of our lawmakers but they will have none of it. Deterrence, they say, is the thing and if the thieves will not be deterred by the hanging of a dozen then we shall have the hanging of a hundred." Worthing fell silent then and drank deeply. Then he looked up and held Thomas' eye. "So, what have you learned?"

Thomas shook his head. "I do not know. This is not the first time I have seen death, but never in this form. I felt great fear, a fear that numbed me, but I think I was more afraid of the crowd." He looked down at his hands and mumbled, "I was afraid of you."

"Of me? Why?"

"I was afraid of you. When the hangman whipped the prisoner at the cart and you cheered with the crowd. I was afraid of you then."

Worthing's face was grim. "That man," he said slowly, "in a drunken rage slaughtered his wife and two children."

Thomas closed his eyes. "That is a terrible thing," he said, "and perhaps he deserved to die. But the whipping? The cheering? The joying in his suffering? That seems something else besides."

Worthing bit at his lip and his fingers tapped upon the cubicle table. Then he said, "You are right, of course. There is much for loathing here and I ..." He fell silent and continued to chew his lip. Then abruptly, bitterly, "I will not talk of this. These are your lessons; mine were taken elsewhere." He drank deeply and Thomas joined him. The liquor flooded his empty belly.

Worthing reached into his pocket and withdrew a packet of tobacco and papers. With practised finger he rolled a slim cigarette, lit it and smoked silently, staring into the middle distance. Thomas had no wish to break his reverie and sat, gazing idly about the tavern, his thoughts and emotions tangled. Much for loathing, he thought, but what is it Worthing loathes? His anxiety diminished with the other's silence and the working of the brandy and was replaced with a kind of agitation as he became impatient with his confusion. So much has happened, something has changed and I sit here like a lost booby. Time passed as a series of waves, breaking upon a thought, then ebbing into dark, empty silence. The conversation from a group of young men standing about an upturned barrel broke in upon his thoughts. Their dress and accent marked them above the poor and labouring men —not that such would have been welcome in this establishment- but below the middle class. Perhaps they were clerks or domestic servants. Or tutors, Thomas thought sourly.

"You fucking cunt," laughed one, "and then he shat on her." The others roared their amusement and Thomas realised they had also come from the hanging. His impatience and agitation began to move towards anger and his face tightened as he stared at them.

"His eyes fair started from his head," laughed the speaker and then, noticing Thomas' gaze, he added in a different tone, "not unlike the stare of this fellow." He was a slight young man, perhaps twenty with plain and sallow features that bore the ravages of a childhood pox. He was also clearly drunk and his tone belligerent as he continued, "do you find some issue with my conversation, sir?"

Thomas stared silently back, his mind crowded with the visions of the hanging, the thud of bodies finding the end of their rope, the roar of the crowd, the screaming woman.

His silence seemed to irritate the drinker further. "A mute, perhaps. Yet his eyes put me in mind of the shitter on the rope. Perhaps they are brothers." His mates guffawed their appreciation and encouraged he continued the line. "Are you his brother, sir?"

Thomas's fists were balled at his side as he heard himself answer. "I would sooner be brother to the shitter on the rope than the shit who mocks his misery." He was vaguely conscious of Worthing's stirring from his black space but his eyes did not leave his antagonist.

One of the man's companions laughed openly and anger replaced belligerence and levelled any hope of repartee. "Call me a shit, you little monkey," he snarled, advancing unsteadily towards the cubicle. His companions called out their encouragement.

The host behind the bar noted the disturbance and his voice thundered out, "Not in here, gentlemen. I won't have my furnishings damaged. Take it outside. There's a suitable alleyway."

"Well? Are your fists as fast as your mouth, or will you cower here?

Now all the chaos of the day finally settled into one place, into gratifying fury and without a word Thomas moved out of his seat. The party headed towards the exit; he heard Worthing behind him, his cane tapping on the barroom floor.

The alley was narrow and dark, greasy paving between windowless walls. The men gathered at the doorway and watched.

The fight began without preamble and Thomas staggered back, his cheek stinging, his head ringing but the pain was distant and of no account. He was caught from behind and thrust forward. This time he was more prepared and deflected the wild blow that came swinging towards him. Then they closed and grappled, slid on the slime and fell among the filth and detritus of the alley. His opponent wrestled and twisted madly, a free arm punching and tearing at Thomas's face but the blows lacked force and at the back of his mind Thomas knew he was the stronger. He thrust the other away and they struggled to their feet. This time Thomas led the attack. His skills were limited but his rage was great and muted the force of fists to his face. Then his own connected and his opponent staggered back, blood flowering about his nose. Again they grappled and fell, Thomas saw his enemy's face close to his, smelled his breath, sensed the fear and then felt teeth closing where his cheek met his jawline. Fury possessed him utterly and he exploded. Then arms were pulling him back and he was looking down at a still, prone figure.

But it was not over as another man suddenly lunged towards him with glinting eyes and a glinting blade. "Bastard! You've done for my brother and now I'll do for you."

Then it was over as the man suddenly froze. Worthing's cane was untipped and a sharp blade lay at the man's throat.

"Hold," hissed Worthing. "Your brother was beaten by a better man. He is hurt but I daresay he will recover. Which is more than you will do if you persist. Drop your knife." The blade clattered on stone. "Now, gentlemen, if you please, clear the doorway. Thomas, you first." Thomas stumbled through the cleared way. "Do not think to pursue us," continued Worthing, "I have forborne on this occasion." Though his voice was calm there was no doubting the intent behind it. Nor, Thomas registered, the ferocity and huge enjoyment.

There was no pursuit; Thomas and Worthing were followed only by a hubbub of voices from the alley doorway, "no, John, the bastard has a sword and I vouch that he knows how to use it," compassion and cursing together, "o God, look at what he's done to your face, God damn the whoreson bastard," muted groaning and a sudden burst of laughter that would doubtlessly inspire further conflict, "you find this amusing, I see." They passed unchallenged through the tavern and out into the street where shadows were beginning to gather, puddling at the pools of light cast by gas lamps. Worthing moved Thomas into a light and studied his face. A puffy eye was closing and blood congealing upon the scratches in his cheek. Worthing gently fingered the wound by the jawline. "It is not serious," he decided. "He did not have the time to take a proper hold."

Thomas shook his head numbly. "He bit me," he said, "he fucking bit me." He stopped, equally shocked by the man's action and his choice of words to describe it.

Worthing smiled. "It was probably to your advantage," he observed. "It turned you into a tiger, by God. If you had not been pulled from him, I believe you would have killed him. What magnificent rage." He shook his head admiringly. "Look at your hands."

Thomas held his bloodied fists up into the gas light. "O God," he whispered, "what have I done?"

Worthing laughed. "You defended yourself against a fool who wished you ill," he said. "That is all. And now we must tend to your injuries. And," he added, wrinkling his nose, "find you some new apparel. You are filthy, Thomas. And you stink."

An empty hansom cab approached and Worthing stepped forward, calling it to a halt. After a swift discussion with the driver, accompanied by the exchange of coins, they climbed in and the cab moved on. Worthing leaned back, watching the evening become night, savouring the afterglow of the excitement, but Thomas was still caught in the rush and fidgetted ceaselessly. "I could have killed him," he muttered to himself. "No, I would have killed him, I wanted to kill him. O God, perhaps I have killed him." And then another terrible thought. "I could hang for this." The visions of the afternoon flooded back and he moaned in shame and remorse and fear.

Worthing took his arm in a strong grip. "Listen to me, Thomas. You have not killed him. I saw him stirring as we left. Besides, you acted in self-defence and there is no crime in that. Now, I am taking you to the home of a friend of mine who lives nearby. All your needs will be attended to."

Lady Evelyn's residence was only a short drive away, but Thomas was barely aware of it; he hung on Worthing's arm as he beat upon the polished knocker.

Then the door opened upon a maid deep in curtsey.

"Good evening, My Lord," she began, then looking up took in Thomas' battered face. "Christ," she said, "'e's been smacked proper."

Worthing brushed her impatiently aside, helping Thomas through and out of his great coat.

"Mrs Peabody," he said tightly.

"No, it's not Peabod –"

"Then it's stupid." he said. "Mrs Stupid, go to fetch your mistress and then see what you can find in the way of medicine and bandages. This man is wounded. And Mrs Stupid," she froze, *hold your tongue.*"

Mary watched the opening scene from a doorway. Here is it is, she stiffened and stared, but not as I had expected. Kendall is injured. Still, it gave her an entrance.

"My Lord Worthing," she glided forward in passing curtsey, but her eyes were full upon Kendall. "My poor man," she said, "what has happened here?"

Thomas shook his head vaguely. He was unsteady on his feet and would have fallen had not Worthing supported him. He ached and his head throbbed.

"Mr Kendall," Worthing remembered himself, "Lady Evelyn, Lady –"

"Please, introductions can wait." She hurried forward and took Thomas from Worthing and helped him into a chair. As she straightened she paused and gazed curiously full into him before sinking to her knees on the rug beside his chair.

Worthing was speaking behind her.

"I fear I make you play the Good Samaritan, dear Lady. And alone, too, for I have a most pressing engagement." He bowed briefly and was gone.

"Poor Mr Kendall, let us see what has been done." She knelt beside him, drawing his hand back gently from his jaw. "You have been fighting with a dog, perhaps," she murmured, "no, no do not answer, I can see it hurts to answer. And I'll warrant your head does pound."

He nodded faintly.

"Here." She moved away and then was back with a glass of red liquid. "This will help you think and will take the pain away." She guided the glass to his lips. "There."

The liquid slid down, warm, caressing his throat, filling his chest. And, truly, the pain did go away, it was at a distance now where he could watch it or close it out.

There were soft fingers about his face.

"You are lucky. It looks worse than it is. The wound will close without stitches; but it will bruise and ache."

But not now.

He was light and clear and also dismayed.

"I have dripped rain and worse upon your rug." He struggled but found his feet and the pain was further away.

"Christ," said Farnwright. "What did she give him? He's coming back to life."

"Our girl was not unprepared," said Worthing. "She has given this thought."

The two were leaning against a panelled wall. The lenses on the other side, lying amongst the books, took in all the room. They were excellent front row seats.

"She's got him down again."

She bound the wound on his jaw and rubbed salve into the bruising around his eye. Pain was a forgotten thing and he breathed in the smell of her and watched the light glitter gold above the auburn.

"Stand," she said and this time he obeyed her easily.

"Now, Mr Kendall," Mary tilted her head, "you can assist with the recovery of my rug –"

"Anything. Shall I go? I –"

"By ceasing from dripping upon it. To which end, sir," she held up an imperious finger, "I must ask you to forsake those sorry rags. Here, Mrs Peaco, body has laid out fresh clothing. Here is a bowl and here are towels. Please do me the kindness of saving my rugs from further ruin." And she swept from the room.

"Wonderful," breathed Farnwright. "How to disrobe the prey? Answer: get him to do it himself."

Thomas tugged off his boots; they were filthy and dripping and now he could smell that they stank. He removed them to a bin by the fireplace and he left his stockings there, too. Horrible things.

Now the rug was softly stroking his bare feet and his shirt was sodden and clammy. Off and into the bin with it. And now the trousers, and now all of it. Off and into the bin.

The water was warm and scented and cleansing, lifting the filth away, taking away the sin. And the towels were warm and scented, too.

He held up the clothing she had left him and watched the light shimmer over it, through it. The last green before black. It was the same garment she was wearing, though the green was darker, stronger. It flowed along the length of him.

Now she was beside him, leading him to the table where Mrs Peacobody had laid out an array of dishes. Then he was in the grip of entirely new tastes.

She smiled at his amazement and brought him more to taste. Wines, he thought, that lay beneath a mist, that breathed and smoked.

"How do you feel?"

"Wonderful." He meant it. "I am overcome with successions of wonder. God is in this place."

Worthing stuffed a handkerchief in his mouth and reeled away from the glass. Through tears he could see Farnwright sinking to his knees, holding to the wall.

They rolled and giggled and finally collected themselves. "God is in this place," said Worthing, and they lost it again.

If Mary heard from the neighbouring room, she made no sign. She smiled at Thomas. "Indeed, Mr Kendall, God is in every place, they say, upstairs and downstairs and," she paused and caught his eye, "and in my lady's chamber."

"What is she saying?" Worthing begged.

Farnwright looked up from where his ear was pressed at the opening. "She's brought her twat into the conversation already."

"The woman is a genius."

Thomas understood a good deal less. But he was buoyant, uplifted, even exotic in his satin gown that was like a cool, living thing about him. He shivered deliciously.

"So much beauty," he murmured.

Have I given him too much? How much did he have to drink before? Damn Worthing.

Please God, don't let him pass out.

"You have other wounds, Thomas. Let me tend to them."

Then her hands were parting his kimono at the ankle and she was exclaiming at the grazing where the alleyway had conquered his trousers. Her fingers were light again; but now they lingered.

He looked down and could see that her kimono had fallen away. Her face was lost in the shadow of her hair as she tended him, but her breasts were full and glowing in the firelight.

"Madonna," he said, then "madonna" again, more loudly this time, then turned his head sharply as a hoot seemed to come through the wall. "I think you have an owl in your wall, ma'am, see, there it goes again. The poor creature, how can we save it?"

Mary was fit to hoot, herself and all. How was she supposed to do her fucking job with those two clowns in the next room?

Perhaps we might have an orchestra, ex tempore, you know.

"Please, Thomas," she came up behind him as he prodded vaguely at the wall and leaned briefly against him. "It is a horny owl," dear God, she bit back a rising, hysterical giggle, "that sometimes gets caught among the eaves. He can find his way out and," she raised her voice, "he can do so without further interruption. Here, have a sip of that brandy you like so much and lean back."

Thomas allowed himself to be persuaded and surrendered to her ministrations. She was very adept.

"Do you know," she asked, "that there is a great concentration of sentiment in the foot? See how if I stroke your foot here, it arches and here, it curls?"

Thomas lay back and closed his eyes.

"And if I bring a different touch, the feeling changes again. What is this?"

"Ah, God, I do believe it is your tongue."

She held his focus to his body, "can you feel the sensation move, can you feel it carried in your blood?"

She slipped sweetmeats to him and taste swirled and mixed with all the others.

Worthing was conscious of growing disappointment. The search for the owl, the poor horny creature had been exquisite, he believed Farnwright might have wet himself, certainly there was a damp stain about his crotch. And the Madonna might have been a defining moment; but it was all going all downhill now.

"She is cheating us," he said. "This is no struggle with demons and angels. She's just got him pissed."

Mary would have argued that there was more to it than just that as she stroked and squeezed, "a little tension here, there, does that relieve it?" She heard the quickness of his breath as she gently eased the ointment into his calf, up behind his knee, up to feather on inner thigh. She let her breast brush against his leg and watched it quiver. And all the time she was talking. "Ah, I can feel your blood racing; and here your heart pounds under my hand."

*Come **on** you bastard.*

She eased him down on to the rug, recalling to push a coffee table from its place where it obstructed the library.

Then she parted his kimono entirely and kneeled over him.

All the other sensations were as nothing to this and Thomas swelled and arched and moaned. Then her hands were busy at the bowl and between her thighs and she was upon him. Almost instantly he shot bolt upright, eye blazing and he caught at her and dragged himself further in. Then he shuddered and moaned and collapsed backwards; he was asleep before he reached the rug.

Now she sat in her chair, kimono gathered demurely about her and awaited judgment.

Worthing was inclined to quibble. "I regret, madam," he said, "that I have learned nothing here."

"O come, James," broke in Farnwright, "you are too harsh. There were some excellent moments and in truth you brought him in damned poor condition."

James was brought up a little short.

"Yes,' he said, "I can see that."

The subject lay insensible between them. His kimono had been closed and a light eiderdown covered him from feet to shoulders. Occasionally he mumbled and grunted and once he farted prodigiously.

"Sir," said Mary, "I gave all I could find, it was the performance of my life. Please." She stared at him.

He grunted irritably and studied his boots and she appealed to Farnwright. "Please, sir."

"The man was barely conscious before the end."

"My Lord brought him in need of treatment and already drunk. And shocked. And you scuffled and you giggled," she was near in tears, "and he heard you, God, I thought all was lost then."

"Yes." Worthing smiled in spite of himself. "The horny owl was a lovely touch and I did deliver him ill-used. Here," he took out his purse and counted out thirty guineas. "It is a provoking number and I think you deserve it."

"For my part," said Farnwright, "I never know how my debts will turn out. Let's see." He inspected his purse. ""Forty pieces." He nodded. "Seems fair."

They left soon after and as the door slammed, the maid rushed in. "Well?" she said, "well? I listened at the door but your voices were low. Well" For God's sake, Mary, how much?"

Mary raised a purse in either hand and let them drop upon the table. "Seventy guineas, Jane," she said. ""Seventy beautiful, fucking guineas."

"Really." Jane's eyes widened. "Let's see, show me, o, wait," she jumped to her feet and ran to the front door; Mary could here her at the bolt. "There," she said, returning, "they hadn't bothered to shut it proper. Seventy guineas and an open door. Go on, then, let's see."

Mary spilled the coins on to the table and brought a candle close to them. They glowed and Jane had to steady herself. "So much money," she whispered.

Thomas grunted and both women started.

"What are we going to do with him?"

"Well, nothing I suppose. You want to carry him somewhere?"

"How long do you think he'll be out?"

"Hard to say. He was drunk when he got here, he's had opium and more alcohol since." She shrugged. "Hours?"

They watched the money winking at them.

"Are all the shutters fastened?"

They hurried to find out.

"Christ, that's a lot of money to be just sitting there. I'd sooner it were out of here."

"I'd sooner we was out of here."

"I'd go mad if something went wrong now, I would, stark fucking mad. If we lost the –"

"–Don't say it."

"O God, let's get out of here. Now. We can pack what we need, he said to take the dresses we liked. Let's take them and get out of here. We've nothing to go back to lodgings for, it's all here. There's a stage at dawn, we can stop at Cranleigh with Tom and Nancy and theirs while we think about what we're going to do. O God, Mary, let's go while we are still ahead. Before something awful happens."

"What'll we do about Thomas?"

"O, we'll take him with us, Mary, you take the arms and I'll take the legs. *What can you be fucking thinking?*"

"Will he be safe if we leave him here?"

"I hope so, I can't see why not and I don't see what possible fucking difference it might make. *Come on.*"

"I have used him badly."

But not so badly that she was unable to flee.

Moititi Island

Secure within the rocky arms of the cove beneath a golden sun the *Venus* rode placidly at anchor. Her master leaned over the railing on massive forearms and watched the wavelets lap gently on silver sands. Further back and on either side of the beach the bush rose in a kaleidoscope of greens, crimson and occasional yellow. Birdsong rose above the quiet plashing of the sea.

Sure and it's fucking paradise. Michael Kelly was well pleased with his lot. Was it not only three weeks ago that he had been a common sailor, mate to an evil-tempered Orangeman whose life had seemed dedicated to finding fault with his crew, to driving them beyond the bounds of all that was reasonable? Not any more. Kelly wondered what he was doing now, probably stuck in Hobart still, ranting, cursing the loss of his ship, his trade and much of his crew. Kelly chuckled. Serve him right. Thought the ship couldn't sail without him, did he? Well, they'd shown him. Him and a few of the trusty lads and the cons. Crossed the Tasman in fine time, sailed the East Coast without a worry. Jesus, she was a fine little boat.

And there were benefits on board a man had never experienced before. The finest cunts he'd known in a while, two snitched from a beach in the far north, three more taken from Korasomething, two from Wangaree and the last, she'd been a surprise bonus, hadn't she now. They had weighed anchor and managed a trade with the local savages, pork, spuds and some green stuff, mainly by mime and some drawings by Smith. Then, seeing there was no point in hanging around they'd buggered off. They were under way before the stupid gets had even noticed. Kelly grinned, remembering the wails and the rush to the rails and over the side they went. Leaving behind one very tasty morsel.

Not so tasty now, though. Still it was only to be expected, considering the service she'd given. Billy Gums, perhaps the ugliest man on God's good earth, couldn't believe his luck and seemed to live in the hold where the cunts had been stored. And old Ned … Kelly's musings were interrupted by movement to his right and glancing around he saw a canoe sweeping around the southern headland. His shout coincided with a dozen others and the deck resounded to the thud of running feet. There was no need for enforced discipline here; the men were very clear that their lives could depend upon their speed and preparation. Cargo nets already hung from the rigging over the sides, making boarding nigh impossible and the men were spread about the deck and across the spars, each holding a loaded musket at the ready.

Kelly relaxed as the canoe drew nearer. Although of a good size it was manned by no more than a dozen warriors armed only with traditional weapons. Flax baskets of potatoes and seafood lay between the paddlers. So the savages were only here to trade. Kelly gestured for the netting to be moved to accommodate a boarder and the man from the stern of the canoe clambered nimbly on board. A movement by others to follow was quickly curtailed by a sharp kahoree and the presenting of muskets.

The man seemed unconcerned to be the only boarder. He gazed about the ship, his eyes wide then burst into a torrent of words. Kelly stood quietly for a while, then raised a hand. "Enough of your fucking jabber," he said, "what do you want to trade?"

The man broke off his welcoming speech and his eyes narrowed at the giant pakeha's ignorance and lack of courtesy. Then he shrugged and pointed to his chest. "Ko Hukere ahau," he said.

Kelly understood that much. "Well, Hookerry, what do you want to trade?"

The trading that followed was ordinary enough but for one aspect. Partway through the negotiations Kelly had a thought. "Hey, Billy," he called, "what's the state of them cunts?"

"Pretty fucked, captain," answered the other, eliciting a roar of laughter at his wit. "One of the lot we took from our second call seems all in. Don't think she'll be of much further use."

"Right then, bring her up."

Billy disappeared into the hold, then returned half carrying, half dragging a young woman. He dumped her at the feet of the visitor.

Hukere gazed impassively at the woman, taking in the bruises and scars, faintly recoiling from the smell of her. "Kei hea koe?" he asked. The woman did not answer and he jabbed her with his foot. "Kei hea koe?" he repeated.

She grunted softly at the blow, then whispered between broken teeth, "kei Tai Tokerau ahau."

"Ah." Hukere was more interested now and squatted beside her, taking her head in one hand and with the other tracing the moko that laced her chin. Then he rose to his feet and nodded assent.

An hour later Kelly and Smith were watching the island fade into the sea. "What do you think they'll do with her, captain?"

Kelly shrugged. "Same as us? I don't know. Perhaps they'll cook her and eat her."

Smith's mouth drew into a tight disapproving line and he shook his head. "Dear God," he said, "them fucking heathens and their godless ways."

Kelly's words proved to be prophetic. Hukere kept the girl, Tawaputa, as a slave wife but later fell into a dispute over her with Te Waru, principal rangatira of Ngaiterangi. Te Waru took her and she was killed and eaten. The same fate befell the other women at the hands of Te Whanau-a-Apanui and Ngati Porou.

Such at least were the accounts that travelled northwards to Whangarei and Kororareka to ultimately fall upon the ears of Te Morenga and Hongi Hika, rangatira of Ngapuhi and kinsmen to the women

Chapter 5

London

Thomas was woken by the bells of London summoning him to church. He grunted his way to his feet, then shuffled through the gloom in search of a chamber. His quest was unsuccessful, made worse by barked shins and a stubbed toe and he took himself out through a side door he had found and used the yard.

Now he shuffled back into the lounge and wondered what to do with himself. He could not walk the streets of London in a kimono, where *was* everybody? Then in the last feeble hold of a dying candle he saw a piece of white paper, light against the fruit. He could not make out the writing and took it to the window where he pushed aside the dark, velvet shade. Light flooded in as he read the letter.

Dear Mr Kendall, I hope you're feeling Well. If you aren't, there is a dark blue Liquid in a silver Tankard that will Clear your Thoughts.

Still reading, he walked back to the table and downed the tankard.

There is Bread and Meat and Wine upon the table, too. I hope you will Enjoy them. Clothes are set out for you by the Bed. They might be a little Large, but I hope you will find them Comfortable and Serviceable.

Forgive my Leaving you like this. Jane and I have Urgent Business.

I am sorry for my Part in your Deception. I am in truth a whore but I am bought out of that now. Ink splotched where the nib had dug into the vellum.

Anyway, I am sorry for what I have done. Still, no laws broken, eh? Don't make too much of it.

I hope you have a good life.

I hope this is our final communication.

The note was not signed.

Thomas nibbled carefully upon a peach as he read the note again. Who was Jane? Mrs Peacobody? *My part in your deception.* There were other parts? Worthing? He delivered me to this. He would need to give thought to this.

He changed into the clothes set out for him. The cuffs gathered at his feet and his hands were near lost in the jacket arms. But the clothes were comfortable and clean and dry. Excellent material. They would, he reflected, sit well upon James Worthing.

His jaw was beginning to ache and he cast over the glasses. There, was that the spirit that helped Clear his Thoughts, no, he'd already taken that, ah here was the red that Took away the Pain. He poured a generous draught and drank it.

His thoughts were gathered upon the Mystery and he neglected to shut the door behind him.

Joseph and Florence were torn between relief at his return and consternation at the sight of him. His diffident, distracted manner did not help.

"What has become of you? What's under this, alright, I won't touch it, but your eye and here and," pulling back his cuffs, "what has become of your hands?"

"He has been fighting."

"And these clothes? Whose clothes are you wearing? Where are your own clothes?"

Thomas watched them distantly as they fussed and fluttered.

"Please," he held up a hand, "I have been ill-used but I cannot understand why."

"You do not know why you were beaten?"

Thomas frowned at the non-sequitur. "I was not beaten," he said. "I left my opponent upon the ground." He touched his jaw. "But I did suffer some hurt. But it doesn't hurt now."

"Upon the ground?" Joseph was staring. "Did he live?"

"Worthing said he did, Worthing said he was a cowardly, scurrilous dog who deserved more than he got."

Slowly the tale was extracted.

"and he screamed 'you fucking cunt' and then he died …

"so we went outside into the alley …

"And then," Thomas smiled remembering and Florence snapped her lips shut, "he took me to this beautiful room and I was given medicine –"

"Medicine?"

"I do not know what it was but it was very effective."

His account became less clear, partly because he remembered it worse and partly because it was keeping him away from finding why. He was annoyed at the Kents' slowness, at their dithering over minor details.

Yes, she was a young woman, yes, there was a maid in attendance somewhere, yes, he would have to say she was attractive, beautiful even, he smiled, remembering again and Joseph shook his head.

"But she was just a whore."

Florence clutched at the back of her chair.

"She was, she said so, herself. See, she even put it in writing."

They pored over the letter.

"Thomas, what have you done?"

He was appalled at the accusation.

"I? I? I am the wronged party here, look, she says so, I am a whore, she says."

"No doubt, no doubt. *And you have been with her.*"

This was not fair. He was not responsible.

"Then who is?"

"Does it matter? My dear friends, I have been ill-used and I find you accusing me."

They would have been readier with excuses for him had he been less ready, himself. Where was the remorse? And he persisted with his wretched mystery.

"What is the meaning of it?"

"The meaning of it, sir," thundered Joseph, "is that among other unsavoury matters you have been with a whore."

"Yes, she would have been paid, I suppose, I wonder who paid her."

"Thomas, Thomas," implored Florence, "can you not look to the deed and say you hate it?"

This became a further sticking point. Thomas was tired, he was starting to become sore again and he felt beaten down by their hostile questioning. His Clarity of Thought suffered.

"I need to sleep," he said.

"You need to face your deeds," said Joseph Kent.

"Can we not do it later when I am refreshed?"

Joseph drew back and took a deep breath.

"Thomas, we are talking of your *soul*, man. You are in deep sin."

But Thomas could not find the moment he was supposed to hate. They were such a fragmented lot, always the lights and, oh, a hand upon his knee.

"Did you know," he said, "that there is a great concentration of sentiment in the foot?"

Thomas.

"Well," he was at the point of tears, "what do you want me to say? I have lain with a whore, I remember, of course I remember. Though I was beaten and drugged. Though I was powerless. Obviously I must be a sinner."

Florence spoke past the self-pity and the sarcasm. "And do you repent of your sin?"

Her hands upon him, his blood roaring with the wind against the glass and the fire in the grate. And then taken in like that, beyond all meaning and experience.

"Do you repent of your sin?"

He shook his head, denying the question. "I suppose I must," he said.

At six the next evening James Worthing lay sprawled in his armchair, toasting his stockinged feet before the fire. On a small serving table to his side was a glass of cognac and a pile of letters. He sipped from the glass then lighted a thin cigar and inhaled deeply. Now prepared, he attended to his mail, deftly slicing open the envelopes and glancing quickly at the contents. Some found their way to the fire, others were put aside for a more considered reading later. One in particular held his attention. He recognised the address –it was Thomas's- but not the hand.

Lord Worthing, he read. No 'dear', no 'sir'? Well, well. *I expect that you will not be altogether Surprised to learn that Thomas Kendall will not be Returning to your Service. He is presently Indisposed and it may be some time before he is Fit for Service of any kind. Sir,* Worthing could see how the pen had scored the page, *you have served a naïve boy a Sorry Turn. I would like to believe it was not as Contrived as it appears but, intentional or not, it has laid him in a Parlous State. I would Urge you to seek Pardon from One more Forgiving than myself.* The note was simply signed, Joseph Kent. A postscript suggested that the beginnings of amends might be found in forwarding any outstanding wages to the address above.

Well, well. Events seem to have taken a more dramatic turn than he or Farnwright had anticipated. Or was it that surprising? Clearly they had been playing with fire and now there were burns to show for it. But had he truly done Thomas that much of a disservice? He had opened the boy's eyes to passions without and within. He had created neither. And, by God, those passions were real. *I would sooner be brother to the shitter on the rope than the shit who mocks him* There was a fine sensibility. And that magnificent rage. Was it to be forever cocooned within the meanness of a tutor of children? No, Worthing decided, he would not berate himself –he would leave that to the Reverend Kent – but he would, of course, forward the remuneration owing with a few guineas besides. And a glowing reference.

The Kents fumed, but they took the money.

Thomas' aches came back along with a painful limp. He sat listlessly in his room, cold and miserable, staring into an empty grate. And if the Kents had previously been aghast at his apparent indifference, now they were overwhelmed by his remorse.

He was, indeed, the most wretched of worms.

A creature beneath contempt need not get up in the morning; after all, he has no useful function to attend. There is no call for him to shave his face or take his slippers from him.

He was, for once, reluctant to talk, for what was there for a worm to say, but nodded continuous agreement.

Yes indeed, he needed to get out, take some exercise, eat a decent meal. He would shuffle off to change and they would find him standing by his desk gazing vaguely at his papers.

"I need to study this," he said. "I must pray for guidance."

But he slept instead.

"Joseph, I say, Joseph," the Reverend Kent started from his reverie, the sun warm on his face, and looked across the kitchen table. His wife was peering closely at him. "Drink your tea, Joseph, before it grows cold. Now, I am much concerned about our young lodger. He has been prone for a week."

"As indeed I know, my love," Joseph replied. "I am at a loss as to know what to do. He must be bullied to eat, to wash, to do anything. He is silent but for some disturbing muttering about sin and being cast from God's sight. I have never seen such despair. And Dr Randell is of no assistance.

The damned, o pardon me, man charged me half a guinea to advise that he needed rest."

"He is taking far too much rest," Mrs Kent observed tartly. "He will rest himself to death." She plucked irritably at her needlework and then put it aside. "Something must be done."

"But what else can we do?" We feed him, tend to him, what else is there to do?"

"We must revive him. He must take an interest again."

"He has suffered a great blow, Florence. He needs –"

"To take an interest. Please do not take this amiss, my dear, but I have watched your efforts and I see little gain."

"It is too early –"

"It will always be too early. His grief is becoming a habit with, I am sorry to say, a strong dash of self-indulgence. He needs to take an interest and if he will not shift for himself then he must be compelled to it."

"Compelled?" Joseph was secretly delighted and generally rewarded by the occasions on which Mrs Kent felt obliged to 'take charge' and he deftly helped her to the role. "I cannot compel –"

"No, Joseph, but I can." Mrs Kent's plump, homely features had taken on an aspect of gravity as she continued. "I have been considering Thomas' needs, not his fantasies you understand, but his needs."

"And they are? Besides taking an interest?"

Mrs Kent drove on unperturbed. "He needs to be comforted. To feel accepted and unashamed. And he needs something to look forward to."

"We have offered all that."

"Not hope, Joseph. And I said that those were his needs, not that we were the ones to provide them."

"Who then? Surely you cannot mean his mother. She –"

"Of course I do not mean Susanna. She would be absolutely the worst thing for him."

"At least we are agreed there." Joseph sighed in relief. "Thomas would insist on confessing and she would never forgive him."

"You're wrong there," Mrs Kent replied. "She would forgive him, she'd forgive him every day, always letting him know the effort it was taking from her to forgive such a sin."

Joseph nodded. "You have the right," he said, "and the weight of her sacrifice and his sin would –"

"Overwhelm him. But you are partly right. Thomas needs a woman."

Joseph sat upright in his chair. "Good God!" he cried, "that was precisely what got him into his present grief."

"And it will get him out again. But I am not talking of a harlot here, Joseph. Thomas needs a wife."

Joseph stared admiringly at his wife. She is a clever woman, he thought, far more so than she shows to the world and I think, dear God, I think she may be on to something here. But he said, "He would turn from any woman now. She would only remind him of the whore."

"Everything will remind him of the whore," Mrs Kent expanded, "she is the cause. But with the right girl, quiet, unobtrusive, kind, his ideas will change. He has entered the world of women, Joseph, whether we like it or not, and he will never leave it. So he must learn how to live in it."

Joseph smiled openly. "It is a fine idea," he said, "But I am not persuaded of any immediate success –"

"Of course not. This will take time."

"As I say, of any immediate success, but it does offer a hope. Something to look forward to. For us, at least." A thought occurred and he stopped, rubbing his chin. Then he said, "I wonder when Thomas will find himself, when he will know enough to try to shape himself."

Mrs Kent nodded. "I wonder, too," she said. "His mother shaped him to be as he is here now, Worthing shaped him to burst into confusion and we must shape him to leave it or, rather, to learn to live with it."

"But we are only the intermediaries, the go-betweens. Do you have any idea of who the next prime mover will be?"

"Certainly." Mrs Kent was emphatic. "Her name is Jane Quickfall."

"An unfortunate surname," mused the minister.

"Joseph."

"I'm sorry. Do you mean John Quickfall's daughter? Plain Jane?"

"The same. I will grant she is not a beauty and that may be to our advantage. Thomas will not manage with beauty right now. Please God, he learns to see another form of it. But I think with a little coaching Jane will be perfect."

Joseph was not feigning as he protested. "Coaching, Florence? This is not a play you are writing."

"It might just as well be," retorted Mrs Kent primly. "At least there is a sensible playwright to hand. And that, Joseph, is Jane's greatest strength. She is sensible. She understands the limits of her ambition and she will be pleased to meet them. There will be no fretting for what she cannot have.

And Thomas is a suitable target for her ambition. He is clever, educated and not without skills."

"Yes." Joseph's hands were busy with his pipe, his tone thoughtful. "He worked a farm for three years before his move to London, not entirely successfully I believe but …" He shrugged.

"He would have done better with a sensible helpmeet."

"Yes, probably. He certainly speaks with affection of the land. His 'country delights', he calls them."

Mrs Kent resumed her theme along with her needlework. Her fingers flew over the petit-point. "So Jane can be assured of a steady provider. Probably best as an educator, I think. Thomas is good with children and he has a passion for teaching. And there is no shortage of employment."

Joseph puffed contentedly but with a touch of apprehension as well. "So now we are determining his career as well as his wife," he said. "When will Thomas begin to determine for himself?"

"When he grows up." Mrs Kent was firm upon the point. "Let us not delude ourselves, Joseph. Thomas is a fine young man, his present fall from grace notwithstanding and I have a great regard for him. But he is a child. His imagination runs away with him –I have watched him discuss theology with you, he bounces about the room as he bounces from one extravagant notion to the next. His emotions often get the better of him, as this last sorry incident testifies all too well. No, for his own sake he needs to be taken in hand by a sensible woman."

As I was, thought Joseph, and it was the saving of me. Aloud he said, "Thomas will confess you know. Probably within five minutes of meeting her."

Mrs Kent nodded. "His candour can be alarming," she agreed, "along with his need for acceptance. But I do not think it will alarm Jane. She is a sensible girl and understands the ways of men."

"Surely," Joseph was quite shocked, "you cannot mean that she would countenance such transgressions?"

"Certainly not." Mrs Kent shook her head and smiled affectionately at her husband. "For all your learning, Joseph, you too can be quite naïve. Perhaps all men are. No, Jane will understand and she will forgive –not that the transgression was against her. But she will forgive him and Thomas will be thankful and take comfort from her forgiveness. And then she will take steps to ensure that it does not occur again. After all," Good Lord, thought Joseph, was that a wink, you saucy wench, "Thomas will have a legitimate and I daresay willing alternative for his," she paused, "his carnal needs."

Joseph heaved his bulk out of his chair and walked around behind his wife. He looked down on the greying hair caught into a loose bun and remembered when it was gold and hanging free. He bent forward, laying his hands upon her shoulders and resting his cheek against the top of her head. She took a hand from her needlework to reach up and pat his and he stood and she sat quietly for a minute or two. The early spring sun streamed through the casement window into the kitchen, lighting golden dancing dustmites and softening the room.

Florence gave his hand another pat, dismissive this time and Joseph returned to his seat. "You have much to do," he smiled, "when does the campaign begin?"

"Tomorrow. Firstly I must wake Thomas up again before he becomes too comfortable with his grief and lassitude. He will, of course, resist it and so I shall compel him."

As promised, Thomas' awakening began the next morning. He was summoned in peremptory fashion from his bed. "No, Thomas, this will not do. The day promises much and I will not have you lying here avoiding it. There is a bowl of porridge steaming on the kitchen table, growing cold as I speak. Get up, get dressed, wash your face and come to breakfast." Mrs Kent left the room.

Thomas dragged himself from his bed, groaning vague complaint and then gasping as he splashed cold water into his face. Half an hour later he was somewhat more wakeful and his belly was full of the porridge Mrs Kent had forced upon him.

"I have need of you this morning, Thomas. I shall be going to the markets shortly to attend to our provisions and also to seek a gift for my nephew, Ernest. He will be ten tomorrow. You will help me with the stores and advise me on the gift. But I will not be seen with you as you are. I would be embarrassed. There is a large bowl of warmed water for you in the kitchen. Please make a point of washing your hair, it is distressingly greasy. And shave. You presently resemble a Spanish bandit. And change those clothes. I will lay out for you a new shirt that I purchased from Mr Lowe, no, do not thank me, o I see that you were not going to. I wish to be gone within the hour." Thomas was dismissed.

Forty minutes later Joseph was leaning on a windowsill, watching his wife and lodger depart in a smart open carriage. Ordered two days ago, he had discovered. And the new shirt. The scheming wench had planned it all before she had raised the subject. He chuckled, then lumbered off to his study. Another day, another sermon.

"The shops will not be open before ten," Florence explained to Thomas, "so we have a little time in hand to take in the air and enjoy the sights." She was sitting upright, looking about with a measure of anticipation and excitement. There was some extravagance in hiring a carriage for half a day and Joseph would not be pleased with the account, so she was determined to extract the fullest amount of enjoyment. "Consider the day." She opened her arms as if to embrace it. "It is quite perfect." The day was indeed unusually clear, the sky crystal blue, cloudless. A light breeze still held a touch of chill and Thomas was glad of his coat. Yet the breeze, the sun and the movement of the carriage, clattering and occasionally bouncing over cobblestone, stirred his blood and brought a touch of colour to his cheeks.

They followed Florence's course through the streets of Mayfair, broad and clean but still and lifeless. "The gentry will not stir for some time yet; they are recovering from last night and preparing for tonight." Florence's tone did not suggest much admiration for this lifestyle but she was determined to be gay and made no further observation. "Look," she exclaimed, "what a remarkable house, see how the sun lights the columns and shines against the windows."

"It is the home of Lord Elgin," said Thomas, "built, I am told, upon the profits of the slave trade." Florence looked startled. What an odd piece of information, she thought, I wonder where he, o, of course. Her lips tightened. Still, it was his first remark of the day and she took heart from it. A clatter of hooves and wheels from the street disturbed her thought.

"Well, well," she said, looking about, "I appear to have been given the lie. Some are yet awake and stirring." They watched a small carriage draw up outside Lord Elgin's house. A liveried coachman jumped down from his perch and hurried to the pavement door. He opened it, bowing as he did so, and handed down a young woman. Thomas stared listlessly at her. Dressed in a white muslin gown beneath a pelisse of black lace she could be seen to shiver against the morning air but her steps up the marble stairway were heavy and slow.

"I wonder what her story is," murmured Florence and then, with a touch of exasperation, "ridiculous girl. Look at how she is dressed. Do you know," into Thomas' continuing silence, "that this winter past a great many women, thousands I believe, perished from the cold. From dressing like that. What a pass we have reached when the dictates of fashion override the demands of health and comfort." She shook her head, tutted and the carriage rolled on.

Thomas remained indifferent to the great houses and indeed there was often little to see behind the great stone walls and iron-wrought gates. But they paused before one where the gates stood open revealing the sweep of a gravel path to the marble stairway. The grounds were a park of stately trees, manicured lawns and well-trimmed shrubs and bushes and Florence noted Thomas beginning to show an interest. She followed his gaze to a pool, set about by smooth sculpted rock and the ubiquitous nymph. On the far side a small waterfall splashed silently amongst lily pads. "How pretty it is," she said.

"Yes," Thomas murmured, "it is very …restful." Nothing further was said but Florence made a mental note to amend the itinerary.

Their passage brought them back towards the shops and markets where life was beginning to stir. Florence was caught by the bustle and chatted on happily. Thomas leaned back and watched the world go by.

Then the carriage halted as a growing crowd swept across the street. The driver stood up on his seat and reported, "a troupe of tumblers, Madam. The crowd is quite thick but if you and the young master was to stand, you should see well enough."

Florence clapped her hands. "Excellent," she said, "help me up, Thomas, whoops," as the carriage leaned under their weight, "no, that will not do, I can only see to their waists, on to the seats." Thomas helped her on to the seat with the coachman lending a further steadying hand.

Now they could see into the cleared space where the tumblers performed. There were six, swarthy, Mediterranean, an older man, forty perhaps, heavily muscled under a tight-fitting cambric shirt and even tighter breeches, three young men in similar attire, strong and lithe, and two young women. The last was no more than a girl, perhaps fourteen years, but she moved with a poised confidence that spoke of years of training and performance. She sped towards one of the young men, driving her foot into cupped hands then rising on the thrust to spin backwards in an open somersault on to the shoulder of the older man. The crowd

72

cheered, some perhaps for the flash of thigh as her light shift opened as much as for the tumble. The older girl followed suit, alighting on the man's other shoulder. And all whirled and spun, building into pyramids that collapsed with sudden precision. A middle-aged woman stood to one side as five golden balls circled about her dancing hands. A boy and girl in multicoloured satin, silk bright red turbans on shaggy locks, ran about the crowd thrusting out their baskets, their cries for coin mixing with the shouts of the tumblers.

Then the woman checked the baskets and evidently decided that the limits of the crowd's generosity had been reached and the show ended as abruptly as it had begun. Florence sank back into her seat, her cheeks glowing. Thomas was more subdued but Florence thought she could detect more colour.

"What a delightful diversion," she said. "And now to our shopping. We are almost there, in fact, I think this will do. Edward," to the driver, "if you would be so kind as to wait here for Mr Kendall's and my return."

She bustled through the shops, Thomas in tow, stopping to sniff in the warm, moist aroma of the bakery before making her purchase, arguing with the fish vendor, "you should take my price before the sun ruins it, thank you, wrap it carefully, please, here Thomas, don't drop it." Past the barrows of fruit and vegetables, "an excellent pumpkin but not at that price, o well, in that case, here Thomas, add this to your bag." Passing by the drapery shop, "o, what beautiful material, wouldn't it go marvellously with the –no, I have already been too extravagant, come along Thomas."

By the time they reached the toyshop Thomas was feeling the weight of the bag on his shoulder. "Our last purchase," she consoled him. "Ernest's gift. Now, put the bag down carefully, here will do, just inside the counter, is that alright, thank you, now look about and then advise me."

Indifferently Thomas studied the toys on display. A top perhaps, a rolling hoop, perhaps not, a rocking horse, too young, dolls, those were for girls. He mooched about the shop while Florence told the shopgirl all about the tumblers and at length returned to her, holding a flat rectangular box. She took it from him and opened it carefully, then said emphatically, "How clever of you. Just the thing for a ten year old boy." She closed the box, handed it to Thomas and turned to the girl to complete the purchase. Thomas tried to remember what toys he had played with as a child. There was an old rocking horse that his father had constructed in a fit of enthusiasm for his first born, in a sorry state by the time it reached Thomas. But beyond that?

Books, of course, for reading, writing, occasionally sketching but they did not really count as toys. He remembered Susanna pulling him away from a rack of wooden soldiers the grocer had carved and painted in his spare time. "We have no time for frivolity," she had said sternly, the message as much for the grocer as for her son. "There is always plenty of useful work to be done." As indeed there was. Study and chores seemed to consume his time and on the rare occasions in which there was truly nothing to do and it was still too early for bed she counselled him to prayer. "You might take a little time to thank the Lord for giving you this leisure." Then he felt the box taken from his hands and the bag back upon his shoulder and he was whisked out the door.

Florence resumed her guided tour, "Ah, what a gorgeous little maid …such a handsome fellow, he thinks so, too …o for goodness sake, how does that woman breathe? she will do herself a mischief in those stays … ah, here we are." She led Thomas into the dark interior of a little shop and sat him down at a table. "You wait here, I shall order." She returned shortly, balancing a tray. Carefully she set it down and unloaded it. "An excellent piece of game pie, I know you enjoy it, coffee, ah, smell that rich aroma. And the piece de resistance, chocolate cake. Eat."

Thomas did as he was bidden and found himself eating with enthusiasm, the venison was delicious and the chocolate descended in black, cloying sweetness. Florence nodded, approving. "Excellent," she said, "now we must be getting back to Edward. There is one more call to make."

Half an hour later the driver reigned in his horses and consulted his watch. "We can only stay some thirty minutes, Madam, if we are to be back by three," he said. "Otherwise I must charge you a further crown."

"Thirty minutes will be ample, Edward," Florence replied. She turned to Thomas. "What do you think?"

They were standing at the entrance of the Chelsea Gardens. They bordered upon Kirmington and the last part of their trip had seen them pass through that suburb. Thomas had looked about anxiously and Florence had patted his hand. "I have given Edward a route that steers well clear," she had said and Thomas had relaxed. It was her first and only reference to James Worthing.

He followed her along perfect pathways between immaculate lawns. About them the work of the topiarist was displayed and Thomas gazed with growing interest. Florence was less constrained. "O look, how clever," she exclaimed, clapping her hands, "that shrub is in the very likeness of a pheasant." She led him into a glass house where Joseph Banks and others had planted seeds gathered from the furthest reaches of the globe, Africa, Australia, New Zealand and they gazed at the profusion of strange, exotic life, vibrant, impossible colour, shapes, dimensions. No place for the topiarist in this lush, unrestrained jungle. Thomas stood besides a small watercourse where a stream ran over glassy rock and thick moss and lichen. The water hung in mist in the artificial warmth and glistened on delicate ferns that arched and dipped and grew at their source into a brown, fuzzy curling fist. Close by a small smooth dark stemmed twisted tree stood in salty mud. A sign stood beside it. Te manawa read the sign, mangrove. He became absorbed and was startled by Florence's hand. "Enchanting, is it not," she whispered. "I sometimes think this is the heart of all things and reaches to our deepest heart. It was here before us and will endure long after our brief vanities are become dust and are forgotten. I find that strangely comforting." She patted his arm. "We must go now, Thomas. You have been standing like a statue for twenty minutes and I would not dare face Mr Kent with further expense." She paused, then asked quietly, "How are you feeling?"

Thomas understood the question and turned to face her. "Better," he said.

That night he dreamed of Chelsea Gardens. He dreamed that he was standing by the stream and he watched it grow and the glass house dissolve and fade away. The stream broadened and deepened and he thought he could dimly see where it became dark, a sinuous twist of serpent. The ferns arched higher, further, growing into one another and strange trees reached from either side of the stream, their branches and leaves folding into a soft canopy, holding out the sky.

He followed the stream in silence until it broke into a wide, open, rocky bowl. The banks reared steeply on either side, held by giant trees with massive trunks and branches that rose up forever. Crowding about them were smaller trees with reddish brown limbs and soft, pinelike, drooping leaves. He gazed at one tree that seemed to have grown as a fern for its leaves grew as delicate fronds along delicate branches and their green gave way to a mass of yellow bells.

On the far side high beneath an azure sky from a thin, smooth lip water fell silently then roaring as it crashed on to the first giant rock step, then swept roaring to fall again into a wide pool. It met the pool in foaming turbulence crashing up in spray that became mist that hung, glistening. Beyond the impact the water was still and heavy save where it flowed into streams that ran silently away into the bush.

He stood upon the rocky outcrop and his clothes loosened and fell away and the sun was warm upon him. Then he stepped into the pool that lapped about him in a cool caress. He moved further in and felt the water rise to his knees, sliding up, stroking his thighs, groin, buttocks and back, flowing over his shoulders. Then he pushed forward and dived into the crystal depths. For a while it was as though he were moving through space, his limbs working, flowing in new rhythms, vaguely surprising him for he remembered that he could not swim. He had no need of breath and sensed that it was being done for him.

As he drove further down the waters darkened but became warmer and more viscous. But they did not slow his movement, rather he seemed to be gathering momentum. Soon it was quite dark but he swam assuredly on. Then he could make out a dully glowing, reddish light and approaching it he saw that it was coming from a tunnel set in a wall of rock. He flowed into the tunnel and as he progressed along became aware that the rock sides were softening into flesh. Ahead the light grew, shifting from rose to gold and as Thomas flowed towards it an aching joy grew within him, enormous wonder and enormous certainty. Knowing that he was where he was meant to be, moving towards what he was meant to be. With the knowledge the colours dissolved and he became still and the dream passed into sleep.

Rangihoua

Perfectly erect, legs crossed before him, Rakau sits on the beach and savours the peace of the gods. Tawhiri has floated away from his brothers and the only signs of him now come with the occasional dark cloud drifting across the face of the moon. Where Rona sits desolate, empty gourd in hand. It will never be filled now. Does she meditate upon her moment of madness when she was human and had gone to fill her gourd from the stream? Does she wonder where the oath came from when the moon dipped behind a cloud and in the sudden darkness she fell over a root? For it was the ultimate curse: *you cooked head of a moon*, she had said. And now she will be forever alone, desolate, empty gourd in hand.

The waters of Tangaroa lap gently at the moonlit sand and they bear their own light, too, a glimmer that covers much of the bay. And in the rising bush behind him, the children of Tane go quietly about their business.

Rakau sits cross-legged in the sand. He discovered the posture many years ago and has learned to find the perfect centre where your muscles can relax, not holding you against tipping either forward or back. And he has learned that that same relaxation can flow into your heart and mind. He inhales the sweet, green salty breath and holds it there.

Three hundred feet above his wife grunts and moans. Sweat pours down her face and over swollen breasts. She squats on open thighs, supported by a woman on either side. They hold her steady with powerful, gentle arms while a third kneels behind and takes her weight. Another dozen girls and women crowd the whare. They breathe with her and grunt with her when a contraction hit home. They share the birth.

It is no place for a man and Rakau is mainly glad of it. Though his curiosity is piqued. He once took the body of a heavily pregnant woman killed in a marauding raid and carefully opened her belly to inspect the state of the child within. He studied its size and the tunnel to light and wondered at the passage.

I do believe the bones must move.

His part will come later. For now he cocks his head to the call of a kiwi, feels his balance shift and restores it. He breathes with the waves and feels his heart slow and the waters wash softly over his thoughts and cleanse his mind.

The birth is swift and easy. Why wouldn't it be? She is fit and in her prime. But it is her first child and, more importantly, it s the priest's child; with both parents of rangatira status the child is particularly important.

From the beach Rakau can hear the people sing welcome to the child; from the songs he can tell it is a girl. He already has sons and grandsons, too so the gender does not concern him.

I shall watch this child grow more carefully than I did the others, he thinks. I will watch her learn and I will teach her, too. She will be a wise woman for Ngapuhi; she will have much mana and her name will be remembered.

He rises to his feet and walks briskly away to the pa.

Later, when the rites are complete and the tapu lifted he carries the child back down to the beach. It is growing light by now and he sits and holds her, resting her head back against his feathered shoulder. And they watch Rangi pale and see Ra spread the colours of dawn over the eastern hills.

She is focussed from the start and Rakau joys in her curiosity. She walks and speaks early and proves to be clever. And she is beautiful although inclined to wide hips. Rakau calls her Tungaroa, Broadbottom.

CHAPTER 6

Thomas began to bestir himself. He rose without summons, washed and breakfasted with the Kents. He was still quiet but there was the beginning of an accessibility about him and he willingly entered into tasks that were found for him, shopping, running errands and more lately assisting with the strengthening of a parishioner's cottage that had been weakened by rot. He did not resume his lessons with his bible class but attended church regularly and seemed to find a kind of peacefulness there. And every day he would walk. He had started once for Chelsea but became unsettled and had turned aside to sit beside the Serpentine. There he found, settled in an opening through the banks, a small pond where ducks gathered and it became his habit to return to this spot, sit upon the bank and cast bread upon the water.

One evening he returned with a touch of excitement about him. "Do you know," he said to the Kents as they sat down to dinner, "I had the most extraordinary conversation today. I was sitting feeding the ducks when this gentleman joined me. He was an elderly man, a retired colonel he told me later, all stiff and brusque and military. Anyway, he settled on to a park bench and watched me feeding the ducks. They are become very familiar with me now and one or two will eat from my hand. Then he said, and Thomas' voice took on a gruff inflection, 'like ducks, hey?' I answered that I did and we sat in silence for a while. Then he said, 'mallards are best.' That's all, just, 'mallards are best.' I wondered for a while then asked him what he meant. He looked at me as though I was simple, then away he went. 'They're all dirty buggers,' excuse me Mrs Kent, I am merely repeating his words, 'they sh-, excrete everywhere, had one once that used to come on to the back porch each morning and poo upon me boots.'" Thomas giggled, then resumed, "'Regular as clockwork. And they're hopeless mothers, lay their demned eggs anywhere, seen 'em do it in a stream. Don't know how the breed survived. But still and withal, mallards are best.' I told him that I like mallards, too, their iridescent green and their funny waddle and he looked at me like I was a complete fool. 'Not talking about their colours, boy, or their wretched gait. Talking about eggs. And meat. Mallards are best.'" Thomas burst out laughing. "I don't know why I thought it so funny, but I was hard pressed to contain myself."

The Kents laughed with him, more in delight at his laughter than at the colonel and that night, as they settled for bed, Florence told Joseph, "I believe he is ready for the next stage."

At breakfast two mornings later she told Thomas, "I shall require you to accompany me on a walk this afternoon. We shall depart at two."

At 2.30 that day they were sitting in the parlour of John Quickfall. The master was out, attending to his drapery business, but Florence and Thomas were welcomed by his wife and daughter. Evidently they had been expected. They were bustled in, divested of cape and coat and seated at a table where coffee and cake were served. Now Thomas sat quietly as Florence and Mrs Quickfall discussed the exorbitant price of corn. Opposite Jane Quickfall also sat quietly. She was a homely girl with ill-defined, almost lumpish features. But her eyes were bright and her smile warm and when she spoke her voice was soft and modulated and her words considered.

Visits to the Quickfalls became another regular feature of Thomas' life and scarce a week would pass without Florence's summons to come with her to call. She never gave any reason and Thomas never thought to ask. Neither he nor Jane had much to say at these visits for the conversation was largely monopolised by the two matrons. But they were seldom unkind and often diverting and Thomas found a comfortable ease in their presence. A silent communication grew between him and Jane. Once, after Mrs Quickfall had delivered herself of a particularly ill-informed observation upon the fashion sense of the young, he watched Jane roll her eyes. He was initially shocked by the disrespect of the gesture but then relaxed as he realised how well it mirrored his own thought. Another pronouncement was greeted by a rueful smile and he found himself smiling back.

The two families inevitably met at church and a seating change that nobody seemed to notice saw them sharing a pew for Mr Kent's sermons. The Reverend Kent was a different man in church. His shyness and quick diffidence seemed to melt away as he strode to the pulpit. He believed in his ordination for the task and performed it with according dignity and confidence. Thomas always enjoyed the sermons. Delivered benignly they were frequently amusing and always to the point. Robert believed the Gospels were there for daily guidance and he wove his sermons into lessons for daily life, praising the virtue of Mrs Brewer for her charitable works ('blessed are the poor'), alluding to committee infighting ('blessed are the meek'). They had assembled to praise God ('where two or more men are gathered in My Name, there is My Church') and they were to be united in that brotherhood, to be kin to one another, kind to one another. Sin of the more extreme kind was left to the bishops and there was no mention of fornication.

The hymns were a joy. Thomas had a pleasant tenor and a quick ear for harmony and was delighted to find that Jane sang beautifully. He contrived to be seated beside her and when they rose with the assembly to sing hallelujah he would seek for a harmony to her part and their voices would blend as one, together, intimate. Quickly it became the accepted seating.

One afternoon in the Quickfall parlour Florence announced, "Thomas and Jane, I think you should go for a walk now. To the park, I think."

Mrs Quickfall nodded her assent. "Take your parasol, Jane," she said, "the sun is passing warm."

Thomas looked up in surprise but saw Jane rising calmly and mutely joined her. The two ladies saw them to the door. "I will wish to leave in about an hour," Florence said.

They set off towards the Hampstead common, a ten minute walk away, and Thomas paced with some anxiety. "I cannot but wonder what Mrs Kent could have been thinking," he said at last. "And Mrs Quickfall, too. For two unmarried people, unchaperoned, at large. I fear for your reputation, Miss Quickfall."

Jane spoke evenly. "I am thankful for your concern, Mr Kendall, but I have no doubt of my virtue and so my reputation is intact. Neither has my mother doubt of it."

This talk of virtue and reputation brought Thomas to a sudden remembrance of his own deserved reputation and he stammered as he spoke. "I meant no disparagement, no doubt. I do not doubt but I ..." His words faded to a mutter and he picked at the buttons of his coat.

Jane turned to face him. "Mr Kendall," she said kindly, "I fear you are upsetting yourself. It is a beautiful day for a stroll in the park and I, we have the confidence of my mother and the good Mrs Kent. What more do you want? Please," holding up her hand, "please, if you do not wish to accompany me you must say so. If not," and Thomas softened under her smile, "let us enjoy the day and the company." She cocked her head and raised her eyebrows in mute question, then nodded and continued on her way. Thomas fell in beside her.

But he could not shake the thought that he was there under false pretences. Mrs Quickfall and her daughter did not know of the stain upon him. Why had Mrs Kent permitted it? Good Lord, she had commanded it. Then he must set it to rights.

When the reached the park he guided her to a bench and with nervous gallantry handed her to a seat. Jane settled her hands in her lap and watched calmly as he paced.

Clearing his throat, he spoke hesitantly. "Miss Quickfall, there is an unfortunate event you needs be apprised of."

Jane bowed her head and answered quietly, "Then pray, apprise me."

"I am not the man you think I am."

Jane held her hand over her mouth. "And who do I think you are?" she asked.

"A man of virtue, Miss Quickfall," Thomas said miserably, "a worthy man, a useful man, a man who deserves his place in church."

"Yes," said Jane, "that is what I had thought. And you are none of these things?"

"None. I am far from grace. I have undone myself in grievous fault and am not fit company for a lady."

Jane stared into her lap. She was already apprised of the circumstances of Thomas' fall, for Florence Kent had spelled it out to her. "Seduced," Florence had said, "as part, I suspect, of a decadent game. Probably drugged. Perhaps he should have known better; he certainly does now. Indeed, he knows it too well and reviles himself for his part in it. He is truly repentant, one might almost say excessively so. That same capacity for indulgence that led him into sin now informs his guilt. He needs to own it but he needs forgiveness more. And yet he cannot, will not forgive himself." She had clucked disapproval. "That same indulgence. Can you forgive him, Jane?"

Jane had been confused. "But he has not sinned against me," she had answered. "Who am I to forgive him?"

Now watching Thomas, abject, wringing his hands, she was no less confused. But his sadness caught at her and she felt a sweeping kindness that unsettled her and made her stammer as she spoke.

"I, I have seen n-nothing to warrant such words. Nor Mother nor Mrs Kent neither."

"Mrs Kent knows." Thomas spoke dully, bitterly, "and I cannot conceive why she has not warned you against me."

Now shame at the sense of deceit plucked at Jane's thoughts and she stared mutely into her lap.

Thomas stammered into the silence, skittering between the drive to confession and the shame of the subject.

"Having p-polluted myself," he said, "I fear to pollute your goodness by speaking of such th-things."

Jane too was no less lost but kindness made her brave and she said, still to her lap, "I have heard that you fell into carnal sin."

"So you knew!" Thomas was aghast. "How can you bear to be seen with me?"

Jane shook her head, wondering, a thousand thoughts colliding. Her own life, content she supposed but only for as long as she did not look too far ahead. A warm, familial circle for now, but one that would inevitably shrink and it seemed likely that there was nothing that would replace it. Shrinking placidity. And the tumult of this man's life that reached to hers in a kind of promise. What was she thinking?

She shook her head again, trying to clear her mind, trying to remember what Florence Kent had said. "He has sinned but I cannot think but that he is more sinned against than sinning."

She spoke slowly. "We are all of us sinners, Mr Kendall."

"But there are degrees of sin and I, I ..."

"God sent His son to wash us clean in His own precious blood. Do you believe that?"

"Of course. But."

"But?"

Thomas shook his head.

Jane was becoming clearer. "I believe that true repentance leads to forgiveness and a new beginning. It seems almost a kind of," she struggled for the word, "perverseness? Is that it?"

Thomas nodded wearily. "Overweening pride," he said, "to believe that one's sin is so great that even God cannot forgive it." He smiled wanly. "I am quoting Joseph Kent."

Jane nodded, clearer still. "Precisely so. It seems to me, Mr Kendall, that you have sinned and that you truly repent. Your penitence shows in your confession and in your torment. I think you are a good man and I am happy to be seen with you."

Thomas breathed deeply and it seemed a kind of peace came over him. "You have the right," he said at last. "Thank you. There is a wilfulness in me that –"

"Please." Jane held up a hand. "Do not start another route." She offered him her arm. "I think we should be getting back now."

Upon their return, Florence sent Thomas on another walk. "It should take at least half an hour, Thomas. Mrs Quickfall and I wish to speak to Jane." So Thomas walked the streets again, but this time with a new lightness.

The three women gathered in the parlour. Florence took in the glow on Jane's cheeks and nodded to herself.

"Well?" she asked.

Jane was awhile in replying. Her arm carried the memory of Thomas' hand and she was caught in an odd mixture of elation and anxiety.

"I do not know what to think," she said at last. "He confessed, as you said he would. Or, rather he tried to. He berated himself, not company fit for a lady, he said, and something about polluting my goodness, but he never actually said what he had done. In the end I said that I had heard that he had fallen into carnal sin."

Mrs Quickfall tutted. "More reticent with the words than with the deed," she said.

"Now, Mary." Florence laid a hand on her friend's arm.

"He wondered how I could bear to be seen with him and I said that he repented of his sin, that I thought he was a good man and that I was happy to be seen with him."

"Good, good. And what did he say?"

He said, 'thank you'. He seemed relieved. And then we came home."

Florence nodded her approval. "Very well," she said. "And now we come to the heart of the matter. Would you marry him, Jane?" She was pleased that the girl did not feign surprise.

"He has not asked me. And I have seen nothing to suggest that he might."

"But if he did?"

Jane looked levelly at the older woman. "Do you mean if you persuaded him to?"

Florence paused, then nodded.

Jane looked down at her lap. "I would wish a man to ask me because he loved me," she said, "but I think I know more than to hope for that. I know I am plain –"

"Jane!" Mary Quickfall broke in. "You must not say –"

"Hush." Florence laid a forebearing arm again. "This is not the time for kindness."

"I know I am passing marriageable age," Jane continued, "and there have been few offers and those from men I do not think I could love."

"Do you think you could love Thomas?"

Jane nodded almost imperceptibly. "Yes," she murmured. "I see kindness and goodness in him. But, Mrs Kent," looking up, "I need to be loved, too."

"Love," said Florence softly. "We women talk of love, some of us live for it and die for it, too, but I think we rarely understand it." She turned to Mary Quickfall. "Did you love Mr Quickfall when he took you to wife?"

"I did not think of it," answered the other. "He seemed a good man with sound prospects. My parents approved."

"Yes," nodded Florence, "and that was the extent of my thinking when I married Joseph. But," she turned to Jane, "I love him now and have done so for many years. And," she added, "I have always respected him."

"Yes," Mrs Quickfall smiled, remembering. "I have always felt safe with John."

"And that," Florence was stern now, "is the issue with Thomas. Like you, Jane, I believe he is a good man. He is doing little with his life right now but he is educated, not without skills and has a great capacity for industry. His prospects are sound. But I cannot pretend to you that he has the stability of a Robert Kent or a John Quickfall. There is a wildness in him, a readiness to run to extremes. He could do great things with his life. But I fear he can be reckless, too."

Mary Quickfall was less concerned. "So can all men be reckless," she said. "They never entirely part company with the demanding little boy. But they can be cajoled and pacified." She nodded, agreeing with herself. "All they need is the steadying hand of a good, sensible woman."

"I pray you are right," said Florence. "But Jane needs to understand this before she decides. So, Jane, are you ready to decide?"

Jane stared into the middle distance. Shrinking placidity, she thought, spinsterhood, loneliness, a cause for charity. She remembered Thomas' hand upon her arm and the gratitude and vulnerability in his eyes when he had thanked her.

"If he asks me," she said, "I will accept him."

That night in the parlour Florence moved Thomas to the next stage of his shaping. With Robert watching gravely on, she spelled out the situation. "You are taking an interest again, Thomas, but you must needs gather further momentum. You must take steps towards a career. And you must take a wife. Clearly, Jane Quickfall is eminently suitable."

She was relieved Thomas did not evade in faintness or in protest. The lightness of being Jane had given him that afternoon persisted and while he was surprised, amazed even by the announcement he was not shocked. But he was speechless.

Joseph spoke into the silence. "Listen to Mrs Kent, Thomas. She is making great good sense."

"You need direction, Thomas, but you need an anchor, too. You need to take more responsibility and learn more of it. I will also speak bluntly and say that I think you need the warmth of a woman, o for God's sake," as Thomas buried his face in his hands, "how can you be so diffident to give or hear words about something you had no hesitation doing?"

Joseph sat back in admiration as his wife continued.

"You and Jane would be a very good match. She is a sensible girl and you need more sense in your life. Her virtue is beyond reproach which is more than can be said for yours. And she has a good heart. You are withal a good man who, I doubt not, would be a faithful provider and loving father. You are eminently suited. Each should be grateful for what he or she has found in the other."

Thomas stammered, "I am at a loss, I had not thought of Miss Quickfall but as a friend. What would she think -?" Understanding dawned. "Of course. She knew about my sin and you and Mrs Quickfall sent us to be together. This is all a plan, a scheme."

Joseph nodded. "And a very good one," he agreed.

Florence pushed herself out of her chair. "There is no more to be said now," she announced, "and the hour is growing late. I must to bed." She crossed the room to Thomas and took his hands. "Do not reproach us, Thomas. You have not been deceived or played, well, perhaps a little, but only to your advantage. Miss Quickfall is sincere. She is, I believe, quite fond of you and could learn to love you. Think on it." She left the room.

Thomas looked helplessly at Joseph. "I cannot keep up," he said, "too much is happening at once."

"I understand," replied the minister. "To tell the truth I am somewhat bewildered, myself. But I have every confidence in the ladies."

"It is not your life that is being planned."

"No, it is not, although," Joseph's eyes wandered left, remembering, "although. Anyway, they are probably right. Where is your life heading? You have studied a little, taught a little, farmed a little and taught again. And now? You have no home."

"I still have the farm. It is leased to Giles Wainwright."

"But you do nothing with it. You live in another man's home, you walk the streets and you feed the ducks. And you are alone."

Thomas bowed his head. "It is true. I am a worthless, useless wretch."

"No." Joseph was firm. "You are not, although if you continue as you are you may become so. You are a good man and there is much usefulness in you. But you must learn to become decisive, active. And indulge yourself less in self-pity."

Thomas and Jane were married two months later and a month after that they moved to North Thoresby. Thomas resumed management of his holding but found that the fifteen acres did not yield sufficient to support himself and his growing family. With his savings from London, including James Worthing's generous gratuity, and the small dowry John Quickfall had settled upon his daughter they were able to purchase the lease of the grocery/drapery store. They did not achieve great success but neither did they fail. They were comfortable and established and within two years were the parents of two girls, Susannah and Elizabeth. Thomas settled to a useful, productive life.

Moremonui

The world feeds upon itself as its parts collide. Along this coast the power of Tangaroa is seldom still: his seas seethe and separate into waves that race with the winds of Tawhiri across green depths. Closer to shore they rise, tower their silver sundering heads, smash into rocks and rip into pebbled sand, clawing and sucking it back.

The cliffs of Tane rise sheer to one hundred and fifty feet; here and there a pohutukawa clings to the uncertain slope, twisted roots exposed; they too claw their way over rock, bury into crevices of dull clay, the blood and flesh of Papa and suck what life they can find. Tangaroa eats at the base of the cliffs, tearing away the weak and Tawhiri howls into the empty spaces. And sends his winds and water too across the faces of the cliffs, clawing and sucking great rocks and seas of clay and gravel that thunder and rush to the beach below. There the rocks become new creatures of earth and sea and air, sucked into their sandy bed, stripped and smoothed, spending half their life in air, the other half beneath the waves. They become the homes for new life as kelp attaches itself as once pohutukawa did and fish drift across their faces and feed from their growth as once birds did. Mussels grow upon them adding sharp edges and intricate new angles. And when the tide recedes Ngati Whatua come down from the bush, sliding through great dunes and clamber over them. They find different shells for different eggs, for it is now kai moana they consume.

At Moremonui the cliffs run into a small valley that feeds its stream on to Rapiro Beach. Harekeke, flax, grows thickly along the stream and reaches up into the encircling hills where it is replaced by toetoe. Its silver plumes dip like waves breaking on the flax and bracken and the valley floor. Cool dawnlight, silver from the distant east that lies behind shadowed mountains, traces the topmost toetoe, but it is still dark in the valley.

Five hundred men are gathered there, five hundred toa, Ngapuhi warriors. They are bent upon war, this taua, out for utu. The take, cause, is a longstanding one but it is always recent, too, built and sustained in conflict. They carry with them pu, the new pakeha weapon, only a few but the men who wield them are gaining in marksmanship. Besides neither Ngati Whatua nor Te Roroa have knowledge of them. They will appear as magic and the roar of their firing alone casts confusion and panic. A great victory is assured and the men of Ngapuhi are hungry for it.

Hongi Hika lays his pu down carefully in the bracken and strokes the smooth, worn butt. He shrugs off a brace of cartridge belts and rotates strong shoulders at the release. He has been a warrior from birth and loves battle, when the senses fuse and the light explodes. He joys with a passion at the imminence of death and does not think of wounds. He loves it all, the cause and the planning that create the reality and sustain it. And soon there will be consummation.

It is quiet in the valley, a careful silence as the warriors rest and a few women and more slaves hurry their preparation of kai. There are no fires; shells are scraped open, strips of fish and pork laid down with kumara, all in a hush that breathes its own tension.

And then the valley erupts and the hills open to scrambling death and the tension explodes. Darting, stabbing, clubbing Ngati Whatua and Te Roroa are amongst them. Hongi flicks on the cartridge belts and roars for his slave. Then his pu is at his shoulder and the world contracts to a naked giant, not to his arms as they plunge and twist his taiaha's point further into a gaping, bubbling chest but to his chest, the enemy's chest and now! His finger squeezes, the pu flashes and the warrior flies backwards, clutching in disbelief at the mess he has suddenly become. The report comes as an exclamation point as Ngati Whatua and Te Roroa freeze with it. Those who see their man fall stay longer in the moment. Then there are further reports, men fall and the screams of the wounded are another layer of sound. The enemy is confounded and quick deaths are taken. Then they regather as the slaves reload and the flood surges and recedes and surges again.

Taoho of Ngati Whatua howls as his mere crushes through skull into brain. Then he howls again as a taiaha slices through lip, breaks through teeth and emerges spurting from the back of his neck He flings himself backwards, jerking his enemy towards him and again his mere is raised aloft, dripping.

Utterly vulnerable, Hongi's slave reloads the pu, cramming in powder and shot, no time for tamping, the butt thumps into the ground instead. His master dances lightly with a Ngati Whatua foe, their taiaha adding a darting, spinning counterpoint. Hongi's eyes are wide and he grunts and snorts as he fights but his face is a blue spiralled mask of concentration. Then there is a flurry of movement and the man is down, stunned by a butt to the side of the head and then he is dead. Hongi takes his pu from the slave and fires again. As the gun flashes he hears a voice roar, down, and the enemy drops to earth and the shot flies harmlessly above them.

The same thing happens with the next volley of shots and the musket's edge is weakened. Hongi sees a large group of men to his left charge into a body of Ngapuhi warriors where Pokaia, their rangatira is fighting. At their forefront is a man with a spear lodged in his face. Yet he roars, roars tangibly in blood and froth. Then Hongi's attention is taken by a wounded foe staggering towards him. A quick, peremptory slaughter and he is reaching impatiently for his gun. He brings it to bear on the heaving mass to his left in time to see the impaled man drive his mere into the face of Pokaia. The roar of Hongi's musket crashes over the huge wail that erupts from his warriors but the shot passes by without effect.

With Pokaia down the fight turns to flight that quickly turns to utter rout. Ngapuhi race wildly to the beach, leaving their dead behind them. Hongi runs with them, taiaha and pu in either hand. Powerful legs launch him over the bodies of iwi and enemy alike and he grunts as he runs. But inside he is screaming with a rage and bitterness that consume him.

Taoho runs with the pursuers. He is exultant but also thinking. It has been a fine battle and there will be great feasting tonight. But Ngapuhi are blood to Ngati Whatua and it would not be wise or tika to take them all. He instructs Teke to close upon Ngapuhi then draw a line in the sand. Pursuit beyond the line is forbidden and such is Taoho's mana, bloody and impaled, that it is obeyed. Three hundred and fifty Ngapuhi are saved, Hongi amongst them. But his brothers are dead. They lie with the dead and their heads are taken to be mounted on poles for display and ridicule and their bodies are eaten.

As Hongi walks stiff-leggedly away there is no room for anything but war.

CHAPTER 7

North Thoresby 1805

Thomas supposed that he had every reason to be happy. Money of course was a concern, as it always was, but he was confident that London brewers would pay a good price for his harvest of hops and that this would see them through the winter. And then next spring he might ... A sudden irritation filled the pause. God, but he was tired of having to think about money. He accepted that as a father and husband he had responsibilities, foremost amongst them the responsibility to provide, to get money, but that made it no less tiresome.

His musings were interrupted by the tinkling of the bell above the door and looking across the room he saw Mrs Fothergill, precariously balanced in the narrow opening, one hand upon the handle, the other upon her cane, Mrs Fothergill whose dumplings had once delighted his father, now old and frail and vacant. He hurried across the room and guided her carefully to a seat by the counter, turning his head from the smell of age and urine. As she bent, settling into the chair, pressure shifted on the gases within her and she belched. She smiled at the brief release, then her eyes closed and her head lolled back against the chair. Soon she was snoring. Thomas watched her, torn between compassion and disgust, praying that she would remain continent during sleep.

He collected her meagre provisions, mainly biscuits and port, and placed them in a small box which he set beside her. Later, if she were still asleep, he would bring his horse and buggy to the front of the store and carry her out to it. Then he would take her to a dilapidated cottage on the outskirts of the village, lay her down on her cot, spread foul, thin blankets over her and leave her there. He had done this often and every time it felt like a betrayal. He had discussed with Jane the possibility of bringing her to their home but both knew they would not endure it. Jane treated this knowledge calmly but it ate at Thomas.

Now he leaned upon a barrel of flour (taxes up, sales down, profits negligible) and watched the thin autumn sun filter through the dusty window panes (must clean them) over boxes, barrels, glinting dully on bottles. And listened to Mrs Fothergill snore. Does she dream, he wondered. Does she think about her life, about what has been and what is to come? Does she even think at all? She barely spoke these days and the little she had to say was addressed to those long gone. Spittle flecked loose lips over toothless gums and she grunted and farted quietly. More like an old dog than human. Beyond reach, care, understanding. Like his father. That thought deepened his growing depression but he did not turn from it. He would see him again tomorrow, he supposed. Sit with the old man he had never known and who now knew him not at all. Talk with forced enthusiasm about Jane and the children, the store, the weather for God's sake. About anything to fill the silence or worse, to block out the old man's bitter words, his profanity and his obscenities. And he would sit with him alone because Jane and the children no longer accompanied him. Thomas would have understood if her tender womanhood had recoiled from the old brute, but it was not that. "He is an old man," she had said, "lost in his dotage. He does not know what he is saying or who he is saying it to. And in the end, they are only words." And she was kind to his brother Edward, now forty and still living in the family home, running the farm in a haphazard manner, surly and distant. So —impossible to believe – it must be Susanna, his sainted mother.

"Why?" he had raged. "You see how much she has to endure. Alone with those two, those ..." Words failed him. "How can you be so careless of kindness, of your Christian duty?"

Jane shrank before his anger, pale, unhappy but resolute.

"Please, Thomas, I do not wish to quarrel with you –"

"We are already quarreling."

"And it breaks my heart. I know my duty and it is my greatest wish to be a good wife to you. And for three years now I have tried, I have really tried, Thomas. But I can't –"

"Won't, more like."

"No, I can't. It eats at me, it makes me ill."

"My mother makes you ill! How dare you! That woman is a saint, she has sacrificed and suffered. She has endured ingratitude and unkindness and she asks so little in return ..."

Jane felt the tears welling and did not try to hold them back. She knew they touched Thomas and softened him. But until now she had had little need of them. Until now they had enjoyed an easy companionship, not without its tensions and anxieties of course, particularly in intimacy, but companionable nonetheless. Each had been keen to please the other and this brought kindness and humility, too.

But from the beginning Jane had struggled with her new family. Old Edward's profanity had initially upset her but soon she had come to see the pain behind it and the more she saw of Susanna the more she understood the bitterness. Young Edward's distance she found unnerving. Then she recognised that there was nothing personal in it; indeed, it seemed an admirable way to manage and she thought she saw a serenity within it. Whereas Thomas saw it as uncaring, surly and utterly lacking in filial duty. And then one day she watched Edward helping Susannah with her first tottering steps and saw the absorption and tenderness and was quite won over.

But with Susanna she encountered an implacable resistance to all the generosity she could muster. The smallest kindness would be turned aside or, worse, somehow converted into something self-seeking or self-aggrandising ('o see how pride informs your judgment, Jane') and she sank into a bitterness of her own. All this she might have managed, even the pious coldness towards the girls, but not the way Thomas responded to it. She would watch him flinch, then close his eyes and absorb the blow or flinch then turn the wound aside. And afterwards he would be terse and cold and shrink from her touch.

Finally, after reflection that turned to brooding and vague letters to her mother and Florence Kent, she had taken her stand. Fearfully, guiltily, but resolute.

"It makes me ill."

She knew better than to try to explain it or call it something else, there was no gentle synonym for malevolence. Instead she called herself irrational and begged for forgiveness.

Thomas had turned to the Kents for support and advice and was appalled when neither was forthcoming. "We do not think it appropriate to take a position on what is essentially a domestic concern," Joseph had written in response to his plea. Nor was the local pastor inclined to intervene. So Thomas had fumed and raged, kicking a chair to pieces then stopping, horrified, as he heard his daughter wail in fright. He implored, he sulked and he thought he had gained some compromise in Jane's agreement to sit with her mother-in-law at church. But then he found himself ensconced in a frosty silence that seemed to utterly contradict the meaning of the occasion. And so church became another matter for endurance.

Susanna was understanding and forgiving. Her own pain at Jane's behaviour was as nothing —she was, after all, well used to cruel and unreasonable treatment and the Lord would give her the strength to bear it. Rather, her concern lay with Thomas and the children and her fear for the welfare of their souls with such an unnatural wife and mother. She had to wonder though whether some judgment might be seen in Thomas' rush to matrimony and in his failure to consult with her. Still, she was not one to carp over past wrongs or carry resentment and she would pray for them all. Thomas was touched by her goodness and did not speak with Jane for a full week. His resolve of silence was finally broken less by an impulse to forgiveness than by his response to her warmth and willingness in their bed. But a barrier had been laid between them and it was a long while before they returned to something approaching their former ease.

The insipid sun sank further in the pale and distant west and cold and shadow spread through the store. Mrs Fothergill shivered in her sleep and Thomas took a blanket from a pile and settled it about her shoulders. She might just as well keep it; they weren't selling anyway. Indeed, nothing much was selling, besides the port and sherry and gin. And laudanum. The medicines of numbness and forgetfulness. Across the channel the war with Napoleon rolled across Europe, taxes rose to meet the expense, the population dropped as young men departed and died and briefly swelled with the return of the maimed and the mad. Here in Thoresby they were largely safe from the epidemics that regularly swept London and the other cities but poverty reached for them too. Thirteen hundred General Enclosure Acts, driving small landholders from subsistence, had been passed in the last forty years; another thousand would follow in the next twenty. Workhouses grew like a cancer and the great factories drew in more and more child pauper apprentices who laboured and starved at the great mechanical looms that swallowed the work of the weavers. And as their employment shrank and disappeared and the crofters' cottages fell empty and those who had worked their own land laboured for a pittance on the great estates, the tendrils of poverty reached upwards and now Thomas, landholder and grocer, looked about the small, dark, empty store and listened to an old woman snore. He was bored and lonely; in sudden, petulant anger he brought his fist down upon the barrel, then stamped across the room and flung open the door. A dirty cobbled street lay empty before empty fields.

I am wasting my time, he thought, and decided upon the instant to close for the day. With new purpose he collected the day's takings –one miserable shilling- then hurried to an adjoining field where he harnessed his ancient pony to a more ancient buggy. Back at the store he carried Mrs Fothergill out and settled her in the buggy, locked the store and urged the pony away. Half an hour later Mrs Fothergill was seated at her rickety table, fire burning in a small grate, port in hand and chatting with ghosts and Thomas was approaching home.

His spirits lightened as the house came in view, a small thatched cottage, simple but sturdy. Smoke plumed from the stone chimney. He released the pony to forage its small field and walked swiftly towards the house. Hens pecked at the dry earth of the front yard and reached their necks through tight fencing that surrounded the vegetable garden. Jane had proved a keen gardener and already rows of cabbage and cauliflower showed a healthy growth. She does more than I, thought Thomas sourly, tending the children, the house, the hens and the garden while I twiddle my fingers in an empty shop.

But as he pushed open the solid oak door the sourness passed quite away. "Daddy!" A small figure raced down the corridor and Thomas fell to his knees, opening his arms. "Daddy!" Chubby arms encircled his neck knocking his wig to the floor, warm chubby cheeks soft against his stubble, his heart swelling and aching in his joy in her, stroking lustrous dark hair, babbling to each other. "Va hens laid eggs and Elizabeff pooed on va bed." "Did they? Did she? Ah, my lovely little muffin."

Then down the short corridor, Susannah in his arms, to the kitchen where Jane stood at the wood stove and little Elizabeth crawled upon the bare boards. The last of the autumn sun streamed through the western window and shafted through the steam from the iron pot. The smell of stew hung in the warm air. And Thomas remembered the reasons he had to be happy.

But later that night, warm under featherdown, the outer world was still there.

"Susannah is growing fast, she needs new clothes."

"I'll bring material from the store."

"Can we pay for it?"

"It's ours."

"Not until it's paid for."

Thomas felt a spurt of anger. "Money," he gritted, "always money. Can you speak of nothing else?"

He heard Jane draw a breath sharply, but she answered quietly, "I am speaking of clothing for our children."

Then Thomas' anger turned to shame but the tension remained and he jerked from the bed. The floor was cold under his bare feet and the chill air reached through his cotton nightshirt. But for a dim puddle of candlelight the small room was wreathed in shadow as he paced agitatedly, sightlessly and caught the leg of the bed. Pain shot through him and he hopped wildly clutching his foot, overbalanced and fell. A snort of laughter broke from the bed and rage consumed him.

"Damn!" he shouted, slamming his hand on to the floor, on to the buckle of his shoe, "damn!' again as the metal cut into a finger. A wail rose from the adjoining room and Jane slipped quickly from the bed, swept up the candle and was gone, leaving Thomas huddled on the floor, sucking his finger in the dark. The sharp pain subsided quickly to a dull throb but despair filled him as he kneeled against the bed, his breath coming in deep heaves that stopped just short of sobs. The air bathed him in its chill but he made no move towards the warmth of the bed; rather he welcomed its icy touch and wished it would consume him utterly.

Then strong hands were at his shoulders, pulling him to his feet, laying him on the bed, drawing the quilt over him. And his head was drawn to her full breasts as she stroked his hair.

"Hush," she crooned, from one baby to another he thought, "you still suffer too much. All will be well, all will be well, we will manage." His anger and shame evaporated with the warmth and closeness of her and he raised his head and fumbled at her nightdress, still open from his son's feeding. She laughed softly and moved away to pull it over her head, then drew him back to her. His hunger soared and his mouth was at her nipple, tasting her milk, and his hand between her thighs, stroking her to readiness; then there was only Jane, her sigh, his moan, Jane, and the slide to oblivion.

He woke the next morning with new resolve, a drive to industry and when Jane arrived in the kitchen she found the wood stove blazing and gruel bubbling in the pot.

Thomas reached across the table and took her hand in his. "I must bestir myself," he said. "I will collect the dray and horses from Edward this afternoon and load the hops tonight. Tomorrow at first light I will leave for London."

Jane nodded. "It will be a relief to us all," she said.

Later that morning Thomas, Jane and the children drew up in their buggy at the church gates and made their way inside. Susanna was already there, kneeling alone in the foremost row. They joined her in silence and settled to the morning service. But there was no joy, no comfort in it and when the baby began to fidget and then cry Thomas found himself wishing to be anywhere else. Jane slipped away with the child but now Susannah became scratchy. "How much longer, daddy?" she asked and Thomas heard his mother click her tongue in disapproval. "Not long, sweetheart," he whispered. Too long, he thought.

A practised flick and the line arcs over the still pool. Edward carefully watches the ripples flow out, fade and merge. He is sitting crosslegged on the grassy overhang, the base of his fishing pole firmly in his left hand, the middle resting on the index and middle fingers of his right. He watches the water and the cork buoy for any suggestions of movement and feels for it through the line. Fat worms slide in a small wooden pail beside him; three stout perch lie still beside the pail.

Behind him sheep graze in stubbled fields that reach back to the Kendall farm. On the other side of the pool and the slow-running stream that feeds it stand birch, elm and oak. Edward inclines his head towards the call of a thrush, just listening. His hair, cut short with kitchen shears stands up in matted tufts, his plain, heavy features are grimed with earth as are his clothes, stout leather jerkin and moleskin trousers. But if he resembles Poor Tom, Edward would see nothing amiss or lacking in reason in his appearance; he is warm and comfortable and the fish are biting. Even if they were not, this is as good a place as any to be. Not that Edward would concern himself with such thoughts, or many thoughts at all for that matter as he sits and baits his hook and watches for the ripples and listens to the birds. If happiness is to be found in being in the moment, he may well be a happy man.

His keen hearing picks up the sounds of an approaching pony and human voices. He recognises his mother's tone but does not trouble to make out the words. He is not interested. But there is a faint flicker of what may be hope as he draws in his line, gathers up his catch and moves to higher ground to see who is with her. The picture of Jane and the children dissolves; there is only Thomas. He listens to the faint thud of his boots upon the earth as they take him to the hedgerow. He waits there until the trap has passed, then follows it silently.

Susanna halted the pony in the front yard, declining Thomas' offer of assistance as she climbed down from the trap. "I may be aged but I am not yet infirm, I thank you." Then, "Edward, what are you doing here? Have you left your father unattended?" Edward made no reply and she stamped away, trailing prayers for assistance with her solitary, unappreciated tasks.

Thomas too looked at Edward impatiently. "Why did you leave him? What have you been doing?"

Edward spoke slowly. "He seemed comfortable when I left him." He shrugged. "What is to be done? He will die soon and will be glad of it."

Thomas knew the words were true but was still unsettled by them. He shook his head but made no answer and busied himself unfastening the harness. Edward came around to the other side to help. "Here are some fish for you," he said, holding up the perch. "Susie likes fish."

"Susannah!" Thomas' tone was sharp. "Her name is Susannah, not Susie." Dear God, he thought, why do I do this? I am offered a kindness and I respond with a snarl. "Thank you," he said, "I am sure she will enjoy them."

They unbuckled the harness and released the pony into an adjoining field, then backed the trap into a small shed. Thomas caught his breath at the sour, stale stench that enveloped his brother but held back the impulse to comment upon it.

When it was done he gazed towards the house. "Well," he said, "now I must go and visit with Father."

Edward looked at him curiously. "Why?" he asked.

Thomas shook his head, disbelieving. "Why?" he said in turn. "Because he is my father and it is my duty." A spurt of anger overtook him. "As it was your duty to watch over him this morning while Mother was in church."

Edward stared back impassively. "I mixed the laudanum you gave me in with his port and he fell asleep. What does it serve to watch a sleeping man?"

In his growing agitation Thomas could find no answer. Then Edward asked, "Do you think a large dose would kill him?"

Thomas' eyes widened and he stammered as he spoke. "I have no idea. Perhaps. Why do you ask? Do you plan to kill him?"

Edward nodded. "Aye," he said. "I think it would be best."

"For God's sake! Do you know what you are saying? 'It would be best' to kill our father? Have you lost your sense? Why? Why?"

"To relieve his suffering."

Thomas stared at his brother and a thousand thoughts squeaked and fluttered against one another. "How can you be so calm," he began, then broke off. Edward waited patiently.

He tried again. "You are speaking of one of the greatest sins."

"I am thinking of a kindness."

"A kindness? To murder your father?"

"Aye. To relieve his suffering."

"Very well." Thomas was a little more composed now. "The intent is well-meaning. But it is not your place. It is for God to decide."

"Perhaps," Edward answered, "but Father is over ninety now and has been in pain for a long time. How much more suffering does your God want from him?"

"My God? He is your God too. There is only one God."

"Why does he want Father to suffer?"

"He doesn't. He loves us all. We are His children."

Edward shrugged. "Funny way to treat a child."

"Do not mock Him, Edward. Do not mock. Your intentions may be good but you are speaking of terrible sin. I forbid you utterly to consider this further."

Edward smiled then, a slow, easy smile. "You sound just like Mother," he said. Then, for there was nothing further to be said now, he concluded, "I will go and harness the horses to the dray. I'll wrap the fish and leave them in it." He moved away.

Thomas called weakly after him, "What will you do?"

Edward paused, considering. "I think I'll do some more fishing."

Later that afternoon Thomas sat in a small, dark, stuffy room with his sleeping father, thankful that that was all that was required of him. What does it serve to watch a sleeping man? The old man had shrunk from the disease that ate him from within and even in repose his features were gaunt and tight and creased in bitter lines.

Thomas bowed his head. Dear God, he prayed, forgive him his sins and bring him peace. Thy will be done but bring him peace. A random thought crossed his mind. God manifests His will through His instruments. Could it be that Edward was such an instrument? Angrily he pushed the thought away. Preposterous. He was thinking like a heathen. He needed counsel. Joseph, yes, on Wednesday he would be seeing Joseph, he would prevail upon him for advice. The thought lightened his mood and he rose to his feet and left the room.

He sat with Susanna, impatient to be gone, away from this bleak house. He forced down the bland, dry cake she forced upon him and listened with only half a mind as she catalogued his father's ailments. When he rose, her mouth tightened. "I am not entirely happy with your taking the dray," she said. "It smacks of labour upon the Sabbath."

"It is only a form of transport. Like the trap and pony. Like walking."

"So you say, and I hope God sees it that way. But I trust that is all you will do with it. You are not thinking of loading your harvest before tomorrow?" It was less a question than a command.

"No, Mother." Thomas kissed her dry cheek and left with the lie heavy on his heart.

CHAPTER 8

London

O God! O shit! O *fuck!*

His back against the slimy alley wall, eyes darting, no one, nothing but crap and junk and two scrawny thirteen year old boys.

"Look. You got it wrong. I done nothin'."

"That's not what Mr Gumball says." An adenoidal twang. "Is it, Mick?"

"It's not." A brogue now. "He says you're a fuckin' thief, Ginge. He says you held back on him."

"I never. I never." The boy against the wall was panting, pale blue eyes wide, freckles bright on white cheeks. "I give him all I had. Honest. Ask Peter."

"And so we have. Course it was hard understandin' what he said, with his teeth smashed and all. But we thought he said you was a fuckin' thief."

The two advanced carefully, watching the third boy's hands for a blade. Adenoids giggled. "You shoulda heard him squeal, Ginge. I thought –what the fuck?" His head turned quickly at the sound of approaching steps, then he relaxed. It was just another kid. "Piss off, you. This ain't your concern."

The kid halted. He was of their age but more heavily built, his simple linen smock tight against broad shoulders and a deep chest. "You must not hurt him," he said slowly.

"No?" Mick was cautious. The fucker looked strong but there was something not quite right about him. A pretty boy but the eyes were vague. "You goin' to stop us?"

The boy nodded gravely. "You must not hurt him," he said again. "It is wrong."

Adenoids laughed suddenly. "He's a fuckin' dummy, Mick. Strong probably, but I bet he's slow. I could smack him silly before he'd know he'd been hit. You watch Ginge. I'll see to the dummy."

He advanced on light feet and spoke with exaggerated slowness. "Now go away, piss off, understand, or," suddenly viciously, "I'll fuckin' hurt you."

The other stared placidly back. "No," he said, "you must not –"

"Hurt him. I know. Don't say you wasn't warned." The punch came with the last word and it took the boy hard on the cheek. Adenoids stepped back to enjoy the moment while the other patted at his face and his eyes narrowed.

"Want more?" Adenoids shuffled up, fists raised and the boy lifted his own in uncertain mimicry. To no avail as a boot, metal-capped and all took him sharp in the thigh.

"Oww." It was what a child would have said.

Adenoids skipped in, dancing, his moment in the limelight, heroic at last. He pummelled the boy's face in short, stabbing, single blows that were no sooner delivered than he was at a safe distance, taunting. He over-reached himself, of course, and as his fist homed in on a bleeding gash his arm was suddenly caught in a grip so forceful that it terrified him. He shrank and then two hands were upon him and they were dragging him in, then fingers lacing at the small of his back and his spine began to bend. He tried to scream but there was no breath in him. Then he was released. He buckled at the knees and something crashed against his head and he was falling unconscious into the leavings of a chamber pot.

Mick fumbled at his jacket pocket, Ginge entirely forgotten, which proved to be a foolish thing. For as the knife came out and he stepped towards the boy Ginge took him hard with a heel in the back. He fell forward on to his hands and knees, then screamed as a heavy boot crashed upon his knife hand, holding it there between broken fingers. Then grunted as Ginge kicked him again and he twisted against his imprisoned arm. And screamed again as the arm broke. But now it was free as the boy released him and moved to catch at Ginge, pulling him off-balance as he steadied himself for a kick to the head.

"No," he said. "You must not hurt him. You can go now." He turned and walked back to the alley way opening. A wheel barrow, wooden frame and iron wheel stood there and he trundled it easily away before him. Ginge scurried alongside.

"Thanks, mate, you saved my fuckin' neck. Those bastards woulda done me proper. Hey, wait up, slow down, who are you? I'm Ginge."

The boy settled the barrow down, then turned and put out his hand. "My name is Richard Stockwell," he said gravely.

Ginge pumped the proffered hand. "It's good to –shit! Ow, let go." He rubbed his knuckles. "Gawd, you got a grip. I can see why Charlie give up." He turned to the barrow, raised it and took a few steps before setting it down again. "That's heavy. Is that how you got so strong?"

Richard shrugged. "I suppose so. I've been pushing it for a long time."

"That right? Where you takin' it now?"

"I'm taking it back to the bakery. I must go now. My father is expecting me."

"That right? Your dad's a baker, eh?"

Richard raised the barrow and wheeled it away without answering. Undeterred, Ginge hurried alongside and chatted into the silence. "So. A baker, eh? I suppose you get fed proper then. That's probably why you're big and strong. That and pushin' this barrer." He prattled on until they came to the bakery where Richard left him.

"Goodbye, Ginge," he said and went inside.

The windows were opened for the cold air from the street and snow had piled in small drifts on the counter and melted on the floor. The room is not warm enough, Richard thought, Father has let the fire go down, Mrs Haslem's order will not be ready. At the back of the room where the air should have been shifting in the dark, John Stockwell stood beside the furnace, lost in meditation.

Richard hurried to the furnace, slipping on a pair of gloves to open its door. The fire was far from dead and could be readily revived but Mrs Haslem's order would not be ready. He loaded coal from the scuttle into the fire and spread it into new flame. John noticed his son.

"Ho, Richard, what are you, o I see, good lad, got the fire back. I must have drifted off for a minute or so. Good Christ!" he was momentarily alert. "What happened to you?"

Richard touched his face and his fingers came away sticky.

"Here," John crossed to the table, took up a rag and dipped it into a pail of water. He patted gently at his son's face. "You been fighting? That's not like you. Did someone try to take the money?"

"Two boys were going to hurt another boy," said Richard. "I stopped them" He was vague about the details.

"Well." John stepped back, bloody rag in hand, you'll carry a scar on your cheek; we'll say it is a duelling wound, a mark of honour and it will be quite romantic."

Richard stared uncomprehending.

"Don't touch it or you might start the bleeding again. Any loose teeth?" A probe revealed a wobbly one in a back corner, "lucky," and his nose was intact, "luckier still. Anywhere else?"

"He kicked me in the leg."

The skin was not broken but already the thigh was bruising black.

"Let's see your hands." His left hand was unmarked but the knuckles on the right were swollen. "Christ, Richard, you hit him hard."

"I'm sorry. I didn't want to hit him but he was hurting me and he wouldn't stop."

John patted him on the shoulder. "You have done well, son. I'm proud of you. I hope the boy you saved is grateful."

"He is, Mr Stockwell, sir, your honour." Ginge scuttled into the room, "gawd, it's nice and warm here; ahh," he closed his eyes and looked as though he would weep, "that smell, that smell."

Ginge provided John with an accurate account of the encounter. He found it needed no embellishment and he told it well. Richard kept the furnace up and turned the bread for Mrs Haslem. It was a fine bake and if Mrs Haslem were put out by the delay she would feel compensated by the quality.

The loaves were ready and wrapped and placed in the barrow.

"Love to help you, mate," said Ginge, "but pushing a barrow's a one man job." He turned to John. "Anything I can do here to help, Mr S? To show me gratitude?

John shrugged. He had been woken alert by Richard's return and diverted by the boy's story but now he was becoming vague again.

"Make my father a cup of tea," said Richard. "Make yourself one, too." He pushed the barrow out through the doorway.

He returned an hour later and the last batch was nearing readiness. Ginge slipped on the gloves and opened the oven doors with a flourish and Richard lifted it out.

"We thought this should be the last order for the day, didn't we, Mr S? Take it nice and easy, mate, no hurry, you've had a hard day."

It was growing dark when Richard returned. He trundled his barrow into the store and set it down by the counter. His arms were very tired, his leg throbbed and he peered over swollen cheeks through puffy eyes. He saw his father settled in his old chair, leaning back, toasting his toes in the last warmth of the embers. He held a mug of tea on his stomach with two hands. Ginge sat beside him, tea in one hand, a fresh crust in the other. He waved the crust at Richard. "Just in time," he said, jumping up. "kettle's boiled," he searched, "shit, only two mugs, never mind, here, have mine, I'd finished it anyway. And a seat, Richard, have a seat, here, here by the fire …"

Richard settled by the fire and carefully nibbled at the bread Ginge offered him and softened it in hot, sweet tea. Ginge sat on the counter and Richard noticed that it was clean and dry. The shutters, he also registered, were closed and a small lamp added to the embers to light the room.

John had opened his eyes at the sound of voices. He stared at Richard as if remembering.

"How are you?" he said.

"My face hurts, my leg hurts, my hand hurts."

Ginge was concerned. "I'm concerned, Mr S," he said, "Richard is not well, he needs rest. And food." He turned back to Richard, "your dad says there's cold meat and cheese at home and veges, too. That's what you need, mate." And back to John, "Food and rest, Mr S. Shall we be going now?"

He saw John and Richard out of the bakery and stood beside John as he locked the door.

The walk home was only a short one and Ginge was still concerned as he helped Richard through the door and on to a seat. "A blanket for him, Mr S while I start the fire?"

Under Ginge's prompting John found Activity again and began preparing vegetables. Ginge laid an old newspaper and some damp kindling on to the grate. The fire was slow to take and he lay in front of it and blew into the sparks.

"I know more about cleaning the bastards."

With slow, careful precision John sliced the pumpkin and potato and poured them into the pot. He was beginning to move away but was still close enough to listen to the boy prattle on.

"There, got you. Now, Mr S, do you have any rags?"

John motioned to a corner.

Ginge selected the thickest piece and took it outside. He was back soon and the rag was wrapped about a number of small icicles. "Here, hold this against your cheek, mate, it'll keep the bruising down."

John might have been an intelligent man once and that intelligence recoiled. *This is all a performance, this is all horseshit. This boy is no friend to Richard, nor to me.*

"... I see you fancy pumpkin, Mr S, I know where I can fetch one tomorrow, I'll bring it to you. In thanks for your hospitality."

I would be an idiot to let him into our lives. Look at what he has brought already.

Richard spoke through puffy lips. "If you cannot kip here," he asked, "where will you go?"

Ginge swallowed. "I got nowhere, mate. I can't go back to Gumball, you've seen what waits for me there." His voice trembled. "I suppose I'll just have to look for a hedge or a bridge and hope I don't freeze to death." He looked up at Richard with moist eyes. "That can't be right can it, mate?"

"No," Richard was firm. "It would be wrong to turn you out." He turned to John. "Wouldn't it, Father?"

John might have been a compassionate man once and it was not a night to put a dog out.

"Yes, Richard," he said, "it would be wrong."

Richard was still tired and sore the next morning but he sipped between swollen lips the gruel Ginge had prepared for him.

"Now, are you bundled up warmly? Good, good, God, that's a warm coat you've got. Now you take it easy today, Richard, don't push him, Mr S. And I'll see you both later."

When Richard and his father returned home that evening, Ginge was waiting for them, a satchel slung over his shoulder. He bustled in with them and deposited the contents on the kitchen table.

"See what I brung you, a fresh pumpkin, mates. And leaks. And for dessert," he flourished, "three apples. And I ni-, got some more tea. And another mug."

He was still talking as he cleared the table away.

"You got a mum, Richard? Got a missus, Mr S?"

John was lost in the fire, so Richard answered. "My mother died when I was young, I don't remember her. Michael went away and hasn't come back."

"Michael?"

"My brother."

"I remember my mum," said Ginge. "Fuckin bitch, sold me to a chimney sweep, what a bastard he was. I hope the cunt burns in hell forever."

John gazed placidly into the flames but Richard was upset. He spoke without prompting for the first time.

"You should not curse, Ginge. It is wrong to curse."

Ginge was relaxed from the fire and a full belly and he forgot himself. "That right?" he said, "well, fuck you, too." Then he remembered and was instantly contrite. "Sorry, mate, sorry," he said hurriedly, "didn't mean no offence to you." He watched anxiously.

"It's alright," Richard said at last. "The words just came out."

"That's right, that's right. And he was such an evil bas-, man. He had two of us, you know, worked us together. Beat us together, too. And starved us." He was becoming agitated again and Richard laid a hand upon his arm.

"What happened to the other one?"

Ginge shook his head. "Dunno. She died, I suppose. She was already coughing up blood and shit when I scarpered." He closed his eyes, remembering and his voice was harsh again.

"God, I hate him." He opened his eyes to see Richard shake his head sadly and remembered himself again.

"It is wrong to hate," they chorused.

Ginge chuckled but Richard continued to look gravely at him. The eyes weren't right, there was a vacancy there but the vacancy was placid, it wanted little and mostly got what it wanted.

"Can I hate his deeds then?" Ginge asked.

Richard considered. "It must be right," he said at last, "to hate an evil thing."

"That's right, that's right, that's what it's there for."

"What's there for?"

"Hate, Richard, we have it for hateful things. So I hate what the evil cunt, sorry, man did and I hope he burns in hell forever. Nothing wrong with hope, is there?"

John sniggered in spite of himself, the self that saw the mocking, well, perhaps not mocking but the boy was certainly playing Richard. And him. But of course Richard didn't see it, so what was the harm? And the little weasel was amusing. *Nothing wrong with hope, I hope.* He smiled at his embellishment.

But it wasn't right. The boy was not here as a friend to Richard, he'd be kind to him for as long as it suited him but he'd never be a friend. The thought drifted by that he was hardly one to speak of friendship.

Would Richard even care if the little sod buggered off? He'd never seemed to miss Michael and he hadn't grieved for his mother; he probably wouldn't even notice.

He stirred as a mug of freshly brewed tea was set down on the tray beside his chair and wriggled his stockinged toes in front of the fire. It was hard to know what to do.

I expect it will all turn out badly, he thought, but, and he shrugged mentally, what is there to be done?

CHAPTER 9

The last light was fading behind a leaden sky when Thomas reached London. Three days of interminable plodding with breaks to rest and feed the horses when time had stopped altogether, a persistent miserable drizzle that softened the road to slush and slowed the plodding to a creeping, stiff and aching joints … Dear God, he was sick of it.

But now the glow of London reached through the umbrella of smog and journey's end was within sight. Soon the horses would be settled at the ostler's yard, the hops unloaded for the brewers' auction and he would be leaning back in a soft chair, in front of a warm fire, in dry clothes, port in hand and the splashing thud of hooves would turn to Joseph's kindly tones. He sighed in anticipation and let the memories wander. Dear Joseph and Mrs Kent, their warmth and kindness, the pleasure of their conversation, the stimulation, the excitement of new ideas; and outside there hummed the vibrancy of London life, the bustle of its streets, Lady Evelyn, the whore. He jerked upright and grunted as the memory struck with sudden, awful force. Evelyn. He had thought he had forgotten her and here she was again, cream and jet and pomegranate. He rolled his head, denying, and a soft groan escaped him, lost in an aching flood. He had not forgotten Evelyn, the sin was still in his daily prayers but he had –until now- forgotten how he had felt. And now the memories soared and swirled and danced in a mad tarantella and the reins fell from his nerveless hands. The horses seemed not to notice and plodded on, uncaring of the driver who sat bowed and unseeing beneath the cold, grey rain.

He had wrapped everything that was Evelyn into a shroud of guilt, sin and unworthiness and so she had left him alone during his time with Jane. And when Jane had seen how he had shrunk in his shame and remorse it had been easy for her to pity him. It was not as if she had had to manage with his longing for another woman; there were no tears for a lost love. And he was appealing in his vulnerability, loveable in his need.

At the first, shame had made him shrink from her in their bed but Jane was sensible enough not to see this as rejection and with time, hunger, port and encouragement he had found his way into her. And here the shroud served them well for the pleasure he found with Jane was not diminished by any other memory.

They had fitted well together and with the knowledge of her affection and the certainty of her loyalty Thomas had gradually expanded. Why now, utterly unbidden and unexpected, should That Night be alive again?

It was the thing that he Should Hate most but as he remembered he could find nothing to hate. He had seen past this world, *it was the drugs, Thomas, the alcohol, the shock, you were not yourself,* indeed not, I saw beyond myself. The light was perfect, quite perfect, textured, it breathed of smoke and pomegranate

Say that you hate what you did

And all my pain went away, it shrank and faded and went away and I felt the presence of great goodness and peace

God is in this place

I fed upon ambrosia and I supped upon nectar and I saw beauty, no, I absorbed beauty, no, I *knew* beauty, God, I was part of it.

Say that you hate what you did.

I suppose I must, he had said. And so he had accepted it with the same lassitude that he had accepted everything. And the shroud had taken it away, along with a great deal else and he had forgotten it.

Til now. Now it wrapped upon him like a snake in the night, the knowledge of that beauty, that truth. He raised his head and opened his eyes and there it was again, the lights, the yellows and the dark smoke, seen as through a veil of silver.

Like the rain.

He had never been so alive, so complete, merging in turn with each sense, praising the god that had put it there.

To rest a wine upon the tongue, to feel it slide through the flesh for closer inspection, to slip between its light and shadow, hear it sinking in your tongue, my tongue, our tongue, there is only the glow that surges within me, that shines through the pores of my skin.

Thomas, she drugged you. Please. Say that you hate what you did

And she shone, her skin was golden and alive and she breathed through my blood and her hands were a breeze then a wind that blew within me. And then, O God, when she, when she

You stammer. You cannot say the words yet you rejoice in the memory.
Obdurate boy, you will suffer for this.

But I am the victim.

You hypocrite, how can you call yourself a victim so long as you love your sin?

I did not know

But you know now. And you cling to it

It clings to me.

Listen to yourself.

I was seduced.

And you loved your seduction. Worse. You still do. Say that you hate it

Thomas pounded his fists blindly on to his knees and the horses pulled up, surprised by the flapping reins. "Why do you do this to me?" he screamed.

The cry exhausted him and he sank back into his seat. Then, slowly, he pushed himself erect, clicked the horses on and thought dully about the cancer he bore within, the stain he would not cleanse.

Later, as he sat warm and dry in the Kents' parlour he had no recollection of driving to the yard, leaving instructions for the care of the horses and the unloading of the hops or of trudging through the rain. The intensity had gone, leaving him dull and vague, a void within a void. Occasionally he would shudder and close his eyes.

He had eaten reluctantly under Florence's stern eye and nursed an untouched glass of port. The Kents sat helplessly. It had taken some time to extract an explanation for his condition and neither knew what to make of it or what to do with it.

Florence however was clear on one point. "I know you are in no fit state to consider, Thomas," she said gently, firmly, "and we will talk more tomorrow when you are rested and are more yourself. So I will say only this, just this one idea at the outset and I hope you will hold fast to it. You are not to tell Jane. No matter how much you ache to confess, to unburden your soul, you will say nothing of this to Jane. Do you understand?"

Thomas nodded and silence fell again upon the room. Joseph busied himself with his pipe. He was surprised by his wife's words but judged it wiser to refrain from comment or query.

Then Thomas pushed himself to his feet. "I need to walk," he said. "No," as Florence made to protest, "you need not worry." He buttoned his coat and quietly left the room.

Joseph nodded to the departing back. "God keep you," then to Florence as the door closed, "why did you demand his silence? You know how secrets eat at him and Jane is an understanding girl."

Florence shook her head. "Not that understanding," she answered. "No woman would be. Nor man neither, I suspect. Could you?" She saw that the question had thrown Joseph off balance and she saw anger there, too. She hurried on, "such knowledge would do nothing more than hurt Jane sadly. It should not be her responsibility."

Joseph nodded, back in agreement again. "You're right," he said, "it's the least he can do for her."

Thomas plodded blindly, holding his thoughts to the progress of his feet, to the cold and the rain upon his face and the empty streets. He passed by a tavern, dimly registering shouts and the snatch of song, then there was only rain upon the cobblestones and his thudding feet.

Then, in the distance he heard voices in chorus, in muted harmony and found himself headed towards them. They came from a small chapel set briefly apart from the surrounding tenements. It glowed faintly behind the rain, the yellow of candles and a smudge of red and purple through a small round stained glass window. As he neared the voices became clearer, one in particular, a woman's clear soprano rising purely, effortlessly.

The Lord is my shepherd, I shall not want

The notes were silver, crystal, pure in the dark and Thomas felt his heart lurch.

He restoreth my soul

Carefully he crept towards them, near holding his breath and found his arms opening in supplication.

I shall fear no evil for Thou art with me

Then he was at the door, very still, his mouth partly open; to drink the words? to breathe them?

Surely goodness and mercy shall follow me all the days of my life

He leaned against the doorway, now aware of a stillness upon him, an aching simplicity of being, a quiet breathing space in the dark and the prayer.

The psalm ended and in the rustle of movement within Thomas slipped in the door, gazing over the small congregation settling into their pews to a bare table and simple cross that were the altar and the man who stood beside it. He was a striking figure, handsome, patrician features, silver locks falling to his shoulders, tall and slim in his black cassock. He did not raise his voice but the sonorous tones filled the church.

"Do you feel alone?" he asked. "Apart? Even though you sit in the bosom of your family, are you lonely? Are you incomplete, is there something missing?"

He paused and Thomas thought, yes, these are the questions I must answer. And he found a comfort there for if the man knew to ask the questions that went to the heart of him did that not mean that he must also have the answers?

"Do you carry a sense of purpose?" asked the man. "Is there a reason for your days? Or do you labour through one day to no point other than to obtain that which is necessary to survive the next?"

This is my life in Thoresby, thought Thomas. But what of Jane and the children? I labour for their well-being, too.

"You may think your efforts are for the benefit of others," said the man, "and they may well be so. But ask yourself this: was your life different before them? Would it change if they went away? You do not become a baker to support a wife and children; you become a baker, then you gain a wife and children and you employ your baking to support them. If they went away you would continue to be a baker, labouring through one day to survive the next."

The questions were having a strange effect upon Thomas, disturbing, challenging, but inducing nothing of his usual excitement or agitation. Rather, the voice soothed and the stillness that had come to him at the church door seemed to expand, holding him open, receptive. There were no thoughts and he waited without anticipation as though enveloped in a cloud, a cloud of peaceful unknowing.

"You may know what you are doing but do you know why you are doing it? Is the purpose of serving the needs of tomorrow enough to give meaning to today? My friends," the man stepped forward and slowly paced the aisle, "my friends, I lived like that once. And I thought I lived well. Every day I attended to my concerns and I supposed I was successful; certainly I was not in want. I had many acquaintances who I called my friends and I took my pleasures from a variety of sources, some of which it would shame me now to name. I told myself and the world I was a happy man. But there was an emptiness in my life to which I could find no answer because I could not find the question. It came to me through the lips of a child. In the street one day I watched an anxious mother in argument with a little boy. "What do you want to do?" she was demanding, "what do you want to do?" The child was confused and tearful. How was he to know? And he said, 'I want to do what I'm supposed to be doing'." The man paused and folded his hands in prayer. "'What I'm supposed to be doing.' And it came to me, was I doing what I was supposed to be doing? Was I answering my purpose?" The voice rolled on, smooth and warm, lapping at the cloud but the words faded as Thomas closed his eyes. Perhaps it was candlelight but he thought he saw a distant door glowing faintly in the dark as at the end of a tunnel. He felt no sense of movement towards it but knew with deep certainty that it would some time, soon, open unto him. Then there was dark and peaceful waiting. Voices and movement echoed faintly then faded to silence.

He became conscious of a presence close by and opened his eyes to discover the chapel dim and empty but for the preacher watching him. He made to rise but a strong hand was on his shoulder, holding him to his seat. "Gently, my friend," said the man, "be still. I think you have been in a special place. Do not rush from it."

Thomas nodded and closed his eyes again. When he opened them the man was still there, watching patiently.

"How long have you been watching?" Thomas asked.

The man smiled. "A little while," he answered. "I was initially concerned that you might not be well but you seemed in no discomfort. Quite the contrary, you looked very much at ease so I thought it best to wait while you rested."

"Thank you," Thomas said, "you are very kind. And you are right. I am at ease but very tired. I have travelled far these last two days." He paused then added, "but much farther these last two hours."

"I hope it has been a beneficial journey."

"Indeed, but …" Thomas raised his palms.

"Quite. This is not the time to speak of it. Have you lodgings for the night?"

"I am staying with friends nearby and I must return soon or they will fear for me."

"If it is nearby, may I accompany you to see you safely home?" "Thank you." Thomas smiled and shook his head. "Nearby? Yet I spent hours getting here. I must have been walking in circles."

The man laughed softly. "A dozen homilies present themselves for that," he said, "but I shall resist them." He took Thomas by the arm and led him from the church. On the brief walk back to the Kents' home his conversation was light and easy. His name was Basil Woodd and he had been pastor at the Wesleyan chapel for three years now, although he also spent time travelling and preaching, along with an administrative position at the Church Missionary Society. At the Kents' door he shook Thomas' hand. "Sleep well," he said. I shall be at the chapel at eleven tomorrow morning. Will you come to see me? I think we have much to talk about." Thomas agreed and slipped quietly into the darkened house. He tiptoed past the Kent's bedroom, "is that you, Thomas?" and up the stairs.

Kneeling by his bed he prayed, "I thank Thee, Lord, for having brought me here and for showing me my confusion. Please, show me Thy will, let me be Thy instrument. Help me to find what I am supposed to be doing and where I am supposed to be."

That night he dreamed that he was standing by a cottage in a lush valley beneath a hot, bright sun in a vast, clear sky. He did not know the place, the bush grew dark and green in dank and hungry, almost violent richness that was quite unlike the forests of England or the fields of his home. He was approached by a group of men, gypsies he supposed by their dress, bright, baggy pantaloons, coloured silken shirts with flared sleeves, kerchiefs, bandannas, golden hoops of earring. An older man with a sparse white beard and laughing eyes pointed to a line of painted caravans. "You will come with us," he said.

"Yes," Thomas answered. "Where are you taking me?"

The old man chuckled and clapped him on the shoulder. "To te manawa," he answered.

Then he was inside the cottage, lying on a simple bed. The air was dark and smokey and he could barely make out the shapes of people standing about. He became aware that he was lying next to a woman but could not turn to see her. He did not know who she was but was aware that there was profound intimacy between them. He was comfortable with his unknowing and lay quietly, patiently in the dark. Then a woman was standing over him. Sunk in shadow he could make out only her outline and long, black wavy hair. I am the twin sister of the woman who lies beside you, she told him. My name is Wendy Iro. Thomas understood that there was no more to be said and he gave himself up to the dark, back to sleep. At breakfast the next morning the Kents were relieved to find their guest calm and clear in his thoughts. He told them of the night's events and of his intended meeting with Basil Woodd that morning.

"Woodd," said Joseph, rubbing his nose, "I have heard of him. A man of integrity, I believe. I should like to meet him."

"Of course." Some of Thomas' old eagerness had returned, "but this morning I think ..."

"Naturally, naturally. Some other time."

"So I understand, Thomas," said Florence, "that the meeting is to, how did you put it, to clarify the direction and purpose of your life?"

Thomas nodded. "Yes," he answered, "and I am hopeful of an outcome. I hope this does not sound presumptuous or vain but I believe that Divine Providence is lighting a way for me. My being in London, finding my way to the chapel, the vision, the feeling of a guiding, loving hand –this is more than coincidence."

He did not see her roll her eyes to Joseph and missed the edge to her voice as she spoke. "I pray that you are right, Thomas, but I also pray that you do not allow impulsiveness to rule you. Remember, you have a wife and children."

Thomas smiled at her. "I will not forget," he answered, gathering up his coat, "and now I must be gone. To seek my destiny."

Joseph stared in a kind of quiet despair after the retreating figure and shook his head. "There he goes again," he said, "another dream, a new mentor." He tamped the tobacco into his pipe, then added, "at least one can hope for a more benign influence from Basil Woodd than from James Worthing."

Florence nodded. "That is something," she agreed, "but, O God, Joseph, he is such a child. And I fear for Jane and the children."

An hour later Basil Woodd was beginning to have similar misgivings. "Thomas," he urged, "please believe me, I delight in your enthusiasm but pray, do not abandon moderation entirely. Do you truly intend to leave Thoresby upon the instant and move to London?"

"I must." Thomas' voice was calm but his eyes glittered. "Here is where I must be, where I am supposed to be. The painted caravan will bring me here."

"But your wife and children? How will you support them?"

Thomas clasped his hands. "The Lord will provide," he answered.

There was more than a touch of asperity in Woodd's voice. "The Lord may expect you to take a measure of responsibility as well," he said. "Let me tell you a story, a joke but pertinent to your situation. A man, a pious man who believed deeply in the providence of the Lord was fishing from the rocks when a sudden wave swept him into the sea. He did not panic or cry out or even try to swim for the shore although he was a strong swimmer because he believed that the Lord would provide and that he only need pray for salvation. So when his companion made to cast a line to him he said, 'do not bother yourself, my friend. The Lord will provide.' And when a man in a passing boat offered to take him on board he made the same reply. The man drowned, Thomas, and arrived at the Pearly Gates in a state of indignation. He complained to St Peter, "I have been a good Christian all my life. Why did the Lord not answer my prayer?"

'My son, 'replied St Peter, 'the Lord provided you with a strong body and skill in swimming. He gave you a friend who cast a line to you and He sent a boat to save you. He answered you three times; why would you not listen?"

Thomas was silent for a time. Then he said, "I take your point and I will take steps to provide for myself and my family. However, I know I must be here and take my place in this congregation. And learn from you." He looked at the preacher almost accusingly. "It was your words that began this movement."

"And I am glad that you hearkened to them. But how are you to manage? What do you do in Thoresby?"

"I lease a little land but am primarily a grocer. I have no liking nor talent for the work and business is going badly."

"Very well. So a change in career might be a sound move. But what else can you do? Have you always been a grocer?"

Thomas shook his head. "No," he answered. "I farmed for three years when I was younger. I enjoyed it but cannot claim much success. Then I became a schoolteacher."

Woodd's eyes widened. "A schoolteacher," he repeated. "And did you find satisfaction in that employ?"

"Yes." Thomas was more enthusiastic. "I believe I was suited to it and I have references that testify to my performance."

"So why did you leave?"

Woodd watched in sudden alarm as Thomas bowed his head and shook it slowly from side to side; his right fist clenched and he beat it slowly upon the table.

"Thomas? Is all well?"

Thomas looked up and all the excitement was gone from his face.

"I fell into sin," he said dully.

Woodd waited, then prompted, "what kind of sin? Come, come, man," seeing Thomas' reticence, "I cannot help you if you are not square with me. Did you steal from your employer?"

"No." Thomas was indignant. "I was tempted by a woman and I fell."

"Was she a married woman? Did you commit adultery?"

"No." Again Thomas' tone was sharp. "She was a whore and I was deceived."

"Does your wife know?"

"I sinned before I met my wife. But yes, she does know. And has forgiven me."

"Mm." The minister steepled his fingers against his lips and his tone was grave. "And have you repented of your sin?"

Say that you hate it.

"It was a vile and wicked deed."

That is not quite the same thing.

And then, because he could not help himself, "But it was not entirely my fault. I was played by wicked people, I was hurt and drugged and ..."

Say that you hate it.

"And I was barely conscious ..."

Thomas' eyes were filling.

"Please." Woodd took Thomas' hand. "I can see the grief that just the recollection brings you."

"It was a shameful, shameful thing."

"Indeed. But we have all made mistakes. I –"

"This was more than a mistake."

"Very well. If you insist. But if we repent then we can rest secure in the knowledge of God's forgiveness. Did He not send His Only Son that we might be washed clean in His blood?"

Thomas knuckled his eyes and nodded mutely.

"So. And there have been no further," he paused, "incidents?"

"No. It only ha-happened once."

"Well then. I think we can leave it behind us." A worrying thought occurred. "There was no publicity, no scandal?"

"No, it was a private matter. It is not spoken of."

If you don't count Lord Farnwright pounding his fists upon the table and roaring in delight as his good wife regales the company with the story of the horny owl.

They sat in silence while each tried to gather his thoughts. Woodd was struggling with a growing discomfort. Lord, he thought, if he takes on so about one act of youthful folly of his own what would he think of -? No, that was no matter. Not any longer. At last he said cautiously, "Your repentance, if I may say so, seems somewhat," he flapped his hands, "excessive, given the isolated nature of the event and the years that have passed since. You seem to," again he dithered, "to hold on to it. I am sorry if that seems harsh …"

"No." Thomas seemed more composed now. "It is a common enough observation."

"And yet you –"

"Persist with it? That is Mrs Kent's judgment and, I daresay, a wise one. Perhaps I need more than human counsel."

"I see." Basil Woodd thought he might be beginning to. "And that is why your response to my sermon was so," he considered, "intense."

"Perhaps. I had not thought of it in those terms. But I do know this. I was lost and alone and I prayed for comfort and a voice answered, the Lord is my shepherd. I prayed for a meaning to my life and a preacher spoke of the purpose of my days. And in your church I found a home and I believe God touched me for the peace I found there was beyond anything I have ever known. I must not lose it."

"Amen." Woodd was moved and in the silence he remembered the serenity on the young man's face that had stayed his hand from waking him. "I believe God has a plan for us all and it does seem that in His mercy He is making yours manifest." A quiet excitement touched him. "For I think there is more to follow. Thomas, you spoke of your need to move to London and I of the need for attending to your wife and children. You answered that the Lord would provide and I replied with a sermon on self-sufficiency. But perhaps you were right. You see, I know of no positions for farmers or grocers but I do know of one recently arisen for a schoolteacher."

————

Thomas' eyes widened as Woodd continued, "and what is more, it comes with lodgings suitable for a small family."

Thomas threw back his head and the glow was upon him once more. "Hallelujah!" he exclaimed. "The Lord has provided."

The glow stayed this time along with a driving momentum. Basil Woodd undertook to make enquiries of the teaching post – "I believe I may have some small influence in the appointment"- and Thomas could not be held.

Panting, radiant he burst upon the Kents and his account tumbled out with prayers, praise and laughter. Then he was gone, "I will return within the week", ringing in the parlour.

The hops forgotten he drove the horses to near collapse and was at his father's home by the next nightfall. Even his mother's stony reception of his news could not dampen his enthusiasm nor detain him.

Jane was initially appalled. "Thomas! The hops! How could you forget them?" But then she became caught up in his enthusiasm and could not resist the joy she saw upon him. Besides, while she feared for the profits cast away and worried about the liability their stock had become, the promise of a steady, comparatively substantial income allayed much of her concern. And it would be wonderful to get away from Thoresby and Susanna and back to London, to her family and friends. She had missed them sorely. Finally, sensibly, she saw that nothing could deter Thomas and that she would be a fool to try.

Thomas made good his parting promise to the Kents. Within a week the grocery stock was largely disposed of in a sale that further compounded their debts, the house leased for a pitiful income and the Kendalls were established in a comfortable tenement house, a short walk from the parish school where Thomas presided as headmaster.

Truly, thought Jane, the Lord has intervened and Thomas has found himself.

CHAPTER 10

As Thomas' fortunes rose, those of John Stockwell continued to decline. War and taxes gripped the market by the throat, wheat became a rare commodity and the price of corn soared. Wealthier customers fled the swelling discontent of London for country estates, frequently leaving substantial debts behind them and along with many others John watched his profits disappear. While others raged against their fate and marched and shouted and plundered, John sighed and inexorably, like an old clock, he wound down.

He lost interest in food and gave up washing himself or his clothes; scrawny and stinking he shuffled from one moment to the next and having got there found no interest in it. For a time he continued to walk to the bakery even though it was now bare of ingredients. Once there he would sit and when Richard arrived for his deliveries he would send him away. At the usual time he would shuffle home and sit. The larder was bare and Ginge was now their provider, returning in the evening with various provisions courtesy, he said, of mates in the markets.

Finally one morning he simply stayed in bed. There was no choice or decision in it and only a touch of fear. It was just something happening to him, holding him there. He watched Richard and Ginge standing at the foot of the bed and saw the fear in them and then he registered a dark, consuming sadness and regret at being the author of his son's unhappiness. But there was nothing to be said or done. He felt Richard prop him up and the wall against his back. Later he felt a mug of tea at his lips, fingers at his mouth and warm liquid passing down his throat and dribbling down his chin. And further away he felt the flow of urine puddling between his thighs.

Richard set the mug down and turned to his friend. "Ginge, what is the matter with my father?"

Ginge was direct. "He's fucked, mate. I seen it coming a while now."

"What is to be done. I must call a doctor."

"Won't do no good." Ginge saw the distress in Richard's face, his smooth, even features creased in growing panic. He suddenly looked much younger than his thirteen years and the little Cockney felt a rush of sympathy. "Come into the kitchen, mate," he said, taking Richard's arm. "Better to talk where your dad can't hear us."

"Hear us?" asked Richard. "Can he hear us? Father," turning to the bed, "can you hear me? Please, answer me."

His father stared vacantly back.

"Come on, mate." And Ginge led Richard unprotesting from the small, dark room to the kitchen where he sat numbly, silently as tears coursed.

Ginge paced nervously. "Look, mate," he said, "I can see you're all upset and I want to be kind but you got to understand. The doctors can't do nothin and if you get one, if you manage to get one here, it'll just make things worse. They'll put him in a madhouse, mate, and no one will care if he lives or dies. If he's lucky they'll bring him food or the shit they call food and if he doesn't eat it they'll just leave it there for the rats. They'll leave him lying in his own shit and he'll die, mate, he'll die. You listenin to me, Richard, you listenin?"

Richard straightened and knuckled the tears away. "I'm listening," he said.

"And they'll do for us, too. They'll stick us in a workhouse and we'll live like fuckin slaves. This is the truth, mate, I'm not shittin you."

Richard stared at him mutely, his lips trembled. At last he whispered, "This is like a very bad dream. I do not know what to do."

"But I do. Like I said, I seen this comin and I been thinkin about it. You're not goin to like this but you got to promise to listen. Will you do that?"

Richard nodded.

"Right, then. Now you know how I was bringin stuff home, food and that?"

"Yes. It was given to you by kind friends in the market."

"It wasn't, mate." A pause, then, "I pinched it. Go on, tell me it was wrong."

Richard nodded.

"Right. So think on this. If I hadn't nicked it we'd of been goin hungry for a while now. We'd of been fuckin starvin."

Richard stared and Ginge pressed on. "So listen. I'm not talkin about fruit or the odd bit of fish here. You got no idea how much some of them rich whoresons have got. They eat off golden plates, one of them would keep a good man alive for a year. That's if you could get a fair price from the fuckin thievin fences," he added sourly.

Richard shook his head unhappily. "Are you saying we should steal, Ginge? That's –"

"Wrong!" the other broke in angrily. "Well, it may be, but it's not as wrong as some rich cunt eatin from a table that would keep half a dozen starvin families. Christ! Where do you get all this wrong shit from, anyway?"

Perhaps because the question took him from the immediate horror Richard found the words to answer. "My father put me into school for a while. My teacher was Mrs Dallimore. She was very kind and looked after me when the other children were cruel. I could not learn to read but she taught me other things. Thou shalt not bear false witness –that means to lie. Thou shalt not steal."

"That right, eh? Well, I learned some stuff, too. How about this? Thou shalt not starve."

Richard was silent.

"Look, mate," Ginge continued in a kinder tone, "as I see it, we got no choice. Either we starve and your dad dies or we steal. We'd not be hurtin anyone, them rich bastards wouldn't even notice, they got so much. And we could keep the house and look after your dad, feed him, keep him clean and dry. He might even get better after a while."

There was a touch of hope in Richard's voice. "Get better? You think he might get better?"

"Why not? At least you'd be lookin after him. Don't you want that?"

"Yes. I must look after my father."

"Alright then. So you got to steal to do it."

Richard looked helplessly at his friend. He shook his head slowly as he tried to make sense of it. Then he said, "I do not know what to do, Ginge. You must tell me what to do."

"I will, mate. You can count on me."

Within a month Richard and Ginge had a thriving business on their hands. Or rather, Ginge had, for he ran every aspect. But through his father

Richard was able to provide him with something no one else could, a safe base from which to operate. Richard also offered loyalty and dependability and Ginge treasured both.

The capers as Ginge called them were straightforward compared to the attendant precautions and organisation. What we need, Ginge had told Richard is an adult, some codger we can work through. They found their man in William Reade. Reade was an educated man, the youngest son of a successful merchant. But his ambition had exceeded his station within the family and that combined with a taste for alcohol and opium to see him fall utterly from favour. When Ginge had discovered him he was living in poor lodgings, using the last of his charm in giving French and other lessons to a small group of bored and unattractive ladies.

He was lying fully dressed on an unmade bed watching dust mites in golden arabesque in the morning sun when there had come a tap at the door. Mrs Mellors, he thought, come to dun me for the rent. But the languor of the night's opium dreams was still upon him and the thought did not produce its usual agitation. Still, it was pleasing not to discover the grasping slattern; instead, two boys stood in the darkened corridor, one scrawny and freckle-faced, the other taller and strongly built with the face of a vacant angel.

"Mornin, squire," said the smaller. "I'm Peter and this is me mate, John. We was wonderin if you could spare us a few minutes of your time. We'll pay you for it." He reached into a shabby overcoat and produced a small, silver tankard.

Reade had taken the cup, turning it over in his hands.

"This is a rather fine piece," he said. "I wonder if I should ask whether you came by it honestly."

The boy had fixed him with clever eyes. "Do you care?" he asked.

Reade smiled then. "Not particularly," he said, "come in." And the grounds of accomodation had been laid.

"We can bring you good stuff, squire, nothin too flashy, nothin to raise questions. You probably know pawnbrokers or the like who'll be happy to deal with you. If you don't, I can give you names. You hand it over and keep a cut. Easy. Everybody's happy."

"How will you know that I am playing square?"

Peter had shaken his head. "Not a problem, not a problem. I know what the stuff'll fetch. If you can get more, good luck to you. Keep the difference."

Reade was impressed. "And if I decline to part with any of the takings?" Peter had nodded approvingly. "A fair question," he answered, "glad you brought it up. Now if you do, you'll only do it once and that'll be the end of your future earnins. And of course we'd be pissed off and you can be pretty sure that one night when you're staggerin home all pissed and that we'll be waitin for you." He grinned. "And none of us wants that." Reade had grinned in return. "You have a persuasive tongue, Master Peter," he said. "But why do you require my services at all? Why not handle the transactions yourself?"

Ginge had laid a finger along the side of his nose. "You're a gentleman, Mr Reade," he answered. "no concerns about a gentleman fallin on hard times and floggin off some of the family silverware to meet debts. You should suggest to your dealer though that he flogs it privately. No public displays, like. He'll understand. It'll drop the price but it'll keep you safe. But it's your worry. Me and John, we'd rather stay out of the picture."

"So I take all the risk?"

"That's what you're bein paid for. Me and John, we take the risk in getting the stuff and you take the risk getting rid of it."

"Very well. And when do we begin transactions?"

"Now." Ginge and Richard had opened their pockets and produced a small pile, several ornate plates, cutlery, another tankard and a golden goblet. "It's worth thirty quid on the closed market. Your fence'll give you ten. You keep two. But we do it now. Don't want to give offence, Mr Reade, but, like, we know your habits and havin this lot lyin around would be dangerous for all of us."

The transaction had been completed within the hour to the satisfaction of all parties.

Now, two months later there had been two more. In each case the amount had been comparatively small but still, Reade told himself, he had made seven pounds for only a few hours work. He was well pleased. Mrs Mellors was off his back, he had eaten well and the residue had financed some memorable nights. He was also impressed by Peter's caution. Each transaction had taken place with a different fence, "no need to become familiar, Mr R," Peter had said, and the goods were not distinctive, no outstanding quality or identifying marks. "No need to ask questions." He knew nothing about the boys, where they came from or even, he suspected, their real names. All to the good, he thought, showed a professional approach. But he quite liked them, well, Peter anyway, quick and clever and sometimes quite amusing. He had never heard John speak and wondered what purpose he served. Perhaps some kind of bodyguard. He shrugged, what did it matter, and poured himself a generous draught of brandy.

A mile or two away Ginge was a good deal less comfortable in his surroundings. He was actively afraid and his hand shook as he lighted the taper from the smouldering embers in an ornate grate. Damn, he thought, doesn't matter how many times you do this, it always scares the shit out of you. This is why good people don't steal, not because of their fuckin morals; it's just because they haven't got the fuckin nerve.

This was a theme dear to Ginge's heart and more than once he had tried to explain it to Richard. "See, mate, rich geezers don't steal 'cause they don't need to." He corrected himself. "I mean, they do steal, they steal their workers fuckin blind, but they don't steal like us, in the window and nick what you can, straight-up honest thievin. And why? 'Cause they think it's wrong? My arse! Because they'd be too scared to, that's why. Creepin in the dark in a strange house, knowin one wrong move could mean the noose. What I'd like to see is for some fuckin righteous judge to shimmy up the brickwork, slip in, nick somethin, anythin, knowin he's for the high jump if he's caught, then sneak away with it. If he done that, then give it back, then he can say stealin's wrong. But he wouldn't. Why? 'Cause he hasn't got the balls."

Richard had gazed back uncomprehending and Ginge sighed. It was not that Richard was stupid, sometimes he was quite wise, but he did not manage well with possibilities. Nor did he retain information for long. Ginge had tried to teach him card games and was delighted when Richard grasped the point and even played a thoughtful hand or two. But after several days he would have forgotten the rules.

Physical learning was different. Ginge had decided that for all his strength Richard's ignorance of tactics would hamper him severely in a serious fight. So he undertook to teach him. "You got to be light on your feet so that you can move away from what's comin. Watch everythin, the whole body. See, I shape to punch with me left but it's what's called a feint. I want you to act on that so you'll leave yourself open and I can smack you with me right. Or kick you in the balls. Let's try. Slow, easy. Now, I lead with me left, block, good, here's the right, block, that's right, now what could you –ow! Shit! Gently, you bastard. But that's good, let's try again."

But that was practice in the kitchen, here it was horribly real. Here there was no way of talking your way out of trouble, successful flight was improbable and a noisy fight would attract more attention. The only hope was getting in the first blow with your cudgel and hoping the bastard fell quietly. There was nothing to lose. They could only hang you once.

Shit! He'd nearly tripped on a loose rug. Look around, where are you, what is there, light, small enough to tuck in a bag. Here on the table, a pair of tidy gold? gold-plated? candle holders, a crystal decanter, stop it firmly, wrap it in loose rags, a crystal wine glass, no, too fragile. Stealthily Ginge crept about the dining room, carefully packing the bags. His heart raced and he felt his bowels shiver. That's alright, he could hold it this time. There had been other times when he couldn't and the owner's outrage at the theft had soared with the discovery of the thief's leavings.

Then he was back at the window, feeding out the cord, lowering the bags to the courtyard below. Then squirming through the gap, dropping into the night, into the cold, driving rain.

Thirty yards away, his back against a dripping elm, Richard could barely make out the dark shadow dropping. He was cold and wet but did not mind. He was serving his purpose, watching the house and gate, ready to warn Ginge of any arrivals or signs of movement within. A small pile of loose gravel lay cupped in his hand. "First chance you get, mate, lightly against the window, then back into the dark." He knew these inclement conditions were the best for the job in hand. There were many reasons. "The rain on the roof and the windows muffles noise in the house. But that's not the main reason. It also means people are unlikely to be out in the grounds. But that's not it, either. No, it makes our gettin there and gettin away safer. See, it's on the streets, 'specially these streets with their high fuckin walls and no alleys to whip down, where it's most dangerous. Some bastard comin home from a ball, sees us skulkin along, bags on our shoulders, what's he to think? Couple of fuckin thieves, that's what. So he stops, him and the driver and perhaps a mate or two, fuckin swords and shit, we're right in it. Dark night, rain pissin down, no one's goin to notice and even if they do they probably won't be bothered stoppin. Same thing when we get back to our neighbourhood, some likely lads spot us, hullo, what's in them bags? Got the picture?"

Richard got the picture, though its details became blurred after a while. But that did not matter. He was clear about his task, he knew what to do.

Even in the dark rain they hugged the walls and hurried past the gas lights. And on their home turf they were just as careful, using alleys where they could, sinking into doorways, their cudgels ready.

It was only when they were home at last, loot secure beneath floorboards, changed into dry clothes, warming themselves before the fire that Ginge would accept that the danger was past –for the moment. But the tension would stay with him and long after Richard had found his way to bed and easy sleep he would pace and sit and fidget.

The caution that attended the thefts and the disposal of the goods pervaded their lives. All other stealing ceased and purchases were made with coin, preferably of small denomination. "Don't want people wonderin how the likes of us come by a sovereign." They were never extravagant and while their clothes were now clean, warm and intact they remained cheap and simple. They spread their purchases over a wide area so that they would not be seen as steady customers with cash at the ready. To that end Ginge would occasionally beg credit when there was no need and complain at the invariable rejection. And John would be brought into the conversation – "what else did your dad tell us to get?"- to confirm that the money came from a working man and was not the property of boys with idle hands.

Richard was content with his lot. He had not entirely dismissed the lessons of Mrs Dallimore and the knowledge of what they were doing sometimes made him sad. But mostly he did not think about it, for however ill-gotten their gains might be they ensured their survival and the welfare of his father. John now lay warm in his bed under woollen blankets, purchased one by one at different locations and transported, along with other provisions, in Richard's barrow under a pile of stinking sacks. He slept in a clean linen nightshirt and when he soiled it there would be another to take its place. His appetite was small but he did not resist feeding and the food was nutritious. Richard's patience was endless. He would feed and clean his father quietly without complaint while Ginge would stay away. "Christ, mate, don't know how you can bear the fuckin stink." And he would talk to him. That had been Ginge's idea. "Seems to me he's fucked off somewhere else. See if you can bring him back. Tell him about your day, about what's goin on in the streets." Monologue did not come easily for Richard and he was slow and hesitant and his speech was punctuated by lengthy pauses. But gradually he found a kind of momentum and a growing fluency.

It is cold outside today. It is snowing. It makes the streets muddy and slippery. Lots of people have fallen over in it. It makes them wet and angry and sometimes they are hurt. Other people laugh at them. They think it's funny. Lots of fires are burning and there is a lot of smoke. It hangs above the roofs like a cloud and makes the snow dirty.

There is no rain or snow today but it is still very cold. I am glad I have my overcoat, it keeps me warm, but lots of people are cold. Ginge says people are dying from the cold. Mr McGregor came for the rent today. He said to tell you we are his best tenants.

Today I saw a big crowd of people. They were listening to a man. He was very angry and he shouted a lot. He said the gov, gova, government was to blame for people being cold and hungry. The people got very angry too and there was lots of shouting. Then soldiers came on horses and they rode into the people. There was lots of screaming and many people were hurt. I saw one man fall down near us after a soldier hit him with his sword. I wanted to go and help him but Ginge told me I mustn't. He said we would be ar res ted and then I would not be able to look after you.

So Richard assisted Ginge and tended his father, content that he was doing what he was supposed to. And his ministrations enjoyed some success. One morning he came to his father's room to find him out of bed, standing by the window. He had pulled aside the old sheet that hung there and was gazing out on to the street. By his bed the chamber pot was full and steaming in the cold air.

He never fully returned but it was enough for Richard. Once again his father was with him and with the edge taken off his earlier indifference and replaced by a more placid vagueness he was easier to live with. He would sit quietly in the kitchen watching his son prepare their meals or baking bread. He offered no advice, indeed he rarely spoke, just watched as Richard patiently explored possibilities, discovering, learning, forgetting and then discovering again. With time and without pressure he became a more than passable cook.

By the end of spring he had adventured outdoors and with Richard he would walk the busy streets. Colour returned to his cheeks but he had become an old man and passers-by might have mistaken them for grandfather and grandson, sitting by the pond, feeding the ducks.

Rio de Janeiro 1809

... the man is Bitter. He impresses as One who has been –or Believes he has been– Often and Grievously Wronged and is Ever on the Watch for Further Offence. He is naturally of a Stubborn Temper, very obstinate and rude in his manner. He will require to be held in with Bit and Bridle till he understands his real Situation.

Samuel Marsden laid down his quill and sighed; his gaze strayed from the heavy table overflowing with papers and ledgers to the profusion of shape and colour in the garden beyond. Below the harbour glittered in the hot South American sun. The temptation seized him to lay down his work and take a turn in the garden but he resisted it firmly. Industry before pleasure. He returned to his ruminations upon William Hall and the dilemma he presented. It seemed to Marsden that either his disquisition upon Hall erred, and this was not a line of argument for which Marsden had any liking, or that he and others of the Church Missionary Society had erred in their selection. Another unattractive route. He bowed his head in a silent prayer for guidance and the answer came. He took up his pen again.

Nevertheless, he wrote, *he is Pious and Resilient and most certainly possesses the Skills for the Great Purpose. Mr Barnes has Testified that he has shown a quick and thorough Grasp of the Rudiments of Boat Building and he is an Industrious and Efficient Carpenter. I cannot but Conceive that the Lord has placed him in our Hands that we may guide him to Upright Conduct in All Things.*

There was a peremptory tug at his trouser leg and he glanced down in sudden annoyance. But the furrowed brow meant nothing to the child standing there and he tugged again.

"Father, there is the most wonderful bird in the garden. Come and see it."

Impatience left Marsden then and he chuckled indulgently. "Very well, Charles," he answered, "but only for ten minutes. Then I must return to my work." One could hear the capitalisation of the last two words. He rose and with a grunt swung the boy on to his ample hip and carried him out to the garden. There were indeed a number of wonderful birds with improbable beaks and feathers of all hues and for ten minutes father and son stood and admired them. Then Marsden placed the boy down and returned to his table.

John King is not Resentful, he wrote, *but there are Aspects to his Character that Trouble me. He is quite the Reverse of Hall, Timid where the other is Forceful, even Abrasive. I pray his Diffidence reflects Humility but I fear it may suggest Weakness. Still and all, his Skill as a Ropemaker and Cobbler is beyond Question and he is a Pious man. He is become the Lord's Instrument and the Lord will bring him Strength and Wisdom.*

By and large, Marsden was pleased with how matters were developing. Most particularly he was delighted by his discovery of Ruatara and the treasure he contained. Here the Lord's hand was at its most evident. Born of rangatira standing at Rangihoua Ruatara had been enchanted by the pakeha waka and had developed the passion to travel upon one, to sail to England and meet the king. At the age of sixteen he had put the plan to action, embarking as an unskilled hand upon a passing sealer. Marsden shook his head in wonder: what could he have been thinking? Taken upon a floating pa that could beat against the wind and sail across the oceans of the world. For all he might have anticipated, it could have risen to the currents of the sky and sailed upon the winds of Tawhiri. Certainly the waka was magical, even the humble sealer. What amazing courage, what an incredible lack of imagination. And did he think of the society he would keep, of the lives that played out on the slippery decks and the circumstances that had conspired to put them there? Lives of violence and survival that equipped them well for this task, if for few others. But at sixteen Ruatara was no novice in death and violence. He had killed upon the field and he had eaten his foe, too. But did he ever think of loneliness, did he imagine that the ship would form a whanau deep of his knowing that would replace the life he knew at Rangihoua? Surely he had not thought at all; rather with the fearless impulse of youth and the authority of a man, and a chiefly man, he had simply had his way.

Which proved a long and bitter one. Ruatara soon found himself on a rocky sealing ground with a crew of sixteen others. They were provisioned with stores for a stay of three months. They remained for ten. Ten months sheltering beneath the longboat propped on its side, gradually, angrily, building extensions as the months slipped by. The catch was bountiful and the skins mounted up as the gulls fed upon the bare, red carcasses on the rocks. Early there had been eggs and there were always fish and of course an endless supply of seal meat, but greenery was scarce and their health suffered. They were cold and wet and bitter. They depended upon one another for their survival but they did so without liking or kindness and each man retreated in the hard grey metal winter, hid before the hardness of it, the sea and the rocks and the sound of the wind and the cries of dying seals.

Ruatara was quite lost in the sharp, angular world. No circles here, no simple conjoined set. For the first time in his life, he was apart. These men did not laugh and their conversation, so far as Ruatara was coming to understand it, had little sense or meaning to it. Like all the men he missed the warmth of female flesh. Some had looked longingly at his smooth clean lines and had thought of substitution but the ferocity of Ruatara's response had persuaded them that there would be death in it and they had not persisted and he was left alone to his own, sad ministrations. Sometimes he felt his own death upon him, a lassitude that came with understanding how much had been taken from him. But there also came strength as he remembered the mana of his family and his own mana. Sullenly he survived to be lifted from the killing grounds.

To add treachery to abandonment he was soon after cast from the ship as she stood off a Tongan island. He swam ashore with nothing but his mana and the Tongans recognised it and he was treated well before boarding a passing vessel six months later.

Numerous passages followed and eventually Ruatara found himself cast up upon the port of London. But there was to be no visit with the king. The master kept him at work until the vessel was discharged and he was placed upon the 'Ann', a transport carrying one hundred and ninety three convicts, bound for the penal colony of Australia. Here he was discovered by Marsden and it was as well for him that he was for in his recognition of the failure of his quest, six years of toil and deprivation for nothing, he despaired and fell ill. Marsden took him from the cramped, unventilated sick bay, gaunt, listless, sucking air through inflamed lungs, and deposited him in his own quarters. His ills were tended and gradually he recovered.

The wonder of it, Marsden wrote, *is that his Nature has been quite Restored. Where one might quite Reasonably have Anticipated a Virulent Hatred and Distrust of the White Man and his Ways, there is instead a Remarkable Candour and Generosity of Spirit. He is much attached to Mrs Marsden who has been most Solicitous of his Health. For my part, there was little of Conversation twixt us for the first Month of sailing as I was laid very Low by Sickness of the Sea. But once I was Recovered enough, I found a very Cornucopia of Knowledge. Truly, my dear Doctor Good, how can we doubt the Success of our Mission when here, at its very Knockings, the Lord has Seen Fit to place within our hands such a Powerful Connection to New Zealand? But it was a Near Thing. For several days after we sailed I was Apprehensive that he would not Recover. This gave me Much Concern as his death would entirely defeat the Object I had in View.* Marsden had learned much. He and Ruatara would settle into conversation in English and Maori and the chaplain compiled a working vocabulary. Grammar largely eluded him but he soon had enough to begin his study of the ways of the Maori.

Do you know, he penned excitedly, *that Ruatara has told me that his People believe the First Woman to have come from the Rib of the First Man? What further Proof need we enquire that God has already brought the Beginning of Revelation to the Heathen?*

For three days the 'Ann' sat at anchor, host to an endless stream of smaller craft, bearing provisions and spars and rigging to answer to the damage of a sorry time of it in the mid-Atlantic. Passengers plied to and fro, grateful for firm ground after three months of toss, pitch and wallow. The decks rang in a cacophany of beating hammers, the hissing anvil, shouting sailors and, ludicrously, the bleating and clucking of livestock, shifting and fouling within their narrow pens, crowding for shade but breathing fresh air. And the clank of chains from the shuffling convicts taking their daily ration of light and air.

John King gazed across the harbour in disbelief and wonder. Nothing in his twenty five years of England had prepared him for this. Beneath a perfect sky the sea was blue and green and transparent. The town drew back from port and pier into a clutter of colour; the jungle was an encroaching mantel. There was an opulence here, a voluptuousness in the rampant growth that reached across the glittering tide and touched him and made him shiver. And over the salt and the brine and the cowshit there breathed the occasional fragrance that he held to the extent of his own breath.

There are tigers here, black tigers that spring from shadow. And giant snakes, thirty feet long that envelop their prey and squeeze the life out of them.

He heard a heavy step approach and turned to face his fellow mechanic. He gestured with an arm, taking in this radiant new world.

"I am amazed," he said.

"Aye," Hall nodded. "I thought I was dreaming at first; all those colors I'd never seen before."

"I would love to see it at closer hand," said King wistfully. "To smell the flowers."

"To stand on dry land."

They were quiet for a while, leaning amicably on the railing, but King noticed Hall's fingers beginning a heavy rhythm. This was one of his many signs of anger and King sought to stave it off.

"Do you know, William, the anaconda is –"

Too late.

"This is not good enough, John. We should be on land, I should like to see the markets."

The words came slowly, heavily, deliberately. What might have put a quaver in a voice went instead into drumming fingers and now a tapping foot.

"Alas," King affected to speak lightly but there was a quaver here. "Duty before pleasure."

"Aye," Hall chewed the word. "Our duty and Master Marsden's pleasure."

King hesitated to argue, he hoped only to cast a little damp on the ember. "Our immediate duty," he said, "is to the families we serve. And it *is* paying our fare."

But Hall would not be dissuaded from his course. "That fare should never have been, John."

King took refuge in agreement. "It was not right to dun us of our passage." But, back to soothing waters, "that was the vote of the Society. It was none of Mr Marsden's doing."

"Says Marsden."

There was that finality, Marsden had it, too, the man who would be Right.

"I heard Dr Ingram tell the captain that they would be disembarked for the afternoon. Perhaps they will wish you to accompany them."

"As their beast of burden. Carrying madam's parcels, sweating in my jacket. I can't wait."

King sighed. There would be no relief here and he looked about for a means of escape.

He started as Hall took him by the buttonhole.

"We should just *go*, John, just get into the next longboat going ashore," deliberate, no excitement but the cheeks were darkening in more anger.

How does he do this to himself?

"There's always plenty of room. Who's to stop us?"

"Dear God," King stared at him. "You cannot be serious."

"And why not? I reckon I know what I'm entitled to, I'm still a free Englishman."

"You have an obligation –"

"To God. And to my employers, that's true. *And they have an obligation to me.*

Everything came back to obligation.

"William, I beseech you. Marsden would see such a thing as wanton defiance."

"Let him. What can he do?"

"He can dismiss us from the Society." King screamed the last words and a group of seamen looked around sharply.

He stepped back, holding up his hands in supplication, panting to steady his breath, to gather himself.

Hall looked at him scornfully. "You let Marsden walk all over you," he said. "All of them, the captain, the Ingrams."

"They are my superiors. It is my place."

Why did it happen so often, when Hall was angry with Marsden and vice versa, that King ended up apologising for himself?

It was his place, he knew it, it was his last place, too; there was no place else to go. This was his life.

He tried another approach. "If you, we are dismissd from the Society, the ship's directors will sue us for the passage. We could be bankrupted. There will be nothing from the Society. And," he caught himself to stop from screaming again, *"we will be in Australia."*

Hall hawked and spat prodigiously over the side. His rancour was not eased but he would not take himself to Rio de Janeiro. Perhaps he wouldn't have, in any event. "You're right," he said at last. "I must be the servant. But I will not bow and scrape; they will know they are talking to a man."

His fist thumped the railing rhythmically, underlining each word.

"I will not be wronged.

CHAPTER 11

London 1810

Dear Emmeline,

> *My great Love to you and John, all my Thought and Cares are with you as you enter your first Confinement. I have had three now with another due soon and, Praise God, all Thrive and Prosper. But you must know, Emmeline, it is a Hard Time. Avoid Surprise and Anticipate a Hard Time. And when you are Hurting and Crying out do not let yourself believe that it is Anything less than a Hard Time. Do not charge yourself with Weakness nor Cowardice. They are Meaningless here. You will come through your Confinement, Emmeline, and you will hold your Child afterwards. You will know Woman's Greatest Blessing.*

Jane reread the opening paragraph and her eyes widened. Lord, she thought, I am writing a sermon, warning and encouragement together. Pompous but kindly meant. The kind of thing dear Mrs Kent would say. She smiled at the image.

The past four years have flown by. Susannah is six years old now and Elizabeth is five. Thomas will soon be three. All enjoy Good Health and I daily thank God for His Kindness, particularly when I see how many others Suffer. The last winter was a Hard one and in the poorer quarters there were many Deaths. Thomas says that we have been Unduly Blessed. I try to remember this when sometimes I am tired and the children fractious.

Mother also enjoys Good health but sadly I must report that our Father does not fare so well. His Lungs are failing and he struggles to Breathe. His Quality of Life is very poor; he must needs even foresake his pipe which has been such a Comfort to him over the years. Thomas blames the London climate, this pernicious blend of Smoke and Fog that we must daily breathe. Truly, Thomas has become much Disenchanted with London and regularly catalogues its Faults: the Disorder in the streets, there was a great Disturbance lately which saw much Loss of Life, the Poverty and Hunger and Illnesses that sweep through the poorer quarters. He also rails against Crime. But recently a member of the Congregation was set upon in the streets in Broad Daylight and robbed of all he had. The poor man also endured a savage Beating.

Jane laid down her pen and thought about Thomas' Disenchantment. It seemed to permeate his thinking and had brought with it a kind of sourness that was uncomfortably reminiscent of his mother. A child could not but cough without his launching into a diatribe against the weather; a shortage of bread at table would be an invitation to discourse upon taxes, the cost of living, the war with France that had now run for near a lifetime.

I wonder, she wrote, *whether this View might in some part inform his Desire to become a Missionary.* She paused then, uncomfortable, feeling a prick of disloyalty in the thought. Worse, almost a kind of blasphemy. Thomas' movement towards the Mission was nothing other than the will of God. It had been a long time coming, he had told her, but now that he looked back over his life he could see a pattern there. There was the time, for instance, when in early childhood he had fallen into a stream and would have perished but for the fortuitous intervention of a farm labourer. Was it just good fortune? I was saved for something else, Jane. His fall was part of the pattern, too. Because he had been blind to his nature, not knowing what he did not know, he said, it had been necessary that he fall, for only then would the scales be lifted from his eyes and he could seek redemption. And it came, Jane, it came: the Lord led me to the Bentinck Chapel and to Basil Woodd and delivered me to salvation.

And they were good years, Jane thought, we were happy then. Another disloyal thought. We are happy now.

And then another revelation. Three years ago he had read the CMS Report and the Way had opened before him. He saw the blessings of his own life, a fulfilling, rewarding vocation, a loving wife and family and the wider family of the Church; and against this he saw the dark and wretched world of the heathen. His children were born to know the love of Christ, their salvation was assured, but what awaited the pagan child? Savagery and degradation and in the end, unknowing, they would be cast down howling. A new awareness had overwhelmed him, once again the scales were torn from his eyes and he was ashamed of his happiness. The soul of the heathen, he said, is as valuable as my own and Christ is ready to save him.

He had prayed long and hard and had taken to calling frequently upon Basil Woodd to explore this further revelation and torment. One night, after Jane had settled the children to bed, he opened his Bible and pointed out a passage to her. It read:

And it shall come to pass in that day, that the Lord shall set his hand again the second time to recover the remnant of his people which shall be left, from Assyria, and from Egypt and from the islands of the sea.

See there, Jane, to recover the remnants of his people from the *islands of the sea*. There is a significance here, a meaning that we cannot deny.

He had continued to seek after the meaning and inexorably it became plain. God had prepared him for a purpose, had He not made him to be a teacher serving out his apprenticeship here in London? And had He not delivered him to Basil Woodd and thence to the CMS? His way, his purpose was clear.

Initially Jane had been alarmed and, to her shame, bitter, too. This inevitable movement, she had thought, from London to Thoresby where he had failed and become discontent to London where he had thrived and become discontent. Would nothing ever be good enough? And where might discontent lead him next time? Where does one move from living amongst savages? To living with them?

For the first time since leaving Thoresby they had quarrelled.

"The children, Thomas, the children. Will we not be placing their lives in mortal danger?"

"You exaggerate, Jane. You fright yourself with things which are not."

"Which are not? Thomas, these people *eat* people. And you talk of things which are not!"

"They practise cannibalism, it is true. But only on their own kind, prisoners they have taken in battle. It is a terrible sin and we must turn them from it."

Thomas was calm, serene in his understanding and conviction, gently pitying Jane her foolish anxieties.

"But how shall we survive? Where shall we live?"

"Dear Jane," Thomas smiled, "we are not sailing straight to the bush to set up camp with savages. We will sail to Sydney where Dr Marsden and the Society are well established. He serves as a magistrate, you know, as well as chaplain and he consults with government. We shall live in comfort, you, the children and I in a house with walls and ceilings and all the modern accomodations. And we shall plan the mission to New Zealand from there and it will grow gradually and safely, Jane, safely and it will be as a beacon shining in the pagan darkness, a light to the glory of God."

"And my parents, my sisters, my *family*. I shall never see them more."

Now Thomas had no easy answers. His father had died two years before at the age of ninety one. For a man who had endured chronic pain for years his end was surprisingly sudden. No decline, just immediate death. He died of asphyxiation, which the doctor called a failure of the lungs inducing a failing of the heart. Thomas called it suffocation and patricide. He did nothing but could not face his brother at the funeral.

Edward and Susanna had shared the house, that is, they shared the spaces and the silence. For Edward they were much as they had always been. He had lost his father long before he died but it had come in slow and generally easy stages. Firstly he had lost the companionship of shared endeavour working on the farm, the awareness of other. That had come not quite so easy and for a while Edward caught himself beginning remarks –'would you pass the … have you seen the …'-and had known the sudden touch of fear as his words fell into empty space. But after a time he adjusted and became comfortable with the new silence. And when pain took his father finally to bed, cursing and moaning, he had become the agent of a new silence. Thomas had acquainted him with the properties of laudanum and he had traded for a regular, growing supply, primarily for his father but also for himself. Susanna had complained at its liberal use but there was nothing she could do. Edward just ignored her, indifferent to her unreason and unconcerned about the reasons that lay beneath it. He tended patiently, gently, even affectionately to his father, cleaning and changing him when Susanna became unable. But he did not sit with him –'where's the use of it?' he had asked Thomas – and when in the end laudanum had lost its power, gently, even affectionately he had smothered him with a clean, fresh pillow.

Thomas became excluded, dismissed from his mother's life. But for a while the old bonds had remained intact, held in the occasional letter.

The Neglect which has attended my life has now become Complete. I am Prisoner in the house in which I sacrificed my Hopes for the Well-being of others, dependent on one Unkind man and ignored by Another.

Thomas had writhed under the words. He could not offer her the shelter of his own home; there was little enough space for the five of them as it was, quite apart from the certainty of Jane's utter resistance. Nor did he believe that his mother would have accepted any such offer. But it galled him bitterly that he could not even make it.

He visited when he could and berated himself for the infrequency. Conversation was strained. He would tell her of the children, the grandchildren that his wife had stolen from her, of his school and she would shrug and turn away, of his involvement in the congregation and his Sunday school class.

"I am glad you are doing some good," she said, "although it is a shame it is not within the true church."

Telling her of his decision to enter the mission field became an excruciating task. He longed to tell her yet at the same time shrank from it. Finally, buoyed upon a bottle of port, he broke the news.

She nodded vaguely. "There may be some good in it," she said. "My appetite is almost gone; I eat like a bird."

Edward was much more interested.

"I have heard something of New Zealand," he said. "I am told it is a land of vast forests filled with the most beautiful birds and with streams and lakes that team with fish."

Thomas was caught by his attentiveness and for a full hour he declaimed and invented.

Edward shook his head, wondering. "It sounds like paradise," he said, "still and peaceful. A man could lose himself there." He looked at Thomas. "I think I should like to go there with you. What do you think?"

Thomas shook his head. "No," he said.

Edward was a poor instrument for Susanna's focus, poorer even than his father had been as he had lain unconscious on his bed. Susanna's complaints dissolved upon indifference and fell pittering away into a void. There was no spark for her here, not with a man so soft and distant in his port and laudanum, smiling at the way the leaves had eddied in the shadows of a stream. And his utter indifference dissolved her connection to the moment and others began to intrude. One day as she was reading her Bible, bent over a magnifying glass, she paused upon the twenty-third psalm. She lowered the glass and closed her aching eyes and then she was nine again in her pretty, muslin frock and the grass was soft beneath her toes. She lay down in her father's garden and the air was full of lavender. Then she was flying on a swing, flying through a fresh breeze as the world swept and turned beneath her. Edward had found her some hours later, still at her desk, the lines about her face gentle now and her cheeks wet with tears. He walked softly back to the kitchen and carefully, quietly prepared the evening meal.

Her strength and purpose left her together as she played in the woods of her childhood. And as movement left her command the dreams became stronger. Here she was, helping mother in the kitchen, clown-faced in dabs of flour, the air warm and sweet with baking bread, here she was exchanging smiles with Mary Mercer and later with Jimmy Wainwright, so strong and straight, so clean and young. And here she was –it seemed so real – held in the strong, loving arms of her father as he carried her to bed. Her fingers traced the heavy, muscled shoulder and the hard mass of upper arm and she smiled in the security of her utter safety.

She died in gradually declining stages and Edward nursed her because he had to, patiently, gently, caught in the pervasive sadness of aloneness, melancholic and carried on the movement of her death. He voyaged with her, watching the loss of colour as of falling leaf and as she became still more silent she became less alone. Edward retained a steadiness of being but the rest of the world did not. Thomas had become an unwelcome intrusion, a distraction, flapping, bothering, talking too loud and too fast. She disliked his grief and his fear and his anger and wished he would stay away. She was unaware of the spark he carried that might rekindle old, dark flames, only dimly aware that there was an offer to old engagement. But she disliked it anyway and said nothing. She did not wish to disturb the slowing stream, to blow skittery words upon its surface. Somewhere, dimly, she might have thought it would be unkind. So she murmured meaninglessly and flowed away on her stream of shadow to a kind and easy end.

In confusion Thomas watched her die; he darted in the shadows of Edward's vessel and whimpered at the dying of her light. His own small craft bucked in the eddies and scrambled through rapids while Edward and Susanna sailed serenely on. Alternately he watched his mother's face and wondered at the gentleness, listened to her sigh in Edward's arms and marvelled at the tenderness and felt his own exclusion and was bitter at the injustice.

So when Jane lamented the loss of her family he was taken alternatively severe.

"We must not think of ourselves like this, Jane. You are weighing trifles, matters of comfort and convenience and self-interest against the Will of God and the salvation of our Immortal Souls. What doth it profit a man to gain the whole world if he should lose his soul?"

Alternatively tender.

"I know what I am asking and I know how hard it is. I know it is harder for you than for me; I have little left to leave and you have much. I am sorry, so sorry."

Alternatively mute

It was left to Jane to try to make some sense of it.

His mother's Death has placed Thomas at a Loss, she wrote, *he scarce knows how to grieve, nor for whom he grieves. Deep inside he is Unsettled and I doubt not her Departure is somehow close to his Desire to be a Missionary. Why must he reach to such Extremes?*

She could not sustain resentment against Thomas. Apart from all other considerations his vulnerability touched her too closely. So even when he had swung, on the nights when doubt had assailed him and he had clung to her with swamping need she, dear God, she had comforted him. What else was to be done? So she had looked to Basil Woodd, the man who had awoken Thomas and who would be the namesake of their fourth child.

I do believe it is Basil Woodd who has Turned Thomas to the Dream and who Sustains him in it.

She had turned initially to her mother for advice. But Mary Quickfall had moved as swiftly from her near infatuation with Basil in the beginning to seething dislike when he had encouraged and supported Thomas –'driven him to it, more like'- in his drive to join the mission. So her advice served little in either case.

Florence Kent had a wider view and steered Jane from making Basil a monster. "If his motives matter, they are probably as they appear. He sees God's hand in this; he believes Thomas is the man for the mission. It is not a position that requires discussion." She sighed. "I believe he is quite persuaded by Thomas' enthusiasm and shares, perhaps partakes of it."

"How exciting that must be for him." Jane's sarcasm was savage. "To partake of the Great Venture, share in the spread of the Word of God and keep oneself comfortable in London while so doing."

"Precisely so." Florence was unperturbed. "Basil is adventuring through Thomas, it is true. But if one's adventure is also the will of God ..." She raised an eyebrow.

"So I must not think he is insincere. Let him do for us in full sincerity?"

"It has not yet happened, Jane; perhaps it never will. You know how Thomas can turn."

But that was in the early days and Thomas had not turned. And now Florence could only look at Jane in sadness. ""I'm so sorry," she would whisper, "so sorry."

Everyone is sorry, Emmeline, and we stand and watch our Sorrow draw near as though it were Something that lived Apart from us. How can that be? We say, "I'm sorry," and we stand and watch or go to Join our Sorrow.

Chapter 12

"The *Swallow* has come in sight, sir."

"Excellent." Samuel Marsden did not look up from his papers. "Keep an eye on proceedings and advise me when the passengers disembark. And, Jones, this is not an invitation to idle about the docks all day. Check on the hour. Go now."

He listened to the door close, then stretched back mightily in his chair. So the new man was here. Excellent. His curriculum vitae promised much, an Oxford graduate no less, ordained by Dr Rumpole himself no less. Of excellent stock. His father, Joshua Egan was a pillar of the community, a successful man, an upright man and a generous benefactor of Oxford.

Ah, they would do such fine things, he and Egan; they would make order out of chaos, they would fill the churches again. There would be another responsible voice echoing Marsden's sentiments. There would be posts for Egan to take, under Marsden's advisement, significant posts that would help shape the way the colony developed.

He was not likely to be a farmer. Horticulture would not be found among divinity papers. That was a shame. The life of the farmer was an enduring example, even an enactment of the principles of Industry and Progress. Still, Egan was obviously an intelligent man, he would doubtless be a quick learner and under Marsden's tutelage ....

Marsden smiled, then straightening his shoulders he turned back to his desk and his paperwork.

Port Jackson was aglow in the last of the sun when the *Swallow* finally docked and released her passengers. They were comparatively few, the *Swallow* was primarily a merchant trader but Marsden was still at something of a loss as he watched them. The CMS had not thought to provide a physical description. Never mind, Egan would know him, he need only stand and wait. Or rather sit, he eased his bulk on to a crate and gave his attention over to the price of wool.

His thoughts were interrupted by a weak cough.

"Mr Marsden?"

Marsden stared at the man before him. Gaunt and frail, his clothes hung from him like a scarecrow. Marsden could see the outline of bone behind stretched cheek and the darkness puckered beneath his eyes. His grip was weak.

"May I present my wife?" The voice was soft and tired but the accent was that of a gentleman.

Mrs Egan was a lesser version of her husband. She was such as one who had lived for months with discomfort and exhaustion, keeping her husband alive. She had survived better because she had to; if she had fallen ill both would have perished.

But her smile was full and open and Marsden was charmed by it.

"My dear sir," he was all solicitude, "I can see that you have suffered terribly."

Egan inclined his head. "I have," he agreed.

More than he would have believed possible. And he was not inexperienced in pain.

"I would have died," he said, "had it not been for this good woman here. I shall be forever grateful."

"Amen. A loyal and caring spouse is a great blessing. Now," Marsden took charge, "Jones, fetch a carriage immediately, say who it is for and bring any argument to me. When you've done that, convey my compliments to the master of the vessel and arrange for Mr and Mrs Egan's belongings to be sent to the parsonage."

Jones tugged a greasy forelock and scurried off. In almost no time a carriage was drawing up to them and an anxious driver was making his obedience.

"Good evening, Mr Marsden, your worship, Smithers at your service, your worship."

Marsden ushered them into their new home.

"It's been somewhat neglected since we left it, ten years now but I hope you'll find it serviceable."

After the *Swallow* a hole in the ground would have been welcome. Joanna was enchanted.

"There's so much *room*, isn't there, George, well there is to me."

"And this is Mrs Bishop who will be looking after you. Having met you, I am very glad she is. Besides being a midwife and knowledgeable about health, she is a fine cook. Elizabeth, Mrs Marsden recommends her highly."

Mrs Bishop stood quietly in the third person, examining the Egans. "You do not look well," she said and Marsden made no demurral at her not waiting to speak. "But I think you will find that a diet of fresh food and rest will do you wonders."

"There." Marsden rubbed his hands. "The diagnosis is complete. And I must be about my business. Oh," he paused and raised a hand, "Mrs Marsden sends her kind regards and hopes to meet with you soon. When you feel up to it."

He brushed aside their protestations at his kindness. "Not at all, not at all. Your health, dear Sir and Madam, that is the thing. You cannot serve any if you cannot serve yourselves. I will call upon you in a fortnight."

He bowed stoutly and was gone.

It was a joy to wake in a soft, spacious bed and George stretched and almost moaned for the pleasure of it. Joanna was already up, standing by the window, a cape draped over her nightdress. She turned and her cheeks were flushed with excitement and suddenly she was young and pretty again.

"Come and look at this. Hurry! It's fucking amazing."

George raised an eyebrow and looked towards the door.

"Sorry, I forgot. But come and look at it."

He crossed the floor to join her, carefully, his sea-legs had not yet left him.

"There. Look at that."

He looked across the verandah and out on to a field that went on forever. Its grasses were faded under the sun but close by the house was a stand of gum and acacia and in their shade the grass was lush and green.

"There. In the shadow of the verandah."

"Dear God, it is a dragon."

It was a face from mythology, he had seen many a replication but still he could not believe it. Ridiculously he felt a giggle start.

It was altogether remarkable, not just the creature but that he was here, looking at it.

Joanna squealed as the dragon suddenly rose on to its hind legs and the skin about its neck expanded to a pointed blue ruff. It looked around towards the sound and for a moment it seemed to be looking directly at them. He shivered then the giggle became a laugh. Joanna joined him and they pushed the window open, uproarious and watched the beast race away, its pointed scaly tail steering scaly pounding thighs.

"God," whispered George, "it is like opium but more focused, more real."

They could not wait to be out of the house and short strolls became longer walks became exploration. A carriage was engaged and it took them to the beaches where they waded, trouser and dress above the knees in the warm water. As their strength returned they cautiously climbed on to the beginnings of the rocky coastline that separated the beaches. There they found pools in the rocks, still, like glass and they watched tiny fish flit after invisible things and eyes on stalks that stared from the sand.

"You will be wanting your own house and land." It was not a question. "The better parcels about the town are long gone, my own farm is stationed thirty miles away in Paramatta. But there are some smaller and, I believe, very feasible blocks due to be opened shortly. Jones will take you to see them."

They visited the blocks like excited newly-weds looking for their first home. Up at first light and quickly away before the sun became serious. Smithers would urge the horses on and they would lean back, cushioned beneath the hood and study again what passed for a description of the land. Then they would be driving and walking and climbing about it, looking for this, remarking upon that. They could always find shade from the full heat of the day. Invariably there would be stands of bush, sometimes by a stream where they could take their picnic. Over lunch they would rate the land against Marsden's criteria: is there available water, might the land be subject to flooding, is there a suitable house site …? Then as Smithers snored from a distance they would play with possibilities.

"I want hens, George, I really want hens. Wouldn't they be brilliant, clucking and pecking?"

"And laying eggs and flavouring the broth."

"I can't imagine what it would be like to have animals. Have you had animals?"

"Yes, I had a dog once I was very attached to, various cats. And horses at different times." He nodded, remembering. "I had a lovely mare named Bess, she was a -. Anyway," remembering again, "yes, a few."

"We will have a dog and a cat and a horse. I will learn to ride. Will you teach me?"

Marsden commended their choice. "Now the house," he said. Again they put themselves in his hands or rather, through Marsden they placed themselves in the hands of Mr Bull, an emancipist of some years standing. In his former life he had served a builder and had picked up enough of the trade to pass himself as one now. He had built for Marsden before and the chaplain had been impressed.

"Solid workmanship, nothing clever but sound. Your roof won't leak and the house will hold together. He gets the best out of his men, too. Doesn't take any nonsense from them."

Marsden arranged the payment of materials and labour and George was penniless and in debt against future earnings. He had no idea when the money from England would arrive; it would depend upon ships and conditions and the vagaries of his father's temper. No, that was unfair, it would be here within six months. In the meantime he would have to borrow again but that was not a problem. They would manage.

A different problem emerged.

"Now that you are looking so well and the land is settled and the house is under way, we might turn our attention to Matters of the Parish."

Marsden thought it would do very well if George were formally introduced to the congregation by taking the lesson. They discussed the theme.

"Best, I think," declared Marsden, "if you take a stand at the Very Outset on Virtue in life."

"Virtue in life?" asked George faintly.

"Yes," the chaplain was grim. "You need to know that Moral Standards here are not what you would have been accustomed to in Oxford. The emancipists do not change their Progligate Ways when they change from convicts. Intemperance is their curse. You need to understand, sir, that I am a Mortal Enemy of the demon drink. May I ask your position?"

George had recovered himself. "I do not drink," he said a little severely. "I have vowed that alcohol will never cross my lips."

Marsden nodded approvingly. "I respect that," he said. "Now, their Profanity is a commonplace and there is a shocking Lassitude of Morals that manifests in a growing population of bastards. I have established an orphanage for girls that they might live in some safety and acquire some useful skills." He paused.

"A most worthy endeavour," said George obediently.

"And they do not Observe the Sabbath. Numbers in church are a great disappointment."

George cleared his throat. "So you would like me to speak –"

"Preach."

"-preach against obscene language, immoral sexual behaviour and profaning the Sabbath?"

"And idleness and sloth."

"And idleness and sloth."

"Succinctly put. I am looking forward to your sermon already. And don't hold back. The Lord saith, 'the Wages of Sin is Death'. They should be thinking to the Hereafter. This Sunday should do very well. I will see you then, say at thirty minutes after nine. Madam." A bow and he was gone.

The next day the Egans stayed at their lodging and George brooded at the kitchen table, immersed in a pile of sermons. He skimmed quickly through them, "I should have started this sooner," looking for lessons on the theme. Given its breadth, all touched it in some way.

By mid-afternoon he was beginning to worry.

"I don't know if I can do this, Jo," he complained. "Hellfire and brimstone, the wails of the damned and the sniggers of the self-righteous. It's obscene."

Joanna bustled helplessly. She could not help him yet.

George was beginning to work himself up. "The very idea is an obscenity, imagine wishing an *eternity* of torture upon anyone. The thought alone is the product of an utterly evil or utterly mad mind. It is the ultimate spite, the ultimate malice. It makes me sick to think on it."

"Yes, but you can't *say* that."

"What can I say?"

They worried together, then Joanna said, "I've only been in a church a few times, funerals mainly but it seemed funny how the preachers spoke only of evil."

George nodded. "They revel in it," he said. "Here, look at this," he held up a sheet of crabbed writing. "On fornication, one of Marsden's themes. 'And she,' the whore of Babylon, that is, 'shall be burned utterly with fire. And the kings of the earth who have committed fornication and lived deliciously with her shall bewail her and lament for her when they shall see the smoke of her burning.' Why are they so absorbed in other people's sex lives?"

"Yes, but you can't ask that. Hang on, here's a thought. How would it be if you talked about virtuous stuff?"

"The language of virtue? Yes, I could do that. Don't know about the language of chastity, though."

"It doesn't have to be chaste. Just not unchaste."

"This is getting silly."

Silly or not, it was a direction and by the next morning George had a draft. Now Joanna could help.

"Everything," she said, "is in the delivery."

Two days later she sat in the foremost pew, hands folded in her lap, chaste and demure in her grey bonnet and dress. Her eyes were downcast but she listened attentively.

Don't clear your throat.

"Friends," his baritone was deeper and resonant against the high wooden walls. "In settling upon today's lesson," he paused, "my first conversation with you," he smiled and nodded faintly, "I took advice of our Good Chaplain." George bowed slightly in Marsden's direction and from the corner of her eye Joanna saw Marsden nod in return. "Mr Marsden shared with me his concern at the Poverty of Moral Standards," across the aisle Joanna heard a sigh, "and suggested I address the issue of the virtuous life. Specfically he spoke against profane language, unchaste living and breaches in the Observance of the Sabbath.

"Of course I heeded his wisdom but I did wonder: would I not be preaching to the converted? After all, are you not here, virtuous people in the bosom of your families, taking your place in church observing the

Lord's day? What can I say that you do already know? So I thought and mused. What is the language of virtue, I wondered and where do we hear it? Friends, the answer seemed to me a simple one. The language of virtue is the language of kindndess and since my good wife and I have arrived on your shores we have heard it continuously in its simplest and purest form. 'Good morrow, sir, I hope I find you well. May I help you? Here is fresh fruit for you, a loaf of bread, side of meat. May I advise on good land?"

George continued in a similar vein, outlining the kindness of the congregation and Joanna heard them settle in their seats and saw the smiles.

"...and for those who have fallen from the wayside into unchaste and thoughtless lives, what would be the point to our condemnation? We have heard, 'Judge not lest ye be judged'. How much worthier is the helping hand, the orphanage for the innocent victims ...

Be careful, George. You're starting to sound like Jesus. Marsden liked the acknowledgement for the orphanage, though.

"... and here we are in church together in observance of the Sabbath. What will we do with the rest of the day? I think we should first observe the beauty of it, feel the sun and breeze against our skin ...

Careful.

"Think of what we have here, remember what we have left behind, be grateful. Perhaps true observance of the Sabbath is in the act of conscious gratitude."

He smiled at the audience and the congregation smiled back.

Marsden stood beside them as they shook hands and conversed with the parishioners.

"Uplifting, Reverend. Gratitude, that's the ticket."

"I suppose I shouldn't say but it was a delight to listen to your voice, sir. An agreeable gentleness, persuasive, not abrasive."

Marsden narrowed his eyes.

"Good day, Mrs Egan, such a pleasure to meet you, ma'am."

Marsden was not entirely settled. There was something about the *tone* of the sermon, he could not put his finger on it, that was not quite right. But the congregation had taken to Egan, he had seen that, him and his wife, too, with her sweet demure smile. He watched William and Dinah Hall pass by, they nodded curtly and his face soured at the comparison.

And he eyed the Egans more closely. Perhaps, like Ruatara they had been put in his way to Further the Mission. Something Unexpected.

So altogether he deemed the sermon a success, or he would have had he been a judgmental man. As it was, he let his judgment be known in a judicious nod and a firm shake of the hand.

CHAPTER 13

London 1811

The hulks lay in the muddy estuaries of the Thames. When the tide was out and the fading sun picked crimson and gold out of the water's sheen they could be very beautiful. At a distance the stump of mast reflected in turquoise was only a delightful marriage of colour and line. Closer the image of the coffin was irresistible but there was life of a kind within so something quicker must be found, like a beast that roots within the mud and feeds on flesh, like a joining of dragon and mangrove. But most people saw them as just part of the landscape and gave them little thought. And even less to those that dwelled within them.

These were the convicts, the outcasts of England. Sometimes their crimes were cruel and barbarous but rarely capital; they had earned less than the rope. Mostly they were thieves who had stolen for a variety of reasons of which necessity was commonplace. Often they had left others dependent upon their fortune who might now starve, particularly the children, to be given over to the workhouse or sold to a sweep for a guinea.

They had usually come from a barbarous world. Not always; witness the merchant who became mad when his business failed and ran to his rival with a pistol to claim the money he believed stolen. He gibbers at shadows now. Unlike the merchant or the scrawny tutor who Forgot himself in a Frenzy of Frustration (vide the 'Gazette') and thrashed into unconsciousness one of his pupils for idleness, insolence and a prodigious stupidity. The boy was the younger son of a magistrate and now the teacher chants his conjugations without fee. But to most this place was known before they came here, through messages and guards who would discourse for a pint of the landlord's best. The hulks lay beached beneath the shadow of Newgate as a likely end.

They had one hope but that as dreadful as their present circumstance. The hope took them from the mud and the hulks to the sea and a transport, a floating hulk. Their world would be exactly the same but for the certainty of days in which heat would suck the life from them, water would be scarce and their rations could be gone. When their world would roll and plunge and hurl them to the end of their chains. When the incessant tossing and wallowing made the stomach twist and spasm and move the bowels without warning and they would roll and plunge in the shit and the vomit and moan and wish to die.

It remained a hope nevertheless. They would die where they were or they would die on a transport. The transport offered greater horror but it was measuring the same death. And despite the great numbers lost most, they were told, did survive. They got to walk God's earth again, grass beneath their feet, stand in air, listen to a singing bird. So if they prayed, they prayed for transportation. Let it be done with, one way or the other. For the moment their conditions were tolerable. The weather was mild and time on deck in the sun and fresh air brought a kind of peace.

The rations were reasonable and better than that if you had friends on the outside and an agreeable guard on the inside.

But the nights were something else…

A young man sat hunched upon a narrow cot, gazing at the floor between his feet. The cot was attached to the curving wall behind it. Along its length ran a steel bar; a chain ran from the bar to his wrist. The chain was not fixed but could slide along the bar, leaving the captive free to shuffle a dozen or so steps to his right or left.

As he was now obliged to do.

"Hey," a hand was on his shoulder, "move along. Trembath's got to go to the head again."

The young man rose to his feet and became one of a line of a half dozen men. Together they shuffled along to the deep cesspit where they huddled together, allowing room for the last man to drop his breeches and attend to his business. And then they shuffled back and the young man resumed his study of the floor.

Even here he retained his place on the outside. There were no connections he could draw on to establish his place, nothing or no-one he knew that might be of value. Even if there had been, it would not have occurred to him to try to take advantage of it. He was, he knew, in his proper place and there was nothing to do other than just accept it. Beyond that, nothing needed to make sense. Like the conversation and the stories his fellows told. They spoke too quickly and interrupted and contradicted themselves. He had mused upon their tales, but still they made no sense.

A hand tugged his chain. An old man of forty, wrinkled, bent, with long silver greasy locks and beard gazed fixedly at him.

"I tell you about my son," the man said. "My son is a very good boy, very loyal to his father. Not a day goes by but he will be planning …"

The young man had heard the story before, it was the fence's only theme. His freedom would be shortly purchased as soon as his son … The young man could understand what the man was hoping but not why he kept on saying so.

Perhaps he was waiting for the right answer.

"Can you imagine a worthier boy?"

The young man could not imagine the boy at all or at least not as his father had portrayed him. But then he did not know many boys. He thought that if the boy were that clever and concerned he would have effected something by now. His father had been here a long time. But nothing. Not even a parcel slipped by a purchased guard.

"Perhaps he has stopped trying. Perhaps something has happened to him."

The fence was enraged. "What! What's that you're saying? Not trying? Something has happened to him? You godless, fuckin whoreson! My boy is worth a hundred of you." And he was away again, chanting his litany and shoring up the walls of his belief. After a time he was restored, but spiteful.

"You got a father, boy? You taking care of him?"

The young man might have said, something happened to me, but he recoiled instead; his head hunched as he pulled in his shoulders and shivered down his spine. Dark in his gut anxieties twitched. But there was a prayer on hand.

"My father is dead, sir," he heard himself saying, "he has gone to join my mother and rests in the arms of Jesus."

"Dead, eh? How did he die, I wonder. In the arms of his loving, fuckin son?"

The venom in the fence's voice poured acid on the darting fears and they screeched and whirled and multiplied. But the prayer persisted while the young man rocked and grunted. The fence was excited by this change and hungry for more of it. He leaned forward and hissed triumphantly, "You abandoned him didn't you, you whore's get, you –"

The words ceased abruptly as a large, heavy hand encircled his throat. Blood roared in the fence's head and his body screamed for air. His hands tore desperately, ineffectually at the fingers that dug deeper into his throat and he was suddenly, screamingly aware that he was about to die. Then the pressure relaxed and the hand was holding him up as he coughed and spluttered.

The young man's eyes were dark pinpricks but the distance had left them and there was a terrible focus as they held his tormentor. His voice was raised, as though over other voices, like a deaf man, "no more, no more words." His hand dropped and he sank back to the struggle. Gradually the grunting ceased and his breathing became more even. After a time he murmured, "my father has gone to join my mother and rests in the arms of Jesus."

CHAPTER 14

Paramatta 1811

It is not consistent with Morality, Religion or Sound Policy to nominate men magistrates who have been convicts and who are still openly living in Profligacy. What the governor's motive can be I cannot conceive. He issues public orders in Favour of Morality while he appoints men magistrates whose general conduct and example militates as much as possible Against it.

The final stop speared into the page, black ink splattered and the chaplain muttered in exasperation as he reached for the blotting paper. Then he pushed the letter from him where it joined a sea of papers overflowing on the vast oak desk. Briefly he bowed his head. *Lord grant me the patience to deal righteously with these wretched men.* But the indignation stayed with him as he paced his study. Dimly lit by a single narrow casement the height of a man, walls of cedar lined with shelves crammed in books, papers and files, it was the workplace of a man with too much business upon his hands. He lowered his squat bulk on to a black leather sofa but his irritation would not settle.

They are a trial sent to test me, he thought, as the Lord tested Job. But Job was required only to endure the Sabeans, the wind and fire, whereas I must resist and overcome wickedness. And where are my Eliphaz, my Bildad and Zophor to sit with me and counsel me? Those who should join with me appear to take the Adversary's part and do his work for him. In sudden fury he hurled a cushion the length of the room, flying into a shelf of deeds and documents and sending them fluttering to the floor.

Samuel, Samuel, see how the sin of anger attaches to you and will send you to despair. See how you lament of loneliness while your children play within your house and dear Elizabeth waits to comfort you. Wilberforce will hear your words even at twelve thousand miles and he will stir on your behalf.

Gradually he quietened and the fire faded from his heavy cheeks and the drumming in his temple faded.

And yet, and yet ... to overlook iniquity is to conspire with it. When Macquarie the governor, the man whose every move should inspire to Proper Behaviour, had chosen to appoint Andrew Thompson, thief, convicted felon, pardoned after only six of a fourteen year sentence, when Macquarie had appointed Thompson justice of the peace, Marsden had not spoken out. And what had that served? It had served to encourage further excess. Thompson had not changed. He had continued to amass wealth –not that that was a bad thing in itself. Marsden would not deny the man the fruits of his industry although profits derived from the illicit distilling of spirits called for condemnation. It was the source of much evil in the colony. But worse, the man continued to cohabit with Sara Jones, convicted thief and madam, emancipated now but no better than she ever was. A painted creature with sly eyes and pouting lips, dressed in gaudy silk that fell low cut to swelling flesh and ... o, it was outrageous.

His public silence had encouraged Macquarie. When the governor had approached the chaplain to serve as a commissioner for the turnpike road he planned to run from Sydney to the Hawkesbury, Marsden had consented. It would be more work of course, but he conceived the plan to be a good one, opening communications that would further the development of the colony and Marsden always knew where his duty lay. But when the issue of the *Sydney Gazette* came out at the end of March he discovered to his horror that he was to share the duty with the same Andrew Thompson. And Simeon Lord! Another convict freed early from penance. Who, like Thompson had amassed great wealth, in part Marsden would acknowledge through careful planning and much industry but also through surreptitious trade in spiritous liquor. Who now sat at table with the colony's administration and strode the streets of Sydney in London fashions for all the world like a gentleman. His doxy on his arm. Coquette! Whore, pretending to be a lady. On one occasion, in the governor's mansion no less she had dared to approach the chaplain's wife and speak with her as though they were equals. Elizabeth, bless her meek, forgiving heart, had not turned away (a fault she had later confessed to her husband) but was clearly discomforted. Marsden had been enraged and it had taken all his great self-control not to berate the simpering wretch upon the spot. He had had to content himself with crossing the floor in thunderous silence to take his wife's arm and lead her away from the contagion. And Lord had watched, had taken in the chaplain's mottled features and clenched fist. And had smiled! The memory sent a rush of blood through Marsden and the vein in his right temple throbbed dangerously.

Worse was to follow. Rumours had spread through Marsden's beloved orphanage for the abandoned daughters of the convict and emancipist worlds (see how premature forgiveness leads to further sin) that Lord had enjoyed improper relations with two of the girls. An enquiry had been called and Lord had been closely examined by the committee. And there he had stood, languid and evidently bored, dabbing at disdainful lips with a scented handkerchief, prevaricating, evading, lying! Nothing had come of the enquiry for the girls had further compounded their vice with protestations of innocence. It was apparent that Lord's promises had overcome Marsden's calls for righteous disclosure.

Macquarie knew all this for Marsden had advised him in detail when he had declined the commissioner's office. It is a degradation of my office as senior chaplain, he had said, and totally incompatible with my sacred functions. And Macquarie's response? He had told Marsden that the advancement of emancipists was laid down in His Majesty's instructions and then, unbelievably, that it was as well for Marsden that his commission had been changed from a military to a civil one or he would have been tried for disobedience by a court martial. At which point Marsden's self-restraint was lost to righteous fury.

And now Lord was elevated to the bench. *What the governor's motive can be I cannot conceive*, Marsden wrote to Wilberforce. But he could conceive and in his heart he knew that it was wickedness and spite.

And it was everywhere. Amongst convicts and emancipists alike who drank and gambled and blasphemed and whored their lives and souls away. Who knew no respect for the Lord's Sabbath nor for His representative among them. He could see it in the faces of the soldiers when he preached to them, yawning, uninterested, attending only out of duress. Even in the free settlers. Empty pews, their occupants sleeping off the effects of last night's revelry or scratching at their disordered gardens. How could they have so little regard for their souls and for the souls of their wives and children? Be so insensible of the wrath to come? Marsden feared the judgment that lay ahead for many and sometimes came near to despair. A lone voice crying in the wilderness. But, as Elizabeth had so often assured him, he need not berate himself for want of effort. As chaplain he had carried the Word throughout the province, exhorting, warning and if they would not unstop their ears … As administrator, agent, lobbyist and magistrate he had fought the liquor trade, he had thrown his weight behind public morality orders, particularly observance of the Sabbath, and had enforced them with righteous zeal. And had borne the opprobrium of the ungodly with steadfast patience. Let them call him the flogging parson. He knew where his duty lay. He had struggled to advance the movement of civilisation, calling for schools and proper non-denominational, that is, protestant worship. His orphanage was a model for all the world. And he was humble enough to acknowledge failure, though he could find no fault of his own in it. The aboriginals were a case in point, primitives who appeared to see no reason for the uses of civilisation and so defied the Missionary Society's policy of salvation through technology. Shameless in their nakedness, depraved in their habits, they stood apart from the growing settlements and showed not even a touch of curiosity at the wonders of the white man. Marsden wished to be charitable but he sometimes wondered if they were truly human. Certainly the white community regarded them as another species and treated them as such. Marsden lamented it and cast his hopes of a new flock further afield, across the Tasman.

"Mr Marsden." A thick, Yorkshire brogue broke into his meditations and Marsden sprang in sudden shock from the sofa, glaring at the open doorway. Mrs Bishop was unperturbed. In her plump features beneath her housekeeper's bonnet there was even a touch of amusement at the great man's discomfort.

"I'm sorry to have given you a fright, sir, but I stopped to see if you'd like me to bring you a pot of tea. Soothing for the spirit."

Marsden waved her offer away. "Thank you, no. I have not the time for it." Then he pushed past her and stomped down the corridor and out into the garden. The parsonage loomed behind him, a plain grey two-storeyed box. He drew in a deep breath of the cool mid-winter air and his racing heart slowed to an even pace. The sky was a pale, crystal blue unbroken by cloud and the hard straight lines of the house forgotten. But there was order here, too. The bare branches of apple and peach and pear were carefully pruned and the shining green of citrus leaf tidy and compact. No errant stragglers here. Further afield beyond the neat regular lines of fencing the Australian plains drew endlessly away but here the English grass grew thick and verdant. Sheep and cattle dotted the tidy pastures and lowing and bleating mingled with the mad laugh of the kookaburra. Here at least there was order and progress, the fruits of industry to nourish a growing settlement.

Marsden turned towards the sounds of hammering from a nearby barn and his head was full of business once more. He moved down through the slope of the orchard, pausing to pull delinquent broadleaf from the base of an apple tree (uncontaminated seed, indeed, he would have a word with the dealer), then on to the solid gate. The tidy gravel path glistened in the last of the morning dew.

He paused at the open door, watching Hall at work on the final stages of a dray, admiring his precision and economy of movement. For all his wilful obstinacy there was no doubt that the man was a skilled and industrious craftsman. And pious, too. Neither he nor his wife and child were ever known to miss Sunday service, although Marsden harboured doubts that the remainder of the day was spent in prayerful meditation or in study of the Maori language. Marsden had heard the Halls' dwelling was stocked with more furniture than one family would require and rumour had it that he engaged in private trade. Always an eye to filling his purse. Marsden sighed into a sudden silence and the carpenter turned swiftly to face him. A tall, wiry man with dark, almost Romany features and hard eyes that glittered briefly at the sight of his visitor. He laid down his hammer and nodded towards the chaplain but made no move towards him. Marsden nodded in return. "Good morning, Mr Hall," he said. "I trust I find you well." He nodded towards the dray. "A sturdy piece of work."

"Aye." Hall wiped the back of his hand over his mouth. "'twill serve well enough to cart your grain to the mill."

Marsden sensed the rebuke behind the words and his lips tightened as he answered. "The word of God is best received by men with full bellies, Mr Hall. We must nourish the colony."

"Aye." Now the rebuke was overt. "And line our pockets as we do so."

This was too much. The man's insolence was insufferable and all the earlier grievances flooded back. Marsden's voice shook as he answered, "You forget your station, Mr Hall, you would do –"

"I forget nothing." Unbelievably the man was interrupting him And contradicting. Marsden's face turned purple with rage and he gasped for air. Hall continued and now the pent-up resentment was evident in his voice, too. "I was engaged by the Missionary Society to bring the salvation of our Lord Jesus Christ to the heathen. I understood that were my station and I would dearly wish to occupy it. But I began as your servant on the *Ann* and I continue as your servant still." Self-restraint left him then and his voice rose in fury. "Brothers in the Lord, you said! A godly mechanic, you said! Your humble flunkey, more like. Have you seen where I live? Where my wife and son live? O no. It would be beneath you to stir from your home –a palace by comparison- to visit with your brother in Christ. And where are the heathen we were brought to save? I've barely seen a one and none in church. They stay away, they ignore us. And we ignore them! I am not here labouring for the Lord and serving Him. I am here labouring for you, serving you, enriching you while I live in poverty. I tell you, sir, it is a shame."

He paused for breath and Marsden exploded into the moment. "I'll tell you what is a shame, sir," he roared, pounding a fist into an open palm, "and that is your sinful pride. How dare you presume to judge me? I will not dignify your contumacious manner and outrageous charges with an answer. I am answerable to our Lord and to the Society, not to the likes of you. But I will tell you this. It is by my good grace that you are engaged in worthwhile endeavour and by the good grace of the Society that you are paid for it. You should be thankful that while the Lord has placed impediments to the mission in New Zealand you are being paid at all."

The two men glared at one another in silence, then Hall turned to the dray and began to gather up his tools. Marsden watched, the vein in his temple still throbbing but a thread of unease slipping through his anger. Then Hall spoke, bitterly but with control. "Then you will be pleased," he said, "that I intend no longer to be a drain upon your precious funds." He watched the chaplain breathe deeply, reaching for self-control, and was pleased and soothed by a sense of the upper hand. "Mr Shearer has offered me a position at his dockyard," he continued in a milder tone. "I sent message that he would have my answer within the week. He shall have it today." He opened a sturdy canvas bag by his side and began carefully to place his tools into it.

Marsden's business sense found sway over his passion as he assessed the situation. Hall was paid well, he thought, one hundred and twenty pounds a year was a good sum but he was probably well worth it. Marsden would be hard pressed to replace him and now with the Society's approval for extensions to the church in Sydney … Marsden sighed and reached for a more conciliatory tack.

"We have both spoken in anger and not in the spirit of good, Christian men," he began. He found he was addressing Hall's back as the man wrapped a saw in an oiled cloth and swallowed rising bile. "I have represented your endeavours in a favourable light to the Society," he continued, "and they are pleased to offer you continuing employment."

"In what capacity?"

"As a builder and craftsman. You know," he went on quickly to forestall the inevitable retort, "that since the unfortunate business of the *Boyd,* which I believe was initiated by the cruelty and thoughtlessness of the captain and crew, since that unfortunate business, I say, passage to and from New Zealand has become impossible. To the extent that I am presently raising with the Society the idea of purchasing a vessel. We will establish a mission there, Mr Hall, but we must be patient."

Hall turned to face him and Marsden sighed at the stern, closed face. "When the mission is established," Hall replied, "you will find that I am your man. And I will labour faithfully for it. But not," he held up an admonitory finger, "as your farm worker."

Marsden swallowed. "I understand," he said between gritted teeth, "but there will shortly be work to be done upon St Phillip's in Sydney. What say you to that?"

Hall paused, stroking his dark jowls. "At what rate?" he asked eventually. "The present rate. One hundred and twenty pounds a year."

"No," Hall answered shortly. "Mr Shearer has assured me of one hundred and fifty pounds a year with time to develop projects of my own. I do not think you can match that and even if you could I would not accept it. I am not content in your employ, sir, and doubt that I ever shall be." He picked up his bag and left the barn.

Marsden watched him go, his fists balled at his side. Then he fell to his knees, praying for forgiveness for his impatience and fighting the urge to ask that Hall trip over his headstrong, wicked pride and break his damned neck.

Aotearoa, 1811

Opara lies on the southern banks of the Hokianga Harbour nestled between rolling hills to the east and west. Between the hills a glittering waterway reaches out two kilometres to the harbour proper. The water is clear and pure and deep. In these days a three-masted schooner might easily sail from Opononi nine miles south-west at the mouth of the harbour to Mangamuka, another twelve miles north-west. The hills hold together, bound by a vast network of roots; the great forests of kauri, the children of Tane, stand as they have for hundreds, thousands of years, reaching up from the fern and bracken, the manuka and twisting rata far into the domain of Tawhiri. Within the next few decades English civilisation will grasp Rawene, a mile or two to the north-east and will establish its mills there. The forests will be felled, fuel for the insatiable hunger for masts, spars and building material. And just be cleared for the sake of it, for a vision of English farms and righteous order. Many of Tane's children will rot where they lie, others sliced into logs and planks to be borne away for homes, buildings, vessels and churches for the greedy, alien god. The dust from their bodies will sink into the mangroves and lie there, slowly, very slowly putrefying. In two hundred years time the smell of their decay will mingle with the mangrove. The roots will die and rot and Papa will weaken and dissolve, her flesh running with the rains into the waters, mixing with the dust, rising up through the depths to grasp at a three foot keel. While about the naked hills will lie and slip in open scars of bleeding clay, red and yellow against the brighter yellow of English gorse.

But now the forests flourish, no opossums yet, and are alive with birdsong, no stoats or weasels yet, and the waters are deep and clean. Great shoals of fish rush and turn in moving silver forests, the children of Tangaroa, kai moana for Ngato Korokoro, the people of Opara.

Evening is settling in, the waters to the east of the narrow inlet reflect the gold and crimson of Ra as he sinks behind the western hills. Wahine nurse their babies on flattened bracken, toddlers, tuakana, splash in the warm shallows under the careless eyes of their teina, older brothers and sisters. The men are gone, paddling east in their waka. They will have left them beached on the upper reaches while they head inland, travelling east to Tokerau to exact utu upon Ngapuhi.

The wahine talk together, smiling at the succulence of the oyster and flounder that have made their evening meal, recalling, not for the first time, some mishap that befell a sister and laughing fondly at the memory. They do not dwell on the absence of the men, on the likely outcome of the taua, but neither do they avoid it. They do not know how many will return, almost certainly not all, nor the condition they will be in. They must know that soon each of them will have been personally affected for the brother of one is husband to another and father to a third. They must know their family will soon be diminished and that death will spread to them. When the taua returns and the losses are counted who knows which woman or women will go with knotted vine to seek a sturdy branch?

This knowledge is part of their being as war inhabits their lives. Ngati Whatua and Te Roroa to the south would have their lives for past wrongs as they would have the lives of Ngapuhi, kinsmen to Ngato Korokoro to the east. And Ngati Korokoro would also have utu from Ngapuhi; their men are presently bent upon that very purpose. Alliances come and go but war goes on forever. And none would think to question it; there is no Lysistrata here. But if acceptance drives the contentment of this present gathering, that does not mean they will be stoic in their loss. Shrieks and wails will greet the news that may be only weeks or days or hours away; they will rip open their old scars with new ones and any slave brought back from the killing fields is likely to perish under their righteous rage. They, too, will have utu.

Seven miles away to the south-east the valley of Waima lies golden under the setting sun. The Waima stream meanders between the mangroves, still and peaceful; birds call and forage on stilts at its edges, mangroves plop and suck at the shallows. Then the stream stops and the waters swell and spread over the banks, drowning the bracken and circling spindly trunks. The buzzing of flies sizzles through the air here along with the screeching and chattering of birds as they feed upon the flesh that blocks the stream. For a time this spot will have a new name, Waipuru, blocked stream.

The Te Roroa taua who did this are gone now. Walking, limping, lying on litters they move from their triumph up towards the reaches of the Hokianga. Diminished in number, some in agony, probably all hurting, their spirit is uplifted, their mana enhanced. Gorged for the moment, their hunger is never far away.

On the harbour banks they discover the waka that Ngati Korokoro have left. Thanks be to Tu, they can make the journey back by water. They paddle past Rawene towards the Whirinaki River that will carry them south to their home. And discover the waterway leading to Opara.

The warriors from Ngato Korokoro will have to walk all the way from Tokerau now. And when they return to their village they will find it bare, the whare razed, dogs and birds tearing at the mouldering flesh of what is left of their family. They will not have to search long for the identity of their enemy. Utu taken in anonymity is no utu at all. The triumph, the slaughter of women and children will be celebrated in story and song and will move throughout the land. Ngati Korokoro will lament their loss and plan revenge.

CHAPTER 15

London, 1813

"A glass of port before the service, Reverend? To fortify the spirits? I know my own could do with it. Not my favourite time of the week."

Stephen Killick nodded sympathetically. "Nor mine, neither," he replied.

"No?" The governor seemed surprised. "My predecessor advised me that your punctiliousness was a model for all preachers. Never missed a service in two years, he said." He turned to the sideboard and poured two generous measures. "To punctiliousness."

Although it was near eleven in the morning and the curtains drawn from the large stern window, the cabin remained dark and gloomy. To the west the waters of the Thames were flat and grey under a dull winter sun. The governor followed the chaplain's gaze. "A dark abode," he said. "I have given thought to having a window set in the northern wall but, truth to tell, I am here so seldom it hardly seems worth the bother." He shivered. "Wretched place."

Stephen drank deeply, savouring the liquor's warmth. "Indeed," he agreed, "but a great deal less so than the berths below."

"I wouldn't know," answered the other flatly, "and make no apology for my lack of knowing. All the knowledge and concern in the world would make not a tad of difference to the conditions. If I must oversee hell, I would prefer to do so at a distance."

Stephen nodded again. The governor's indifference to the lot of his charges was at least candid, a refreshing change from the previous incumbent who was, in truth, no more involved but sought repeatedly to

167

justify it. The godless beasts below had brought their fate upon themselves and now must suffer the consequences. No, the position was a sinecure, no more, no less, and but for the occasional report that would doubtless be filed and forgotten in some secretary's office nothing further was required. Let the man take his money and keep his distance. The hulk would run as well or as badly without him.

The governor interrupted his reverie. "But you," he said, returning to his earlier theme, "you find no joy in your message of hope and salvation?"

Stephen shook his head sadly. "I do not have the gift for inspiration," he answered, "nor can I frighten men to repentance. I do not think they understand me, nor do I understand them. We have no common language."

"And yet you never miss a sermon?"

"No, I do my duty and there is sometimes little kindness in that. Often I think on a cold winter's day I would be doing them a greater service by staying away." He drank again. "But I don't."

The governor looked down at his manicured nails, touched by the sadness in the chaplain's voice. A good man, he thought, who can find no useful purpose for his goodness and is ashamed of it. He suddenly remembered Crookshanks, a tutor from his youth who had daily stood before a group of gentlemen's sons and tried to teach them Latin. God, how ignorant and arrogant they had been, mocking the man from the heights of their teenage omniscience, joying in their contempt of all he held dear. For two years –the same time the chaplain had held his services but Crookshanks had endured it daily. He saw again the grey watering eyes and heard the querulous pleas, please, boys, please. He had made nothing of them, but what had they made of him?

He refilled their glasses. "I think you are unkind to yourself," he said, "and unfair. Lost as they may be and, I grant, often bemused, very well, bored by your sermons, I think they take something from the kindness that informs them. I have watched such men being sermonised by others and have seen the fear and anger on them at the promise of hellfire and damnation. I have watched them shiver in their rags while a well-fed parson in his greatcoat, in love with the sound of his own voice, drags his lesson on and on. At least you see their need and when the wind bites hard you cut your lesson short."

Stephen shrugged. "It would have been kinder still to stay away."

But the governor was determined to drag in some comfort. "Very well," he said, "but if you have not brought succour to the body corporate as it were you will concede that you have comforted individuals."

Stephen sipped carefully and seemed to cheer a little. "Perhaps," he agreed, "I have brought a little peace, a little hope."

"You have done better than that. I know that from your own pocket, very unprofessional, my predecessor thought – you have brought food parcels and clothing and you have endured the stench and the racket to sit with a man in his hour of need."

"I have helped keep them alive, is that kind? And more often I have had them brought to the mate's cabin for prayer and conversation. Their quarters make me retch."

The Governor sniffed. "You are determined, I see," he said, "to keep all credit to a minimum. But, surely, they must gain from it; meetings are not compulsory. Why else would they attend?"

Stephen smiled sourly. "For the warmth and comfort, I imagine," he said. Then, relenting, "and there is some spiritual relief. One at least appears to find comfort in the Word," he paused. "for all that he understands it. In fact," he continued, "I had been meaning to bring him to your attention. His name is Richard Stockwell. He has been here two years now. He was sentenced to transportation for theft but what with the war and the demand for ships and parts there has been little movement."

"Do I not know it? We are overcrowded to bursting point. However, I believe that will change very soon. But tell me more of this Stockwell. Why has he taken your attention?"

The chaplain stroked his long angular nose. "Richard Stockwell," he said, "is a convicted thief, convicted properly I should add, there is no doubt of his guilt. He had been living for some years in quite comfortable circumstances on the fruits of his profession, he was lucky to avoid the noose. He is, or rather was, we have made some small progress, completely illiterate –"

"As are they all."

"- and is quite simple, no, that is not right, but he is a very slow learner. God," animation was creeping back into the chaplain's voice, "the number of times I have gone over a simple, blindingly obvious point with him to the point of apparent mastery and then, a week later, completely forgotten! But he never despairs and he never stops trying."

"So. A simple, excuse me, slow, convicted felon. There must be more."

"There is." Stephen nodded eagerly. "He is also the best, the most Christian man I have ever known. There is not an ounce of malice in him."

"Ha!" The governor gave a barking laugh. "I cannot believe but that there are those amongst his victims who would say otherwise."

"Indeed, and Richard would agree that they are in the right to hate him." Stephen paused, remembering the pale face and heavy, faltering words. "I have done wrong, Mr Killick, very wrong. God says thou shalt not steal and I have stolen. They are right to hate me and it is right that I am punished."

"Well," the governor gave a twisted smile, "that is certainly a departure from the norm. My understanding is that the great majority either protest their innocence or claim duress."

"Richard does neither, although it is my belief that he could well claim the latter.

He –" Stephen broke off at a tap on the cabin door and the appearance of a leathery, whiskered face.

"Beggin' pardon, Governor, your Warship, sir, but the men are gathered for service and it is past eleven."

"They can wait. The weather is clement, is it not?"

"Cle-?"

"Fine, pleasant. The men are comfortable?"

"O indeed sir, your Honour. A little cool, but warming nicely. They're glad to be above and are in no hurry to return."

"Very well, then. The Reverend and I will attend at our leisure." A pause. "That will be all." The door closed. "You were saying?"

Stephen emptied his second glass and waited while the governor refilled it. "From what I can gather," he continued, "Richard lived with his father and another youth. Richard knew him only as Ginge. Evidently in the fracas that attended the arrest he seized the opportunity to flee. He must have returned to their home because when the constables arrived the floorboards were up and the valuables gone. Only a few items were retrieved but they would have been sufficient to secure a conviction." He shrugged. "Not that evidence was necessary. Richard pleaded guilty from the outset."

"What became of the father?"

The chaplain's voice became gloomy. "By the time Richard came to my attention and apprised me of his father's plight the events were in the distant past, over a year I believe. Richard was arraigned, tried, convicted and sentenced in a day. And left to languish. None would hear him nor stir on his behalf. God, he must have suffered. I think the only thing that kept him going was the belief that this Ginge would act for his father. It was like a kind of prayer. Ginge and me are mates, he would say over and over, Ginge will do right by my dad."

"And did he?"

Stephen closed his eyes and shook his head. "No," he said. "When I arrived at the address there were new tenants and they told me the story. The old man must have been distressed by the constables' search and you can depend upon some officious bas-," he checked himself, "fellow telling him that his son was for the noose. A week or two later the landlord was concerned by the absence of rent and came to check. He found the old man in his seat, staring towards the doorway, sitting in his frozen excrement. Dead of cold, pneumonia, starvation, dehydration, despair." He shook his head again. "Take your pick."

"Christ." Both men drank, then the governor asked, "what did you tell Stockwell?"

"I told him," said Stephen flatly, "that Ginge had taken the best of care of his father but that he had caught cold and died. Peacefully in his bed. That he had sent Richard his blessing and appreciation for all that he had done for him. But it was now time for him to rejoin his wife. We chanted it together, over and over, my father has gone to join my mother and rests in the arms of Jesus."

The governor nodded. "A kinder lie I have never heard," he said. Then, "how did he come to your attention in the first place?"

Stephen picked up the lighter tone and smiled faintly. "His singing," he answered, "he sings quite beautifully. And he remembers the words, too, forgets everything else, remembers the hymns. He told me that he would often pass time in the back of a church, he didn't understand the sermons but memorised the hymns. Anyway, at the conclusion of the service I offered to speak with any who wished to hear more of the word of God and he was the first to volunteer. We have been in regular communication since. And will be til -." A thought intruded. "You said something earlier about a movement in transportation?"

O yes." The governor was rising, straightening his impeccable cuffs, checking his timepiece. "God, look at the time. I fear we can delay the service no longer."

"Transportation?"

"Yes. A number of men have been selected for transportation to Port Jackson this coming May. Upon the *Earl Spencer*." He paused. "Would you like me to ensure that Stockwell's name is upon the list?"

"Please. That would be very kind. A further thing, could you recommend Richard for any duties that might take him out of the convict quarters? He is, I believe, a capable cook and adept with a thread and needle. And. I warrant my soul, utterly dependable."

The governor smiled. "A dependable thief." Then seeing the pain in the chaplain's face he added gently, "I will write the letter this evening and I will make two copies, one for Stockwell's records and the other directly to the captain. Does that satisfy you?"

"Immeasurably." Stephen took the governor's hand and pumped it warmly. "May God bless your goodness."

Then with a jaunty and slightly drunken step the chaplain made his way to the foredeck to lead in prayer and worship.

CHAPTER 16

London 1813

Thomas sat upon a mildewed bench, it was probably staining his breeches, could he detect a creeping dampness? Ah well, it would either wash out or it wouldn't. He gazed indifferently at the pond, its waters pallid and greasy under a feeble, watery moon. Two a.m. and he was deeply weary but sleep continued to elude him. Jane had snored softly, spread easily while he had lain along the edge, tight and resentful. He had prayed for sleep, commanded it and then finally with a kind of bitter defiance he had slipped from the bed and made his way into the streets.

Further away the cobblestones rang under iron hooves and iron wheels as London society continued its rounds. But here it was still and silent though neither peaceful nor safe. Roaming footpads and thieves might well pass through the common and the sight of a solitary man would be a ready invitation. The thought did not perturb him as it should have; indeed he played with it, breaking it into two appealing scenarios. In the first he fought with two burly assailants, leaping and ducking with amazing speed and assurance, mocking their clumsy efforts with a disdainful smile, then striking with sudden terrifying force that laid them senseless. Sighs of admiration rippled across the waters of the pond and whispered in the trees. In the second he stood impassively before them but there was something in his eyes that held them still. Then he reached into their damaged souls and through him they felt the flow of the Loving Kindness of the Creator of All Things. They fell to their knees and owned their fault and tears of pure repentance flowed down their grimy cheeks. And sighs of admiration rippled across the waters of the pond and whispered in the trees.

Thomas grunted, partly in laughter but mostly in contempt and tossed a pebble into the pond. My life, he thought, my wretched life, all our wretched lives. Cast at random, throwing up a brief impression of effect, an inevitable sameness of reaction, ripples running across the surface as they were bound to do by the impact of the stone, pretty perhaps, if anyone happened to be watching or interested but gone almost as soon as they had begun. He tossed another stone, there, the same plop, the same flow, the same nothing. A handful of gravel for the chimney sweeps and a rock for Napoleon. Lost to sight immediately, all gone to the mud beneath, down, down, brief pebble. A flat stone skimmed, half a dozen skips, half a dozen tiny circles and a final crash into the bank to fright a sleeping duck. Now there was a life with some impact.

This interminable waiting. Eight years of it. They also serve who only stand and wait. My God, if that were true, then he had given good service. But now the waiting was over and he hardly knew what to make of this new certainty. Why was he not rejoicing? It seemed to Thomas that there was a very inexact balance of pleasure and pain here. No, not just here, it permeated lives in all their large and tiny moments. But particularly in their large ones. Please God, let the child be born sound in mind and body. And let the mother be well. Knowing that if neither is the case, my cup of sorrow will overflow through the rest of my days. But how soon after a successful delivery, mother and child both well, had the event slipped into the past with barely a sigh of relief? Where was the joy to answer the sorrow, particularly in the cries of a healthy baby at four a.m.?

Like the imbalance of pleasure and pain, waiting had taken over his, their lives. A life on hold, a static anticipation. He had watched pupils come and go to new stations, to further progress while he had stood and waited. There had seemed no point in seeking preferment to a more established, better appointed post and then the roll had shrunk, funding became tighter and his position had gained nothing in security. For the same reason they had remained in lodgings; then the population swelled with returning servicemen, new taxes bit and with due apology and explanation the rent had risen. But there had been growth within the waiting, five children now and accomodation shrank while expense expanded. The years accumulated; Susannah would be nine at the end of this year and Elizabeth eight. And he would be thirty five. Sometimes the simple chapel ringing in rich brown harmony of promise realised and salvation attained seemed an impossible distance away and he had berated himself for a fool, clinging to an empty hope. The vision of wheat fields bending in a southern breeze and storehouses laden with the assurance of a generous land all faded and he had stared at the leaden English sky, wondering if he would ever behold another.

Waiting had grown into a wider uncertainty. The Committee had noted it in the March 11 interview. And it had been Basil of all people who had brought it to the table.

"We need to be assured of your resolve, Thomas," he had said, "and this," tapping the note that lay before him, "would appear to suggest otherwise, that your, and I quote, 'zeal for the work' is abating."

Thomas had stared, open-mouthed and Basil looked away.

Josiah Pratt weighed in. "This is not an inquisition, Mr Kendall, and at this point our concern is as much for you and your family as it is for the unfortunate heathen. This will be an arduous mission and if you have any doubts …" The sentence trailed away.

Thomas stared, still caught in sudden alarm, anger pricking at its edges.

"That was a confidential letter," he began, then stopped.

The Deputy spoke into the silence and as happened so often in parliament his words soothed and settled. Men might detest what he had to say but it was hard to hate the speaker with his twisted frame, sweet angelic features and golden voice.

"Thomas, may I call you Thomas? We are all brothers here, united in our common cause, and there are no secrets between us. It was out of his love and concern for you that Basil, Mr Woodd brought your letter to our attention. You must believe that, Thomas."

Caught in the spell now Thomas found himself becoming ashamed and nodded mutely.

The Deputy continued. "Yours is a very special calling and I am sure I speak for us all when I say that we sit in awe, yes, in awe at the magnitude of the service that God has laid upon you. We do not question it, but we must know that you do not, either."

Thomas gazed about the table, at the great men gathered there, ('we are all brothers here'), the President, Lord Gambier, stern and thoughtful, next to him the Secretary, Josiah Pratt, watching carefully over steepled fingers, then Basil silently pleading, his friend, his very dear friend. And back to the Deputy, the saintly Wilberforce.

———

"The benighted Maori need us, Thomas, they need *you*. They are fallen from God's grace in that strange Eden of theirs. They live in perpetual war and savagery, they are flesh eaters. And they practise slavery." Wilberforce was well into a speech. "What greater indignity can befall a man than that he fall into slavery? That his very existence should hang by the thin thread of another's whim?" He bowed his head in brief, sorrowful prayer. Then, looking up, he said, "We have with us the Word of God," laying his hand upon the bible, "and are blessed to know His commandments and to serve them. But the Maori lives in darkness." He opened pale, perfect hands in supplication. "Are you the man to bring them light?"

The words were tangible. Thomas could feel them stroking gently at his cheeks, raising the hairs on the back of his neck. Certainty flooded him then, yes, my Lord, I hear You, thank You for the purpose You have given me, for the meaning You have assured my life. He pushed back his chair and stood before the board.

"I am your man," he said simply. "I do not deny the occasional doubt but it is an inconsequential thing, a fly that buzzes and distracts but cannot penetrate neither my coat nor my skin to sting at the heart of my faith." He was dimly conscious of the awkwardness of the metaphor (and the double negative?) but pressed on.

"Perhaps the delay in my taking up my part implies doubt on my part." That was definitely awkward and he stammered as he reached for further persuasion. "Wh-when I wrote that I, what was it, o, yes, that I c-could not look at the difficulties before me I did not mean that I did not consider them."

He saw the doubt in Gambier's eye and worry in Basil's. Did not look but yet considered?

"I did not dwell upon them because," yes, this was the tack, "because I know that I can depend upon divine support in the trials which I am not prepared to expect. And if my strength is not sufficient to the purpose, I know, I *know* that He will hold me up and carry me through."

He had struck the right note. The Calvinist roots of the Evangelical Movement scorned human strength. Man was but the vessel of God's will and if the vessel should prove frail then God would make it strong. With true faith success was assured.

Further waiting followed and Thomas continued to soar and sink and wallow. Then suddenly, a year later, Liverpool gave way as Secretary for War and Colonies and all was agreed. Marsden wrote to Pratt suggesting that the Kendalls settle initially in New South Wales and plan the mission from there. A month after receiving the letter Wilberforce and Thomas Babington met with Lord Bathurst, the new Secretary and gained the assurance of free passage and a land grant.

Even Jane was excited. "How much land, Thomas?"

"I'm not entirely sure but it could be hundreds of acres."

"*Hundreds?* Thomas, we will be rich."

"Did I not say so?"

More months rolled by but now Waiting turned to Preparation and Thomas maintained momentum. There were, of course, drawbacks. The free passage turned into something less free.

"Three years teaching for both of us to work off the passage?"

"It is vexing, I know, but not all the wages will be set against the fare. And we will be paid well. Twenty pounds for me, twenty for you and ten pounds for each child. That's ninety pounds, Jane! Annually. We will save and prosper."

"I am to raise five children and teach as well."

"The girls will help you, I will help you." Thomas smiled winningly. "And God will bless your efforts and give you the strength and knowledge to fulfil your purpose."

Jane said nothing but was thinking, three years of servitude also meant three years of safety and growing prosperity. Dear God, they *would* make something of this.

The remembrance swept away the uncertainty of the past few nights and Thomas was fortified again. His gaze returned to the pond and as it did so a single shaft of moonlight broke through ragged cloud and drew a line across the waters. Thomas sank to his knees.

Thank Thee, Lord, for this Thy sign, pray, keep me true and steadfast, Thy humble servant and instrument of Thy mighty purpose.

A yawn escaped him and he felt sleep beckon.

Pakenae, 1813

To the south south east of Opara, little more than half a dozen miles as the kereru flies, the pa, Whiria runs sheer and high, ringed by dense palisades. The women and children are clustered at the top behind the final gate; the warriors and slaves are set at different levels, each crouched behind a wall peering across the cleared space to the palisade below. Most are armed with traditional weapons, the taiaha and the mere but here and there is the glint of the new pakeha weapon, the pu.

Hukeumu has a gun and he excels with it. He found it late in life, he is an old warrior now, and he was brilliant almost right away. A discovery that amazed him and delighted his people. He is putting it to good use now. Three times he has retreated to higher ground, racing to a sudden opening in the fence that will close again quickly, defences rammed in. Each time in confusion as Hongi breaches a line and they fall back before him. His last shot for now, he and his slave retreating to the next line to begin again. He is among the first to retreat for, although he aches to close with his enemy with club and spear, his purpose is with the gun. In the hiatus of the close of one battle and the beginning of the next, as Ngapuhi tear down the fence and prepare for the next charge, there are many opportunities for a marksman. His taking of them lie with a dozen Ngapuhi warriors.

Hukeumu is extraordinarily alive, his senses glow. In the pale dawn he sees the dark outlines of men clearly. They seem to move slowly while he spins and aims with utter authority, his arm rock steady, finger gentle on the trigger. He does not wait to tamp the powder but beats the butt upon the hard earth and his gun, his excellent gun fires true.

They are blocking the palisade now as all but the last of the surviving group crash through to momentary safety. One man is isolated but three Ngapuhi are between him and drawing in upon the opening and the barricade slams home. Ngati Korokoro watch between the slits as their brother fights on. Ah, he's fierce, his eyes stand out in pukana, tongue erect, he roars out his defiance. Does them all proud. Hukeumu shoots the man who kills him.

Hongi calls his men back. They are reluctant to turn, their blood is up and they can see Whiria's peak before them. Hongi too knows the hunger, the abandon but he is also a general and losses are mounting. That man with the gun has done a lot of damage. So he snarls as he calls them back.

Then he steps apart to think, baring his teeth at the cheer from further up the hill.

"Hey, Ngapuhi, why are you stopping? Two more stops to the umu. They are prepared for you." A roar of laughter and shouting follow the taunt, followed by howls of frustration and rage from the foe.

Hongi's problems are mounting. Seething, he hears a man tell him that Tuoho of Ngato Pou, northern neighbours of Ngati Korokoro, has struck his, Hongi's undefended pa at Pakinga. There has been a great slaughter and most of the women and children are dead.

Hongi must explode and the slave who has brought the message collapses, clutching at his shattered face.

"They are kin to us, the treacherous dogs, Ngati Pou are kin to Ngapuhi."

He rages and storms and none speak. They are all of a mind with him, his rage is their rage. As one they turn, Whiria suddenly forgotten, turn towards Mataraua, nearest home to Ngati Pou.

A shot rings out and a careless Ngapuhi slave jerks in a sudden heap.

Mataraua pa is less imposing than Whiria with fewer numbers and those tired from the hurried march from Pakinga. There will be no pausing to count the dead here. The assaults are remorseless and Hongi runs free with his men. The world explodes again and he is wild in the light. His last shot takes Te Tihi, rangatira to Ngati Pou and there upon the battlefield, in the very midst of it all he takes the time to take Te Tihi's eyes, to rip them from their sockets and devour them. One less pair of stars for Rangi's oceans of night.

But the rage of Hongi and Ngapuhi does not end with Mataraua. It is a huge and vibrant thing and it will never end and it carries them on to Mataerangi, pa of Tuoho. Ngapuhi are invincible and feed upon Ngati Korokoro in the ashes of their home.

At Pakinga, Whiria, Mataraua and Mataerangi there is stillness or there is mourning. The bodies lie in their dozens, perhaps hundreds overall. Karakia will be offered for them and songs made out of their living deeds. They are tupuna, ancestors now and they continue in a greater whanau.

Twelve thousand miles away the plain of Vitoria twists and shifts, taking on new lines and shapes as she is possessed by the armies of four nations. Behind one hundred and thirty eight cannon sixty thousand Frenchmen gaze like Hukeumu down the barrel of a gun. None is here for utu, nothing more than generalised rancour. Some may believe the propaganda of the utter degeneracy of their enemy, others find it convenient to say so and only later come to believe it as a wild-eyed Englishman drives his bayonet home.

They would think nothing of mana but their love of courage may not be so very far away. But none wants to be here the way Hongi wants to be at Mataraua. These men are mostly just doing their job, doing it for the money, the uniform, the rations. For the companionship. Because there is nothing else they can do. Because the wife and kids are starving and the wage keeps them just alive. Because the old man showed you the door and you went to join your brother. Never found him, though.

Some will break in battle and more quickly and in greater numbers than Maori ever would; Hongi and Hukeumu would both be amazed to see the officers firing after the deserters as they flee. Most will fight stolidly to a point and then begin to find a kind of love in it. Howls of pain will be drowned by a scream of exultation as another man finds the world and sense exploding.

Fifty thousand British, Portuguese and Spanish troops march towards the guns and the earth shudders beneath them. Smoke sweeps the plains as the guns roar, then roar again in answer. Too soon for rifle fire and the men march on. No wild haka for them, no rush to battle. They hold their formation and march while death explodes in pockets about them. An arm flies into the face of a Welsh corporal. He dashes the blood from his eyes but does not break stride. They march to the drums, to the call of the drummerboys, perhaps ten, eleven years old, faces like old men riveted over the terror, staring their way to the next step. Within range now, a voice barks and they fall to one knee, muskets at the ready. Then they wait, they kneel and wait and fire upon the order. Then loading, tamping, marching to the drum.

On this occasion the French break, break spectacularly. They abandon their guns, their position and their dignity as they head for the hills, north to the Pyranees. The two commanders decamp with such alacrity that all is left behind, personal possessions and the marshal's baton. A prize as no head ever was.

At Vitoria there is brief stillness. Until the details for the mass graves and burnings are organised, there is no time for mourning. The bodies lie in their hundreds, in their thousands, in their tens of thousands. Prayers may be hurriedly muttered but there will be few songs for the dead. They are nothing now and their children are orphans.

CHAPTER 17

The Atlantic, May 1813

In the history of ships and the sea perhaps no vessel has been more maligned than the transport, the floating hulk. At a time when the dregs of ships were needed for the wars with France and the dregs of men impressed to crew them, the transports were taken from the very bottom of the maritime barrel. Not for them the glory of battle nor the chance of a rich prize. Therein lay their safety for they were beneath regard as a prize themselves, bearing as they did the refuse of their land. They were the container ships, the floating dumps that scrabbled and wallowed their way across the oceans of the world to the cesspits of Australia.

Thomas had been much alarmed when he learned that the *Earl Spencer* was to be the Kendalls' home for the next six months. He had pleaded with Pratt, argued with Basil and written lengthy letters in which scripture, economics and social niceties were knotted together into a tortuous, impenetrable case. Nobody was impressed. Basil was annoyed.

"Do you not think," he asked with some exasperation, "that you might be blowing this up out of all proportion?"

"The well-being of my family is a large proportion."

"But where is the danger? *Earl Spencer* is an older vessel, I grant you but seaworthy for all that. She is not a swift boat and I believe she has an awkward gait. But she is still a safe boat, or as safe as any that you will find. Thomas, we are talking about *discomfort*."

But Thomas was earnest and persisted. "It is the discomfort of the soul that concerns me, Basil. Two hundred and forty convicts crammed together in a makeshift prison."

"They are well guarded and held securely. You are in no danger from them. For God's sake, Thomas, what is this? Not the onset of Doubt, I hope."

"No." Thomas was indignant. "My mission, God's mission for me is to bring salvation to the heathen. I am steadfast. But I spoke of discomfort to the soul, Basil. These men carry their corruption with them. And the sailors are scarce better. How many *are* sailors, not just men who were drunken thieves yesterday? My children will be subjected to the sight of convicts exercising on the foredeck. Who knows what they may say or do, I mean the convicts, who knows what they may do? And the sailors, I have heard about them, my children will be daily subject to their vile speech and manners. And Jane, too. Basil, this is not good enough!"

Basil sat through the diatribe in growing anger. This was when Thomas was at his least charming. Hedging a subject he found deeply disagreeable but could not escape, his tone and manner became querulous. It was too intense to be a whine but it was shot through with complaint working its way to anger. His cheeks were red and he breathed in deeply through flared nostrils. God, thought Basil, if this is how you are going to respond to the depravity of the Maori you may truly be in much danger.

He waited for Thomas to settle, forcing himself to patience, closing his eyes, breathing carefully Then he said, "Listen to me, Thomas. We do not have a fleet of vessels for you to pick and choose. Passages are few and we must take what we can. If you," he gestured, "decline this one, God knows when the next may be. And it could be worse." Then solemnly, "If you think the coarse language of seamen will be such a trial, perhaps you should consider your intent towards your larger purpose."

The finality of his tone shocked Thomas. Dear God, he thought, he means it. Basil did. He owned a part, a fairly large part he would concede, in Thomas' movement into the field. And he knew that he had ridden on it, caught in vicarious enthusiasm and hope. He had not anticipated the downward rush of the swing and he became gloomy and depressed when Thomas doubted. Then his protégé would recover his spirits and Basil would away again to the South Seas and the light of Christ in heathen darkness.

But he had become tired of the round and when Thomas had stopped calling he felt relief and the beginnings of the old, easy contentment. So now when Thomas ranted, despair became annoyance and impatience and Thomas was caught short by it.

Now he was beginning to apologise.

But as he stood by the rail and the dark Atlantic heaved and rolled beneath him and swallowed the last of Africa, the apology and undertaking to maintain a broader vision were quite gone.

Jane and the children were below deck, trying to make something of their cramped quarters. Thomas could not abide it there and had found his way unsteadily to fresh air. Clinging to a backstay he leaned over the rail and emptied his convulsive stomach. His temples throbbed and his body ached. He sank to his knees still holding the railing and curled into a ball. Almost immediately the throbbing turned to a killing pounding and he scrabbled back to his knees and leaned his head against the greasy rail. He now knew one thing and it was all he needed to know: remain upright.

While he was so engaged, Jane was sitting in the mate's cabin looking despairingly at him. The third would-be maid was being escorted back to her quarters.

"But they're *dreadful*, Mr McGregor," she complained. "Never mind the rags and the stench, that can be cleared up. But her *eyes*, did you see her eyes?"

"A forbidding lass, 'tis true. None too savoury a record, neither. But then what can you expect?"

Jane grimaced and scratched her head. (Have I caught something?) "You said that there was one specially recommended?"

"Aye, but he's a man."

"Can he be so much worse? May I see the reference?"

"Aye, it's here, not too long. I'm not much of a one for reading, here, you have a look." He passed it over.

Dear Captain Newby, she read, *at the Behest of my Chaplain I am writing to recommend the Services of one Richard Stockwell. Mr Killock my Chaplain asserts that he is Everything a fine young man should be. We may Wonder what a Fine Young Man is doing in such Company – he is convicted of Theft – but the good Mr Killock Assures me that he is notwithstanding an Upstanding fellow, Reliable and quite without Malice. He is further equipped of some Domestic Skills and Mr Killock urges that he would constitute a Very Agreeable Servant. I have the Honour to Remain, etc.*

Jane put down the note. "I should like to see this Mr Stockwell," she said.

She watched him warily, looking for the involuntary flash of spite that she had seen in the women. Nothing. He stood, hunched a little by the crossing beam, eyes downcast, slow and reticent. The position on offer was a prize, regular rations, freedom of movement and she remembered the protestations of the would-be maids that she had soon dismissed as lies. But Stockwell made no claims.

"Sir Josiah writes of your domestic skills."

Silence. She tried again.

"Do you have domestic skills?"

"Yes," then after a prod from the mate, "ma'am."

"And what may they be?"

"I know how to cook and bake."

"Anything else?"

"Yes," pause, "ma'am."

"And that is?"

"I can do a little sewing, not like making stuff. But I can patch and darn."

He stumbled over his history and made no attempt to excuse his crime, nor to engage in any kind of pleading. "I have done wrong," he said. "God punishes me."

Jane searched the impassive features, the distant eyes. Has he no feelings, she wondered, can he be without humanity?

"Have you family?" she asked.

And there it was. A slight tremble, a widening of the eye, the shadow of great sadness.

"My mother died when I was a child. My brother went away. My father lived but then he died. He has gone to join my mother and rests in the arms of Jesus. I don't know where Ginge is."

"Ginge?"

"Ginge is my mate. He took the best of care of my dad."

Jane stared at him trying to imagine some animation on the still face. What would he look like if he smiled? Or wept? God, he would be beautiful then.

Richard was dismissed and Jane gazed helplessly at the mate. "What do you think?" she asked.

The mate pulled at his beard. "I dinna ken," he answered. "He's a strange one, isn't he? You wouldn't know where you stood with him. Mebbe wake up with your throat cut."

Jane shook her head doubtfully. "I don't think so," she said. "He owns his fault, accepts his punishment, acknowledges Christ."

"Perhaps he is a canny actor."

"Do you think so?"

"Nay." The mate was more definite. "Or if he is, he is wasted here. He should be on the boards. But no, I do not think he acts. But he could still be dangerous. He's big enough. Perhaps he's mad."

"Or very sad."

"Aye, the two go often enough together. But still, you don't know where you stand with him."

Jane nodded her head. "You have the right," she said. "But I believe I do know where I stand with the women. They will hate me and mine and cheat us if they get the chance. I do not want them about my children."

"And you want Stockwell?"

"I don't know. I do not feel he is a threat but I need something more than that before I place my children in his charge."

They sat for a while in silence. Then the mate held up his hand. "A thought occurs to me," he said. "How would it be, do you think, if you took Stockwell on trial? Keep a close eye on him and at the first hint of trouble he'll be back in irons."

Thomas spent the first two weeks of the voyage in purgatory, experiencing everything through sea-sickness. Lying in his cot when his head permitted he was dimly aware that neither Jane nor the children were suffering as he was, a little whimpering perhaps, the occasional retch but as nothing to his misery. Feebly he thanked God for it.

He also registered from time to time the appearance of a silent young man. He was very handsome and at first Thomas thought he might be an angel, come to deliver him. Alas, not even a message was forthcoming.

By the time he was more recovered, Richard was firmly established. Jane was delighted.

"He is perfect, Thomas. Always willing, never complains. Never says much of anything, come to that. The children adore him and I believe he has become fond of them."

Thomas made to rise but sank back on to his cot with a whimper. "I am not yet fully recovered."

Jane patted his shoulder. "Do not disturb yourself. Everything is in hand. I have every confidence in Richard, he comes with references from the governor and his chaplain."

Thomas relaxed a little.

"He is very quiet and rather slow. But he is keen to learn. The Reverend Killock had begun to teach him his letters and now Susie has taken up the role of teacher." Jane smiled. "She is a very demanding taskmistress."

"My daughter teaching a convict. What has become of this world?"

Jane nodded. "It is a very different world now, Thomas. But there is much goodness in it, too. The sailors have been very kind. They have taken little Thomas up the rigging to see over the whole boat. Now he wishes to be a sailor."

Thomas shook his head. "My daughter instructs a convict, my son gambols with sailors in the riggings –the *danger*, Jane, the danger."

Jane looked at him sternly. "Now hear this, Thomas Kendall," she said. "It was your wish that brought us to this world and I am doing with it the best I can. The children are content and are even beginning to enjoy the voyage. Richard has been a godsend. He amuses the children, plays with them and takes them on walks about the ship -."

"On walks about the ship? Have they encountered convicts?"

"Probably." Jane was terse. "For God's sake, what did you expect? That they would spend six months cooped up in here with nothing but prayer and instruction? They need exercise and the fresh air and I am confident of their safety when they are with Richard. They have made no mention of sailors and convicts other than to say that people are kind to them. Such has also been my experience. It is enough."

Thomas eyes her sourly. "For you, perhaps," he said, "I shall have to see for myself."

That afternoon the Kendalls walked the decks of the *Earl Spencer*. Thomas walked carefully beside Jane and the girls. The boys had gone ahead with Richard, little Thomas scampering about his heels, Basil close ahead. Thomas had felt a sullen flash as he watched Joseph, not yet two, reach out for the lowering convict. "Wichard carry me," he demanded and sank against the heavy chest.

The day was fine and warm and though the deck groaned and shifted beneath him Thomas breathed easily. His stomach was settled and his head was nearly clear; only a dull ache persisted. The ship was alive with activity. Aloft men sprang carelessly in the great shrouds, below they sat in knots tending to cordage, patching canvas, scrubbing greasy deckplanks. Voices boomed. Thomas wondered vaguely whether their ears had filled with salt or whether it was long practice competing with the wind and sails for speech rarely sank below a shout.

But there was goodwill here, he would grant that.

"Morning, Mrs K, hey-oop Susie lass, Bessie." Thomas prickled at the familiarity. "Hey, watch what tha's doin with barrel. Tha near took fuckin head."

Thomas bristled, then felt Jane's hand on his arm, hurrying him along. "Pray," she murmured, "do not be provoked. It is only their way."

"It is a godless way," Thomas gritted, "and one that clearly provokes me more than it does you. And what about the children?"

Jane shrugged. "You get used to it," she said.

But Thomas did not get used to it and his head began to throb again. His mood sank and he was barely civil as Jane paused to chat with an elderly, bearded Scot. Afterwards she upbraided him "Mr McGregor has been a good friend to us, Thomas. He has been very kind. We would do well to mind him."

The stroll went from bad to worse as the noise rose, interspersed with the clanking of chain. Thomas could make out the form of their servant, the perfect Richard standing by a rail, still holding Joseph. Little Thomas and Basil pressed against him as the four stared down on to the foredeck. Thomas hurried to join them and gaped in shock at the scene below.

Under the watchful eye of a half dozen marines, rifles bayoneted, at the ready, a group of about thirty women, were they women? shuffled about the deck. The ankle chains that held them together banged and clanked and slithered like a grey, metal snake. Greasy faces, greasy hair, filthy cotton smocks, stained and torn, one hanging in strips over bony shoulders, flapping over bare, withered dugs. Thomas closed his eyes.

A woman looked up towards them. From her face she could have been any age but her body, though lean was firm, her breasts high and full. She waved gaily.

"Hey-oop Richard, lad. Tha makes a fetching maid."

Richard stared impassively back.

Another woman took up the call. She was smaller than the first with wild black hair and glittering eyes. There was venom in her voice. "Happen tha'st something for the lady that we girls lack." Shrieks of laughter attended the remark as the woman gyrated her hips in frenzied mime.

Richard stared impassively back.

Horrified Thomas sought out the faces of his children. They were animated and curious, now Richard was crouching down, Joseph still secure, to hear something Basil was shouting in his ear. But there was no horror or fear there. Thanks be to God, their innocence had kept them safe. Then across to Jane, looking for the pallor of shock, ready to move to her, comfort her, lead her away from this barbarity. And she was pale, her eyes worriedly on Thomas but dear Christ! was that the beginning of a smile twitching at her lip.

Rage possessed him then and ignoring the pain in his head he bellowed at the women below. "Harlots!" he roared, pounding a fist upon the railing. "Witches! Jezebels, have you no shame? Have you no fear of the pit that awaits you?"

There was more laughter, then a high, clear brogue. "None whatever, sweetheart. Sure and we've been livin' in it for the past lifetime. Why don't you drop down one evening and see for yourself? There might be somethin' in it for you."

"Aye," screeched a cockney. "I've got a lovely pit meself."

Thomas railed against the blasphemy, the ridicule, the contempt but his words were lost in the women's voices. Then a sudden shot ripped through the tumult and "a nice stiff cock" trailed off into the silence.

"Enough of your bloody racket," snarled the sergeant of marines. "Shut your goddamned mouths, you filthy whores. And you, sir," looking up to where Thomas stood mutely, fists clenching and unclenching, "I'd take it as a kindness if you'd refrain from taunting the trollops, working 'em up, like."

Thomas gaped like a goldfish and then Jane was steering him away. "O well done, Thomas," she murmured. "What an impression you have made."

Later that evening he sat wearily on his cot, hands limp in his lap. Hunger nipped at his gut but he could not entertain the thought of food. Besides, the dining quarters for the passengers were closed for the night. Jane and the children were returning now, Susannah and Elizabeth lost in earnest chat. Richard had returned to his quarters. Thomas felt very much apart.

Then a small hand was tugging at his trouser.

"Father," asked Basil, "why did you shout so at Megan and Peg?"

Thomas stared. "Megan and Peg?"

"I suppose he means the women on the foredeck," Jane supplied. She did not look up from the nappy she was wrestling on to Joseph.

"Megan and -." Thomas swallowed. "How is it that you know their names?"

Susannah took up the answer. "O we have spoken with them before," she said, then grandly, "probably *dozens* of times."

"And what do they say?"

"Nothing much." Elizabeth's turn. "They like to look at us, especially Joseph, they *love* looking at Joseph."

"Then why," truculent little Thomas spoke up, "then why do they cry if they love it so much?"

Jane supplied the answer. "I suppose Joseph reminds them of their own children, dear, and they are sad to be away from them."

Events continued to outrage Thomas' sensibilities. The next morning he dined well, a great relief from the biscuits and tea that had sustained him thus far, and took to the deck with his wife. The girls had joined Richard and the boys elsewhere; perhaps they feared another outburst. He breathed in the clear tang of salt air and removed his jacket and unfastened the buttons at his throat. He spoke politely to Mr and Mrs Dobbins, enquiring gravely after their health and wishing them God's blessing for successful settlement at the colony. He also wished God's blessing upon a passing tar who was civil enough to wish him good morrow.

Then he was undone.

Twenty feet above a pure tenor broke out in song.

O it's hard upon a six month cruise,
Without no titty, without no cooze
And the only thing a man might choose
Is a hand, my lads, a hand.

And the sailors roared in chorus.

Heave away, haul away ...

Thomas clapped his hands over Jane's ears and fled.

He had regained his composure in time for the evening meal. But he wrestled with it. Jane's wilful refusal to be as shocked as he brought back to mind her apparent ease with his father's profanity and added to the measure of blame.

But now he was calmer, buoyed up by the approval of the other passengers at the captain's table. The men were a little muted in their agreement ('quite right, Mr Kendall, quite right, shockin' business, a fine piece of beef don't you think, bit salty perhaps but there you go'). The women were more intense in their support ('it's a *disgrace*, Mr Kendall, that's what it is and within the hearing of ladies and children! o it is too bad'). Mrs Darrow, Mrs Sparrow Jane called her and he supposed there was something in the name, the quick, pecking speech, the glittering eyes and the curving beak over thin, tight lips. But it was disrespectful nonetheless and quite in keeping with this new Jane. Mrs Darrow now, she could appreciate his distress.

She was speaking to the captain. "Surely, sir, there is some manner of order that can command these beasts to more Christian behaviour."

Newby chewed on the rebuke. Damned women, he thought, all prim and precious, and damn that old woman of a schoolteacher for rarking 'em up. If it wasn't bad enough missing a commission to the Mediterranean and being stuck with a filthy transport, now he had to endure this horse shit. Christ, what did they expect, fucking *psalms* in the rigging?

He chewed on sullenly while Mrs Darrow warmed to her theme. "My father was a navy man, you know, a captain like yourself. He was proud of the order on his ship, nothing like a tickle he would say to keep them in their place. A tickle," she tittered behind her napkin, "such a quaint way of putting it."

And if he made such a damn fine job of it, thought Newby, why is it you sit at table, you and your shrinking man, in a transport on your way to the end of the earth? He eyed her grimly.

"Have you ever seen a man 'tickled', Mrs Darrow?"

Mrs Darrow's eyes glittered back. "More than once, Captain Newby," she replied. "A most distressing occurrence of course, but for the obdurate wretch who cannot be brought to heel by reason," she cocked her head to one side, "what else is there?"

Well, well, thought the captain, here is a lady who does not shrink at blood. He noted that Thomas had fallen silent, poking aimlessly at his meal.

"Mr Kendall," he resumed, "would you join with Mrs Darrow in calling for a flogging?"

"Sir!" Mrs Darrow protested. "I must object. I did not call, as you so inaptly put it, for a -."

"You did. And you may get your wish. Is it also your wish, Mr Kendall?"

Thomas' mind was full of Newgate as he shook his head. "No," he answered, "I do not think that I could bear to see it."

Mrs Darrow clucked.

"But surely there are other means to command more decent behaviour."

"O yes." Captain Newby was a trifle more relaxed. "We can clap 'em in irons, not much help sailing the ship from there, of course. We can cut their rations though there's not a few that might prefer a few stripes to losing their toddy." He winked at Thomas. "Hanging's a bit trickier, full enquiry, paperwork, King's regulations. Lot of bother."

Macgregor was enjoying himself. "A thought occurs," he said to the captain, "perhaps we could just remove their offending tongues?"

Jane heard the mockery and looked worriedly at Thomas as Mrs Nicols turned pale and had to be supported.

Mrs Darrow heard it, too, and caught her breath in hissing intake at the insolence.

Newby bit back a chuckle but thought Macgregor had probably gone too far.

"Ladies, gentlemen," his hands opened to the full table. "I appreciate your distress and if I thought it might serve your purpose I could command a flogging. But, believe me, it would achieve little." Like cutpurses at a hanging, flogging for obscenity was equally insane. Lashed to the rigging, howling at each stroke, O Christ! O shit! O *fuck*! "I will command that the convicts refrain from song when they take their exercise. A rifle butt to the side of the head will knock the melody from 'em."

Jane caught her breath at sudden, inner dialogue. Mummy, why did that horrible guard smash his gun on Megan's head? Because your father wished it, darling.

"I will not command it when they are below. Impossible to enforce and anyway you can hardly hear 'em. The sailors are another matter. For the most part I don't think that they can help themselves and if I locked each oath away the whole ship would be in irons, including Mr Macgregor and myself. But I'll put the word out for 'em to watch their mouths when there's passengers about and the midshipmen will remind 'em." He spread his hands again. "I can do no more."

That night Thomas hunched over a chest of drawers, an ink bottle in his left hand, his right competing with the roll of *Earl Spencer* to maintain an even line.

The Captain has, he wrote to Basil Woodd, *at my request desired the Convicts to desist from singing obscene Lewd Songs. He also Desires a Higher standard from the Crew but seems to hold out little Hope. So the Situation is as I Warned it would be. The sailors' sea language, Expressions not Proper to be named and the most Dreadful which can be conceived pervade Alas! the whole Conversation amongst this Useful body of men. And These will be the men who bring Civilisation to the Heathen! I fear Greatly for the Damage they will do.*

The captain's words bore some fruit. Profanity during the convicts' exercise periods diminished although a certain irony attended the process.

O let's sing a ditty to a nice firm titty –

Crack! Ow, shit!

Shut your filthy fuckin' mouth.

And the sailors seemed to make some effort, with similar reminders from the midshipmen.

But Thomas was not content. On the first Sunday that he was able to stand without too much fear of disgracing himself he brought his family to the ship's service. It was not an uplifting affair. Newby and his officers stood about the altar, an overturned chest, swathed in a Union Jack. The ship's chaplain stood before a makeshift pulpit and mumbled into the wind. Convicts stood grumbling and shuffling in the biting air under the bayonets of the marines. Sailors crammed the empty spaces, some hanging above in the rigging. Nobody could hear a word and the close of service was deduced only when the captain jammed his hat back on and stumped off to his quarters.

Funeral services were peremptory and, as *Earl Spencer* plunged further into the turbulence of the Atlantic, more frequent. Fears of a Newgate fever proved groundless but mortality was still high. Chained below in the foetid unmoving air there was no escape from the movement of the ship, no steady horizon to hold to and over the first month seven men and one woman died. Unable to hold the contents of their guts they died of starvation and dehydration.

The size and intensity of the service varied. An item might elicit the appearance of nobody; Thomas tried to make a point of attending.

"And so we commend to Thy care the body of what's his name."

But the service of a popular midshipman who fell in a gale to shatter on the deck below saw a full complement and, Thomas noticed with some surprise, an open and general grief.

He brought his concerns to the chaplain.

"Some greater volume, sir, to bring the word of the Lord within earshot. A bullhorn, perhaps. If there is not one available, I'm sure it could be fashioned."

The Reverend Fisher was uninterested. "Those who have ears will hear," he said.

He raised the matter with the mate.

"Not my concern," said Macgregor.

Thomas prayed for patience and forbearance but it was a struggle and one made no easier when he discovered some of the domestic arrangements.

"Mr Macgregor, sir, a word, I pray."

The mate was surly. "Make it a quick one," he said, "I must be seeing to the hands on the spanker." He had become impatient to the point of intolerance with the wittering, would-be parson, standing there wringing his hands, all pale and prim and proper.

"I noticed yesterday one of the convict women coming from the cabin of one of the officers, Mr McLeod, I think. May I ask, what business did she have there?"

What business do you have to ask, Macgregor wondered, why don't you attend to the affairs of your own cabin? Aloud he said, "Aye, that would be McLeod. He applied to the captain for the lass to be given partial release to serve as his maid." He shrugged. "'tis not an uncommon practice."

Thomas pursed his lips. "So I gather. She is not the first I have seen."

Macgregor shrugged again. "So your question is answered?"

But the catechist was upon Thomas and he would not so easily be rebuffed. "I must ask about the nature of the service," he said sternly. "I have a fear it may not be a proper one."

"Well then." Macgregor saw a window to some entertainment. "You fear improper behaviour amongst the ship's officers. You must take this to the captain. Here," he fell in alongside, "I'll take you to him."

As Macgregor well knew, Newby was in a foul mood. An aching molar had not responded to the unguents of the surgeon and he was steeling himself for its removal. Thomas had barely finished explaining his concerns before the captain exploded.

"Damme, sir, is there no end to your complaining? The language of the items and the jacks, the sermons of the chaplain and now the arrangements of my officers! No, you listen to me. This is a perilous mission, sir, I have in my care the safety of five hundred souls and I have neither the time nor the inclination to endure any more of your holy nonsense. Neither here nor at my table. If you cannot curb your tongue, sir, at least have the goodness to keep it away from me." Thomas was dismissed.

The storms passed and now *Earl Spencer* hung motionless on the equator. The sun blazed and the decks grew warm. Below the temperature soared and the convicts lay naked and sweating in their chains. More deaths followed.

Above the sailors and marines grew morose and irritable. Suddenly habits that had once vexed now became matters of intense concern.

"Do you got to keep moaning that fuckin' dirge?" Give it a rest, for Christ's sake."

"I'll sing if I like. Who the fuck are you to tell me to stow it?"

"Who the fuck am I? I'll fuckin' show you."

Scuffles between the men were initially overlooked but after a diminutive Irish swabby was delivered to the sick bay with a broken arm and three cracked ribs Newby took a stand. All hands were piped to deck to witness it. Thomas turned and walked away, feeling Mrs Darrow's contempt upon his back as the malefactor's back was shredded. The screams rang over the ship.

"O Christ! O shit! O *fuck*!"

He passed his time in a daze, caught in this constricted community, his family about him and felt utterly alone. He would sit the children down for daily lessons but the cabin was stifling and they grizzled and could not concentrate. And on deck there was always something to distract them. Richard was their constant demand, Richard and the sailors who told them stories and hauled up buckets of sea water to empty over them. They looked like bedraggled waifs. After a while Thomas began to lose track of them. He pored over CMS tracts and struggled with a chaotic and contradictory Maori vocabulary taken from the writings of Marsden and others. But the words swam and his depression grew.

Jane was no comfort. Freed from the constant demands of the children she gave herself over, rather self-indulgently Thomas thought but was too kind to say aloud, to her growing pregnancy. She lay upon the bed, pale and uncommunicative. And when her spirits revived, she would prefer to take the air, to converse with the other passengers or sit with the children and chat with the sailors.

They followed Marsden's course and took brief respite at Rio de Janeiro. Then it was about the Horn and endless days of driving into iron winds and biting spray, rearing, plunging then rearing again. Thomas took ill again, Jane and the children with him this time. He lay or kneeled (be upright!) helpless in pain and worry and shame. Richard moved silently amongst them, removing and emptying buckets, holding a damp cloth to a sweating brow, gently urging, just a little, see if you can keep it down. Thomas blessed him and resented him.

The Pacific was more accommodating and for a time they made good speed again. Then they wallowed and sweated in the doldrums and prayed for wind and rain.

Earl Spencer staggered and reeled her way down from the heat of the equator, south west into the grey autumn winds of the Tasman Sea. On October 10, 1813 she docked at Port Jackson.

Rangihoua

It is such a day as any man might be commanded by his god to go forth and fish.

The sea is so placid that the waka is left to float freely in the reef, taking no more than the occasional brief bump. Below, terakihi flash by, darting for a baited hook?

Ruatara is intent on his line, feeling its weight through thumb and forefinger, his head cocked as though he might hear the fish approach. Rakau is less absorbed and he lets his attention wander as he gazes about him. And back to Ruatara. His face is clear of the swirls of the moko but it has other lines now. Something had been taken from him during his time away and he did not seem to be finding it again. Except at moments like these.

Ruatara is lame somehow, uncertain in his movement. He looks as though everything is not quite right, the world is out of balance. His uncertainty seems like a distance and sometimes it keeps people away from him. It is unsettling and it is sad.

You see more now but it has not added to your vision. You have seen the way the pakeha see Maori. You have lived with the comparisons. I only see Maori as we see ourselves. I have no comparisons. Do the pakeha see us as weak, do they wish to fight us? Do they wish to be friends? Would we wish to be friends with them?

What did you do for aroha among the pakeha, Ruatara? Where was your whanau, your turangawaewae. Your mana had to live alone. You were abandoned in rock and wind, betrayed and thrown overboard; and you were held captive away from the end of your quest. What utu have you taken, would you take?

Inland, in the rich soil of Kerikeri young corn has broken free and a trail of yellow bells tell of new pumpkin. Between the mounds of potato and kumara a regulated stream keeps the roots moist. New fields are opening, trees felled by the axe, the ground broken by the pick and hoe. The runes of this canoe were carved with a pakeha chisel.

Perhaps that was your utu; you took from the pakeha his knowledge and his tools and you put them to your own purpose. But it was not enough, the balance is not redressed and you still limp.

Hei! Ruatara has a fish and a good one, too; the sinews on the back of his arm knot as he takes the strain and begins to draw it carefully in. Hei, another one and he near loses the line and Rakau laughs. Then Rakau's attention is taken by a striking fish. He draws it swiftly in; then carefully, almost tenderly he holds it still against the bottom of the waka and draws the barbed hook from its lip. He holds it for a moment in both hands, smiling at it, then he slips it over the side. His lips are moving soundlessly as he watches the fish swim away.

Tangaroa is generous today and soon they have their fill. They paddle idly back towards Rangihoua, they are in no hurry and they stop off at a sandy cove. There they beach Rakau's canoe and swim out to a mussel-encrusted little rock. They find rounded corners for their rumps or they squat on leathery heels and prise open the dark and cream and orange flesh with fine British steel.

A shout and they look up to an approaching canoe, gliding under ten paddles, sliding to a halt. The foremost paddler waves to them. "Ruatara, e Rakau, see what we have." Ruatara and Rakau stand and look into the canoe, at a pile of rough clothing, canvas pants, a couple of shirts, pots … "From Whangaroa," says the paddler. "We went back again after Mata's tangi for utu on Tamati."

They have been on a muru raid, seeking redress against the man who was unlucky enough to lose his son. They had mourned with Tamati, for loss in the whanau is loss in the hapu, the greater family and Mata was of their blood. They held Tamati in their arms and his tears were their tears. Then they bade him farewell and went away.

Within two days they were back in a different part. They found Tamati waiting for them by his whare, staring away at the headland. It rose grey and brown above the dark green and it was where his son had died. Shattered and drowned. Since the death he had been thinking about tapu and noa and utu, looking for a connection between his son's death and his own fault. What had he done to invite such a consequence? He was none the wiser now as he dully watched his wife's kin plunder his house. His fault was acknowledged in the raid, it was the point of the raid; and now it could begin to go away.

His kin did not greet him on arrival or departure. He was still an unlucky man. But neither did they harm him. They just dispossessed him of the little that he had and now he was a man with nothing. Now he could start again, perhaps work his way to being a lucky man.

"He had some choice stuff," says the paddler. "Look." He holds up a shining steel blade.

As they paddle off, Ruatara inspects his own knife. "Pakeha will be here soon," he says. "Not just passing by, but to live here."

"You will permit it? Ngapuhi will permit it?"

"I think it is the wisest thing to do; it may be the only thing to do."

He expands on the way home, talking quietly to the waka's bow, to the sea ahead. "Their power is beyond belief, e Rakau; their technology calls us primitive and they can summon a hundred men for every warrior of ours. They would slaughter us. We would resist and we would be brave and we would hurt them. But they would slaughter us."

"Have they done so to others?"

"I believe so."

"A dark outlook then."

"Ae, but there are good things, too."

He is thinking of the new horticulture, of farming. There is much Ruatara values in the pakeha world, a warm jacket, canvas leggings and dry boots, a sharp knife, an axe and a pot. He admires their houses, they are warmer and drier and more spacious than the Maori whare; he is presently designing one for himself. And he loves their working of the land. Of all the years that he spent with the pakeha the only time that had been good for him had come at Paramatta when he had recuperated with the Marsdens and had learned about farming.

He had sat over drawings of plants and their root systems, plants at different stages and he had seen how the field was laid to take from the sun and avoid the wind. He had watched manure taken from the horses and the sheep and the poultry and laid in the soil to feed the plants. He liked the circularity of it.

He loved to handle the plants, to make a soft, rich bed for them and ease them gently in, to hold them healthy and erect in one hand, patting them home with the other. Then, early in the morning before the heat of the day was upon them, he would water his garden with an old watering can that he had found. There were easier and more effective ways but they could not make the leaves drip and glisten.

He found peace in the garden and in the fields and he walked and sat and lay and listened and watched.

One day he sat against a gum, watching a lizard scratching at a log. He stood to address it.

"Tena koe, rirate," he said. And he told the lizard his whakapapa.

He loved watching the lizard. There was no question that it was a taniwha, but it was a diffident one and also comparatively small. The horse was something else altogether. He had seen them before, of course, drawing wagons along the docks, bearing the pakeha away on their two-wheeled waka. But he had never seen one at close hand, looked at its eyes, felt its warm breath and hairy velvet lip as it ate from his hand. He had placed a hand upon the massive muscles and thought of the laden wagons and carriages and had near worshipped at the animal's power.

"An awesome power."

"Eh?" Ruatara is at a sudden loss

"The power of the pakeha."

"Oh. Yes." He is silent as the horse gallops away. "They are here already, e Rakau. Their ships line the shores of Korarareka and Hongi is glad to trade with them. They bring wealth and Maori will have it. So we will have them here and see what they have for us."

"Mm," Rakau lets his paddle trail, "it is always wise to know your enemy. It might not be so wise to invite him in."

"You are assuming pakeha are the enemy."

"Yes, of course, I suppose we don't know that yet."

"But we do know that Ngati Whatua and Ngati Korokoro and all the others are our enemies."

"Yes," Rakau nods, "we wish one another harm; that is enmity."

"So the pakeha tools have made our lives easier and more enjoyable. Their guns would make us stronger and safer."

"You have been talking with Hongi."

"Ae, he is anxious to have pakeha at Waitangi and has told Matene so." "And you think that if the pakeha are to be here, then you would rather they were at Rangihoua where you can keep an eye on them. And watch the end of Maori."

Ruatara drops his paddle into the waka and pushes off his knees to turn and sit in the one movement to face his friend.

"How would it be the end of Ngapuhi?" he asks. "We would be stronger than ever."

Rakau shakes his head. "I'm not talking about slaughter," he says. "Ngati Whatua would be far more inclined to slaughter us than the pakeha. But there will be an ending here; when we stand in pakeha clothes, unable to light a fire without a tinderbox." He gestures, "unable to open a mussel without a knife."

Ruatara nods slowly. "Yes, we will change, we have changed. We are better fed now and we will have more and be better fed still. We are more comfortable and we love it." He holds Rakau's eye. "Does it matter so long as you have the knife?"

Rakau smiles. "A very fair point," he says. "And, as you say, we will have it." He closes his eyes and shakes his head. "I am enormously curious," he says, "about how this will all turn out. There will be so much to see." He registers that Ruatara has turned to the front and feels the waka move forward. "It's exciting, isn't it?" he says to Ruatara's moving back. The shoulders shrug without breaking rhythm.

Now Rakau puts his shoulder to it and the waka flies, riding on the surge around the last headland before the pa. They wave their paddles and cry kia ora to the children playing on the rocks.

Chapter 18

Port Jackson October 1813

"Like folk lined up to meet the squire." William Hall ran a finger inside his tight, starched collar and peered sourly along the line of those assembled to meet the schoolteacher. Marsden headed the line (of course), his bulk a little bent as he declaimed to his wife about, who knows what. Hall's gaze moved on to John King, anxious as ever, nodding urgently at the words of the great man.

Now the gangplank was lowered and a crush of bodies pressed about the exit. Hall could see a small, stocky man, clad in the ubiquitous black, moving to the front. Beneath a stained wig his face was pale and eyes were rimmed in black circles. But Hall could sense the excitement in him as his gaze flew about and across the faces of those waiting. It settled on Marsden and the man raised his arm in sudden, exuberant greeting. Marsden waved back and Hall could see that, despite his abiding consciousness of his importance and dignity, he too was hugely excited.

The schoolteacher was followed by a woman in grey; she was evidently heavily pregnant and leaned upon the arm of young man. Four children traipsed about their feet, the eldest, twelve perhaps, carrying an infant.

The teacher skipped ahead, nearly losing his footing as he hurried over the last boards. For a moment he teetered wildly before clutching at the chain rail. He giggled suddenly, high and nervous in his relief. Hall's mouth twitched in disappointment.

"Mr Marsden. Sir. What joy, what delight in meeting you, sir. I can hardly begin –"

Marsden cut smoothly in. Holding the proferred hand in both of his he smiled benignly down on the smaller man.

"Mr Kendall. Let us praise God for your safe deliverance. And that of your good wife and family." He released Thomas' hand to gesture inclusively at Jane and the children. The wave enlarged as he opened both his arms, as if to embrace them all. Then his hands closed in prayer as he bowed his head. "O Lord, our God, hear Thy humble servants as they offer up their thanks to Thee for Thy deliverance of Thy servant, Thomas. Grant, we pray, that he may prove himself useful and worthy in Thy holy work. And grant Thou strength, patience and humility to all Thy servants here gathered. Let them learn to do Thy work, putting all self-interest aside –"

Hall snorted, then quickly turned it to a cough. Well, I suppose I know where that is aimed, he thought. As if his own eye is ever far from the main chance. But he said nothing and his eyes remained fixed on the planking beneath his feet.

Marsden's voice rolled sonorously on. "May they learn that true worth and reward is to be found in the soul that glorifies Thy Name." He paused, savouring the silence. "Amen."

"Amen." If Thomas was a little puzzled by the prayer, it was lost in his buoyancy. "Ah. Praise the Lord. I can hardly begin –"

"Praise the Lord, indeed." Marsden laid a hand about Thomas' shoulder and moved him closer to the others. "May I present Mrs Marsden?"

"Mrs Marsden, ma'am. What a pleasure to meet you. May I present Mrs Kendall?" the two women smiled cordially, "and my children." The children shuffled their feet and Mrs Marsden smiled kindly.

"And this is Mr Hall, our carpenter. Mr Hall, may I present Mr Kendall who is here to school the heathen in the ways of the Lord."

Hall's lips tightened at the comparative banality of his role but took the proffered hand. Thomas's grip was fierce and urgent and for an instant Hall felt the impulse to respond with all of his considerable strength.

"Mr Hall. We meet as brothers in God's holy work. May his light guide and inform us."

Hall grunted. Guide and inform us? The man is preaching at me. He looked across at Marsden who smiled triumphantly back.

"Indeed, Mr Kendall," said the cleric. "An apt prayer." He nodded significantly. "Let us seek guidance."

At the last words Thomas flinched as Hall's grip suddenly tightened to the point that it was hurting. He pulled his hand away and stared at him. He was now consciously puzzled. There was a meaning here but he could not catch at it. What was Marsden saying? And what underlay the anger in the man before him?

Hall was seething. It is as I feared, another pompous, self-righteous … He has already taken Marsden's side, you can see it. And he will become Marsden's creature, his lapdog, no, his terrier, yapping at my heels. He looked at Kendall's hands, pale, elegant, soft and smooth. Hands that have never seen a day's honest toil.

He looked into the puzzled, enquiring face of the schoolteacher and felt the closing of a wall of dislike.

Then Thomas was bowing to a handsome, rangey woman, taking the easier grip of a hesitant man and bowing again. He was caught by Hall's intensity and his attention wandered.

Then Marsden was saying something and he was shaking hands with James Worthing. Thomas jerked away, staring, rubbing his eyes and staring again. Now the man was not Worthing but, dear God, he was like. The same height, though this man had the heavier build and was tanned where Worthing was pale. Their features were not dissimilar but it was in the air of languid confidence that Worthing was identified. And the easy tones of an educated gentleman.

"Mr Kendall, I do hope you are well, sir."

"Yes," Thomas gathered himself, "yes, I thank you. A momentary dizziness. Forgive me. I am pleased to meet you." He thrust out his hand and it was taken in a strong, brief grip, then he was bowing to Mrs Egan who was a fine match for looks and confidence. Thomas blushed.

Marsden was concluding something. "Mr Egan," he said, "is a fine example."

George saw Kendall's confusion begin to return and interposed smoothly. "The Chaplain," he said, "is speaking kindly of my farm. He does not say that most of its growth and good fortune have come from his good offices and generous advice."

Thomas smiled and instantly liked Egan.

Marsden swept them along, away from the docks. He marched at a good pace, with the gait of a fat man who has climbed many steep hills without loss of breath. On new, unsteady land legs Thomas stumbled and ran to keep up.

Marsden gestured and declaimed as he walked. "There," he said, "look at that, streets running into one another, running nowhere. 'No planning,' I said to Macquarie and to Hunter before him. 'Think to the future,' I said, but they sat and twiddled their thumbs and the town has grown like Topsy."

After London and *The Earl Spencer* Thomas thought the streets like barren avenues. But he held his tongue and gazed back over his shoulder, watching his wife and children falling further behind.

Marsden returned to his earlier theme in which Egan was a fine example. "This is the place for a man to show what he's made of."

Thomas heard a challenge that startled and partly unnerved him.

"A man is God's Instrument wherever he is," he replied.

And Marsden, hearing Opposition, answered sternly.

"A good and pious answer, Mr Kendall," he said. "But piety without industry is not a great deal. It is in industry and in the measurable production of that industry that a man will show what he's made of. 'Thou shalt know them by their fruits,' said Jesus. And he was right."

George watched Kendall shrink under the Admonishment, but he saw too his eyes glare as he looked away. He continued to watch curiously as Kendall became contrite.

"Your servant, sir," he said to Marsden.

The remainder of their party was lost to sight now and Thomas thought anxiously of Jane. He should be with her, no, he shook his head and Egan watched that, too; no, this is where he was supposed to be. Besides, she had Richard.

"Not all stand up to it," said Marsden. "Not all can say, 'here I stood firm against the Adversary.' Some who would come to save are themselves in need of salvation. Avarice, Mr Kendall, you will see it. And Sloth." He was speaking in capitals now. "And Pride. Pride Is Very much With Us. Beware Against It."

"I will," said Thomas humbly and Egan bit back a laugh. Later he would re-enact the conversation and he and Jo would laugh at the irony but for now he must behave. He strode along, eyes cast down as Marsden inveighed against the iniquities of man in general and Hall and King in particular.

Thomas could not contain his astonishment.

"I am astonished to hear you say so, sir. I am astonished."

Marsden stopped and smiled approvingly. "You are right to be astonished, Mr Kendall, and to have the good sense to say so. You are not a man to say one thing and mean another." He wagged a finger. "You will be steadfast. I can see it. I have a nose for an honest man, have I not, Egan?"

George assured Thomas that the Reverend's nose was revered throughout the colony.

"And so," continued Marsden, "it is only proper that you should immediately be acquainted with the Situation."

It was not quite as Marsden had put it to the minister but the message was the same. George had sighed and sympathised; he might have spoken of Job. But he had stopped short of offering any help. He had already declined suggestions that he might himself consider joining the mission. His doing so had not pleased Marsden and the chaplain had not quit easily or gracefully.

They continued along at Marsden's pace as he expanded upon the Situation. He wanted Thomas to understand that Hall and King were good men, men whose piety and moral character were beyond any reproach. But there was no getting away from a certain lack of Industry in King, his Output was Disappointing. And he was given to Complaint. Marsden pointed at Thomas as they walked. This could constitute a Major Problem in the new colony. None could ascribe Sloth of any kind to Hall, a very industrious man but he was Wilful and Proud; qualities that might threaten an harmonious and communal life.

Thomas felt the last of his excitement ebb away.

Then they were at the Egan's lodgings, a plain but spacious rectangle, ringed with verandas and blessed shade.

Thomas sank gratefully into a welcoming sofa. Though not yet summer, the heat had become quite oppressive. Then he thought of Jane and his earlier anxiety returned with redoubled force. He pushed himself erect and headed towards the door.

"I am concerned for my wife. This heat and her condition ..."

"Of course you are." Marsden crossed the floor and laid an affectionate arm on Thomas' shoulder. "You would be a lesser man if you were not. But, please, be reassured. She is with Mrs Marsden and, of course," bowing towards George, "Mrs Egan. She could not be in better hands." He steered Thomas towards a dresser holding decanters, bottles and a number of glasses. "There is no usefulness for you there, Mr Kendall. Have patience here." He placed a glass in Thomas' hand. "Egan does not drink, so you must drink with me." He raised his glass.

"To the Prosperity of the Mission and the Salvation of the Maori."

Then there was the sound of horses and wheels and voices at the door and sudden relief that turned to sudden alarm as Jane was carried in. Her face was wet and flushed, her eyes closed and she wheezed and panted.

"Dear God." Thomas pushed to her. "What has happened? Jane, speak to me."

She lay still in Stockwell's arms but an eye opened and she tried to smile but gasped instead.

Elizabeth Marsden stepped forward and took Thomas by the arm, none too gently and he felt the anger she was too well bred to show. "Take Mrs Kendall to your room, Joanne," she said. "I will be with you directly. Now, Mr Kendall, your wife is ill. She has been so for some time and I cannot conceive how you failed to notice it."

Thomas stammered, "She has –"

"Taken a turn for the worse and will need proper attention and nursing. Mrs Egan has kindly agreed that she can stay here for her recovery. I have sent instructions to Mrs Bishop to move here directly. She will know what to do." Then she turned and walked away. Thomas made to follow but was taken by the arm again, gently this time.

"Please, Mr Kendall," Egan said quietly, "you need to settle yourself before you can be of any help to anyone else."

"Perfectly right," said Marsden. "There's no usefulness for you there." He gestured towards the five children, whimpering softly by the doorway. "They might benefit from some comfort and refreshment."

"Of course." Egan was stepping forward, smiling at the children. "Now I don't want you to worry about your mother. She's feeling a bit tired and needs a rest. But," holding up a finger, "I bet you are hungry and thirsty. Eh?"

"I starve," said Basil.

"I'm starving," Elizabeth corrected.

"Well!" Egan threw up his hands, "you'd better come with me. We've got sweetmeats, lamb and chicken and biscuits …" He swept Joseph, the toddler from Susannah, "give your arms a rest, eh?" and led the children off down the hall.

"And biscuits and cake and cold fruit drinks and …"

Like the pied piper, thought Thomas. Why are some people so much *easier* with things?

He stood helplessly in the centre of the room, peering constantly to where his wife and children had gone.

He was distracted from his uselessness by the Halls' and Kings' concern. He was thankful for it but he remenbered Elizabeth Marsden's Admonishment and then he saw their disapproval.

He creeped down the hallway and no one tried to stop him. He found his children seated around a low table packed with delicacies, doing them full justice. Egan was with them, watching as Susannah spooned mashed savoury to the youngest.

His uselessness compounded. He and the children and Richard were accommodated in lodgings closer to the docks where they were left to their own devices. Elizabeth and Susannah and Richard managed the children and the house very well and Jane was in the competent hands of Mrs Bishop.

So Thomas was left free to worry about his wife and revile himself for her neglect.

He hurried to her now, caught in stabbing fear, dear Christ, if I should lose her. And there was the child! He kneeled by her bed and wept and poured out his shame and his remorse.

And made excuses. I did not see how ill you were. Ah, Jane, you are too brave.

He apologised to any one who would listen.

"Mrs Marsden, you were right to charge me with neglect of my duties." He paused, hoping for some denial perhaps. It didn't come and he continued on. "I should have seen how ill she was, I should have made closer inquiry. I should not have believed her when she said she was well. But I was so busy with –"

"Now you are making excuses."

"I am trying to explain."

"I'm sorry; I thought you were trying to apologise."

"And so I am. You are right again. I am guilty and there is no excuse. I am a worm. What can I do to atone?"

Elizabeth was no less exasperated but she was less angry. "You might start by thinking," she said.

"Yes, thinking." Thomas was all attention. "Along what lines?"

"You might think to the purpose of your visits. Are they to bring Jane comfort and concern?"

"Of course, of course."

"Then you might think to what your outbursts achieve. For Jane, that is."

"I am apologising to her."

"Then you are indulgent in your apology. It does not aid her."

"So what should I do?"

"What you can, sir. Look to the mission."

But there was nothing much to look to right now. It was mid-spring and unseasonably warm and Marsden was looking to his farm. Hall and King were similarly engaged.

There was no call to teach.

"I would not consider it," said Marsden. This may have been because he had not considered it and the year was drawing to a close. "Your concern must be with your wife and children."

So he sat at Jane's bedside, hunched under accusation. But he minded Mrs Marsden's words and tried to keep his guilt out of the conversation.

For her part, and she was ashamed of it, Jane wished he would just go away. At first she had been too weak and in too much pain to attend to him; now he was an intrusion on her peace.

She had never known a place like this. Nor had she ever known a time when she could, should, was commanded to lie still and do nothing. That that was all she was capable of did not lessen the wonder.

Peace, quiet, a cool, dark room and the right diet were Mrs Bishop's prescriptions. And while Jane did not flourish she regained the strength to sit upon the verandah and walk in the garden. Mrs Egan forbad any thought of her returning to her family.

"Her time is near; it is best she pass it here with Mrs Bishop in attendance."

The weeks before her delivery were hard. Although colour had returned to her cheeks and she breathed easy now, she was too light for her time of term. She could feel the child within and it was sluggish where the others had kicked and twisted. It dragged down on her.

But there were times, too when she lay on her bed and felt at peace. Beyond the open windows Port Jackson went about its business, but here it was still. In another place there were children but here it was quiet and undemanding. The silence was a tangible thing; she breathed it.

She had never known people like the Egans. Elizabeth Marsden she had known before in Florence Kent. Mrs Bishop was special but still familiar. George was a more distant figure and he was absent most of the time, the toddler with him.

"The farm is demanding at the moment," Joanne explained. "And he enjoys having Robert with him. Sometimes I am quite jealous."

Jane was embarrassed. "I am keeping you from your husband and son. You are staying here on my account."

"Of course." Then she saw that Jane was becoming distressed and laid her hand upon her arm. "Please understand, Mrs Kendall," she said, "it is my great pleasure to do you a good turn. Particularly in this company." She saw the puzzlement on Jane's face and smiled Jane was charmed.

Everything about Joanne Egan was delightful, she thought. Her voice was delightful, husky and confiding, a mixture of the English lady, a brogue and something else. Jane thought it exotic.

She was the easiest of visitors, stopping by with a pot of tea and the *Gazette*, chatting easily but knowing how to hold a silence. And she knew how to sit with pain and weakness and measure the right amount of laudanum. And how to listen. She was a most accomplished lady.

It was a chance remark from the accomplished lady to Mrs Bishop who passed it on to Elizabeth Marsden who advised her husband that settled Thomas.

"Perhaps," she had said, "Mr Kendall might turn his scholarship to the Maori language. He has little enough to do and it would distract him from his worries."

"Mrs Egan thought Thomas the Twit might distract himself by learning Maori. It would give Jane a break and it would give him something useful to do for a change."

"Mr Kendall appears to have time on his hands. Can you think of some way in which he might be Usefully Occupied?"

Tui arrived with a letter designating his Purpose. Marsden would cover all expenses, for this was CMS Business and Thomas would use Tui and this time for the study of the language.

Thomas thought he had never seen a human being smile as often or as expansively as Tui. There seemed no point to the smile, it was more like a reflex; the man would catch your eye and he would smile. It was unnerving. But then Thomas came to see that it was just Tui's way. He valued the moment of connection and he smiled to show it. Thomas found himself smiling back.

Marsden must have been impressed by Thomas' enthusiasm. He would rise early, often before sunrise and would climb a small hill to sit and watch the day begin. Then back to the house, to the shed to rouse Richard and Tui. They would start the fire and every day would begin with a nourishing bowl of porridge. Thomas was attentive to their meals, 'ensure that your children are Fed Sensibly,' Mrs Marsden had said and he would oversee lunch and dinner as well. And every day he would read to them from the Bible and ask them questions. For the rest he was somewhat vaguer. The children appeared healthy, were always cleanly dressed and dutiful. They held tightly to one another and were happier together. And they were happiest with Richard. So he would oversee the cleaning and the tidying and perhaps dandle Joseph on his knee or tousle Basil's hair. But he would not delay their leaving. Sometimes he asked where they were headed, sometimes not. They would be safe with Richard.

And now he was free.

If the wind were up or rain threatened they would sit at a table in the kitchen. More commonly they would sit out under the verandah and Thomas would instruct Tui in his instruction. He quickly realized he had no idea what he was doing. But, by God, there was a measureable production here: thirty words this afternoon, a dozen phrases this morning. And his notebook was filling. That was something to show for his labour.

But he continued to struggle with how the language worked and when he found some of the structure it made even less sense. He looked at a drawing of a dog running to a green house. "The dog is running to the green house," he said to Tui and wrote down the translation. 'E oma ana te kuri ki te whare kakariki'. Oma was to run, te kuri the dog, ki to, te whare the house, kakariki green. Odd, the adjective 'green' followed the noun instead of preceding it, like it should. 'Like the French,' Marsden had said. 'E …ana' must set the tense of oma. So, literally, runs the dog to the house green.

"This is a remarkable thing, Jane," he said later that afternoon, "the action precedes the actor. Marsden says he knows of this in no other language, no civilised one, anyhow. It shows us how the primitive *thinks*. The individual is only a part of the action, he follows it. It is tribal thinking. And the words they have for 'you' or 'we', 'koe' if there is one of you, 'korua' if there are two, koutou if more. Showing your connection to the thing you have, *toku* matua, my father, superior, *taku* kuri, my dog, inferior. It is the language of relationship."

Jane gazed tiredly back at him. This new enthusiasm was an agreeable change from the neglectful worm but it was still more intense than she would have liked.

Thomas saw the pallor on her and reproached himself. "I am sorry," he said, "I am talking too much and too loudly. I am distressing you."

"No." her voice was weary but a smile tugged at the corners of her mouth. "I am pleased to see you so," she hesitated, "involved."

"O I am, I am and there's so much more." He checked himself. "How are you feeling? How much longer?"

"Mrs Bishop can't tell," said Jane. "We can't place the time of the conception," Thomas closed his eyes against that conversation, "but I think I stopped menstruating," she was too tired to think of another word, "in February. So it could be any time. But I am not well, Thomas, this does not feel like the others and I know Mrs Bishop is worried."

Thomas immersed himself in study and filled his head with Maori.

Then a chink would appear and panic close in.

What if she should die?

There is no usefulness in such thinking, he admonished himself and chanted aloud from his growing text.

Ko Edward toku matua

Ko Susannah toku whaea

Ko Jane taku wahine, toku wahine hoa...

He could not imagine life without her and now he catalogued her virtues as he had earlier catalogued his faults. And the panic increased.

Thought served nothing for there was nothing to be thought about. There was only this corrosive fear that hunched his shoulders and clenched his fists and whispered to him in the dark. He fought to hide it from others, particularly the children, "mother will be home soon, sweetheart with a new little baby," and from Jane. He did not have to be told this time.

He prayed with her, silently, for which all were grateful, he oversaw the Nutritious Diet that Richard and the girls purchased and prepared, he studied and he held the fear at bay.

Only when the word came that her waters had broken and the carriage was clattering through a warm, dark rain did he feel its breath full upon him. He clung to the door for support as much as balance and he shook his head from side to side. "Dear God," he moaned, and Smithers heard the agony in it and urged the horses to greater effort, "dear God, this, if nothing else: let her live."

He ran into the house without waiting to knock and hurried to the master bed-room. There he found Jane much as he had left her, pale against white sheets and pillows. Her belly was the same small bump. He hesitated in the doorway.

"Mr Kendall," Elizabeth Marsden spoke from a chair by the bed, "you come upon us precipitously, sir."

"My apologies, Mrs Marsden," Thomas bowed, "Mrs Egan, Mrs Bishop and oh," he broke off as he faced a man by the window. His tanned and leathery features told him for a sailor and his eyes were distant. "Surgeon Biggs, may I present Mr Kendall, husband to Mrs Kendall. Mr Biggs is a senior surgeon with the fleet, Thomas; Captain McQuarie has kindly offered his services."

"I'm sure they won't be necessary," the words were faintly slurred, "Mrs B knows what she's doing."

"Thomas," Jane seemed very calm, "thank you for coming, but there is nothing for you here."

Then Joanna Egan was taking his elbow and steering him back to the lounge.

"She's quite right, Mr Kendall, Mr Smithers has been over-diligent, there is nothing you can do, here, take a seat, now I insist upon a brandy for your health against the night air."

It was a warm, late November evening but Thomas made no demurral.

"And here is Mr Biggs come to join us. Mr Biggs, may I offer you a glass to fortify the spirit? Excellent. Now, gentlemen, if you will excuse me, I must rejoin the ladies." And she left them to it.

"So," Biggs pointed wth his glass towards the bedroom, "she has been seasick. And the baby, too. Interesting business, sea sickness," he took a draught, "it's different from land disease. It gets at the mind." He sipped more slowly this time. "Christ, that's good."

"Your language, sir." The reproof was automatic.

Biggs was unconcerned. "Sorry," he said, "now, the first thing about sea sickness is that you know exactly what's causing it and exactly what to do about it. And it's easy. But your knowledge is useless because you're trapped. And you trapped yourself. You bought the ticket, you walked up the gangplank. You put yourself there. And you hate yourself for it." He tapped his temple. "Gets at the mind, see?"

Thomas stared at him.

"It's the same thing with pregnancy."

Thomas stared again. "What is?"

"The self-hate, sir, for putting yourself in the shit. For example, did you think for one minute about getting your wife pregnant before a six month sea voyage around the world?" There was no virulence in his tone, just polite inquiry.

But Thomas was aghast. "I do not believe my ears," he exclaimed, "you tell me that my wife and I hate ourselves for our misfortunes, then you inquire into matters that … Your behaviour is outrageous, sir. I fear that you may be mad."

The surgeon looked perfectly sane as he sipped upon his brandy and his words were calm, reasonable, utterly passionless. "Yes," he said, "I have sometimes considered that I might be mad. But," he shrugged, "it seems to make no difference to what I do."

Thomas scrabbled silently for coherent thought while Biggs ambled to the walnut dresser for further spiritual fortification. Then suddenly Jane moaned and it came through the wall, slow and shuddering and Thomas was clutching a broken glass. Brandy and blood ran together.

"My good man, look what you've done, o the waste. And you're bleeding on Mrs Egan's carpet." Biggs crossed the room swiftly, surely, removing a stained handkerchief from his pocket. "Here, step away from the rug, now, give me your hand, God, I could do with a pair of tweezers right now, hang on, I've got my tools here. Wait a moment. Keep this covered." He hurried from the room.

Jane moaned again, low and sad that ended on the beginning of a cry and Thomas clenched his fist, then moaned himself as the glass drove deeper into his palm.

The self-hate, sir, for putting yourself in the shit.

Then Biggs was back, tutting over the new injury and his fingers were quick and sure as they drew out the glass. He splashed some brandy on to Thomas' palm, "I suppose this is a shocking waste but somebody told me once it was good luck and the men whose wounds are washed in alcohol do seem luckier than –"

This time Jane really cried out and the pain in her seemed to tear at Thomas' insides. He gestured helplessly at Biggs.

The surgeon was puzzled. "Don't follow that," he said, then, dawning, "o, of course," and he brought Thomas a fresh brandy.

"No," said Thomas, "that's not it." But he took the drink anyway and it seemed to help a little. H e set the glass down carefully on the mantelpiece. "You should go home," said Biggs. "Don't know why they called you in the first place. There's nothing you can do."

Thomas heard an accusation. "I can pray," he said. Then the cries started again. They came like a series of waves and then a waterfall, each one splashing on Thomas and he fell to his knees and clapped his hands over his ears. But the cries came through, muffled and he prayed aloud as much as anything to drown them.

"Dear God Almighty, Sweet Loving Jesus, spare my wife this pain. Deliver her safely. And the child, too." His voice rose as he broke into a hymn and he sang and Jane screamed together. At the conclusion he uncovered his ears and listened to the silence.

"Thank Thee, Lord."

Biggs was taking off his boots. "If you won't go home you might as well get some kip," he said. "The ladies will call us if there's anything to be done." His jacket followed the boots to the floor. "Ahhh." He unbuttoned the stiff buttons of his shirt and scratched through his vest. In grey stained underwear he crossed to the dresser, "a wee nightcap, perhaps."

"I will not leave her."

"Suit yourself." Biggs settled himself under the blanket and further reply was lost in another onset of wailing.

"How can you *do* that?"

"Do what?"

Thomas snatched up his jacket and fled the room, "shut the door behind you," and into the night. He could not be in the house a moment longer with that madman and Jane's cries.

I will not leave her.

He prowled away from the house and stood beneath a dense plane, watching through the rain. Then he reviled himself for his cowardice and hurried back inside where Biggs mumbled through his snores.

He stayed on, pacing the verandah, praying and singing over her cries, prowling the lounge, fortifying his spirit.

There was no will in the child to be born. Neither did it resist but lay passively while panting, inch by inch Jane drove it into light. In the end he suffered to be born as he suffered to be washed clean, swaddled and taken to his father.

Thomas watched his son as he lay in Mrs Bishop's arms and knew that he would lose him soon. The child had starved along with Jane during the voyage and the flesh was thin upon his tiny bones. He seemed to sleep for his eyes were closed but he did not sleep easily and his breathing was ragged.

"He does not fare well," said Mrs Bishop.

Thomas shook his head mutely as tears gathered. Then he leaned forward and kissed his baby boy upon the forehead. He straightened then shook his head again and shrugged meaninglessly.

"Thy will be done," he said.

Then he turned away and walked into the master bedroom. Mrs Bishop followed.

Jane was propped up against pillows. She was pale and her face was deeply lined but she spoke clearly enough.

"Put him to the breast."

"Jane," Elizabeth Marsden spoke. "We have engaged a wetnurse who will be here shortly. You do not have the wherewithal, my child. You should sleep now."

"Put him to the breast."

Mrs Bishop laid the baby on Jane's breast and it was empty and dry; but the boy lay there uncomplaining, dragging in his breath.

Love in moderation for children die sometimes and the grief is proportionate to the love. The advice Jane's mother-in-law had taken from her own mother had passed through generations of women and was applied of necessity even more in the new colony. And John had died before his family came to know him, so the grieving was further diminished. Basil and Joseph sulked as for the loss of a promised toy and were upset by the general sadness but soon forgot about it. Young Thomas and the girls wept for a little longer, then returned to the adventures of the new land. Jane remained in convalescence for another month; she grieved silently and without fuss. Thomas sat with her and stroked her hands and told her continuously that the child had gone to a Better Place.

Privately he was less assured; he could not set aside the ominous quality of the first child to be born within the mission to be taken so abruptly.

Marsden heard him out but was dismissive of his doubts.

"Children die, Mr Kendall, I have suffered my own losses and I understand your sorrow. But it is the will of God and it is not for us to question it. Indeed, to do so smacks of Impiety. Look to your usefulness, man, and lose your grief in industry."

The Halls and the Kings offered due sympathy and attended the child's service.

Jane was restored to her family and they moved to Paramatta. Mrs Marsden was a neighbour now and watched with approval as Thomas atoned. He was kind and attentive to the point that Jane sometimes thought that a little neglect might be a good thing. He scratched ineffectually at the hard-baked earth and he continued to study. He also met regularly with Marsden and with Hall and King, too, and swiftly became embroiled in the deep antagonism that now enmeshed them.

"I cannot believe it," he complained to Jane, "they accuse each other of self-interest and station. Marsden says that Hall is led by avarice and Hall says exactly the same thing about Marsden." He shook his head. "What do you think?"

Jane was touched by his vulnerability and laid her hand upon his. Nobody else asks me questions she thought, well, the children of course, Joseph incessantly, why, why, but no other adults.

In part this was a product of their isolation. Paramatta lay some thirty miles from Sydney and the Marsdens were their nearest neighbours. While she had been convalescing there had been Mrs Bishop for company and from time to time Elizabeth Marsden had called upon her. But with her recovery Mrs Bishop had been recalled to her duties on the Marsden estate and Elizabeth's visits had diminished. The girls and little Thomas spent their days at the parish school, leaving Jane with Basil and Joseph. And Richard, of course, now assigned to them for three years. But Richard was not adult company. Nor a child, neither. He stood somewhere between, utterly dependable as no other adult was, including Thomas, but also profoundly apart. Only with the boys and Tui did he appear to open. Yet there was no doubting his devotion, particularly to Jane.

She had had no further contact with the Halls or the Kings and was not sorry for it. She had found little of warmth in either couple. Thomas was her companion, she missed him when he was away, as he frequently was, and was glad of his company when he returned. And they shared the loss of the child.

So now she stroked his hand and said, "Is either in the right?"

Thomas' bafflement grew. "That's the thing," he said, "I think they both are. Hall says that Marsden is demanding and overbearing. He says that soon after their arrival here, when it became apparent that the mission to New Zealand would be delayed because of the *Boyd* tragedy, that Marsden with-held all CMS funds and insisted that Hall and King fend for themselves. Then, Hall says, he resented his, I mean Hall's success, he has apparently done very well for himself, and complained that he would not give any time to learning the Maori language or anything about them."

Jane nodded. "I can understand Mr Hall's complaint," she said.

"Exactly. But Marsden says that the CMS initially provided for them and funds were only withdrawn when it became apparent that there was no immediately useful service to put them to. And that further it was evident that there was other work available. Which Hall and to a lesser extent King manifestly proved. Then when it was time to put the mission back into action Hall and King declined because there was not sufficient profit in it. Evidently an exploratory trip to New Zealand was set up but Hall refused to participate."

Jane mused. "One would think," she said after a while, "that there must be grounds for compromise. After all, they share a common purpose. Can you not mediate?"

Thomas shook his head. "I have tried," he said. "I have tried to persuade each that the other has a reasonable position, but I fear I have only succeeded in antagonising both. They will all be right, Jane, and any suggestion to the contrary ..." He shrugged.

Jane reached across the table, took up the port and refilled their glasses.

"Poor Thomas," she said. "You are caught in a parlous position."

Thomas drank deeply. "I am," he said. "The mission is what I am here for, it is the meaning of us all, it is such a great thing, Jane, and it is becoming petty. Avarice and envy and pride, o, particularly pride. I think it is pride more than anything else. Hall and King envy Marsden his greatness and they envy me, too, humble as I try to be, they envy me my superior position. 'Marsden calls us mechanics,' King told me and he resents it. Yet that is what he is. And Hall, too, 'godly mechanics' Marsden called them and there is no shame in it. Yet they would have it that we are all equals. I said to them, 'Dear Brethren, we are all equal in the eyes of God, from the greatest to the meanest, but in the eyes of men we have our appointed stations. Can we not accept that?' And Hall said that I was arrogant." Thomas rolled his eyes, despairing.

Jane could see it, Thomas sincere, pleading, sinking his foot deeper into his mouth, trying to please, yet very clear about his own elevated status, catechist, teacher, instructor, not for him menial labour, blind to the affront he bore. But the pain on him, his need of her understanding and approval touched her more deeply and she stroked his hand and murmured her sympathy.

"We will triumph, Thomas," she said. "You are God's man and He will not let you fail."

"Yes." He was settling now. He emptied his glass, then rose and walked about the table to stand behind her, stroking her hair. "We must surrender to His will and be His instruments." His hand moved down past her shoulder and came to rest upon her full breast. She reached up and held it there.

Then all the years of delay abruptly ended. Marsden was the architect and Thomas the catalyst.

"I am much impressed by Mr Kendall," Marsden told his wife. "I sense in him an urgency so sadly lacking in Messrs Hall and King. The plight of the poor heathen touches his heart and he is bent upon their salvation."

"Certainly," Elizabeth agreed, "he is a most intense man."

"Indeed." Marsden missed the edge, "an essential attribute if the mission is to succeed. But equally importantly, he shows a willingness to take counsel. And that bespeaks a humility and wisdom his fellows lack." He paused. "I fear their stubbornness and their eye for a profit will lead to difficulties for Mr Kendall. I pray he will have more success in guiding them than I have done." He waited for some demurral from his wife. But it was not forthcoming and he clicked his tongue before continuing. "Be that as it may, I believe the time is now ripe. The purchase of the brig is complete, the repairs are done and I am much out of pocket, two thousand pounds, a serious sum, Mrs Marsden. But I doubt not that trade will see it back and more besides." He paused again. "What was I saying?"

"The time is ripe."

"Ah, yes. The Lord has seen fit to bring all circumstances together. Hall has responded to my letter —and a similar one, I believe, from Mr Pratt – and has at last recognised his duty. He will sail with Mr Kendall upon the fourteenth."

This time the sudden movement did not unsettle Thomas. Rather, he was elated. Things were closer at hand now and the distance and vagueness that had shrouded his hopes in England quite evaporated.

So he was buoyed up as he left the final meeting. The *Active* was ready, Peter Dillon engaged as captain and the sailing date was barely a week away. Finally, finally he was about to realise his purpose and employ the talent which God had given him. He was become an Instrument, his faith and trust were secure and he had no doubt but that for all his shortcomings he would succeed. He had spent much time over the last five months in discussion with Tui and thought he now possessed a rudimentary knowledge of the Maori language. His knowledge of their customs was a good deal less; after all, there was little point. Once the heathen had embraced the Word –and how could they not – their dark ways would be swept away in Christ's light.

After lengthy talk, much of it heated, it had been agreed that this first voyage would be exploratory in nature, 'to promote a friendly Intercourse with the Natives' Thomas wrote later to Pratt. And only two would be making the trip, Thomas and William Hall. Hall's agreement had not come easily. He was bitter at the reduction of earnings it would entail and resentful that, with allowances for children, it would be considerably less than Thomas'. His position as mechanic as opposed to catechist was also a source of rancour. Yet he had consented. Publicly he had stood by his word to Marsden.

I said that when the mission was begun, I would be your man. And so I shall.
Other considerations were shared privately with Dinah.

"I will stand by my word to Marsden and my promise to God," he told her. "I would think too much less of myself if I did not."

Dinah nodded in sombre agreement. "You are a worthy man, William Hall," she said.

"I try to be, my love. But listen, we will undertake the mission and with God's help we will succeed. And there may be another kind of success there as well. I would expect that, as here, there will be grants of land. And, as here, the first to settle will have their pick. In the meantime we can lease our house and land and if the venture fails we will have something to come back to."

John King did not have the same options. His skills were not in demand and he was struggling to keep afloat. It was decided that he should remain in Sydney with his wife and child and wait upon the results of the expedition.

So it would be Kendall and Hall to lead. The thought was not depressing. Right now, nothing was depressing. Certainly Hall was a man with a grudge but he was also, as Thomas had written to Josiah Pratt, a man of acknowledged piety and integrity. Once the mission with its distance from Marsden was established, Thomas was confident that the holy purpose would sweeten even Hall's nature. The frustrations of the past few years, the circumstances that had conspired to keep him from his work, would melt like dew under the morning sun and he would find himself.

Thomas was infused with a warm serenity. The frustrations and failings of his life dissolved; he felt a blessing upon him. Now he would repay the sacrifices that had been made for him, now he would realise the purpose for which he had been made. Warmth spread through him and tears pricked at his eyes. This, he thought, is what happiness is.

He did not wish to lose the moment and carried on past his lodgings and down to the harbour. The lamp lights of a dozen ships played upon the waters but he did not see them. In his mind, brown smiling faces turned to him, faces lit in the knowledge of certain salvation, voices raised in praise of an all-merciful saviour. Clad in modest, Christian garb, they laid their weapons down and turned their backs on war and savagery. Above the sky was a perfect blue and the sun's rays bent upon them a golden shaft of promise and acceptance.

A little less than three months later he might have believed that he was in heaven. The rigours of the voyage, the run to Van Dieman's Land to unload cargo, we will take profit where we can Marsden had said, the tedium of the delay there, recurrent sea-sickness, the boorishness of Dillon, all this lay behind him now as he leaned upon the ship's rail and gazed at Rangihoua Pa. Like a crouching lion, he thought, facing inland, its southern flank dropping sheer into the waters of the vast bay. Islands, some no more than rocky crags, were clusters of green and stone in the deep blue. Early into the southern winter, the day was near still, warm by English standards, delightfully cool after the cruel Australian summer and autumn. The *Active* heaved slowly through the placid sea.

"So this is to be our home then." Turning, Thomas saw William Hall a little further apart, also leaning upon the rail. He nodded affably enough. Relations between the two had improved on the voyage, largely inspired by Hall's decision that it really was about time that he started learning the new language. Thomas had proved a willing teacher and Hall a surprisingly apt pupil. He was not a man of words or letters but he brought to his studies the same remorseless care and determination that had made him such a fine craftsman. Thomas' readiness to share the readings of the service on board had further softened relations.

"And here comes the welcoming committee." A large canoe shot away from the shore and raced towards them, a fleet of smaller craft in its wake. As it drew closer, Thomas could see that the tremendous speed came from upwards, he estimated, of forty paddlers. A single figure stood by the raised ornately carved prow.

"Ruatara," said Hall.

Behind there came a rush of noise, shouting, bare feet pounding the boards.

"Cargo nets down," roared Dillon. "Men, take your positions."

Turning, Thomas saw nets dropping from the mainstays along the flanks of the *Active*; more fell over the stern. A dozen sailors stood at the ready, muskets in hand.

"Captain," he called, "these men are our hosts." But as he looked down over the warriors, the protest died away. The affable Tui, in seaman's jacket and jaunty beret, puffing on his corncob pipe, was little preparation for this vision, glinting eyes in tattooed faces, carved spears lying by. Many of the men he noted with a shudder of disgust were quite naked.

"That may be, Mr Kendall," Dillon yelled back, "but they can keep their distance. The security of this ship is my concern and I will not be found wanting."

The canoe, 'waka' Thomas remembered, came to an abrupt halt beside the *Active* as forty pairs of arms simultaneously back-paddled. The man Hall had called Ruatara stood still, impassive, his eyes roaming the deck. Then 'tena koe, Wiremu," he called and smiled and raised his arm in a salute.

There was no smile from Hall but he raised his hand in answer. "Tena koe, Ruatara," he said, "haere mai."

Ruatara gauged his distance, then leaped for the netting. He quickly climbed it, drawing himself up on powerful arms. Another man followed, then a third and a fourth but fell back, muttering and glowering as muskets were presented.

Ruatara appeared not to notice the guns or the men who pointed them as he vaulted the rail and gazed about the ship. He was joined by the other man and the two stood quietly, watching, waiting. They were dressed alike in flax skirts that stopped an inch or two above the knees, their shoulders draped in short cloaks of grey feathers. Ruatara was the taller, broad shouldered and deep chested, a powerful man, a chiefly man. His face was unmarked and the even, regular features could almost have been those of a well-tanned young Englishman. But it was the other man who seized Thomas' attention. He was older, perhaps fifty, sixty or even more although it was hard to tell because his face was hidden behind a blue swirl of moko, tattoo, that reached up from his chin and disappeared into black, feathered locks. Thomas had seen moko before on Maori in Port Jackson and he remembered how Tui had described the process, how the lines were chiselled into the living flesh and how even the strongest man could bear only so much. The pain that must have come with the carving somehow added to the ferocity of the final effect. Thomas shuddered.

The two Maori stood and waited. Ruatara spoke quietly to his companion and Thomas could make out the word *haruru* but it meant nothing to him. Then the men were stepping forward, their right hands reaching out. Suddenly conscious of his position Thomas hurried forward, brushing past Hall and took Ruatara's hand.

"Kia ora," he said, "welcome."

Ruatara smiled affably and returned the greeting, then offered his hand to Hall and Thomas was left facing the tattooed man.

"Kia ora," he said again and offered his hand. The man took it and his grip was strong. He continued to hold Thomas' hand and stared into his face and his eyes were penetrating behind the blue mask. Then he released his grip and laid his hands upon Thomas's shoulders. Thomas stood still, confused then suddenly alarmed as the man took another step forward into Thomas' space and their noses were pressing against one another. It was the closest Thomas had ever been to another man and it took all his resolve not to flinch. The moment dragged on and the presence of the man enveloped him. Then, in the mingling of their breath he felt a loosening of his spirit, a warmth and the sudden unnerving impulse to weep. The old man's hands were strong upon his shoulders and his own rose from his side to hold the muscled forearms.

"Kia ora," said the man, "ko Rakau ahau."

Then Ruatara was speaking, the words came quickly and the confidence Thomas had taken from his slow, stilted conversations with Tui washed away. Behind him he heard Dillon mutter, heathen jabber, and he felt a flash of anger.

Ruatara's speech closed and Thomas spoke nervously into the silence.

"Tena koe," no, that was wrong, there were two of them. "Tena korua," he corrected himself and his confidence was bolstered by the approving "kia ora" from Ruatara. He staggered through the greeting Tui had taught him and the two Maori watched him, nodding, smiling, occasionally baffled.

Then he reached into his pocket and took out the letter Marsden had given him.

"Tenei he korero o Marsden," he said.

Ruatara smiled. "Use the English words," he said.

Thomas relaxed and read the message aloud.

Ruatara king,

I have sent the brig Active to the Bay of Islands to see what you are doing; and Mr Hall and Mr Kendall from England. Mr Kendall will teach the Boys and Girls to read and write. I told you when you was at Paramatta I would send you a gentleman to teach your Tamoneeke's and Cocteedo'es to read. You will be very good to Mr Hall and Mr Kendall. They will come to live in New Zealand if you will not hurt them; and they will teach you how to grow corn Wheat and make Houses and every thing.

Then he passed the letter over and Ruatara carefully opened it. Thomas was surprised to see his eyes move across the page and he wondered if he was reading it.

A table had been brought on to the deck, laden with a variety of meat, fruit and vegetables. It is important, Tui had told the missionary, that you feed them well. Manakatia, hospitality, will give you mana. Thomas had taken this to heart and had argued with Dillon that they should feed as many of their guests as possible. Dillon had been steadfast in his refusal. The security of this ship, he had said, and Thomas had stopped listening.

So only four sat down to table. Dillon watched from the poop. It is not my function, he had said, to break bread with savages.

Thomas folded his hands and bowed his head. Lord God, he prayed aloud, bless this food and these Thy servants who take sustenance from it. Sustain also, we pray, our souls and give us the strength and wisdom to bring all Thy children to Thy love and forgiveness.

Ruatara and Rakau sat quietly, silent.

Throughout all the proceedings the men in the canoe sat patiently still and Thomas forgot all about them. Then he heard a splashing and looked down to see a warrior standing, urinating over the side. He felt a tremor of repulsion and remembered, for all the placid agreeableness of the two men at table, the enormity of the task that lay before him.

"Will you come on shore," Ruatara asked, "and come to the pa?"

Thomas, Hall and Dillon had discussed this possibility earlier. The security of this ship is my concern, Dillon had said, and the safety of the men. If you wish to place yourselves in the hands of the heathen, that is your concern, but you will do it alone. I will not risk my men. Marsden had also urged caution. *Ruatara is a fine man and I would trust him with my life. But it is three years since I have seen him and who knows what changes may have taken place. Besides, while he is a chief, he is still only one of many.*

But as he looked at the rangatira and the tohunga Thomas could see no menace and he thought that to commence dealings on a note of suspicion could be folly. And was he not the instrument of the Lord; where could he find greater safety? He looked enquiringly at Hall and read agreement there. *This is what we came for.*

Gifts were exchanged, fish, pork and kumara from the Maori, materials, cotton, calico and tools and pots from the pakeha and then Thomas and Hall were clambering awkwardly down the netting and into the waiting canoe.

Then there was exhilaration as the waka flew across the bay, strong arms carrying him clear of the small, lapping waves and the sand blessedly still beneath his feet.

They crossed a small beach and climbed to the first ring of palisades, to be greeted by the wild, high keening of the karanga. *Haere mai nga manuhiri*, let the visitors be welcome. Ruatara and the warriors left them there and moved ahead, past the women up through the gates to the summit. Rakau stayed with Thomas and Hall.

"E korero ana ahau," he said, and Thomas understood that he would speak for them.

As they climbed, following the calling of the women, passing through one gate in the palisade, crossing open ground to the next, the *Active* further away, further beneath them, Thomas felt himself sinking deeper and without retreat into a new world. Each gate closing seemed to signal the end of one level of being and the opening of another, darker and infinitely more dangerous. His thoughts swirled in wild fancy, ascent became descent, the rings of barricade became circles, circles of purgatory. His sense of vulnerability swelled, yet strangely he felt no fear, rather an almost delicious sense of abandonment and surrender. I am utterly in God's hands, he thought, now truly I am become the instrument of His purpose and in this peril I am safer than I have ever been. Each step became a momentous metaphor, a movement to new certainty; words were clothed in exalted meaning, this man, Hall, is my *companion* in Christ and this man, Rakau, is my *guide*.

A great peacefulness was upon him as he stood at last upon the summit and gazed at the sea of brown faces. The weapons did not alarm him and their nakedness made him uncomfortable but did not repel. *They will learn better and I will be the source of that learning; they will know their dependence upon God as I know it now and they will reap with me in Heaven.*

They walked behind Rakau through the village, past storehouses, faced by carven boards, faces and figures conjoining, fixed upon a single pole, past whare low to the ground under thatched roofs. Then they were led into the whare nui, the great meeting house, stooping through the narrow single entrance. They followed Rakau to the right and sat on the hard earth floor. The walls were hung in panels stitched in regular design and the poles that held the roof's spine were figures mounted on figures, glittering eyes of paua, protruding tongues, three-fingered claws. The reproductive organs were carved in detail and Thomas looked away.

He sat and listened as Ruatara addressed the meeting, walking to and fro, gesticulating, his words flowing in practised oratory. He was followed by two further speakers, courteously they did not exceed the numbers speaking for the manuhiri. Each speech was followed by a waiata, a song in which all joined, men, women, children. Thomas could discern little of melody but the rhythms ran and crossed and he found his hand tapping in time. Then Rakau spoke and while Thomas could make out words and phrases here and there most of the general sense was lost to him. But there was a completeness to the speech in the rhythms and cadences and he found himself nodding to a meaning that eluded but somehow charmed him. At the conclusion of the speech Rakau broke into a chant and Ruatara and the others joined, supporting him where the missionaries could not. Then he turned to Thomas. "E korero ana koe, e Keni," he said.

Thomas was on firmer ground here. Tui had schooled him assiduously in his greeting on the marae and he spoke with a confidence that was enhanced by murmurs of approval. He addressed the god, the dead, the whare and the people. He told them who he was.

Ko Edward toku matua.

Ko Susannah toku whaea.

Ko Jane taku wahine.

Ko Susanna, ko Elizabeth, ko Thomas, ko Basil, ko Joseph aku tamariki.

Ko Thomas te ingoa.

He moved into the chant he had memorised and as Rakau and then the others joined with him he felt a swelling in his heart that near overwhelmed him. *This is where I belong. This is what I am supposed to be doing.*

Hall's speech was much briefer; but he was firm and resolute and at the close Thomas joined with Rakau. *Kia ora, Wiremu.*

Then the people gathered in a line and Thomas and Hall greeted each individually. By the end all sense of personal distance had vanished.

The *Active* lay at anchor for two another two days while the missionaries continued their exploration of the Maori world. With Ruatara and Rakau they travelled inland to Motutara where they were shown the kumara and wheat fields. Two crops of the latter had already been taken and Thomas was impressed by the extent of the cultivation, but somewhat dismayed by the idolatrous stones and the way in which the success of the crops was attributed to the heathen deities. He tried argument with Ruatara.

"If," he said, "it is your gods that make the crops to grow here, why do they grow in England without their blessing?"

Ruatara smiled. "If," he said, "it is your god that makes the crop to grow in England, why do they grow here without his blessing?"

Thomas turned to another subject, one that, despite his relaxation at Rangihoua pa continued to trouble him.

"God teaches that nakedness is a great sin," he said.

'Sin' proved a difficult concept and they became bogged down in immoral, wicked and evil and tapu and noa. But Thomas ploughed on, never for a moment pausing to wonder at the Maori's readiness to discuss the subject, to listen and to ask for clarification. He did not consider the position an Englishman would take were the conversation reversed, were he presented with the argument that nakedness was a good thing, the instant, disdainful and utter rejection.

"Do you sin," asked Ruatara, "when you bathe, when you take out your cock to mimi?"

Thomas blanched at the word, but let it go. "That is different. It is necessary and anyway should be done in privacy."

Ruatara was puzzled. "But I have seen many English sailors bathe naked in front of their fellows. And piss and crap, too."

Thomas flushed under the brutal words. "If there were only men present," he said, "that could make it different."

"I have heard this talk from Matene," Ruatara mused, "but I could not understand it. He seemed to say that men and women should hide their nakedness from one another."

"Yes," Thomas was quick to answer. "That is correct."

"But why," Ruatara persisted, "would your god make the wahine such a fine thing to look upon and then make it shameful to do so?"

Unbidden the vision of Evelyn the Whore rose burning in Thomas' mind. He shook his head dumbly and the conversation ended.

On the evening of the second night Thomas and Hall spoke to Dillon about moving on to Kororareka, stronghold of the great Ngapuhi chief, Hongi Hika. Dillon was initially resistant.

"If it is as short a distance as you say," he grumbled, "why do you not travel there with your heathen friends?"

"Because," Thomas tried to be patient, "we have gifts to convey."

"Take them in the canoe."

"There may not be room. Besides, we wish them to see the *Active*, the great technology we own."

"The bay is full of islands and crags. I do not know these waters."

Hall intervened. "It is a common anchorage for whalers and sealers," he said. "Surely your seamanship is the equal of theirs."

Dillon consented but not without qualification. "We will have to wait for a good wind. I will not just drift on the tide without the means of sudden avoidance."

The next morning a good wind blew in from the sea, a sign from the Lord, Thomas told Hall, and the *Active* was prepared for passage. Ruatara and Rakau were to sail with them along with three others, Dillon's maximum concession. The rest of the Rangihoua contingent would travel in the large waka, preceding the *Active*, showing the way. With the prevailing wind they would be able to run in a straight line and a quick and easy trip was anticipated.

Ruatara had hoped to revisit his old sailing days and lend a hand with the ropes but Dillon would not have it. "I don't trust the bugger," he told Thomas, "who knows what foolishness or skullduggery he might get up to."

So now Ruatara leaned on the bow railing with Thomas and Hall and Rakau and spoke about Hongi Hika. Their connection was a close one. "He is my matua," Ruatara said. Thomas was confused and further conversation followed before the missionary understood that in this case the term indicated uncle, rather than father.

"He is a famous warrior," Ruatara continued. "He has taken many deaths."

Thomas shook his head. "God teaches that killing is a great sin," he said.

Ruatara nodded. "So Matene said," he agreed, "yet I have heard that your great rangatira, Neroni, the sailor, killed more in a single day than Hongi could manage in a lifetime."

"But they were the French, our enemy."

"So were Ngati Whatua and Ngati Korokoro and Ngato Pou Hongi's enemy. And I have heard the English kill their own warriors for refusing to fight or for running away from battle. Hongi would never do that."

Thomas sighed. "You have much to learn, Ruatara," he said.

Then both fell silent as the *Active* rounded a headland and Kororareka came into view, Kororareka, the hell of the Pacific, home to the worst excesses of European civilisation, where rough whalers and sealers and unprincipled traders could freely practise their vices and introduce them to the Maori. Thomas saw two vessels at anchor and as they drew closer he could make out dark skinned women on deck, bare breasted, pipes in hand, standing amongst the crew. His knuckles whitened and his breath hissed between clenched teeth. Rakau watched his reaction with interest, then spoke to Ruatara who translated.

"Rakau says that you seem angry. He asks what wrong your god finds here."

Thomas' answer was lost as waka sped from the shore and Dillon roared his customary defence.

But as they climbed the hillside through the tightly woven palisades the image of the fallen women amongst the fallen men was still with him and the joy he had known at Rangihoua was gone. The day seemed to echo his low spirits; the sky was overcast and threatening and the wind had lifted, forcing Thomas to hold his hand firmly over his shifting wig. As they reached the summit his heart sank further, for on a row of poles sat a line of heads in varying stages of decomposition. The practice of taking heads was not unknown in England, the head of the assassin of a cabinet minister had recently been affixed upon the tower of Newgate as a general warning. Nor was it unexpected, the trade in heads was well established now, reaching across the world to curio collectors in London. Still he recoiled and looked away. Into Rakau's enquiring gaze. *Does the man never cease watching me?*

Three hours later, the powhiri, meeting, successfully concluded, his mood was shifting again. The cause lay with Hongi, warrior chief, cannibal, savage. He stood before them now in a cream calico shirt, fumbling patiently at the buttons, rotating powerful shoulders under the strange new material. He smiled easily, charmingly at his guests. Then he was bending over the sea chest, picking amongst the treasures. He looked up and smiled a little sadly, gentle in his disappointment.

"Kei hea te pu?" he asked. He mimed raising a musket to his shoulders and sighting along the barrel.

Thomas was at a loss for words. At some level he could not recognise he was profoundly impressed by the man. He was drawn in by the eyes and the hairs rose on his arms and prickled at the base of his neck at the Maori's voice; he felt ashamed that the gifts disappointed. He shrugged meaninglessly.

Hall spoke up. "We did not think to bring guns," he said. "Our God is the Prince of Peace and we do not deal in the means of war."

Ruatara translated, then Hongi spoke again.

Ruatara turned to the missionaries. "Hongi says," he reported, "that your," he struggled for the word, "that your religion does not seem to be fitting for a warrior."

Despite his disappointment Hongi was gracious in his acceptance of the gifts. Perhaps next time, he offered, the pakeha might find it in their hearts to favour him with a gun. Or two. He would be deeply appreciative.

This is a very strange service, indeed.

William Hall looked over the deck and the contradictions there found reflection in his own tangled thoughts. Thomas Kendall upon a chest, quite the parson, looking over his congregation, sailors in their Sunday best to one side, gathered in a knot, tense and nervous, a dozen Maori in flax skirts and feathered cloaks, curious, wondering. Dillon glowering on the poop, folded arms across an open coat, a brace of pistols at his belt. A pair of burly sailors stood on either side, muskets at the ready. Another dozen hung in the riggings, their eyes upon the congregation and the waka that sat about the *Active;* they too were armed. Cargo nets hung from the ship on all sides like tangled skirts.

Kendall and Dillon had argued intensely about the arrangements. The teacher was persuaded, as was Marsden, that the horror of the *Boyd* and the following years of isolation were directly attributable to the ill-treatment of Te Aara by the *Boyd's* captain and crew. Dillon's overt suspicion, Kendall argued, did nothing to promote friendly intercourse. Hall was not entirely persuaded. Even if the retaliation had been provoked, the massacre was out of all proportion. As was the retaliation to the retaliation, the destruction of Te Pahi's pa and the deaths of many Maori. He muttered to himself; there were times when he despaired at the doings of all humans, Maori and pakeha alike.

He could not bring himself to be much impressed by Kendall's present performance, either. All puffed up and full of himself, the little missionary preached with inspired fervour. Ruatara stood by his side, aiding with translation. A cunning move that, adding local authority to the alien message. Yet the message itself seemed trite, given the enormity of the situation, of the gulf between the two peoples.

God made the world in seven days, Kendall proclaimed, and on the seventh day He rested. This we call the Sabbath and as God rested, so should we.

Still, it was a safe way to start and it seemed to be well received. Hall studied the congregation, from the preacher to the captain, from the sailors with bowed heads to the sailors with guns, from impassive Ruatara to smiling Hongi. That man unsettles me, thought Hall. I think there is a part of me that wishes to please him and I do not like that much. And he has captivated Kendall and I like that a good deal less.

They remained at Kororareka for a further two days before sailing on to the south, to Matauwhi, home of Tara and Pomare. Two days after their welcome and acceptance at the powhiri, Pomare invited the missionaries to stay ashore and sleep overnight. Dillon was, of course, deeply sceptical and Hall, too, had reservations.

"We have learned much," he said, "and I believe we are laying the foundations for a successful mission. But do you not think it might be too soon for such a step?"

Thomas might have noted Hall's concern and considered it. But he was once again God's instrument, divine providence assured his safety and enthusiasm over rode graciousness. Hall felt rebuffed, consigned to a lesser role (again) and he withdrew and brooded.

That afternoon Thomas boarded the chief's waka and travelled to the settlement at Matauwhi; and that night he wrapped himself in the great coat his father had bought him another lifetime ago and lay down beside the chief. Sleep came readily and he dreamed of a great waterfall, breaking like a baptism and washing him clean of his sins.

The apogee of the voyage came with the return to Kororareka and the agreement of three rangatira to sail back with them to New South Wales. They were Ruatara, Korokoro and Hongi Hika.

CHAPTER 19

They stayed in Port Jackson for three months as guests of the Marsdens. Now the reality of the New Zealand mission was clearly before him and the chaplain was caught in the momentum.

"I am sure," he wrote to Pratt, "the chiefs will perceive the Opportunity for Improvement and this will have a wonderful Effect upon their minds."

Daily they were taken to view the wonders of pakeha technology. They watched buildings in progress.

"See how the framing is put together. This makes the house strong; it will withstand any wind. See the heights of the walls; they will enable you to stand erect within. No more bending or crouching. These are called windows and are made of glass so you can see out and light is let in. They can also be opened, these are hinges, so that fresh air can be admitted. This is how we clad the walls and the roof; now the house is free of wind and rain. And this is a chimney; the smoke leaves through it. Would you not wish for houses such as these for yourselves and for your people?"

"This is a smithy where we make axes that will cut swiftly through the hardest wood. See how quickly a steel chisel works. Far more efficient than any of your implements."

They viewed herds of cattle, flocks of sheep, fowl runs and pig stys and fields of flourishing crops.

"What a wonderful variety of taste and so nutritious. Stored to meet the needs of winter. Farewell to the fern root, eh?"

"This is a mill. So much more effective than pounding or even Ruatara's hand mill."

"This is a loom. It will produce in no time the material for warm and comfortable clothing that it would take your women months to make."

And each had found something of wonder, some new dimension to take home, explore and develop.

So now Korokoro strode the decks of the *Active* in the manner of Macquarie, mimicking the mannerisms of the governor, even taking his name. Now he, too, would be known as Macquarie, as Whetoi was known as Pomare. Hongi Hika was making a cartridge box.

Ruatara had been less amazed than the others. He had, after all, lived within the white world for many years. But he was impressed by the enormous developments Marsden had made to his farm. Flocks of merino now grazed where before there had been half a dozen. And his fields of crops made Ruatara's efforts look like a child's garden. Ruatara's respect for the man who had saved his life continued to grow.

But there was less for the other pakeha. He had quickly perceived the diffidence, even hostility in the way they treated one another. He watched their eyes when they called each other 'brother' and his mouth turned down at the lie. He watched the convicts in chains as they shuffled from their barracks and he muttered in disgust at the crack of the cat and the howl from the man on the cross.

He realised he had seen Marsden apart from his fellows but now he watched him as he consulted earnestly with his colleagues. He remembered his conversation with Rakau.

"You have welcomed the pakeha here," Rakau had said.

"I have offered Matene a welcome. It is not the same thing."

And Rakau had replied, "It is close enough. One will lead to the other."

Rakau had planted doubt then, but the wonder of it was that it had never really occurred to him before. Perhaps it was the contrast, the kindness and loyalty after cruelty and treachery; perhaps it was the sense of indebtedness, his owing utu or just respect for Marsden's power. Whatever the cause, his suspicions were now real.

And they were suddenly, dramatically even, exacerbated.

One night he had become wearied of the conversation, the endless proselytising, the glories of the pakeha technology and by tacit implication the poverty of the Maori. Though tired and struggling somewhat with his breathing, he had left the house, walking through the clatter of wheels and hooves, suddenly longing for the sound of surf or the call of the morepork. After a time he had found himself outside a run-down tavern and without thought had taken himself inside. A dozen men were seated at rough tables lit in the shadows from a single flickering lamp. A burly man behind the bar eyed him suspiciously but lightened as a shilling was laid upon the counter.

To the manifest surprise of the barkeep he ordered wine, he could not stomach waipiro, stinking water, and stood vaguely by the bar. Then a man was beside him.

"Stand a man a drink, squire?"

Ruatara shrugged, then laid down another coin.

"Bless you, sir, a large rum, I thank you, give the man his fuckin' change, eh?"

The man drank deeply, then wiped a scrawny wrist across his mouth. "Been 'ere long?"

Ruatara shook his head. "Since the end of winter," he said, "but soon we will be going back to New Zealand."

"That right?" Just a visit then. Where you stayin'?"

"We have been staying with Hamuera Martene."

"Who?"

The years away from English had brought back difficulties with the harsh consonants.

"The chaplain," Ruatara said at last.

"Oh. Marsden." The man's eyes glittered. "Mates with the fu-, with the chaplain, are you?"

Ruatara nodded. "He has been very kind to us. He and some of his people are coming back to New Zealand with us. He wants to teach us how to grow crops and build houses."

"That right? Going to help you, eh? Lucky you." The sarcasm was confusing and Ruatara looked at the man more closely. He was an unprepossessing fellow, below middle height and his seaman's jacket hung loosely on a thin frame. But the eyes were quick and clever and Ruatara gazed at the malevolence there.

"You do not mean what you say," he said. "You do not think Matene will help us. Why do you think that?"

"Why do I think Marsden will do for you? Because," the man paused. "How about another drink then?"

Coins exchanged hands and the man drank, more patiently this time. He let out a stupendous belch and Ruatara recoiled from the fumes. The man seemed not to notice. "Ah, Christ, that's good," he said. "Now, where was I?"

"You were saying you do not think Matene will help us."

"That's right, that's right. And why do I think that? 'Cause I never seen it happen, that's why. And I seen enough. I seen the help the English, and that's me too but I ain't proud of it, I seen the help they, we brung to the Indians in America. And India and Africa. And here in Aus-fuckin'-stralia. Ask the abos about the help they got. Helped off their fuckin' land, more like."

Ruatara was very attentive now. He laid another coin upon the counter. "Bring my friend another drink," he said, then, to the sailor, "please continue."

The man continued to drink and his venom grew.

"You seen any abos about?" He saw Ruatara's puzzlement and laughed. "You don't even know who they are, do you? They're the people who used to live here, mate, like you in New Zealand. But you don't see 'em around now. 'Cause we've got no use for 'em. We've got what we want. Their land."

"Did they not fight you?"

"Some of them, a few, not many. They're not great fighters, these abos. 'Sides, for every one of 'em that fought we'd kill a dozen, a hundred. Christ, man, in Van Diemen's Land we shoot the buggers for sport."

"But what," asked Ruatara, "has this to do with Matene?"

The man drank deeply and answered, "Everything. Your Matene is a magistrate here, he upholds British justice, he is a part of it all. Fuck, man, you can't separate 'em. Church and state, different sides of the same fuckin' coin. Sometimes the soldiers come first; they get the natives under control, then the church comes in to change 'em, make 'em thankful. Sometimes it's the other way round. Either way, it's the same result."

One will lead to the other.

Rum was slurring the sailor's words now and he was becoming maudlin.

"We're a treacherous race," he said, "you can't trust us and you have to be stupid to try, stupid and retarded." His eyes filled. "Believe us and you'll be sorry. If we say we'll be your mate and look out for you, don't believe us. 'Cause the moment things go wrong, we'll be off like a shot. And leave you to rot. Ah, fuck it." He pushed himself to his feet. "Stay away from us, mate, that's my advice to you." Then he staggered to the door and was gone into the night.

Ruatara discussed his concerns with Hongi and Korokoro; their response was as he might have predicted.

"If they dare to stand against us," said Korokoro, "we will drive them into the sea." He grinned. "Something to look forward to."

Hongi was no less enthusiastic, but more sanguine.

"Taiaha against guns is not an even contest," he said. "We will need to acquire guns."

Ruatara continued to brood and on the return trip to New Zealand acquainted Marsden with his fears. The chaplain was outraged.

"If I could lay my hands on the calumnious wretch," he roared, "I would have him flogged to within an inch of his worthless life." Then, in more concliatory tones, he appealed to Ruatara. "You have never known me to speak falsely and I pray you believe me now when I tell you I wish your people nothing but good. But," he paused meaningfully, "if you do not, say so and I will have us turned about and return to Australia."

Ruatara believed him but declined the offer. Korokoro and Hongi would be enraged to be stranded in Port Jackson, seeking passage where they could find it with funds they did not have. Te Pahi in similar circumstances had been reduced to sleeping under bridges. Besides, if what the sailor had said was true, the pakeha would come in any event, with Marsden or without him. He was already there and it would be better for Maori if they had some understanding of his ways. He did, however, insist that the settlement be at Rangihoua where he could keep an eye on proceedings. Privately he warned Marsden that were they to settle at Waitangi or anywhere else for that matter they would be plundered mercilessly. Marsden was happy to acquiesce.

Ruatara was caught in a great ambivalence. On the one hand there were his years of experience at first hand of pakeha treachery and cruelty. And now the drunken sailor had cast it into an infinitely wider net. Would Maori follow the same fate as the Australian aboriginals? There was no doubt the English had the numbers and the weapons to effect it, if they chose. Yet he did not doubt Marsden's sincerity –'we are here for good'- so would it not be to his every advantage to be allied with this powerful white rangatira? Hongi's and Korokoro's careless dismissal of the threat - their delight even at the possibility of new and grander warfare- was no aid to resolution.

And finally (and was this not the nub of the issue?) the immediacy of threat did not lie with the newcomers. It lay where it had always lain: in the hands of his fellow Maori. None, as he had frequently told Marsden, could be trusted. He had not lied, although he had certainly exaggerated on other occasions, when he had advised the chaplain against settlement at Waitangi. And further afield, in the districts of Pomare for example, sudden warfare was always a possibility.

His sympathies swung and he could not be still. So he stood by and watched as the chaplain preached the first Christmas sermon and the words rang in meaningless discord, like gulls fighting over a fisherman's leavings. Then the chaplain turned to him.

"Pray, Ruatara, do convey my meaning to your people."

But Ruatara shrugged and said, "They know nothing about it now; by and by they will."

And when Marsden asked him to instruct his people on how they should behave towards the newcomers, instructions clothed in promise and threat, his answer was the same.

"They know nothing about it now; by and by they will."

He watched the missionaries watch the Rangihoua iwi and he saw the contempt in them. He heard their words as they spoke carelessly within his hearing. "Deplorable, wretched, miserable heathen," said John King. "Wanton shamelessness," said Thomas Kendall as he tore his eyes from the high pointed breasts of a teenage girl.

And then he would swing again and his respect for Marsden would swell as he guided the chaplain from one district to another, warning him against the treachery of the locals, advising them to treat the white settlers with courtesy and kindness. Perhaps at bottom there was only this: *these are my pakeha.*

Then when Marsden was gone, visiting other districts, filling his, the Society's vessel with trade, he would view the pakeha with new suspicion. So when Kendall spoke to him of a school for the children he said, "by and by; by and by they will like it, but they know nothing about it yet."

But there was always agriculture. He visited the plantations and watched the new crops breaking out of New Zealand earth and buried his hands in the soil. Here there was certainty. And in building. Here the English clearly had something to offer and he sat with Marsden and planned a village, to be constructed on the English model. For the rest, for their social order, their customs and their god his interest had diminished. He had tried to understand it and had listened patiently enough for Marsden to feel the beginnings of his first conversion, but on his final return to New

Zealand the interest had quietly vapourised. It had all become too much and he could not be bothered with it.

In the event there was no time for reconciliation. The illness that had threatened to take his life in London had never left him. He had suffered a relapse in Port Jackson and now it came again. His breath shortened and his energy failed and he could not stir from his whare. An enclosure was built about it for he was very tapu now and none but his wife Rahu and a few attendants could be with him. He lay there now, the sun pouring through an opening in the roof, panting within his shrunken world, listening to the world beyond.

There was little that Rahu and the others could do for him; he was in the hands of the atua, god, now. So they set down food –potatoes and water– beside him and mourned as they watched him shrink and suffer, shredding his blanket as he fought for breath. The atua was deep in his guts, eating him from within, and all they could do was watch and look for the closing of death; then they would take him to another place and leave him for the final consummation. At one point they thought it was imminent and came to gather him up but Ruatara was not ready. He drew his pistol and warned them away and they retreated to sit and watch and wait.

Outside the enclosure he heard Marsden railing.

"I *shall* see him. How dare you refuse me admittance? You are starving him within, I know it and I shall not countenance it."

There were other voices, placating, Maori and English together, much lost in the translation. And Marsden again.

"Talk to me not of your heathen superstition. I shall see him. And if I do not, I shall have the guns of the *Active* turned upon you. What say you to that?"

Further conversation and then here was Marsden, rage fading to concern and solicitude and bringing comfort of a kind, rice and tea; it slipped down warmly, smoothly and Ruatara seemed to revive a little.

Marsden continued to visit, watching with hope as Ruatara's condition improved and then with despair as he failed again. They spoke of what was to be done.

"My brother will stay with you in Port Jackson."

"Yes. He is becoming more skilled in carpentry and agriculture. I will keep him until his English is better and then return him to succeed you here."

Ruatara half smiled, considering what the rest of the iwi might have to say about that, but said nothing.

Then Marsden was gone, his leave of absence expired, and here was Kendall, pale and concerned, full of prayer and good intentions.

"Here, dear Ruatara, a spoonful of rice water. There, is that not better? I shall take the decanter and have it replenished."

And Ruatara, weakly, "No, Mr Kendall, please do not be so unkind. If you take the decanter away, the atua will kill me this very day."

Thomas wrung his hands and shook his head. Here, he thought, at the very death, he clings to the beliefs that will damn him. Ruatara gave away his goods and left instructions to treat the pakeha with kindness when he was gone. Then he was carried away to the bush.

That night he lay in his solitary whare, truly alone for the first time and that was how it should be, for his death within the village would defy tapu and bring calamity upon the people. He regretted the pain for it weakened his concentration upon holding himself in readiness for his journey. The prayers of Kendall and King that had attended him daily faded as distant bleating, their atua was a mystery that was not for him. After all his time away he was back where he should be, dying as he should. The wind rose and leaf and branch rustled and dipped in its circling embrace, the surf crashed and hissed and the morepork sang its greeting and farewell. Rags of grey cloud scudded and opened upon the dark heavens and the eyes of his ancestors gazed down on him. In a little while he would be with them.

The morning brought with it a soft, grey mist that hung like a shroud over the pa. Thomas sat by William Hall and they watched the mourners tangi for their chief. There was Hongi, sobbing like an abandoned child, Rahu howling through the blood. The next morning she would take a rope to a branch and keep her promise to her husband to join him. Ruatara sat stiff amongst them, his legs bent and tied, his brow garlanded in leaf and feather, his face hidden beneath a scarlet cloth.

Hall grunted. "It is as a scene from the pit," he said sourly.

Thomas could not deny the aptness of the image but he resented Hall his steadiness. For his own part, he was uncomfortably touched and more than once he had fought to hold back his own tears. Particularly when Hongi had approached him, embraced him and wept against his cheek. And he trembled for Ruatara's soul.

"We could not save him," he said. "We have failed him."

Hall shrugged. "What can you expect?" he said. "They are steeped in their heathen lore. It will be a long time before any are brought to Christ."

Thomas bunched his fists against his side.

"How can you be so sanguine?" he asked bitterly. "Do you not tremble for your own sake, to sit here helplessly while Satan calls Ruatara home?"

Hall looked at him curiously, taking in the pallor and fear upon his companion's face. Then he shrugged again.

"I am a realistic man, Mr Kendall," he answered. "I trust myself to God's purpose and do the best I can. But I will not berate myself for not achieving the impossible. Why," he grimaced, "even the great Marsden who had Ruatara to himself all that time could do no more."

But Thomas shook his head. "With God," he said, "all things are possible."

Port Jackson 1815

The Egans had a house now, a fine sturdy house raised on solid posts against snakes and other wildlife. A verandah ran its length, cooling the inner rooms. It stood on a plateau on a hill that sheltered them from a mean southerly that blew in the winter and gave some shade in the summer.

The framework was completed and the mason well along with the chimney when they first saw their home. "Nothing you can do right now," Marsden had told them, "leave it up to Mr Bull. It will be a house to stand. You must build your strength, engage in smaller things. Mrs Cloavis, for instance, has offered to call upon you. Fine woman, Mrs Cloavis, widow to Sir George and a generous contributor to the Mission Cause. A kind reception would be a Worthy Task."

The task was easy as well as worthy and Mrs Cloavis left the parsonage with a smile wreathed about her ample features. Such an utterly charming couple, how kind, how solicitous, how *interested* they were in her.

Other conversations carried a kind of sudden gold.

"I have been thinking about my sister, Mr Egan."

"Your sister, Mary who lives in England?"

"Yes. I hear she has been taken ill and may die. If she has not died already."

"Death comes to all of us, Mrs Smithers. We mourn and we go on."

"It shouldn't be like this, though."

"Like this?"

"We parted on bad terms, things were said …" Her voice trailed off.

"And never unsaid?"

"No." The Australian sun had aged Mrs Smthers well past her years. She squinted from a brown wrinkled face that was usually drawn into lines of petulance and disappointment. But now George just saw sadness and it seemed a pure and fragile thing.

"Are there things you might wish to unsay?" he asked.

"Aye." Mrs Smthers lowered her gaze. "I said, well she did, too, she started it …"

"Are there things you might wish to unsay?"

Mrs Smithers hesitated at the repetition and George waited.

"Yes," she said slowly to her lap, "I said things that were not true and that were said in malice. I wish I had not done that."

"You would like to tell Mary you are sorry?"

"Yes, I would. But she is in England ..."

"You could write to her."

But I can't write ..."

"... so I shall write it for you."

"Would you?"

"Of course."

"She might be already dead."

"So we should move quickly."

"When?"

"Now. I have my notebook and a pencil."

They sat in the shade of luxuriant wisteria while Mrs Smithers made her confession.

"It was quite lovely," George told Joanna later. "She didn't cry, I thought she might but she wouldn't allow it. But she softened. I sat there and drank orange juice and she told me her sad and silly story. That's what she called it. 'This is such a sad and silly story,' she said and I wrote it all down. 'Two grown women, not simpletons and with every reason to love one another. What did we do with it, Bess?' she said. 'What have I done? I'm so sorry, Bess. Please forgive me, I forgive you.' I wrote it all down and read it back to her and she nodded and made her mark. I have left the letter with the church office at the docks. Her husband will see it on to the first ship for England."

Joanna tousled his hair.

"You are a lovely man, George Egan," she said.

Rangihoua 1815

An old man sat a little way from a clearing where his friend sat beneath the earth; not too close, he knew well the boundaries of tapu, but close enough. He heard Tawhiri breathing through the leaves, his soft green breath lifting the old fragrance, cool upon the old man's skin. Moving through the bush, rustling, sighing, lifting the spray from the waves below, silver lace in the moonlight. Greater life moving through the lesser above as worms move through the flesh of his friend below. It was all one.

Rakau draws his cloak about him more closely and the feathers are soft and warm.

Ruatara, what did you mean by going and dying like that? I've missed you.

It's been ten months now, see, I am learning their time, and the last flesh still hangs on your bones so it will be a little while yet before I see and touch you again. Then we will settle you properly.

I've been watching your pakeha, Ruatara, ae, and talking with them, too. It has been most interesting.

They do not seem to know what happiness is. They seldom smile and I have yet to see them laugh, truly laugh like Maori laugh, falling down, thigh slapping, belly shaking, hooting, roaring, gasping for air. Now that I think of it, you seemed to have forgotten it, too. All their pleasure is in their work. If pleasure is the right word. For a while I wondered if they were born that way. But now I do not think that is the case. I have watched young Toma, Keni's boy, run with our tamariki; he laughs and cheers and tears off his hot clothes to throw himself into the tide with the others. Until his mother sees him and he is called back to the fold to practise his lessons in joylessness.

Keni has two older girls, I believe, you would have known them, but they have been left in Port Jackson to learn the English ways from Matene in a home for orphans. Now there is another strange idea —children without a family. Even when their parents live. They will come over here at some later time, Keni says. Then they will have a family again.

Matene ... I can see why you had such respect for him. He is without doubt a man of great power and enormous will. And the will to use that power. Do you think he would have turned his guns on Rangihoua if he had not been allowed to see you? I can't believe it. Surely that would have undone all his intentions here. But he was believed and he got his way. And they did not hate him for it. Now there is power.

Mostly he is all kindness. He sits and listens and nods and does not seek argument the way the others do. And always there are gifts and the promise of more to come.

I have not mastered their language the way you did and I don't think I ever will. I don't like it. It is harsh and the sounds jar upon my ears. Perhaps not understanding I see more. I watch Matene's eyes and hands and listen to the rise and fall of his words. And I do not sense kindness there. I see and hear the shape and the sound of it but it is as a servant to his will, something to be used and discarded when its usefulness is done. He could have turned the guns upon us.

He is the same with the other pakeha; they, too, are servants to his will.

They are strange with one another, these white men. I remember your saying they never touch but in anger and I have seen nothing to contradict that. They are even distant with their children.

Wiremu Hore works like I have never seen a man work before. He is up at dawn, fuelling his body without enjoyment, then marching, he never strolls, to his fields. He has already lifted a fine crop of barley and now prepares for the next. Kepa and Haami are with him and they say he is a good man to work for. He teaches them to use the tools, feeds them well and pays them fairly.

Hore has his own house now. Apparently the pakeha do not like to live together; they also complain about the whare nui that was built for them. It is cold, they say, and lets in the rain and wind and keeps the smoke. Keni and Kingi still live there with their families but say they will also build houses for themselves. They will need Hore's help in this but I think they will be lucky to get it. He plans to move away soon to Waitangi. The land is better there, he says.

He trades with us and I think he gains by the exchange.

But I do not really know him.

I know Kingi even less. His task is to make shoes, a fairly useless article, I think, but then the pakehas' feet are very soft. But he is not a hard worker like Hore and the others complain about him. This makes him angry and now he makes no shoes at all. He does some trading, too, but again he does not try very hard and complains about being in want of necessities. My sons Tara and Ewha have been living with him and his wife and my mokopuna, Ehura, too. Kingi tries to be a good man. He visits with people who are sick and takes them food and drink and says karakia. It doesn't stop them from dying though.

I know Keni best. Mainly this is because he is learning to speak te reo. He asks me the words, then he writes them down and practises saying them until he gets it right. He learns quickly and we are enjoying some fine korero.

Keni is different from the others. They are slow to learn te reo and do not care to know about our history and our ways. I suppose this is because they are here to teach us their ways, how to worship their atua. I think your sailor was right; they are here to change us. Keni, too, is anxious to do this; he is, he says, their kaiako rangatira, their chief teacher, the others are just workers, but he is also very curious about our beliefs. So I tell him stories about out tupuna and he tells me his. Often he tries to join them together.

They are very strange stories and I do not see how they can believe them. Keni says his god is everywhere, even inside us, but I can't see him or feel him like I can see the blood of Papa and feel the tears of Rangi. Everything, says Keni, is the will of his god and we are instruments of that will. But when I ask him if it is his god's will that I should disbelieve he shakes his head and says that is the working of somebody called the adversary. You can't see him, either.

Keni takes us seriously. When I knelt with Kingi in prayer and told him that all I felt was sore knees he was angry and told me that I was too blinded by sin to see the light. When I told Keni that the atua who told his prophet Arahami to take the life of his son sounded like a wairua kino, a bad spirit, his eyes filled and his lip trembled. There is much fear in him.

There is much anger, too. Ewha has told me that while he was living in the pakeha whare nui Kingi and Keni would have great arguments, shouting and threatening one another. One night, he said, after Keni had drunk a quantity of wai piro he brandished a knife at Kingi and perhaps would have killed him had his wife not flung herself between them. And this is the same man who weeps for my disbelief.

So, I am interested in Keni. Perhaps he has taken your place, Ruatara. I always enjoyed our korero. You had much to teach me and you also wanted to learn. Keni is like that. The others are boring: they do not listen – "I am not here to learn of you," Kingi says – and they just keep saying the same things. I think Maori are a bit like that, too. All they think of are gifts and war. They do not think about things, they do not care to learn. Perhaps the tamariki will be different.

I wonder what you're learning now. Did Rahu find you? Are you in darkness or light? Can you hear what I am saying and if you can, do you care?

CHAPTER 20

Rangihoua Jan.1816,

A full moon hung over Rangihoua lighting in the new year, over the whare of the pa, nestled together behind their small enclosures, and over the sprawling mission settlement that clung about the lower slopes of the neighbouring eastern hill. Over the sixty foot whare, sliding from disuse into disrepair, over the shell of the schoolhouse pale and skeletal and over two small cottages.

It flooded through the open shutters of the cobbler's house, lighting the small room where he lay with his wife and child. It floated on a soft breeze that carried the susurrus of waves on sand and shingle, the rise and fall of the morepork's call and the fragrance of bush and sea. And an errant, hungry mosquito. Its drone was impossibly loud for so small a creature, a vibrating malevolence that built to sudden crescendo as it circled the cobbler's face and drove, it seemed, directly towards his ear. In rage and an absurd kind of panic he slapped viciously at it, hard across his cheekbone. Then he was sitting, feet swung on to the floor, lost in desperate hatred for his tormentor, hands cupped then coming suddenly together once, twice, three times.

Clapping like a madman in the night.

Hannah slept on oblivious and Phillip was safe in his crib, his pinced little features criss-crossed under muslin netting. The cobbler looked down on him, caught between a surging love and fear as the boy drew in a rasping breath. *Dear God, this, if nothing else: let him live. All else will be bearable if You but let him live.*

He crossed the room, treading carefully on the rough-sawn planks, picking out splinters was a regular past-time. But it was still an immeasurable improvement on what had been. The past winter in the disused whare had been nothing short of hell. Trapped in a freezing swamp, eight hundred and forty square feet for thirteen, seven adults and six children plus whoever else might be staying, a little over sixty four square feet or a cubicle of twelve feet by five per soul King had once computed in an idle moment. Wouldn't Marsden have been impressed by such a profligate waste of time? Marsden with his fine two-storied house with its plush drapes and carpets, Marsden who gave orders for the mission house and deemed it very comfortable. But Marsden had not had to live in it, he had not had to endure the wind that blew through the chinks in the walls and roof, nor the rain that found its way, leaving no place dry and turning the earth floor to mud. There had been no means of warmth nor drying for the fire was placed outside and the health of the inmates, as King had come to see them, had suffered. Particularly the children; they coughed and sneezed and grizzled and were bored and fractious. Hannah, too, had been laid low and her mother was much perturbed. She shared her worries regularly with King and he felt in them a measure of blame which did nothing to help his shortening temper.

Nor did the company generally. For brethren brought together in Christ's name there was, as King observed to his wife, a marked disunity. Marsden's vision of a communal society where all was shared and no man took his own profit had foundered almost immediately. And the spirit of social and emotional unity had perished in Australia.

Everybody called it pride, everybody believed everybody else had ideas above his station and living on top of one another civility degenerated into endless squabble and accusation. Kendall's endless sermonising made it so much worse. And there was no escaping him. Even as King lay in his bed, the voice rolled on; so he would lie there in the cold damp dark with cotton in his ears holding back the scream. Later he would not be so reticent.

Nothing could have prepared him for this and his cup had overflowed with the bitterness of regret. Yet his faith had remained intact and he had clung to it with a kind of perverse pride like a man before the mast, biting down on the rag between his teeth for the first few strokes. *I will not give them the satisfaction.* But as the blows accumulated the pain overthrew him and he had groaned aloud in prayer.

Dear God, my strength and my saviour, why have You brought me here? Why do you test me so? Were not my intentions good when You called me from my home to bring Your Word to the heathen? Have I not been steadfast? I am Your instrument but Lord, it is a heavy load You have laid upon me.

He remembered the young man bright with Enthusiasm who had stood before the CMS Board and flushed with excitement and pride as they pronounced their verdict. *John King, you are God's man. He has reached out and filled you with His Holy Purpose and you are blessed to receive It and act upon It. We salute you.* He remembered his hands upon the railing of the *Ann*, five years past now, salt spray tingling on his face, gazing resolutely into the west. The dingy, stinking streets of Swerford, Oxfordshire, complaining parents *–when will you make something of yourself, John? –* and the uncertainty of employment at a decent wage he remembered not so well.

Australia had not been easy. Abandoned by Marsden. *The time cannot be deemed Opportune,* you could hear the capitals in his words, the pomposity, the self-righteousness, *not Opportune, I say, for the Mission to Proceed. You must fend for yourself, Mr King, you and Mr Hall. I will aid when I can and when I must but the Society's fund are Limited and the colony Abounds with Opportunity for Industrious men.* So out on their ears they went. It was all very well for Hall, the port cried out for boat builders and he had quickly found his way to profit. But none wanted a flax spinner and there seemed little demand for cobblers and he had struggled.

But the Lord had kept him and although times were hard he had not complained. He had toiled upon his little plot of land and had made do. And when Marsden had sought him out to revile him for not making more study of the heathen tongue he had been dignified. *I hope I know my responsibilities, sir, and labour to answer them. And when my own security is more assured (and I look to you for no support, sir,) I shall be happy to go to your house and study with the natives there.* Unlike Hall who had quarrelled bitterly with the penny-pincher.

And then the tide had turned and brought him Hannah Hansen, daughter of the master of the *Active*. It was a match that suited all parties. Marsden in particular was delighted. King's single status had long troubled him; New Zealand is not a place for single men, he had said. And for King it signalled the end to the loneliness that seemed to have always been with him. That Hannah was much attached to her mother was of no concern. Indeed, it seemed a further advantage as his family expanded. His sense of importance grew, he was a married man now, a connected man. And then he was a father, a family man.

But it had done nothing to raise him in Marsden's eyes. Still the mechanic. Godly perhaps, but mechanic nonetheless. And when Kendall had arrived he had seen just how much. No 'fend for yourself, Mr Kendall.' No, not for a minute. Rather, 'here's ninety pounds for you and fifty pounds for Mr King. You're worth nearly twice as much as such as he.' Marsden said the extra came from ten pounds per child but then Kendall left his two daughters in Port Jackson at the orphanage so they wouldn't be costing him anything. King looked towards Phillip sleeping fretfully and fear fed his anger. How could Kendall have done it? Nothing would have inclined him to part with Phillip.

Marsden had settled Kendall at Paramatta near the parsonage and had begun building a school house for him. Suddenly funds were available. Funny, that. And when Kendall was in New Zealand with Hall the Marsdens had visited with his wife and probably brought her extra supplies, too. No visits for the Kings, though. And then Marsden called them brethren and preached communal living. But there was no equality here.

And Kendall was the first to let you know. From the very beginning he had always known best. In his smarmy, superior way. *If my brother would but bend his ear towards some heartfelt advice.* Bend his ear? What kind of talk was that? What was wrong with 'listen'? And, dear God, the way he had gone on when he was proclaimed magistrate in New Zealand. Along with Hongi and Ruatara, rest his soul, and Korokoro. What a joke. Savages, two of whom couldn't speak a word of English and three of whom couldn't write worth a jot. The proclamation wasn't worth the paper it was written on, Hall had said, and of course he was right but to see Kendall take on, you'd think they'd made him King of the South Pacific. Hannah had seen through him straightaway, she and her mother, too, and through that frumpy wife of his, gazing at him like he was God Almighty.

The simile shocked King and he bowed his head in silent self-reproof. *Forgive me my profanity, Lord.*

Hall couldn't abide the popinjay, either. *He will find I am my own man, Mr King, I will not be his servant.* Hall was his own man alright, with as much of an eye for the main chance as Marsden himself. He'd had crops in, *his* crops, mark, almost before they'd settled. And was trading on his own account. And then he was gone, out of the hell-hole, off to Waitangi. Much better land there, he said, you'll never establish a farm here, he said. They'd established a saw pit there, the timber was better and more accessible. And Hall had built himself a house with proper walls and a roof and floor. And a fireplace and a chimney! Living in comfort while King and Kendall and all remained in the leaky hut. O certainly, timber had been sent over and there was talk of houses at Rangihoua. But that had only come when Marsden, acting kindly for once, had sent over carpenters from Port Jackson. And Kendall was going to join Hall. Until the natives showed their true colours and plundered the sawyers and then the brave would-be parson sat snug. Hall had gone back, though, with his wife and son. More fool, he. He'd learn. King hoped the lesson would not be too severe.

He paused as, unbidden, the image of the settlement's boat, a sturdy twenty footer, came to mind. Hall had built that. He'd used it for himself, of course, but he had not kept it. It rode at anchor now, safe in the lee of the eastern arm of the bay, and it was of immeasurable use. Hall has wronged me, thought King, but there is good in him. I should not be so harsh.

Anyway, praise God, they were in their own house now. Crowded certainly with Hannah's mother and her young son but they were warm and dry and perhaps best of all away from Kendall and his fine words and intentions that were never followed. It was a beginning.

Behind the eastern hills the stars faded and Rangihoua Pa was a sharp silhouette in the pale glow of the new day. The mission houses remained in shadow. King yawned and stretched and scratched himself. He wondered how Hall was faring.

Hall was faring very well. If he had thought about it he might have registered that he was as happy as he had ever been. In the best of places at the best of times. Standing very still on the banks of the Waitangi River watching the mist shift through the colours of dawn over the slow-running waters. There was a purity and clarity here, peace and a sense of eternity. He would have dismissed such notions as fanciful and unproductive but still and all he resonated with it. He stood and waited.

Then there was a stirring and the sound of heavy wings from the reeds on the opposite bank and a water fowl ran on to the surface, flapping itself into flight. Hall's gun was at his shoulder and the explosion split the stillness awakening a rush of squawking life. The fowl was flung back into the water and lay utterly still, its head removed in the fussilade of shot.

Hall grunted in satisfaction, an excellent shot, there would be no picking pellets out of this one. He laid his gun down carefully, then slipped off his boots, trousers and jerkin. For a moment he stood naked in the embrace of the cool air. Then he slipped into the river. The water was cold and he gasped at its touch, then he was paddling awkwardly towards the bird.

An hour later he was striding home, two fowl and a heavy duck bound by their feet hanging from his shoulder. He was pleased with the morning's take although there was such an abundance of life on the river that there was little challenge in it. His breath came easily, the cold dips had not provoked the asthma that plagued him intermittently. Then he was crossing by a field of wheat; it was growing well and promised a fruitful harvest. The barley was also doing well and the potato leaves were a rich, healthy green under the morning sun. He paused by the sawyer's house, vacant at the moment, Conroy was away at Rangihoua helping with construction there, then on to his own cottage, plain and sturdy. A good job. The kitchen gardens lay on either side of the path, a profusion of green and some red. Hall could see that Dinah had already watered the plants for they glistened in the light.

The kitchen was bustling. Haami and Kepa sat at the table, smooth polished kauri, their bed rolls folded tidily away, spooning steaming gruel. Little William sat importantly between them, chattering away. Hall was struck by the number of Maori words in his sentences and by the perfection of his pronunciation. He himself still struggled with the language, labouring over the blends, the awkward 'ng' sound, and communication was usually a mixture of English, a little Maori and a lot of mime. King, he knew, fared even worse, resenting his failure and blaming the language. All of the women struggled. Only Kendall seemed to have found a way in. But then so he should. While Hall and the others laboured that all might survive Kendall visited and sat and talked and listened and took notes of words. At Rangihoua while Hall had laboured in the fields, burning in the summer heat, Kendall had sat in shade and talked and listened. While Hall had bent his back in the saw pit and slipped in the mud from the autumn rains Kendall had sat warm and dry and talked and listened. And when Hall had called for aid Kendall had summoned his servant, no one else had a servant, and kindly offered his time.

We each have our divinely appointed task, Mr Hall. Yours is to build, mine is to instruct. I would not call you from your function. Please do not call me from mine.

And how Kendall had used the fruits of his labours. Hall had moved to Waitangi where he had struggled in the wet and the cold to clear land and build his house. Then he had settled in his family and waited for Kendall to join him.

Later that year he wrote of it to Pratt: *After we had been there some time expecting Mr Kendall to come to us according to his promise, he sent me word that he had changed his mind and that he would not come; and not only that, but he encouraged the sawyers to go away and leave us to the insults and abuses of the natives, which has given me sufficient cause to remember, so that I shall certainly never allow him to deceive me so again.*

But that was all behind him now and doubtless as God had intended for it had turned out for the best. He no longer needed to endure the man's pride and treachery. He was where he was supposed to be and he was welcome there.

He dropped the birds into a bucket and settled himself at the table. Dinah's hand was briefly on his shoulder and a bowl of gruel was placed before him. He attacked it hungrily and ate steadily, silently.

Dinah was back at the fire. It sat back from the wall in its earthen grate, encased in stone and iron and the smoke rose out through the earth brick chimney. Iron rods cemented in the walls on either side crossed above the flames providing a base for the heavy iron pan Dianah was setting in place. *Thank you, Lord, for this fire. And thank you, William, for building it. It must have been a very hard time, worse even than Rangihoua, working in all conditions through an unkind winter, you and the sawyers in your wretched tent. To bring us warmth and dry clothes and hot food. The very essence. And one day, soon, William says, and so it will be for he always delivers on his word, we will have a proper oven.* She broke eggs into the pan and they sizzled in the fat.

"What we do tenei ra?" Haami was asking.

Hall smiled at him. You're a good lad, he thought. A blessing from God, no less. I can trust you and Kepa, too, with my wife and child. With you and Kepa I need not count my tools at the end of the day. A sourer note crept in. Unlike your shiftless brethren.

"Today," he said, "we will work at the pit. We have the boat that Captain Graham so kindly left us for our use while he is here and we have a good supply of timber on hand. We'll finish the parcel today and load it on and tomorrow, if the wind is fair, we'll take it across to Rangihoua. They have a use for it there for the schoolhouse." He turned to his son. "Would you like to sail across with us. You can see Thomas and Basil and Joseph."

The little boy clapped his hands. "Pai ana," he said.

Three hours later Hall was stripped to the waist and dripping. His arms ached as he leaned upon his saw and mopped his brow. Then a call rang out and he turned to see Dinah approaching, a basket in one hand and a billy in the other. Little William marched alongside her, his shaggy locks pulled back in a knot, adorned in dark green feathers.

"Time for a break, lads," Hall said.

Kepa and Haami needed no further encouragement and flopped on to the soft earth. Presently they were all settled to their morning repast, rice cakes, cold duck, hard boiled eggs and hot sweet tea. Away to their left where the river joined the sea there came shouts and splashes and bursts of laughter. A group of young men and boys were gathering tua tua there, although it sounded more like play than work.

"Idle sods," said Hall.

"Ae," Kepa agreed, chewing through his third cake, "very lazy buggers."

Hall sighed. He had tried, times beyond number, to steer the lads away from profanity but there seemed to be something in their nature that kept bringing them back to it. But they meant no harm.

He gestured towards the river.

"Want to cool off?" he asked.

He watched them head off with little William in tow. Dinah called after them.

"E Haami, e Kepa watch the mokopuna."

They sat comfortably in the warm bright day, the tang of fresh sawdust in their nostrils, listening to the sounds of play, little William stridently, "look at me! Titiro ki au!" Hall was content.

"They're good lads," he said, "Haami and Kepa, you can trust them, not like the other lazy, pilfering lot. They have cost us sorely."

Dinah shrugged and smiled.

"Ah, well," she said, "they're children still. They see something and they must have it. And they run with their feelings. If they are unhappy, they cry, if they're angry, they strike out. But mostly they are happy. I have never seen people who laugh so often and so freely. Not like you," she touseled his hair, "you grumpy bear."

Hall grinned and caught at her hand.

"Not grumpy," he protested, "just sensible and a bit serious."

"A bit serious? You are —hello, what's this?"

Hall followed her gaze towards movement on the sawyer's roof. A heavy-set Maori was clambering over it, stooping to tug at a plank.

"Blast." Hall sat upright, then got to his feet, a hand shading his eyes. "I can't make him out at this distance. Silly sod, he'll damage the roof. I'd better go and sort him out. No," as Dinah went to rise, "you stay here and enjoy your tea. I'll be back directly."

It's just like them, he thought, as he marched towards the house. Utterly thoughtless, tug at a plank, pick at the thatching and then wonder later why the roof leaks.

But as he drew closer his mood shifted to one of disquiet. He did not know this man, nor the other four who were now coming around from the back of the house. His disquiet shifted to alarm as he registered that all were carrying weapons. His breath shortened and he felt his heart pump and his blood surge.

"Hey," he called, "what are you doing?"

The Maori moved towards him, tense, eager and there was no friendliness in their eyes. But for their flax skirts they were naked, although he noticed one wearing a shawl draped about his shoulders. In a spurt of fear and anger Hall recognised it as Dinah's.

"Hey you, koe, what are you doing with my wife's shawl?" He stepped forward and reached out. Then his arm was knocked away and he grunted in pain as the haft of a taiaha drove into his back. He staggered forward, clutching at the man with the shawl more in an effort to remain upright than go on with the fight. Feebly he parried a swinging fist and then something crashed against the back of his head and he fell forward into the dust. A foot drove into his side and he rolled grunting and panting on to his back.

A taiaha was at his throat and five faces glared down in unrestrained ferocity, eyes bulging, tongues darting, barking and hissing their contempt. The man with the taiaha burst into a torrent of Maori; the speed of his speech and the roaring in Hall's ears made it incomprehensible. Only a few words came through, taua muru, was that plunder party? tapu, Wairaki.

Then another voice shrieking over it all.

"William! William!"

And there was Dinah racing towards them. Hall tried to call out, to warn her away, but the taiaha pressed into his throat and his breath was gone. He saw her run, her skirts hoisted and then he saw the back of a man closing in on her, a swinging arm and he watched Dinah flying sideways, her face a welter of blood. Her fall seemed to coincide with voices shouting and Hall could make out Haami and Kepa and perhaps a dozen others pounding towards them. He scrambled to his feet and hurried to his wife while the strangers fled.

He kneeled beside her and the fear was back. Dinah's cheek was opened and her face was a mask of blood. Dear God, he thought, holding back the scream that threatened to engulf him, I have lost her. He laid a finger on the artery in her throat and felt it move under a steady beat. He sank back on his heels and bowed his head briefly. *Praise God, she lives.*

Haami and Kepa and the others gathered around him. Their eyes glistened and they panted in their excitement but they made no move to pursue the intruders.

"Not follow," explained Kepa. "Buggers have taiaha and mere."

Hall nodded, then he was all business. He could not tend to Dinah here and she was carefully lifted. Then they hurried back to the cottage.

More grief awaited him there for the place had been ruthlessly plundered. There seemed to be nothing that had not been either stolen or destroyed. Hall leaned against the doorway and groaned in despair. Then he bit down on it and dragged himself together.

"E Haami," he said, "e haere ana koe ki te waka o Captain Graham. E korero ana koe ki ia, whaea Hore is," he grasped for the words, then gestured at Dinah lying still, "very tino sick. Injured. Cut. Need help."

Haami nodded and turned to the door.

"Wait," said Hall, "take Wiremu with you. Leave him there." Then, more to himself, "the bastards may be back." He knew without bothering to look that the guns would be gone. They would have been the first thing.

Then Haami was running down the path with William in his arms and Hall was feverishly searching through the debris. The bedding and linen and much of their clothing was gone but in a hamper he found a cotton shirt and some rags. And then a small wicker basket with, praise God, needle and thread.

"Fill the pot from the tank and ah, this one too and bring them back. Ah, God, wai, put wai in te poti."

Dinah stirred and groaned as he gently washed away the blood. He rejoiced but also regretted it. Without having to look he knew the rum would be gone and he would rather that Dinah was not conscious for the next part.

Her cheek was split from eyebrow to jaw line, torn rather than sliced apart, and her eye was closed, black and hugely swollen. *Please God, do not take her sight.* The other was open and wide in fear.

"William," she whispered, "is William safe?"

Hall mopped more blood away, then laid a strip of cotton over the wound and pressed the sides together.

"He is safe and well," he answered. "I have sent him with Haami to Captain Graham. Help will be here soon."

"Thank God." Her eye closed.

With steady hands he threaded the needle, it was a strong thread, it should hold, it must hold.

Dinah's eye was open again but calm now and her voice was steady as she spoke.

"You are going to stitch my face."

Hall nodded. "I think I must," he said. "I don't know who Graham will send or when." He patted her arm reassuringly. "I have done this before." That was true enough. All the settlers had received some training in medical care in Port Jackson and a good deal of experience since. But he would sooner the ship's doctor were there and he bitterly regretted the missing rum.

"It will hurt," he said. "You must be brave."

Then he removed the strip and cleared the last of the blood away.

"E Kepa," he said slowly, "you must hold Whaea Hore's head very still. Like this. Not move." He prayed there would be no argument, heads and tapu and such nonsense. But the Maori made no demurral and took a gentle hold. Three others were enlisted to hold Dinah's shoulders and waist.

In the event there was no need for restraint for Dinah lay utterly still while her husband stitched her face. Sweat ran down his forehead and into his eyes. Carefully he stitched with intense precision as he brought the skin together. At length it was done and he gazed down on his work. For all his efforts the rip forbad a close join and the skin rose and overlapped and hung loose. Hopefully it would heal well and the lines would smooth. "It is done," he said, "and it will suffice." He shook his head. "But I cannot speak for the eye."

Dinah patted his hand. "You have done well," she said. "God will do the rest."

The wound healed into a pink and puckered scar and Dinah's sight was partially restored. But the raid brought the end of their life at Waitangi.

"We cannot stay," said Hall. "It grieves me deeply to say so, but the danger is too great. There is no protection for us here and we were fortunate to escape with our lives. Had not Haami and Kepa and the others been on hand, we could all three have perished. I cannot expose you and William to the risk."

Dinah nodded. "And yet we did escape," she said, "and I cannot think that it was but simple luck."

"Indeed," agreed her husband, "we must give thanks to the all-powerful providence of God."

But it was hard returning to the whare, back to the cold and the wet when the wind blew through the walls and the rain seemed to find them out wherever they sheltered. For thirteen weeks they lived there, while Hall drove himself to the point of exhaustion, sailing at every opportunity to Waitangi, carefully demolishing his house there and returning it to Rangihoua. He found support in John King who travelled daily with him and laboured alongside.

Bless the man, he later wrote, *I hope I shall never forget the kindness of him and his family towards us when we were most distressed.*

But it was hard and even when they moved into the new home it was hard. They felt most keenly the want of bedding, sleeping under flax mats and whatever the settlers could afford, praying for the return of the *Active.*

Rangihoua 1816

"Why are Maori so lazy, Papa?"

Rakau looked fondly towards his daughter, his beautiful girl. Jet hair, dripping and sleek upon smooth brown shoulders, wide inquisitive eyes now squinting in concentration as she felt beneath the little waves, fingers probing through the sand. She was anything but idle; her flax kete was more than half-filled with tua tua while barely a dozen lay in his. He leaned back on his elbows and the water washed over his belly, across his chest and lapped about his throat. He watched a gannet circle in a clear sky, then drop in sudden dive, wings folded, beak leading, a white arrow and barely a splash as it pierced the bay. Does it dive straight at its prey, he wondered, where the fish is now, or does it drop to where it will be? Does it calculate in some way the distance of the fall, the movement of wind and current and the speed and direction of the fish? If so, is that thinking? A surge interrupted his musing and a wave broke upon his face. Spluttering he sat up, laughing with his daughter. *Why do we laugh at the discomfort of others?*

"Why are Maori so lazy?" the girl asked again.

"But you are not lazy, Tungaroa," he answered. "Look," gesturing at her kit, "it will soon be full." He laughed. "And then you can fill your lazy father's bag."

The girl's brow furrowed. "That is not an answer."

"No," agreed Rakau, "it's not, not yet anyway." Then he asked, "who has told you such things?"

"The pakeha. They say we are all lazy." She pursed her lips and took on an aggrieved tone. "There is a time for play, my child, and that time is after the work is done."

Rakau laughed at the precision of the mimicry. She had the teacher off well.

"What else does Keni say?" he asked.

"He says that the children do not pay attention and that they will not learn."

Again Rakau protested. "But you have learned very well," he said. "You have been in his class for little over a year now and already you can talk just like a pakeha."

Tungaroa nodded. "Yes," she said proudly, "I am learning all the time. But Matua Keni is right about a lot of the other children. They do not listen and they talk when he is talking. And they are often away. When there was no food nobody came and when Ra is smiling they run away to play and swim."

"Does this make Keni angry?"

"No." Tungaroa shook her head. "Even when some of the children are rude and say bad words he does not get angry. Well," she hesitated, "he was nearly angry with Ewha when he said fuck." She giggled. "Matua Keni's face went very red, his lips were all tight, like this," she pursed, "and he snorted through his nose like a hoihoi. The children thought this was very funny and they laughed and laughed. And Ewha said fuck again. I thought the matua might burst but then he closed his eyes and said god give me patience and he waited for the laughter to stop and then he said we must not listen to the convicts working with the blacksmith, they were bad man and they did not love Jesus and if we talked like they did we would not go to heaven to be with Jesus when we died."

Rakau smiled. "I can imagine it," he said.

"I felt sad for the matua," continued Tungaroa, "and I told Ewha to shut up and be polite."

"Did you?" Rakau was impressed. "And what did Ewha say?"

"He told me to fuck off."

Tungaroa filled their bags and they left the water and walked up the beach, or rather, Rakau walked while Tungaroa ran on ahead. Rakau watched her run, sighing at her energy, delighting in it. She was still a child but womanhood was not far away. She would make a fine wife to some fortunate man and would bear beautiful children.

When he reached her, the driftwood they had gathered earlier was blazing. Set about the fire were four small rocks and resting on the edges was a heavy iron pan Rakau had traded from Keni for a plump pig. Tungaroa had partly filled the pan with fresh water from an earthen jar, also traded from Keni. As the water rose to the boil she dropped in two handfuls of tua tua.

Now they sat in the warm sand, prising open the shellfish with a pair of sharp knives. I am becoming a man of property thought Rakau. The sun was warm upon him and the tua tua were sweet.

"So Keni is a patient man," he said. "I am surprised. I had thought him readier to passion."

"He is patient with the children, with the Maori children anyway. I have seen him angry with the pakeha children. But he gets very angry with the pakeha grown-ups."

"Indeed?" Tungaroa was in an excellent position to report on this for she had been living in the settlement for a number of months now, sleeping with the Kendalls, attending school and learning sewing and cooking from Hanna Kingi and Heine Keni. Rakau pressed on with his inquiry.

"What do they say?"

"He says that Hore is a greedy man, that he is only interested in getting rich and that he does not love the Maori. This makes Hore angry and he says that Keni is a lazy man, all he does is talk when he could be helping others. Keni says that he *is* helping others, that he is teaching them about Jesus and how to read and write and speak the pakeha tongue. Then Hore says that the schoolhouse is empty half the time and he can't see that Keni is teaching anything useful. Then Keni gets really angry and they shout at each other. Sometimes I think they might fight." She sighed. "They never do, though."

Rakau shook his head. "What an example," he said, then, "Does Kingi argue, too?"

"O yes." Tungaroa nodded her head vigorously. "He is always angry. And his wife and her mother, too. They are always complaining. They say that Keni and Hore keep all the trade for themselves while Kingi and his family go without. But they are really silly, Papa. There is lots of food and they do not share. Sometimes each family trades a pig and it is too much for them all to eat and half of it goes bad and is wasted. Why do they not share?"

Rakau shrugged. "I don't know, e hine. Perhaps because they do not like each other, perhaps because they are too proud."

"But Matua Keni says that pride is a great sin."

"And so it is. It is also usually very stupid. What else do they say?"

"Well, let me see if I can remember. Wait." She reached into the bag. "Do you want more tua tua?"

Rakau smiled. She is a great treasure, he thought. I wonder why other adults don't spend more time with their children, pakeha as well as Maori. Everyone's too busy.

"Thank you," he said. "A few more would sit well. They are very tasty."

Tungaroa dropped a handful into the pot as she thought back over the last pakeha meeting. She wanted to get it right and please her father. Now, there was Hore, quiet, unmoving, arms folded, listening but not really listening. Kingi was busier, fidgetting, clinging to complaint like a koura to a rock. And Keni, pale with passion, trying to be reasonable.

"If my brothers would but consider the possibility of a unified approach. Let me quote from Mr Scott in his address to the CMS. Here it is. Remember, remember, I say, that Satan's grand object is to divide those who seek the subversion of his kingdom. Be fully and constantly aware –"

Then Kingi, "We are not natives in need of a sermon, Mr Kendall."

And Hore, "I am my own man, Mr Kendall. I need no direction."

And Keni, still trying, "We all need direction, brother, and I –"

"Not from you."

Then Keni exploding, "You stubborn, unreasonable man, I speak with the authority of His Majesty's government, I am magistrate, I –"

"That does not set you in command over us."

And then shouting, chaos and the men storming off, each in his own direction.

"What do their women say?"

"Whaea Kingi says what her husband says. Whaea Keni and whaea Hore don't say much. They just look sad. Often I hear whaea Keni weeping." Then, "you still haven't told me why they think Maori are lazy."

"I don't know, e hine. Shall we try to work it out? What do you think?"

The girl was pleased. It was good to have an adult take you seriously, particularly when the adult was your father and tohunga and the wisest man in the iwi.

"Well," she said, "I suppose they think the children are lazy because they do not like to do their work. They are grasshoppers."

"Grasshoppers?"

"Matua Keni told us a story about an ant and a grasshopper. During the summer and autumn the grasshopper sang and played while the ant was very busy and worked hard, gathering food for the winter. So when winter came the ant had lots of food stored and the grasshopper had none. The grasshopper went to the ant and asked for food but the grasshopper said, 'during the summer and autumn you played and sang. Now dance.' The grasshopper starved because it had been lazy and not done its work."

"And also because the ant was not willing to share. Let us look at this another way. The Maori children do not like to do the pakeha work. What about other work? Do the girls work in the fields when they are told? Do the boys practise hard with the taiaha?"

"O yes," Tungaroa agreed quickly. "They work hard then."

"So then perhaps they are not so lazy. They just don't like doing what the pakeha say. Perhaps they think it is boring or has nothing to do with them. And now I think you should be getting back." He smiled. "There is probably work for you to do."

After Tungaroa had left he sat and watched the gannets. He thought that he had put her mind at rest although he also hoped that she would not share his observations with the teacher. He would do that later, himself.

So, Maori were indolent grasshoppers and the pakeha industrious ants. Mean, grasping ants who would take but not give. No, he corrected himself, that was not fair. They gave of their knowledge, their time, their medicine. All three families were known for visiting with the sick and for offering food and assistance. Particularly Keni whose ointments had brought much relief to those suffering from sick eyes. But they would not share amongst themselves. No, that was not true, either. Kingi had given his time and labour to Hore when he was moving his house and Hore had helped build the schoolhouse. But then earlier he had refused to help the other two build their houses and Kingi would not make shoes for them. Rakau's brow furrowed. They would not keep still.

The Maori then as lazy grasshoppers. Certainly they loved to sing and dance and would leave off their work to do so. But he could see the pakeha enjoyed it. They would watch and smile and sometimes clap their hands in time. And afterwards they would applaud. And then complain about the Maori singing and dancing when they should be working.

And it was not true that the Maori would not prepare for winter. Ruatara in particular had worked in agriculture like the most industrious ant and many acres of land now stood in fine crops awaiting the autumn harvest. Onions, cabbages, turnips, potatoes, the list went on. And many others had followed his example, particularly Hongi. Rakau himself had a fine garden.

And who was more industrious than the Maori when it came to war?

Rakau shook his head. The story was too simplistic. And yet, he rubbed his chin, and yet there was something about the images that resonated with some kind of truth. The laughing, thoughtless, carefree grasshoppers and the ant, in its ubiquitous black, scurrying busily, joylessly, from one task to another, declaiming on its own virtue as it finally found a kind of pleasure, standing piously back from the grasshopper as it starved.

Dark rain clouds moved slowly above the northern hills. They would bring heavy showers within an hour or two but now there was only a light, steady drizzle drifting through the cold grey air.

It was the kind of day that filled the school house. Completed at last, it was warm and dry and a recent visit from the *Active* meant that there was food to be had. From two of the crossbeams a pair of lanterns pooled dull light over the bare boards of the open space. Maori students, from children of six to young men and women of sixteen sat at rough sawn benches or on the floor. At the far end on a raised platform stood the schoolmaster's desk and benches for the pakeha children. The room was full of continuous movement as older children went to assist younger ones or, more regularly, stopped to converse with their peers. The sound rose and fell like waves, from moments of blessed stillness to cacophanous levels where it seemed that all thirty were talking or shouting at once.

Thomas sat at his desk, steadying himself. The trick, he knew, lay in maintaining perspective. This was not London where the children bent assiduously over their books in silence, their obedience assured by the master's switch. He had swiftly learned that that kind of discipline was not available here. You could not strike these children, for all that they might strike each other. Their leaving in sudden fury and outrage was the least of the likely reactions. You could not make them learn. But neither was this the whare where his first classes had been assembled, cramped in damp space between the canvas partitions that lay between the other settlers' quarters. Here at least he did not need to sacrifice teaching for constant vigilance, ensuring that the children remained within their appointed area, that they had not slipped away to explore, tutu with the settlers' possessions and on occasion purloin them.

Here he had his own domain, humble as it might be. And here, irregular as attendance might be, there was a steady, growing roll. Maintaining it, certainly, was an enormous chore and he bitterly resented the time and energy and drain upon his own resources that went into ensuring that enough food was available, along with a collection of small prizes and rewards to keep the pupils' motivation going. If Marsden were not so disorganised and so mean with his resources. One hundred pounds a year and he would have enough to buy all the cooperation he needed. He could transform the place. Thomas caught his mood blackening and snapped down on it. This was not the perspective he sought. This was the way to resentment and anger and sometimes, he feared, to madness.

Here was the beginning and he should be rejoicing in it. He looked across the classroom and his spirits rose and fell. There was his boy, young Thomas, Toma the Maori children called him helping Moka with his letters. *Good lad, Thomas, you are a credit to me.* And there was Maui for once bent over his book, a picture of concentration. *Thank you, Lord, You are bringing him round.* He hurried over to the boy, ready with praise and encouragement. To find Maui drawing lines and circles over a precious blank page. Thomas drew a deep breath, holding down his anger at the wanton vandalism.

"He aha tena? What is that?" he said at last in the mildest tone he could muster.

"He moko tenei."

So he was drawing moko. Hongi had done the same thing on the *Active*, reproducing his own with startling accuracy to serve as his signature. But this was not the place for it and paper was in short supply.

"E Maui," he said, "this is not the place for moko. You should be practising your letters."

The boy made no answer and continued with his design.

He is ignoring me.

The insolence was like a slap across the face and Thomas snatched for the pencil. But the boy was too quick. He jerked his hand away and stared at Thomas with glittering eyes.

Don't touch me.

Thomas felt his heart begin to race and his breath shortened. Then a hand was tugging at his sleeve. Looking down, he saw Tungaroa holding up a book to him.

"Titiro, e matua. I have finished my letters. Have I done them properly?"

The writing was laboured and Thomas could see the care that had gone into it. Each letter sat neatly on its line, a clear finger space between each word.

Kapi ta Hara no God. Kakeno ta Hara no Tungata.
The way of God is good. The way of man is bad.

He looked down on the child's anxious face and his anger washed away in a surge of affection and almost pathetic gratitude.

"You are a good girl, Tungaroa," he said. "God loves you."

CHAPTER 21

One hundred feet away between the foreshore and a steep hill stood the smithy, a simple box built about a fireplace. On two sides the shutters were open as was the door, yet the heat within was intense. It rose from glowing coals into the dark and acrid air, bending the dark in a shimmering haze.

The bandana about his head was long since soaked and sweat ran down his face and into a drenched smock. But he barely noticed it, nor the aching in his arms. All his focus was on the glowing steel gripped in iron forceps as he lifted it from the fire.

"Good lad. You've picked the moment well. Now, on to the anvil, just so, hold it steady now, good, now with the hammer, firm but don't beat the shit out of it, remember how I showed you."

Hammer fell on steel and the soft metal spread and thinned into the shape of a blade

Walter Hall stood in the open doorway where the air was cool upon his back and watched his apprentice with admiration. Patience, that was his virtue. Most youngsters, if they didn't wilt from the heat, would pound away, wear themselves out and ruin the shape. And then be too tired and pissed off to start again. Not Stockwell though. If anything, he was too careful and worked slowly. But his patience and endurance more than made up for that.

And bugger me, thought Hall, I do believe he enjoys it. Not that he showed it, he didn't show much of anything, but Hall had seen the way he fingered the finished product and tested its edge and he thought he detected a kind of pride there.

Now he was dipping the axe head into a bucket of water; the steam gushed up, hissing, threatening to engulf him. And then he was laying the head on to a work bench where it joined a half dozen others.

He seemed to feel the aching now as he moved towards the smith, to the cool air, rubbing his right bicep. Hall clapped him on the shoulder.

"Well done, lad. You must be stuffed."

Richard shook his head. "I'm alright," he said. "A bit tired."

"So you should be. You've done a power of work. Hungry?"

Richard nodded.

"Right then. I've brought some bread and a few slices of bacon. What we need is some nice fresh eggs. How about you pop back to your place and see if you can snaffle us a half dozen. I'll put the billy on and brew us some tea."

Richard stepped out of the heat into the cooling drizzle. At first its touch was delightful and he paused to remove his bandana and tilt his head to the sky. But then the cold seeped in and he shivered and hurried along the foreshore; past the convict huts, the schoolhouse, the old whare, John King's house. Then climbing to a small plateau where the Kendall house stood. He stopped by a small hut. This was his home and he had built it himself with some help from one of the convicts. He had never built anything before and he was proud of it. Well, not proud because pride was wrong but he had enjoyed building it and he liked being there. It stood ten feet by ten feet with six feet walls with a big window that looked south over the bay. There was no glass in the window but shutters fitted neatly over the space and kept out the wind and rain. It did not have flooring and probably never would have but Richard did not mind; the ground was level and the earth hardpacked and dry. The few clothes he owned were folded away neatly inside a wooden box; from a peg on the wall above it hung a fine linen shirt. Mrs Kendall had sewed it and given it to him at Christmas in appreciation, she said, of all his kindness. His first Christmas present, since… His first Christmas present. On the northern wall was a narrow shelf. Shells lay there, and stones, a blown tui egg in a cracked saucer and a polished deep green bottle he had found on the beach. On the eastern wall a piece of bleached driftwood hung by twine from two nails. His bed was against the southern wall beneath the window, rush matting and two woollen blankets. He had a pillow, too, a small sack stuffed with feathers and down. It was a fine house and Richard was thankful God had given it to him.

He stood by the doorway, removed his sodden shirt and wrung it out. He laid it on the box then dried himself with a blanket. Then he took the linen shirt from the peg, pulled it on and hurried over to the Kendall house. It was a grand affair with two bedrooms and a kitchen and living area. And wooden flooring and a fire. He tapped on the door and waited.

There was a call from within, "haere mai," and he opened the door and stepped in. The room was very untidy, he thought, clothes spilled out of a hamper on to the kitchen floor and on the table unwashed dishes were piled on top of one another and pushed to one side to make space for sewing. Mrs Kendall sat there, needle in hand, a pile of clothing about her feet. Her features were pale and drawn, her eyes red rimmed and Richard wondered if she had been crying. But she smiled in recognition and the smile was warm and welcoming.

"Hello," she said, "what are you doing here?"

"Walter Hall asked me to pop back and snaffle us a half dozen eggs."

"Of course." She stood up, kicked away the clothing and crossed to open shelving. "Here, somewhere, I'm sure, I know I, ah, here." She brought back a small flax basket and took out six brown eggs.

"How will you carry them? Shall I find you a container?"

Richard did not answer but held out two large hands in a cup and she carefully filled it.

They were silent for a moment, then Richard said, "I would like to stay to help you tidy but Walter Hall is expecting me back."

"Of course," she said. "You must go. Could you remember to go to the fowl run later to replace the eggs?"

Richard furrowed his brow. "I will try."

"Here, I will help you remember. Hold out your arm."

She walked over to a desk covered in books and paper and rummaged about. Then she took a goose quill, dipped it in ink and returned. She pushed back his sleeve and wrote upon his inner forearm. The nib tickled and the hairs on his arms rose in response.

"There, I have written 'eggs'. And here is a picture of an egg to help you remember. Hold a moment, let the ink dry."

They stood for a moment or two and she held his arm, holding back the sleeve. Then she released it.

"There. It is dry now."

Richard nodded and left the room. She followed to close the door and watched him walk away.

Apart from Thomas, you may be my only friend. You may be even more a friend than he, for you are always here, always available, ever helpful. While Thomas is so often gone away, away visiting, planting seeds of wheat and religion, he says. Tending to the sick and needy. Visiting with ships' captains, trading, talking, drinking. And even when he is here, it is sometimes as though he were not here. Distant, brooding, unhappy, writing endless letters, talking to Marsden, to Pratt, to himself in his journals. And less and less to me.

Richard hurried back to his house. He carefully set the eggs upon his bed and removed his shirt. He hung it carefully on its peg and put the sodden one back on. Then he gathered back up the eggs and headed back to the smithy.

He arrived to raised voices. Standing in the doorway he watched the smith and King in fierce debate. The little cobbler's face was screwed up and he pounded his fist into an open palm.

"I am not here to argue," he shouted. "I am here to collect my axe heads."

"I am sorry, sir," Hall did sound at all sorry, "but those heads are all spoken for. Mr Kendall has given me my orders and I –"

"Kendall! And who does Kendall think he is to give you orders? The trade was settled last week, Hall, and the fish will be here as soon as the lazy sods bring them. It is not my fault they are delayed. And I will not be done out of my trade. Not again! Not this time!"

Hall shook his head. "I am sorry, sir," he said again, "but I cannot let you have them."

"You cannot let me have them?" King's voice broke in incredulity. "And who are you to tell me what I can and cannot have? Remember what you are, Hall. You are a convict. You should be thanking God that you stand in open air, not shackled to a cell wall. You and Kendall's simple brute here."

Richard looked at him curiously. Why is he angry with Hall, he thought. And with me? We have done him no wrong. Yet he behaves as though he hates us. He carefully set the eggs on the bench beside him.

Hall was beginning to become angry, too.

"When I lay me down at night," he snarled, "my aches tell me that I've done an honest day's toil. And," holding King's eye, "I've got something to show for it. I don't doubt *my* usefulness."

King spluttered. "How dare you!" he roared. "How dare you! Suggest that my work is of no use! Marsden will hear of this."

"I suggest nothing," returned Hall. "I only say that I do an honest day's toil. And that I cannot let you have the axes." He reached for his bellows and turned back to the forge.

But King was not done. "I will have them," he said and seized the two nearest. With one in either hand he hurried to the door then halted abruptly as a heavy hand fell on his shoulder.

"You must not take them, Mr King," Richard said. "They are for Mr Kendall."

King stood still, quivering as hatred bit hard at him. But his rage was not so great as to entirely deplete his reason. There was no way he could physically resist Stockwell and now Hall stood beside him.

He hurled the axes to the ground.

"You have not heard the end of this," he promised. "You will rue the day you dared lay hands on me."

Then he turned and walked out into the rain.

Chapter 22

Rangihoua 1816

There is stillness here. Better than prayer and meditation where the borders never hold fast. They always fray and stretch and rip and a trickle of other things becomes a flood. Sometimes they skitter briefly like squeaking bats and are gone without being fully seen. Harmless, distractions merely, like snatches of a sailor's song. Sometimes they are things that creep on the edges of shadow and are then only the shallows rushing back to join the deep. Sometimes they hold a place like the line of a song that will not go away, the Lord is my shepherd, I shall not want, shall not want, shall not want the Lord. Shifting intimations that clamour for their place and batter at the stillness but will not reveal themselves.

I am Yours, my Lord and my God, bring me to Thy blessed peace. Still the doubts that assail me, close my ears to the taunting of the Adversary. Take away the anger that rushes me to spite and shame; let my will be to do Thy purpose. Give me meaning.

And for a moment there may be stillness, a sense of something huge, of vast promise; and then an answer biting in.

Don't touch me.

But mostly stillness is lost in the tiresome, inane repetitions of brooding. A wrong visited and revisted. Conversations run and re-run. *We are not natives in need of a sermon, Mr Kendall, we are not natives, you are not in command.* And the only intimation of thought comes with invented responses (that are always clever and cruel) and with the further invention of the wrongdoer's paying any attention. They all fall under the head of What I could have said, should have said. When the spite that is received is

271

paid back tenfold. It is a round of self-pity and anger that feeds upon itself, a writing creature of accusation. The Adversary, the Father of Lies must rejoice in it for it is attended by nothing of truth or kindness.

This is what people do when they sit alone with their hurt and anger. They do not think at all for brooding is the antithesis of thought. Brooding never asks questions or explores alternatives. It is centred upon its rightness and its sense of injury and, like the invented response, the only direction imagination ever takes is towards revenge.

It is lonely, so people brood together. This is the place for the loyal friend whose function it is to agree with the brooder. *O I know, I know, you're so right, I know, he doesn't deserve you, I don't know why you put up with it, you're too forbearing, that's your problem, I know, I know.* There is some advantage for the friend here: he or more commonly she is honoured by confidence and vulnerability. She is invariably told how good she is, *you understand me, I can talk to you,* and her own security is proportionately reassured. She must, however, keep silent and that is not always easy, particularly if she thinks the brooder might be in the wrong. To say so would be betrayal. *O my God, you're taking his part. I thought I could trust you (to agree with me).*

People brood together in groups, reinforcing one another's sense of rightness, elaborating on the Other's wrongness. It is very satisfying and exciting, too, and they shout one another down, adding to their pool of rightness. *You're right, mate, they're naturally lazy, they'd rather live on our taxes. I knew this whole, bloody family ...* The pool deepens and they gather together at its edges, swelling in the brotherhood of indignation. A bounty of brooding and not a thought between them.

There is another form of brooding where the brooder turns his anger upon himself and dwells on his own deficits. Others generally find this very disturbing and try to avoid it and those who practise it. They call it morbid and unhealthy and they may be right for it can lead to abnegation in apology or suicide. So here, instead of rushing to agreement, they attack the very process. *You mustn't think like this.* They're wrong, of course, to call it thought. There is no more thought here than there is in brooding. But there is more imminent danger for here the enemy is at hand.

When Thomas reaches for stillness and finds brooding instead he is liable to move to either style. Villifying Hall or King or Marsden or Maori. Or himself. But either way it is villification and there is no peace in it.

But here there is stillness and a silence that does not threaten. The ship shifts beneath him but he does not feel it, the creaking of timber is distant and is only the creaking of timber. Across from him a man sits silently, head bowed, and he is only a man. Everything is constricted to the board in front of him, all the possibilities are contained there. He may not see them, he may retreat from the wrong threat or move to false hope and be undone. And then his gut will tighten with anger and that anger will inform his next move and probably he will sink more deeply into error. But, win or lose, the possibilities will reveal themselves and he will at least be able to understand his undoing. And then the board will be cleared and reset and he may try again. It is not final and there is always a hope of redemption.

He studied the board carefully. He thought he could see what Brind was up to. He was hot upon attack now and his attention had narrowed. If he had read Thomas' last move as simply a defensive response and did not focus upon the opening it created for the bishop ...Thomas held down his excitement and refilled his glass. Then Brind was reaching across, *excellent, excellent, you are moving too quickly.* Thomas drank deeply and sighed at the rum's rush. He held the glass, fighting the urge to leap to his move and made himself consider the new possibilities. The situation was as he had hoped for, no, damnit, had played for; the game was his. The bishop slid across the diagonal.

"Check."

"Damn." Brind sat up in surprise and alarm and Thomas exulted. "I forgot. Now you can, o shit, and there's nothing I can do stop you." Brind brooded over the board, craggy weatherbeaten features lost in smoke wreathing from a stubby clay pipe. Then he was laying the king down and a large paw extended across the table.

"I knew it was there," he said. "I'd seen it before and told myself to keep it in mind. But then I got carried away and forgot all about it." He drank and wiped the back of his hand across his mouth. "Story of my life."

Buoyed on rum and triumph, Thomas grinned at him. There were things about Brind that worried him. He did not concern himself enough with his men's morals; indeed there was talk that he had a Maori wife himself somewhere. But he was a kind-hearted man, a liberal host and a worthy opponent. You could only hope for so much.

Brind was resetting the pieces.

"How is life on shore?" he asked.

Thomas grimaced. "We remain divided," he answered. "Events conspire against us and we conspire against ourselves. Marsden preaches communalism and self-sufficiency and leaves us in Rangihoua."

"Aye," Brind grunted, "I wondered at that. Steep clay hills. What did he expect you to grow?"

"Lord knows. We have planted nothing there. We've got flourishing crops at Waitangi and Kerikeri and Matauwhi. But a lot of time is spent getting there and back and they are not always secure." Thomas shrugged. "So we turn to trade and compete with one another."

"And you are not getting along."

"No." Thomas drank and registered that he had become drunk. Ah well, he was entitled to some comfort. "We cannot agree. Hall and King make no concession to my being named magistrate. They are, they say, as good as I –and I make no argument with that, we are all sinners, none more so than I, the thoughts I ..." He trailed off. "What was I saying?"

"Um." Brind scratched his grizzled beard and then held up a finger, remembering. "You are not getting along."

"That's right. They will take no direction from me, nor heed one another, they quarrel bitterly. And so we go our different ways."

Brind fell into agreement mode. "You will make no progress that way," he said. "There can be but one helmsman."

"Precisely so. Ah, it is a comfort to talk with one who can understand."

The praise stirred Brind to further wisdom. "One captain," he said, "one helmsman, men for the harpoon and men for the oars."

"Each in his appointed place."

"Exactly."

"I crave unity, William, and I do all I can to promote it ..."

"I'm sure you do."

"... but they will not heed me. They are headstrong and obstinate, Marsden knows, he said so, but he provides no leadership, he is mean with his resources, he tries to do everything and completes none of it."

"A very disorganised man."

"Exactly."

From the deck outside the captain's quarters came voices and the sounds of a ship's boat being lowered. Then a burst of laughter, high-pitched laughter. Thomas looked at Brind suspiciously.

"That laugh," he said, "it sounded like a woman's."

Brind shrugged.

"That would not be right," Thomas said uneasily. "One of my functions as magistrate is to bring to an end the vile habit of white men," he paused, "taking advantage of Maori women and leading them into prof, profligate behaviour."

Brind was bemused. "You mean fucking 'em?" he asked.

The rum was no protection for the brutal directness of the word and Thomas blushed. "I mean wanton and depraved behaviour," he said. "And language, too."

"Ah." Brind nodded. "Well it's like we was just saying. Each man has his appointed place and the jobs that go with it. One of yours is to stop men and women enjoying one another, no, no," he raised a hand as Thomas made to break in, "call it fun or profli- what have you, it's the same thing. My job is to catch whales and I drive the men to do it. They think I'm a hard bastard, sorry, taskmaster but they think I'm fair, too. And in their way they're loyal and they stay with the ship. I need them to stay that way so I'm not going to piss, upset them more than I need to. And trying to stop them getting with the women would really upset them. Here," he filled Thomas' glass, "have another drink. This is a harsh place Thomas, and you do what you must to get by." He nodded. "You're going to have to learn that."

The ship's boat was long gone now and the deck was silent. Thomas stared morosely into his glass. Brind was right, he reflected, you do what you can and you pray that change will come. Right now any further remonstrance would be futile and would only invite ridicule.

He leaned forward and advanced his king's pawn two spaces.

"Your move," he said.

While Thomas stared vaguely at the swimming pieces, Jane sat at his desk in a fog of her own, on to her third attempt at a letter and her fourth glass of port. The first letter, now lying in a ball in a corner, was such as one was expected to write; later, perhaps, it would be retrieved, ironed into shape or rewritten and sent on its way.

Dear Emmeline, it began, *I pray that all is well with you and your Family and* blah, blah she had thought as more of the same followed. Not that it was untrue; her sister was daily in her thoughts.

The children all Thrive; the boys are fit and active and Baby Samuel is a picture of Health. Thomas has spoken of adding to our house so that there may be room for Susannah and Elizabeth. They write regularly from Port Jackson and blah, blah.

You would be impressed by how far the Mission has developed. We all have our own houses now and very Comfortable they are and the school house is largely complete. More details about the buildings and the accomodations, blah, blah.

Thomas has become quite fluent in the Maori tongue and when he is not teaching the children he spends much of his time visiting other tribes, tending to the sick, planting crops and spreading the Word of Our Lord. He has also compiled a Dictionary of Maori Words and Phrases and is very keen to have it Published. It was such a letter as would bring a smile to her sister's face. So Jane was safely and comfortably settled and perhaps soon the family would be complete once more. New Zealand was clearly another Eden, free of poverty, pollution, crime and disease. She would be able to envisage Thomas sitting among eager upturned brown faces smiling with the joy of the knowledge of God's love.

And there was truth in all of it. Yet Jane had scrunched the letter into a ball and hurled it from her.

She had tried again.

I will not pretend that all is Perfect. Disagreements persist among the settlers and Thomas has been drawn into some Unpleasant Exchanges with Mr Hall and Mr King and their families. I had supposed that when we were all crowded into that Draughty Hut, enduring such Privation, we suffered dreadfully then, Emmeline, Living on top of one another, I had supposed, I say, that a measure of Ill-feeling was Inevitable. But it has followed us into our Homes and is attended by such Vindictiveness that I cannot but Wonder at it.

We Live with separate Hopes and Fears. Even our sense of Danger is different. William Hall and his wife have the greatest Cause to be Apprehensive of Maori after their dreadful Experience at Waitangi but they do not seem much Affected. Mr Hall goes readily amongst them and is a most Astute trader. Mr King and his wife are much more Fearful. They Fasten upon accounts of Atrocities and look for their Enactment here. While Thomas sinks further into the Maori World and seems to feel Safer there than with his Fellows.

We are all well-meaning Christian Folk. Why can we not live in Peace and practise Kindness towards one another as Our Saviour taught?

Then back to the mandatory form.

Do not be Dismayed, Emmeline. There are Good Intentions here and much has been Achieved. We are Safe and Secure; there is so much to be Thankful for.

Jane pushed herself back from the desk and walked to the window. The moon was full over the bay and lit the beach in a silver glow. *All is calm, all is bright.* The house was warm and dry, the children slept soundly and the larder was full. *What more do you want?*

She threw the letter aside and thrust the quill into the inkstand. The ink blotched and spread as she wrote.

I think I may go Mad from Loneliness. I am so Unknown I think I may be turning Invisible. Nothing makes sense, Everyone is changing. Even my children are growing into Something Else. Young Thomas and Basil, they are Toma and Pehi now, are turning Brown and speak a Language I do not understand; they will not come Home after school to their Mother but run laughing to an Alien world. And Joseph cannot wait to join them. I might in another Time and Place have been friends with Dinah Hall but her Husband and mine are at War. Hannah King will not speak with me, nor her Mother neither. I sit sometimes with Maori Women but understand Little of what they say. They are always laughing and sometimes I think they laugh at me. I cannot remember when I last Laughed.

I cook and clean and sew and bear children and that is my Life. I do not resent it, it is my Lot and I am Thankful, truly I am, to Serve. But I need some Recognition.

My Husband is become a Stranger to me. His Moods have always spun but never like this. And whether he is Triumphant or Despairing, it has Nothing to do with me. His classes excite his Passion, Hall and King excite his Passion and the World of the Maori consumes him. At his desk he mutters and I do not understand him. Sometimes he speaks to me or the boys in Maori. And they answer him!

He is never Cruel, he has never Struck me and when he shouts and rages it is not at me. It is at Hall or King or Marsden or Ewha. Sometimes he sees my Grief and then he is Kind and berates himself for his Inattention. But even then I do not remain in the Picture. He is the worthless Creature, he the undeserving Wretch. And then he is Distant and gone again. I cannot make him happy the way Ewha could make him happy by learning his Lines.

He does not see me, I am Invisible, I do not belong here.

She underscored the last line several times then thrust the letter away. Panic fluttered at the edge of awareness and her breath came panting. But she caught at it and forced it down, her mouth tight and teeth clenched, dragging in the air through her nostrils in careful measure. She sat immobile then and slowly the room became very still; even the light from the candle seemed to fade into stillness. She watched her hand reach for her glass and followed the warm glow down her throat. Then she took the letter and slowly fed it to the flame. As the heat reached to her hand she dropped the paper on to the desk and watched it curl and shrivel. Then her finger was dipping into the wine and rubbing the remains of the letter into paste and powder. She drew a cross into the mess then stood up and walked across the room, through a pile of clothing, past the sleeping infant and out into the night. For a while she stood before sinking down and scratching vaguely at the bare earth. A morepork called from the bush behind and she gazed dully towards the sound. The bird called again and the cry seemed to echo inside her head. Death, she thought, Thomas says the Maori believe the morepork sends messages of death. Thomas, she thought dully and the thought faded away.

Then everything faded and the earth was somewhere below her and the sky somewhere above and she sat in the emptiness between, her arms wrapped across her chest, hugging her shoulders, shrinking. Neither tired nor wakeful she sat, cocking her head towards the thoughts that fluttered but would not settle. There were no words in them, nor shape nor meaning but she shrank from them. Then a word came, loss she thought and became aware that a kind of teror was at hand.

Then she was on her feet and stumbling towards Richard's shed, now pushing open the door. The shutters were wide open and the moon flowed in, glowing on the shells and the shirt and the tui's egg. She crossed the room and sank to her knees beside his bed, pushing at his shoulders, urging him awake.

"Richard. Richard."

He came up from sleep quickly and easily but was startled to find her there and stared uncomprehending.

"Richard. Richard."

He sat up and the moonlight put silver and shadow on his face and bare shoulders; he saw the fear and need on her but had no words to answer them. So he watched her, waiting as she watched and waited, too, for whatever it was to be said.

Her voice was a breathless croak.

"Who am I?"

Richard stared. "You are Mrs Kendall," he said, "Mr Kendall's wife."

Her hands clapped him into silence. "No," she muttered, "that's not it."

"But you are," said Richard helplessly. "Ah," a thought came, "you are mother to Toma and Pehi and Hohepa and Hamuera. And Susannah and Elizabeth," he added.

The terror she had sensed outside abated here, the earth was hard beneath her knees and her heels solid against her rump. But anxiety fluttered close by and panic was only a little further off.

"I need more," she said. "Who am I?" Then quickly, "please do not say 'Mrs Kendall'."

Richard shook his head, perplexed. He was worried to see her like this, pale and shaking. "I wish I could help you," he said. "I wish I knew what you want to hear."

The anxiety receded a little further and Jane managed a half smile. "Thank you," she murmured, "that helps." She picked at the blanket, feeling the coarseness of the fabric, a thread catching under a nail. Richard's face was in shadow but close and she could hear him breathe. The world settled about her and she became aware of the night air reaching through her nightgown. Richard saw her shiver and he tugged the upper blanket free. He passed it to her without speaking and she settled it about her shoulders.

"Thank you," she said again and then, almost with a touch of petulance, "I don't know why I'm here."

Richard nodded, agreeing.

"I lost touch," she went on. "I don't know what's real." And then the touch of petulance again, "do you?"

"Do I what?"

"Know what's real? What matters?"

"Everything is real," Richard said, "everything matters. In its own way."

Jane looked at him closely. His features were calm and placid, no twitch at the corner of a mouth here, no darting, evasive eye. He held her gaze evenly and his eyes were kind and concerned. Then she looked away, down at her hands picking at the blanket.

"I am Jane," she said. "My father is John but he is dead now and I miss him. When I was a little girl he made a swing for me. I would sit upon the wooden seat and hold the ropes and he would push me away, little pushes at first. I would rise up and hang for a moment, quite still and then I would swing back. I would feel his hands upon my back holding me steady and his hands were big and strong. And then he would push me away again." She closed her eyes. "That was real, all of it, the creaking of the ropes against the branch, the seat beneath me, the ropes in my hand worn smooth, flying, hanging, falling back, back to my father's hands.

"And now it is gone, it is really gone and my father's hands are fleshless bones that lie still in the earth."

Richard watched her bowed head, the thick, tangled hair falling forward, the strong hands, chipped nails picking at the blanket. He felt sad for her and cast about for words that might help.

"Your father has gone to Jesus," he said at last, "One day you will be with him again and he will push you on your swing once more."

But he could see he had brought her no comfort because she raised her hands to her face, her shoulders shook and she was taken in weeping. He watched, helpless, worried; his hand reached towards her, fingered the air then returned to his lap.

She spoke as she wept, words that were hiccups and gulps.

"No," she sobbed, "the swing is gone forever. Even if I do see my father again, the swing is gone forever." Then she raised her head and her hands pushed back her hair. Her face was streaked where earth had become mud in tears and mucus, her mouth hung open and her eyes were wide.

"No," she wailed, "never again, never, gone, gone." Then her hands were at her face, clawing at her cheeks and Richard was leaning forward, catching at her wrists, drawing them away and pulling her towards him. The wail grew into a howl that filled the room and rushed out through the shutters into the night and broke the sleep of John and Hannah King.

He held her hard against him, taking both wrists in one large, strong hand and stroking her hair with the other. She collapsed on to him and her grief was without restraint. When he released her wrists her arms encircled him and her hands clenched and beat against his back.

At length her sobbing subsided and her arms fell to her sides. He continued to hold her, murmuring, soothing until he realised she had fallen asleep. A gentle shake failed to awaken her and he was reluctant to do more. Carefully he extricated himself and lowered her upper body on to the bed. Then he rose and went to the clothes box. He pulled on a pair of breeches then returned to the sleeping woman, lifted her and carried her from the room, across the earthen divide and into her house. There he lowered her on to her bed, holding her upright in one arm while he tried to arrange the tangle of bed linen with the other. The result was not entirely satisfactory but it would have to do; he laid her down and covered her over. Then he took up the blanket and returned to his shed.

CHAPTER 23

He was not hungover which was just as well because the volume of noise in the school house was high. It irritated him but he was too seedy and tired to bother intervening. So he sat at his desk and stared glumly.

Few of the students were on task; they milled about laughing, arguing, two boys appeared to be squaring off, a group of girls were practising with poi, others were … who cares. Thomas rubbed his eyes and sighed. This is a thankless task, he thought, worry and disappointment outweigh reward; they do not appreciate what I do for them. No one does. Am I proud or vain to ask for a little recognition? And some respect? But there is none. If I stand and shout they will resent me for it and if they do fall silent and return to study it will only be for a little while. He took his watch from his waistcoat. Near noon. They're waiting for the mid-day kai; they will scoff it and then be gone. I might as well feed them now and be done with it.

He became aware that the room had fallen silent and looked up to see the students quietly returning to their places under the placid gaze of an old man standing in the doorway. Wearing only a flax skirt, his chest was deep and his belly flat, the body of a much younger man. A flax kete hung over a shoulder and he held rather than leaned upon an ornately carved cane. Thomas stepped down from the platform and picked his way through the benches and bodies to greet him.

"Kia ora, e Rakau," he said and they pressed noses and their temples met. "What an impact you have on the students. I wish I could persuade you to visit more often. We would make great progress."

Rakau smiled. "You are impatient, e Keni," he answered. "Think of where you were a year ago."

"Ae," Thomas nodded. "I am an impatient man. I dwell upon the faults and forget the blessings."

"Then let us concentrate upon the blessings," said Rakau. "Show me what the students have learned."

"Willingly." Thomas turned to the class. "Whakarongo mai, tamariki," he said. Then, holding up a book, he said in English, "Waima, what is this?"

A stocky boy stood up. "Tat," gulping back the vowel that rushed to follow, "is a puka, a puk."

"Kia ora," said Rakau admiringly.

Thomas produced a series of questions, what is this? what is your name? where are you from? and the children furrowed their brows in concentration as they answered. Many struggled with the difficult consonants but here and there a voice piped up in clear English. Finally Thomas turned to Tungaroa. "What can you tell me," he asked slowly, "about the ways of God and the ways of man." The little girl stood and spoke confidently with an accent that might have come straight from Thoresby. "The ways of God are good," she said, "the ways of man are bad."

Rakau beamed his approval. "Kia ora, Tungaroa," he said, "he taonga koe." Then to Thomas, "dismiss your class. I have something to show you."

Thomas followed Rakau through the bush. The times when he had stayed behind on walks while Liddiard and the portly Marsden had driven ahead were gone now, but even so he laboured to keep up with the old man. Rakau glided, wasting no time or energy in a stumble or a re-directed step, bending and turning only as much as was necessary. At one point he stopped and said, "take off your coat and shirt, e Keni. They weigh you down and overheat you, they are not necessary. We will collect them when we return."

Thomas slipped off his coat and hung it on a manuka. He could discern no track but did not doubt that Rakau would find it again. He could not bring himself to part with his shirt but unfastened the buttons and pushed back the sleeves.

Bracken and fern had grown into forest and the sun filtered through canopy lighting green and silver, then it was bright and hot as they forded a stream, then dark and cool again. The air hummed with insects; a piwakawaka fluttered about, feeding from the disturbed air, a tui piped silver chimes. Thomas absorbed the sounds and slid into the rhythm of the march, and time moved apart.

Then they were stepping from foliage as through a curtain and the earth turned to rock. To their left and right the bush rose sheer and thick. Before them, a hundred feet above, water flowed over a smooth rocky lip and dropped in a shining, translucent wave to the pool below, crashing into a million drops and rising, hanging in mist.

Thomas stared.

"How did you know?" he whispered.

"Know?" Rakau was puzzled. "Know what?"

Thomas gestured at the waterfall. "You have brought me to my dream." He shivered. "This is magic."

"Ah," Rakau nodded, understanding. "This is an old and special place for you. But there is no magic in knowing that, e Keni. It is an old and special place for anyone who can see."

"But I have dreamed this."

"And so have I and so has anyone who can remember his dreams. It is a very old but a very common memory."

Thomas gazed for a long while, from clear sky to bush and earth and rock to shining water. "It is perfect," he said at last. "Look," pointing to where the water hung, "te aniwa, the rainbow. God's covenant. There is a promise here."

"A promise of what?"

"Of redemption. When God destroyed the earth because of man's wickedness, He made His covenant in the rainbow that He would never do so again."

"That he would never again destroy the earth?"

"Never again by water."

Rakau pulled at his nose. "That is not very reassuring, e Keni," he said. "Perhaps next time he will destroy it by some other means. Like fire."

Thomas shook his head. "You do not understand," he said.

Rakau chuckled. "I have noticed before," he said, "that pakeha often say that, particularly when they are confused."

Thomas began to answer, then let it go and sat and watched the rainbow.

Scattered on the rocky base lay piles of dry, bleached branch and twig that had fallen there in past winds. Rakau gathered up several armfuls and broke them into smaller pieces. Then he took from his bag two pieces of pale wood, one flat and grooved, the other a pointed stick. He held the stick between his hands and began to spin it into the groove, pausing now and then to drop in leaves. As they began to smoulder he added more, along with small twigs. Soon a fire was blazing.

"A flint and taper are more effective," said Thomas.

"Indeed," agreed Rakau, "and I carry them for occasions in which I am in a hurry. But I like to do it this way, too. This is the tree that swallowed the last of Kahuika's fire. It is good to see that her legacy is still with us. More helpful than a dodgy promise in a rainbow," he added slyly.

Thomas shrugged. "You cannot provoke me, e Rakau," he said. "This is too beautiful a place to argue."

Rakau stepped back from the fire and took a small billy from his kete. He took it to the edge of the pool, filled it, then returned to settle it above the fire.

"Not at all," he said. "This is an excellent place for korero. It is full of promise and shifting meaning."

"How does meaning shift? Where?"

"There." Rakau pointed to the mist. "There, where your promise shines. The mist came from water and is water but is no longer of water. It hangs in air but is not of air. But it means both and where the colours shine it means something else. To you it means a promise. Perhaps redemption or a pot of gold beneath the pool. Who knows?"

"At least we know that we don't know," murmured Thomas, then stopped, surprised by the thought and unsettled by the associations it brought. More meaning.

Rakau looked at him sharply. "Yes," he said, "that is exactly what I mean."

They sat on the rocks and Thomas fed Rakau tea and biscuits and they watched the fire die. The smoke drifted across the pool and disappeared.

"Nothing is settled, everything changes, everything passes," said Rakau.

Thomas found himself unsettled by the idea and reached to contradict it. "The love of God is changeless," he said severely, "as God is changeless."

Rakau recognised that this was not a subject for discussion and changed direction. "Why did you tell Tungaroa," he asked, "that Maori are lazy?"

Thomas' severity left him and he blushed. "I did not mean all Maori," he said. "Tungaroa is the most conscientious student I have ever taught. I certainly did not mean that she is lazy. It was a foolish generalisation and I am sorry I said it."

Rakau smiled. Keni's capacity for retraction, he mused, set him apart from the other missionaries and apart from many Maori, too. He patted the teacher's arm. "I am not offended," he said, "but I am curious. Why do you think that Maori are lazy?"

"Well," Thomas trod carefully. "The children do not seem to like study and avoid it when they can. They would rather play. And the adults, too, not all you understand, but a good number would rather sit and talk or sing and dance than labour." He looked at Rakau anxiously. "It is just an observation."

"Ae," Rakau nodded judiciously, "and perhaps a fair one. But why do you hold work in such high regard?"

"Well." Thomas was nonplussed. The value of labour was a given, almost an article of faith. What was it that Marsden had written? *Occupy every spare moment in manual labour or some other useful occupation; if you indulge in idleness you will be ruined.*

"It is not one of your god's commandments," persisted Rakau, "yet you behave as though it were. Why is that?"

Ah, Rakau, you always do this, you ask questions that are almost absurd, the answer is so obvious. But when I reach for it there are suddenly no words. Why do I need to work so hard? I work to save my soul.

He shook his head helplessly. "We work to glorify God," he said at last, lamely. "We," a thought interposed, "Jesus said thou shalt know them by their fruits. So we work to bring our Lord a bountiful harvest."

"I see," said Rakau, "so you measure your worth in what you have achieved. By that account, Marsden must be a worthy man, indeed. Or any wealthy man, for that matter."

"No," Thomas shook his head vigorously. "It is not about accruing wealth. It is also written that it is easier for a," what was the Maori for camel? "for a hoihoi to pass through the eye of a needle than it is for a rich man to enter the kingdom of God."

"So all his industry is to no avail?"

"I suppose it also depends upon the use to which the industry was put." Thomas thought of the wealthy men and women he had seen at prayer at St Paul's. The jewellery upon a single hand might have kept a large family for a year or more. And these were among the pillars of the church.

"So it is also a matter of intention?"

"Obviously."

"So if a man labours with the best of intentions but fails, how do you judge him?"

Thomas was on firmer ground here. "Judge not," he said, "lest ye be judged."

"And yet you judge Maori to be lazy."

Thomas stared at the old tohunga. *You play with me, Rakau. You, an uneducated, illiterate savage who has killed for the joy of it and eaten of the flesh of men, you take my most profound beliefs and play with them. Are you my serpent? Marsden and Hall and King would say so, yes and Josepht Kent and Basil Woodd, too, and they would dismiss your questions. But my faith is not strong enough to do that and I cannot help but think you wise.*

He wrung his hands and stared miserably at the smiling priest. "I cannot answer you," he said. "I am here to instruct you, to lead you into the light and I cannot find the words that will take you there." He looked away to where light shifted in air and water. "I am a worthless, useless wretch."

"And now you judge yourself."

This time he did not even try to answer but gazed back towards the waterfall. Its movement seemed to slow, then freeze so that the silver arc became still and hung like a transparent painting. He was dimly aware of Rakau's hand upon his shoulder but that was far away and his words seemed to come from a great distance.

"Of course you judge, e Keni. That is a part of your function. You are a magistrate and judgment is required of you. It is required of all of us and we could not survive without it. We judge that a storm is brewing and that it would not be safe to go out in our boats to fish. We judge the amount of water our crops will need to give us a good harvest. And we judge one another. You judge that Tungaroa is an industrious student who is deserving of your praise. Would your Jesus have you withold that judgment? And as I speak you are judging the truth and meaning of my words. You would be less than human if you did not do so."

Thomas shrugged meaninglessly and continued to stare.

Then Rakau's hand was taken from his shoulder and he could hear him getting to his feet. "I judge," said the tohunga, "that the water will be cold and that I will gasp and shudder as it passes over me. I also judge that it will refresh me and when I stand again upon the rocks my blood will sing."

There was the sound of a flax skirt falling, rustling, then Rakau moved forward into Thomas' vision and into the pool. He stood in the shallows for a moment then threw himself forward and disappeared beneath the surface. The sound of the impact rose above the fall then merged and was lost in it and the ripples spread. Then Rakau was rising, roaring, "oue! It is colder than I had judged," and he was driving hard towards the turbulence. Thomas watched him swim beneath the fall to emerge standing on the other side. He could vaguely make out the brown arms waving to him and raised a desultory hand in reply but if Rakau were speaking he could hear nothing of it.

Rakau dived again beneath the fall and swam back towards the bank. When he was waist deep he stopped and stood. "Haere mai," he called, "haere mai te kaiako, the teacher, haere mai te mihinari, the missionary." Thomas gazed at him dully and shook his head. But Rakau was insistent. "You must," he said, "there is something here for you." Again Thomas shook his head and again Rakau insisted. "You must, e Keni, if not for yourself, do it for me." His eyes were hard and uncompromising. "I will be very angry if you do not."

Thomas pulled off his boots and stood uncertainly.

"Now your shirt." The sun was warm upon his pale skin.

"Now your breeches. Your breeches, e Keni. It will be a painful walk back in sopping trousers. They will chafe you cruelly. The breeches, e Keni."

Thomas turned away and unfastened the buttons then hesitantly, awkwardly, near stumbling on the uneven rock he pulled his trousers off. He turned back, hands over his groin and stared at Rakau.

The priest held back the laugh and gestured, beckoning. "Haere mai te tama."

The pool bit at his ankles and calves, jerking him back into the moment and he shuddered at it. The rocks and pebbles were slippery beneath him and he stumbled, then caught his balance.

"Pai ana. Now," pointing towards the waterfall.

"But I cannot swim."

"No," Rakau nodded, "but I can. I will hold you up." Then, before Thomas could argue further or resist he caught him around the waist and plunged towards the depths.

The water closed over his head and took him in an icy grip. He kicked down frantically for the bottom reaching for a place to stand but it was gone. Then Rakau was bearing him up and his head broke the surface and he roared in pain and shock and fear. He struggled wildly but Rakau's grip was strong and through his terror he could hear him shouting into his ear. "Be still, e Keni, I have you, you are safe, be still." It took all he had but he managed, he held down the fear, he silenced the scream and he lay shivering in Rakau's arms.

The old man's voice was soothing now. "Pai ana, you are a brave man and you are safe, too. Now, on to your back, tilt back your head, so and so you are safe, you are floating, the waters hold you up. Feel what it is to float, see how the cold recedes." And so it did as the blood rushed in a warming torrent from his pounding heart.

He lay still upon his back and the moment was huge about him. Rakau's hands were under his shoulders, fingers closing against his arm pits as he kicked slowly, easily towards the fall. "Hold your breath and close your eyes." Then a deluge fell upon his face with tremendous force, pushing his head under but before he could begin to panic again it was gone and he was standing, rock against his back and beneath his feet and he was staring through a silver curtain back at the shimmering bank.

The roar was deafening but it was magnificent too and Thomas was caught in a kind of exultation. He turned to Rakau and saw that his eyes were closed and his lips moving but he could not make out even the sound of words. He stepped cautiously forward, feeling for a foothold with great care and reached out his arms, extending his palms upwards into the waterfall. The water was a solid wall and the initial impact drove his hands down and near unbalanced him. But he recovered and again, rigidly, he reached into the fall. And found enough strength to keep his arms up and he watched the water break upon his hands and divide there.

His thoughts flowed away and he became very still and there was only the fall and the roar and the distant cold and the sun on the pool. The rainbow was somewhere above and out of sight.

Time passed and then he felt Rakau's hand upon his shoulder and saw him point back to the rocky bank. He nodded, then a yell exploded from him and he plunged through the fall, turning on to his back, raising his knees and paddling palms downwards. He hung there for a moment, exulting, then Rakau's arms were beneath his shoulders, drawing him back to the shallows.

Rakau stopped and he stood and picked his way back. There he reached for his clothes but Rakau took them from him and laid them down by the dead fire.

"You must dry first," he said. "Lie here and let Ra dry you."

Some of the old feeling began to emerge and he lay awkwardly, his hands over his crotch. Rakau lay beside him, grunting as he settled; soon he began to snore. Thomas became more comfortable then. He sat up and folded his shirt into a pillow then lay down, easing his body into the smooth rock. It was warm upon his back and the sun was warm upon his front. The occasional cry of a bird or a movement in the encroaching bush obtruded upon the continuous roar but after a while they became a distant accompaniment. The stillness was a force in itself and Thomas became vaguely aware that it had reached into his mind. There was no thought there and its absence was delicious. He sighed and his hands fell away as he slipped into easy, empty sleep.

Later he was aware of Rakau's hands shaking him awake and he looked up to see the sun disappearing beneath the lip of the fall. The rainbow was gone. He dressed in silence and in silence they walked back into the bush and back to the settlement.

CHAPTER 24

Rangihoua Autumn 1817

And we know that all things work together for good to them that love God, to them who are called according to His purpose.

Carlisle's voice was soft and the words slipped below the murmur, the shuffling and the outright conversation. Once the cobbler might have fastened the offender with an accusing glare but he had learned and now he only sighed and strained a little harder for encouragement and comfort. Then another voice, Kendall's, rose in its place, louder and more insistent and the congregation quietened. But the words were in Maori, quick and fluent and their meaning was lost. Paul spoke to the Romans again.

Moreover whom He did predestinate, them He also called: and whom He called, them He also justified: and whom He justified, them He also glorified.

How can I measure the meaning of my days? But to hope for that which I cannot see, trudging from one moment to the next, glancing back over my shoulder, doubting that which was, fearing that which will be? Holding to my faith as to a lantern, holding back the dark certainty that all this meaning will soon be caught within the confines of the grave.

One day we will be the people who lived long ago.

What shall we say to these things? If God be for us who can be against us?

And if my faith is strong and bright —and daily I attest it is – what is there to know of fear? Yet I fear and doubt and blame.

Such were John King's thoughts —colliding in less coherent form – as he sat in the school house upon this Sabbath, giving ear to the word of the Lord. His eyes rested on William Carlisle's slight, dark figure as he strained for the words of redemption.

Who shall say any thing to the charge of God's elect? It is God that justifieth.

He knew nothing of Carlisle. How could he? Carlisle was here to assist the school teacher, he was Kendall's man and so he was a stranger. And there was William Hall, austere and distant looking ahead past the reader. Another stranger, a pious man who would not bow his head. How did he measure the meaning of his days? He carried a certainty with him that must reside in something, probably, thought King sourly, in the accumulation of wealth. He and his wife tended parsimoniously to their own needs and he had a gift for barter, trading with the Maori for provisions he would in turn barter with the captains and crews of the vessels that thronged the bay. It was common belief that he was becoming a wealthy man. And he did not care to share.

Who shall separate us from the love of Christ?

And Kendall, he had his measurements, too. Here in this makeshift church that was *his* school house, no matter that Hall and King had laboured in its construction. He had measurement in the fluency with which he translated God's word, in the growing school roll, in his influence with Marsden and the Society and in his healthy, growing family increased by his two daughters back from Port Jackson. He need not fear that his only child might not survive the next winter.

His influence extended to the Maori too, Rakau, Hongi and Pomare and to the ships' captains with whom he drank and ridiculed the settlers. His trade thrived; he had no need to depend upon the reluctant kindness of a critical father-in-law.

King took in the teacher's face, pale and gaunt with heavy shadows beneath the anxious eyes. And yet, he thought, unconscious of the satisfaction which the thought brought him, and yet he is not a happy man. There is a kind of torment here. He remembered the wail that had broken in upon his sleep.

For I am persuaded that neither death, nor life, nor angels, nor principalities, nor powers, nor things present, nor things to come, nor height, nor depth, nor any other creature shall be able to separate us from the love of God, which is in Jesus Christ our Lord.

The reading was complete and the congregation rose to sing, accents and pronunciations blending to make the words more than usually incoherent. Then they spilled outside and each went his own way.

Susannah and Elizabeth were heading back to their sleepout. There they would sit and read or write long letters back to Port Jackson, to friends from the orphanage who could understand what it meant to be a young woman. Their joy at being united with their family had swiftly turned to acrimony. With no companions but each other and no prospects of further society they railed against the constraints that enclosed them. They were properly bred young women, graduates of Marsden's piety, the daughters of a missionary and they knew their place. But they railed nonetheless, passively and constantly. Against the father who had brought them here, who had joyed at their return and then despaired of it, who daily read accusation in their eyes and did not know what to do with it. And against their mother, too, who had found a new distance of her own. They belonged only to each other.

Thomas leaned against the doorway and watched them leave and his heart ached for their unhappiness. There was no society of children and games for them as there was for the boys; the Maori girls of their age were fast becoming women and their pursuits could not be entertained. *Be careful where you let them walk,* Marsden had written and it was a narrow and a lonely path.

He had no answer for their silent accusation and so he fled from it.

Now he watched the backs of the other settlers and his own sense of loneliness compounded. Even Jane seemed to be in a space he did not know. He had tried to talk to her about the girls but seemed to find accusation there, too.

"It is their lot," she had said.

Where is the peace that comes from knowing I am doing the Lord's work? And I do labour at it, at the school and the dictionary, tending to the sick, looking after my family. And sometimes there is peace. But it is such a fleeting thing, and frail, too. A harsh word or an angry look and I feel my demons stir. And too often they get the better of me.

I do not know where I belong. Every resting place has been only that, a pause before the next movement. It is written that God is in all things, but I do not see Him the way Rakau sees his world. Before he would take a tree he would propitiate Tane, he sees the hand of Rongo in his crops, he returns the first fish to Tangaroa. And when we lay upon the rocks it was Ra who warmed us. He shrinks from nothing and does not fear death as I do. He does not fear his god as I fear mine.

There was no peace in church for me this morning. Nothing of justification, nor of glory. Dear God, I did not even feel called.

Haere mai te kaiako, haere mai te mihinare.

Haere mai te tama.

There was peace at the waterfall, no justification, no glory, just peace, a wholeness in the goodness of being. Like the peace in the Bentinck Chapel the night the Lord brought me to Basil Woodd. I cannot separate them.

Bubbles of anxiety stirred within his gut and he became aware that he was standing very still, his breath coming in shallow snorts. He shivered in the morning sun. Without moving his head, his eyes crossed the empty space about him. To his left, almost out of his vision stood a woman dressed in grey, silently waiting. Before him in the shallows of the bay a group of perhaps a dozen men were gathered about a waka. They were Ngapuhi preparing their return to Waimate.

Thomas turned to the woman in grey.

"I must go," he heard himself say. "I have some business with Hongi."

Jane nodded briefly. "Very well," she said. "If you say so."

She watched him walk down the beach, his gait was odd she thought vaguely, somehow trudging and hurrying at the same time. He spoke with the warriors, then moved quickly up the hill to their house, to emerge almost immediately with a bag slung across his shoulders; he was always ready packed. Then down to the waka, a brief wave and he was gone.

She viewed the proceedings with a dull fatalism. So be it; now her alternative life would begin again. Outwardly it would only differ for a little while but inwardly it would inform her every moment in anticipation and dread.

Slipping baby Samuel into a sling against her back she walked towards the poultry enclosure. At present it was well-stocked, the hens were breeding and the *Active's* last trip had brought two score more. But the numbers were never a certain thing as visits from other whanau or hapu members always increased the level of depredation. Only the other night King had chased off a couple of thieves, firing powder into the air above their heads as they fled. There would be no consequences. Even if King had recognised them the next meeting would pass as though nothing had ever happened. The accusations and denials were not worth the trouble.

Without bothering to remove Samuel from his sling Jane cornered a pair of plump hens and wrung their necks. Then she looked through the laying boxes, through the damp, soiled straw (it needs changing, I might send Richard down later) but found no eggs. First come, first served.

She headed back up the hill, a pair of scaly claws in either hand, pausing by Richard's hut. In late summer it was a profusion of colour. He has done well, she thought, and has worked hard to do so, turning this heavy clay into rich, dark beds. Seaweed had been spread and left for the rain to wash the salt away. Then it would be cut into small pieces and mixed with sand. Two small bins of chicken and pig manure stood to one side, each one gradually filled by the single bucketload. Every day when he had returned from his labour he had brought with him another contribution. And there was a barrel Thomas had given him to be filled from the spring by the same laborious process. A larger bin of rotting materials completed his resources. He had learned that flesh and entrails should not be added after the Kendalls had complained of the stink of maggots and now they were put directly into the soil. By trial and error he had mixed his elements and now they fed the shrubs and flowers that grew about his house and twined up the walls on flax trellises. He was kneeling in the earth now, gently settling a cutting of karaka into the warm, black soil. He was utterly engrossed and Jane passed him by in silence.

There was no silence at the house. Thomas and Basil stood outside the girls' sleepout, truculent before their sisters' reproaches. There was little of affection between them. Three years was a long time in the life of a child and their separate lives had made them forgetful. The children saw Jane approach and instantly she was brought into the conflict.

"Mother," Susannah was all resentment and righteousness, "will you tell the *boys*," it was a term of abuse, "to keep away from our house? They are *annoying* us."

Thomas muttered something.

"And tell them not to speak to us in Maori. I am sure they are being *rude*."

They probably were, thought Jane. She had some grasp of the tongue but nothing of Thomas' or Basil's fluency. Nor Joseph neither. Another barrier.

Tungaroa emerged from the house. "I have put away the dishes, e whaea," she said quietly. "I am going to see my koro now. I will be back tomorrow perhaps."

"Thank you, Tungaroa. E haere atu."

"Whaea," shrilled Elizabeth. "Doesn't whaea mean mother? Why does she call you whaea? You're not her mother."

"Mokopuna call all old women whaea," Thomas said. He spat contemptuously. "Girls don't know anything."

Jane recoiled from his action and his tone but held back the urge to smack his cheeky head. "You will not speak like that," she said angrily. "And you will not spit. It's disgusting."

Thomas was unrepentant. "Everybody spits," he said.

"Better out than in," added Basil and giggled.

Jane stared at them, despairing. *What am I to do with you?*

Shouts rose up from the beach and looking down Jane could make out a group of young Maori.

"There are Matai and Marama," said Thomas. How could he see so clearly? "Can we go and play with them?"

"Yes," piped up Joseph, "me too."

"And me," from John.

"Very well," said Jane, anything for peace. "But go with Richard. And tell him I want you back in two hours for lunch."

"Richard can't tell the time." This from Elizabeth, scornfully.

"He can, too," retorted Thomas angrily. "He can tell from how far Ra has moved across the sky."

"Ra," said Susannah. "You sound just like a Maori."

"Enough!" Jane was pale and the children suddenly registered that a limit had been reached. "Girls, go back to your hut to do," she paused, "whatever it is you want to do. Just do it quietly. Thomas, two hours, don't forget. Now go."

She went into the house and laid Samuel in his cot where he fell into an easy slumber. Thank God he was so placid. Then she readied the fire and placed a pot of water above it. As the water began to bubble she dunked the hens then sat heavily on a wooden bench, a bucket between her legs and pulled the feathers from the hot, dripping birds.

This is how the rest of the day will pass, cooking, cleaning, perhaps firing up the copper and standing soaked in steam and sweat, no, that would be to profane the Sabbath. Tending to six children and a baby. Then at the end of the day the evening meal and thanksgiving. Thanksgiving for what? For the close of night and the beginning of silence as the children went to bed and left her alone.

And then the alternative life. She shivered in a moment of hungry anticipation. For a time she could be Jane, a woman, for a little time with a long time to repent.

She had gone back to Richard's hut with no intent other than the need not to be alone. She had talked in a dull monotone, losing herself in anecdotes about her childhood, restoring her sisters and parents to a more substantial dimension. The stories crossed and folded, a word from one leading to elaboration in another. Richard had listened quietly, sometimes barely comprehending and this had led to an evaporation of self-consciousness, of any idea of what was appropriate and what was not. So she might talk of the onset of menstruation, comfortable in the vagueness of his nods. Sometimes her words would fade away and she would sit silently, remembering. And he was easy in the silence, too.

She asked about his life and learned of his father and of Ginge. Only when he began to talk of his sin did she intervene.

"No, Richard. I have had enough of sin and judgment. Just tell me what happened."

She listened to the tale and made no judgment on Ginge's goodness as she had made none on their sin. Things just happened.

As Thomas' absences had increased, she had met with Richard more often. There was a pleasure in that time that would have been hard to define, had she been inclined to attempt it. As it was, she simply enjoyed it. She felt herself expand and grow with an alien freedom. Tomorrow the world would shrink again but for now the stars were brighter.

One night she leaned against the wall, her legs drawn up, her bare toes wriggling idly against the dry earth. The moonlight swam in through the open shutters and reflected on an empty bottle. Richard sat opposite on his bed nursing his glass, his eyes a little bright from the effects of the port. He had little liking for alcohol, it slows my thoughts he complained and only joined in a glass out of a wish to please.

"Do you have friends?" Jane asked.

Richard considered. "I have not thought about it," he said. "I suppose so."

Jane stared at him. "Do you know," she said, "I've never thought about it either. It's a term we all use as though we understand it and as though everyone else understands it, too. But we don't." She sipped her wine and mused. "Like 'love' and 'happiness', What do they mean? Little Thomas loves to swim, the Maori love to fight and Thomas loves to suffer." She stopped, confused.

"You love your children," said Richard helpfully, "and I love Jesus."

"Do you?" asked Jane. "Do you? And what does it mean, to love Jesus?"

Richard shook his head. "I don't know," he said. "I just do."

Jane nodded. "Very well," she said. "Let us explore this. How can we, yes, that will be a start." She looked at Richard and saw his face in light and shadow, the beauty and the dullness. You are a good man, she thought. *And there is another word.*

"What do friends do?" she asked.

Richard furrowed his brow.

They do what you are doing now. They see their friends, they hear the question and they try to find a truthful answer. They do not hide in worn cliché and dogma. They know when they do not know.

"They talk," he said. It was more a question than an answer.

Jane shook her head. "We all talk," she said, "all the time. And our talk includes lies and boasts and threats."

"Perhaps friends do not lie or boast or threaten."

"And mostly we talk about nothing, about the weather or the latest gossip. Talk that could be had with anyone. There must be more."

She held his eye for a long time and more questions surfaced.

Then Richard smiled and she thought she could fall into that smile.

"Friends play," he said.

Jane considered and then she was swinging once more and although she was unsure whether there were strong hands waiting, waiting to steady her and send her away flying again, her hands were tight about the ropes.

"And who do you play with?" she asked.

Richard looked at her curiously. "I think I may be playing now," he said. Then he shook his head, baffled. "I do not understand what I just said."

Jane smiled. "I don't, either," she said, "but I think you may be right."

Have we forgotten what play is? I think it may be worse than that. I think we may have reduced it to sin. Something that might be tolerated in a child but is to be utterly eschewed in an adult. It is vice and indulgence, the road to perdition. So we watch the Maori as they sing and dance and promise them damnation. Are we so afraid of pleasure?

When did I last play? What is there of pleasure in my life?

Now there was a touch of anger in her and a harshness in her voice as she raised her glass. "To play," she toasted.

Richard drank with her and the unaccustomed alcohol ran through him, warming him, fuzzying him and inducing a touch of the reckless. He watched her sprawled against the wall, her dress falling in folds between her thighs, the curve of her throat and the full breasts. There was tightness in his chest and his breath shortened. And now there was a heat in his groin and it was in his head, too, blurring his thoughts, searing his doubts and uncertainty, burning away all objection, leaving him only with the lushness of her.

Jane drained her glass and the tension in the little room flowed into her. She saw his eyes upon her and she ached where they settled. There was a momentum here that brought her to her knees and brought her hands to the buttons of her dress. She felt her fingers unfastening them while her eyes never left his face, drinking in his defencelessness. And she was defenceless, too as her dress fell open and she pulled it back to show him who she was.

He fell forward from his cot to his knees and she gasped as his encircling arms drove the breath from her and his mouth was upon her breast. They clung to one another for a long time, then Jane pulled away. Richard's face was almost stricken and he seemed at the point of tears. He made to speak but she laid a finger across his lips.

"Hush," she said. Then she removed her dress while he stayed kneeling, staring. Naked, she raised him to his feet and gently undressed him.

Then they lay upon the cot and she knew him and gave herself up to being known.

Throughout the following day she moved as if in a dream. While the older children took their lessons from William Carlisle she sat beneath a pohutukawa by the beach. John dug in the sand and Samuel crawled in the shade.

She tried to think but reason evaded her. There were only stark certainties. By any standards, Maori or pakeha and particularly by those of her husband she was a fallen woman. Nor did she allow herself excuses: *I know I have sinned and, God help me, I also know I will go on sinning. I cannot, will not let this go. Should it be the death of me, I will not let it go. Because it will be the death of me if I do.*

Thomas did not return that night and after the children were put to bed she went to Richard's hut. She had not seen him that day; he was gone before the children left for school and he had stayed at the smithy to take his evening meal with Walter Hall. She doubted that he had spoken of the preceding night.

Now Richard sat and stared at her and now the fear was uppermost.

"We have sinned," he said. "God will punish us."

Reason had returned and she knew how she would use it. And here was a greater betrayal, greater than the one she had delivered to Thomas.

"I have sinned," she agreed.

"Thou shalt not commit adultery."

Again she agreed. "Thou shalt not commit adultery."

Then she said, "I want you to listen, Richard and try to understand. You must tell me if you do not understand."

He nodded.

"There was once a boy," she said, "who loved his father. But his father became very ill and could not look after himself, nor his son. The boy knew that God had said, 'honour thy father' and he knew that God loves life. For He had said, 'thou shalt not kill.' Do you understand so far?"

Richard nodded.

"So the boy knew that God wanted him to look after his father, because if he did not then his father would die. And God did not want that.

"The boy had two choices. He could sit and do nothing and watch his father die. Or he could steal."

Richard's eyes were wide. "You are talking about me. I am the boy."

"Good. You understand. So the boy stole and his father lived. And he was grateful to his his son and he blessed him. And God was pleased."

Jane paused. A part of her hated herself for what she was saying. But her choices were no less stark than Richard's had been.

"The boy became a man, a good man and he shone in the eyes of God. One day he met a woman who, like his father, was near death."

"You are that woman. But you are not near death."

"There is more than one kind of death. On the outside I am alive but on the inside, here," she laid her hand on her breast, "my spirit is dying. It is dying of loneliness, from being unknown."

"I do not understand."

"No, because you do not suffer from loneliness. But it is very real. It is like," God, how far would she take this blasphemy, "it is like being utterly tapu. You have seen how, when a Maori offends the atua he may become so tapu that there is no life left for him."

Richard nodded. "I have seen it but I do not understand it."

"No more do I. But it is no less real. And my loneliness is real, so real that I thought I might die of it. I do not want to die."

She sat quietly then but her eyes were steady on him. He barely understands, she thought (I barely understand myself) but he wants to. A dark thought occurred. Of course he wants to. He senses that here is a way he can be freed of his sin, here is redemption and, more than that, he can be free to sin again. And he wants that every bit as much as I do.

"I do not want you to die, either," he said at last.

Her eyes were still on him and now he held her gaze.

"You see me," she said. "You let me show me to you and you show yourself to me. And in that showing and knowing you brought me life again."

The words were just sounds but the sounds had their own meaning and the gazing held more still, meaning that was translating and spreading through him as his body found its own explanation.

"Your small sin brought your father life. And your sin with me brought a greater good. Ask your heart: what is right?"

He fed from her eyes and his hunger grew.

"It feels right," he whispered.

"Yes," she said and crossed to him. She took his hand and laid it on her breast. "Does that feel right, too?"

"O yes, o yes."

They gave themselves up to the moment and with the freedom of utter hopelessness she was able to show him her every need. And their cries rose like wild birds fleeing through the shutters and into the night, breaking in upon the sleep of John and Hannah King.

CHAPTER 25

Waimate

A heavy stone stood within neat fencing, an acknowledgement to Rongo and a constant prayer to his good will. And such, thought Thomas sourly, was clearly evident in the rows of vibrantly healthy wheat that covered the field. Had the crop been a poor one, of course, this would have been equally clear evidence of Rongo's displeasure. Either way, he was very much with them. The success of the crop was also aided by the way the rich soil had been prepared and nourished. Hongi had learned well from Ruatara. But Rongo would take the credit. Further away stood fields of golden corn and potato in tidy mounded rows. It was a sight that would have brought a smile to Samuel Marsden and heartfelt thanks that western technology had been so thoroughly and effectively embraced by the heathen. The first step was taken: the next was an obvious movement towards acceptance of the Christian god and his love and mercy.

Thomas knew better. Western agriculture had served the Maori well. The mortality rate had dropped markedly and they were free at last from dependence upon the fern root. But their glowing health and time for leisure had not brought gratitude to the pakeha, nor had it turned them to Christ. Quite the opposite. An abundance of food meant they were now able to pack up baskets of kai and take it with them. They could travel further and for longer, travelling like Napoleon's armies on their bellies. And their intent was just the same.

The benefit of white technology was apparent to them and they held out their hands for more. But they did not hold them out to Christ; they held them out for guns.

I bring not peace but a sword.

Yet there was a quality of happiness here, of generosity of spirit that he seldom saw among the white settlers. There, by the northern gate a group of half a dozen women and girls were raising the heavy planks that served as a dam for the irrigation channels that had been dug from the stream. The job did not require that number and the missionaries would have looked with disapproval on the four standing by as two stalwarts slid the planking up between the posts that held them in place. But how were they to measure the contribution of amiable society to the task? A dark, stout woman sat and watched, recounting an anecdote that reduced her companions to helpless laughter. The work stopped as they hooted and slapped their thighs. Then the stream was released and the women watched and smiled as the water ran between the rows.

This was their turangawaewae, the place where they stood and the sense of belonging was boundless. They belonged to one another, women were whaea and men were matua, they belonged to the earth, Papa was whaea to them all and the world of the spirit permeated every aspect of their lives. Tapu or noa inhabited all things and actions and gave them meaning. The lives of their ancestors crowded about their daily living and lit their paths in the night.

Is there a word in te reo for loneliness?

Thomas had heard of white settlers, isolated traders who would risk everything to avoid the Maori winter, the long, cold, wet days and nights when there was nothing to be done but sit and scratch and listen to interminable stories. And drink themselves into oblivion. They would leave their posts with no idea of what would await their return to flee to Port Jackson for any kind of change, anything to break the maddening monotony.

Is there a word for boredom?

Perhaps that was one of the charms of war. Certainly it enriched Hongi's life. It drew together the threads of distant time and space, weaving them into the details of his day and shaping his future. It told him his purpose and determined who he was. Was there some dark love in that? Certainly by any civilised standards Hongi was a monster. But there was a kindness in him, too and a regard for others that was almost tangible. Thomas recalled his grief at the passing of Ruatara and when his elder brother, Kaingaroa had died Hongi had had to be restrained twice from taking his own life. And he joyed in his children in a way that

Thomas envied. The restraints upon his own love seemed to increase daily and now he would watch his daughters from an uncomfortable distance and ache for the memory of a chubby little figure racing down the hall. *Ah, my lovely muffin.*

"E Keni."

His thoughts were interrupted by the arrival of the women from the dam. They were watching him curiously, their eyes crinkled in concern.

"What are you doing by yourself? Are you sick?"

Thomas smiled at their solicitude. "Kahore. I am well. I just want to be by myself for a while."

They stared uncomprehending, then shrugged and went on their way, clucking at the strange habits of the crazy pakeha.

They are so certain of themselves, so untroubled. They do not doubt for a moment the meaning or value of their lives. As Marsden, Hall and King, yes and Basil and Robert and everyone, they do not doubt. None question, all are certain. They are too busy to doubt and have not the time for fruitless meditation.

He suddenly remembered James Worthing; now there was a man plagued by doubt. And Rakau, he was forever questioning. Thomas shook his head, caught between a groan and a laugh: *fine company I keep.*

He clambered to his feet. *This will not do; this is idle self-indulgence. I must be up and doing.*

He marched resolutely back to Okurapete pa, past the neatly tended fields, smiling, waving to the greetings that rang about him. Up the hillside, past moat and pallisade, strong, deeply entrenched, this would withstand an artillery barrage, and on to the village.

And there was Hongi, standing with a group of keen young toa, deep in instruction.

"However pressed you are, take time to aim. A wild shot is a wasted shot."

He saw Thomas and beckoned him over, handing his musket to a young man, then laying his hands upon the missionary's shoulders. Their noses pressed and they stood still for a while as their breath merged.

Then he was stepping back and his smile was warm and welcoming.

"Kia ora, e hoa. We did not have time to korero last night. We will do it now. Inside, I think. Come."

He led Thomas towards his whare, barking orders to a woman on his way. She hurried ahead.

As they settled in the shade the woman ran up bearing two plump cushions. Hongi gestured and she laid them down.

"I think I must be ageing, e hoa. Once the earth was soft enough but since I have discovered feather cushions it has become harder."

The two men settled themselves comfortably.

"Take off your jacket, e Keni. Unbutton your shirt, remove your shoes. Be comfortable. I cannot understand why you pakeha dress yourselves in such discomfort."

Thomas did as he was bidden and his toes wriggled free and the breeze was a delight. The woman approached again and set down before them two cups of tea and an assortment of biscuits.

"How does the school progress?"

Thomas shrugged. "Well enough. Some learn, some don't and the provisions to keep their attendance and attention are always in short supply. It vexes me that I must spend so much time on administrative matters when I should be teaching."

His fellow-magistrate nodded. "Nonetheless," he said, "you turn a handsome profit."

Thomas was nettled. "I do not administer for wealth," he answered stiffly, "but to ensure the survival of my family and myself. And I lament the nature of it."

He was speaking of te pu. He had long since made up for his initial breach of etiquette and he had bathed in the warmth of the chief's appreciation. So he continued trading and his family and then his school had flourished. And Thomas had accused and excused himself.

In the beginning it had been a small thing. The occasional weapon, like the musket to Hongi was more an act of coutesy and diplomacy than anything else. But when he discovered that William Hall had traded a half dozen muskets for supplies and labour it had become something much larger.

Marsden's disapproval hung over them all. "A vile trade," he had declaimed, "and those who deal in it deal in death and betrayal of the commandments of God."

Hall was not ashamed and had dismissed the charge out of hand. "Let him near starve in a leaking, freezing hut; then he can talk to me about the ethics of trade. I am not Marsden's subject."

While Thomas swung between accusation and excuse and longed for an understanding ear. And there was Rakau.

"Marsden says that I must not sell guns to Ngapuhi. He says that Hongi will use them for war."

"And so he will."

"Yet I am here to preach of peace."

"Preach away. Perhaps Hongi will listen."

"You know he will not."

"Is that your responsibility? Are you responsible for Hongi's choice? That might be considered rather disrespectful. Not to speak of dangerous."

"Of course I cannot choose for him."

"But by withholding guns, isn't that exactly what you are doing?"

Without the possibility of sin there can be no virtue.

Lead us not into temptation.

Thomas had seized hold of the idea and had taken it to Jane. "The Maori are a sovereign people; who are we to make their choices for them?" "I suppose you are right but, o Thomas, the choices they will make!"

Rakau was not helpful. "These are just words that accompany the events," he said, "you know you're going to do it anyway."

"I must. How else can I feed my family and fulfil God's purpose for me?"

Hongi was more considerate. "Guns defend as well as attack," he had argued. "Who would dare attack well-armed Ngapuhi? And so the pakeha are safe. Why would Matene not wish you safe? He should be pleased that we are doing it for him and saving him the trouble."

Like I provide for the school and save him the trouble.

Hongi had sensed agreement and pressed his case carefully. "What is it that keeps the English people safe? Their God and his ministers? You can believe that. But you can see the warriors and the ships and the guns. What keeps Matene safe in Port Jackson? The goodwill of the people or the guns of the soldiers? He is safe behind the gun; why would he not wish the same for you?"

"Marsden cannot, will not defend us, Jane. How can he resent Hongi's doing so? I think it may be that he fears our independence. He will not accept or take responsibility for our dependence yet he is resentful if we turn to another. We are not safe without Hongi."

"And who will defend us against Hongi? Or men who are drunk or out of control."

You have not fought with a Maori but you have fought with John King. What kind of defence was called for then?

"The danger is probably closer at hand," said Jane. "Remember what happened to William and Dinah Hall."

But Thomas would have none of that, for he was quite captivated by Hongi. He felt the chief's mana as a physical thing. He swelled at Hongi's praise or appreciation and he felt safer than he ever had in his life before.

Rakau saw the respect and reinforced it. "You are Hongi's man, e Keni, there are none who would dare to do you or yours harm."

Unless they're so pissed or angry that they've stopped thinking altogether.

So he went on doing it anyway.

But even now, with the trade into its third year Keni continued to protest and apologise and explain, often all at once. Hongi was alternatively amused and irritated and always a little saddened at the pain the missionary brought upon himself. Still, he was impressed. Keni alone of the settlers understood rangatiratanga. Only he had really sought to learn their language and understand their ways; Rakau had taught him well. He did not despise the Maori gods, Rakau said that he thought Keni feared them, he was respectful. He understood mana.

He even knew the rage of the warrior. Hongi had not seen Keni fight Kingi but he had heard that if Keni had not been restrained it could have gone to the death. Nor had he seen Keni threaten another but he had seen the fury as the missionary recited his ill-treatment and did not doubt that he had.

Yet here he sits, safe in the heart of Ngapuhi, pigs and pu traded to the satisfaction of all concerned and he declaims against warfare. Hongi shook his head in silent disbelief.

"If you would but turn to Christ and turn your swords to ploughshares."

It was a familiar appeal; perhaps he thought one day it might magically take. There was no doubt he believed it passionately. But Rakau was probably right; he thought that Keni hoped the prayer would end his obligation. He had preached against guns and Hongi had exercised his god-given gift of choice; leaving Keni free to negotiate the next deal.

Hongi smiled at his friend, all woe-begone and wringing his hands. "Speaking of ploughshares," he said, "what did you think of the new fields? We are hoping for a bountiful harvest."

Which will leave you free to stock your waka with more provisions so you can seek death further and further afield.

Hongi saw his face darken, read the thought and continued. "With all the new varieties we are growing there will be many new words for your dictionary. How is it going? Is it any closer to publication?"

You know it is not, thought Thomas, how could it be? The dictionary sits in Rangihoua and Professor Lee is in Oxford. But he just shook his head.

Hongi nodded sympathetically. "You need to be in England, e Keni."

Thomas looked at him sharply. He had spoken with the rangatira a number of times of his need to be gone. *If I could but meet with Professor Lee and show him my work; he would know its value.*

They had been through Thomas' anxieties and Thomas had persuaded himself that Jane and the children would manage perfectly well without him. *She will be under Hongi's protection and Rakau will keep her and the children safe. She will be well provided for, the Society pays me directly now and Marsden cannot stop it, she is an efficient if untidy housekeeper, she trades well, the girls and young Thomas are a great support... Carlisle can manage the school without me, he will have Thomas and Basil and Tangaroa to help him ...*

But Marsden would forbid it.

Here the conversation had ended for Hongi. The mana of a rangatira, even a pakeha one was an inviolable thing. And Hongi respected Marsden, respected the iron will, the great power at his command and his readiness to use it. Unlike Thomas, he believed that Marsden would have turned the guns of the *Active* on Rangihoua.

So what was he saying now?

"I have been thinking about rangitiratanga, e Keni. I have asked myself, how far does the authority of a chief reach? Does Matene's mana reach across the sea to tell you your duty? Here, in the heart of Ngapuhi where you live or die at my wish his mana can command you? Ngapuhi rule here, e Keni, we are a sovereign people, you often say so yourself. You are here, manuhiri to our land and we have taken you to our whare and fed you and kept you safe."

"None know our debt more than I, e Hongi. But I do not see where this is leading."

Hongi tapped his chest. "To me, e Keni, it is leading to me. I command here."

"Of course, but –"

"You obey Matene because I wish it. He is rangatira there, I am rangatira here." He pointed to a young man walking past. "That slave lives because I say so. Perhaps I might stop saying so and who will hear you when you cry, 'Matene forbids it'?"

Thomas shivered, afraid that Hongi would order the death or more probably take it himself. And his point would be well and truly made.

"None can forbid you, e Hongi," he said quickly. "Matene's mana depends upon yours. But I still don't see what this has to do with –"

"I think I might like to go to England; it would be good to make Ruatara's journey, to finish it for him. I could meet the king and inspect his armies. There may also be a way to secure more muskets."

Always war.

"You would come with me, of course. I will not speak the pakeha tongue, so you must speak for me." He watched Thomas blink and shake his head and laid a kindly hand upon his shoulder. "E Keni, why do you look so bewildered, isn't this what you want?"

"It is, o yes, but, but …"

Hongi smiled. "You need to be alone with your 'buts', e Keni. You should go back to Rangihoua to listen to them. Perhaps your god will speak to you. There is no hurry. And," his hand slipped to close about Thomas' upper arm and draw him to his feet, "I think you should go now. There will be a feast this evening that you would sooner avoid."

Thomas was dismissed.

He hurried (was hurried?) home, on horseback to the bay and into a waka and across the water. The trip passed in a blur as random ideas jostled for space with random feelings. He was only marginally more settled as he stepped ashore at Rangihoua. The beach was empty and the only sound was the small waves. He stood undecided then started walking slowly through the sand, occasionally pausing when he stood and stared at his feet. They took him further along the beach away from the settlement, up into the scrub. There he sat and tried to focus.

He had understood the promise and the threat at once. The journey to England was suddenly intensely real and he understood that he had never really meant it before; he had wished for England with all his soul but he had never intended it. He had always been waiting for it to happen.

Like Hongi had said, it was all that he had wanted and Hongi thought he had given it to him, had freed him from Marsden's command. But of course he hadn't, not that it would be politic to tell Hongi so.

The threat was also intensely real. What might be the consequences of defying Marsden? What if the Society should take his part? What if Professor Lee declined? But how would the Society know Marsden disapproved if Marsden didn't even know he was gone? They'd find out. Eventually. Would the Society want letters of authority? Would they consider his ordination without Marsden's agreement?

But clamouring over them all: what if I am dismissed? My pay stopped? Trapped in England?

He softly pounded his fist on his knees, near in tears with the frustration of it all.

It is my choice. Hongi will not command me to make the trip against my will.

It is my choice: to risk everything I have for everything I want.

This is unfair. It is too much to ask.

Perhaps your god will speak to you.

Thomas pushed himself up on to his knees and folded his hands before his chest. Lord, he prayed, guide me now; bring me to ordination and the acceptance of my work. Let me hear Your Words in an English church in an English tongue. But keep me safe, Lord, and Jane and the children, too.

He opened his eyes and the sea was rolling in like it had always done and the air was warm in the autumn afternoon.

There was no answer but once again there was an answer in that. "I know that I do not know," he said aloud and wiped his hands on his jacket. "I don't know," he said again and then roaring at the indifferent sea, "I DON'T KNOW." Then he was caught in the release and he stamped and pounded fist into palm and roared and roared again.

Some thirty feet away three boys sat and watched the crazy missionary dance and rage.

"He is doing a haka."

"What for? Who for?"

"E tino riri ana ia," said the third boy. His skin was as dark as the other boys' but there was blue in his eyes. "He is very angry. When he gets angry he acts like this."

Thomas was very tired. His thoughts were clear of all but one, there is nothing to be done right now. I will wait upon the Lord and he will show me the right path. He bowed his head briefly then began to make his way down to the beach.

I will go home now.

He opened the door to a new house. The floor was clean and freshly scrubbed, the walls and ceiling clear of cobwebs and the dishes stored away. Jane was sitting at the kitchen table engrossed in needle work. But she looked up as he entered and nodded briefly.

"You are returned safely," she said. "I trust your business with Hongi had a satisfactory outcome."

Thomas smiled. An English voice. "A momentous meeting," he said. "I hardly know where to begin." He broke off as he registered that her head had bent back to her work. Her lack of interest seemed almost a palpable thing and he hesitated, suddenly uncertain again. The silence hung heavy between them.

At length, almost lamely, he said, "The house is looking very well; you have been busy."

Jane nodded. "Thank you," she said. The silence resumed.

Has she always been this silent?

He became aware that his shoes were sodden and he could see his footprints on the floor. He gestured vaguely towards them. "I am a mess," he said. "I need to wash and change my clothes. I have not been out of them for three days."

Jane did not raise her head. "Clean clothes are in the bedroom," she said, "and there is a fresh towel in the washing room. Put your dirty clothes in the hamper and I will attend to them as soon as I am free."

Thomas walked into the strange, new bedroom with its clear swept floor and neatly made bed. He opened the dusted dresser for shirt and undergarments and took a pair of trousers hanging from a rack. The alien tidiness was unsettling as he carried his clothes to the washing room without further word.

The little shed was as tidy as the house. Even the grate beneath the copper was cleaned. Thomas stood and stared and tried to collect his thoughts. He should have been delighted for the mess they lived in had been a source of longstanding bitterness. But this neatness seemed to carry a kind of menace and this sense was somehow emphasised by the distant, industrious woman working at her table.

He stripped off his clothes and with a handful of leaves, also neatly stored, he lathered his body. Cleanliness had become something of an ethic for him, an unusual idiosyncracy for one raised in a society where personal hygiene was of little consequence, where the poor lived in grime and the rich covered it in scent and powder. Paradoxically it had come from his association with Maori who bathed more often, or at least spent more time in the sea, but rarely washed their clothes. Their filthy, stinking rags called for frequent comment in his letters to the Society. So now he took pleasure in cleaning himself in the warm and soapy water. He felt a stirring as he soaped his groin and there was an image of Jane's breasts and belly, swelling in the early showing of the next pregnancy. He thrust the thought away in near anger and doused himself in cold water. Then he took the clean, dry towel from the rack –such a change from damp towels on the floor – and rubbed himself dry. He dressed and emptied the copper and laid the towel outside to dry. He stood there, gazing back at the house. It would be good to talk with Jane, to tell her of this new development. They could pray together and seek direction. But not now. She seemed a little ... what? Now he needed to get down to the school to see how things were coming along.

Chapter 26

There was little to do as the long golden days called the Rangihoua people to their summer encampments where they swam and feasted on the gifts of Tangaroa. Neither were the few children who remained in any evidence. "This is not the time for school," they said.

They exulted in the season, awake to all its invitations. And as the kereru gorged its passion for the red, succulent berries, Ngapuhi seized the time for passion of their own and war was all their glory. Taua regularly departed for retribution from the north, south and west. Sometimes they would stop at Rangihoua and then the stillness would be shattered as the warriors drawn from their scattered hapu converged. They brought with them an intensity that was focused on death, they were hungry for killing and the settlers shuffled aside and held their tongues as property vanished or was destroyed. Most did not fear for their own safety but still knew better than to argue with a man who was aching for savagery. Hongi heard their complaints and shrugged them away.

But witnessing the return was worse.

One morning Thomas was sitting on deck with the captain of the *Dromedary*, chatting and negotiating when a call from the topsail alerted them to a dozen waka returning from the south.

The captain turned his glass upon the canoes. He was not unduly worried for a direct and unprovoked attack —although what was taken as provocation was any white man's guess – was unheard of.

"Here," he thrust the telescope into Thomas' hands. "You know these people better than I do. Do you recognise 'em?"

Thomas swept the telescope across the waka. He felt a touch of alarm as he picked up quite unfamiliar faces paddling at the front of the nearest canoe. And sitting behind and between were several women and children. But only men had travelled on the last expedition. Even Turikatuku, Hongi's principal wife had stayed behind. He scanned further and ah, there was Mana and there, standing at the stern, one hand on the great canoe post was Hongi himself.

He passed the telescope back. "There is no danger," he said. "Ngapuhi are returned." But his tone was grim for he knew what was to follow. "Have you any men ashore?"

"No." The captain shook his head.

"Keep it that way," said Thomas. "What is to come is not the place for pakeha. Or any God-fearing soul, for that matter. But I must return to my family May I prevail upon you to have me delivered back to the settlement?"

Soon he was hurrying towards the school house. To his left came the sound of voices raised in excitement and fear as the remaining inhabitants of the pa streamed down towards the beach. Then the school house door was opening and Carlisle and his students emerged, the children of the mission and two Maori, Tungaroa and a curly-haired boy who was staying with the Kings.

"Mr Kendall." Carlisle was pale and uncertain and his relief at seeing Thomas was apparent.

Thomas wasted no time on greetings. "Quickly," he said, "you must return to your homes immediately." He had to raise his voice to be heard above the shouting on the beach. Manu, I would like you to go to Kingi's and Tungaroa to come with me."

Tungaroa shook her head. "I am sorry, matua but I must go to my kin now. And Manu should come with me."

Thomas groaned as they hurried away. So apt a pupil and so close to welcoming Christ into her life. How the Adversary must smile to see her speeding back to sin.

Carlisle was gone, too, back to his wife and child. Was there ever a more appropriate time than now for the missionaries to come together in his school house, to join in prayer and hymn and witness their faith? He had raised the issue and before and had stammered in anger at the blank-eyed obstinacy. And Satan had smiled again.

The tumult on the beach was growing, increased by answering calls fom the approaching waka. Thomas shepherded the children away and up toward their home. "Quickly now, tamariki, there is no time for delay. Elizabeth, *move*, remember Lot's wife."

The girl began to argue. "I can't see why we –" but was silenced by her father's glare. "O very well then." She lifted her skirt above her ankles and hurried after the others.

He ushered them into a room darkened by curtains that were woollen blankets hung across the front window, blocking out the view of the beach. Jane sat at her table in the tidy gloom.

"Mother." Elizabethe tried an alternative source. "Why may we not watch the warriors returning?"

Jane's face was pale but her voice was even as she answered. "Because the killing is not yet done, child."

The voices from the beaches grew louder still as the canoes beached and their questions were answered. Now there was the certainty of loss and their rage erupted into a pandemonium of shrieking and howling. *This is what hell must sound like.* And added to the women's voices came the scream of a male. The women needed more immediate redress than their own blood could provide and had taken a prisoner to answer for their loss. With sticks, shells, stones and their bare hands they were tearing the life from him.

Now wailing was within his own room as Elizabeth and Susannah clung to one another and Joseph and Samuel to their mother. Basil's hands were over his ears but young Thomas's were by his sides clenched in fists and his face was pale and grim.

Thomas collected himself. "To your knees," he ordered, sinking down in example. Then his voice was rising above it all.

O Lord who so loved the world that He gave His only begotten Son that we might have eternal life, bring these poor heathen into Thy Light and away from the darkness of their abominations. And give us the strength and fortitude to bear their wickedness and to serve Thy Holy Purpose.

Then still on his knees he raised his arms towards heaven and forgiveness and led his family in hymn.

The Lord is my shepherd, I shall not want …

Similar scenes were enacted in the other mission houses. John and Hannah King were joined by Hannah's mother and her young son as together they too kneeled in prayer. Hannah's hands were over their little boy's ears as he coughed and panted in his crib. *We pray for the life of this, our second son but I cannot but think that he will soon join his brother. And all about us other lives are casually cast away. I cannot understand it.*

William Hall had stopped his ears and his wife's and son's with wax as they sat in silence. His hands guided young William's in the patient, careful sanding of a kauri table.

On a small plateau some thirty feet above the beach a half dozen convicts sat in a tight knot and watched. Violence of all kinds was known to them but this was something new. They had shuddered and gasped and breathed hissing between their teeth as the prisoner was battered and ripped and fists had clenched as a young woman suddenly aware that she was a widow had near opened her breast with a mussel shell. Like the missionaries they too mouthed the names of God but theirs was a different prayer. *O Christ, o Jesus, will you look at that, she's, o God.* They were caught in the horror, appalled by it but they never looked away.

Richard had seen such a homecoming once before and had thought it cruel and stupid. It would make God sad, he thought, and perhaps angry, too. He had thought to intervene but had been dissuaded by his mates. *This is not your place, you can't save him and you'll only make things worse for yourself. And for all of us.* He remembered Ginge saying something similar as the redcoats had driven their horses into the crowd and he had nodded and walked away. Now as he stood at the forge all his attention was on bringing the hammer down with exactly the right amount of force in precisely the right place.

CHAPTER 27

"Checkmate."

Thomas stared at the board. There was no way out, no further possibilities. He should have seen it coming, he had seen it coming but his responses had been ineffectual. Even as he had made them he had known they would not be good enough. Anger bit at him but he held it down as he reached across and toppled the king.

"Congratulations," he said.

Brind scratched his beard. "I dunno," he said. "Seems to me you lost the game more than I won it."

"As I have been doing all night." *As I have been doing all my life*. He tapped out his pipe into the laden paua shell and set about refilling it. Brind filled his own and for a while the two men sat and smoked silently. The cabin was wreathed in an acrid haze.

Rum and victory had put Brind into a mellow mood. He enjoyed triumph and resented defeat like any man but with little of Kendall's intensity for either. Funny little fellow, he thought, you never see him relax. Always competing, always worrying; but a well-meaning chap for all that. He filled their glasses.

"Your mind is elsewhere," he said at last. "You seem worried."

Thomas drank without answering and idly reset the board. Then he heard himself ask, "Are you ever lonely, William?" Strange, he thought, I didn't mean to say that. But he waited anxiously for the answer.

"Dunno," said Brind. "I haven't really thought about it. Am I lonely? I don't know that I've got time to be. Hard to be lonely on a boat. There's always someone to talk to."

Thomas' eyes were still on the board. "It's not the same thing," he said.

316

Brind scratched again. "You've got all kinds of company," he said. "Your colleagues, your pupils, your family. Man, you're surrounded by people. What about your wife? You can always talk to her."

Thomas shook his head. "I can't," he said. "She's changed, it's like I don't know her." He shrugged. "Anyway, she doesn't want to talk to me."

"Really?" Brind was puzzled. For a man of God Kendall seemed to find conflict everywhere. He also wondered briefly why a man would complain of a silent wife. But he kept it to himself and asked, "Is she angry with you? Have you done something to offend her?"

Thomas raised innocent palms. "Our life is as it ever was. I provide, she keeps house and attends the children and assists where she can. Indeed, she keeps the house much better than," he paused upon the point of disloyalty, "than was her wont."

"She does not complain or give you the evil eye?"

"No. She barely speaks at all and she will not look at me. I feel an accusation but cannot learn what it is."

Brind marvelled silently at a woman who would keep a tidy house and her peace at the same time. He measured his words for the next question. "Is she still agreeable?"

"Agreeable?"

"To your er," how to put it without offending the little prig, "to your, er husbandly needs?"

Thomas studied the chess pieces closely, moving each to the centre of its square. He was deeply embarrassed but at the same time understood that the question was only too relevant. For where Jane had once given herself willingly, even with an enthusiasm that had sometimes troubled him, she now lay like a corpse, enduring him, suffering his demands. Resenting him. "She is," he murmured, his eyes still on the board, "compliant." *Which is to say, obedient and bitterly so.* "But," he continued so softly that Brind had to strain to hear him, "she is …hostile, resentful. She says nothing but she accuses me."

"Mm." Brind drank and topped their glasses. "But English women are like that, Thomas. Not like your wahine who –"

"Please." Thomas raised a hand. "I do not care to hear of …" Words failed him.

Brind was unperturbed. "Your loss," he said amicably, then quickly to preempt a lecture, "have you asked her if she is troubled?"

"Many times. She will not look at me, she looks away or down and says she has no cause for complaint. And falls silent again."

And then I do the same thing and the silence consumes us. The children are uneasy and quiet and keen to be somewhere else. Even John and Joseph. And I don't know what to say to them either. It doesn't matter whether I'm quiet and gentle or strident and angry: she looks away and says she has no cause for complaint.

He stared miserably at Brind. "The silence is driving me mad, William. I need to be heard."

"Have you told her that?"

"How could she not know?"

"But have you *told* her you need her. Women love that. That and being told they are beautiful."

"Jane is above such shallowness. And I would not beg."

Brind filled their glasses and made no answer.

It is pride, Thomas. You betray yourself with 'I would not beg'.

He remembered Jane's begging him for attention and how he had dismissed it. *She is punishing me.* And then the silence and the unspoken complaint and the punishment that had filled his parents' house.

The last glass had toppled him into drunkenness and words were slurred. "I shall tell her that I have wronged her and ask for her forgiveness. I shall tell her that I need her. Not because it is a ploy but because it is true." He pushed himself to his feet. "And I shall do it now."

He made his way unsteadily to the cabin door then paused to look back.

"But I shall not tell her that she is beautiful."

Brind watched the canoe weave an erratic course to the beach, torn between amusement and concern. Then he turned back to his cabin and forgot about it.

Thomas staggered up the hill. Thoughts and memory collided and were as a whirling blur at the back of his mind. But he clung to an intention as to a prayer: *I will be humble. I will not be righteous. I will own my neglect and will atone for it. I will be open and acknowledge my need.*

And if she looks away I do not know what I will do.

The house he saw was in darkness. *Of course, it is the small hours of the morning and she is not expecting me back tonight.* His fault clutched at him *She will expect that I am drunk and sleeping on Brind's boat.*

As he drew near Richard's shed he noticed that the door was ajar and a dull light shone within. He stopped in surprise. It was a late hour to be entertaining. Unless … his mouth tightened in anger. Unless some shameless wahine from the pa was … and he would not be surprised. The blond hair and powerful frame had elicited many a vile invitation but he had thought better of Richard's resolve. This was outrageous, it was not to be tolerated. And with the house and the girls' sleep out only a short distance off. The righteousness that he had cast aside returned and his breath hissed between clenched teeth.

This would be sorted forthwith. He stamped up to the shed and flung the door open. His suspicions were instantly realised: there was a woman, there, a naked slut and she was, O Christ, she was his wife.

His eyes widened and in a moment of awful clarity it all made sense and he understood the accusation.

And then there was nothing but the roaring of blood and a consuming hatred. He saw Jane frantically clutching her dress before her, hiding her shame and wickedness. Richard did not move. He sat still on his bed, his arms hung limply and he slowly shook his head from side to side. His eyes closed and his mouth hung open. Thomas lurched towards them, his hands clenching and unclenching, scratching at the air and there was a scream building in his pounding heart that was driving up to explode as the accusation of his own.

But then the room spun and his knees failed and he fell forwards towards the earthen floor and the scream dragged at his guts. He fell on to outstretched arms and the rum and the food and everything that was within him cascaded out and down his arms and on to the floor. And long after he had emptied himself he continued to retch and now there was only the pain of ripping, the gasping for air and the groan of relief as the last spasm passed and the groan of fear as the next began.

At last he lay utterly spent in his waste and strong arms were lifting him up. He tried to strike them away and curse the man but had not the strength for either. At a distance he was aware of his clothes, his filthy stinking rags being stripped from him and a damp cloth and then a towel at his face, his hair and over his body. Stars wheeled across a black sky and a vast moon shrank and shuddered and a wind was cold upon his distant back. Then he was lying shivering on something soft and his face was wet and his heart pounded and then he was sinking, then falling into blackness and he was thankful for it. The hope stirred that this might be death.

If there was daylight he could not see it. So the glow by which he picked his way must come from the forest itself, pale on the underside of fern, grey on rock, burnishing dark red and green on berry and leaf. Damp air enveloped him, flowing across his shoulders and running down his chest and belly. Grass and rock were beneath his feet, now mud that sucked at his soles and squished between his toes. And yet his step was firm.

There were no edges to the forest. It breathed gently, silently on him and its touches from the mud beneath to the ferns that stroked his face were soft, even tender. When he reached out to steady himself he laid his hand upon a branch that was as warm flesh that yielded to his touch.

Ahead the glow intensified and he made his way towards it. It shafted through the canopy and as he approached it bent towards him until it was shining full in his face. He turned his head away and as he did there was another shaft that lanced through the back of his skull. He groaned and opened his eyes.

Across the room Jane was sitting in a high-backed chair with the morning sun behind her. Her face was pale in shadow and seemed almost carven in its stillness. She watched him impassively.

He made to speak but his throat was dry and his words a croak. Jane pointed to the bedside table but made no further movement.

Carefully he eased himself to sitting and reached for the glass of water that sat beside him. He drank deeply then set the glass down and turned to face her again. And he was as silent and as still as she was.

Maui and Hine nui te Po.

"Tell us a story, e papa."

Rakau smiled fondly. "Any particular story, e hine?"

Tungaroa considered. Then, "tell us a story about Maui," she said.

"Ae," agreed Ewha. "Tell us about the end of Maui."

"The end of Maui is the end of us all."

"Then tell us about the end of us all."

"Very well." Rakau stretched himself on the sand, still warm in the day's last light. "After Maui had dealt to Irawaru —what did he do to Irawaru, Tungaroa?"

"He turned him into a dog."

"Pai ana. And why did he do that, e Ewha?"

"Because Irawaru had caught more fish than Maui."

"Excellent. Now, after Irawaru's change his wife, Hinauri who you will remember was also Maui's sister threw herself off the rocks. Maui decided it would be wise to move away for a while so he went to visit his parents –"

"Who lived in the country of the manapau trees," said Tungaroa.

"Ae, so they did. Well, one morning Maui's father –e Ewha?"

"Ko Makea tutara. Could we have no more questions, please?"

"Very well. Makea took Maui to one side. 'My son,' he said sadly, 'I must tell you that when I performed the tohi ceremony over you I made a mistake and missed out part of the prayers. I fear that means death for you.' Now up til then death had had no power over man."

"E papa," Tungaroa interrupted, "I have thought about this. If there was no death, how would Makea know what it was and how would Maui know what he was talking about?"

"It doesn't matter," said Ewha. "We do. Get on with the story, ow!' as Rakau cuffed him none too gently.

"It is a good question," Rakau said, an astonishing question, he thought, for a thirteen year old girl. It was also the same question he had asked Keni when the teacher had told him the story of Adam and Eve. "I am surprised by their reaction," he had said.

"You are always surprised," Keni had answered, "but why this time? What reaction would you have expected?"

"Well," Rakau paused and then pointed towards a circling gannet. "You must not eat of the gannet, e Keni," he said, "for if you do, you will gerbil."

"What? Gerbil? What's that?"

"That," said Rakau," is the reaction I would have expected." But if Adam and Eve's reaction piqued his curiosity, Keni's amazed him. For the missionary suddenly became downcast. "That's right," he said after a while. "If there was no death how could they have known what God meant?" And he had trudged away, muttering to himself.

"But Ewha is also right," said Rakau, patting the boy's arm. "We know and we need not be concerned how Makea and his son came to know.

"Maui was not concerned. For while he knew that Hine nui te Po had left Tane and the world of light and retreated to the underworld in the hope that one day her children would join her, he also remembered that his mother had once told him that one day he would overcome Hine nui and then death would have no dominion.

"Maui shrugged. 'Well,' he said, 'then I shall take away Hine nui's power just like I took away Ra's.' He considered further. 'How will I know her?' he asked.

Makea pointed. 'There,' he said, 'there she is, she is the mountain in the setting of the sun, her body is a woman's but her eyes are greenstone and her hair is kelp. Her teeth are like the barracuda's and they also line the place where men enter her, teeth of obsidian and greenstone."

Ewha shuddered. "Ouch," he said.

"Early in the morning Maui assembled his companions for the journey; there was Tiwaiwaka, the fantail, Miromiro, the grey warbler, Tataeko, the whitehead and Pitioitoi, the robin. Maui stood amongst them naked but for the sacred jawbone of Muri ranga whenua which was tied about his waist. Ah, he was a handsome fellow and his hips and thighs glowed like a mackerel's skin, carved by the chisel of Uetonga.

"After a time they came to the place where Hine nui lay sleeping, sprawling on her back, her great thighs open. And it was as Makea had said for within the folds of her vagina were set rows of cruel, flinted teeth. "Maui then explained his plan to his friends. 'I will crawl,' he told them, 'into her centre and shall pass up through her womb and out her mouth. Then Hine nui will die and man will be freed from death. But,' Maui/ Rakau held up a warning finger, 'whatever you do, you must not laugh. For now she sleeps but if you laugh and wake her, her vagina will close and I will be stabbed to death.'

"Then as Maui stood his shoulders narrowed and hunched like this, and his face extended like so, and he was a rat. 'No,' said Tataeke, 'you will never succeed like that.' Then all his features faded and his arms and legs dissolved into his body and he was Toke, the earthworm. 'No,' said Tiwaiwaka, 'that will not do; Toke is kai. Be something else.' Then the flesh of Toke folded into segments and bristled and glowed black and green with stripes of kowhai and he was Moko Huruhuru, the caterpillar. The birds agreed that he looked very fine, indeed.

"Have you watched how Moko Huruhuru moves? A forest of steps for every move, jerking himself along between Hine nui's thighs. Tiwawaka stared and raised his wings over his beak to hold back his mirth. He closed his eyes but immediately opened them again and Maui's head was disappearing into Hine's folds. He looked away and aue, alas, he saw that Miromiro was doing the same thing, staring, wings folded over her beak. Tiwawaka lost all control then; he broke into wild chirruping laughter, leaping about upon his perch and flapping his wings."

Rakau held his arms out, parallel, bent at the elbow, wrists turning extended fingers to interlace as the teeth closed. Neither Ewha nor Tungaroa recoiled from the cruelty of the image; their eyes were as wide as Tiwawaka's.

Ka mutu te korero.

CHAPTER 28

He could not look at her without remembering what she had done. And then the revulsion became a physical thing and he had to look away. It weakened him, too and his anger flapped like a fledgling against its cage. He could barely bring himself to speak to her.

"How could you?" he murmured weakly.

"I have sinned," she agreed.

"The betrayal ..."

"My sin is great."

The scream that had torn at him in Richard's shed was a whimper now. "How could you?"

Richard was equally penitent and so lost that Thomas could not discover the anger to even strike him. But nor could he abide the sight of him and none argued when Richard was returned in chains on the next ship to Port Jackson

His wife, the mother of his children was a ruined woman, cast down and scrabbling at the edges of community....

William Hall was a man of plain, blunt speech who did not shrink from niceties. He said what needed to be said without fear or favour as much as his wife wished fervently that he would not.

"I saw Jane Kendall," the honorific was gone, "in church today. Seemed unfitting."

Dinah sighed. "Or," she suggested, "the most fitting place. Where better to repent and seek forgiveness?"

William grunted. Asking for forgiveness was, he thought, like asking for an undeserved favour. "It's a lot to ask," he said. "Her deeds call for condemnation. Jesus said, 'thou shalt know them by their fruit' and this is rotten fruit."

The Maori could see the pain on her, the women saw the dying of her spirit and it frightened them and they tried to call it back.

But Jane was becoming mute. She had found little call for speech; after all, what has such a woman to say? She scrubbed her floors and polished her windows in silence. She cooed and murmured baby Samuel to sleep in lullabies without words. Joseph of six followed Basil of eight who followed young Thomas of ten who ignored his teenage sisters. The children needed only nourishing food upon the table, a warm clean home and dry clean clothing. Jane could do all of that and none of it needed discussion. Sometimes she felt she should intervene as the children's pain became anger became incessant conflict and spite. Young Thomas was becoming more and more inclined to rule with his fists and she was saddened by Basil's and Joseph's tears. The girls became a single creature and she shrank from it and its resentment. She saw its tears and they made her sad, too. But what might such a woman say? Who was she to call for forebearance, patience, for Christian virtue? So she held her tongue and spoke only when spoken to and then reluctantly, hesitantly, certain only in her unworthiness.

She was a woman who had been cast down and scrabbled at the edges of community. She learned the world at ground level, to identify a man by his boots before his speech, his mood by his gait. And she found a kind of miserable safety there.

Thomas' duty called him further afield. Trade summoned him to ships' captains to secure the livelihood of his family and to gather supplies for a last stand against a falling roll. He traded with them and more muskets and ammunition changed hands; he urged them to a life of Christian virtue and then they drank themselves insensible.

And God called him further afield, to Kerikeri and the outreaches of the Hokianga, to Waimate and to Hongi.

While Jane sat at home in her silence and her shame. And there was none to wash her feet.

CHAPTER 29

Port Jackson 1818

"I will be saved, won't I?"

*And what else is there to say but, 'of course you will'? It is the smallest
kindness at such a time.*

"Do you repent of your sins?"

"O yes, o yes."

"Then you shall be saved."

Who could say otherwise?

*In truth, I have no idea whether you will be saved or not. I don't even know
what salvation means. All I know is that life will cease and you will rot. And yet
I am expected to declaim authoritatively upon an eternity —the very word makes
my mind shudder – upon an eternity of joy.*

And out of fear and kindness I will do so.

Fear drives us apart and aloneness stalks the chamber. Rheumy eye and
foetid breath and blood upon the counterpane. The wife already in black
at the end of the bed, wringing her hands with fears of her own. *What will
become of us? How will I feed my children?* The surgeon shrugs and sighs and
all eyes turn to the man of God.

George Egan has been here many times but it has not become easier.
The comfort of reconciliation, a note to a long-lost sister, words of discovered
love, these things he manages well and they sustain him but for matters of
the soul and judgment … he is at quite a loss. And as much as he may
sometimes envy the certitude of Marsden, he cannot help but despise it, too.

And doubt it. If Marsden truly believed that infinite bliss awaited him and his, how could there be room in his life for spite and unkind judgment? What could possibly make him angry? How could this knowledge be put to one side, forgotten in daily set-backs and frustrations, to be recalled on Sunday and the death-bed? There was a kind of madness here and George was becoming less and less able to be part of it.

But he whispered, "Go in peace to your reward," and after the final, heaving gasp he kneeled by the bed and closed his eyes. And thought, I have no idea whether you will be saved or not. I don't even know what salvation means.

He had to restrain himself from running to his horse and as soon as the first bend was passed and the farm house gone from sight he tore off his hat and opened his shirt and kicked his mount into an unrestrained gallop.

I have taken this as far as it will go and I cannot do it any more.

Joanna was unconcerned.

"Can't say I'm surprised," she said. "I've been thinking for a while that –" A wail broke through the room. "There you go," she said. "Go and do something useful."

George grinned ruefully and pushed himself up from the table. "What kind of a man would Marsden think me now," he said, "to see me bidden by my wife and waiting upon my child?"

Joanna smiled after the retreating back. "I care not what the great man might think," she said softly, "but I believe poor Elizabeth might wish for such."

Deep blue eyes, wide and wet and staring, damp red cheeks, brown curls plastered down and a wail that hurried George's step. In the cot beside her, little George slept on undisturbed. He pushed the muslin netting aside and swept her up, hand curled at the back of the tiny head, holding her cheek against his, amazed as ever at the rush of tenderness that suffused him.

Other men did not seem to know it, nor women neither; he had seen the raised eyebrows and the curled lip, too. Thinking him a fool, weak, less than a man.

"Fuck 'em," Joanna had said succinctly. "They don't know what they're missing."

Which included perpetual anxiety and a clutching dread whenever a child lay too still, too quiet.

Now he walked from the nursery, its colours dull in the night air and rubbed his daughter's back. He cooed and whispered and smiled at the powerful eructation that escaped her.

Joanna laid her on a towel on the sofa and deftly changed the soggy napkin. Then she opened her shirt, one of George's, so much easier than a wretched bodice and placed the child upon her breast.

George took his place back at the table and sat and smiled and watched. *Surely this is enough. There is immortality right here, right now.*

Who could have imagined it? That he would come to such a pass?

Have you heard about George Egan, you remember, Sir Joshua's youngest? He's landed up, perhaps I should say 'down', heh, heh, in the Antipodes. As God's m' witness, he's livin' in a hut in Australia with a barman's daughter. Fathered a couple of sprogs by her, I believe. Gone quite native. Ploughs fields, digs in a garden, wields a hammer like a navvy. Don't need to, he's been assigned a convict gang for labour; he does it out of choice!

I don't believe it. Dapper George? He was always a wild one though.

It's true. And as for wildness, consider this: he preaches the gospel on a Sunday. Man's a minister.

Well! Who would have thought it? The brandy must have finally turned his mind.

Evidently he no longer drinks. Picture of glowin' Australian health.

Poor George. What a comedown.

"So what are you going to do?"

He looked up, startled. "About what?"

"About the ministry."

George shook his head. "I think I must leave it," he said. "What do you think?"

"Fine with me." Joanna shrugged. "I'm only surprised that you've stayed with it for as long as you have. Why do you think that it is?"

And that was a part of what had maintained them. Joanna rarely bored him and frequently surprised and challenged him. She seemed to hold nothing much as received truth and so was constantly open to new ideas.

Now he stopped thinking about why he might leave and wondered why he had stayed.

"I don't know," he confessed. "I don't think I had made a decision either way. Probably I just waited to see what would happen."

———

"And what has happened?"

"I feel like I am become a liar. And am uncomfortable with it. Strange, it didn't concern me much before."

"Indeed not." Joanna smiled. "You played it as a game. I recall you laughing afterwards at your performances. You were quite the actor."

"As were you, my dear. Joanna Egan as the Pious Parson's Wife, the very Model of Demure Propriety."

Joanna nodded. "True." She stood and crossed the room with the sleeping Elizabeth in her arms. At the door she paused. "I wonder how well we might have managed it if we had not each had an audience to applaud us."

To validate the lie? To turn it into something else?

But he had not lied. He had always been very careful to stay strictly with the truth. *The Bible tells us that Jesus died to redeem you. (I reserve my own opinion.)*

Jesuit! You know what meaning was received.

George sat and wondered at the absurdity that had supported his life and standing in the community. As a spiritual leader, no less.

Joanna returned, buttonng her shirt and crossed to the table. "Here," she said, "I meant to show you earlier but I forgot." She smiled a little sourly. "It may add to your thinking."

The letter was written on a small sheet of folded paper, perhaps torn from an exercise book. The handwriting was remarkable, a perfect replication of examples on a blackboard, each letter perfectly formed and joined, a finger's space between each word, each line like a dark blue carving. Without flourish or personal stamp.

Joanna held up the envelope and pointed at the address. *Joanna Egan,* it read, *Wife of Priest Egan in Port Jackson, care of Samuel Marsden.* George shook his head and returned to the letter.

Dear Mrs Egan, he read, *I am writing to ask you to Help Mrs Kendall. She used to Talk about you and says that you Are kind. Her peeple here Are not kind and she is very lonly and Unhappy.*

Mrs Kendall has become very Noa. That means Unclean and her peeple Will not look on her. She stares at the ground and Wispers to herself.

She Will say Nothing except that she is a Siner who Deserves her suffering. My father his name is Rakau and he is Tohunga at Rangihoua and he thinks that she wispers and talks to herself to keep the voices down. He thinks she might be easier if she knew Richard was safe and well.

George laid the letter down and reached into his pocket for a pipe. After a long abstinence he had rediscovered nicotine.

"Richard?" he said.

"Richard Stockwell, the Kendalls' servant. Jane Kendall was unfaithful to her husband with him. Stockwell was returned to Port Jackson. It's all there and more, but the order's a bit mixed up."

"Stockwell? The simpleton?"

"Yes."

"Good Christ." George thought of dumpy Jane Kendall, all proper and plain. "Good Christ," he said again.

"Apparently Kendall discovered them in fragrant whatsit?"

"Flagrante delicto."

"That's the one."

"God. He would have gone out of his mind. What happened?"

"Tungaroa doesn't say."

"Tungaroa?"

"The girl writing the letter. She has been living witht the Kendalls. Oh, and another thing, Jane Kendall's pregnant. Tungaroa doesn't say who the father is."

George flapped a hand weakly. "God," he said, "what a mess. What an awful fucking mess. And they've got all those kids, too." He paused. "So what are we supposed to do about it?"

Joanna shrugged. "We could start by checking on Richard Stockwell." She smiled suddenly. "Offering succour to a convict, a simpleton," she drew herself up and her voice was deeper and of Yorkshire, "a vile fornicator, sir. A man whose Foulness has tainted God's Work Itself. Mr Marsden will not appreciate any kindnesses to such a man."

"And that," George was grim, "might be motive enough."

The next morning George rode the twenty miles to Sydney. He had business there in any event but he hurried through it and on to the stockade. But the convicts were already gone, had been since sun up; they'd be lined along Macquarie's highway now, or working in the quarry. And many were in private bondage. What was the name? Stockwell? Ah, here he is, stockade, chains, hard labour. I remember him now, big bugger, doesn't seem to mind the work, bit fu- slow in the head, though, doesn't seem to be a problem. Could I ask the nature of your business, sir?

George thought not. He was becoming increasingly uncomfortable in this place. The heavy stone slimed walls, roughsawn planks thrown up in crowded barracks, the greasy, shifty turnkey smiling through black and broken teeth.

"Can Stockwell render useful service? He is not a complete fool?"

"O bless you, no, sir. Like I said, he's slow but he's strong and he doesn't mind the work. He'll keep it up all day, never moans, never says nothin' really. I think you might find him very useful, sir."

"I need to talk to him. When will he be back?"

"Should be in the next hour or two, sir. Can't always be sure. Three's a certainty."

"Very well. Then I shall return in three hours. And thank you for your assistance."

George pressed a coin into the turnkey's hand and the man touched it to his brow.

"He'll be waiting for you, sir."

He watched the gentleman walk away and scratched his chin. Funny business, this. What's a gentleman doing here, eh? Why didn't he get some flunkey to pick the item up and bring it to him? Cos he doesn't want no one to know, that's why. He's one of those dirty sods, like that drunken captain who used to come down and bugger 'em til they bled. He rubbed his hands. The captain's patronage had been an excellent little earner.

It was more like five hours when George returned, dragging his feet; the sun was down behind the blue mountains and the barracks were dark in shadow.

The turnkey's smile did nothing to lighten his mood.

"If you'll step this way, sir. I've had Stockwell moved to more comfortable quarters, private like, where you can," he paused, was that a wink? "interview him at your leisure."

George followed the fellow in silence across the parade ground towards the southern fence where three small sheds stood apart from the cluster of buildings. "This is where the more recalcitrant felons," the turnkey laboured proudly over the fine words, "learn their ways."

"But you said Stockwell was, o never mind." George could not be bothered and watched in morose silence as the turnkey raised the beam from its supports. Then watched from the doorway as the turnkey scurried in.

"A little light, sir. Here we go."

A flint struck and a brace of candles lit the room. It was not unlike Richard's shack at Rangihoua in dimension but there was no window to light a bay and the air was warm and still and foetid. The candles stood upon an upturned crate, glinting their yellow light on a glass and a bottle. "For your comfort, sir; out of me own pocket but I don't doubt you'll see me right." As in Richard's home, the floor was packed earth but it was foul and stained. A small chair stood beside the crate; there was no other furniture. Two staunchions, only a few feet apart, were set against the opposite wall. From each extended a chain that reached to the wrists of the man standing between them.

"Richard Stockwell at your service, sir."

George stared curiously at the figure before him, erect against the wall, eyes downcast upon the floor, utterly passive.

Thoughts came skittering, splintering his focus...*There is an obscenity here, the despair, the helplessness* ... And then ... *But for my father's wealth and influence, this could have been* ...

He clapped his hands suddenly and the turnkey jumped. There was no movement from the convict.

He gestured at the chains.

"Remove them."

The turnkey shook his head. "Can't do that, sir," he answered. "Super's orders."

And now the discomfort was becoming something much more forceful and he near panted as he spoke again.

"Remove the chains. And wait outside. I will call if I require assistance."

The turnkey was approaching alarm now at the staring eyes, the grinding teeth.

"But," he said.

"Do it."

And then the magic words.

"I will take responsibility."

The turnkey nodded and the chains fell to the floor. Then he was gone and George was in the chair, head in hands, trying to think.

After a time his breathing eased and he looked up again. The convict had made no sound or movement throughout the exchange, eyes still fixed upon the floor.

"Please," George flapped a hand, "sit down." His voice was a croak.

Stockwell sank where he had stood, legs crossed, hands in his lap, eyes still down. Like a child on the mat.

"Richard." There was no response. "Richard", again, "I mean you no harm. I wish to help you."

Still nothing.

George struggled for a new beginning. "How do you find it here?"

The blankness of the answering gaze seemed to underline the stupidity of the question.

It is as you see it.

George tried again.

"Jane Kendall," he waited for a response but there was none, "Jane Kendall is concerned about your situation."

Still nothing.

"Would you like to be taken out of this place?"

A meaningless shrug.

George was torn between pity, how could he not know? and exasperation. Exasperation won.

"For God's sake, man, how could you not want to be out of this place? What would not be preferable?"

Ah God, this was not the way to do it.

"Look," he paused, "Richard, I can help you to a better place than this. Don't you want that?"

At last Richard spoke. "I want," he said slowly, "to be where I'm supposed to be. To do what I'm supposed to do." He raised his hands and gestured vaguely about the cell. "That's here. Doing this."

I can't believe this.

"But why?"

Now Richard was more composed. He had his answer ready. "Because," he said, "I have done a great sin and God says I must be punished."

George shook his head, wondering. "How can you know this?"

"The chaplain told me. God told him. I have done a great sin and must be punished."

"The chaplain explained that this was the proper life for you?"

"Yes. He said I have the body of a brute and the mind of a brute so I must live as a brute. He made me say that until I had it right."

"Ah, Christ ..."

"It is wrong to take the name of the Lord Thy God in vain."

George fell forward in his chair and stared at the filthy earth and spoke to it.

"I want to take you out of this place, Richard. To where you can be with kind people and …" He gestured helplessly and the words trailed away.

"I have done this before," said Richard.

What! O God, has he become deranged? More deranged?

"I have sat in a cell like this and talked like this with a man like you. He wrote a letter, too, and I was taken out of the hold to live with kind people." He held up his hands. "And here I am."

And an avalanche of events was reduced to a simple equation.

"It need not happen again, Richard. I will take you out of here and you can come to live with me and my family. You will labour without shackles in open fields, by yourself if you wish. You will feel the soft, damp grass beneath your feet, you can sit in the shade of a gum and listen to the cockatoos and watch lizards in the sun."

There was a new reception in Richard's eyes.

"And you can grow things, fruit and vegetables and shrubs and flowers, too. And instead of a pick you will feel the earth under your fingers."

"And be by myself?"

"If you wish."

"Because, you see," Richard was carefully making his way, "it could happen again."

George stared dumbly.

You think my wife is going to seduce you?

"That is impossible."

Impossible like dumpy Jane Kendall, pious, upright Jane Kendall taking you to her bed?

"You," George flapped a hand helplessly, "you bear a great lust with you? You would take a woman against her will?"

Richard looked puzzled, but there was a new alertness here.

"I cannot imagine such a thing," he said, "but the chaplain says I have the mind of a brute so I suppose it might be possible.

"Altogether," he concluded, "I think it would be best if I stay where I am."

It was his longest speech in a year.

George sat dumbfounded. For the first time in a long time he was completely out of his depth. There was a madness here that was so resolute, so committed to any kind of pain, seeking it out even, that it overwhelmed him. It was all beyond him and it was too awful and he could not abide it. He could not bring this man to his home. He could not have him around his children.

He jumped abruptly to his feet. "I must collect myself," he said, "I need to clear my head." He hurried out of the cell, leaving the door open behind him, leaving Richard staring after him, waiting for the turnkey to come in and tell him what to do. His step became a run and all the anxiety and adrenaline flooded through him and it became a flight from panic. He broke into the open yard and into the dark, gulping at the fresh air. Only then could he collect himself, panting quietly in the shadows.

He strode across the yard and wished the sentry a good night. The man tipped his cap at the courtesy. Then he was alone, marching furiously along the empty street. It was some time and several miles before it dawned upon him that he had forgotten his horse. But there was no way he was going back for it.

CHAPTER 30

A sliver of moon slipped between flapping drapes, lighting on two pairs of knees, one pair clad in a dark skirt that fell to buckled pumps. White kid gloves held a shapeless material bag. The knees opposite were in dark frock trousers reaching over polished boots. These hands were pale in the moonlight, bony fingers under sparse black hairs. The faces were pale now, newly arrived from an English winter, pale and pinched in the shifting shadows of the carriage as it rolled and bounced along a stoney road.

"I thought the evening went well," said the woman. "Didn't you?"

The man ran thumb and forefinger down a long, pointed nose.

"Let us consider," he said, counting points on his fingers, "one, an excellent lamb and an acceptable wine." He looked at his hand. "Perhaps that's two things."

"The service was not all it could have been; you were right to observe it."

"Thank you, it needed to be said but," he was moving into a more expansive mood, "it was only a small thing."

"A bagatelle," his wife agreed, then, "Mrs Marsden is a delightful lady. She bears her disability with great firmness of spirit."

It had been a much easier occasion than their first meeting when Marsden had displayed a most disagreeable disposition. He had not been apprised of the appointment of John Butler as the new Superintendant of New Zealand, nor the stores keeper, nor the blacksmith, nor the unannounced arrival of them all at once. He had stood, letter from the Society in hand gazing up from the words to Butler's face and back again. His face was mottled, his free hand clenched and unclenched and Butler felt accused.

"This appears to be disagreeable news, Chaplain," he said. "I hope you do not hold me accountable for it."

"Of course not," Marsden recovered himself, "I would just sooner," he recovered himself again, "but no matter, no matter, we must settle these things as best we can. Accomodations may be a problem, I don't have houses waiting for unexpected guests to drop in ..." Another recovery. "There is one agreeable set of rooms but the others, I fear, will be cramped."

John had suggested that arrangements be made with reference to domestic standing. Mr Hall, for example, was a single man and Mr and Mrs Kemp were childless. He on the other hand had wife and child ...

Hall and Kemp had not demurred and John was pleased. He had not needed to point out his role as leader and yet he had asserted it

But Marsden's mood had not improved. He had been mindful enough to attend to their arrangements and then had hurried them on their way. "Leaving him free," Mrs Butler said later, "to vent."

No, this last gathering had been much easier. Kemp and his wife were quiet folk; they would know their place and labour with him. Francis Hall was an odd young fellow, a bit wishy-washy. "Mr On-the-Other-Hand," Mary had called him. Bit talkative but respectful; John believed they would work well together. There had not really been a call for leadership on the boat, just the running of meetings for prayer and preparation. But now they would cohere as a beacon for the heathen.

"And you spoke well, John," said Mary Butler. "I could see that Mr Marsden was impressed by your ideas of leadership in the colony."

"Thank you, Mary, I think he was, too." His voice dropped. "But it will be no easy task."

"Indeed not. The settlement sounds as though it were run by the Inmates of Bedlam."

"Sodom and Gomorrah might be more apt. Kendall's tale is an alarming one. The wife of a missionary rogered by a convict retard."

Mrs Butler's lips snapped shut. "As to that," she said, "am I to receive her? How am I to receive her? This will be very awkward."

"Mm," John mused. "Yet it would seem that she and her husband are reconciled, or at least living together. To shun her would be to affront him and him I cannot avoid. I think our judgment must needs be mute."

"And so I shall take her hand," said Mary Butler, "and bid her good day. As her wickedness poisons me I shall smile and take her hand. Ah,

John," she shook her head, "the sacrifices begin even before we get there." Faded kidgloves folded in prayer.

Then there was a yell from the driver and a fightened whinny from the horses and the carriage was jerking and tilting. For a moment, it leaned perilously, two wheels off the ground and Mary plunged forward and sideways from her seat, face first into John's rising knee. Then the air borne wheels thudded back on to the road and she fell into the well between the seats.

He helped her back to her place, torn between anxiety and rage.

"Are you alright? Have you taken some hurt?"

She patted her face, nothing broken, but doubtless there would be a bruise to show for it later, and now he could surrender to rage. He tore open the door and sprang out on to the road.

The horses were still unsettled, stamping and shaking their heads. "Steady, steady." The brake was on and the reins still taut as the driver sought to calm them.

"You stupid whoreson," John roared at him. "What do you think you're doing?"

Intent upon his task, the driver made no answer but there was another voice, up by the horses' heads.

"Do not blame Mr Smithers, he did well to avoid an accident. The fault was mine." A man was standing there, either hand upon a horse's bit, keeping them still.

John was not placated. "Then you are the stupid whoreson," he snarled. "My wife has taken some harm through your actions."

"No, John," Mary was beside him, tugging his arm, "I will be alright, pray, be still."

John thrust her hand away. "No, Mary," he said, "I will not be still. This damned idiot could have killed us both."

The man's face was pale beneath his tan and his eyes were bright. "I apologise," he began.

"Damn your apologies." John shook his fist. "I should – " He stopped as the man stepped away from the horses and clapped his hands, hard and sudden.

"Excellent," he said, "the very thing."

"What? What are you babbling about? Are you drunk as well as stupid? What very thing?"

The man rubbed his hands. "The very thing," he said again.

And now the driver interceded. "Hello," he said, "is that you, Mr Egan? Are you alright, sir? You took a nasty tumble there, what were you thinking, marching down the middle of the road in the dark and all. Didn't you hear us coming?"

John stared. "Do you know this man?" he demanded.

"Indeed, sir. This is Mr Egan, he is a church minister, sir."

"That only makes it worse. What is a minister doing, staggering drunkenly down the middle of the King's Highway, a danger to all – " He stopped as the man pointed at him.

"Fuck you," he said.

"Oo," shrilled Mary. "What is this?"

"Yes," said the man, "and fuck you, too."

John's fists were balled and he was advancing on the wretch, but his movement was hampered by the driver on one side and his wife on the other.

"No, John," she hissed. "Recollect yourself, *look at him.*"

In the light of the carriage lantern, John could see his antagonist clearly now, a tall man, matching John for height, but more heavily built. But it was the face that stopped him, the eyes wide, unblinking, lips drawn back over a hungry, feral grin.

He submitted to his wife's arm.

"I can see you are not well, sir," he said through gritted teeth. "I would urge you to seek assistance." Then he took his wife's hand and helped her back into the carriage. "To our lodging, Smithers," he said. But Smithers was ignoring him, crossing to the wretch, speaking quickly, urgently. Then he was back at the reins and John was steadying himself against the lurching carriage.

He breathed deeply while Mary patted his hand.

"You did very well, John," she said. "To walk away from such provocation showed firm control and good judgment."

They sat in silence now or rather in the scattered rhythms of iron hooves and wheels. Then they were pulling up at their lodgings and Smithers was at the door.

"There we go, madam. Shall I take the bag?" he reached forward.

Mrs Butler drew back sharply. "Do not grasp, man," she said. "And give me room."

"My apologies, madam," Smithers knuckled his forehead and stepped back. But he was clearly anxious to be gone, shutting the carriage door behind John before he was barely out of it. John's lips tightened and he seemed about to speak and then to think better of it. Instead he said, "You did well tonight, Smithers. Had you not pointed the man out I might have thrashed him unknowing."

"Indeed, sir, good evening sir, madam." Smithers touched his hat and clambered back to his seat. John and Mary watched him urge the horses on but instead of continuing on to the ostlers' yard he was backing and turning them.

John flung up a hand. "What are you doing? Where are you taking the carriage?"

"Back to Mr Egan, sir. I do not think he is well; he may need help."

John was suddenly angry. "He needs a smack in the head," he said, "the foul-mouthed drunken, he was quite drunk, you know –"

"He must have been," said Mary, "to behave so."

"I do not think he was drunk, sir, but he is not well." John and Mary both stared at the contradiction. "I need to go now."

"Well," said John, "perhaps you don't."

"Would you have me leave him there?"

"I don't see why not," John began, then broke of as his wife squeezed his wrist. "What Mr Butler means to say, Smithers, is that we are conscious of the Christian example that is required of us. Now that Mr Eganisthatit? has had time to settle himself and is less likely to become overexcited by strangers, it would be a worthy deed to attend to him." She patted her husband's hand. "Is that not so, Mr Butler?"

"Yes," he agreed. "What is holding you, man? Be off with you."

Alas, the Chaplain did not share Mrs Butler's estimation of her husband's qualities.

Two days later he was sitting with Elizabeth before the parlour fire, brooding, finding less and less to like about the new man.

"Perhaps you ascribe to him some of the Society's fault," she said.

"Mmph," Samuel grunted. "He made the same point the first time I met him. But this is a matter apart. The man's a bully, Elizabeth, thoughtless and proud."

"Certainly," Elizabeth agreed, "his manner towards Mr and Mrs Kemp and young Mr Hall was not courteous. And I was not pleased by the way he spoke to Mrs Bishop."

"Indeed, I was hard pressed to refrain from reproaching the fellow."

Elizabeth nodded. "I am pleased that you did not."

Samuel leaned across and patted her hand, her right hand, the hand that could respond.

"I thought Mr and Mrs Kemp very pleasant people," she said. "Sensible people. I would expect Mr Kemp to run the stores in a thorough manner. And Mr Hall is a good young man."

"Bit talkative, I thought. Wishy-washy, not what you'd expect from such a strapping lad."

"He is a good young man."

"This will be the settlement's third Hall, you know; Walter Hall, blacksmith, William Hall, builder and now Francis Hall, a blacksmith again."

"Walter Hall" said Elizabeth. "Wasn't that the man who tried to shoot Thomas Kendall?"

"Only after Kendall tried to stick a chisel in him."

Elizabeth's smile was lopsided. "Lord, Samuel," she said, "there is farce in this."

"Aye." Samuel did not smile in response. "But I fear there is more of tragedy."

"Yes." The smile was gone. "Kendall, Hall, King and Butler. You can't see them being at peace."

"Yes." A shake of the head. "And we will find out soon enough. I must return to Rangihoua, Elizabeth and it will be a lengthy stay. McQuarrie has agreed to six months, I am perplexed that he has authority in this, but hopefully we will not need that long anyway. It began again as soon as my back was turned."

Elizabeth understood he was speaking of the trade in muskets.

"We should be gone in six weeks. Take Butler and Co with me, and then we will see what happens." He sighed.

"I am sorely tested, Elizabeth."

She gave a lopsided smile. "As you have been before. And yet you prevail. You can only do the best you can and trust in the Lord for the rest."

Samuel smiled. "My wise wife," he said. "So," he heaved himself out of his chair. "I will away to my study to do the best I can. There is correspondence I must tend to. Is there anything you need? Shall I send for Mrs Bishop? No? Well, your bell is at hand." He bent down and kissed the fine, grey locks.

He entered his study with resolute purpose. He crossed to his desk to raise the wick on the lamp and the light folded across the drapes and glowed on dark panels. A brighter halo lit a pile of letters and he took them up, glancing at each in turn. There was one addressed in an unfamiliar hand; legible enough but it could have been written by a child.

Dear Mr Marsden, he read.

"I regret to advise that my Husband has suffered a Collapse. Surgeon Biggs calls it an Indisposition of the Nerves but he cannot Guess at how long it will Endure. He Fears that it might be Quite Some Time before Mr Egan can Perform his Duties again. At the moment he is Subject to Much Anxiety and Begs that he be Released from his Ministry. Surgeon Biggs concurs that this would be best both for Mr Egan's Health and for the Health of the Parish.

The chaplain's fists clenched over the letter. So, Biggs, agnostic and not the least ashamed of it, had Opinions on what was best for the parish, did he?

His temper showed no improvement for having to fold the paper out and press out the creases.

At the moment Mr Egan is in a Fragile Way and is best left Undisturbed. Surgeon Biggs has recommended walks in the countryside and perhaps some undemanding work in the fields. I shall report any progress.

I have the Honour to Remain

Your Obedient Servant

Joanna Egan.

Samuel stared gloomily down at the childish hand. Another sorry pass. He wondered what condition Egan was in, what was a 'fragile way'? Perhaps he should, no, she had said he was best left undisturbed. What could have brought it on, he seemed perfectly fine the last time they met, a little pensive perhaps but he had always been a thoughtful chap. How would Joanna and the children manage? No, that was not a problem, they'd had a fine harvest and their work gang was the best in the colony. The farm could run itself. And Joanna was eminently capable.

So what was this 'nervous indisposition'? Damn the woman, she'd told him next to nothing. Release from the ministry? Surely not, surely Egan was over-reacting. By the same token though, a man in a Fragile Way would be out of place in a pulpit.

So. He was losing Egan and gaining Butler. It was altogether too bad. Abruptly he seized the malevolent letter and thumped from the room.

"But Samuel, this is terrible news. Poor George. And what of Joanna and the children? We must do something."

"Aye, but what?" He read, *cannot guess at how long it will endure... best left undisturbed ...progress to be reported.* "Sounds like 'stay away' to me."

"This is so unlike Joanna."

"It's so unlike Egan. "Nervous indisposition', man's as fit as a buck rat."

"I must write to Joanna immediately; I must know more." Then she fell silent and her eyes closed.

She is praying for them, thought Samuel and he closed his own eyes. *Lord, tend to Thy Servant Egan. Bring him clarity and strength of mind again. Make him well so that he may serve again in Thy Name.*

Amen.

CHAPTER 31

Hokianga Winter 1818

John King was unclear about what to pray for. Had he thought about it, a soft dry bed and easy repose would be agreeable, but hardly worthy of prayer. So he lay on the damp manuka and buried his face behind the collar of his great coat, breathing away from the acrid air. His clothes were tied tightly at throat, wrist and ankles but there was no defending his face or hands and he scratched at the itching on his neck.

The flea is a creature of God, it has its place and purpose. It bites without malice or meaning but I cannot help but hate it.

But it was a feeble hatred without intensity or direction and like the pain on his neck it seemed to stand at a distance from him. He muttered and turned and the manuka scratched lightly at his cheek. Near the centre of the whare some half dozen men were seated around the last of the fire. Caught in the light of winking embers and wreathed in shadow and the smoke of their pipes they might have been wraiths, warrior tupuna in feathered cloak and moko. Except for the small pakeha, sat cross-legged on his coat. His eyes glittered red from the fire and smoke, deep in dark circles as he pointed and gestured in the passion of his korero.

King had a greater grasp of te reo now but the man's speech was low and swift and the snores of those who lay between them muffled its sense. Yet a few words came across, te aroha o te ariki nui, the love of God Almighty, and King understood that he was listening to a sermon. Kendall never stopped, he could resist no opportunity to advance the word and the yawns and a man lying where he had sat served only to intensify him.

King wondered at the energy. These days he could find little of his own. He called it lethargy and a sin and would have berated himself for it. But he lacked the inclination so he merely looked at it and carried on. In truth, he would not have been without it for the numbness carried a quietness and kind of peace.

He was not without feeling but it was more contained now and had been so ever since the death of his son. While Hannah and her mother and sobbed and railed like bereft wahine, and King had feared that they might even mutilate themselves, he had sat quietly beside the still, small boy and felt a part of himself die with him.

And everything came to mean less. Particularly his own understanding. He could not understand why God would take his boys away. He thought perhaps he was being punished, that there was utu here, or that he was being tested like Job. But it was all rather vague and he could not follow the thoughts through. So they hung like dust in the sun and he watched them and shook his head in helpless sorrow. He did not curse God, he did not even blame God because it was all too much for him.

He simply set about his work as best he could because there was nothing else to do and nothing really mattered anyway.

So when Kendall had spoken of the expansion of the mission and had asked for a man to accompany him to the Hokianga to explore the possibilities there King had raised his hand. Kendall had looked at him in some surprise, then had smiled and nodded.

"Thank you, brother," he said and thought, perhaps this might be the means to restore you to yourself. Perhaps God has brought you to me that I may help you become whole again.

Over the next few days as they had crossed fields and picked their way along scant trails through the heavy, twisting bush he had engaged his brother in earnest talk. King had listened for a while but then had tired of it and listened to the birds instead. Kendall's words beat like muffled wings behind their song, occasionally intruding.

"Sometimes our deepest sorrows may seem as a cloud that hides us from the love of God. And in our loneliness we may be tempted to despair. Turn from despair, my brother, and look to the light of the Lord."

And then a tui chimed and the words flew away.

"I know what it is to lose a child."

But you do not know what it is to lose all of your children.

"We have our purpose, John, and it is our salvation. It will lead us to oneness with God and then you will see your boys again."

Then I must die first.

The thought was not a disagreeable one and though King would have shrunk from wishing it, he would also have understood the words being penned a world away …I have been half in love with easeful Death.

Kendall could not remain silent. He prayed and sang and that was pleasant for he had a good voice and King listened for a while. There was more talk of purpose but King's was now confined to placing one foot carefully before the other and ducking before the embracing rata.

Then he was watching vast kauri that reached into the sky along the water's edge and the silver drops that flew from the paddles. And always at the back of his mind he was remembering, my boy is gone. He had learned that it was important to hold to the memory; on occasion he had become immersed in the silhouette of a tree on the sky line or the sun upon his back and had quite forgotten. Then when the memory returned it had come as a hammer blow and he had near fainted with the horror of it. So it was important to guard himself and he wore his sorrow as a protective cloak.

It was harder to block Kendall out now, for he was not deterred by the absence of a listener. He did, however, tend to lose direction and his monologue fragmented on his own concerns and he moved into incautious soliloquy.

"Do not despair, my brother. It is the final sin, for to despair is to deny all hope and that is to deny God. Rather, we should rejoice in our trials for in our endurance we may prove ourselves worthy of His Love and salvation."

King stared impassively at the water.

This is a death bed sermon. I have used it, myself.

"But," and there was a break in Kendall's voice, "there should be something, not a miracle, we do not ask for that, but something for our support. We struggle and sacrifice and endure and endure and at the end there is the taste of ashes and the laughter of men. You take your gifts, humbly thanking God and you use them to do His work. You burn the midnight oil, you put your sight at risk, and you produce the beginning of an understanding of the heathen tongue. This is no small thing. It is no great thing neither, I would not be so proud, but it is a key to communication that may turn the locks of the heathen heart. Is it unworthy to ask for a little recognition? Should I sit in humble obscurity while others take credit for my work? I do not ask for praise but surely, dear God, surely I am within my rights to *assist* in its production, to ensure that the labours done for God's love are not wasted. It would be wrong, a rejection of my responsibility to do otherwise."

King understood that he was speaking of his dictionary. He had taken little interest before, thinking the teacher boastful, and he showed none now. The words beat away but something of the tone remained.

"The school has failed," Kendall nodded to himself, "and I have failed with it. It is my failure, not Marsden's, though a pittance would have saved it. The lessons are gone and the children forget; Christ is quite forgotten as they watch their fathers war. I stand on empty ground and call my message to the air. And none hear me. Even Jane, ah Christ ..." Then his face was in his hands and his shoulders shook.

In the same way as King's hand had raised to volunteer, now it settled on Kendall's arm.

"Do not despair," he said.

CHAPTER 32

"Another letter from the chaplain."

George stared at it gloomily.

"Ah, shit," he said. "I hate this."

They sat in silence and jasmine beneath the southern cross, sat on the veranda of their spacious home, looking north across rolling, moonlit fields.

The years had been kind to them. For one not long since laid low by a nervous indisposition, George was a picture of health; tanned, lean, fit. He and Joanna both. The new Australians. But now his brow was lowered and his tone spoke of complaint.

"It'll be the same thing," he said. "In everyone's prayers, speedy recovery, return to duty …"

Joanna nodded. "True," she said, "he means well."

"And that's half the problem. He leaves me nothing to resist."

"You're not thinking of going back?"

"God, no." George paused. "That was vehement, wasn't it? Just the thought. But we hadn't thought how to escape from this bit." He sighed and raised his hands in supplication. "So how the fuck do we handle this bit? What are we going to do?"

"About Marsden?"

"About all of it. But yes, in the first place, about Marsden. And I am all over the place with him. I respect him, I despise him, I am beholden to him and I resent him for it, I feel hostile, I feel defensive."

Joanna finished it for him. "You feel lost."

"Yes," George nodded. "I do feel lost. And I feel like a coward, too." He looked at her sadly. "We're not free, Jo. We're still trapped within lies."

"And we've added to them," said Joanna and George loved her for her understanding and agreement.

"We are popular within the community," he said slowly, "and there are many who would account us friends. But they're not. We have no friends. Who would forgive us for our deceit, out fraud?"

"You have made fools of us," Joanna spoke for the community. "And we have made liars of us. But it didn't matter before. Why should it matter now? Can't friends have secrets? Must everything be shared? Damn," as a wail broke in, "feeding time." She rose from her easy chair and headed into the house/

George gazed into the night as his thought wandered back.

To his father's ultimatum.

The man sat behind a dark, mahogany desk (always at a distance) and his face was pale in the lamp light.

"This cannot continue."

More control and distance and George prepared himself for a lecture.

"I have seen no change in your behavior since our last conversation and now I cannot but believe that none will be forthcoming."

George smiled behind his hand. Cannot but believe? Such convolution. Why must he talk this way?

"And I can tolerate it no longer. The idleness, the insolence ... and now in the public eye ... reports of tavern brawls ..."

His voice faded and George moved scarred knuckles to his lap.

"And so I am resolved. I will fund this lifestyle no longer. You are on your own."

There was a finality to the tone that brought George to a new level of attention. His mouth was dry and he licked his lips, looking towards the cabinet where the wine was stored. His father followed his eyes.

"The cabinet is locked, sir, and will remain so. There is no refuge for you there."

And now a softer tone.

"Ah, George, can you see what you are doing to yourself? You have so much ability, you could be ... (was that a break in the modulation?)... Anyway, it is as I have said. You must go."

And now George was all attention (*Christ, he really means this*) and his mouth was very dry.

"Where?" he croaked.

"I don't know. Anywhere. But not here."

And the tone softened again.

"I would not see you destitute and will assist you. But it must be into change. I have given this much thought and there are three options that may work. One," he counted off a finger, "you could take a commission in the armed services. The army, I think. You ride well and are more than a passing shot. But it would need to be overseas."

George stared mutely as his father continued.

"Two, you might find a place in the diplomatic corps. Three, you could join the church."

George stared.

"You think I am mocking you. And given your views on religion, I will grant there is some irony here. But consider: it is secure employment and may provide a gateway elsewhere. And so long as you are out of England, I will provide support that may speed you to that gateway. And you know enough of church doctrine to mock it. Perhaps you could put it to more positive use."

"And be an utter hypocrite? Preach that which I disbelieve?"

His father shook his head. "I don't know. Perhaps there will be no call to preach. Perhaps you could preach what you believe." He paused. "You must believe something. Anyway," suddenly abrupt and final, "you will need to give this much thought and I'll give you time for it. There may be other options you wish to explore, letters to write, counsel to take. I don't know," suddenly muttering, "how the hell could I know? Anyway," pulling himself back on track, "consider it. Goodnight."

The conversation had ended then and George had left the house with 'you must believe something' playing in his head.

Over the next few weeks he found himself moving to a new space. And it was strange because instead of the fear and resentment that might have been anticipated, he found excitement.

And a confirmation of loneliness as his drinking companions proved not to have a single, worthwhile idea between them. A lot of understanding and sympathy, of course (*how dare he, what could he be thinking, he's your father, for Christ's sake*) but nothing of any use.

He also realized that he needed to make some far-reaching decisions and that alcohol was not assisting the process.

He felt quite alone and thought that he found a kind of freedom in it. And the excitement continued.

Perhaps, most strangely of all, in the midst of all this chaos, he made a friend, a most unlikely friend.

George had always liked Joanna Kelly. Where another bargirl might simper and faun, she was direct and straightforward. He thought he could believe what she told him.

She was attractive too and more than once he had given thought to proposing a more intimate connection but something had held him back. Perhaps he had valued the liking and had not wanted to risk it.

Her reaction to his dilemma brought a perspective that aligned with the one he was developing.

"Well, well," she said, "what an adventure."

And perhaps that was at the heart of the new excitement. For when he looked back at his life, it seemed little more than a series of distractions, anything to break the monotony.

You must believe something.

"You think I should go along with my father's plan?"

"What other choice do you have?"

"Very well; and which career should I pick?"

"How the hell should I know? What do you think?"

"Well," George considered. "I think we can immediately exclude the army. The idea of a career based on keeping the natives in their place holds no appeal. And the diplomatic corps would amount to the same thing and that within the web of a bureaucracy." He shuddered. "No, thank you."

"Which leaves the church."

"Which is the most preposterous."

"Why?"

"Why?" George stared at her. "Because I don't believe a word of it."

"Really?"

At this point George realized that Joanna was taking a serious interest in the conversation. She was asking questions, for God's sake. Nobody asks questions: they just wait for you to stop talking, so they can tell you something.

"Well," he said, "I suppose I don't have any issues with the teachings of Christ, the parables and all that, but as for the rest of it, the trinity, divinity, salvation and," his voice rose, "what the church has done with it…" He flapped his hands and relapsed into silence.

He watched Joanna as she considered his position.

She is giving this thought. How unusual. Most people have an answer ready before you've finished framing the question.

"I think," she said at last, "that the church is your best option. You can leave it if you want, probably with less difficulty than you would with the army or the diplomatic corpse, why do they call it a body?"

"The word is corps, no 'e', pronounced core."

"Ah," she nodded. "And the money from your father along with your pay from the church might set you up for some new chance."

"That's what my father said."

"A sensible man." She pointed a finger. "Not quite the bastard you have made him out to be."

George was beginning to agree. This new space was throwing up all sorts of new considerations. "I suppose I have brought him some grief," he said. "And he has been patient." He grunted. "Up til now."

"So what drove you?"

George shook his head. "I really don't know. The best I can come up with is that I was bored and the drinking and all that was a way of distracting myself."

"Boredom? That's all?"

George grinned sourly. "It was enough for Young Werther to top himself."

"Young who?"

"Werther. A character in a novel." He waved the thought away.

"A penny for 'em."

"Eh?" George looked up, startled.

"So where were you?"

George smiled. "I was sitting," he said, "in a common pub with a buxom Irish barkeep, planning my life."

"Ah," Joanna nodded, "I remember her. And how has it worked out?"

"Surprisingly well." He grimaced. "Up til now."

And surprisingly quickly and all within his father's time limit. The final decision had been a mixture of cynicism and avoidance: take the position his father would negotiate/buy for him, settle in, fudge for as long as possible, accumulate funds, then look to see what other options might be available and …

Which left one last issue.

Sitting in the snug, sober, sipping upon coffee. Without any conscious decision or vow (that would come later) he had stopped drinking alcohol. Listening, sober, to the conversation of drunks had added to the process and he was surprised at how easy it had been. And now his mind raced with a thousand possibilities and an excited anticipation.

"There is one more thing," he said. "I have been considering the make-up of the society I will be entering. It will be a shrunken one, harder, more primitive, shaped towards survival. There will be no theatres, concerts, libraries …"

"Ah," said Joanna, "you think you may be bored again."

George considered. "I suppose I might," he answered, "but that was not the concern." He looked away from her and studied his hands. "I think I might be lonely," he said softly.

"That," said Joanna, "I do not understand. You've told me you have no friends here –"

"I have one."

"Thank you. I like you, too. But why should that be a concern? It hasn't mattered so far."

"I don't know why, but it has become important."

I have known many people; some would say we were friends, others would say we were enemies. It's easier to be clear about the enemies. And one after another, I have walked away from them, sometimes in abrupt rejection, sometimes in indifference. And it is always indifference in the end.

I have never sought out companionship. It has arisen incidentally, connecting to where I was and what I was doing. And when I was no longer there or doing that, the connection was gone. I never wrote nor inquired after those I had known.

And my relationships with women were much the same. Arising incidentally. And just as empty.

Joanna had watched him closely through the silence. And now she said, "You are accusing yourself."

George's eyes rose to her face. "I am," he said. Then, "how did you know?"

Joanna smiled. "It's a common enough sight in a tavern," she said, "the face of a man lost in accusation. Normally it's directed at someone else and most end up that way. But that's not what you're doing. There's a sadness upon you, and fear, too," the brogue became more pronounced, "and now you're looking away and there is shame in that. No," she was clear, "you are accusing yourself."

George smiled wanly. "So I am," he said, "should I now give my confession?"

"The papists say it is good for the soul."

"In which I do not believe. But still," he spoke to his hands again. "Forgive me, Joanna, for I have sinned. I have been a poor friend and an uncaring son. It would seem that I do not care. I take, but I do not give." He shook his head and closed his eyes.

His vulnerability called to her and she fought the urge to lean forward and take his hand. Then she thought, fuck it, and took it anyway.

"Listen," she said slowly as she tied the thought together. "A man who cares that he does not care cannot be said not to care."

Like the trouble with people who do not know do not know that they do not know.

George smiled. "Kind and clever," he said. "And, I hope, true. But when I look behind me, I see nothing of kindness. Nor of cleverness, neither."

"Alright, then," Joanna agreed. "It would seem that you have been a right royal prick."

Another rush of another feeling.

This was not how it was supposed to go.

But now there was no escape.

"People have been the vehicle for my purposes." He saw her confusion. "They have served a purpose or they have not. Men and women both."

"Yes," she broke in. "I have seen you with women, seen you compete for them, take them as prizes." She paused, then continued. "I have wondered, God, I can't believe what I am about to say, but what the hell, have wondered why you never approached me that way."

George smiled again. "I have thought about it, of course," he said. "You are an attractive woman. But I think I know the reason why I never approached you; it was because I liked you too much."

And now it was Joanna's turn to be unsettled.

"Well," she said at last. "There is some caring in that."

"But it was all in my own interest."

Joanna tutted and her tone became sharper. "You are determined, I see," she said, "to stay with the prosecution."

"I need to stay with all of this." Joanna could hear the underlining of the words. "This is … huge. It cannot be ignored. I must stay with it."

They sat in silence for a while as George considered. Then he said, "I have given this much thought. For the first time in my life I am required to take a stand. I must make a momentous decision that will shape my life; and it is one that I cannot retreat from. And with all this, I found a new need: someone to talk to. Someone to listen, to understand."

To be on my side.

"And you have been here for me, Joanna. How many times have I taken up your time with my troubles? Taking you from your work? Your father will not be best pleased."

"My father is delighted with the arrangement. His prices for coffee are outrageous."

"Really?"

"And, if you hadn't noticed, custom is declining. There is no need of me at the bar."

She became aware that her hand was still on his, but did not make to move it.

"To the point then." He looked directly at her. "Will you come with me on this adventure?"

Now Joanna was truly unsettled and stared at him.

"As my wife, of course," George continued. "I can't imagine the church's being comfortable with my turning up with –"

"Your whore." She finished the thought.

Joanna took the proposal to her parents where, of course, the concern lay with security.

"You could be abandoned, penniless, at the ends of the earth."

"He says himself that he is an uncaring wretch. How can you trust him?"

"Do you even care for him?"

"I think I am fond of him."

"You think?"

"Alright then. I am fond of him."

"Why?"

"I don't know. He touches me somehow."

"And that is enough for you to ruin your life?"

In the end they decided that the security concerns could be dealt with: George could guarantee her a measure of financial independence, at least enough to return to England, should the need arise. Or a settlement could be made upon her parents. Or something.

And in the end she found the answer to it all was a simple one.

For all his faults, I like George. He interests me more than any man I have known. I learn from him and I like that. I believe he is fond of me.

But more than anything, I am caught up in his adventure. And I want it, too. If I stay here, marry into a measure of security, raise a family with ... who? A man who might bore me? A man I cannot talk to? I do not think I could spend the rest of my life wondering, what if.

I have to know.

And so it was settled. George and Joanna married in a small ceremony, attended only by her family; qualifications were negotiated, a position was found and tickets purchased.

And then they were gone.

And, thought George, it had worked out, and better than they might have imagined. For a match based upon such a mix of pragmatism and wishful thinking, the marriage was a success. And that –and the boys- had made it all worthwhile.

But now what?

So George proposed a second time. He held Joanna's hands in his as he spoke. "I think," he said, "we need to run away again." He waved an arm, encompassing the house and the fields. "Can you leave this?"

"For what?"

"To start again. Somewhere. Anywhere. But not here. Somewhere where we can say who we are and be easy with it. To be known for who we are ... to have friends."

She squeezed his hands. "So long as I have you and the boys," she paused, "and freedom, that will be enough. So, George Egan," and suddenly she was smiling broadly, "let's run away again. Let's have another adventure."

And so they did.

CHAPTER 33

Hongi sat in the darkness and gazed down at the bones. Below a grey sea rolled and broke on rock and washed away again. He sat in less a cave than a crevice but it was a sacred place, very tapu, because it housed the bones of his third father-in-law. They had lain in the earth for a year before being scraped clean and taken to their final resting place.

But word had come that their home had been profaned and worse, that the bones had been broken and removed and fashioned into fish hooks. If this were true the insult was intolerable and only blood could restore the balance. And this was at the heart of Hongi's purpose. From an early age he had known that the mana of Ngapuhi was central to his life. Steeped in the lore of his tribe and trained in all the arts of war, he was the true rangatira toa, the warrior chief, and his passion for his task was legendary.

It is a wonderful thing when a man's love and talent and meaning fuse together; and such was Hongi's luck. And now as he gazed down at the poor pieces of what had once been his father in law, a few ribs and a part of a skull, he trembled in the purity of his rage and in the anticipation of vengeance.

It would not be a grand affair, not like the recent trips down to the East Coast when great waka filled with hundreds of fighting men had redressed the balance of Ngapuhi mana by taking the lives of those who had defiled the women taken from the *Venus*. That had been a long wait, like vengeance for Moremonui had been a long wait. There had been others that had been longer; it was only time.

But this would be swifter.

Hongi looked again at the bones and the memory of the old, grizzled warrior washed over him and his eyes filled with tears.

"We will right this wrong, e koro," he murmured, "we will take your mana back." Then he eased through the narrow opening and climbed down to the rocks below where his men awaited him.

They edged nervously away from him for he was very tapu now. Later Rakau would perform the correct rites to lift it from him but for the moment any contact could, almost certainly would bring disaster upon the tribe.

"It is as we were told," Hongi told his men. "Tomorrow we will take utu." Then he gestured to the old tohunga and they moved away across the sand and into the bush.

Later they sat on a grassy knoll and watched the moon slip from silver cloud across Rangi's dark sky.

"We will need restraint tomorrow," Hongi said.

Rakau looked at him curiously. "And why is that?" he asked.

Hongi scratched irritably at the sand. "I have told Matene that we will not fight while he is here," he answered. "Fighting offends his god."

Rakau was none the wiser. "You are concerned not to offend his god?"

"No." Hongi shook his head. "I have no regard for his god. His religion is a soft, creeping thing fit only for slaves. But I would not offend Matene.

The pakeha are arriving all the time and others are bidding for them. Te Morenga is trying to persuade Matene to move settlers to his land. I have told Matene that he is not to be trusted and that the settlers will be safest with us. I would not lose their trade, e Rakau, and I would certainly not wish to see Te Morenga secure it."

Rakau nodded, understanding. "By trade," he said, "you mean guns."

"And grain and iron and tools and clothes, but yes, above all, guns." Hongi grinned. "There is already a shipment on its way from Port Jackson that Keni has set up. But I have plans for many more, enough to arm every Ngapuhi warrior. And then, ah Rakau, and then we shall see war and the mana of Ngapuhi will light the land." He paused, then changed tack. "Would you care for Keni's family if he were not here?"

"Ae," Rakau inclined his head. "He has already asked me. I said 'yes'."

They sat in silence for a while, then Hongi rose and Rakau followed him back to the men on the beach.

"Soon," Hongi told them, "Rakau will perform the rites to prepare us for tomorrow. We will travel with the blessing of our tupuna and our deeds will redress the wrong and bring glory to the mana of Ngapuhi." The men shivered in their excitement and stroked the barrels of their guns. "But," Hongi held up an admonitory finger, "there will not be much killing." There was a mutter, a grumble from the warriors but Hongi was unperturbed. He waited quietly, then continued in the same conversational tone. "Ngati Pou are kin to us and Te Pere is much respected throughout Tai Tokerau. We will show our strength and exact utu but there will not be much killing. We will take no heads and we will take no slaves."

It was here, thought Rakau, that Hongi showed the completeness of his mana. There was no bluster, no warnings and there would be no argument.

"We will approach the village in a single, wide spread line. There will be ten paces between each man. Seven will fire upon my command, eight will hold their fire, ready to shoot if we are charged. I do not expect that this will happen. Then we will leave."

An older warrior raised his head. His name was Tipene and he was the veteran of many battles, not the least amongst which was at Morenui when he had fled along the beach with Hongi.

"So eight," he said, "will stand and watch."

"Ae."

"And who will they be?"

The tension was palpable as Hongi gave the names. Yet the men sat silently. But Rakau could see tears welling in the eyes of Pare. A young man, not yet sixteen, this was to have been his first battle. He had dreamed of it and talked endlessly with friends and whanau. Now there would be nothing, no danger, no glory, no wounds. Rakau watched as the tears ran silently down the boy's cheeks. Then he said, "E Hongi, my old eyes do not see so clearly now and my hand is not as steady as it was. Might I exchange my part for Pare's?"

Hongi nodded and the boy's eyes widened and his joy was a tangible thing.

Rakau smiled at him. "You'd better not miss," he said.

They moved silently through the night and into the dawn and then they were upon the Ngati Pou village. Hongi said nothing, there was no need to repeat his instructions and there would be no haka. They slipped like shadows through the pale green light and then on to their bellies as they reached the clearing.

To the villagers they appeared as ghosts rising out of the land, still and grey in the morning light. A child whimpered in the sudden silence before she was hushed against her mother's breast. silently the villagers rose and moved together to stand and wait.

"You have taken the bones of my father-in-law," said Hongi. "You have taken them from their resting place and you have turned them into fish hooks."

A keening sigh swept through the people and they huddled closer together. But none spoke.

What answer could they make? Whether the accusation was true or false, the outcome would be the same. What conqueror had ever retracted the grounds for conquest?

So they moaned and clung to one another and the moment grew and enveloped them all.

Then a young man broke from the crowd and moved towards Hongi. Eyes wide and staring, his tongue licking against his lower lip, he walked stiff-legged and snorted and hissed. A wail broke behind him and swallowed his challenge. Hongi smiled his approval, then shot him through the heart. The shot served as a signal and the young warrior was still flying backwards as the fusillade broke. Four men pitched back under the force of the heavy balls and a girl dropped, fainting, clutching at her shattered shoulder. Pare's shot flew harmlessly through the space where a man had stood a second before and he stared in disbelief at the ground. His mortification was complete.

"And then," said Hongi, "everything was suddenly still. And out of the silence a kaumatua stepped forward. 'Will you stop now?' he asked. 'Is your utu satisfied?'" He raised a fine china cup to his lips and sipped his tea while his words were translated. He smiled vaguely but was listening intently. Refusing to speak English gave him a nice edge; time to consider, time to check and time to retract an ill-chosen word. "I said," he continued, setting his cup down, "that our mana was restored. There was no further korero and we returned home."

Samuel Marsden steepled his hands over pursed lips and closed his eyes. Dear God, he thought, it could well be true.

Like the Whangaroa villagers he made no answer. He could not bring himself from any perspective to accept the situation. He could not countenance the desecration but neither could he endorse the response.

It also rankled that Hongi had deceived him.

"You promised me you would not fight," he said.

Hongi shrugged.

"I only discovered the truth after we had spoken," he said. "Would you have had me ignore it?"

Yet you went looking for the truth with fourteen armed warriors, thought Marsden. But he said, "Will not Ngati Pou seek utu in their turn?"

Hongi shrugged again.

"They have not the strength for it," he said.

And this was at the heart of the matter. Whether or not Ngati Pou had accepted the deaths as legitimate satisfaction, and Marsden was privately inclined to doubt it, it could well be only for the moment. Later they might view it differently.

But there was no point in worrying about it now. The take, causes for war, were as many and as varied as the men who followed them. Only when they accepted the teachings of Christ would the savagery end.

So he said, "I am sorry for the deaths."

"Their deaths were necessary," said Hongi. "What else would you have had me do?"

Turn to Christ and find a new necessity.

"Their offence was a grievous one," said Samuel Marsden, "and they have paid grievously for it."

"Ae," said Hongi, "that is utu."

CHAPTER 34

For all that Marsden had said of Hongi –and there had been a good deal- John Butler still gazed at the warrior chief with a kind of disbelief. He had been prepared for the moko and had hidden his repulsion behind a toothy smile. Then the disgust had faded and he had found himself warming to the man. He had blanched at the account of the raid but that too was not unexpected and he had tightened his jaw and maintained, he thought, a stern resilience.

All these were aspects that could be held apart. It was the man's tone that brought them together; he spoke, John thought, of the taking of life in the same way that he might speak of taking off his boots. And then everything was bizarre and real and horrible all at once.

He looked about to steady himself, to find a familiar horizon but there was none and he began to wonder if he was dreaming.

What am I doing? I am sitting atop a hill that looks like a crouching lion that looks over a great, glistening bay. I am sitting on a flax mat on a dirt floor with two of the most powerful men in the South Pacific. We sip fine English tea elegantly from bone china cups and chat of this and that, the excellence of the brew, the weather, the slaughter of some local villagers, only half a dozen this time, didn't want to make too much of it.

He choked back a breathless giggle and coughed into his hands instead.

I am dining with a man who has dined on man.

He leaned forward on to his knees and breathed deeply.

I wish Mary was here.

No, it is better that she is not here; I would not wish her to hear this.

He looked up from his knees across the floor of the whare nui to the faces of Hall and Kemp. They were pale and drawn and John thought he saw tears in the eyes of the blacksmith. Beside them Carlisle, the settlement's only representative was shaking his head.

John's breathing became easier but now he felt the heat and closeness of the place and he longed to be away.

Could he do that? There was a hiatus in the conversation right now while Hongi considered a response. But surely it would be insulting to just get up and walk out. Yet others were doing it.

He pushed himself forward on to his hands and knees and shuffled forward a little way. "Carlisle," he hissed, "is it acceptable to leave for a time? I need fresh air."

"Of course. Just move quietly and don't step over anyone. Are you not well? May I be of assistance?"

"No, thank you." John pushed himself to his feet, grunting as stiffened joints moved. "Thank you," he said again, then crept from the building. "The evil trade in muskets," he heard Marsden say as he stepped outside.

The air came on a cool breeze and he leaned against the doorway, taking it in, recovering himself. Everything became clear in that miraculous light and he set off with some small certainty in his step. Like Thomas Kendall seven years ago, he walked with an averted gaze; the nakedness of children was one thing, the nakedness of their parents quite another. The carvings were a further affront. He hastened his step, heading towards the southern end of the pa. There was a break in the palisade here where the ground fell away into sheer cliff. He found a pleasing spot and laid his coat down on the dusty earth. Below and beyond the bay stretched away forever, murmuring behind occasional birdsong. John took off his wig and scratched a receding hairline; he wondered briefly at the forked pole that stretched out over the cliff's edge.

He sat quietly and breathed carefully, evenly. *Take in the beauty, John, consider God's work, have you ever seen such light, such pure colour?.*

"This is, this is," he whispered, shaking his head. But the words eluded him.

It is too many things at once and they will not keep still. Even people will not keep still. Take Marsden, autocratic, pompous, Always Knowing Best. And there he is, attentive and respectful to a man confessing murder. Not pleased, you could see that, but mastering himself to an entirely new extent.

John could not believe the Chaplain was intimidated. *So it must be that he respects him. Perhaps he likes him.*

Too many things at once.
I wish Mary was here.

Yet John could not help but be impressed by the Ngapuhi chief. His grip had told of strength and restraint, the eyes behind the mask were kind and thoughtful and you could not help but return the smile. And his utter confidence was somehow reassuring even as he told the most unreassuring of tales.

Marsden was a powerful man. He had held men's lives in his hands and he had taken them too, along with their freedom and their pride when he had them flogged. (John had never known that power but he had assured himself, and more than once, that when the time came he would exercise it with dignity and diligence.) But Marsden was a part of a process, his power was prescribed within that process and he was always at a distance from its final workings.

Not so Hongi. He *was* the process; at Whangaroa he had found the fault, determined retribution and he had taken it with his own hands.

And then I shot him, an excellent shot, straight through the heart. He showed much mana in his dying, that young man, and more that his death was at my hands.

And Marsden had nodded polite agreement.

"You must understand," the chaplain had told him, "that in these bays Hongi holds an authority that Nero might have envied. Although unlike Nero, Hongi would never abuse his power."

The poor people at Whangaroa might take some issue with that.

"So we are safe?"

"With Hongi's good will."

"So we could live or die at his whim?"

"Not at his whim. Hongi has the power to kill you where you stand and who would restrain him? But he would not do so. He is a thoughtful and learned man and he only acts with due tika, that is, correctly."

"He is acting correctly when he kills and takes slaves and feeds upon human flesh?"

"Of course." Marsden was beginning to show exasperation.

"But that's outrageous. How can you say such a thing?"

"For God's sake, sir!" Marsden's fist had thumped upon the captain's table. "I say it because it is true. It is a terrible, evil thing but it is also utterly in accord with his customs. It is required; he is acting honourably. This is the evil thinking that we are here with Christ's light to address. It is why you are here. And it is not," and his voice had boomed across the cabin and out on to the deck, "to call judgment upon my understanding. I will not have it, sir."

Through gritted teeth John had apologised for any misunderstanding. To the same man who now sat all courtesy to a cannibal.

He scratched into the earth and clawed out a small stone; and watched it arc and drop and disappear.

This was not what he had left St Alban's for; he shook his head, remembering. St Alban's. Now there was a place where things were as they seemed and people didn't change. It had been a good time he thought and looking back he believed he had been happy. Granted, there had been those on the Church Board and others in the Congregation who had pleased to be Difficult, men and women, too of Complaint and Argument. But John and Mary had been resolute and would not turn from their position. And it seemed that others heard of their resolution and found it admirable and John was called to the office of Lord Gambier, himself.

My Lord explained that John had been spoken for by Lord Gresham; his estate stood near by St Alban's and he was the most eminent member of the congregation.

"He called you Steadfast, Mr Butler, one not readily swayed, a man who would Hold True, these were his words, while others faltered. He believed you might be Suited to the Mission. This," he pointed a bony finger at John, "is a calling for strong men, men of character and will. Lord Gresham declared you to be such a man."

John blushed. "Thank you," he stammered, "so unexpected …"

"It was such praise," he told Mary later, "that quite took my breath away. And there was more. Lord Gresham had said that should I look with favour on the Mission, the Board would cover passage and settlement costs. The parish, he said, would mourn our leaving but would understand a calling to Higher Office. Mary," he grasped her arm, "I shall be the *Superintendant* of New Zealand."

Mary had been delighted and horrified and resolute.

And here he was, the Superintendant of New Zealand sitting on a rock and, hello, his head turned at the approach of a chanting girl. She was moving into womanhood and John took in the firm brown breasts and the rounding belly.

She broke off her chant when she saw him and raised a hand. "Kia ora," she said.

"Kee ora," John answered and watched her go past, walking away towards the jutting pole. She clambered easily along it while John stared and held his breath; but then she was safely settled, squatting in the fork. John watched in puzzlement and then in shock as he saw what she was there for.

He clapped his hands over his eyes and turned to flee back to the whare.

While Jane Kendall sat in an easy chair, set at an open angle to the southern window. The sun glittered on the bay and its light and warmth flowed through spotless, shining glass and on to a shining kauri floor. Where little Samuel sat and played with dough. The newborn was asleep at her breast and carefully she eased the nipple free.

The house was silent and immaculate in the sun, Samuel was engaged and the baby was asleep. She reached into a pocket in her dress and withdrew a folded envelope.

Dear Jane,

I have received news of your Circumstances from Tungaroa. What a Clever Girl she is to think to write to me, how Devoted she is to you.

Richard Stockwell has been taken in by a Kind and Understanding Employer. He enjoys his work and is showing great interest in tending sheep. He is becoming a prodigious shearer.

He seems to be finding Peace.

It was a brief letter, particularly given the hours that had gone into its construction.

"The need to advise," George had complained, "is almost overwhelming. Even when you know the problem is completely beyond you, you worry at it. There must be *something* I can say, you think, and there isn't."

After half-filling a basket with crumpled beginnings, Joanna was inclined to agree with him.

"I don't know what to say."

"Tell her Stockwell is fine."

"I've already done that, but I can't think of anything else."

"Then wish her peace and be done with it."

"Alright. Ah God, this awful."

Quickly she scrawled the last words.

I hope you can do the same.

Your friend

Joanna Egan

She had read it dully the first time, staring at Richard's name and thrusting the paper away. But she had kept it and now, as she read it again she was familiar with every word.

She understood that her sin was no less than it had ever been, yet there was an easing.

CHAPTER 35

Waimate 1818

Marsden's fears for Butler proved well-founded. He joined a voice to the acrimony of Hall and even stirred John King to remember resentment.

But in Kendall he met a passion he had not known before. He had heard of and partly witnessed Marsden in a rage; but while the chaplain's anger was a fearsome thing, it could be measured. It had shape and cause and there were limits to it. None of these applied to Kendall and there was a volatility here that threatened to unnerve him.

From the moment he had proclaimed his leadership Kendall had opposed him. There was an obdurate spitefulness to the man. Sometimes it might suddenly soften and then he would become remorseful and penitent and this was almost equally unnerving, particularly the first time. But mostly it sat there, brooding and flaring, consuming the man. Butler thought he might be mad.

It was such a night that might wake the elemental within you; such a night when you might sit before the fire and lose yourself in the flames. You might see ancient towers and dragons or taniwha and the shifting mountains of a new land. And find absorption without thought. You lean forward and hold out your hands and it is a kind of supplication.

The rain crashes in solid sheets upon the shingled roof or is driven by a howling wind against the windows, shaking the shutters and rattling the glass. You might step away from the fire to peer between the shutters, to see the writhing bush lit in sudden light and the image of bending trees and dancing branches lingers after the lightning is gone. Then the sky shudders in thunder.

It was such a night when you might snuggle into your bed and exult in the warmth and comfort, wriggling like a five year old in the overwhelming safety.

Or you might shudder as the house shakes, cringe at the creaking of a nearby tree and wait for the roof to lift and the world to crash in upon you.

Or the storm might call to you, summon you to fling back the door and run into the heart of it; to howl against the thunder and reach up for the light.

It might reduce you to the full extent of your insignificance as you kneel or grovel in submission. Or lift you to a fine and wild defiance.

Either way, you know there is a godhead here.

All of this would have struck John King as whimsical at best and dangerously pagan at worst. The sort of foolishness Kendall would trouble his head with.

The rain meant a wet walk home and the danger of flooding in the wheat fields. And the winds and thunder were an intrusion, breaking in upon the meeting and making it difficult to hear the speakers.

Which was not altogether a bad thing. For while the meeting had been called to attend to God's work, it seemed to King that it had little of the Christian spirit about it.

There was William Hall, arms folded, lips drawn, eyes narrowed. A good man, King believed, and one who spared himself nothing in his work for the mission but there was not much kindness there. Perhaps that was an unkind thought, what had Jesus said, *judge not lest ye be judged?* So he tried hard not to judge.

And there was the new man, Butler. He was an angry man, that was no unfair judgment, for it was clear for all to see.

And though he was some months returned to Port Jackson, Marsden was there, too.

Butler had tried to fill his space but he was too small, too angular and the spirit of the chaplain sat with them yet, leading them in judgment. The meeting had been called at his behest and attended to his cause. And they were all guilty but none more so than the man who now paced the low stage like a wild, caged thing as he attested to his innocence. Or rather, refused to be judged.

"Who are you," he was asking, his eyes hard upon the Superintendant, "to bring your judgments here? What do you know of the reality of this land? You cannot understand a word the natives speak, you know nothing of their beliefs and customs." He paused, panting, before breaking into a torrent of Maori. His voice dropped to a growl, his fingers fluttered and his eyes widened in pukana. Butler stared back in disbelief as his own rage soared and balled his fists. Glancing about the hall, he could see the settlers and mission people lean forward into the tension and he realised that most could understand at least a part of what this wild man was saying. A large bearded man at the back was grinning broadly and Butler was at a loss to understand who the man found the more ridiculous.

Then Kendall fell silent but for his panting breath and Butler took his turn.

"You have the right," he answered. "Clearly I have not the intimate acquaintance with heathen savagery and language that you so clearly manifest. But," and his voice rose to forestall rejoinder, "I do have some knowledge of the Holy Bible and the edicts of the Society that brought us all here. And I speak with authority from that Society when I say that you do evil, sir, you and all who would trade muskets to the heathen."

John King felt a touch of shame and of resentment, too. Certainly he had traded muskets to the Maori, as had all the others. But it had never been a matter of choice; not if they were to survive and continue the work. He saw Hall move to speak, then bite back his words. Of course. While he had been the one who spoke out against the ban and was unapologetic about his part in the trade, he would not speak now. Not if it meant taking Kendall's part.

Kendall appeared to stagger under the enormity of the charge. Or perhaps it was the effects of alcohol or laudanum. His face lost the last of its colour and he gasped wordlessly. Butler pressed his advantage.

"We are here to do God's will, sir, not yours. And God has surely told us, 'thou shalt not kill'. And that is surely what the benighted savage will do with his acquisitions from this devil's trade."

This was too much even for Hall and others and Butler's voice was lost in the uproar. And then, rising above it all came Kendall's response at last. He stormed about the stage, for all the world like a small war chief rousing his troops. He glared and stamped and waved his arms.

"'Thou shalt not kill'," he screamed, "'thou shalt not kill'? Have you thought to post that on the gallows at Newgate? Or tell it to the armies of Christian Europe as they slaughter one another in their tens of thousands? Will you advise Marsden 'thou shalt not kill' the next time he sends some wretch to meet the hangman? You stupid, ignorant man! You sanctimonious," he gasped, reaching for his full of condemnation, "you sanctimonious *fuck!*"

Butler recoiled under the single word and visibly struggled with the urge to physical response. But Kendall was not finished.

"What do you think the Maori do with the steel you so righteously trade them? Have you seen the work they will set an axe to? Of course not! You know nothing but in your ignorance you bray like a damned donkey, 'thou shalt not kill'."

King had moved away with Butler's appeal to the will of God. *Was it the will of God that a child should die because someone made fish hooks of someone's bones? That my beloved sons should die while others live in neglect. Jane Kendall was delivered of a child last year and I see she is pregnant again. How many will that be? Eight? Nine? Is it the will of God that we should stand in this place and condemn one another in His name? We all of us claim to know the will of God, but we cannot all be right. Is there anything that happens that is not the will of God? There must be nothing or God's omnipotence is in doubt. Therefore everything that happens is at the will of God and the words are meaningless.* He shook his head sadly, *it is too much for me,* and returned to the debate.

"The Maori are a sovereign people, sir, a free people and they will make their choices as Adam made his and we make ours. They may choose poorly and then it is for us to teach them wiser ways. But," pounding his fist on the table now, yelling again, "*it is not for us to make their choices for them.*"

"And so they choose for you," Butler hissed the words, "and you are become their thing. Hongi's creature. He holds you."

Kendall became very still as he drew a long shuddering breath. Then he exhaled slowly and his eyes found a middle distance. He appeared puzzled as a man seeking other bearings.

"Ae," he said, "ko ahau te tane o Hongi. I am Hongi's man; and it is you and your kind who have made me so. Hongi has mana, I can see it, I can breathe it." He shook his head. "But I can't see yours."

Butler felt insulted though he did not realise the extent of the insult.

"You can see this mana as you term it," he snapped, "in the Church Missionary Society? In Samuel Marsden?"

Kendall nodded.

"Ae," he answered distantly. "I can see mana in Marsden; he has a kind of power. And I can see power in the Society but it is not mana. Only people have mana."

Butler was exasperated by the man's perversity but the quietness of his speech softened his own.

"You traded muskets to the Maori," he said. Then fell silent.

Kendall nodded again.

"I did," he answered, "but I did not make that choice for them. I argued against it but Hongi paid no heed. They would have taken the muskets anyway, with or without assistance."

You're a liar, thought Butler and then, because he was the kind of man he was, he said so.

And Kendall lost his place altogether. He lunged at Butler and was barely restrained by King and another. William Hall hurried to assist and the three men struggled to restrain the little missionary while Butler struggled to restrain himself.

"You have no mana," roared Kendall, "you are a food basket and I do not recognise you." Then he became still and his voice was more controlled when he spoke again. "Let me go," he said to his captors. "I have nothing more to do here. I will leave now."

They did as he asked and he walked with measured steps to the end of the hall, tugged open the door against the wind and disappeared into the storm.

There seemed nothing left and the formal inquiry into the trading of muskets fell in upon itself. Butler stared out after the departing settlers and missionaries. I am lost, he thought.

He was prophetic. Three months later he was to write 'gifts blind the heart' and begin trading muskets to the Maori.

He remembered his dreadful passage from Thoresby to London, a lifetime ago; hunched upon a wagon in the rain, despairing. And then the epiphany, the Bentink Chapel, Basil Woodd. He was a young man then, but now his hair was thin and grey.

What epiphany could there be here where failure and loss of redemption beckoned at every hand?

I fear I am going mad. Can there be enemies everywhere? Is there no one to share a thought with me?

I am accused at every turn. Hongi accuses me because of my God, Jane accuses me in shame and loss, Marsden …

Why am I counting up my failures? If I am being tested, dear God, it is a heavy burden. If I am not being tested, that is even worse.

The rain and his thoughts blinded him, but he did not slow. Then a pebble loosened by the rain slipped in the clay beneath his foot and he plummeted forward on hands and knees into the muddy path.

There is a godhead here.

I can go no lower than this. This is my limit. Thought will not avail me here. I need Something!

England.

London in the rain came back.

Dear God, I need to be in London. I need someone to share a thought with me. Dear Basil, dear Robert… I am an alien here. There are those who care for me and they are all Maori and those who are dear to me and those who are bound to me. But there are none to understand me. And I barely understand myself.

I need to be in London. I am dying here, the earth is sucking at my spirit and the earth is looking different to me now. I need to hear the voices of good Christian men and I need them to hear me.

I am driven from my feet. I crawl, I kneel in the mud while the rain comes down on me. My strength is gone. This is my place, here on my knees. I need to stand. But I cannot stand here, must I wait for help to come to lift me?

Then he thought of Butler and Hall and pride came to his rescue and he struggled to his feet.

I need to be in London.

Jane was bent over a sheet of paper, chewing at the end of her pen, when she heard Thomas at the door. In one movement she scrunched the paper and dropped it into a flax woven bin at her side. She made no further movement but sat quietly as her husband entered the room.

He looked dreadful; thin, grey locks plastered against pallid cheeks, dark and heavy bags beneath red-rimmed eyes. He dropped his sodden coat upon the floor and reached into a hamper of soiled clothes sitting outside the boys' room. He took out a mud-stained shirt and dried his face and towelled his hair. The mud ran with the rain and he looked like a scarecrow.

He was muttering to himself.

"O my anger, my anger. What has it led me to, now? I called Butler a, o now I cannot say the word. Sorely pressed, I was sorely pressed, but even so. O, it was a terrible thing to say."

He hurried to the fire, holding out his arms before him. Jane watched him quietly.

"I must beg his forgiveness, though provoked, dear God I was provoked." He nodded vigorously, agreeing with himself for want of anyone else, someone to share a thought with.

Jane sighed.

"Thomas," she asked. "What have you done?"

"I have spoken in anger," he groaned, "I have spoken in anger and have said unspeakable things, I called Butler an unspeakable thing." He shuddered. "And, o God, I said this before the entire committee. And then I was physically restrained and sent into the night." He shook his head almost wondrously. "My downfall is complete. God has cast me from Him."

As the meaning of his words came to him, he began to shrink. Back to his knees in the mud. And the same Answer.

"London," he said, "I must go to London."

"When will you go?"

"Soon, soon, tomorrow if I could. There is much to be done, my dictionary, I will assist Professor Lee with my dictionary. It shall be published and well-received. And ordination, I must receive ordination. These years I have stood and preached the Word of God, they need acknowledgement, I am entitled to the part."

He did not say, "I need to escape, I am drowning here. I must save myself."

"And the children?"

"There is provision for you and the children. My salary will continue to come through, though I have drawn on it to meet expenses. Marsden would not dare stop it. It would not look good."

Jane closed her eyes. "Indeed," she said, "it would be a poor look."

"And you are under the protection of Hongi. Though he will be gone, too, his mana reaches across the world, he will be still great here. But more particularly you have Rakau and Tangaroa and many others. You and the children will be their whanau and Rakau will guard you and help you like he would his own. You will be well."

There was one more thing.

She stood and stroked her swelling belly.

"Thomas," she said, "a baby sleeps in a crowded room and I am with child again."

His scarecrow face folded in sudden grief but it gave way before the Answer. "I will bear the loss of greeting the child with the knowledge that you are all safe and well."

And there was nothing further to say.

Now London became everything he could think of, the only thing he could think of. It lay behind his flushing apology to Butler and the others for his outburst. The angry worm begged forgiveness.

Inevitably he spoke of it to others, cautiously at first as if his plans were anything other than common knowledge, then more openly as they became firm. Passages were booked, for himself, Hongi and Waikato, a young man of chiefly descent who was kin to Hongi.

The settlement was torn between their delight at seeing the departure of Kendall, their consternation at his leaving behind his ruined wife and brood and their horror at the thought of Hongi gone. Their most assured line of protection gone. We will be open, they wailed, to the most wanton and incessant depradation, perhaps to the extent of our lives.

William Hall was less concerned.

"I cannot think," he said to John King, "that we are as at much risk as is made out."

King scratched at a persistent flea and raised an eyebrow. "Hongi will be gone."

"Ae," Hall rejoined, picking up a rhythm, "but we live among Ngapuhi and there are no chiefs who wish us ill. And they would not cross Hongi, even in his absence. We are safe, well," he amended, "mostly safe. But we can expect some boisterous times."

"The chiefs will not hold the men as Hongi did."

"No," Hall nodded. "but I think they will keep them from killing. So long as we are careful. But we should expect boisterous times."

King nodded. "And this," he asked, "you perceive as safety?"

Hall did not answer but stared aside and stroked his beard.

"Hongi may not go if Kendall does not go."

"No, John," Hall shook his head, "No, I am sorry but I can find nothing but liking for Kendall's going."

"Even if it exposes us to danger? The women? The children?"

Hall returned to his thoughts and his beard. "It is not so bad," he said at last, "I cannot think we are at as much risk as is made out."

But anxiety ran high through the settlement and Butler was prevailed upon, particularly by the women to approach Kendall. Sensing in their situation an acceptable line of approach, he agreed.

"If you would but spare a thought for the children, sir, and the women. Your very own wife is with child. How can you think to leave her unattended?"

"She will not be unattended and neither will my children. They have their tasks, they know their responsibilities and Mrs Kendall is a most resourceful woman. And they have Rakau and his whanau. They will be safe and well." The finality drew Butler up short.

The man is consumed, he thought. He sees only what he thinks will save him. So for want of anything better he wrote to Marsden about it.

Reverend Sir, he wrote stiffly, *I think it my duty to draw to your attention ...*

Marsden crumpled the sheet and hurled it from him. Damn the man. Was he entirely beyond reason? Up until now he had largely supported Kendall in his squabbles with the others settlers; perhaps Kendall had come to presume upon that support, perhaps it had gone to his head, but what he now intended outran all presumption. It was a kind of treason. The outburst at the meeting was bad enough, although it was nothing new. And rage in the face of any kind of accusation, justified or otherwise, had become almost a commonplace. Amongst all of them.

But to place his settlement at risk like this went beyond all comprehension.

He pushed himself out of his chair and paced. His fists clenched and unclenched and his face became mottled.

Betrayal and testing.

He lumbered out of the study and stamped through the house, from one empty room to the next as the servants heard his coming and fled from it.

Idle vagabonds! Could he not depend upon compliance and industry within his own four walls?

By the time he found Elizabeth in the drawing room his sense of outrage was near complete and he did not pause to greet her and inquire after her health.

"It is too bad, Mrs Marsden, too bad," he boomed.

Elizabeth looked up from her book. "Why, Mr Marsden," she smiled, "whatever can be the matter?"

He did not see the smile and she sighed. He must be really cross.

"I must be gone, I cannot leave them for five minutes to manage themselves."

"What has happened?"

"Kendall has happened. O, I have tried to be kind, to overlook his faults. But the devil is in him, Elizabeth, and he goes from excess to excess."

"What excess is this?"

"He will away to England and take Hongi with him! Hongi has a fancy to meet the king." Marsden gesticulated helplessly. "It is foolhardy and dangerous to the settlers and God knows what damage he will make at the Mission Society. And," his voice rose to a crescendo as he addressed the greatest sin of all, "he has done all this in wilful defiance of my known wishes." Panting, he slumped into a chair, huddled in his fury, driving fist into open hand.

"So you will go to New Zealand?"

"As soon as passage can be secured. Within the week, I hope." Marsden sighed. "What more can the man do to me?"

The man could do nothing but live upon a knife edge of anticipation. All thoughts, all consequences must be put on hold. He must away to England.

His children watched him in varying degrees of interest. To the younger boys, from Basil down he had become progressively a stranger. Even when he was home, he was distant. He was quieter than he used to be, slower to anger and quicker to despair. He carried something with him that kept the boys away. And they could not see how their mother's actions impacted on them.

Whereas Susannah and Elizabeth could only see their father through their mother's shame. And the resentment they already bore him hardened in a mixture of grief and disbelief. They blamed Thomas for the blame they bore their mother.

All the children watched their parents feel their way about the house. It became somewhat easier as Thomas came to understand that Jane's subservience was inviolable; he came to depend upon it although never really trusting it, either. Two shrinking, civil ghosts.

Dinner time was excruciating as they sat at table, the older ones silent, simmering, the younger sullen and getting used to it. Thomas sat shrinking under the accusations and there was no response but silence.

They would watch him hasten to his desk at the close of the meal to become very busy with his books and journals. Sometimes when the house was settling between cleaning dishes and preparing for bed he would almost creep to the baby's crib at the foot of their bed and watch the child sleep. He might find a kind of delight there, losing himself in the perfect skin and the perfect tranquillity. But then the child might cry and he would pick it up and deliver it to Jane or the girls and hurry back to his desk. Or, more commonly, rogue thoughts would intrude, *you will be walking when next I see you* and he would hurry back to his desk.

Only Thomas Surfleet knew him now. But the knowledge was limited to their travelling together, by foot, horseback and waka, working the gardens together, eating and sleeping cramped in a flea-infested whare. Yet it softened the eldest boy's response; he would miss their father most.

Two weeks later Marsden was discovering what more Kendall could do to him. He was standing on the foredeck of the *Dromedary*, overseeing the unloading of the Mission's cargo. It was a fine March morning and sloop stood placidly at anchor. Men worked without their shirts swiftly and efficiently in the easy conditions. God's good day and industry together touched him and he leaned over the rail, watching the bales hanging from winches, dropping into the waiting longboats. The sea about the *Dromedary* broke and sparkled under two score of oars and paddles.

"Beg pardon, sir."

He turned in faint shock to face a burly seaman.

"Sorry to disturb you, sir, but the captain says there is cargo for Mr Kendall and he understands the gentleman is gone and what should he do with it?"

Marsden grunted. For a moment he had forgotten Kendall. Which was the best thing to do at the moment, seeing the wretch was gone. He had made good upon his threat and with Hongi and Waikato he had fled to England. That's all it was, flight, all this talk of his dictionary and ordination, just excuses. And his own poor ruined woman. Marsden gritted his teeth and God's good day took a sudden turn for the worse.

"Sir, sir?"

The sailor was waiting. "What answer shall I give the captain?"

"Right." The chaplain nodded briskly. "I'll go to see for myself. If you would show me the way? Step along."

The sailor hurried along the deck to the cargo hold. Here the industry was excellent, men shouldering boxes, slinging ropes and netting about the larger consignments. And the collective pause as the load rose in smooth ascent, the sigh as it settled safely in the longboat.

Captain Roberts was at his side, pointing to a large crate in its net. "That one there, that's for Kendall, but he's gone, isn't he, so should I land it?"

Marsden peered down at the crate,

"Does it bear any description?"

"No, I already checked. Just 'colonial supplies'."

"That could be anything. O well, it's for the colony. Let's have it."

Roberts gestured to the men and they leaned into the hawsers and the cargo rose. "I'll tell you this," he shouted, "it's damn heavy 'colonial supplies'. Watch out, you fool," as a rope slipped from a sailor's hand and the cargo tilted. The men swung upon the ropes and the cargo swung upward, leaning, then it was over the lip of the hold and dropping, banging on to the deck.

Roberts hurried to the crate with Marsden close behind him. "If the crate's survived that, I'll be hanged," he said, "yes, see there, the corner is quite smashed, hello, what's this?" He stooped to prise the broken boards free and reached inside. He froze there for a moment, then drew out his arms. And held up to Marsden a brand new musket.

And Marsden erupted. No patient forbearance would hold him this time and Job was the furthest example from his mind. He drove his heel with fury into the sturdy deck, then the other while he crashed his fist into his hand. His eyes stood out in a pukana any warrior would have been proud to claim and the blood stood out in his veins.

Roberts beckoned to the men nearby and they moved cautiously away. He had seen rage such as this before and it had never stopped at violence. Marsden spun on them.

"Muskets! Good Christ, these are muskets! And they are on consignment to the mission." He drove the heel of his hand into his forehead. "Macquarie will have me for this, this will go to the Society, Macquarie will *question* me." He roared aloud in his fury and wildly looked about for something to destroy. Roberts and his men moved further away, leaving the rifle on the deck. Marsden seized it by the barrel and grunting and cursing swung it at the crate; then used his boots to finish off the broken boards. A musket fell free and he seized it again by the barrel and smashed it until the barrel bent and the stock broke. Then he lent upon the devil's trade, panting, his face flushed.

Gradually he began to recover himself. But a toxic connection was irretrievably set. He would have Kendall. He prayed, sincerely he hoped that God would forgive Kendall but for his part he could not do it. He had been wronged beyond forgiveness. More to the point, he would act upon his judgment. Vengeance is mine, saith the Lord but Samuel Marsden was in no condition to listen. He would have Kendall for this.

If I can, Kendall, I will ruin you.

Unless you ruin yourself first.

CHAPTER 36

For the first seven days the man who would be ruined lay in his cabin, cursing all the forces of motion. Slowly he began to recover and to venture up on deck. After a time he found his place, high up on the foredeck where he could lean upon the railing, gripping securely and watch the ship's bows cleave the sea. He would feel the surge, the slide in his feet and hands, rarely in his stomach now and he felt the world expand. The sea and sky met ahead and he would be at that place soon. His destiny was at hand, the years of struggle, deprivation and betrayal would see some recognition at last. Jane would be so pleased. At the thought the world shrank again and for the first time, now that the path was irrevocable, Thomas managed to think about Jane.

Distance had extended time and he was pleased to find an easing of his bitterness. He was even more pleased to find a kind of pity for her.

Poor Jane, I miss your companionship, the friendly ear, someone to share a thought with. Our Saviour preached forgiveness; who am I to withhold mine?

But can I ever recover from the blow? Can I rise above the mistrust, the loss, the constant, disbelieving shame? I still say, 'can this have happened'?

But to dwell on the thing is to blame and blame again. I must not think on it. By putting it from my mind, I can move ahead. And think upon the future.

And the world expanded again.

"…and all who sail in her. We ask this in Christ Jesus' name, amen."

The rich tones rolled away and then were back again as John Reagan led the congregation in hymn. There were some who did not sing, Hongi noted the furtive gazes wandering, looking for an eye to meet, but most did, and some of them with an enthusiasm that might have been best watered down; wide eyes, straining throats, bellowing their anthem to the Lord. Here and there a true voice appeared, like Keni beside him, but none had the utter authority of the voice that led them. Each note was like a bird, Hongi thought, alighting perfectly on a new branch. Some of the other singers, he grimaced, missed it entirely and went plummeting down or were flung sideways in a wayward gust.

The gentle congregation was gestured to their seats while the sailors stood behind them.

Reagan stood before them in the silence that followed, like a man about to take a bow. His face glistened and his arms reached out. Then slowly they dropped and he appeared to shrink and pale and there was a slight tremor on him. The captain hurried across from his seat and whispered a few words. And Reagan grew again.

"There were two men," he said as one telling a story and Hongi watched the congregation lean forward, "and one was a good man and the other a thief. It was the cold small hours of the morning," his voice dropped, "and a drizzle of rain lighted silver against the gas beacons. Beyond the silver light lay stone and darkness.

"The way to their homes ran through filthy streets and dark, stinking alleys, quiet in the rain but listening," he cocked his head sideways and cupped an ear, "listening for a life."

"The thief leaned close against the slimy stone walls as he crept silently forward."

Reagan slid sideways against the wall he had described, his hands were at his shoulder as though carrying a sack and his features were pinched and mean.

"'I 'ave me plunder,' he said," and the rich smoothness turned to a Cockney rasp, "'and they must bear the loss'."

And then he was Reagan again, full and urgent.

"He hurried through the dark rain and had begun to believe that he would be safe when a hand," his arm shot out rigid, "when a hand with the strength of many men reached out and gripped him still while another held a blade to his throat."

Hongi had ceased all audience observation and was as entranced as the rest.

"Out of the shadows a voice spoke." It had Reagan's bass but was the voice of a beast.

"'Curse your god,' whispered the voice, 'curse your god or I shall take your life this moment.'

"Desperately the man thought but his thoughts were chaotic and he could not assemble them. Only one idea stayed with him.

"'No,' he said, 'I will not lose my hope of heaven.'

"'As you will', said the voice and the man's throat was sliced apart."

Reagan fell to one knee, hands at his throat and on his face a beseeching fear that dragged a moan from the congregation. Then he rose calmly, dusted off his trousers and continued.

"The thief died in the gutter in filth and ruin.

"The good man followed on. He was thinking about his wife and children and how he could provide for them with his day's takings. He was not as careful as the thief and it was easy to catch him.

"'Curse your god,' whispered the voice, 'curse your god or I shall take your life this moment.'

"The man thought desperately. He was a pious man and the thought of the curse was terrible to him, but if he perished so too would his wife and children. Surely God will understand, he thought if I *pretend* to curse Him. Then I can look after my family and make my repentance of words that were never intended.

"'Choose,' said the voice.

"'I curse God,' said the man and his throat was sliced apart.

And the valediction in the gutter's voice.

Now I shall send you to hell well and good.

The audience released its breath in a huge sigh. Though the story was a common one, a favourite of the captain's, they were as enchanted as when they had first heard it.

Hongi was more enchanted than most. Finally, a story about the pakeha god he could relate to.

"It is a story about mana," he said.

Thomas was not listening. The sermon had quite thrown him and he was struggling for composure. While it had seemed a simple if brutal exposition of the first commandment, it kept throwing up questions.

Did the thief go to heaven?

Thou wilt be in paradise with Me this day.

Did the good man go to hell?

Did God understand? Of course He understood. What did He understand?

The good man put his family ahead of his soul. Was this blasphemy? Or heroism? What kind of love was this?

And the absorbing theatricality of it all. Did it add to or subtract from the meaning?

What meaning? Which meaning?

He clutched his head then turned and pushed his way blindly through the sailors. Hongi watched him go then returned his attention to the show.

Which, sadly, was winding down. The final hymn was over and the benediction was a brief farewell. There would be no encore until next Sunday.

But it had lifted Hongi's spirits and he left the deck in a fine humour. Back home autumn would be moving towards winter but here in the mid-Pacific the tropical sun beat warm upon his back. Beneath his bare feet the deck hummed and the sails were full from the following breeze. The sea was blue and inviting but for the occasional black fin that cut the surface, following the ship in the expectation of offal and scraps. He leaned over the rail and watched the sea, watching for a whale. He had seen them before, from waka and twice on the journey to Port Jackson but never as close as from the *New Zealander*. Two days ago one had broached barely two chains from the vessel. It had blown and the spray had covered the deck and Hongi had wiped the moisture down his cheeks, then touched his finger tips to his lips.

The magnitude of the ocean was inspiring and Hongi thought he would like to see it at its most complete. Above the crow's nest beckoned and he stepped on to the rigging.

"Oi," a voice broke in on his meditation. "what you think you're doing, eh?"

Hongi stepped back and turned to face the sailor. He understood perfectly well what the man was saying but chose to feign puzzlement.

"Kia ora," he said politely.

"Kee ora yourself," said the man and Hongi understood he was not returning the greeting. A spark lit but he held it down and pointed aloft, making signs of climbing.

"Ah, no," the man shook his head and a pigtail jiggled over a broad shoulder. "No," he said again, "too dangerous, eh? You might fall down and break your fuckin' neck."

There was no response and the man tried again. "Too dan ger ous," he said slowly, then turning to the men standing about, "does anyone know their heathen jabber? No? Shit, look," patiently and very slowly, "no climbee, not good, very bad."

Hongi was fed up, piqued that this common oaf should presume to instruct him and he turned away to take hold of the rigging again. He sensed as much as saw the hand reaching for his shoulder and spun away furiously. The fool had thought to touch him, to violate his tapu. He should take his head.

The sailor stepped back, raising his hands placatingly against the raw rage. "Alright, alright, I'm not going to fight about it. Jesus."

Hongi turned his back on this man without mana and climbed the rigging.

While Hongi lost himself, turning in slow circles in the epicentre of the vast circle about him, Thomas wrestled with demons on the foredeck. The sermon seemed to present a terrible question he could not recognise; but somehow, he knew, it went to the heart of his quest. He ached for someone to talk to, Robert or Basil, even Rakau. Hongi, he knew, would laugh at him.

It came to him that he had not thought to approach the preacher. He wondered at his reluctance but could not deny it either. He did not warm to the look of the man, a gaunt spider with pale, almost cadaverous features and long, stringy hair but it was the performance, there was no other word for it, that repelled him; that and the voice which was like a thing apart from the performer. He stepped back from the railing and smacked himself sharply on the forehead. What a worm he was, judging without understanding. He would deal properly with the matter forthwith and he set off to find the ship's master.

Captain Munro's response was diffident.

"Why do you want to speak with Mr Reagan?"

Thomas was a little miffed. "Why would I not?" he asked. "Surely for a man of the Church, I am due for ordination, you know, to want to converse with another is not an unusual request?"

The captain tugged at his beard while he considered.

"Well," he said, "I can understand that, perfectly reasonable, but you see, Mr Reagan has been poorly of late and may not feel up to receiving visitors."

"He seemed quite well at service this morning," said Thomas stiffly.

Munro's diffidence moved to irritation.

"I am not accustomed, Mr Kandall –"

"Kendall is my name."

"Mr Kendall, then. I am not accustomed to having my word doubted on my ship. Or anywhere else. Nor to being interrupted, neither."

The confusion that had been washing over Thomas for the past hour channelled itself into a familiar focus.

"It seems to me, sir," he said, "that you are putting obstacles in the way of what you yourself term a perfectly reasonable request."

"It seems to me that it is less of a request and more of a demand."

The two men glared at one another as Munro moved further on to the offensive. "Perhaps," he said tightly, "I might make a request of you. Perhaps you might see fit to have a word with your," he hesitated, "companions to amend their behaviour."

"And in what respect do you fault their behaviour?"

"The younger man –"

"Waikato."

"Whoever, and you are interrupting again, Mr *Ken*dall, whoever he is, he has threatened my cook with violence and the other," holding up a hand, "I do not care to know his name, has just now refused to follow a lawful order from Mr Darcy and has taken it upon himself to ascend the crow's nest." He pointed and following his hand Thomas could make out a tiny figure above the topmost shrouds.

"He is a rangatira, a chief," Thomas protested, "he –"

"Could be Jesus Christ for all I care. He'll do as he's told aboard my ship."

Thomas stiffened at the blasphemy but Munro had not finished.

"That is all, Mr Kendall. If you would be so kind. I have my duties to attend to."

"And Mr Reagan?"

"I'll let you know when he's ready to receive visitors. It could be a while."

Thomas was now resolved to speak with the preacher and he scoured the *New Zealander* in search of him. But after three days he had not caught so much as a glimpse of the man; nor was he to be found at evening meals. Inquiries of the ship's officers proved them to be less than forthcoming and he saw Munro's hand in that; the puzzle was becoming a mystery was becoming a plot.

And then there he was. Simply, undramatically, leaning on the rail just a few feet from Thomas' place, smiling vaguely at the sea. A young seaman stood quietly at his side.

"Mr Reagan," Thomas exclaimed and moved towards him. Reagan stayed as he was but the seaman turned sharply and his eyes widened as he saw Thomas.

"Mr Reagan," Thomas said again and tapped him lightly on the shoulder.

Reagan started and turned.

"Mr Reagan," Thomas said, proferring his hand. "My name is Thomas Kendall and I am very pleased to meet you."

Reagan looked at the outstretched hand for a moment then hesitantly, it seemed, offered his own. It was limp and cold and Thomas shuddered slightly at the touch.

"Do I know you?" said Reagan.

Thomas stared. The voice was less than a shadow of the one that had held the audience spellbound; it was pale and soft and distant.

"No," he answered, then became aware of another hand, tugging at his sleeve.

"Excuse me, sir," said the seaman, "Mr Reagan isn't supposed to be talking to the passengers. He's been feeling poorly. Come along, Mr Reagan," and he took the preacher by the arm.

"Wait." Thomas took Reagan's other arm. "Let's ask him. How do you feel, Mr Reagan?"

The same dull voice. "I'm alright."

"There you are," said Thomas. "May I speak with you, Mr Reagan?"

"Alright."

The seaman shuffled anxiously, but his hand was off the preacher's arm. "Cap'n won't like this."

"Let him. Now, Mr Reagan, about your last semon."

Reagan gazed at him.

"Remember, the sermon about faith?"

There was no response.

"Mr Reagan," Thomas was becoming agitated, "you preached a powerful sermon, one of the most powerful I've ever heard. I need you to explain it to me."

Reagan stared at him.

"Do I know you?" he said.

It was weeks before Thomas saw him on deck again.

But he continued to lead the congregation at the Sunday service as well as conducting two brief funerals, one for a child and one for a sailor who had fallen from the ship and been lost. An empty casket plunged into the sea for him. There were no sermons, no eulogies, just the reading with rich tones and utter kindness.

One Sunday John Reagan stood beneath a leaden sky on a deck that rolled slowly in the one place. He stood as he so often did at the close of the hymn preceding the sermon, diffident and uncertain. The captain crossed to him and spoke urgently in his ear, holding him firmly by the shoulder. Reagan half turned, watching the captain back to his seat, then he became still. He seemed to shrink yet at the same time his lean frame filled with a sudden energy. Then he turned and looked levelly at the congregation with placid, young eyes; his voice was unbroken.

"Today," he confided in the congregation, "is a special day. Today my father is going to take me with him into the mountains. We are going to sacrifice to the Lord. I feel very proud that my father will share this ceremony with me. Perhaps he thinks I am growing up.

"Father is the most important man in the land. He communes directly with Yahweh and is the instrument of His messages.

"To be with such a man is in itself the highest honour. That he is also my father ... I hope I don't do anything to shame him. I will pray to Yahweh to help me, for He is my father, too."

The preacher lowered his head and clasped his hands before him as he silently prayed to be the best son he could.

Then he looked up and spoke again, but now the voice was breathless against the climb and his shoulder sagged as he trudged on, steadfast.

"Father is an old man now, see," pointing, "his hair and beard are like tangled snow. But he does not tire. He hoists his heavy robe with the one hand and his staff in the other and he strides, he strides up the mountain.

"We are above the clouds now and the mountain glows in the sun. But I am spent."

Reagan fell to his knees. "Father," he panted, "I am sorry but I must rest. I need water.

"Father stops but he does not turn. Nor does he answer and we gaze together at the place God has brought us to. It is a large cave, opening on the mountainside like a grey yawn. It is all rock apart from a heavy thicket along the far side. But Father's attention is upon the great slab of rock that lies alone in the centre of the cave.

"His face is still away from me as he whispers softly but his voice shakes and I can hear tears in it. 'Ah, no,' he says, 'not an altar.'"

Thomas was becoming agitated.

This is all about testing and obedience. Again. Has the man no other theme? And how he lights upon the cutting of a throat. There is mockery here. Somewhere. I do not want to hear this.

I am thinking very loudly right now. I have managed to block out the demented preacher. I do not want to hear of fathers sacrificing their sons. Tra-la-la-la....

Hongi was becoming agitated, too. He did not like this story about the mad god the white men worshipped. A father losing a son to a mere in battle would seek utu but there would be no shame in the boy's death and he would grieve accordingly. If he had fought well, his father would take pride in it. But to slaughter one's own child?

"I would not do that," he said to Thomas, then realised the man was entirely inattentive. His hands were over his ears, his eyes were closed and he seemed to be mumbling something. Tra-la-la? Hongi shook him firmly by the shoulder. "I would not do that," he said again. "I would tell your god there is no mana in what he is doing."

Thomas regained attention in time to collect the last few words.

No mana in doing what? No mana in my leaving New Zealand? No, he said 'he', no mana for the preacher he means. Ah, Hongi is wise; he sees that the man does not praise God; he does not love God as he should.

And then he was caught by the story again.

"My father's shoulders are shaking and he seems to be arguing with someone. But there is only silence. He sinks to his knees and falls upon his face on the rock and his cheek begins to bleed and he pounds his fist into the rock until it bleeds, too. And all the time there is this silent scream."

Reagan tore his hair loose from its ribbon and suddenly he was an old man. His mouth hung open in exhausted, utter defeat and his eyes were wide with fear.

"I cannot think," he stammered, "this is so awful I cannot think about it. No room for thinking here." He giggled meaninglessly and the giggle became a laugh became a – he snatched back at himself. "I can neither obey nor disobey, both are unthinkable."

At which point Thomas turned and stumbled away, pushing through sailors riveted by the drama, dragging himself along the railing, hurrying to his place. He did not see, as Hongi did, the finale, the son torn into terror, the father an automatic thing with a sudden dagger, then frozen into immobility as the merciful God stayed his arm.

Thomas felt compelled to speak with Munro again. He would come apology in hand, he had been abrasive at their last meeting and he would ask pardon for it. He was not there to judge or complain. He just needed someone to talk to.

Hongi had not been helpful, though he had not laughed either. Indeed, he had seen nothing amusing nor instructive in the story.

"Yours is a cruel and greedy god," he said dismissively.

There was only Munro.

He received Thomas cordially, accepted his apology and proffered one of his own. Then a glass of rum was in their hands as they toasted the king.

Thomas steadied himself. "The minister, Reagan," he said, "he unsettles me."

"He's a powerful presence, alright," said the captain. "He's unsettled many in his time and most would say they were the better for it." The broad Yorkshire vowels lent a certitude to his words, turned them into a pronouncement. Of course Munro had had this conversation before. Not a trip went by without some complaint or concern; he expected they would continue.

Now Thomas was unsettled by the ready agreement and tried again.

"The theatrics, sir," he said, "are they not more in place on a stage than from a pulpit?"

"I take your point," agreed Munro again, "but remember, he preaches to simple men who may not follow the spoken word, particularly the holy, biblical word, as well as you or I. So he moderates the language for them. Right accommodating, very conscientious of him. And for those who can't hold their focus like you or I, he brings in a little drama to help their understanding.

"And they listen to him, Mr Kendall, these roughnecks attend to John Reagan, they attend to his every word, sir, and they talk about it, I've heard them, profane tars, you know what their language is like, discussing

Sunday's sermon, trying to understand it. Now isn't that spreading the gospel?"

Thomas' head was spinning and he gulped at his rum; the fierce spirit brought him back to remember himself. He was not here to judge or complain.

So he judged.

"The man is unsettled in his mind, sir, he is deranged, he does not know who he is."

"And do the rest of us?" asked Munro. "And when he speaks on Sunday he has a shining presence who knows who he is."

Thomas stared. "This is ludicrous," he said, "you are letting a madman preach the word of God. And you are defending it with great good sense."

"Mr Kendall." The captain spread his hands before gesturing at Thomas' glass. "Why are you so set against Mr Reagan? Would you have him confined in Bedlam? Where he will die. Or here, where he lives and expresses his unique gift to the glory of God?"

Thomas shook his head.

"Take more time to think about it," said Captain Munro. "Listen to the reverend. Listen to your heart. Then come back to me."

The following Sunday hung heavy on the Pacific and *The New Zealander* hung like Mr Coleridge's painted ship. Not for much longer though, the crew assured themselves and anyone else who would listen. Soon they would have lurched their way to the Horn and soon they would be longing for days such as these.

John Reagan hung over the pulpit like a ragged crow. But his face shone with kindness and his voice was soft, assured, soothing.

"Dearly beloved bretheren," he said. "Today's story comes from the Very First Book of All. It is our oldest story.

"In the beginning the earth was without form and void and darkness was upon the face of the deep."

He gestured towards the endless ocean.

"What an appropriate place this is for our meditation.

"And out of the darkness He brought forth light and life.

"Eden was a state of perfect innocence, translucent in the dawn of time." He raised a hand to the sailors at the rear of the congregation. "It *shone*, my lads. And it was deathless.

"Every creature followed its nature and its nature was as God had decreed. They lived in perfect obedience.

"No," Reagan wagged a finger at the congregation. "It was not perfect because it was not exacted. So God created Adam in His own image to provide perfect obedience."

He leaned on the pulpit and spoke over the seated gentry to the sailors again. "If something can't help but obey you, there can be no obedience. You might as well command a stone to fall, then let it drop from your hand and tell yourself that it obeys you."

There can be no virtue without temptation.

"So of all the creatures Adam was given the faculty of disobedience. Along with enough intelligence to understand what disobedience meant.

"But he had no moral sensibility. He did not know his soul from his life. And he was quite without care.

"But Adam moped. He would sit listlessly for hours staring into a shaded pool, gazing into the soft, reflecting waters. And God would watch him and see how his eyes turned at every small thing.

"He is looking for something, thought God."

"He wahine," said Hongi to himself. "He is looking for a woman. How can't you see that?"

"So God grew a woman from Adam's rib and called her Eve. And Adam and Eve were made rulers of the earth.

"It was all there for them, boys. Never a thing to trouble them: food fell into their hands, the conditions were so perfect there was no need for shelter. So they fed and slept but, strangely, they did not mate.

"Now God laid the circumstances for disobedience. 'There is a tree,' He told them, 'which bears a different fruit called the knowledge of good and evil. You are not to eat of this fruit for on the day you do you will surely die.'"

Reagan cocked his head quizzically.

"God sounds as though He is expecting it, doesn't He?

"Then He brought into the garden a serpent and the serpent's part was to tempt."

Reagan stared at the congregation with dead eyes. Slowly his head turned and his tongue flickered. His voice was a rasping, hissing whisper that slid across the congregation and settled in every seaman's ear.

"'Why did the Lord tell you not to eat of that tree?'

"'He told us that if we ate, it would be a sin.' She was radiant in that first forever morning, serene beyond dissembling.

"'What is sin, Eve?

"'He is afraid, Eve. He knows that if you eat you will become as He is.'

"'But we will die.'

"'What is death, Eve?'

She realised that she did not know.

"'I have been frightened by threats I do not understand.'

"'If you eat of the tree, you will understand them.'

"'I might be happier if I did not.'

"'What is happiness, Eve?'"

The final hiss faded away and the preacher shook his head in sorrow.

"The serpent seduced her, friends. You must judge for yourselves how she was persuaded. But persuaded she was and she did eat.

"What must it have been like when she took that first bite of the forbidden fruit? To pass in an instant from unknowing into knowing? To touch that first understanding, that first golden starburst of pure thought. And she knew: *I am a sinner.*

"Now I know what sin and death are.

"And what did she do with that knowledge?" A harsh touch was creeping into Reagan's voice and he seemed to shrink within his black cloak. He hunched into bony shoulders and stared malignantly at the ladies in the congregation, passing from each to the next his bitter judgment.

"The very first thing she did was to tempt Adam into joining her in her sin. She knew what she had done, o, she understood it very well now; she knew that she would die.

"'So if I must die, then I shall be sure to take him with me.'"

Now I shall send you to hell well and good.

Reagan shuddered and the men with him, joined in outrage at their betrayal, their horror at the viciousness of women. Small wonder she was to become the mother of the first murderer.

"So Adam fell, taking us all with him. And what was his first thought, what ushered in his new godhead?

"I lust.

"And the Bible would tell you that his first response to this awareness of woman was to run into the bushes and cover himself with leaves. Well, perhaps so. Or perhaps the writers were considerate of our delicacy. My personal thought is that they would have been at it like rabbits."

Reagan thrust his hips suggestively and there was a cry of dismay from the ladies. Captain Munro half-rose to his feet and gestured to two seamen standing close by.

But the moment was past and Reagan was grave again.

"And so they –we – were banished from Eden. They understood the threat now, they knew what sin was and they knew that they would die. And they traded immortal innocence for that knowledge. They invited in hell just to see what it was like."

He raised his arms, holding his hands on either side of his head and his face and voice were perfect tragedy.

Knowledge. Self-awareness. What's it fucking good for?

CHAPTER 37

Cambridge, November, 1820

Near seven years ago to the day, he had sat by water and waited on a sign from the Lord. In near despair he had prayed and his prayer had been answered in a silver ray of moonlight suddenly opening from behind a black cloud (the Cloud of Doubt) to shine a path across murky waters. He had told his vision to Rakau, the Ngapuhi tohunga, his friend and dearest enemy and the man who now held the safety of his family in his bloodstained hands. Rakau had laughed. "Omens often mean what we want them to mean, e Keni," he had said and Thomas had stopped listening.

But Rakau had been wrong. For the promise that Thomas had read in the moonlight now stood almost entirely fulfilled.

God had set his feet and those of Hongi and Waikato upon the oceans and He had sent temptation in the mad priest, Reagan. But Thomas had held to his faith and he had prevailed.

God had sent him to Samuel Lee and now his grammar and dictionary were barely weeks away from publication.

But more than anything else, Thomas was vindicated and all his doubts washed away. For now he was a priest. Only yesterday he had kneeled before the Bishop of Ely in a still and solemn and *English* church and had entered priests' orders.

Moreover whom He did predestinate, them He also called; and whom He called them He also justified.

Thomas was justified.

The process had been as rapid as his admission to the Church Missionary Society and departure for Australia had been; barely three months would see the business done. And like his admission and departure then, his ordination had followed years of waiting, despairing, then waiting again. Neither had been easy; that sudden doubt of the Committee last time (*are you the one to bring them light?*) and his reception this time.

Thomas had been indicted. The fear of it had never been far from him, yet when it came he was like a man living in a nightmare, caught in the reality of his own awful predictions.

An indisposition to act in subordination, Pratt had said; and Basil had looked down but he had not demurred.

Your submission to be ordained is rejected.

He had stood before them alone, eyes downcast, hands clasped before him. Behind him Hongi and Waikato were seated, prominent amongst the few dignitaries and bureaucrats who attended. Gambier had welcomed them on behalf of the committee and Thomas had translated. A gracious speech of course, welcoming, haere mai but it was brief and no waiata followed. Hongi had spoken at greater length and more to a point. He was specific about his demands which Thomas translated as requests: a party of men who would dig up the ground in search of iron, a hundred settlers, blacksmiths and carpenters and soldiers under Hongi's command. A large dog would also be nice.

He was enough of a tactician not to mention guns directly.

The committee responded with polite, meaningless applause.

Then the welcome had been over and judgment had begun.

Their faces had told Thomas all he needed to know but he had not anticipated the pang that came when Basil looked away.

With the shame came more fear, are my worst thoughts to be realised? He barely dared to look past his boots and he could not trust himself to speak.

To act in subordination to Mr Marsden and Mr Butler.

To act in subordination to unreason and ignorance, Thomas nearly said. Then he caught himself with a gasp and his fingernails drove into his palms, reminding him where he was.

"Kia ora, e Keni," said Hongi and "kia ora," said Waikato.

Their voices quietened him and he had stood in silence, absorbing judgment.

Something had to be done with them, so they were taken to Cambridge, to Professor Lee and the dictionary.

It had proved a blessing. Thomas plunged into the work, consuming it; it calmed him and he was able to reflect upon his position.

Where are the pebbles? There must be pebbles. Ah.

The stones skidded across a grey, greasy stretch of water that was caught between being a pond and a boggy fen. The land lay low here and gathered and held the winter rain in swamp and wetland and puddled cobblestones. Always grey in a steady drizzle and a kind of snow held away by a broadbrimmed hat and a new coat and mantle.

Thomas had admired Lee's work and reputation and almost immediately he admired the man; an extraordinary scholar, self-educated, then as protégé of the CMS going on to university honours, a professor at 25, an ordained priest. And a quiet and thoughtful gentleman.

"Thomas," he said one morning, "you are trying too hard. The work will take form and intensity will not hurry it. You weary yourself."

Such an ordinary man. Of average height, he would have stood an inch or two above Thomas but it was not apparent. Clean shaven, a commonplace, sandy face, ordinary. His accent told of his humble origins and he made no attempt to disguise it; he was, after all, a linguist. It was comforting to hear those broad vowels again.

And his quiet, intelligent concern.

"I am thankful," Thomas told him. "And you are quite right, I am intense in my considerations for the dictionary; it helps me put aside other idle, unconstructive considerations."

"It is not helping you; the considerations will still be there."

"I know." Thomas put down a sheet that had come to resemble a moko, Hongi's moko. Thomas could forge his signature now. "I can see how I have upset the Society and I know I have been censured. I have been shamed, my mana has shrunk." There was an edge, a bite of something, then Lee saw him clamp upon it and silence it. "And I am rightly censured. My mind was much afflicted, there was some wickedness there."

"Please." Lee raised his voice but it was still kind. "There is too much accusation here. A lack of judgment is not a sin, misguided is not wicked.

And," he pointed to the sheets littering the table, "this is no small task, but we shall master it."

"And I thank God for it. To have something to offer, some atonement. I am a worthless creature."

Samuel was startled. Such a ready confession was most unusual. Indeed, he could remember no occasion where any member of the CMS or any society for that matter had ever admitted to anything. He saw vulnerability and penitence, too, too much penitence, he thought. Then not enough as another side of the missionary came through.

"You are ambitious for office, Thomas. You call yourself a wretched, wicked creature, yet you seek office that would put you above, further above other men. You do not bow your head."

"You think I am a hypocrite?" Thomas'voice rose, shaking on the words; then he abruptly fell silent.

"I am wondering what kind of recognition you seek in ordination."

"I wish to serve the Lord. I wish to use the gifts He gave me to bring His message of forgiveness to the heathen."

And yet you sell them guns. Samuel had been told a good deal about Thomas Kendall; but he did not doubt the man's sincerity.

"But you do not wish to be subordinate to John Butler."

"John Butler must be my master."

"And you will not serve him."

"I will not lie to you."

He was warm in his new coat and dry under the wide brimmed hat. The drizzle was almost beautiful, he thought, misting silver on to the grey waters. No ducks, no mallards. There was a random thought.

Why am I not more elated? There was divine coincidence here; Basil Woodd at the Bentinck Chapel who brought me here (and who now turns away and will not demur from censure. *Stop that!*). And now Samuel Lee at Cambridge who takes my part and persuades the Committee to ordination. (Reluctantly and with conditions, particularly that Messrs Kendall and Butler will tend to their own Separate Parishes and Neither will interfere in the Business of the Other.)

And the office of priest did not extend beyond New Zealand.

\ He had readily accepted the conditions; he was more than content with them, but that they were there in the first place somehow reduced the meaning of it all.

Why was he not more elated? He should feel differently. Things should not be so different. Basil should not turn his head away and Joseph Kent should not fall asleep during a conversation and Florence should be able to remember it. They had parted almost casually, a pat on the shoulder from Robert and another question from Florence. *That was a poor farewell, a mean poroporoaki; my dearest friends and I part forever without a parting word.* He leaned against the door after it had closed on him. He nearly knocked on it, he nearly hammered on it, he nearly roared through the letter box. Instead he had knuckled the tears away and hurried to the CMS to learn that Samuel Lee awaited him at Cambridge.

I should be getting back. Cambridge was not a town to walk alone and even less so the fens and soggy woodland. The armies of the homeless streamed through its gates, slept in its streets and lived however they could, to the point that the Lord Chancellor himself had advocated some legalising and control of begging. At other seasons they might swell Cambridge's population by a third; now as winter closed in their numbers were fewer and their desperation greater.

They intimidated Thomas in a way the Maori never did; they were his brothers and he pitied them and was ashamed of them.

Samuel Lee had listened to Thomas, had understood him –ah God, I am talking to an English priest in England- and had intervened on Thomas's behalf.

"I can see that you are resolute, Thomas." Resolution and guilt about the same thing are odd bedfellows, he thought, but somehow they prop one another up.

"Resolute to do God's bidding."

"But you will determine what that bidding is." Samuel paused. "Might God bid you to bow the head to John Butler?"

He saw a smile tug at Thomas as he answered, "I cannot imagine that He would."

But if Samuel saw the intransigence and marvelled at the penitence that went with it, he also saw a confused man who meant well even as he missed the mark. A man who tormented himself more than he tormented others.

And a liability and a potential embarrassment.

"There is no doubting his sincerity, Josiah. It is just that it won't keep still. He castigates and excuses himself in the one breath and he means them both."

They sat, the three of them in easy leather chairs, encircling a vigorous fire. Samuel Lee sipped from a glass of tea while Josiah Pratt and Basil Woodd nursed brandies.

"He's always been like that." Basil stared into his glass and breathed the fumes. "No," he corrected himself, "not usually at the same time. Still," he paused to drink, "it's been seven years."

"Seven very hard years," said Samuel and looked at the CMS secretary.

"Enough to daunt a more stable man," Josiah Pratt answered. "It's taken hold of all of them, in William Hall as he declaims and complains, in John King as he complains and despairs and now begins another lonely path. In Marsden's passion." He trailed off and turned his attention to his glass.

"You wax quite lyrical, Josiah; another lonely path. Yes indeed, I think Thomas Kendall is one of the loneliest men I have ever met." Samuel sipped his tea delicately, precisely.

"He's so damn desperate to do the right thing," said Basil, "that …" he lost the thought.

"He is just as likely to do the wrong thing." Samuel finished it for him.

"And that," said Josiah Pratt, "is the nub of it."

"Made worse," added Samuel, "by the fact that he is –whether he deserves to be or not- a significant man. More significant in this context than Marsden.

His power over the Maori.

They knew that Hongi understood a great deal more English than he acknowledged and that Waikato was passably fluent. Still, they spoke to the Maori through Kendall with no way of knowing what he was telling them. Significant, indeed.

"I think Hongi holds Thomas more than Thomas holds Hongi." Basil shook his head. "He always lets himself get captured. God, this is depressing." He raised his glass, "to the soul of Thomas Kendall. I think I might get drunk."

"Before you do," said Samuel, "you might decide what you're going to do about him."

Josiah scratched his beard, shot through with grey, much of it turned in the service of the CMS. "I said Kendall would leave this country in the same condition that he entered it. But I'm starting to wonder what that might achieve."

"It will make him angry," said Basil, "and he will share that anger with whomever will listen."

"Like Hongi and Waikato?"

"Exactly like Hongi and Waikato."

The drizzle seemed to have lifted for the moment but the sky was as grey as it ever was and darker now as evening approached.

I must be getting back.

The thought came with the sound of a footstep behind him and he bounded like a coil, forward then twisting with clenched fists to face the man who had come up behind him. A pallid, foxy face hidden under tangled beard and hair bound in a tattered shawl that was neither bandage nor turban but something thereabouts.

The man jumped in fright and something clattered behind him on to the pathway.

"Steady, guvner, steady, Christ, I near shit meself with you leapin up like that."

"At you creeping up like that." But Thomas relaxed, the man was alone, gaunt and shivering, holding himself in a threadbare coat over a threadbare jacket. His whole being cried hunger. "You poor man," said Thomas, "you need aid. Can I help you to some place for comfort?"

Behind the beard there was almost a smile in a decayed mouth. "And where might that be?" it asked.

"Well," Thomas flapped his hands. "Where did you stay last night?"

"I stayed under a bridge, it was sheltered there, then this burly great bastard and his doxy and they had food and they wouldn't share and they kicked me out." He stopped and his teeth chattered in a spasm of shivering. "Your coat," he said, "give me your coat."

Thomas' fingers splayed over his chest in a burst of protectiveness. "What?" he said.

"You heard, give me your coat."

"But it's mine." Thomas was dimly aware of the childishness of the answer.

"You can do without it. You can get another. I'll die without it. Give it to me."

He's quite right. I'll get another, the Society won't like it but they won't let me freeze.

Like this man will freeze. Is freezing.

What would Jesus do?

Thomas spread his hands. "Look," he said, "can we find some peaceful accommodation here?"

"Certainly. As soon as you give me the fuckin coat."

Jesus left.

"That kind of language," said Thomas, "is unlikely to aid your cause."

"Fuck," said the man, disbelieving. "You think I'm askin you, I'm fuckin telling you." Then he was bending down and reaching around behind and Thomas was upon him and the club went flying to one side.

The man was bony under Thomas' grip with no strength to resist it. The he began shivering again, more violently than before as the icy puddle Thomas was holding him in poured through his clothing and froze against his skin.

Thomas registered that the man was not struggling and loosened his grip and stared at the chattering blue grey skull. Then he was panicking, pulling the man from the puddle and casting about for a dry spot to lay him in. He could see none and the man curled into a ball now, twitching, shivering, chattering.

He will die.

Frantically Thomas tore at the buttons of his coat.

"Here. Have it. Have the damned thing."

Then abruptly all thought ceased.

Ordination had finally proved a simple matter of logic and expediency.

"It has been fifteen years since the *Boyd* went down and there has been nothing like it since. Surprising really, you'd think with the greater white population, proximity, guns ..." Josiah shrugged. "It seems that the Lord must be with them – at least to an extent."

"Have Maori the capacity?"

"Certainly. They have always had the capacity, indeed the appetite, oh dear, for it. Hongi has had it since the first days. He holds order in the north, the mission proceeds at his will, but I do not think there is danger,

Hongi would not endanger his resources, but he has a control that is beyond my understanding. And he is a prophet of war."

"And yet," said Basil, replenishing his glass and leaning forward to poke further life into the fire, "he is a charming gentleman."

"Certainly he has charmed Kendall."

"And Kendall, he."

"So," said Samuel, "we have established that given cause in Kendall's eyes —and none of us has that vision- he may well be capable of influencing Hongi against the mission. Hongi's power is such that any turning by him could create a situation of the Gravest Concern. Poetentially disastrous. Kendall is unsettled enough to advise Hongi and Hongi is powerful enough to act upon it."

"I suppose," said Josiah, "that we must make the bloody man a priest."

Basil laughed. "So Thomas has become dangerous," he said. "I wonder if he knows."

"I am sure he does." Samuel was earnest. "He knows very well the power the language gives him. The problem is, he seems to have no idea what to do about it. But he can be malignant, usually impetuously so, later regretting it. He has spoken with shame and justification together about turning Maori against settlers, particularly William Hall and more lately John Butler."

But I spoke only truth, Thomas had finished his confession.

"He does not wish to rule so much as he will not be ruled."

"And yet," said Basil morosely, "someone is always ruling him. But it won't be Butler. Thomas and Butler were born to hate one another. Butler is the greater bully, as I have said before-"

"Indeed as you have said before, Basil, and more than once. And you were quite right, his appointment was an error of judgment that all could see. But you also know very well that support for his preferment came from a high authority." Josiah was irritated. "It was not done wilfully, nor ignorantly."

"I am sorry." Basil leaned forward and solicitously filled his friend's glass. "I mean no blame."

"Butler's appointment is probably irrelevant now," said Samuel. "He is there and he is waiting. Could he be recalled?"

"No," Josiah scowled. "High Authority was very specific. Position and duration. Do nothing to remove him."

"And Kendall cannot be kept away?"

"No, of course not. The man's family is there; he must return."

Samuel nodded. "I understand unsettling forces are at work within his family. His wife," he waved the words away. "I should not have said that."

"Lord," said Basil, "do you think your information was confidential? Their marital difficulties are popular knowledge. Still," he shook his head, "I would never have thought it of Jane."

"Thomas has changed," said Josiah. "Why would not Jane change, too?"

"It seems to me," said Samuel, "that your choices of action are no choices at all." He ticked the points off his fingers. "Kendall must be released to New Zealand. Butler must stay there. You will gain Kendall's good will —which will maintain as far as possible good relations with Hongi- by ordaining him. Restrict the ordination to New Zealand, keep Kendall and Butler apart, perhaps separate parishes." He shrugged. "Do nothing for as long as possible, keep the peace from moment to moment." He shrugged again. "What else can you do?"

Basil pointed at Josiah Pratt. "He's quite right, Josiah. You'll just have to make the bloody man a priest."

And so they did and now the bloody man was moaning his way back to consciousness, shaking awake from his own shivering, shrinking under the cold and terrified by it. He pushed himself to his knees, hugging where his coat should be to keep him warm. To further awakening as he saw the man lying curled up at his feet, quite dead. Then his body took over and he jerked to his feet, stamping *–ah, damn his thieving soul-* on stockinged feet.

He lurched his way across the wetland, splashing through puddles, near falling but holding to his balance. His feet became numb and his teeth chattered uncontrollably as he panted in fragmented prayer.

Th-the L-L-Lord is m-my she-shepherd.

But he was a man accustomed to physical endurance and he made his way back to the cottage he shared with Hongi and Waikato. They were away in London and he was thankful for it as he snatched with shuddering fingers at his freezing, sodden clothing, grabbing blankets from the bed.

He had near wept in frustration as he knelt at the ready made fire, trying to hold his hands steady enough to make a spark. The fire started at last and now he sat dry in spare underwear, a pair of blankets clutched to him and watched the flames give new depth to the amber in his glass; watching the fumes fold into the shadow of a frozen face.

The incident would be barely worth reporting. Another frozen vagrant, another fallen sparrow.

You attacked a man and he died.

Ridiculously he heard himself say, "he would have died hereafter."

Then, "he was set to rob me, to murder me, it was self-defence."

Of course it was.

And my beautiful coat is gone.

The light went out of the day.

Hongi and Waikato were in an entirely different place, one that was flooded in light and colour and opulence. Above great polished beams vaulted across the ceiling; you could place two wharenui beneath it and there would still be room to spare. Below were polished floorboards, here exposed, there lying under a handworked rug. Where the floor met the sweeping balustrade it merged to marble.

But it was cold; the great fire in the centre of the far northern wall glittered off diamonds and gold and crystal but lent no warmth here.

This was the palace of the English king who was even now deeply engrossed in conversation with the king of New Zealand. The theme was never far from his thoughts, nor indeed from those of much of the population.

"A royal wife," he was saying, "is a royal tribulation." He saw their puzzlement and drew a slicing movement across his throat. "A bad thing," he amended, "a rotten thing, a bad wife is as rottenness to a man's bones."

Through Waikato Hongi asked, "What is a bad wife?"

The king was pleased to elaborate. "A bad wife," he said, "is a woman who cannot know her place unless it is under or on top of a man, any man," his voice rose, "a shameless, spiteful creature who would meddle and thwart in matters of state." His eyes stood out, Hongi thought, in creditable pukana. "Do you know," he continued, "that she has appeared in limerick in the *Gazette?* Some guttersnipe wit; 'tis not a truth for ducking'" he quoted, "'that the Queen is fond of fucking.'" Then he recollected himself. "Mr King Shungee," he asked, "do you have a wife?"

Hongi nodded and held up five fingers.

The king was astounded.

"How on earth do you manage 'em?" Beneath the incredulity there was a touch of resentment.

Waikato translated, then asked, "what is 'manage'? They know who they are and what they will and will not do."

"They will do your bidding?"

"There is no need of bidding."

"The queen will not be bid, sir; she will have her way."

"Are your way and hers not the same?"

The king shook his head. "She will defy me and disgrace herself, as rottenness to a man's bones."

"You are describing your enemy."

"And so she is enemy to me and to this country, too."

Hongi and Waikato stared at him. The man must be raving, there can be no such thing.

"And she has friends who have Influence and the dogs in parliament who would intervene, agitators who stir up the masses until they too think they are entitled to an opinion."

"You are surrounded by enemies."

"You understand." The king uplifted a glass of brandy from a silver salver, held in obedient, ever-present white gloves. "How ironic that I should find understanding in," he hesitated and corrected his imminent error, "in a man with five wives who do not hate you, who would not undermine you, who, I suppose, would mourn your death."

"I would expect," Waikato translated, "that upon my death they would hang themselves."

Hongi watched the king stare into his glass and saw his lips move. His hand, he noticed, was fiercely gripped about the stem and he wondered if he might break it.

How could your wife be your enemy?

As he stood watching, he became aware of the movement of bodies, the hum of conversation, the clink of glass, an oboe and a flute crossing. The king was shaking his head now and his mouth was tight with anger. Then he saw Hongi watching and placed a bejewelled hand over his stomach. "A trifling indisposition," he said, "please excuse me." He walked off and Hongi heard him muttering.

"Fucking *hang* themselves."

The departure of the king was a signal for the throng to move in upon the Maori. Both were relaxed in European clothing, particularly Hongi who wore his military uniform with flair and confidence and treasured its warmth. He looked about his admirers and smiled agreeably.

Ruatara, he thought, you were cheated out of an amazing display.

But the palace for all its wonder did not amaze him the way the armoury had. They had stood with the king and courtiers on a turret watching the troops exercise in the parade ground below. Hongi and Waikato had followed the precision of the movements with expert appreciation. He had gazed impassively at the rows of rifles and gleaming bayonets and in quiet meditation had laid his hand upon the great cannon; imagining the impact of cannon on a pa, on a body of warriors, thinking of a thousand muskets in the hands of Ngapuhi.

A man was speaking earnestly to him —with no introduction, how boorish. He stammered as he spoke and Hongi could not be bothered to try to understand him. He looked away to see Waikato in conversation with a tall, lean man, elegant in black but his calves were shrunken under dark stockings and his hands were bony on a tapered cane. His face was pale without the benefit of powder.

Two young women were scrutinising him, giggling behind lace fans. The women here were very different from the pakeha women in New Zealand and utterly different from wahine. They walked as though there were no strength in their legs. Perhaps there wasn't. There was no way of telling as all sight of leg was lost under lace and satin. And they seemed to have no strength in their arms, too. They were not the sort of women for a warrior.

Not that their men impressed as warriors. Half of them acted like their women, all small movement and delicacy. And there were those with a bulk that would stop them, gasping in mid-haka. Yet he remembered the click and snap of twenty rifles, men dropping, kneeling, aiming all with utter precision.

Sir John Mortlock, his very good friend from Cambridge was speaking slowly in his ear and Hongi understood that he was being introduced to the knight's nieces. He held their hands in his and smiled kindly. "How do you do, Miss Annabelle, how do you do, Miss Margaret?"

Then Sir John was being taken in hand by My Lady Mortlock, "how do you do, Mr King Shungee," and whisked away to have words with her uncle.

Miss Annabelle and Miss Margaret continued to stare and Hongi began to think them rude. But this was not his marae and women knew no better here. They were standing closer to him now and Annabell was pointing at his face. "See," she said, "Stephen said they are not painted on, they are dug in with a *chisel*."

Margaret smiled at Hongi. "Imagine the pain," she said.

Hongi understood and thought the pain his moko had brought him was not a fit subject for women. He was aware of becoming angry, but also aware of where he was and how he would need to manage it.

Now there's a fitter subject than wives for management.

He closed his eyes for a moment, then opened them abruptly as a finger snaked down his cheek, crossing over the circling moko.

"Stephen's right, Annabelle, you can feel the ridges."

Hongi stepped back and glared at them.

"Oo," squeaked Annabelle, "we've upset him." And they giggled behind their fans.

I do not wish to be here; I will not participate in this.

With even steps Hongi walked away to where a row of plush, armless chairs sat against the wall. He placed three together, then lay across the single surface, his face buried in the crook of his arm.

There was a hubbub of voices and movement and Waikato hurried through it to where Hongi lay.

"Don't touch him," he said, "he will be angry if you touch him."

Sir John wrung his hands. "What has happened?" he asked.

"Margaret touched him," said Annabelle.

"I am sorry," said Margaret, "I didn't know not to."

"Dear God," said her uncle. "Who do you think he is, what do you think he is?" Then, suddenly aware that Hongi was listening, he turned quickly to Waikato.

"What should we do?"

"Nothing," said Waikato. "He will come back when he is ready."

So Waikato returned to his conversation with the pale gentleman and Hongi removed himself further. He thought about the chain mail coat the King had given him. He had lost his aplomb for a moment then; holding the coat out before him, delighted by the precision of the interlocking, glittering scales. He was further delighted that night when he tried it on.

"It could have been made for me, Waikato. See how it moves on me," he rotated his shoulders, "like a second skin. Let us see what it can withstand." He took a solid brass candlestick holder and swung it hard into his chest. Metal rang and he staggered back, grinning broadly.

"Pai ana, that would have broken a rib without the armour." He picked up a thin, steel knife lying on a platter of fruit and with sudden force thrust it towards his belly. The point twisted, trapped between the scales and there was only the barest of pricks to show for it. "It might turn a sword or an axe," said Hongi. "I wonder how it stands up to a bullet."

This time he brought more caution to the experiment. A pillow was stuffed into the jacket and he shot it at point blank range. The shot brought cries of dismay from neighbours and some hammering upon their front door, to be soothed and comforted and sent away by the Welsh manservant. But the jacket held together under the bullet, a flattened, dented scale, weakened perhaps but intact.

I will keep this coat, Hongi decided and I will wear it to war. He would not part with it as he would later part with all the other gifts. They were a generous collection; the King, aristocracy and fashionable people had raised their mana in an array of extravagant, expensive and largely useless gifts. Hongi could not always understand their value but through Thomas he was well aware of what they would fetch. All were carefully packed and stored for the voyage to Port Jackson where they would become something else.

Long after the fire was lit, he continued to shiver. But his teeth ceased chattering and when he held up his hands for inspection they were quite still. Yet he continued to shiver. Strange. Perhaps it was his eyes that shivered for the room would not keep still. He pulled the blanket closer about him and gazed into the shivering fire.

Snatches of thought, parts of pictures and random words on scraps of paper skittered about and crowding darkly on the edges was an encroaching sense of menace. He pulled the blanket closer to him and tapped his foot to hold the anxiety out.

There was a pop from the fire as a log broke apart and released a pocket of flame. It rose up but in the instant before it dispersed he knew it was a head. Now that he knew what it was he could continue to see it clearly. There, dark, curling locks ringing a brown ochre face and wild black eyes.

It is the head of a giant, he taniwha nuinui and he means my death. But I am ready. There is a round, smooth, heavy stone in my left hand. I searched a long time for that stone and when I found it I knew what it was for. My slingshot is in my right hand and now the stone is in its pouch. And I am whirling my sling with a strength I never knew I had. And even as the giant nears me I am very calm because I know that God will guide my aim. And so He does. The forehead of my enemy splits under my Holy Stone and the legions behind him are frozen in amazement. And now I take the sword and I take his head and here it is, dripping in the fire.

He watched, exulting as the head toppled to one side and now it was lying on a silver platter. And a proud king was handing it to his daughter because she had danced so well.

Now there were two heads, both crowned, and he knew the first was Charles of England and the second was Louis of France. And they joined with the first two heads, then other heads, the vagrant's head, to sit impaled upon the fence before Hongi's marae.

He shook his own head in confusion and then the fire was just a fire again.

At another fire in a London snug, sitting at a table where glasses and bottles glinted off the steady flame and the paler light of candle were two …what? First inspection might have thought them a part of Thomas' vision: a pale, cadaverous face with dilated eyes gazing vaguely through the coiled smoke of candle and tobacco at a round, fat face, falling to chins over lace and silk, a white, powdered face with scarlet rose-bud lips and mascared eyes. Like a corpse and a painted frog.

"I have been in attendance upon the king," said James Worthing. He paused to draw heavily upon a hand-rolled cigarette and then the conversation paused again as he broke into a fit of coughing.

My Lord Farnwright took advantage to push home the last cream bun, patted his lips with a silk napkin and regarded the empty plate.

"And did you find anything of interest there?" he asked.

"To my surprise, yes. I engaged for near an hour in stimulating conversation with a cannibal."

"Indeed," Lord Farnwright burped delicately, "and what did you learn? What did he tell you of the taste of flesh?"

"Somewhat like pork, I believe, cooked over hot stones."

"Fancy."

Worthing's eyes narrowed. "Ah," he said, "that easy, studied flippancy. But can you imagine the reality of it?"

Farnwright sipped his brandy and burped again, this time not so delicately. "What would I gain from that?" he asked.

"Some breadth of vision, perhaps."

"It is a vision I would sooner do without. Was there anything else of interest?"

Worthing nodded. "There was," he answered, "I was brought up to date on the doings of a former acquaintance of ours. Thomas Kendall."

"Kendall? The name rings a bell."

"Madonna? The horny owl?"

"Christ," Farnwright appeared to wake up, "the tutor? What has he to do with cannibals?"

"He has lived amongst them for eight years, brought two of them back to England to meet the king. He's a priest now, a missionary and father to a tribe of his own."

"Christ," said Farnwright again, "he has a cannibal wife. He certainly wasn't put off by the great experiment then."

"No," said Worthing, "his wife is an English woman, though I wonder whether … Anyway, can you imagine his life?"

"A fairly uncomfortable one, I should think."

"That's it?" Worthing was clearly irritated, "the man has crossed the world to live in the heart of savagery and you wonder whether he has a stuffed sofa in his lounge."

"Ah, he has a lounge then?"

Boney fingers drummed upon the table.

"That bumpkin has crossed the oceans of the world; you and I occasionally cross the channel. He has, according to Waikato –"

"Waikato?"

"The cannibal chief. He has climbed mountains, forded rivers in the flood-"

"How disagreeable. I prefer the comfort of my carriage."

"Fuck you."

"Unfuck you."

"He has sat with savage priests and discussed their lives, their beliefs. He speaks their language, for God's sake."

Farnwright snapped his fingers and a pair of white gloves materialised. "Some more of those delightful buns." Then, "why James, I do believe the bumpkin has made you angry again."

"He has been working with an Oxford don to publish the first dictionary of the language."

"And what cause for anger do you find in this?"

"I'm not angry with him, I'm annoyed with you, with your glib easy answers that mean nothing, with your indifference to anything that can't be crammed into your overflowing belly."

"My thanks for the reminder," Farnwright helped himself to a bun and sent it on its way. "My answers are as they have always been; why should they be so annoying now?"

Worthing made no answer and Farnwright continued. "Last time you were angered by his hypocrisy. Is he still a hypocrite?"

"Probably. Waikato said he preaches peace and trades guns. He seemed to find it amusing."

"But you do not?"

"I do not find it amusing, I said I found it interesting."

"Ah, there is a difference then?"

Boney fingers drummed again.

"I see what Kendall has done with his life –"

"-and what you have not done with yours."

"Very well. I see that callow, virginal prude staring at my wife's tits, distraught by the thrills of Newgate; now I know of a man who has travelled, a scholar, a priest who has traded weapons to savages, who speaks with them in their own tongue, who has experienced God knows what while you grow fatter and I grow thinner..."

"Ah, so you are envious then? Now I am not so sure how interesting that is, but it is certainly amusing."

Worthing's lips tightened then and his fingers drummed upon the mahogany. Then he paused and shook his head, wondering.

"Is this a conversation?" he asked.

Farnwright was puzzled. "What else could it be?"

"An exercise in vanity. A procession of quips and repartee."

Farnwright went to reply but fell silent as Worthing continued.

"What do we learn? What do we inform?"

"Nothing much. What does it matter?"

"It matters and has done so now for some time. It matters that Kendall seeks and may even find meaning in his life and we do not. It matters that I don't like you and I don't like me and yet we ..." The words trailed away.

Farnwright patted a napkin over crimson lips.

"You are moving to philosophy, I see," he said. "Which I find neither interesting nor amusing."

"And there you go again. No," as Farnwright made to reply, "you have made your point. And I think it may be the only point you have. And it's not enough. None of it is enough."

"Enough for what?"

"Enough to go on with."

Farnwright smiled. "Back to Young Werther, then," he said.

"Yes," Worthing nodded. "I am tired of pain and pointlessness, of you, of me, of all of it."

Farnwright watched in silence as his companion laboriously pulled himself to his feet.

"Ah well," he said to the retreating back, "have a nice trip."

CHAPTER 38

Kerikeri October 1821

The Journal of Francis Hall

It is well past a month since Hongi left. I don't know whether we are better off with him or without him.

When we were without him, when he and Waikato and Kendall were away, the people were not as disorderly as had been feared. (The odd theft and a scowl but mostly they went about their business.) *And the chiefs held them in and none of us went in any real fear of physical injury.*

It had been a fair autumn and a full crop had been lifted. The people had dispersed to their hapu and whanau to attend their own crops and provisions for the winter. After such a season, they were well provided.

The hostility shrank from want of numbers and there were friendly visits to the villages. Sitting outside if the night was warm, perhaps a friendly fire, a cup of tea with a family you have met and if korero was a matter of mime and guesswork, there was still a warmth here.

The bush quietens in autumn but it is still the same bush, tired now, a little faded, ready for a moi. There was a stillness then.

Then Hongi came back and the stillness was gone. He came back angry and his anger set off the hostility and quickly it became something huge and implacable. The hunger for killing became a palpable thing and we could not believe that we were safe. Hongi was indifferent to our pleas. 'It is our way,' he said.

And as their way became more manifest, the settlers shrank from it and avoided it. Gone were the days of friendly mime and guesswork but the meaning was clear. 'We are taking back our mana,' Ngapuhi said. 'Now we will show you who we are. We are paramount.'

The mission shared in Marsden's lie. "Your king does not know you," Hongi said. "He does not know Matene." He had paused for dramatic effect. "But he knows me. And he has shown his appreciation of who I am. He has set a helmet on my head and given me a coat of mail for my protection and a musket in the one hand and a sword in the other. His mana has touched these taonga and I will bring them more mana.

"And he says he knows nothing of your claim that the trade in muskets is unlawful. 'Here,' he said, handing me my musket, 'I must be breaking the law. I wonder if Mr Marsden will come to arrest me.' And he laughed and I spat.

"So now I know your lie and I know how your Society tried to weaken my mana. For while the king and the lords of England, the true rangatira, respected my mana with their gifts, the mean koha from your Society told another story. It tells me you are slaves to King Hori and that he does not know you."

Francis sighed and scratched at brown curly locks that regularly threatened to unseat his wig. At bottom he was an affable man with a liking for peace. The explosions he had witnessed since his arrival in the new world, Marsden, Butler, Rewa and many others, William Hall, more self-contained but no less virulent, these explosions had embarrassed more than alarmed him. And exasperated him, too.

How can anything be achieved in all this squabbling, this utter failure of fellowship?

He corrected himself; this was altogether an extreme judgment (*dear God, am I becoming like them?*).

There had been much kindness here. James Kemp, for example, was a fine fellow, an easy man to work with, and the two had done well as they brought order to the holding and distribution of mission stores. And Mrs Kemp was a good, sensible woman and a wonderful cook.

William Hall on his own could be agreeable. In his garden, away from the warfare, he gave Francis generous and useful counsel. He spoke of the families he visited, the men he traded with, the men he worked with.

"I've been working with Kepa for six years now. It's a pleasure to work with him, he has become an excellent tradesman."

"You have taught him well."

"Yes," with a slow smile, "yes, I suppose I have. And Haami, too. He's not in the same class as Kepa but he's steady; and you should see some of the carving he has done. Perfect lines."

He spoke with pride of his son. "Good, solid lad. Great help to his mother while I'm away. Speaks the language like a native, never neglects his duties. He's a worker, strong lad."

And John King was a good man, too, less disengaged than he had been at the beginning, although always at a distance. A sad man, but a good man, too.

But Francis could not be at ease with John and Mary Butler. Everything was always in the context of a Dispute, resistance to someone or something. Even when they attempted to be agreeable and invited him to dine with them the conversation remained Dispute. They seemed to be constantly angry and Francis could find no sympathy for it.

This has been my first experience of a Building towards War. There have been others before my time but none, I am told, of this Magnitude or Intensity. The mood is one of Vengeance and though it is bent on the southern tribes, yet there is a portion of Anger for us. None walks safely abroad and no one is encastled here.

As John Butler had stood challenged in his own home, Mary behind him, her left arm steadying a whimpering child, her right hand holding a poker, imploring him to submit for their lives. And John's hands had moved in submission and placation, his eyes dropped and his voice was soothing. Perhaps it had saved them from immediate violence. And then they were saved, as Rewa stormed in, utterly naked and utterly enraged; he had roared at the intruders and then at Butler and then they were all gone and the missionary and his family safe and only partially plundered.

We have our Health and our Faith and a Community that mostly serves. And even within these Dark Times there are moments of Respect and Kindness.

And as the numbers reduced, there was more respect and more kindness.

On a call to Rangihoua Francis had made the acquaintance of the old tohunga, Rakau who had taken Kendall's family into his own.

Rakau must be Advanced in years now, he recalls battles of over fifty years ago. He is much given to Korero and through the good offices of his Daughter we have had friendly and informative Discussions.

It is a new, quite powerful communication to speak with another through an interpreter. It can be confusing to begin with as you find yourself earnestly listening to the interpreter putting your words into another tongue, listening for the occasional word you might recognise, to nod hearty agreement, ka pai. After a time you realise that this is pointless, you either trust the interpreter or you don't. Either way there is no point in listening to words everyone knows you don't understand. So the time for communication draws out as every story is told twice and the space between is twice as long. You start to listen to the other's voice and watch his hands and eyes and mouth as Rakau had watched Marsden's and you begin to hear the stories in between.

On a clear morning before the birth of spring when the bush swelled and deepened and the sun was warm in a cloudless sky, Francis sat in the sand at Rangihoua and had korero with Rakau. Around them stood a dozen or so Ngapuhi, attending with varying degrees of attention.

The sun lifted off the bay and the light that enfolded them was a holy light, Christ's light brought into the darkness. It flooded Francis with utter certainty, I am an apostle in paradise.

He smiled at the old tohunga, cross-legged in the sand but addressed his words to the young woman who sat between them. He enjoyed the opportunity to look at her, to watch the waved, jet hair glistening in the sun off the sea lying against the smooth, brown neck on smooth, brown shoulders. She was quite perfect and that she spoke English with an accent straight out of Thorsby did not make her ridiculous.

"Why must Maori war?"

"All men war."

"My people do not war with you."

"No, we are too strong."

Francis thought of the English navy and Rakau recalled what Ruatara and Hongi had said of British military force and both left the point alone.

"The English King does not go to war for utu."

"Then why does he go?"

"To keep his people safe, to keep us from invasion."

"Have you ever been invaded?"

"Not for a long time."

"And during the time that you were not being invaded, did you invade?"

Francis was too educated to deny it.

"But only in defence, I am told."

"Of course, it is much more agreeable to defend yourself on enemy soil. As Hongi is doing."

"I think," said Tungaroa for Rakau, "we often find the same causes for utu. Sometimes from the same event, and sometimes our utu is the same."

"I cannot imagine such a thing."

"Then I will tell you of one. Two years ago Te Morenga took a large band of taua down the east coast to engage with Te Whanau-a-Apanui. Te Morenga was very angry and had a number of reasons, but one of them he shared with the English.

"Eighteen years before, Te Waru of te Whanau-a-Apanui had bought a Ngapuhi woman from a mutineers' ship and he had killed and eaten her. "Te Morenga and Ngapuhi took utu against Maori; the English had already taken utu against the English. And it amounted to the same thing."

The face of the ugliest man in the South Pacific was by definition memorable. Insipid, stupid eyes peering over an oft-broken beak and the defining portion: short, fat lips pulled clear of yawning gums.

"I'm certain it's him, sir, can't be another like him."

They found Billy but they took him alone, the *Venus* and the others gone together. Ngapuhi stood by and watched them take Billy with the same placidity that they had watched the others decamp.

To begin with, Billy was most outraged by the treachery of the betrayal. That he had no recollection of its circumstances, nor the circumstances of anything very much, in no wise weakened his outrage. That he was where he was was evidence of betrayal. How else could he be there?

Where he was, was on the deck of a substantial trader. And the captain was brother-in-law to the master of the *Venus*. He was not much concerned by the fate of the women, although of course he abhorred it, but he was very much troubled by the fate of the vessel he had come so close to retrieving. And all he had for his rage and his loss again was Billy Gums.

Billy wailed that none had ever been killed by them, it was the Maoris who killed them and ate them, they just bartered. And he had never wanted to be on Kelly's crew in the first place. He joined with a gun at his head.

"You can't say 'no' to him, Your Worship."

"Nor to me, neither. Quite apart from your vile deeds with the women, you have mutineered against your lawful captain and taken his ship."

Thus the captain clarified his take, his cause.

And then pronounced utu. "And now, you son of a bitch, I'm going to hang you."

With urgent new clarity, Billy had cried out that he was not bound to this ship, the captain had no lawful authority, it would be murder, only a military officer could order death, it would be murder.

"They hanged him anyway," said Rakau through Tungaroa. "And because the captain and the officers hated mutineers worse than any other thing they weighed Billy Gums light and the knot was tied loosely."

Rakau spread out his hands.

"Billy took property from the English, Te Whanau-a-Apanui took life from Ngapuhi; the English killed Billy, Ngapuhi killed te Whanau-a-Apanui. Take, utu, balance."

"Surely to God there is all the difference in the world between the execution of a single, foul and guilty man and the slaughter of a tribe, men, women and children together."

"But the tribe is everyone, men, women and children together."

They lay in the warm sand at Rangihoua Bay in Christ's perfect light and they talked horror.

The words were Rakau's but the voice was Tungaroa's, soft and clear and she told the story with her own expression. Francis was captivated.

"Te Morenga came upon Te Waru suddenly but the Ngaiterangi chief was not alarmed; this was, after all, a populous area and there were many of his own people, armed and hungry for conflict.

"So when Te Morenga taxed him with the death and the eating of his niece, Tawaputa, Te Waru stared him down."

She fixed her eyes on Francis and they widened in pukana and drew him in.

"Te Waru mocked Te Morenga. 'There is no satisfaction here for you here. Perhaps I will kill you and eat you, too. Will there be satisfaction in that?'"

She breathed quickly through nostrils flared in Te Waru's defiance.

"Te Morenga invited him to join in battle the following day and Te Waru agreed.

"Ah, what a fine sight it was.

"Ngapuhi stamped as one man and their cry reached up to Ra. And Ngaiterangi with mighty numbers of their own stamped their answer. They charged Ngapuhi, mere strapped to their wrists, taiaha in hand. And as they neared, some of those taiaha became spears and a Ngapuhi chief went down."

Her hands followed those of her father, pressed against her breast, showing where the spear had entered. Rakau watched the young man's attentive eyes.

"But then Ngapuhi, only thirty five of the seven hundred, fired into the approaching Ngaiterangi and the foremost twenty fell.

"Ngaiterangi fled and Te Morenga was satisfied and did not follow. Besides the dead blood he also had the living blood of Ngaiterangi, Te Waru's wife and children. He attempted to sue for peace.

"But Te Waru would not surrender.

"He retreated to his pa, reassembled his men and led them against Ngapuhi. And the thirty five marksmen emptied round after round into them and they were slaughtered."

Tungaroa raised her eyebrows in inquiry.

"Great stubbornness and an inability to learn, don't you think?"

Francis had no idea what to think.

"Te Waru escaped the battle into the Tauranga bush where he prowled like a wild thing. He prowled to the edges of the settlement and he saw the bodies piled high. Four hundred dead they say and another two hundred and sixty to become slaves. And he saw how those who had built the umu were now fed to the hangi.

"He leaned against a tree and he watched a young Ngapuhi man lash the wrists of a headless teenage girl, then fling them over his shoulders to bear her to the umu. He watched a man, evidently of some wit who found and gave amusement in impaling severed feet with taiaha and marching them about the village."

"He watched the doings of hell." Francis was aghast. "How can you tell such a story?" he asked Tungaroa.

She asked her father and, interpreting, answered, "it is a story you should know. My father also says that I know the story well enough to tell it in my own words."

"I don't like this story."

"No," said Tungaroa, "of course you don't. Now, Te Waru crept through the bush, lost of all reason. He did not exist, everything had been taken from him and he moaned in his nothingness. He did not sleep or eat, he prowled like a tiger from India.

"He saw that there was no mana in him, it had been taken away and burned upon the ovens and it lay in scattered limbs that had already begun to stink. And he knew that he must take it back.

"He prowled along the bushline and found a lone ngaio at the edge of the sand. This will serve as kindly shade, he thought and he climbed the tree and crouched concealed in its branches. After a time Te Whareumu, a man of the ovens, came walking along the beach and stopped to shelter in the shade. Te Waru dropped upon him, knocking the breath from him and as Te Whareumu fought to breathe his hands were lashed behind him and his own taiaha was at his throat.

"Holding the taiaha was a crazy man. His hair stood up unbound and unkempt at all angles from his face and there were twigs and leaves in it. He had bled or was bleeding from a hundred scratches he had taken in his prowling.

"But there was reason in his voice.

"'Stand up,' he said and Te Whareumu obeyed. 'Now,' said Te Waru and the taiaha shifted against his captive's cheek to turn him, 'walk back quietly through the bush, think to be concealed.'

"Te Waru walked Te Whareumu to the threshold of what had been his pa and was now the graveyard of Ngaiterangi."

"The doings of hell."

"Then Te Waru untied Te Whareumu and returned his taiaha to him. 'Now,' he said, 'you will bind me and I will be your prisoner.' Te Whareumu did as he was bade and led Te Waru into the heart of Ngapuhi. Immediately they were beset by young toa, engulfed by the thought of the head of a Ngaiterangi rangatira and Te Whareumu was hard pressed to hold them at bay. Yet he prevailed and then Te Morenga himself was calling for quiet as Te Whareumu recounted his tale."

Rakau spoke and Francis watched her listen to him and then watched her as she spoke.

"What do you think Te Waru has to say, Mr Hori? What would you say?"

"Truly," Francis shook his head, "I cannot begin to imagine."

"At first he just looked at them and his hands were tied behind his back and he faced the ovens where his people lay and where he would probably soon lie and his shoulders were straight, his head was up and he was a proud man again.

"He told them who he was and where he was from and Ngapuhi sat among the horror and gave him ear.

"'I will not skulk about my pa like a starving dog, hiding on my own turangawaewae, waiting for you to go, to curse your backs.

"'I was not dragged here by the feet. I walked here. This man,' gesturing to Te Whareumu, 'was not my captor, he did not bring me here, I brought him, the whole man, I could have brought his head but I brought him entire.

"'Now I stand on my marae and I am a rangatira of Ngaiterangi and I salute my people, nga mate o Ngaiterangi, and I look in your face, Te Morenga, and I say, have you had satisfaction enough?'"

Francis held up a hand to stem the story. "Please," he begged, "a moment."

Tungaroa was pleased her story was having such an impact. I must be telling it well, she thought and looked to her father for confirmation.

Francis was overwhelmed. He had left the golden bay and behind closed eyes he could not hold out the open ovens, smoke and flame in the stygian air, humanity eviscerated and become flesh again. And tattooed, naked demons exulting in their own damnation.

Tungaroa watched with concern. He had become pale and was breathing shallowly.

She leaned across and tapped his knee. "Listen," she said, "this is a fine story. For Te Morenga and all Ngapuhi could see Te Waru's mana. And they restored his wife and children to him and they made peace with him. And unlike Ngapuhi's other alliances which were always broken, sometimes immediately, this peace has prevailed. We pass through their lands as we go to meet Waikato and we pass in peace."

Peace being the gaps between the wars.

Francis knew that Rakau and his family, particularly Tungaroa, were close to the Kendalls. She had lived with them for years off and on and had become fluent in English under Kendall's tutelage. What else do you teach someone when you teach them a new tongue?

It was Tungaroa who decided that Francis should visit with Jane Kendall.

"She needs to talk to a kind pakeha."

Francis had already given thought to a visit but with a certain diffidence. He had heard of her fall from every source and the general animosity towards her absent husband was perhaps the mission's only common thread.

And himself a single man.

It was a point upon which Marsden had experienced Forebodings.

"The temptations of the Adversary are prevalent in the Pacific Islands and they are harder upon the single man. And when he is a young, fit man, they are harder still.

He paused, waiting for Francis' agreement and apology.

Francis felt that he was apologising for being male, young and fit but apologised anyway.

"God will give you the strength. You are His Instrument."

Now Francis was touched and his gratitude was genuine.

"And to help you in your resolve, you will have only to look about you to see the Wages of Vice."

And Francis had understood that association with the very source –and her husband away- would not be a clever political move.

Tungaroa registered his reluctance but persevered. The church people at Rangihoua do not talk to her, even though she is sad and lonely. She is quiet during the day and she cries quietly at night.

Francis stared unhappily at his boots, then looked up, feeling Rakau's gaze on him. The eyebrows were raised in silent enquiry.

"Of course I will meet her," he said. "When?"

"Now." She stood up and he watched her brush the sand off her thighs. "My matua wants to be alone now, so I will take you to her."

The suddenness of the move brought some trepidation –Unannounced, Mr Hall, no Thought to preparation, there are Steps, sir- but then he forgot about it as they walked together across the beach and up to the Kendalls' home.

Past a derelict shed, torn open, the door and shutters gone, fed to the family fire by an angry cuckold, vines twisting through the openings as Maui had once crawled into Hine nui te po. The colour of the exotics long gone. In their place, sheltered by the shed against the cold south salty wind, there crouched lines of cabbage and cauliflower, spinach waving above them, a small peach tree readying itself for its spring flourish.

It was an awkward meeting, made none the easier by the presence of her eldest son. Thomas Surfleet was a taller, leaner version of his father but he had his uncle's eyes. They flickered across Francis and returned to the knife he was sharpening.

Just before he met her Francis realised he had no idea what Jane looked like. He had never thought to ask and given her theme it would probably have been regarded askance. When he saw her, he dimly realised that he had nonetheless imagined a kind of presence because he was disappointed by the emptiness of her.

No woman had ever looked less like Jezebel.

Francis struggled to make something of the visit. He asked after her health and the health of her children ('we are all well, we have nothing to complain of'), he inquired after their comfort (not entirely comfortably –the woman has Traded Arms to the Maori, sir. Just like her husband) and learned they were entirely comfortable and had nothing to complain of.

Francis waited for her to ask something of his history but she had no questions and the silence grew. He tried to draw her son into the conversation but he too seemed to have little use for it. In growing desperation he complimented Jane on the orderliness of her house and the productivenesss of her garden. She seemed to brighten a little then, so he pressed on.

And learned that the garden had been built by another who had gone away. Before he went he had brought up prodigious amounts of food for his garden, seaweed and sand together, the carcasses of fowls, the entrails and bone of pig. Once at dawn he had single-handedly heaved a ravaged marlin across the sand to bury in his garden. He had taken the run-off from the roof to a tank and then to other run-offs and other tanks that lay above the garden.

Francis became alarmed as he realised that she was talking at length of the convict Stockwell with whom she had – Could this in Any Wise be construed as an Appropriate Conversation, sir! Yet she was utterly impersonal, just telling what she knew.

Well done, Jane. You told Mr Hall that praise for the garden was not for you. You didn't correct him, you were just honest. And truthful. Well done. But he's looking a bit agitated, isn't he? What can you have said?

Francis asked again about the children's health and she sipped her wine and became easier again and a little more expansive; that is, she said 'all well' in different ways and at greater length.

Tungaroa was speaking. "Whaea Keni needs to hear you talk. Say stuff."

"What stuff?"

"How should I know? Tell her where you're from."

So Francis talked into the silence about his home and family and recognised sadly that this was the first time anyone had shown an interest. He talked about the father he admired, a man occasionally given to absolute judgment –the only difference between a petty thief and a bank robber is a lack of nerve- but a fair man, a good Christian, a man of peace.

He told Jane how he missed his brothers, particularly John; the most even-tempered man I have ever known, a second father in the early days when our father began to fail.

He stopped on the hiss of a sudden intake of breath and looked across the table to meet the narrowed eyes of Thomas Surfleet.

"And what," asked the young man tightly, "was your father's failure?" Francis wondered at the tone and the emphasis on the second word but answered levelly enough, "an infection, sir, that slowly spread through him and eventually took his life."

"Ah," Thomas Surfleet looked momentarily confused, then without a word took up his knife and left the room.

Francis continued to visit, sometimes with Tungaroa, sometimes alone. He learned that he need not take Thomas Surfleet's aggression seriously but that the younger boys should. He decided that it did not matter what he decided about the girls, which was a good decision seeing that he was quite lost. Were they children or spinsters, were they angry or sad or content, we have nothing to complain of. Why when they were present did he become so ill at ease, so conscious of Female? Yet it was when he was alone with Tungaroa that he was at his most relaxed.

"You bring whaea Keni comfort."

"Yes, I think I do. But she says nothing."

"She hasn't anything to say yet. But she will."

"I am not the man for her confession."

"She has already done that, a thousand times. She does not need to be heard yet. But she needs to be seen."

So they sat together in the sun and drank wine and Francis cared not a jot for Marsden's Forebodings. He spoke with a young man's nostalgia for his youth, his mother's cooking, fishing with his father, wrestling with his brothers. He smiled to himself in the details, remembering. And Jane heard the affection in his tone and the longing, too, as she sipped her wine and peered into the shadows.

Paramatta April 1821

An old lady sat in the autumn sun and watched the world go by. Beneath a broad-brimmed hat her hair was white and thin, pulled back in a coiled bun from a pale, lined face. Her eyes were pale, too, but they were clear and focussed as she watched the world with careful attention.

Past the orchard, harvested now and the leaves turning gold, across the fields and down to a long, narrow shed where William Hall and her husband had once fought over payment due. Now a set of wagons could be built within that shed. It was a sensible, practical building as were the shearers' quarters that adjoined it, but there was little charm in it and her gaze moved away across the fields.

She had ridden those fields once and now, with most of her life behind her, she knew that those had been the best of times. It was probably a sin to hold them so and doubtlessly she would pay for it. For if she had ever made Faust's bargain, she would have been caught on a wild ride.

Her sense of the wild was long gone now and for all that she had joyed in it she would not have had it back again. Now her pleasure was in peace and stillness and the colours of autumn and birdsong. She had become accustomed to the failure of her body and accepted the use of one arm and one leg as she had once accepted two. Others had admired her patience and forbearance but she held it to be no great thing. It was how it was and that was all that there was. One could be a cripple and still be thankful. And it had brought a different kind of freedom.

She sat in the shade of a liquid amber diminishing by the hour as its leaves floated down to carpet the lawn. Samuel had ordered the gardener to sweep them away but Elizabeth had countermanded him.

"Let them lie," she had said, "they bring a colour to the grass and as they rot they will feed it. It is as it should be."

The leaves also fell on to the extensive gardens that ringed the house. She missed gardening more than riding and had tried on occasion to tend to it. But she could not control her balance and had ended up sprawled among the cabbages. "Not a becoming position," she had said, "for the wife of a chaplain" and she had given it away. But she had maintained direction of the preparation, the planting, the maintenance and the harvest. Amongst other things, it was her connection to Ruatara. She had awoken the gardener in him and still thought it one of the best things she had ever done.

Suddenly the peace was broken by the slamming of a door, then boots scrunching the gravel path, then the sound of hooves driven to sudden gallop. She sighed and sat and waited.

Now there was a second set of boots, slower, heavier and angry, she could tell, making their way towards her. And the rubbing of hands.

"It is too bad, Mrs Marsden, it is just too bad."

"Your meeting with Mr Kendall did not go well?"

"There was no meeting here. I cannot imagine why the man bothered to come at all."

Because you ordered it, she thought, but said nothing.

Samuel stood behind her and rested his hands on her bony shoulders. The touch seemed to calm him and his breath came easier. Elizabeth reached up with her good right arm and patted his hand.

"You might have expected," Samuel continued, "that having achieved every last da- thing he set out for, he might have shown a touch of, what? Gratitude? Grace? Repentance? But not a bit of it." His voice shook and she patted his hand again.

He squeezed her shoulder lightly, then she felt his hand withdraw. He was, she knew, counting off points on his fingers.

"One, he has been ordained without qualification and through manipulation and blackmail." Elizabeth sympathised but without much feeling. Ordination, she knew from long experience, neither reflected a man's character nor changed it. "Two, his dictionary will be published. Professor Lee reports that Kendall's contribution was invaluable. He is, I think, too kind —as well as charmed and deceived." Samuel paused to draw a breath. "Still," he added charitably, "it is a lesser matter. Three, he has been granted new authority by the Society, again the work of manipulation and blackmail." This, Elizabeth knew, truly rankled; again she sympathised but again without much feeling. Could Kendall be that much worse than Butler? "Ah, but the fourth thing, Elizabeth, the fourth thing ..."

Now he had her sympathy and intensely so. For what Kendall had done was, even for a forgiving Christian woman, beyond forgiveness. He had armed Ngapuhi. All the gifts that England had lavished upon Hongi —with the exception of the helmet, coat and sword- had been converted to cash and the cash to muskets. And as before, as he had ever done, Kendall would have been in the thick of the trading.

"... and probably lined his own pockets into the bargain."

Elizabeth remembered the wretched little man, wringing his hands, all guilt and repentance at his wife's bedside. At the time, although she had found him ludicrous, she had accepted his repentance, his love and concern for his wife and she had softened. And when Jane had betrayed him she had pitied him. But the leaving of his family to advance his ambition and now this ...Like her husband she judged him and condemned him.

Samuel fell silent and into the silence there came the clopping of hooves and steel-rimmed wheels on a stony road. Two teams of four horses were dragging carts laden with rock and gravel down the roadway that ran from the main highway to the shearing sheds and quarters. Last winter between the heavy rains and the flooding plains the road had begun to fail. It remained passable, barely, but would not survive further such treatment. Samuel had explained to the prison superintendant that while officially the road might not be designated as public, still the welfare of the state was dependant upon it. How else would the rich merino fleece reach the docks? What effect might this have upon the state's economy? The superintendant understood that this was more about the chaplain's pockets than the state's but he had not demurred.

They watched the teams move slowly down to where the road had become part of the field. There the horses were released to graze where they would and Samuel tutted. Unlike sheep which nibbled neatly at the tips of the grass, horses would grip it with their tongues and uproot it. With that and their greater weight ... Still, there was plenty for all and the ground was firm after the dry summer; it was no matter.

Now the men were unloading the wagon, heaving the larger rocks into position to shore up the sides and retain the road. Smaller stones and gravel were emptied into the spaces between where they were broken under sledgehammers and crushed into the beginning of a flat surface.

The three guards retired to the thin shade of a lone eucalypt, laid their muskets down, unfastened their tunics, filled their pipes and appeared to lose all further interest in proceedings. Samuel tutted again. There was, he would have conceded, probably no need for further attention and the men were capably driven by a belligerent foreman. But it was a poor look all the same. An Affront to Industry.

As you are being idle, a voice whispered, *you should be up and doing.*

"Look, Samuel," Elizabeth was pointing at the gang, "see that man, the one nearest the right hand wagon." Samuel watched but could see nothing of interest, just a tall, lean man with a shaved brown head and a bare brown back. He began to say so, but Elizabeth hushed him. "Just watch," she said.

After a time Samuel took her point. The other men laboured more or less to the commands of the foreman, pausing frequently for breath or water, and who could blame them for it was brutal work and the day was warm. But this man worked unceasing, methodically moving from rock to rock, laying his sledgehammer down only to take up a smaller hammer to crush the smaller pieces.

At last the man did stop and turned and walked towards them to the large water barrel that stood between the wagons. Samuel squinted, straining, there was something about the fellow... Then he remembered.

"It is Richard Stockwell," he said.

"Stockwell? The Kendalls' servant? The one who ...?"

Samuel nodded, then remembering where he stood grunted agreement.

Stockwell. He had not given the man a thought since upbraiding him in the Port Jackson stockade these four? five? how many years past? Nor had he ever thought about what it was that had taken him there to speak his condemnation. Yet he remembered the interview clearly, the sullen brute, dumb to begin with, then, when driven to speech, making no protestation of innocence, no excuse. For reaons he had also given no thought to this placid compliance had enraged Samuel and he had reviled the man, then forced him to chant a disclaimer of his very humanity. He would sooner now that he had not remembered.

"Stockwell," Elizabeth mused, "I would have thought that his sentence would have expired by now."

Samuel grew more baffled as he registered a strong disinclination to tell her that he had extended it.

"He is clearly a good worker," Elizabeth persisted, "quite Herculean really. I wonder why he has not been signed out to work on a farmstead."

Samuel grunted meaninglessly but still Elizabeth was not done. "Stockwell," she said again, "what a coincidence to see him on this very day when you have just met with," she stopped and reached up to her shoulder with her good hand.

The unspoken name brought Samuel a quick shot of resentment but it was preferable to the uncertainty.

"The day is growing warmer," he said, "and the shade is moving." He reached around the back of her chair and grasped the seat from either side. Effortlessly he lifted the chair and his frail wife and carried them closer to the liquid amber. Then he hurried back to the house to return immediately with a chair of his own. It so happened that the trunk of the tree stood between Elizabeth and the convict gang and he faced her with his back towards them.

Elizabeth was concerned. She had seen many moods reflected in her husband's face, pleasure in accomplishment, concern, kindness, tenderness even, obduracy, spite, anger and rage in the face of defiance or setback. But she had never seen him so unsettled, dear God, was this uncertaintly? Doubt?

"You are concerned about your meeting with Kendall?" she asked. The lack of title was very unlike Elizabeth and Samuel received it as sympathy. His thought returned to the past hour and he relaxed into a more familiar, angrier space.

"The man is beyond all reason or conscience," he said to his boots, nodding in agreement with himself. "And he has changed, Elizabeth," looking up, "he was as a stranger to me."

"What did he say?"

Samuel closed his eyes, remembering. "I taxed him with his offence, of course," he said. "I asked him how one so newly ordained could so readily defy the requirements of his station."

"And he said?"

"He looked at me quite calmly, dispassionately, so unlike the Kendall I have known, and asked me what I meant. I said that I hoped he would not be rogue or fool enough to deny his part in the trading of muskets on the *Dromedary* and he interrupted me, he interrupted me, Elizabeth, quite calmly, mark, to say that he thought I was speaking of events subsequent to his ordination. His words were polite enough but his tone was utter insolence. I told him that I would not quibble and adverted to the sale of Hongi's gifts and their conversion into guns." Samuel paused as he brought his breathing to a more level pace.

"Did he deny it?"

"How could he? The conversion of so much wealth into so many muskets, hundreds I understand, is known throughout the colony. They are on display for God's sake! I am told that Simeon Lord's execrable doxy will flaunt an emerald bracelet to any who will regard it. 'A gift from the King of England to the Queen of New Zealand,' she says. Even the governor's wife is said to pour her wine from a crystal decanter, courtesy of the Bishop of Ely."

"Samuel, you must calm yourself."

"Yes, yes, let me take a minute." He breathed into cupped hands. Then, more calmly, "No, Kendall did not deny the deed. But he denied blame."

He closed his eyes and there was Kendall, pale but composed. Samuel thought he even detected the touch of a smile at the corners of the rosebud mouth. "'Tell me,' he asked, 'have you reviled Hongi for his amassing of arms, have you rebuked him for the use to which he will doubtlessly put them?' He did not wait for me to answer, knowing full well that Hongi and I have argued bitterly. 'Have you rebuked the traders who sold him the guns, will you take their profit from them?' Then he pointed his finger at me, he pointed his finger ..."

"Samuel!"

"..and he asked me if I intended to rebuke the Bishop of Ely and the King of England. 'After all,' he said, 'they are the ones who gave Hongi the means.' All the while in quiet and measured tones."

"He has rehearsed his argument."

"Yes, of course, he must have. He was so damned, forgive me, glib. 'Why,' he said, and he was mocking me, Elizabeth, 'do you discount all the principal players and attend only to the part of one who would oblige a friend and maintain the favour upon which the safety of the settlement depends?'"

"And *that* was certainly rehearsed."

"I could have struck him, but I did not. I asked God for patience and explained to the miscreant that I had no authority over the gunsmiths who had broken no laws, nor over English royalty and nobility who had also broken no laws and who had acted in good faith. And he was ready for that, too. 'Indeed,' he said, 'yet the king provided Hongi with arms from his own hand. To what use do you suppose the King supposed Hongi would put them?'"

"His insolence is horrible," said Elizabeth, "quite horrible, and yet," she paused, "there is some dark logic in it."

"Pshaw. Royalty confers gifts of that sort all the time; it is a ceremonial thing."

"Even to Hongi?"

Samuel was silent and Elizabeth came to his rescue. "You are right, of course," she said. "Even if His Majesty had given it a thought, you can't start a war with a suit of armour and a brace of muskets." Samuel nodded, wishing he had thought of the rejoinder. Instead he had fallen prey to Kendall's next question.

"And what," he had asked, "is the law that I have broken, for which all others stand excused?"

And of course Samuel had answered, "the law of God, sir. The law that says, 'thou shalt not kill.'"

"Yet Hongi will kill."

"Indeed, and it is a terrible sin, one that it is your function to end, not ennable."

The new priest was more composed now than when he had faced the same charge from Butler. But his answer was the same.

"I do not kill, Mr Marsden," he said. "I have never killed," he faltered but Samuel was too vexed to make note of it, "and I have pleaded endlessly with Hongi to amend his ways. I have told him time and again of God's injunction against killing, as my station requires. But I cannot compel it. God gave Hongi the power to choose and I cannot undo that. I cannot compel him, sir, any more than I can compel you when you order some poor wretch to the gallows."

The chaplain could scarcely believe the man's audacity and his resolve for patience crumbled utterly.

"You twisting snake," he roared, "when I give sentence I act within the law."

"The law that says, 'thou shalt not kill'?"

"The law that says society has the right to dispense justice, preserve order and stability, to check lawlessness, to secure its citizens' safety and security of property."

He paused for breath and Kendall broke in smoothly, "As when a fourteen year old girl is hanged for the theft of a loaf of bread?"

"I would not countenance such a deed."

"But others have, others more highly placed in the judiciary than your good self, they have passed such sentence and they have done so within the law."

And cry hallelujah to fucking British justice.

And the Christian armies of Europe, they have killed in their tens of thousands, in their hundreds of thousands.

As Saul killed in his thousands but David in his tens of thousands.

"Ah, Samuel, he was well prepared for this. And he has avoided defence through offence."

Her voice brought Samuel back to himself. "You are right again," he said, "he was most deeply offensive and I, like a fool", good God, Samuel, what did you say? "I continued to defend."

"Justice and security may be terrible things, but we cannot hide from them. Nor can we hide from the responsibility that calls for the ultimate sentence when faced with the ultimate crime."

"Is it not written, 'vengeance is mine,' saith the Lord?"

"We need to have balance in society. If malefactors are to escape free from judgment, they will only rack up more crime and sin. Their deeds must be balanced."

"Ae," said the missionary, "Hongi knows that law very well. He calls it utu."

Samuel looked up and Elizabeth thought she had never seen him so tired. If a fat man could be gaunt. "There was more," he said.

"War is a way of life for Maori," Kendall had said, "and there are no innocent parties. All adhere to it. The men whose heads Hongi has taken would have willingly taken his and those who have taken death at his hands would have found mana in it. It is their joy. Perhaps it is ours, too. England has been more at war than at peace during my lifetime. To lay down one's life for one's country we call patriotism and afford it the highest honour. Are we so different? And perhaps there is a greater purity in Maori who fight selflessly for the mana of the tribe as opposed to the Englishman who fights for pay."

Elizabeth shook her head. "It is a speech," she said.

"He said, 'so if we are to have war, perhaps the civilised musket might be seen as preferable to the savage axe.' And I said I would readily admit the force of his argument provided he could arm all the population of New Zealand."

"O Samuel."

"And then he said that it seemed that my objection was not to the Maori slaughtering each other but to their not doing it on equal terms."

"Of course he did."

Still Samuel could find no foothold. "I told him that he was turning Maori against the mission, that he had slandered me personally to Hongi to such an extent that when I saw Hongi in Port Jackson last week he raged and told me not to come to New Zealand again.

"And he shook his head as if in pity, I swear he was enjoying this, Elizabeth, and he said that Hongi said that King George told him there was no edict against trading muskets to Maori. "So it was Hongi's conclusion that when you and others of the mission told him it was against English law, there was a lie in it. I told him that you and the others were opposed to the barter; would you have had me say otherwise?"

There had been silence in Samuel's office at that point and there was silence in the garden now.

CHAPTER 39

Tamaki Makaurau September 1821

It was the most basic piece of engineering and the planning had been minimal. The extraordinary thing was the way two thousand men had built it. Digging into the rich Tamaki soil, sinking holes, deep but not too deep because it would be planted shallow and had no need to stand for long.

Four strong, straight children of Tane were taken, felled by the white man's axe, stripped to their trunks and planted shallow. Men climbed makeshift ladders and dragged on flax ropes over steel pullies and lighter lengths of trunk and branch rose to sit, lashed across the posts and it had become a frame.

All the time they toiled, three continuous days now, they conversed with Ngati Poua. The distance between them had called for precision, just beyond the range of an angry rock but well within musket range. They left Ngati Poua in no doubt of their intentions.

"We will be the death of you."

Inside the pa a small girl whimpered. Something large and dark and very frightening was growing outside her home. There was always noise, shouting voices, different voices, some strident and angry, others drier and mocking. Some of the voices she knew, her koro roaring at the scary thing, the higher tones of her whaea screeching defiance.

The monster had come suddenly but they had been ready. There was plenty of kai, the winter crop had been lifted and stored, leaving Ngapuhi to feed themselves. Large gourds stood full to the brim with fresh water. But she could not go out of the pa, to the gardens or the villages or to the beach with her mothers and sisters. You could not go past the earthworks because that was where the taniwha was but everyone still had to poo and the smell was frightening, too.

She did not see it arrive because she could not see over the palisade, so she did not know what it looked like. But it was very loud and it made sounds she had never heard before, sudden, loud, angry and then the sound of things smacking into the walls. She heard people calling out, nga pu, nga pu, but she did not know what a pu was.

Hongi was a priest now. He had been a chief when Ngapuhi and their allies had laboured together as one man. And when he had called a retreat from the palisades as shot after shot buried itself uselessly in the defending earth, he had been a general. The new route they were creating had been his vision.

"We cannot breach them directly. If we cannot approach them by land, then we shall come from the air."

At the beginning Ngati Paoa had felt safe. But as they learned the size of their enemy a creeping fear began to settle. The child felt it all about her. Then it had lifted as Ngapuhi had retreated and they had thought, we are impregnable here. They will become hungry and dispirited and then they will go away.

So when sentries reported that Ngapuhi were digging holes into the ground they were more puzzled than alarmed. They watched the poles heaved in and the frame begun and still it seemed pointless. But there was a remorseless purpose behind everything Ngapuhi did and the frame had become a danger well before it had become a platform.

Ngapuhi did not need surprise for Ngato Paoa had no retreat. The swamps of the estuary lay as all escape lay beyond them and open cultivated fields.

Two thousand toa waited for them. Some waited less easily than others and those not needed for the platform danced before the earthworks and howled their challenge.

Hongi was a priest now; priests were for waiting and he would wait the last few hours as a priest. There were no bad omens, everything would soon be done and then the waiting would be done and then he would be a warrior.

The world glowed about him in the birth of spring. All around gardens were greening on new-turned soil. There will be no help for you, he said to them, not this year and perhaps for many years.

He was wearing his military jacket, muddy and stained now, scarlet in a sea of brown bodies. His breeches were stained, too, and his feet were bare. The earth was like flesh between his toes.

He sat apart from the others for he was very tapu now but he watched them closely, as he had watched them build the platform. Breathing on the collective grunt, watching sweat glisten on bunched muscle, loving the way they drove themselves, loving the way they danced before the palisade. Not far off, Rewa was sitting alone. As he watched Rewa turned his head and their eyes met. Hongi saw the longing in him, the enormous excitement and the two men grinned at one another.

Hongi had no wish to fight, you understand. You remember when we all met in Australia Hongi asked Hinaki whether he was for peace or for war and when Hinaki said he was for war Hongi urged peace.

The chaplain remembered it altogether differently. He remembered the meeting at his Paramatta home of the chiefs, Hinaki, Te Horeta, Hongi and Wharepoaka, now Hongi's apologist. Hongi was newly arrived from England and Hinaki and Te Horeta were hoping to emulate his visit. Samuel had been aghast. Papers that arrived with Hongi and Kendall on the *Speke* left him in no doubt of the Society's view of the visit just ended. He urged them to reconsider – it is a cruel and dangerous climate- but they were anxious for the gifts Hongi had gained. Ironically it was Hongi who dissuaded them.

"Look, I have brought my guns to show you. I have named them, too. This is Te Waiwhariki, this is Te Kai-a-karoro; and there are more."

Hinaki and Te Horeta understood much better than the chaplain what Hongi was saying. Each of the guns was named after a Ngapuhi defeat, each was a statement of intent to those who had inflicted it and the statement was, we will have utu. And, more precisely, this is the order in which we will take it. Te Waiwhariki was the slaughter by Ngati Maru, invading the north some thirty years earlier. Te Kai-a-karoro was named for the defeat at Moremonui when Ngapuhi had lain in the scrub and the sand, waiting in piles for the seagulls.

"And this, o Hinaki, is Te Waikahu which will travel to Tamaki with me. I think you should hurry home and prepare your pa for war."

No, no, Hongi would not have said that. And when the chiefs shared passage back to New Zealand, Hongi tried again and again to plead for peace. But Hinaki would have none of it.

And now Hongi sat at Tamaki in the morning sun and thought, this will be finished with most of the day to follow. All we need is light.

Inside the pa the mood had shifted again. Ngapuhi had no need of surprise as they called out the platform's purpose.

"See how high it rises. Higher than your palisade. It will hold thirty of us at a time. Thirty of us with our pu."

Even with understanding, Ngati Poua still barely believed it as fire rained down over the palisade and they began to die.

Hongi had ceased being a priest by then. His exaltation became a more visceral thing as he strapped on his coat of mail. A steel helmet over dark, curling locks, ringing a brown ochre face. His sword buckled at his side and in each hand a musket.

He had been among the first to mount the platform.

It was as though the taniwha had seeped through their defences and was among them now. Its tendrils touched them and they clung to one another and would not be drawn apart. But there was a woman slumped against the whare nui, sobbing and wailing, her tears pouring over the baby at her breast. And there was a little girl sitting in her whare, crying for her mother. But her mother was outside with a spear that she had fashioned and sharpened herself. Her eyes were wild and she panted, her need for battle overwhelming.

But she had no opportunity for it, for in the first fusillade from the platform a musket ball near blew her chest apart. Volley after volley poured down; it was target practice and random shooting together as when a shot passed through the flax wall of a whare and blew a little girl's brains out.

But Hongi was never the aggressor. When he first saw Hinaki in his village his heart saddened for he could see that Hinaki was dressed as a soldier. But even then he was so desirous of peace that he sent his own son with a chief and a few others to parley with Hinaki. Even after Hinaki shot the chief Hongi remained desirous of peace and went himself with Rewa and myself and others to try to talk Hinaki out of war. It was in this talk that Hinaki treacherously attacked and would have stabbed Hongi had Rewa not intervened and deflected the blow. In the following action Hinaki was killed but not at Hongi's hand.

The roaring fire swept down over the palisades and now added to it came the screaming of those who had been shot but had not died yet. Shelter might be found up against the wall Ngapuhi were shooting over. There was a safe triangle there. Or you might find shelter behind the ancestor, pressing your back against him as he took the shot meant for you. But what could you do other than cower there? There was no resistance, only waiting as the rain kept pouring down and people kept dying.

There was nothing to hold Ngapuhi back as they scaled or broke through the unprotected walls and were upon them. And while the slaughter remained one-sided, taiaha and mere do not fare well against a musket at thirty paces, there came at last an opportunity for resistance as distance closed.

Yet even here they were at a disadvantage as Hongi led his men in a flying wedge that held its shape and turned and flanked and Ngati Poua's confusion grew. They fought alone or in groups and sometimes through good luck or good management they made a little headway and Ngapuhi joined the dead and wounded. But it remained a slaughter.

Some say Hinaki met his death at the hands of Hongi Hika, others say it was Rewa or another. But all agree that Hinaki died and that Hongi drank his blood. He opened the veins and the blood gushed and when he rose his face was a mask of blood, Hinaki's blood on him, within him, joining with his own blood and now he had subsumed a part of Hinaki and would be safe from Hinaki's atua. He took Hinaki's head and the blood gushed again as he raised the head up to the sun.

It was not an utter slaughter. Not all perished. Why, I myself carried off several of the children of the Tamaki chiefs and hid them in safety. After the battle –in which brave Ngapuhi perished– I restored them to their families.

Survival depended upon being a very young boy or a very beautiful woman. The boys would be taken back as slaves and they would grow in Ngapuhi without memory of their beginnings and so without rancour. As they grew to men they would fight for Ngapuhi. The women were for breeding, extra wives for Ngapuhi. They had no use for the rest.

CHAPTER 40

Opononi November 1821

Everything is happening too quickly.

And there is a pattern to it.

Years of waiting for the Lord to show me my purpose.

And a fall before my eyes were opened to my error.

And then suddenly the way opened and I was a missionary. I was called and I was justified.

And then years of waiting.

And then suddenly the way opened and I was a priest. I was called and I was justified.

But all the while it was gathering speed. And now I can barely keep up with it.

Everything is happening too quickly.

It would have been close to a year since he had stood by the fens of Cambridge and meditated upon his life. Now he sat upon the rocks at the south head of Omapere and looked across the narrow bar that separated the quiet harbour from the rolling sea.

I left England with such high hopes. I believed –and still believe - that God had touched my endeavours and as I left my country's shores for the final time my sadness was subsumed within the joy of knowing I was His instrument.

I journeyed back in peace and knew there was a divine power upon me. I felt it there when I confronted Marsden in his den. When he roared and clenched his fists the Lord was with me and He made me gentle. He guided my words as He had once guided David's aim and I was able to show Marsden the beam in his eye as he raged against the mote in mine.

And yes, I helped Hongi procure his arms but I was reassured by the society of Port Jackson who also recognised his right to choose. Indeed, like the King and the nobility of England, they contributed more substantially to his cause than I ever did. I kept the settlers safe and only Marsden accused me.

Behind him the cliff rose sheer, gulls drifted across its face, riding on the coiling winds.

I was so full of hope as I returned to Rangihoua, to my family, my friends, my congregation. To my parish.

But as the land moved from the golden days and harvests of autumn into the grey, wet winter, so too did his expectations pale and fade. Any hope that old hostilities might have softened with time vanished on his first encounter with William Hall ('I will not take your hand, Mr Kendall; things are as they ever were'). And the idea that others might find a kind of pride in his accomplishments … Even Thomas knew better than to expect that. But he had not anticipated the resentment.

"Your title of priest carries the same weight your magistracy did."

His family was no less guarded.

Rakau, Wharepoaka, Tungaroa and the others in their whanau were pleased to see him and he supposed that would have to do.

There was the new man, Cowell and his wife; they seemed good-hearted people who were not inclined to judge. And there was kindness in Francis Hall and Thomas was thankful for the support he had brought Jane in his absence.

Ah, Jane … I wrote to tell you how God was helping me towards forgiveness and I hoped the news might help lighten your darkness. And you welcomed me back as a good wife should and you came to my bed as a good wife should and now our child stirs within you. And so I know that God has blessed our union. Yet even as we conjoin I sense distance and accusation and there is more loneliness.

Dispute pervaded all their lives, Maori and pakeha alike. Ngapuhi prepared and practised for war, all their thought was with the killing to come, their stories and conversation dwelt upon their grievance and the causes for utu and the winter months dragged on. With Hongi's anger at the mission's deceit, the mood spilled over on to the settlers who went about their daily lives in fear and resentment of their own; towards the Maori and towards those of their own who had fuelled it. They reviled Thomas for his part in turning Hongi against them, they cursed the whalers and sealers who had provided Ngapuhi with the greatest proportion of their weaponry and then they joined with Thomas as he wrote in defence of the trade. We have no choice, he had written to Marsden two months before; Maori can procure what they want independently of us, hatchets and axes which are the Society's stock-in-trade will be put to the purposes of war. Pratt, he wrote, will not consider the difficulties we face and you are equally ignorant, unreasonable and harsh in unwonted criticism. Both settlements had concurred with his views and the letter was endorsed because, they said, it expressed so just a view of their difficulties. For once they had joined but it was in dispute, accusation and condemnation and after the letter was sent they returned to their own fights and Thomas was alone again.

They fought over supplies; a separate store was established at Rangihoua but soon broke down. Butler attacked Francis Hall for partial storekeeping at Kerikeri. And the mood became uglier still as the winter months dragged on.

As rancour spread across the races, so too did it pass down through the generations. There were few who attended school when it re-opened and those who did brought their own hostility with them. Where Ewha had once resisted and cursed, there were now a dozen to do it. While Ewha himself polished his musket and sharpened his knife.

I could have done more, I should have done more.

But he hadn't. Instead he found himself moving further and further afield, itinerating he called it, bringing the gospel to villages that might otherwise remain in dark ignorance. He preached mainly to women and children for many of the men had already left for Kerikeri or Whangarei where they would combine in the greatest taua Ngapuhi had ever produced. The hearts of those they had left behind were with them and there was little inclination to give ear to the wandering pakeha priest and his foolish talk of peace and forgiveness.

Judgment pervaded Rangihoua and it reached across from Kerikeri, too. Somehow the settlers had managed to reconcile the general trading of muskets to Ngapuhi with condemnation of Thomas for his part in it. Perhaps not entirely unreasonably; for they had now called a halt to it while Thomas persisted. "I would as soon trade a dollar as a musket," he had said. It was a part of his refusal to be ashamed.

The failure of the school was also held to his account and here more than anywhere else their judgment cut at him.

I could have done more. I should have done more.

If the fool would persist in his folly he would become wise, the poet had written; and so they persisted in their folly but it brought no sign of wisdom. And as eight years of preaching salvation had found no convert within the bay, so the solution must be more preaching, but further afield.

Thomas decided to take the message to Hokianga. That his last trip there with John King had found no willing ear was no matter.

Surprisingly, seeing that he shared in the general condemnation, John King was willing to undertake the journey again.

"There is nothing here for me right now," he said to Hannah. "Our crops need little attention and we are well provided for."

"Do you think you will achieve more than you did last time?"

"No," John shook his head, "but I must not allow doubt to determine my actions any more than I should let my dislike of Kendall sway my decision. All I know is that I am asked to take the word of God into the darkness. Should I refuse because the messenger is not agreeable to me?"

Hannah King had patted her husband's arm.

"You are a good man, John King," she said.

All this self-recrimination is achieving nothing. I must be up and doing.

He jumped to his feet and headed off towards the Pakenae gorge. Behind him to the west the sun poured gold on to the great rolling dunes that stood high between the wild Tasman sea and the placid Opononi harbour; to his right stood Whiria, a pallisaded cone rising high above the flat lands. The stream that watered the pa and its surrounding gardens ran south into the Pakenae gorge.

The sun had not yet reached its zenith but already the day had warmed and he sweated under his jacket. His shirt, five days in the wearing now, stuck to him. He turned and headed along the pathway beside the stream. The bush thickened here in fern and palm and the shade was welcome. How pleasant it would be to lose these filthy, stinking rags for just a little while and wash away the traveller's grime. But while it was quiet here, with only the sounds of the stream and birdsong, there was no guarantee of privacy. Still, he found himself leaving the path and picking his way down the steepening slope to the water's edge. There he divested himself of his boots –there was no shame in bare feet- and jacket and picked his way to a smooth rock rising out of the shallows. He kneeled and drank and doused his head, then rolled up his trousers and sat and watched the water flow about his pale legs. A fantail alighted on a nearby branch and in a sudden surge of tenderness he smiled at it.

Tena koe, piwakawaka, kia ora, e manu iti. Do you still laugh at the memory of Maui the caterpillar crawling into Hine's —? Enough.

Peace and loneliness seem to go together for me. There is no one to antagonise me here.

The journey with John King had not been an easy one.

He seems much recovered from his earlier gloom –and I would like to believe I had a hand in that– but now he has even less to say to me. He disapproves, I know it, but he cannot be bothered to even say so.

When their hosts had told them of the white man who lived here, King had shared none of his interest.

What would I have to say to him or he to me?

And now Thomas pulled his feet from the cold water and sat hugging his knees, wondering what he had to say.

He was distracted by a swirl in the stream as a fat eel coiled between the rocks.

Kia ora, e tuna roa, do you regret the time you nosed your slippery way into the tene of Maui's wife?

Dear God, is all Maori belief rooted in the obscene?

Abruptly he jumped to his feet and picked his way back to the bank.

The renegade's home stood on the eastern side of the stream in enough of a clearing to let in the sunlight. A thatched roof of tightly plaited flax stood at a height that would allow a tall man to walk erect beneath it, a brief chimney, lengths of lashed manuka formed the walls, the chinks between were stopped in gravel and mud that had hardened to brick *(why did we never think of that at Rangihoua?)*. In front of the house there stood a small, rough-hewn table where a man sat on a stool, bare brown back to the sun, bent over a journal. He turned and rose in the one movement at Thomas' call.

"Well, I'll be damned, a parson's come a-calling."

Thomas flinched at the profanity but moved to take the outstretched hand.

"John Callaghan."

"Thomas Kendall. What makes you think I am a parson?"

"'Tis the way you dress, man." The brogue was pronounced. "All close and uncomfortable on such a glorious day."

He stood there, half a foot above Thomas, hair pulled back from a clean-shaven face, dressed for the glorious day only in canvas breeches, falling just below the knees of bare legs and feet.

"What can I offer you? Are you foe to the demon drink or will you share a fine Irish whiskey with me?"

Thomas assured him he would be happy to share and they walked back into the house. The room belied his first impression of the man; a glass window opened to the north and the sun streamed in on order and economy. A mud brick fireplace, pots and pans hanging over the grate, flax matting on an earthen floor, a single shelf, books, (Thomas saw a thick, leather-bound volume of Shakespeare's works), journals and writing materials, a seaman's chest with an open box beside it. The Irishman crossed to it now and reached in to retrieve a bottle and a pair of glasses. There were no tables or chairs, the one outside must serve, and in the corner a stuffed mattress, blankets and pillows lay on a low bed frame. Dimly Thomas registered that the bed was a good deal larger that a single man would need; then his mouth turned down as he noted on the shelf a plaster cast of the Virgin Mary. A crucifix was pinned to the wall above it.

Callaghan had followed his gaze and noted the reaction.

"You guess aright," he said, "you are in the lair of a papist. Will you still drink with me or will you flee from this den of unrighteousness and idolatry?"

The words were mocking but the tone was friendly and Thomas' answering smile was not contrived.

"I have drunk with worse," he said.

"Sure you have. Now," he swept up a box and led Thomas back to the table, "take a seat, make yourself comfortable. And for the love of God, will you lose that jacket and those boots. It makes me hot just looking at you."

Thomas did as he was bade.

"Now," said the Irishman, raising his glass, "what shall we drink to?"

"Well," said Thomas, "I am here to explore the possibilities of a site for the Church Missionary Society. Perhaps we might ask a blessing for –"

"Please," Callaghan held up a hand, "don't think me rude but let us keep this easy." He lifted his glass. "Let us drink to this glorious day."

Their glasses touched and they drank and Thomas marvelled at the smooth and golden warmth. "It is like drinking from the sun," he said.

Callaghan slapped a hand against his knee and pointed an approving finger. "Now there's a toast," he said. "Let us drink to the sun and to the men who made this golden drop."

He was, Thomas learned, a man of many parts, clear about some, vague about others: an educated man with a love of words and imagery, an epicure, something of a philosopher, a man of some means though very vague about the source, possibly a family man, obviously a papist but reluctant to discuss his beliefs ("let us keep this easy") and a generous and genial host.

The sun shone down, the level in the bottle sank and Thomas found him charming.

"How do you come to be here?" he asked.

"Well then," Callaghan filled their glasses, "that is a story I am happy to share. I first set foot here about two years ago and while the ship sat at anchor and the captain went about his transactions, I had time to walk about the place. I thought I might do some sketching, perhaps even paint a little if I had time. The light, the colours ..." He paused to drink, then tugged at a long nose. "I had an epiphany. Or rather, I think I had one."

"How can you not be sure?"

"'twas a wordless revelation. How can I put it? Have you ever gone somewhere –to a place you've never been before- and been consumed by recognition?"

Thomas thought of the waterfall and nodded. "I have," he said, "and I know what you mean by wordless recognition. It's like it speaks to you, deep in your soul and what it has to say is of absolute significance-"

"And you know that you already know."

"But you can't find the words for the meaning."

"Exactly." Callaghan thrust out an arm. "Shake my hand, Thomas Kendall." Their eyes met with their hands and each thought he was beginning to know the other.

"There was a man at the pa who had some English and through him I was able to ask the chief if I could stay on. He was agreeable –Maori are second only to the Irish for hospitality- and I bought a fair collection of stores from the captain, for trade and my own survival. And here I was.

"For all my liking of the natives I was reluctant to live among them. I'm a man who tends to find peace in solitude and sometimes I am a melancholy man. And I need to be alone with my melancholy.

"So. Some of the lads came down to help me and we whipped up my little castle in no time."

"How did you communicate?"

"Surprisingly easily. Of course we were putting up a hut, it wasn't like we were discussing Aristotle and there was mime and," he jumped up from his box, "I'll show you." He went into the shed to return with a pair of thick journals. "Look."

Thomas opened them curiously, then stared. The pages were full of words along with a great many sketches. There was a wood pigeon, a brief sketch and without colour but indisputably a pigeon. 'Kerry-roo' was written alongside it. And there was a scowling face with 'reeree' printed neatly next to it. "This is a dictionary," he said.

"Aye, there's quite a vocabulary list there and I've learned a lot. But I've barely got my head around the grammar. God knows what I'm saying half the time. Still," he smiled and drank to his journal, "they seem to get my drift most of the time. How do you manage communication?"

"Well, I've been here a good deal longer than you and I've had exceptional teachers. In fact I've just returned from England where ..." Thomas explained his work with Samuel Lee, recognising with a pang that he had never declaimed to so attentive or appreciative an audience.

"You are a scholar, Thomas Kendall," declared Callaghan, "you have performed a mighty task and it will live on after you and all the rest of us are gone."

Tears were pricking at Thomas' eyes as he thrust his arm across the table. "Shake my hand, John Callaghan," he said.

They carried the table into the shade on the eastern side of the house and sat and chewed on bread —fresh from last night's baking- and lightly fried flounder.

"Have you ever floundered?"

"Many times. I am forever floundering."

"You are pleased to jest. I speak of the fish. You should try it. It is one of the most beautiful, perfect things you can do. Let me paint it for you. You paddle with a friend who must be able to keep his peace. And you sit in the shallows of the mighty Hokianga, it is a still night and the waters are a dark, shining glass lit by the moon and a million stars. You hold a burning brand in one hand and a spear in the other and you sit in silence with your friend and gaze into the waters. Perhaps you have scattered crumbs about your waka to attract your prey. And you sit in the cool night air and you are alive and thankful and the waiting is like a prayer. The torches draw the fish to you as moths to a candle, they rise like pale ghosts to the crumbs and then," his hand flashed down, "they are squirming on your spear. And you exult, Thomas, and you thank your god you are a man and not a flounder."

"You have been here for two years now?"

"Aye, but not continuously. I took a passage last winter to Port Jackson. I feared I might go mad with boredom and drink myself to death. Which reminds me." He filled their glasses.

"You were not plundered in your absence?"

"No."

"And you have suffered no indignity, no threat?"

"None."

Thomas thought of the mood of Ngapuhi which had crossed the island, attracting many of the young men of Whiria to Hongi."

"I wonder why that is."

"Well, I'll tell you then." The Irishman settled back to tell a story. "'twas a glorious summer day and I was sitting out front of my castle, it had just been finished, contemplating my choice of pleasure for the day when along the path comes Rewi, he's the rangatira here as you doubtlessly know and about twenty of his lads. Buck naked, half of them but bristling with weapons, mere, taiaha and a few dodgy-looking muskets. My English-speaking mate was with them and he told me that a war party of Ngati Whatua had been up to mischief -"

"Murder and mayhem."

"Indeed." Callaghan did not appreciate the interruption. "Anyway, they were not strong enough for an assault on Whiria and would skirt about it. Their path, I learned, would take them past my own fine whare.

"So. Rewi suggested that I scoot up to Whiria for safe-keeping while he and his lads dealt with the raiders. Well! I was deeply insulted and told him so in no uncertain terms. I popped back into my whare, collected my musket and some powder and shot, strapped on my sword and away we went."

"You went to fight with them?"

"Of course I did. They were threatening my hosts, they were threatening *me*, what else could I have done? Besides, I was delighted for the chance –hadn't been in a decent donnybrook since … Anyway, they moved along at a fine clip and I was hard-pressed to keep up with them.

"There's a valley about two miles south of here and we met them there." Callaghan closed his eyes, remembering. "They stood in line and waited for us. I was wondering if there might be some crafty buggers hiding behind trees with their muskets —we would have been easy pickings —but no, they were all there waiting. About twenty five of them, even numbers.

"And then —I couldn't believe it – they started dancing, stamping their feet, smacking their chests, all in perfect time. And then, God bless me, Rewi and his lads started doing the same."

"They were performing a haka."

"Of course they were, but I didn't know it at the time. But I'll tell you this much, it got to me and before I knew it I was dancing with them And there was another epiphany, not wordless this time, they were shrieking their heads off but of course I couldn't understand a word of it. And then I was shrieking, too, roaring and stamping and I couldn't understand a word of that either." He opened his eyes and looked at Thomas levelly. "But I loved it. I was part of something huge and dark and golden and it consumed me and I fucking *loved* it."

Suddenly he bounded to his feet and slapped his hands against his chest and when they came away there were red handprints against the brown. His eyes bulged and his tongue thrust out from an open mouth.

Then he was back in his seat and filling their glasses.

"'twas a good fight, though I'm ashamed to say my marksmanship gave us more than a fair edge. And then it was close quarter stuff and I laid my musket down and took up my sword. Ah." He closed his eyes again and smiled.

"Have you ever fought in battle, Thomas?"

Thomas shook his head.

"But you've thought about it, haven't you? You've wondered what it's like to abandon yourself utterly to the call of the blood and touch the deepest, darkest part of your manhood."

Thomas made no answer.

"There is a glory in it, you know. Pro patria mori and all that. To lose all restraint, ah God, there is an absolute freedom in it. A divine madness."

Thomas' hand was shaking as he took up his glass. There was a crawling on his skin and a deep shudder threatened, but he had to ask, "Did you take part in the next proceeding?"

"No." Callaghan shook his head. "I was more than sated by then. Was it Ovid who said, 'post coitem omne animale triste est'? Seeing Thomas' blankness, he translated, 'after coitus every creature is melancholy'. I've never found a grain of truth in that but 'post bellum (that means 'war', my scholarly friend), Callaghan triste est'. So I left them to it and returned to my home. But before I went, Rewi laid his hands upon my shoulders and pressed his nose to mine. 'Ko taku teina koe,' he said."

"He called you brother."

"So he did. And so I have been since, which might answer your question, why I have never been plundered or disrespected.

"I walked along the beach and sat and watched the sun go down and I thought about death. Then I came home and ate my loaf and my fish −and because I am a whimsical man I drank red wine −and sat in front of my house and listened to the bush and watched the moon go by.

"I heard footsteps coming through the bush and then a maid, all wrapped in a feathered cloak, came out into the moonlight."

"I do not wish to hear this part of the story."

"Indeed. Yet you listened to the dance and the bloodshed and you asked after the desecration and I daresay you would have listened to that. And so you will listen to the resolution. You sit upon my turangawaewae, you have accepted my manaakitia and now you will hear out my korero."

There was a glint in the Irishman's eye and menace in his tone and Thomas sat in silence.

"You'll laugh −well, perhaps you won't but many would − when I say that at first I wondered what she was there for. Remember, I was new to the land. Perhaps, I thought, she is come to escort me back to Rewi for some purpose.

"So I said, 'kia ora' and she said 'kia ora' and I sat and she stood and I looked at her and she looked at me.

"Her hair glinted black in the moonlight and her skin shone. With the feathered cloak and the stillness and the silence she could have been a spirit of the wood and I thought that I would like to paint her. Even if I had known her tongue, I would not have known what to say.

"All the while she was watching me intently and then she smiled and her eyes widened and she raised her hands to her throat and unfastened her cloak. Like a shadow slipping down a hill, Donne said −or words to that effect − and so it was. She was naked under her cloak and she was perfect in the moonlight."

Thomas stared at his hands upon the table and his mouth was dry.

——

"This is how a woman is supposed to be, broad, strong feet for gripping the earth, not your angular, cramped Englishwoman's feet crushed into their leather coffins like your crippled Chinese, strong legs that could take her up and down Whiria a dozen times a day, not like Your Ladyship tripping from her sofa to her carriage." His eyes were closed again as he moved into reverie and Thomas thought he could probably get up and move away undetected, leaving Callaghan to talk to himself. But he stayed. "Her arms were strong from chopping wood, paddling a canoe, tilling the gardens, good, honest toil, not like your effete lady of the court who might blanch before the weight of a plate of scones. She had beautiful hands, slim fingers with close cropped nails, not like the talons of Your Ladyship who advertises her power to have others do her bidding by making herself helpless. Fingers that might soothe a child or please a man or wield a spear. No poison pen for her. Broad child-bearing hips and a glorious arse, a rounded, soft woman's belly, but there was no fat on it, full woman's breasts that needed no tying up. She stood and smiled and shone in the moonlight, no paint or powder for her to hide anaemic skin or the ravages of a pox. But she had her decoration and it was of a nobler kind, chiselled in perfect lines into her chin. And I'll warrant there were no tears or wailing, no swooning or crying out for her salts. He wahine toa ia.

"And she came to my bed like a warrior, too. She gave and all but by Christ she took, too. And I was glad of the taking and though it was some time since I had been with a woman I contained myself and I lay back under her and watched her explode in the moonlight. And then, my pious parson," and his eyes were suddenly open and blazing, "and then we found a common tongue as we groaned together. And the explosion and the crying out was not such a far cry from warfare."

He looked hard at Thomas and all the earlier affability was gone. "You sit there all pious and precious, Thomas Kendall, and you think idolatry and debauchery but you know," he pointed a finger, "you know whereof I speak. Or rather you would if you were not so afraid."

Now Thomas was pricked to anger and his cheeks were flushed. "I do not fear you or any man, John Callaghan," and the whiskey spoke, "and I'll prove it upon you this very moment if you wish."

The Irishman's mood seemed to soften and he nodded his head. "That's better," he said, "that's more like it. But I can see," and he wagged a finger, "I can see a man who terrifies you."

"And who might that be?"

"Yourself. Now piss off."

Thomas was dismissed.

He snatched up his jacket and boots and left without a word. The ground was rough beneath his feet, sharp bracken and fern and stone but he marched on regardless of the discomfort. He would not give Callaghan the satisfaction of seeing him lace up his boots. It was only after he had crossed the stream and gained the path beyond that he sank to the ground to rub his feet and dry them on his jacket and curse all degenerate papists. Then he sat and hurled stones and tried to collect his thoughts.

He registered with some surprise that much of the day had passed and that he was sitting in shadow. He also realised that he was quite drunk and likely to be so for some time. "Which means," he addressed himself to a mossy boulder, "that I should not go back to the pa. John King will disapprove and I have had enough of disapproval for one day." Which brought him back to Callaghan. His anger had eased now and he shook his head sorrowfully. *You are too charitable, Thomas. Or perhaps you are just naïve. God knows there were signs enough of what he was, he even said so, you are in the lair of a papist, he said, and then he took advantage of my tolerance and courtesy to force that tale upon me. But I did not take offence. I had every right to do so, but I did not. He took offence and for what possible reason?* He shook his head sadly again. *Clearly this solitary life among the natives – engaging with them in their horrid practices – has unhinged him. He was probably unsettled to begin with; remember that bitter diatribe against Englishwomen.* He bowed his head and prayed for the soul of John Callaghan.

Now what to do? He got to his feet and went to find out.

An hour later he was close to where he had started from, sitting in tussock and watching the sun set over the Opononi bar. To his left were the cliffs of South Head and across the bar from them were the great dunes; the waters of the bay between glittered red and mauve and purple.

It would be nice to light a fire here, not for the warmth for it was a balmy night and he had his jacket, but there was comfort in a fire. Not far from where he sat, in the soft sand and tussock above the high-water mark lay a partially burned out log; others had shared his fancy there. He got up and wandered along the beach gathering driftwood, twigs and sticks and heavier pieces. He laid them in the lee of the log, set to work with his flint and watched the kindly fire grow.

How long ago was it that I watched heads revolve in a Cambridge fire?
Things are happening too quickly.
I am drowsy.

The sun was gone now and the waters shone in the last of the day and the beginning of the night.

Build up the fire, it is licking at the log now, tasting it and soon it will begin to consume it. Shadows dance their haka about the umu, shivering black shadow over the soft, dark sand.

Words floated like ghost writing, silver whispers, *the waters are dark shining glass lit by the moon and a million stars, where did I hear that? Doesn't matter...*

Then he was drifting, floating, rising and sinking on velvet waves. There was a sensuousness in the motion and he smiled as he slept.

The waters were smooth and viscous, like blood, like flesh and he trailed a hand, stroking them and for a moment it was hard to tell where his hand ended and the waters began; he could see smoke and shadow on them, glowing red from the flame of beacons, but he could not make out their source. Both his hands were free, no brazier or spear for him evidently and he wondered vaguely what he should do with them. Pale shapes drifted ghostly through the deeps; he supposed that they were flounder but they might have been women. There, see one broach, stirring the surface into rippling folds of black cream honey, was that not a curve of hip? And coiling through the folds a long, fat eel, kia ora e tuna roa, with its questing phallic head.

And the air was viscous, too, but through it he could see at the prow of their waka a kneeling man, brown back arching as he bent over the side and he was holding a burning brand of dark dripping oil in the one hand and poised taiaha in the other. His back glistened down to muscled buttocks, chiselled in deep blue moko. Thomas spoke aloud into his mind, why did you carve your backside so, and Callaghan answered, as I gave myself to war and love I gave myself to pain and these tattoos say, this is a man who never once cried out at the wrong time. Then his spear flashed down like David's sword and he snatched up the head of Medusa.

Their waka gathered speed, racing, slicing through the water's flesh and Thomas clung with both hands to its sides, things are moving way too quickly, but there was more elation than fear in the rush. Even when the sea began to twist and boil and it was all he could do to remain aboard, there was only elation and curiosity. And now the air was twisting, too, rags of red and purple and black ripping free from its fabric to coil and twist and rip again. And was this spray or rain or something else that drove and splattered and broke on him and he threw back his head and opened his mouth and drank it in.

Then the sky was alight in flashes of white and yellow and he could see ahead to where rocks thrust up through the surge like dragon's teeth and a thousand voices were roaring in his mind, you need to steer us now, Thomas, you need to get us through this, and there was the tiller between an outstretched arm and body thudding against his ribs. Without looking down he knew it was not a wooden tiller but flesh pumped into erection by coursing blood and he seized it with both hands. He was flooded with mighty strength then and he held the craft to the line of his will and they flew past the rows of teeth and he gripped and pulled and they veered and flew past another row and then another and then they were gone and the voices cheered his power.

But his work was not yet done. Ahead, bathed in sudden, brief light he could see the waters curling and circling in a vast, dark moko and now he could feel their craft sliding sideways towards its heart. And for all his strength – he forced the tiller until it was lying sideways across the stern – he could not hold back the drawing in. Look into the water, the voice was Rakau's, and there floating within reach were lengths of dark rata. Your mother has sent them, Rakau told him and he thought Susanna? surely not but there was no time for further thought and he released the tiller and reached into the sea and grasped a vine. There was no thought either as he swung around to set his feet against the stern and heaved. The touch of the vine awoke an even greater strength and he felt his muscles swell and bunch and his feet and legs were rocks against the stern. And the craft held still.

It was a long and demanding haul and more than once he thought how much easier it would be to abandon the boat and drag only his own weight to safety. But the voices called, Thomas, you need to get us through this and he knew he could not leave them.

He felt the pull of the maelstrom weaken and then he was free of it and they drifted in the shallows of a dark mangrove swamp. An old promise floated past – I will take you to te manawa, the gypsy had said – and he released the vine and made to climb from the boat. But something whispered caution. So he took up the spear that now lay beside him and probed the waters; he watched the spear slide through and into the mud and it kept on sliding, then was sucked from his grip and disappeared.

They drifted along and the mangroves sang to him, haere mai they called, you are arrived now. Their song was as nothing he had ever known, rustling leaves that shifted pitch, merging into minor chords that floated and dissolved and flowed together again, the bass of the mangrove waters, skittering scales piped through old, dead bones and, so faint that he had to strain to make it out, the pure high keening cry of the lonely woman. Haere mai, e Keni.

You should not hear this. This is not a song for mortal man.

But I must.

He staggered forward to the mast and wrapped his arms around it and closed his eyes, then rata was lashing his wrists, binding him to the mast. So now he was free to struggle and twist and tear against the protecting vine until he bled and he wept in his need to join the woman.

They drifted on and finally the song faded and the bonds dissolved and he sank to the deck thinking, I can never again be content.

Now the air was still and the waters of the mighty Hokianga were dark, polished glass lit beneath the moon and a million stars. And the boat was a waka again and in its prow a man kneeled, holding a brazier over the side to light the way to the bobbing crumbs.

And the waiting is like a prayer.

There is something holy here.

He bowed his head and closed his eyes.

"Well then, young Thomas, and what are you making of your life?"

He looked up with a start at the voice. Like everything else, it was hugely familiar but he could not place it. Then he felt the waka rock and gripped the sides to steady himself. There was a hiss as the brazier was doused in the tide, a light thud as the spear was laid down and the man in the prow was turning to face him. The movements were slow, cautious, steady.

Thomas gazed into the face of his father.

"I am dreaming," he said.

"Of course you are," answered Edward. "I have been dead near twenty years. So. What are you making of your life?"

"There is no short answer to that. But," looking around at the peace and the perfection, "I must be doing something right to have arrived at such a place."

"But this is a dream. Let me be clearer. What are you making of your waking life? Are you content with what you have wrought?"

In this place of truth and beauty there was no place for lies and Thomas could answer only, "no."

"Do you think you will ever be content?"

Thomas remembered the song of the lonely woman and answered, "no."

The old man nodded. His face was as Thomas had seen it last, thin, whispy hair, white against a grey, drawn face, strong, protruding nose over thin, grey lips and pale blue eyes, blind behind a milky film.

"Can you see me?"

"I can see you now. I couldn't then."

They sat in silence in the softly bobbing canoe and Thomas heard himself ask, "what is it like to be dead?"

Edward nodded again and smiled faintly. "I cannot tell you that, but I can tell you what it was like to die."

"Tell me."

"The atua had been busy inside me for a long time and it was a voracious thing. The potions your brother gave me often held it at bay and then I could dream but they always wore out and then the atua would return to its work.

"Have you ever known pain, Thomas? Not the kind of pain you make for yourself when you are lost and lonely but the pain your body makes, regardless of your will?"

Thomas tried to remember. There were toothaches, headaches, once he had torn a ligament and had been surprised how much it had hurt. Then he remembered the screams of men lashed to the mast and the final sobbing howl of the man dragged behind the Newgate cart. He shook his head.

"There is pain so intense and so horrible that you would cut your own throat upon the instant if you had the strength. I have known that pain many times in my life and what I remember of dying is that it was taken away. There was panic and dread in suffocation but it was a brief thing and my last living thought was to bless the man who took the pain away.

"Where is your brother, Thomas?"

And Thomas remembered Cain's response and could not answer.

During the night the prevailing westerly wind got up and Thomas woke with the taste of sand in his mouth. He was also hungover and made his way slowly along the beach before turning towards Whiria and creeping up the mountainside. There he found John King and announced that their work was done there. King shrugged and acquiesced and they began their return to Rangihoua within the hour.

CHAPTER 41

Kerikeri December 1821

That first surge as the breeze fills your sail and you point your craft to take more of its blessing, that surge can fill you, too and you sigh into it and slide away on the bosom of Tangaroa. Everything is like a caress, the waters smacking gently against the bow, then sliding, stroking along the sides, canvas yielding, swelling under the breath of Tawhiri and he breathes on you, too, cool and salty, perhaps ruffling your hair like a fond father.

She trudged rather than sped but with a quiet sea and a kind, prevailing wind her progress was steady and she picked up enough of a momentum –about four knots, he estimated – to warrant a line. Twenty, thirty feet astern, weighted to about a fathom, paua shell carefully affixed to a barbed steel hook spun and sparkled its invitation.

John Callaghan would have found in Francis Hall the perfect floundering companion. He was pleased to be away from the noise of humans and found another kind of conversation in the creaking of wood, the splashing of water, the shifting of the sails and the mewing of gulls.

His hand jerked as the trailing line pulled hard and took and he knew the fish was hooked. Excellent. He held the tiller between his left elbow and body, leaving both hands free to draw in the line, carefully maintaining the tension. With the same care he lifted it over the side, a fine kahawai, glittering silver in the sun, four, maybe five pounds. He slid his fingers beneath the gills, holding its head still in his right hand while he gently worked the hook free. Then he dropped it back into the sea and watched it swim away. He knew that there was some kind of blasphemy in this recognition of a Maori god and that the deed could not be excused in this case as a political gesture to attending Maori for there was no one here to applaud the cultural sensitivity. It was at some level an act of defiance. But he did it anyway –there was a charm to it, a recognition of who and where he was, there was humility and gratitude in it and it was done in the promise of abundance.

But it annoyed him that it was a secret and that his brethren would call it a shame.

The thought brought other images –James Kemp shaking his head worriedly, Butler pointing his finger. His bony pointing finger and another condemnation.

Wake up. He smacked himself smartly across the side of his head, let out his line again and turned the boat across the wind. But the affairs of men stayed with him.

Like Marsden, kindly James Kemp had Forebodings. "I know you mean well, Francis and I don't doubt your integrity but there has been comment and I daresay it may have found its way to Mr Marsden."

"What would you have me do, James? Leave her in her loneliness and despair? She has repented, you know and are we not here with the message of forgiveness?"

"Don't preach at me, Francis. I am not looking at this from a spiritual perspective –"

"Perhaps you should."

"Thank you, I am admonished."

"O James, you know I don't mean –"

"Yes, yes, I know what you mean. And you know perfectly well what I mean. This is not about Jesus and Mary Magdalene; it is about your reputation and maintaining what little equilibrium there is among these divisive people."

"I understand. And thank you for your concern. But I'm going to do it anyway."

Her husband had been and gone and been and gone again. But he had met with Francis once or twice and indeed had expressed his gratitude for the support. He would soon enough have other rumours to deal with, like the story that Butler had deflowered his eldest daughter.

Why can they not attend to the big things?

Francis had come to discover a measure of comfort with Jane that he could find nowhere else. There was such a lack of judgment in her and so little chance that she would share her thoughts with anyone else, least of all Marsden that he could speak his doubts and anxieties with her as he could with no other.

He had told Tungaroa that he was not the man for Jane's confession but as it turned out she was the woman for his.

As proved to be the case on this visit.

He drew up the centre board and dropped the sail and the skiff scrunched gently into the sand. To his left the stony, crouching lion that was Rangihoua pa stared away to the west. New buildings grew out of the rising bush before him for the settlement was slowly growing; there was the school house, bereft of students now but still serving as the church for Sunday service. Closer to the pa was the smithy, wisps of smoke coiling grey in the bright, clear day. But there was little sign of life along the beach, apart from a dozen or so plump, black hens scratching above the sand line and the day was quiet and still. Tangata whenua and manuhiri alike would be away at their gardens or gathering kai moana. And waiting.

Francis gathered up a satchel, slung it over a shoulder and then, with trousers rolled above the knee and stockings and boots in hand he clambered over the side and made his way ashore. He laid the articles down in the sand then returned to the boat, drawing out an anchor on twenty feet of rope from the bow before pushing the craft out and burying the anchor in the sand. The tide was going out but he would have returned well before the boat ran aground. Then he sat on the beach and waited for his feet to dry before putting on his boots and heading to the smithy.

He found William Hall within, a kerchief tied across his mouth, bending closely, very closely Francis thought over a spade. He looked up at Francis' greeting and grunted a reply before turning back to his work. Ah well, Francis thought, it is only his way.

"I have brought mail from the *Active*," he said, "it must have been missed on your delivery and found its way to Kerikeri. I told Captain Hansen I would save him the stopping and bring it myself."

"Ah," Hall laid down the spade and made his way out into the day. He removed the kerchief and drew a deep breath before bursting into a fit of coughing.

"Civil of you," he said when he had recovered, "you've given up a lot of your time to save Hansen a little of his."

"Ah well," Francis shrugged, "there was not a great deal else calling on my time and I was glad of the chance to go for a sail and run a line."

"O yes," Hall was rummaging through the mail, peering closely for each name. "Any luck?"

"Mm," Francis nodded. "I followed the gannets and sailed into a school and pulled in four good kahawai." Five, he thought, if you count the first but he would not mention that. "I thought I might take a couple up to Mrs Kendall with her husband's mail." He pointed at the remaining letters. "Would you mind disposing of the rest?"

"No point." Hall straightened up, stuffing a handful of envelopes into his trouser pocket. "Drop 'em off at the schoolhouse, everybody checks there." He snorted, "good that it's not completely useless." He turned back to the smithy, thern paused to throw back over his shoulder, "you might take care with the company you keep, Mr Hall."

I will not buy into this, Francis thought sternly, but he said, "do you have some objection to it, Mr Hall?"

Hall turned and pointed a grimy finger. "You know what I'm talking about. You judge a man by the company he chooses."

Francis thought even more sternly, I will not buy into this. And said, "what happened to 'judge not lest ye be judged'?"

"Are you judging me, Mr Hall?"

"Are you judging Mrs Kendall?" Francis, he thought despairingly, what are you hoping to achieve?

There is a local disease and I am catching it.

And Hall retorted as he had done many times, "Jesus said, 'ye shall judge them by their fruits.' And there is rotten fruit here."

"Jesus also spoke of repentance and forgiveness. How long has it been now –five years? How much longer do you intend to persist with condemnation?"

I am not an angry man but by God I am angry now

"Damn it." Hall crashed a fist into an open palm "I do not persist with past offence, sir. I speak –and pass judgment – on offences that began on day one and have continued to this day. From the beginning we have endured pride and deceit from a man who would place himself above all others. 'Mechanics' he called us in the early days and now the slander has progressed. Cooks! He tells Hongi that King, Butler and I and the others, you too, I would expect, are but cooks while he stands high above us like some kind of chief."

Francis held up a hand. "I am not speaking of Mr Kendall."

"Well I am. Do you not think that we tried to live in peace with him? He was to bring his family to Waimate where we might have flourished. But he did not come and he turned the local Maori against us as he has done ever since. He called out for assistance for his wretched school and I helped him to build it. So that he might neglect his charges and call us cooks to Hongi.

"And there is an injustice to it that eats at me. He defied Marsden to his face and yet the Great Man took his part. He fled to England leaving his wife and fulsome brood to fend for themselves and, I might add, she managed –as he had done – by trading arms to the natives. And yes, before you point your finger at me, I have traded, too, as have we all, but it was done out of necessity and in moderation. And it has kept us and the mission alive. But," and now the finger was stabbing, "it has made Kendall rich."

Hall was not finished. "So even after the defiance and the flight, he found support and his dictionary was published and he was recognised as a scholar and I do not resent him for that for it was a signal achievement and worthy of recognition but," and now his voice was rising, "in the name of God what inspired the Society to ordain him? So that he could come back and look down on us from an even greater height?"

The diatribe came to a sudden halt as he was taken in a sudden fit of coughing that became a wheezing and then he was fighting for air. Francis hovered helplessly and his anxiety turned to panic as Hall's lips turned blue and his fingers clawed at his throat. He bellowed for help but there was no response. What should he do, should he pound Hall's back, but might that not make it worse and drive what little air he had from him? Perhaps he should run for help, Hall's home was no great distance away, but he was loath to leave him. God help the man, he implored, then fell to his knees and prayed with a fervour he had not known since he kneeled by his father's bed.

Gradually the wheezing eased to be replaced by long, shuddering breaths and he opened his eyes to see Hall seated on the ground, his back against the smithy wall. The constriction must have passed for slowly his breathing was becoming more even and Francis closed his eyes again to give thanks.

"Water," Hall croaked and pointed to the smithy. Francis rushed in to return with a pannikin which he held to Hall's lips. Slowly the day moved into silence as the roaring in Francis' ears faded to let back in the slapping of the waves and the gulls' mewing.

"You prayed for me?"

"I did. And it seems my prayer was answered. Are you recovered? Is there anything I can do?"

Hall was struggling to his feet and pushed away Francis' efforts to aid him. "I'll be alright, I can stand." The words came more easily now and he even managed a wry smile. "Asthma and the smithy are a poor combination."

"So why do you -?"

"The work must be done." Then the tone softened. "Thank you for your concern and for your prayer, Mr Hall but here is nothing further you can do. You should go back to your boat and check that the gulls have not plundered your gift to Mrs Kendall."

Francis felt bound to protest. "At least may I see you to your home? Assure me that you are done with the smithy for the day."

"Be assured. I'd just finished anyway."

His breathing was even and his colour had returned.

"Very well then." Francis nodded and turned to go.

"One last thing, Mr Hall. You have prayed for me and I would like our meeting to end on a kinder note." He paused, gathering his words. "I do not hate Mrs Kendall. I hate what she did but, as you say, it was long ago and considering what effect her husband has had upon many in the settlement, who knows what effect he has had upon her. Anyway, I wish her well and you may tell her so. But I have judged Thomas Kendall with good reason and I have condemned him with good reason and I shall always detest him." He stretched out his hand. "Again, thank you for your prayer and good day, Mr Hall."

"Good day, Mr Hall."

William Hall need not have been concerned for the fish, they were lying safely in a bucket with the top lodged on firmly, but Francis was pleased to be away and back to the boat.

He sat in the sand and thought about the encounter. At one level, he supposed he should be pleased. After all, dispute had been resolved in the handshake of fellowship and William Hall had –astonishingly – extended well-wishing to Jane Kendall.

But the enmity was as implacable as that between Ngapuhi and the southern tribes and with considerably less likelihood of even temporary alliance. And for all the good reason of Hall's judgment and condemnation,

Francis thought he could see other causes that were not so noble. Like envy. For years the tale had been that William Hall had cornered the market, indeed it was a common accusation that for him mission work had always been a secondary consideration. Yet here he was pleading poverty and for all that Francis could not warm to the man, he would not think him a liar.

The argument over standing in the community had been there before the mission had begun, had never shown signs of easing and the arrival of Butler had only served to exacerbate it. It baffled Francis. For his own part, he had never sought power over others; sometimes he wondered whether this might be indicative of a personal failing, perhaps residing in weakness or the avoidance of proper responsibility. Perhaps, he thought, this grasp for power and status was nothing more than the habit of men brought up in the rigid English class system where every man was supposed to know his place and render unto Caesar. But it made for a difficult life where every man would be Caesar.

The Maori had their own class system and it covered a wider range than the English. Within the one village ranks might move from king to archbishop to slave to untouchable. But they seemed content with their lot.

For all the horror of their wars, their daily lives are not attended by dispute as ours are. Living with interminable bickering and complaint.

There was something else. 'Fulsome brood' Hall had called Kendall's children and Francis wondered whether it was part of a generalised resentment (the sins of the fathers) or whether there might be something more specific here. Hall was, Francis knew, a devoted father to his only son and John and Hannah King remained childless. Might this also be part of the injustice that ate at Hall?

He removed the fish and set the boat again. Then he turned into the schoolhouse, hollow and still, dropped off the mail and headed up the hill towards the Kendall home.

Jane Kendall's house was a very poor advertisement for the Wages of Sin. Sitting at his father's desk overlooking the bay, Joseph was bent over his letters, not with a great deal of enthusiasm, it seemed, for with a certain regularity the towelled head would lift and he would stare vacantly off into the middle distance.

At two and a half Lawrence was still the baby of the family, sitting up at the kitchen table, squishing dough into shapes and planting it with blocks and utensils, all the while chatting quietly to himself, here is the garden, here is the whare nui. John, namesake for the child who had died in Port Jackson all these years past, now rising four, sat with Samuel, eighteen months his senior, the solicitous older brother. Between them, and Francis smiled to see her there, was Tungaroa, cross-legged on the floor, a large picture book in her lap. "There," she pointed, "can you see the star shining over the stable? And aren't those funny horses the kings are riding?"

"They're not horses," said Samuel with a certainty direct from his namesake, "they're *camels*."

"And so they are," said Tungaroa. She looked up at Francis, smiled and raised her eyebrows, tilting her head, then returned to the book.

Jane was bent over the wood fire, setting the last of the sticks in place. Dressed in her customary grey, a straying bonnet holding back whisps of greying hair, she looked tired as she glanced over her shoulder to greet him. "A moment, please." She did not resemble a woman barely forty.

She offered him a glass of wine and Francis accepted. He noted with a touch of concern that the bottle was half done but her hands were steady as she took the fish from him and her movements were deft as she skinned and filleted them. As ever, the house was spotless.

"This is a haven, Mrs Kendall," Francis said. He gestured about the kitchen and living room. "A haven of peace and quiet domestic industry." And ironic, he thought, that all of this is more in keeping with the charter of the mission than much else I have seen. Then, because he was a scrupulous man, he amended, yet I suppose the households of the Halls and the Kings are not such a far cry away.

In the background he could hear, "and they laid him in swaddling clothes. Do you remember what swaddling clothes are?"

"Yes," said Samuel authoritatively, "they're bandages."

Francis found himself in a moment of peace but it was shot through with sadness.

"How do you manage," he heard himself asking, "with all the turbulence without?" Then, without thinking, he added almost abruptly, "William Hall sends his regards."

"Really?" Jane looked up. "That is kind of him." Then with no alteration of tone she added, "Joseph, will you take these fillets out and hang them in the smokehouse?" The boy snatched himself from his meditations and was swiftly at the table and swiftly out the door. Francis suspected that the task might prove to be a lengthy one.

He asked again into the silence, "How do you manage with the turbulence?" Jane drank from her glass and Francis wondered whether that might be part of her answer.

"I am not aware of it," she said finally, "my duties are here, within this haven as you call it," and for a moment Francis thought she might smile, "it is easier not to think outside it. Everything is here," and she patted her belly. "I am with child again."

Francis heard Marsden tut and flicked it away.

"You are blessed," he said.

"Well," Jane paused, "I am not so sure. I have been blessed nine times now and …" The words trailed away.

Good Lord, thought Francis, we are having a conversation. He vaguely realised that the room was silent now, the story had stopped and Tungaroa was listening, too.

He leaned forward in his seat. "Go on," he said.

Jane sipped thoughtfully. "Well," she said, "I have lost one child and the last was not easy. And Samuel is often sickly. I wonder if we should stop now. But I suppose," she looked down at her hands, "the decision is not mine to make."

And what is the response to that, thought Francis and they sat in the growing silence.

Then, "I am tired of this story," from Samuel.

And, "Me, too," from John. "Tell us another one."

"Yes," demanded Samuel, "tell us the story of the ant and the grasshopper."

You have no decisions to make other than follow the will of God. And how do we determine what that is? Is it God's will that Mrs Kendall should refuse her husband his God-given rights and fail in her duty as a Christian wife or continue to breed until she dies of it and leaves a dozen orphans? And if she does breed and she does die do we then say that because it happened it must have been the will of God? It is a nice point, one that a thousand theologians might pick over for a thousand years. And in the meantime women breed and their children are neglected and then they die and their children are orphaned. Marsden's response would be the simple one: this is not an Appropriate Conversation, Mr Hall.

"And so because the grasshopper was lazy and the ant was lacking in all charity and compassion the grasshopper died."

Francis drank deeply and shook his head. "I do not think I have your powers of endurance, Mrs Kendall. I think I may have to leave this place."

"Well," said Jane, "that is your decision."

Is it? Is it? Is it my decision? Is it God's will? Why is it that as a man here to teach forgiveness and redemption, I have not the slightest idea what God's will is?

Thou shalt know them by their fruits, Hall said. And what are his fruits? Or Kendall's? Or Marsden's? Or mine? I have been here for eighteen months now and what is there to show for it?

What has the mission brought to Maori? Not one convert in all these years. And all the civilising technology we have brought has been turned to the advance of war and the fruits are slaughter and slavery.

Francis spoke to his lap. "You must think me weak," he said. "I do not have your capacity for endurance, I do not, do not ..."

Then he was rising to his feet.

"I must pray for guidance," he said and left the house.

CHAPTER 42

Kerikeri December 1822

The sky was dark and threatening the day the fleet returned. It swept past the islands of the bay, silent, majestic with all the glory Nelson had brought from Trafalgar. It was no longer the flotilla that had gathered at Whangarei as allies had turned off and gone their own way but still it turned into the bay like a massive bugle call.

Thomas Kendall sat readied at Rangihoua with his family. The shutters were closed and the curtains drawn, no triumphal flags for you, Hongi. The same tableau was played out throughout the settlement. Dark curtains and candles to hold out the day, *we are in mourning.*

Francis Hall did not know better and was waiting on the shores of Kerikeri with James Kemp. A little to his left he saw John Butler standing alone and the men nodded to one another.

The banks of the inlet were crowded, gripped in a vast excitement, not yet discriminating, that would come later as women, children, old men, wounded men and sick men clamoured and jostled, pushing against one another, vibrating against one another. They sighed as one when the first waka rounded the cape and as more followed they began to jump upon the spot and wave their arms and shout and cry.

Over it all rang the wild keening of the karanga.

Haere mai te iwi, nga whanau, nga ora, nga mate.

A single canoe was manoeuvred to the front where it floated quietly, rocking on the tide. Although Francis could see the paddlers sitting erect in their places it had no movement of its own and as it was nudged towards the shore by the waka around it he could see why. This was the waka of nga mate, the warriors who had fallen and now returned home. They sat upright, lashed to their places, staring sightlessly towards their waiting families. Some were recognisable, others were not but all had been taken by corruption over the journey back. The stench of them reached out with dark and slimy fingers and Francis thrust a bunched kerchief over his mouth and nose. He heard John Butler retching.

The waka of the dead sat and bobbed while the others sat quietly about it.

Then another canoe flashed past to settle halfway up its length in the sand. Paddles were dropped as the crew leaped out, snatched up their taiaha, mere and more besides and roared their greeting to the crowd. Naked they danced up on their toes, knees lifting high then stamped, hands smacking across chests, upon thighs. Thirty spears rose as one in salute, then Francis was closing his eyes and shaking his head as they waved their trophies.

Then the heavens opened and the rain crashed down in mighty sheets and still the dance went on.

Finally the warriors slowed and sank to their knees, sweating in the rain and silence fell upon them all. The fleet moved slowly up to the beach and their prows settled in the sand. Then the silence was sliced in a piercing scream and a wild-eyed woman was racing across the sand while her husband sat stiffly in the slowly revolving waka of the dead. A taiaha was in her hand, then reversed its haft was thudding into the carven figure that adorned the great canoe. The woodwork broke beneath her rage but she found no satisfaction here and looked about wildly for more satisfying prey; she found it in a young woman crouching in the front of the waka. She wrenched the woman unresisting from her place and beat and tore at her. Other women followed, snatching young boys and comely girls from the canoes, punching tearing, biting.

Then Hongi was amongst them and King George's good sword was slicing and dripping and Butler, Hall and Kemp together fled.

The storm that had marked the fleet's return had passed and the day was fair and clear. But its effects were still there and ground was soft and clinging, adding to the reluctance with which they dragged their feet.

They trudged along slowly and their faces were set and grim. Ahead, Waimate pa rose and shone in the new day.

"I do not think," said Francis Hall, "my spirits have ever been so low." He was deeply tired for he had found no sleep the night before but the grey weight that dragged him down was not of the body.

James Kemp nooded but made no answer.

In their path ahead lay a small boulder and Francis pointed to it. "Let's sit for a while," he said, "I need to gather myself. I am not at all prepared."

James grunted agreement and they settled themselves. James reached into his pocket and withdrew a stubby pipe and a packet of shag. He loaded and lit the pipe, then sighed into the grey plume.

"I wish I smoked," said James, "it seems to bring you a kind of ease."

"It gives me something to do."

"I cannot shake the image of Hongi and those slaves," said Francis. "They were just *children*, for God's sake."

James nodded and puffed.

"And now we are to visit him, to offer our condolences for his loss. What can I say that is not an utter lie?"

"You can say that you regret the deaths," said James. "You needn't say which ones. And you can offer your sympathy for the loss of Tete and Apu."

"Yes," Francis nodded, "that is true enough. Tete in particular was a fine young man. But offering any kind of sympathy to Hongi seems to imply some recognition of humanity in him –"

"And there is."

"No," James shook his head, "not right now. They were just children, for God's sake."

"It does not help to dwell upon it, Francis."

"No?" As Thomas Kendall had once resented William's Hall placidity at Ruatara's tangi, so was Francis now offended by Kemp's. And his rebuke was the same.

"How can you be so sanguine?"

And Kemp's response was the same as Hall's had been.

"I am a realistic man. I trust to God's purpose and do the best I can."

But Francis could not let it go and as they picked themselves up and headed off towards the pa, anger was now mixing with despair.

The bodies of the fallen sat in rows, upright, knees bound to their chests, their weapons lying by their sides.

And there was Hongi, his face a mask of grief, standing, shaking in the embrace of a short man in a dark coat. Kendall! Banned he may have been from officiating at Waimate, but the new priest could not have been kept from Hongi at such a time. His eyes were red-rimmed and his cheeks were wet.

He offers Hongi a sympathy that I can only feign. How can he do that?

Yet as he approached the Ngapuhi rangatira, the fear that his revulsion would overwhelm him dissipated and he hongied without a shudder. Still, he was pleased to get away and after mumbled condolence he moved away from the marae to sit in the shade of a storehouse.

He looked vaguely back to where the dead sat quietly and the living lamented them.

"There seem fewer women than I would have thought," he said absently, aloud.

"Some have gone with a rope to find a branch to follow their kin; others may be trying to dissuade them, or are perhaps assisting."

The voice was soft in his ear and he jumped with shock, then turned to see Kendall regarding him gravely.

"I'm sorry if I startled you," said Kendall, offering his hand. "This is a sorrowful meeting."

And one, thought Francis, in which you have played a sorrowful part. He studied the outstretched hand for a moment, then took it.

I have pressed noses with Hongi; why would I not shake Kendall's hand?

"So," he said, "there is to be more death. They take their own death with the same ease that they take another."

"Ae," said Kendall, "they do not fear death as we do. That is why we find no conversions here. Most men are afraid of dying, so the promise of immortal life is irresistible. But if you do not fear death …" His words trailed off and he shrugged.

Then what are we doing here, Francis thought, then wondered whether he was speaking aloud again, because Kendall was answering him.

"Why are we drawn to this darkness? Why do we live with wickedness and horror, in deprivation and danger when we could be taking our ease in our own country? He paused and Francis wondered whether this was to be a conversation or a sermon. "We live with wickedness, Mr Hall, so that we may rise above it and by the examples of our lives show a better way." He added softly, almost to himself, "And in so doing we assure our own salvation."

"And what," asked Francis, "are the fruits that show us our salvation? For as I sit here in this horror, Mr Kendall, I cannot see what we have done to lighten the darkness."

Kendall laid a hand upon his arm. "I know whereof you speak," he answered. "I, too have been afflicted by doubt and I have prayed for certainty."

"And were you answered?"

Kendall nodded. "In some measure. I felt alone and useless and I begged the Lord to give me direction. And He answered me. He set my feet on English soil and my work upon the Maori language was brought into the light; and He affirmed the rightness of my going with ordination." He looked at Francis steadily. "I was called and I was justified."

This is self-serving nonsense, thought Francis and nearly said, I can see how you have profited, Mr Kendall but I cannot see the profit for Maori. Instead, he gestured back towards the lamentation and asked, "And how has that served to lighten the darkness here?"

Kendall gnawed his lip. "I suppose," he said, "that is not immediately clear. But the ways of God are mysterious. I only know that we are the instruments of His light and we are here to face the wickedness and rise above it."

"Lead us not into temptation," Francis said and wondered, why did I say that? His musing was cut short.

"What?" Kendall was abrupt. "Why did you say that?"

"Truly," Francis answered, "I don't know. It just came to me. Has it upset you? You look pale."

"No, no," Kendall waved it away. "it just," he fidgeted and gnawed his lip again, "it just put me in mind of a conversation I thought I had forgotten."

Francis remembered his earlier question. "How can you embrace Hongi, knowing what he has done?"

"Yes," Kendall nodded. "I have often asked myself that question. I have told myself he is a monster, for he has done and continues to do monstrous things. And then I have wondered, to be truly a monster isn't it necessary that you know you are?"

Francis was appalled. "Are you saying he is an innocent? That he should be forgiven for he knows not what he does? Of course he knows. How many times have you and Marsden and all of us pointed out to him the evil of his ways?"

"Yes," Kendall agreed, "we have, but doesn't that only mean that he knows we believe his deeds are evil? Is not the hallmark of evil that it is done in secret and covered up with lies? Hongi acts in the light of day for all the world to see and his people applaud him for it. And not just Maori. Our king put in his hands the sword that he used to such evil effect yesterday and he gave him a coat and helmet for his protection – which, I might add, has saved his life on more than one occasion." He shook his head. "I sometimes wonder if evil is such a simple matter."

"That I should live to hear a priest say such a thing!"

Francis and Kendall both jumped at the intrusion and turned to see Butler and his bony finger. It jabbed at Kendall then back to the silent warriors. "That is the work of evil, Mr Kendall, and it is a simple matter." The finger jabbed again, towards the umu this time. "And as you debate the complexity of evil the flesh of man is being laid in those ovens. Do you find some virtue there?"

Francis saw with alarm that Kendall's eyes were blazing, his fists were clenched and his breath was coming in short, panting breaths. Quickly he placed himself between the two men.

"I cannot think, Mr Butler," he said, "that this is the time or place –"

"Can you not, Mr Hall? Perhaps you think the gospel should be reserved for Sunday services. But I am here to tell you that it is the function of the Christian man – and I am assuming you still declare yourself to be such – to speak out against evil wherever he may find it. And it is here, sir, and it is –"

Wherever else it may have been was lost with his breath as a heavy hand gripped tightly about the back of his neck.

"Turi, turi, e tama." Wharepoaka took his hand away and Butler stood aggrieved but silent, his hand rubbing at his neck. The Maori's eyes were blazing like Kendall's but his breathing was steady and his words measured. "Your quarrel is out of place here. We are at peace, we are in mourning and we will not hear your condemnation." He pointed towards the gate. "You need to go now. Haere atu."

Butler was dismissed.

Then Wharepoaka enveloped Kendall and the two wept together while Francis stood uncomfortably by. At length they parted and Kendall made the introductions. "Wharepoaka, this is Francis Hall, he is no blood to William Hall at Rangihoua. He has joined the mission to bring God's message to you. Mr Hall, this is Wharepoaka, he is son to Rakau and brother to Tungaroa. He is," and his eyes flashed warning, "just returned from Tamaki Makaurau with Hongi."

"Good day, Mr Hall. How do you do?" Like his sister, like Kendall he spoke with the accent of Thoresby.

"Very well, thank you, Wharepoaka. How are you?"

Their noses pressed and their breaths mingled. Then they stood apart, Frances offered his condolences, Wharepoaka graciously accepted them and silence enveloped them.

Francis had never in his life been at such a loss for words. Snatches of small talk suggested themselves, each more ludicrous than the one before – did you have a pleasant trip? Any sights that you might recommend?

What do you say to a man whose name means Pigpen, who is your host and a courteous gentleman and also just happens to be a murderous cannibal? What's on the menu for tonight? Get a grip, Francis, you're going to giggle in a moment.

Kendall came to his rescue.

"Wharepoaka is preparing an account of their journey for Mr Marsden," he said. "Tungaroa will transcribe it for him."

And won't that make entertaining reading for the chaplain. I wonder what he will make of it.

Then Kendall was speaking swiftly in Maori to Wharepoaka, they bowed and made their departure and Francis was released.

For all his subtle musings upon the nature of evil, his compassionate and wise understanding of Francis Hall's anxieties, his gentle encouragement of the young man, for all the calling and justification, Thomas was again beset by doubt.

There were of course all the usual reasons, the cruel and uninformed judgments of Marsden and the mission, the failure of the school, the depravity of Maori, their defiance of the word of God, a sense of alienation from his wife and family … But he had ridden these out before, he had risen above them and ultimately his faith remained strong.

This was different, the cause was deep within him, a hungry lizard gnawing at the very fabric of his belief, whispering surrender. Temptation sang to him and it was hard to resist because he could not see where the urge would take him. There were no words to the song, or rather no words that he could understand, but the poignant appeal seemed to touch the very root of him. Like the song of the lonely woman, ah God, now there was more of a shape to it, it would draw him from his craft and then, he knew, it would take him down and swallow him. And yet he longed to be consumed.

I know not what thou sayest.

I do not know the man.

He stood at the makeshift pulpit and looked about his church that had once been his schoolhouse. The windows grimed and streaked with salt, cobwebs gathered in the corners and sand and dust upon the floor.

I must remember to speak to the girls about the upkeep.

The congregation sat on the rough-hewn planks that had once served the children of the school and they were grey and dusty, too. William and Dinah Hall sat with their son, upright and dutifully attentive, John and Hannah King, Cowell and his wife, a handful of convict labourers who had not yet lost hope, a bearded sawyer, Leigh, the Weslyan visitor, the new smith, Jane and the children occupying much of the front row – *have I bred the majority of my congregation?* There were no Maori to be seen.

He had sat at his desk the night before, trying to decide upon the text for the day. But after half an hour his mind remained as blank as the sheet of paper before him, but for an intricate, detailed moko. He poured another glass of wine but there was no lubrication there and in a wave of fatalism he opened the bible at random and let an index finger fall on the page.

I know not what thou sayest.

Apt, he thought. And he had laboured to bring some meaning, some message of hope from the story of Peter's denial.

"Three times," he said into the heavy silence, "thrice before the cock crowed the first of the disciples had denied his Christ. He did it knowingly and he did it with forewarning. Could there be any excuse for him?"

His eyes roamed across the congregation and settled upon William Hall, staring ahead, arms folded, a man not known for his readiness with excuses. "Perhaps," said Thomas, "we would struggle to find forgiveness. But," he raised a hand, "God did. And Peter went on to be one of the great apostles, one of the great martyrs."

And who, wondered Hall, is this plea for?

As if answering Thomas gestured towards Rangihoua pa. "These are dark days, my friends. We are faced with horror on all sides, enough to make the strongest heart become faint. And we would not be human if sometimes our natural repulsion did not impel us to condemnation, perhaps even flight. And then we need to remember the words of our Lord on the cross: forgive them, Father, He said, for they know not what they do. Let us remember their souls are as dear to God as ours are..."

He carried on in a similar vein, vaguely aware that he was largely repeating himself, that it had all been said before and that nobody was particularly interested anyway. The grey and dusty church and the lifeless, disapproving congregation – *waiting for me to stop so they can go home* – seemed to suck at his energy and he wound the sermon down, led a spiritless rendition of the twenty third psalm and stood and watched them leave, filing out at the conclusion of the hymn. There was no waiting for the priest to take his place at the door, to greet and bless each one in turn. Even Jane and the children were gone, leaving him standing at the pulpit, wondering what it all was for.

At the church, no, its function was done for the day and it was a school now, no, that function was done, too; at the hall door he stood and watched the last of the congregation dissipate. Behind him a dull, dusty, ultimately meaningless space; before him throbbing and vibrant the colours and abundance of the new land. Beneath a crystal, blue vault, the waters of the bay sparkled and the bush glowed green and yellow and red. He drew in deep breaths and felt a new energy, sweet and salty, surge within him. He stepped off tussock into sand and it slid and crunched beneath his boots. Then he was walking east along the beach to where the sand ended in rock rising to scrub and bush growing south into the bay.

Perhaps it was because he had no idea of where he was going or how long it would take him to get there that he gave new attention to the movement itself; feeling calf muscles bunch as he stepped up, lengthen as his boots took their purchase, leather bending about the contours of the rocks. He watched the way his arms moved independently of conscious thought, keeping him safely balanced; his wrists and hands strong and sure, moving from rock to rock as he climbed sideways, spiderlike up the short face. He picked up the pace as he moved along the ledge, nimble, lithe, like a cat he thought as he sprang from one smooth surface to another, bending, steadying before the next step. Where the rocks turned and moved into the next bay, the ledge became narrower and in places he was obliged to hold to the rock face, arms spread, his face only inches away, feeling for the next foothold, the next handhold. His face closed in concentration, all there was was the next grip, step, pause, then the next. He gathered himself for the final leap from rock to sand and landed with a kind of elation.

He sat in the sand for a while and watched it trickle through his fingers and listened to the softly breaking little waves and the cry of the gulls and he was quite without thought.

Then he was up and striding along a short stretch of beach before he was up on the rocks again.

Ra was approaching the end of his ascent when Thomas removed his jacket, tied the arms about his waist, unbuttoned his shirt and pushed up his sleeves. For perhaps the first time he became conscious of being fit and strong and he was pleased and thankful for it.

Past the third beach the ledge around the rocks opened into a wide platform and he discovered a pool set within it. Roughly rectangular, about twenty feet by twelve, sinking to a depth that would have covered Thomas' head, it was quite perfect, a self-contained microcosm. Refreshed twice daily by the incoming tide, life added or perhaps withdrawn, it lay protected amongst the rocks, serene and glowing. For all that it was salt, the water was as clear as any fresh water pond and the sand that carpeted it shone. Kelp hung as though painted and the small fish that moved through its folds appeared to float in air.

Thomas settled himself carefully on a smooth rock and lost himself in the pool, watching a crab edge across the sand, creeping out of sight into a friendly crevice, a grey spreadeagled starfish joined to rock. The sun was hot upon him now and absently he removed his shirt and then his boots and stockings. Then he lay upon the rock and felt its warmth stroke his chest and belly; he cupped his hands into the pool, lukewarm upon the surface and tossed the water into his face. Then he stood and removed his trousers and lowered himself into the shallow end. Beneath the surface the water was cooler, a sudden touch upon his groin and he leaned back on his elbows and let his legs float up and now there was warmth against his back and the sun upon his face.

The spell broke with a rumble in his stomach and the realisation that he was hungry.

I should be getting back.

And that, he realised with a start, was his first conscious thought since he had left Rangihoua bay. It soured him that it had begun with 'should'; how pleasant it had been to spend some time away from it. He climbed out of the pool, dried himself on his shirt and headed home.

The return was long and arduous and he was weary when he reached the house. As he opened the door his nostrils filled with the aroma of roasting pork and for a moment he thought he was back in Thoresby. But there was no bouncing child to greet him, no tales of the day's doings. He had passed John and Basil on the beach, building castles against the incoming tide. He had thought briefly of joining them but he was tired by then; besides, neither boy showed much interest. To John at five he would have been near a stranger, gone altogether for over a year and only an intermittent presence since. The older children were absent, at Kerikeri he supposed; Lawrence was engaged with dough and Samuel was nowhere to be seen.

"He has been coughing and has gone to bed," said Jane. She was seated at the dining table with Tungaroa, fingers flying over their needlework and she did not look up as she answered him.

Thomas nodded and turned to the boys' room. It was a sensible, airy and colourless space, warm in the late summer afternoon but the little boy shivered under grey blankets. "Mother," he croaked.

Thomas kneeled by the low bed and took a glass of water from the nightstand. "Here, son," he urged, "try a sip of water." But the boy pushed his hand away. "Mother," he whimpered.

Don't touch me.

Then Tungaroa was beside the child, kneeling, stroking his hair and he was sipping from the glass she offered him. He swallowed with some difficulty then drank again, more easily this time and she lowered his head back on to the pillow as he closed his eyes.

Thomas retired to his desk and papers and here, as ever, there was a kind of comfort. It was not the same easy comfort he had found when he had compiled the dictionary. Then he could be sure that every session at his study would produce some yield, some further forward movement. This was altogether different and as he sought to clarify Maori religious belief he ran into difficulties which he recognised yet could not surpass and difficulties which he could not recognise and which made the whole exercise ultimately meaningless. He recognised the Maori association of the spiritual with the sexual and was fascinated, appalled and struck dumb. 'A public relation,' he later wrote, 'could not be endured amongst Christians, or only those at least whose professional office leads them to study midwifery, anatomy, etc.' He did not recognise that his every discovery was filtered through evangelical assumption. So he was frustrated before he began and for all that he could see that he was accumulating an abundance of information without any meaning to go with it, he could not leave it alone. And vanity went with it, too. He had shared his ideas with Lee and Pratt amongst others and could see that they could make no sense of it and he understood that that was because he could make no sense of it. But I will, he thought. I shall persevere and God will lift the scales and then I will be the first to understand. He did not recognise how much he needed to understand for quite different reasons.

The bay flooded with the shades of sunset and he laid down his pen and watched it glow. *There is meaning there too, and also a kind of promise and both pass beyond my understanding.*

The boys returned and they took their evening meal in silence. Then the children were put to bed, the kitchen was tidied and Jane returned to her needlework and Thomas to his study. Tungaroa had left for the pa.

From the east a full moon angled its light on to the bay; upon the waters phosphorescence glowed and the two lights met in a sparkling brilliance.

I must go down to the beach, it calls me. And I must be out of this cold, grey house and away from this cold, grey woman.

He left without a word.

And now he sat in shadow at the southern end of the beach and watched the bay shimmer and glow.

I suppose there is a logical explanation for the light on the water, perhaps myriads of small fish swim just below the surface and the moonlight reflects off their scales; but I would sooner believe te marama has spread her beams to light the way for a lost traveller.

The night was sultry and he loosened his shirt and removed his boots and the sand was soft and cool.

Someone, I think it may have been Basil, once said, 'they also serve who only stand and wait.' Do I serve as I sit and wait? Wait for what? I cannot wait for a shaft of light from behind a black cloud this time for the whole bay is one glorious shining light. But again I wait for a sign. Will I even recognise it if it comes, will I know what it portends, will I know what to do about it?

What am I supposed to be doing?

The questions drifted back and forth and he poked at the sand in growing agitation. Then there was a faint cough and the rustle of flax and he looked up to see a woman standing at the water's edge, facing out into the bay. Long black unbound hair lay over her shoulders and halfway down her back; a flax skirt swept over full hips and down to the backs of her knees.

Strong legs that would take her up and down Rangihoua a dozen times a day.

Thomas gazed with a kind of wonder, naiad he breathed and then his eyes opened wider as her hands were at her skirt, loosening it, tossing it behind her on to the sand. For the second time that day he was quite without thought, mesmerised, the moonlight on her hair, glowing down her back, cleft and swelling buttocks and thighs. He watched her wade into the bay, the phosphorescence glittered about her, lapped at her and then she was diving forward, her behind rising up and then she was gone, leaving him staring into the broken light that had taken her.

The waters became still and for a moment he thought he might have imagined it all and the thought was like a knife, but there was the skirt and now, some fifteen yards further out, there was her head breaking the surface. Even with the light he could not make her out as she turned and rolled and paddled on her back but he followed every movement with something akin to devotion.

He had not moved, perhaps he had not breathed as she turned at last and headed towards the shore. A final dive and then she was standing, throwing back her hair and she was clear in the moonlight and he could see she was Tungaroa. Her breasts were full and heavy but no infant had ever dragged upon them, drained them and they rose up like a promise and set an ache in him. And as the sea fell away from her – like a shadow slipping down the mountain side – he was gazing at her rounded woman's belly and the dark, luxuriant vee where her thighs joined.

He was on his feet before she left the shallows and she looked up in surprise as he stumbled out of shadow. But the surprise passed quickly as she recognised him and smiled in greeting.

"Kia ora, e Keni. You gave me a fright."

He tried to say "I'm sorry" but his mouth was dry and his tongue seemed swollen to twice its normal size.

She moved forward for her skirt but he was there before her. He lifted it from the sand, holding it tightly and she stared at him. "Are you alright?" she asked. "You look dreadful."

Her choice of words was more apt than she knew for he was staring, shaking and full of dread. He tried to speak but could manage only a croak. "Please," he said.

"Please?" she repeated, puzzled, then her puzzlement grew as she watched him drop the skirt.

"You are wet," he managed at last, "I must dry you, let me dry you."

She stood passively, wondering as he turned her, gathered her hair into a bunch and squeezed; the moisture pattered on to the sand. Then he was taking off his shirt, patting with it at her back and arms and patting, stroking and cupping her tunga roa, then turning her, reaching for her breasts, panting, groaning and she thought he might weep.

Still she stood passively, held immobile by the crossing currents of anxiety, concern, curiosity and a touch of amusement.

Now he had given up all pretence at drying and was on his knees, embracing her thighs, his face pressed into her loins.

"The joints of thy thighs are like jewels," he mumbled and she had no idea what the words meant but she felt his hunger and his need.

He looked up and his cheeks were wet with his own salt, his eyes pleaded and she was caught by his vulnerability; she sighed and stroked his thinning, grey hair.

"Please," he said and this time she understood him and nodded.

"Alright," she said.

He took her hand and led her, or perhaps she led him into the shadows.

CHAPTER 43

At forty-four, some thirty odd years late, Thomas fell in love. And for a man who claimed conversance with the great mysteries of the universe, who was, he said, familiar with the plans and wishes of the creator, he was surprised and bewildered.

He wandered about in a daze, unable to hold his thoughts together; time and again the beginnings of an idea would dissolve into the curve of a woman's breast, the breaking of waves translate into a woman's sigh and he would smile in spite of himself and shake his head in wonder.

It was not surprising that he was surprised. For all that the phenomenon of love reached back to antiquity and had been celebrated in every language, the romantic variety had never served as a proper subject of conversation in either Kendall household. Or any household he had inhabited, for that matter. The love of God had predominated but it was an abstract love, without form or sensation, more allied to duty and sacrifice than it ever was to joy or pleasure.

But even if Thomas had been acquainted with the poets, it would probably not have meant much to him. Love poetry is for lovers, not neophytes and unless you have watched your mistress's gown drift down, the image of the hill and the shadow does not signify a great deal.

As the chemical levels in his brain shifted, his capacity for certainty soared and like most lovers he found enormous, almost cosmic significance in his situation.

"This was meant to be," he whispered.

Along with space – this little room an everywhere – time shrank and eternity nestled in the palm of his hand.

"I shall love you forever," he said and truly believed that she should be pleased to hear him say so.

"Love conquers all," he said, dismissing Jane and the rest of humanity as onlookers in his great drama.

His love was the most precious thing in all the world, divinely ordered and eternal.

He was called and he was justified.

He was of course quite mentally unbalanced but it was a wonderful feeling and he would not have been without it.

But even in the first flush of his madness he did understand that there were no others who could understand it and he held down the urge to cry it from the rooftops. For a man of such candour, it was not an easy thing. And for all that the day shone with a new light, he knew that his love was a secret thing, to be celebrated in the dark and hidden with lies and he remembered what he had said to Francis Hall about the nature of evil and became more disturbed.

Not that it remained a secret for long.

Like a fourteen year old boy with his first infatuation he could not keep his eyes off her; his gaze was too intense, his tone too tender and he stood too close. And it was duly noted, first by the women and then the men looked more closely and saw what the women had seen. It brought the community closer together and there was now new interest in what others had observed, questions began to appear in conversations – "go on, and what did she do then?" – and they joined together in communal brooding. Rumour became fact to confirm what they already believed but they were frustrated by a lack of confession or the kind of clear evidence they could take directly to Marsden or Pratt.

The Maori provided it.

Their knowledge of the situation was much more simply gained. Tungaroa told them. Unburdened by a sense of sin or the need for secrecy and deceit, she shared the information and was happy to satisfy the various degrees of curiosity. There were no particular consequences for her but there were for Thomas and, given his knowledge of tikanga, he should have anticipated them.

The household was quiet; the girls were away at Kerikeri and Thomas Surfleet was also absent on business, taking Basil with him – more and more they were finding pressing reasons to be absent. The boys had gone to bed, Thomas could hear Samuel coughing weakly and Tungaroa and Jane, moving more slowly now as her pregnancy approached its sixth month, were tidying the kitchen.

He sat at his desk, a blank sheet before him and stared out over the darkening bay. Then he was torn from his musing by voices, shouting and laughing and the commotion of squawking hens.

He jumped to his feet and headed for the door. The new fowlhouse, barely a month constructed and placed close to the house for safer keeping, was already under siege. He was faintly surprised by the openness of the raid – he would have expected a more furtive approach – but then his surprise turned to shock as he saw not a couple of young thieves but a dozen men standing about the enclosure. They were locals, he knew them all, but there was no friendliness here; the hostility was a tangible thing.

He was aware of Jane and Tungaroa standing behind him in the doorway and he motioned them back.

"Why are you here?"

"To right the wrong. To take back what you have taken from us."

Still he did not understand.

"You are mistaken," he said. "I have done you no wrong."

The men grunted their disgust at his answer and the spokesman spat.

"You have taken what was pledged to Towhi," he said and pointed at Tungaroa.

Still his thoughts spun but as he heard Jane's gasp and her steps hurrying back into the house they gathered and he realised the enormity of his position.

"I did not know," he answered feebly, "that she was betrothed," knowing that this lack of knowledge had no bearing on anything.

The Maori shrugged and then because there was no need for further conversation they returned to their task.

Thomas stood silently and watched as the fowlhouse was plundered, watched as it became a game and the men cheered as one of their number pursued a frantic hen around the pen, then fell about laughing as he slipped and landed in chicken shit. He nearly cried out as they approached his two asses tethered at their posts – "but I need them to convey me and my supplies" – but he bit it back and watched in silence as they were led away.

At last they were gone and he drew in a shuddering breath before turning back into the house.

Jane and Tungaroa were seated quietly at the kitchen table. They watched him falter at the doorway and Jane held up a hand before he could speak.

"I need," she said, and there was a deliberateness in her voice that he had not heard in near seven years, "to talk with Tungaroa. I would appreciate it if we could have this conversation in private."

He nodded helplessly and turned away from the house into the night. Jane sat and studied Tungaroa. There were no signs of guilt or shame, just a quiet concern and Jane was surprised to realise that she too was calm.

I should be distraught, yet I feel at peace. Why is that?

"Why?" she asked.

"He was so sad," said Tungaroa, "so sad and fragile. I thought he might have died if I had said 'no'."

Jane remembered back to the vulnerability that had won her and she nodded.

"I see," she said, "and that sadness, that fragility has been there on every occasion?"

"It is always there."

"And did you not think that it was wrong – I won't call it a sin – but wrong by your own customs to lie with a man who is married to another?"

"Muru will right the wrong."

Then the real question. "Tungaroa, did you not think that you would be hurting me?"

Tungaroa shook her head. "No," she said. "I thought about that and I talked to my mother and my sisters and we thought I would be helping."

"Helping? How?"

"I heard you tell Francis Hall that you wished for no more children. So if Keni was lying with me, perhaps he would not be lying with you …" She shrugged.

"And how long did you think that would go for? Forever?"

"I don't know."

Jane stared.

This is preposterous, there is no sense in it.

Yet as she knew that there was no sense in it, she also knew, and more profoundly, that there was no malevolence in it, either. And perhaps it was that awareness which led her on to clearer thought, to braver thought.

She is an innocent. Just as Richard was.

It seemed that somehow a door had opened to wider thought. But for the moment it was too much for her, there were too many thoughts, *I should be distraught, this is preposterous, she is an innocent …*

"Are you angry with me, whaea?"

Jane looked across at the anxious gaze and her tone was tender. "No," she said, "you are a good girl, Tungaroa."

The taking of his asses and his fowls did not mark the end of Thomas' debt. Word of the raid and its cause swept across the island to reach other hapu who shared blood with Towhi and so with his grievance.

Within ten days one hundred men had set off from the Hokianga bent on plunder and balance. The mood here was a good deal uglier than that of the previous raid, for amongst their number was Towhi himself. That he had been resident in the Hokianga for two years now, that he had not given Tungaroa a thought in years, that he had a wife and a daughter older than Tungaroa – all of these things were quite beside the point. He had been wronged and he would have utu.

Their mood had not sweetened by the time they reached Kerikeri. Rewa noted it and was concerned.

"I think," he said to Waikato, "that these ones will be looking for satisfaction in more than hens and donkeys."

So they proceeded in a swift waka with a band of their own men ahead of Towhi to Rangihoua where they were joined by Wharepoaka. And it was as well for Thomas that they did. For as the door crashed in and a dozen men broke into his house, snatching up whatever they could lay their hands on, it was Waikato who saved his life, grasping the wrist of a man in the moment before he would have buried his hatchet in Thomas' head. Then Wharepoaka and Rewa were beside the missionary and their muskets were raised and the room was suddenly still.

"E Towhi," said Rewa, "this is your turangawaewae, we are kin and you are entitled to satisfaction. But this man and his family are under my protection – and under the protection of Hongi."

And such was his mana that Towhi and his men acceded.

For the Maori the matter was now closed but for the settlers it was just beginning. While the muru raids provided all the confirmation they needed, they understood that Marsden and the Society might not see it that way. For five weeks they dithered, brooding together, stirring themselves into passions of righteous outrage but holding back from the final confrontation.

William Hall was appalled by their reticence.

"Are we women that we shrink from him and look away from his wickedness?" he demanded. "We sit like lambs in his church and his sin and hypocrisy spill over us. We should be ashamed."

There was a score of them assembled in his house and they were unanimous in their condemnation.

William cut across the chorus of agreement. "So. Are we to take action or continue to cower like frightened children? And think on this." His finger jabbed at a gentleman whose pallor told him for a newcomer and the man started nervously in his seat. "What does the Reverend Leigh make of this?" he asked. It was a rhetorical question. "He would be well within his rights to send word back to his Weslyan Society in England or to the Reverend Marsden that we are led by a vile fornicator and that we cower in fear before him and will not call him to account."

Samuel Leigh tried to assure the meeting that he had neither made nor communicated any such judgment. But William was not finished. "And what does it say for his own reputation that he, an ordained minister, should take his lesson from such a one as Kendall?"

He fell silent then and Samuel shifted uncomfortably in his seat. He had been advised in depth of the depravity and wildness he would encounter in the Maori but none had thought to warn him what he might discover in the settlers.

"Well, Mr Leigh," John King was speaking. "Mr Hall makes a good point. Let me expand upon it. It seems to me that by continuing to attend Mr Kendall's services – and I must include you in this – we could be reasonably viewed as condoning his sin."

"Well said, John," William applauded, "pray continue."

"So," John said, "in the first case we should make it clear to Mr Kendall that we disapprove most strongly of his actions and further that if he does not put the girl away then we must absent ourselves from his services. At which point," and he in his turn pointed sternly, "it would be your duty to fill the gap that he, of his own wicked volition, has created."

Led by Hannah the settlers applauded his speech and John sank back into his seat, well satisfied. I am taking a stand, he thought.

Samuel was distressed by the whole business but was unable to deny the great good sense that Mr King was making. Reluctantly he agreed.

But after the note was duly delivered and duly torn to shreds and the fateful Sunday arrived, his nerve failed.

"It is not for me," he explained miserably to the assembled congregation, "to enter into this. It is a private dispute and I should have no part of it."

"Well then," William gestured about his living room where the faithful were gathered, "here we are, joined together on the Lord's Sabbath without a priest to lead us. What are we to do?"

"Yet we are within a church," said John, "for is it not written, 'where one or two men are gathered together in My name, there is My church'? And the word of God is with us." He held up his bible. "You are our host, William. Read to us."

The congregation murmured its assent.

William needed no further encouragement. He stood and thumbed through his bible. "Hear," he said, "the word of the Lord from the Book of Psalms. 'Blessed is the man who walketh not in the counsel of the ungodly, nor standeth in the way of sinners, nor sitteth in the seat of the scornful. But his delight is in the law of the Lord; and in his law does he meditate day and night –"

His meditation came to an abrupt end as the door was flung open and Kendall was in their midst. Vibrating with fury he stormed through the bretheren, eyes blazing, fists clenching and unclenching he stamped upon the boards and panted and gasped like a drowning man. Cries of distress broke from the congregation and Samuel Leigh found himself leaning forward in his seat, hugging his knees, bowing his head, closing his eyes. Even William was taken aback – *there is murder in his heart* – and stood passively, disbelieving as his bible was torn from his hand.

Thomas Kendall was speaking, growling behind clenched teeth.

"You Will Not Deny Me. You will not take my place from me." His eyes flashed across the listeners, sitting still now, silent, incredulous, apart from Samuel Leigh whose hands were now clasped firmly over his ears.

"You wish to hear from the psalms? Then I shall read to you and it is an apt passage.

"'I was a reproach among all mine enemies, but especially among my neighbours, and a fear to mine acquaintance; they that did see me without fled from me.

"'I am forgotten as a dead man out of mind: I am like a broken vessel.

"'For I have heard the slander of many: fear was on every side: while they took counsel together against me, they devised to take away my life.'"

He was screaming now, fists beating upon the makeshift pulpit and then John King was on his feet, taking Hannah by the hand and leading her from the house. In the silence the others followed and now the priest was silent, too, watching the room empty until at last only he remained, he and the terrified Weslyan who sat in horror but could not bring himself to move.

All his passion left him then and he completed the service in a dull monotone, forgotten as a dead man out of mind.

"If their plan was to provoke me to madness, then they have succeeded."

Francis Hall sighed.

This is all too much for me. Unreason sits on unreason, sin and horror assail from all sides and now madness is shot through with the petty and the ludicrous.

And I am becoming numbed, drained of sympathy for all of them. I sit here as a man entrusted with God's message of salvation and I am starting to think there is none of them worth saving.

My own soul is in peril.

"Mr Kendall –"

"Call me Thomas."

I would rather not.

"Thomas, you cannot put the charges against you to one side and proceed as though they were not there."

"Nothing has been proved."

For God's sake!

"This is not a legal matter to be decided on the production of evidence and clever argument. We are talking of your soul, man. Can you place your hand upon this bible here and swear that there is no foundation to the charges brought against you?"

Thomas scratched behind an ear and his wig fell to the table. He let it lie there. "Who are they to judge me?" he muttered, then jumped as Francis slammed the bible down on the table before him.

"Will you swear?"

"Alright, alright. It's true. Satisfied?"

I see I am not entirely numbed, for I can feel my anger rising.

But he said quietly, levelly, "And what satisfaction do you imagine that I might find here?"

There was a pause, then Thomas nodded. "You are right to be offended," he murmured, "my anger gets the better of me."

For all the good it will do, I shall at least tell him the truth.

"Your anger is not the sin that is under discussion."

Thomas nodded again and Francis saw the touch of a rueful smile. "You are merciless, Francis. But you are right to be so. I -," he broke off and gestured towards the bottle on the table. "May I refill my glass? It seems I need some fortification."

"Allow me." Francis filled the glass and as Thomas drank he said, "You confess your sin to me; will you confess it to others? Have you confessed it to your wife?"

"She already knows."

"But not from you. Have you asked for her forgiveness?"

Thomas' mouth tightened.

"We have not discussed it." He waved a vague hand. "We have not been in the habit of discussing anything for some time now. That's a part of -," he shrugged and returned to his glass.

"I see. But do you repent of your sin?"

Say that you hate what you did.

Thomas pushed the chair back from the table and got to his feet and Francis watched in bemusement as he prowled the room before coming to a halt before the casement window. "The moon is very beautiful on the inlet," he mused, then almost immediately, "Have you ever wondered whether God might lead man to fall so that the scales are lifted from his eyes that might otherwise have remained there? Without awareness of darkness, how can there be awareness of light?"

You seek a means to persist with your sin.

"Thomas," Francis spoke firmly but he was speaking to his back, "you are speaking of that cursed antinomian spirit which says, 'let us sin that grace may abound'. You are seeking justification where there is none." And he said again, "Do you repent of your sin?"

Thomas turned and his eyes were hard. "Very well," he said, "you have withdrawn confession from me – and you were right to do so and I thank you for it. And I see that I must needs publish my confession further abroad." He gestured at the table where an unfinished letter lay. "I see you are writing of developments here, perfectly correct, it is your duty, may I," and he snatched up a blank sheet, "may I add my own contribution? Have you a pen? Thank you." Francis watched without a word as Thomas drove the quill into the inkstand and wrote furiously. Then he took up his wig and jammed it on his head. "Thank you for your time, your hospitality and your wise counsel. I will impose on you no further. Good night."

Francis stared at the open door then crossed the room to shut it. He returned to the table and carefully blotted the note. The message was scrawled between blotches where the nib had dug into the page. It read: 'Neither my Family nor Visitors nor any other person ever saw anything of an Improper Nature between me and my servant, Tungaroa. Nevertheless I feel it my duty to confess my sin.' The message was unsigned.

Francis Hall is a good man but he is young and simplifies that which is beyond him. There are subtle and mysterious forces at work here.
I need to talk to someone who can understand me.
Rakau. I have barely seen him since my return and that only at a distance.
There was a hesitation in his step as he turned towards the Rangihoua pa and disquiet gnawed at him. But, as he acknowledged sadly to himself, there was no one else and nowhere else to go.

As he climbed the slopes, his sense of isolation grew. While most of the people he passed bore him no ill-will for the matter was closed now, he was still an unfortunate man who had offended Towhi and they looked away from his greeting. Unlike the pakeha community there was a variance of opinion in the Maori one. Waikato, for example, was displeased by the turn of events and while he had stood up for Thomas with Rewa and Wharepoaka he remained unimpressed. Hongi on the other hand applauded Thomas' move towards polygamy. Indeed, he was sufficiently pleased that when Thomas in an early excess of doubt had pleaded to flee to the Hokianga away from temptation, he had forestalled him, blocking requests for bearers and guides.

For all that the Englishman in him recoiled from the idea of seeking support and understanding from the father of the ruined maid, Thomas knew that Rakau would see it altogether differently.

I need to talk to someone who can understand me.

He crept into the old tohunga's whare to find him lying on a pallet beneath a pile of blankets. He looked up with a smile and waved a hand in greeting and Thomas thought, he has become old, when did that happen?

Rakau read the alarm in his eyes and answered the question. "I have been old for a long time now, e Keni, but it seems that only now is my body beginning to notice."

Thomas kneeled by the pallet and took the old man into his arms.

"You are going to leave me," he said.

"Ae," answered Rakau, "but not for a little time yet. There is still time for korero."

"Ah," said Thomas, "how can I speak about my own small troubles with you like this?" He gestured helplessly, meaninglessly.

Rakau waved his words away. "What trouble do you see here?" he asked. "Does Tangaroa lament when the tide goes out? Now, make yourself comfortable and tell me about your troubles."

Of course Rakau knew all about the affair, he had known from the beginning, but he was deeply curious about what Thomas would make of it. For all the time he had spent with the missionaries, their beliefs continued to baffle him. He did not dismiss their faith as Hongi did – a religion fit for slaves, he said – but he struggled to make sense of it. It was not just that the stories themselves were bizarre but the meanings the pakeha managed to extrapolate from them and the relevance they brought to their lives had Rakau scratching his head. He understood very well that Keni had offended his god and that his people were angry with him for doing so. But he could not understand how their shouting at one another or refusing to talk was likely to have any correcting effect upon the situation. And what this Abraham that Keni was talking about now had to do with any of it was quite beyond him. He remembered the name – Hongi had told him of the sermons on the trip to England – and he shared his son-in-law's view of the man: a terrible fellow who had banished one son and been prepared to slaughter the other. Nor was he much taken by the rangatira David who had sent a loyal servant to certain death, avoiding battle himself, so that he could steal the servant's wife. Yet both of these men had been favourites of Keni' god and their stories seemed to comfort him.

He realised with a slight start that he had stopped listening. What was Keni saying, Bathsheeba, what an odd name, bathing in the moonlight, Tungaroa swimming in the moonlight, is there a connection, a significance here? The words were meaningless but he heard the fear, the need and the desperation in the missionary's voice.

"E Keni," he asked, "have you enjoyed your time with Tungaroa?"

Thomas stared at him.

Say that you hate what you did.

"Was it a good time?"

"How could it be a good time? It was sin."

"Did you enjoy your sin?"

Thomas nodded. "Yes," he whispered.

There, you have said it.

"And will you sin again?"

Thomas wrung his hands and stared at his knees.

Rakau chuckled. "That means you will but you won't say so. I have heard people say, in situations like this, 'I'll see what happens'. That means they will, but they won't own their will. And then they can say later, 'but I didn't mean for it to happen, I didn't mean to hurt anyone'." He shook his head, "fuzzy thinking. Cowardly thinking."

"So now I am a coward as well as a sinner."

"It seems so."

"What am I to do?"

"What are you going to do?"

Thomas shuddered slightly and looked away. Then he turned his head back and stared directly at Rakau. The old man smiled.

"What are you going to do?"

"I am going," Thomas spoke slowly, breathing between the phrases, "to continue to lie with Tungaroa ... until something happens ... or it becomes so awful ... that I can't stand it anymore ... And then I will flee."

"And so you have your answer."

Two days later Thomas packed two boxes of belongings and loaded them on to an ass he had purchased from the *Active*. Then he fled with Tungaroa to Hauraki's pa at Kaihiki.

CHAPTER 44

Ko Edward toku matua
Ko Susannah toku whaea
Ko Jane taku wahine
Ko Tungaroa taku wahine
Ko Susanna, Ko Elizabeth, Ko Thomas ...

He stood upon the paepae and told them who he was; I am a man with two wives, he said and the congregation nodded its acceptance.

Then they sang together and broke bread and they talked long into the night. And for once he felt no need to tell anyone anything; he leaned against a post that supported the living house and it absorbed him. He listened to the tales of the ancestors who were still here, joining their time to this. There was a warmth against his outstretched right leg and he saw that it had been crossed by the leg of the burly warrior sitting next to him and he was comfortable with it. Tungaroa leaned against him, her head upon his shoulder, her hand upon his thigh and he thought, I could stay like this forever.

The air was warm and heavy and sleep folded like a comforting blanket. Voices faded to the sound of sleep but he tried to hold himself awake, staying with the dying embers and the last of shadow before sinking, sighing into surrender.

Again he was floating, drifting in his vessel of flesh and bone glowing pale against the dark waters. He could feel no breath upon him, yet the sail was filling and he glided over the still, black depths towards a distant star.

Back in the beginning, sliding through silent mangrove, no sound of wind on sail or wood through water, only the occasional plop of dropping seed.

Then he heard the sound of a lifting wind, yet could feel nothing but there it was, rustling the leaves of bush on a bank he could not see. Now there was another sound, faint and distant and he strained to make it out. It seemed to come from below him and he stretched his arm over the side and dipped his hand into the sea. It was clearer then, flowing up through him and he heard it grow within a warm dark bass like breakers, like an organ, a murmuring of pipes of bone between and above it all the pure crystal of a woman's voice. This time there was no one to whisper caution and no restraining vines and he lowered himself into the welcoming sea.

It embraced him, drawing him down and he went willingly, falling, then turning, rolling, surging forward and he was flying, swooping, soaring, dropping a shoulder and kicking, spinning down, floating up on a liquid thermal.

Perhaps the star had sunk into the depths because now he could see a glow ahead; he flowed towards it and he knew it, that opening. It lay between two smooth and rounded boulders set behind a curtain of kelp and sea-moss and the light shone red from within. He stood before it and the mud was like flesh beneath his feet. As he parted the curtain the light became brighter and in careful, sinuous undulation he flowed within. It was as well he came in carefully for now he could see that within the lips there were lines of spikes like dragon's teeth. He held his space between them and as he passed the last rows the thought came to him, I am moving past, beyond death.

Now the tunnel narrowed and the sides were as flesh pressing against him, holding him, then moving him forward in gentle contractions. All the while the light was becoming brighter but it did not dazzle him.

Then the walls fell away and he was swimming into a clear translucent pool where the water was like air and kelp hung still as though painted and small fish floated in space. He drifted up until his head broke the surface and he chose to breathe again, a sweet, green, salty breath. Before him the great waterfall where Rakau had baptised him crashed silently into the depths. He turned and swam towards the stony embankment where Tungaroa was waiting for him.

He stood up in the shallows and he was as naked as she; his limbs were straight and strong and as he pushed his hair back from his eyes he realised that it had grown again, thick and lustrous against his hand.

He stepped up on to the rocks and there in the light, away from all shadow he took Tungaroa in his arms and laid her down on rocks that were as soft as the flax matting of a whare.

And dissolved.

He woke slowly, gradually absorbing where he was and registering that there was nothing to do about it but to be there. So he stretched, luxuriating in the reaching out of muscle and sinew, then letting it go, sighing in the release of tension, surrendering to the wash of drowsiness, smiling as he drifted back to sleep.

And when he did rise, it was only because he needed to empty his bladder. He noted that he was among the last to leave the whare and that was good: there was no one to summons him and nothing to be summonsed for.

He made his way across the marae, warmed by the smiles, the well-wishing, kia ora e Keni, delighting in the acceptance, the recognition.

This is what home must feel like.

This is what turnagawaewae means.

He passed down through the palisades – he would not use the pole – and crossed the fields to the inlet. Then he climbed around the rocks until there was no one in sight and relieved himself against the stony cliff face. After the climb his need had become great and he sighed in his release.

He sat for a while, rejoicing in the day. The autumn was still more summer than winter and Ra spread his rays from a clear, crystal sky. The sea glittered, still, sighing small waves against the rocks and on to the sand. In the fields about the pa and the villages and whare that lay scattered along the coastline and into the bush. Rongo had provided bountiful crops and the tangata whenua would eat well this winter.

It was good to be alive.

It was all very simple.

Climbing back up to the pa he was again enveloped in recognition and he smiled and waved back, just like a rangatira.

For two weeks he lived outside time, outside thought. As long as Tungaroa was with him, there was no other consideration; he may not have been where he was supposed to be, he was only where he was. The enchantment was strong upon him, pervasive and it touched Tungaroa, too.

What else do you teach someone when you teach them a language?

Thomas had opened a world for Tungaroa, a world of ants and grasshoppers and prowling tigers from India and a god who was hung on a cross. He had made her special, the child who could understand pakeha, who could read their books, who stood thoughtfully by as their captains and priests conversed while her elders looked on uncomprehending. He did not teach her how to think – her father did that - but he gave her material for thought.

And he gave her approval that set her aside from the other children. He made her different.

Within the Kendall household she also discovered a new world of feeling as she lived with doubt and contradiction and discontent. Her people knew nothing of these things – they knew with utter certainty the laws of gods and men and there was no distinction between the two. Tapu and noa pervaded all aspects of their lives and once they understood there was no need of further understanding. Actions were not subject to argument; they were one thing or the other.

So Tungaroa watched the missionaries preach one thing and practise another. She knew Matene was their rangatira and she could no more understand how Thomas and the others could rail against him than Hongi could make sense of the English king and his unmanageable, treacherous wife.

She watched whaea Heine become alienated from her bretheren and could not understand how she survived it.

There was so much that was hidden, smiles that were unkind, silences that spoke volumes.

But for all the doubt and contradiction and discontent, there was also much of interest. Books were a wonderful thing and although there was little in the Kendall library for children, she devoured what there was. Thomas would watch her lost in children's bible stories and smile, believing that they were bringing her closer to Christ. He was wrong, of course. Their appeal did not lie in their messages of hope and redemption; it lay in magical stories where a man raised his brother's rod and the sea parted, where another man calmed lions in their den, where people walked in stone castles and a tower grew up into the clouds. And there were other stories where frogs could speak and a princess pricked her finger upon a spindle and slept for a hundred years. Some of the books carried illustrations and where other children might trace patterns for moko, she sat and drew lions and camels and princesses in flowing gowns with jewels about their throats.

With Thomas and Jane and Rakau in her life, questions were answered and encouraged. She was invited into thought and opinion and moved further away from Maori where conversation was direct and rooted in the events of the moment, where there was much to be learned and accepted but little to be questioned or considered. Gradually their korero began to seem obvious and repetitive and finally boring because she was learning a new kind of stimulation.

And as she was seen to be becoming different to that most conservative of all society – the world of adolescence – so began her own alienation.

It was nothing like the alienation she had observed in Jane. She never for a moment had reason to doubt that she belonged; her people were there whenever she needed them. The problem was that she found herself wanting them less.

So as the years went by, she became a permanent resident in the missionary settlement.

None of this was planned; it just happened in the same way that most people's lives just happen, as a conspiracy of circumstance and inattention.

So she became an amalgam of things: a heathen child, daughter of a priest, daughter of a friend, star student, an inspiration, sometimes his only hope, servant, nanny to his children. He did not see her becoming a woman in the same way he did not see his daughters becoming women. And if he noticed on his return from England, he kept the knowledge buried.

And when he saw her emerging from the tide in the moonlight, she became something else altogether.

The enchantment was strong upon him and it touched Tungaroa, too. She had lain with a boy or two before but found it a rough and ready process, a casual and uncomfortable event that she was not inclined to repeat. Her own ministrations were more agreeable.

Thomas swamped her with his need and adoration; and he brought her a pleasure she had not known before.

And the explosion and the crying out were not such a far cry from warfare. For one who attached so much significance to sexuality – to the extent that he could barely discuss the subject – Thomas had little understanding of the nature of the act. He had recoiled from James Worthing's flippant remark about Queen Caroline's being fond of fucking, not just from revulsion at the word itself, but also from the idea that a woman might pursue the act for the pleasure of it. For his own part, it had always been a matter of release, justified by the production of issue. It was an adjunct to marriage and if not a furtive deed, at least one to be performed under cover, in darkness. He had never seen Jane fully naked.

But in New Zealand he had entered a society where overt sexuality embraced life, was the source of life, was a joy, a matter for celebration. And for all that he averted his eyes and covered his ears, it entered him. As he studied their creation stories, their customs, their art, it entered him, reaching past the shame and the lessons of his life to the core of him.

When he had lain with Tungaroa in the sands of Rangihoua and had watched her face contort in the moonlight and heard her moan, he had come by an entirely new kind of knowledge that for a time would bury everything else. He sought that vision, that knowledge again and again. He learned foreplay, to lie back, containing himself as she wriggled herself into the angles and friction that would carry her away, he learned to time his own explosion to hers.

With my body I thee worship.

For two weeks he lived outside time, outside thought and judgment.

Then inevitably thought returned and it was bleak and unforgiving. Who knows what brought it back?

Perhaps it was because the summer had gone out of autumn and winter had intruded. Gone was the idyll of the clear, golden days when he and Tungaroa were free to climb around rocks and stroll along beaches or take out a waka to drop their lines over a friendly reef. Gone was a blanket and a picnic lunch, love in a secluded cove or glen. The sky turned grey and the winds drove a cold rain across the shores and through the bush and confined them to the pa.

Perhaps it was because the continual proximity of others prevented him from enjoying Tungaroa as he would have wished.

Perhaps Tungaroa had begun her menstrual cycle and was not available anyway.

Perhaps it was the growing physical discomfort, the same unwashed clothes, the same smokey whare, finally being compelled to use the pole, clinging wet and shivering over a two hundred foot drop, evacuating his bowels where anyone might see.

Perhaps it was fleas. Or a toothache.

Perhaps it was mental discomfort, missing the quiet of his desk, being caught in tedious, repetitive korero, the continuous noise, the crying of an infant and remembering the child who would be born soon.

Perhaps he had not thought to pack wine in his hurried flight and now his body as well as his mind cried out for its gentle, soporific blessing.

Perhaps all these things brought a remembrance of his home at Rangihoua, of Jane and his children and he fell into the space he had occupied for years now and would occupy for years to come, resenting her when they were together, missing her when they were apart.

Perhaps in what he took to be his returning sanity he found that God had left his life. Or perhaps in some form God returned and taxed him with his sin and asked after his usefulness.

Eli, Eli, lama sabachthani?

But I have not forsaken you, Thomas. You have forsaken Me.

And again he was a worthless, useless creature. He could not bring himself to return to Rangihoua, to the sneers and judgment of the settlers and he could not stay where he was. So he loaded up his ass, bade farewell, mumbled apologies and in the cold and driving rain he fled to Whangaroa. While she was sad to see him go, Tungaroa was also relieved. There had been little joy in the last few days and she was pleased to return to the warmth and comfort of her home at Rangihoua, to Jane and to her father.

CHAPTER 45

Paramatta June 1822

The world without cried power and glory: howling winds that carried torrential rain, hurling it against the house, shattering on the rattling windows: a black sky lit in regular flashes of light that forked into the earth or lit the heavens to the horizons: then a shuddering thunder, the rolling drums of gods and titans.

The thunder boomed *I am*, the heavens lighted death and immortality and the magnificence was such that any man of any sensibility should have been driven to prayer or laughter.

But the rage of the world within cried only spite and meanness.

Samuel Marsden re-read the endorsement that told him why the man was here: *we consider it of the Ultimate Importance that you should have the most Complete Understanding of the Situation* – his lip curled at the implication that his present understanding might be something else – *we judge that this will only be achieved through Dialogue*. He looked with undisguised distaste at the man with whom he would be engaged in dialogue to complete his understanding and his distaste was strengthened by the enjoyment the man brought to his part.

It has been observed often enough that listeners find more meaning in the tone of voice that carries the words than in the words themselves. And one of the most powerful tones is that of complaint and accusation. So as William Hall declared the settlements' charges against the Rangihoua priest the tone dominated the meaning and Samuel began to feel under attack.

And so he was to a certain extent.

"If you had the faintest idea," William was saying, "of the real character and conduct of Mr Kendall since he came to New Zealand you would no more have ordained him than you would have ordained his shoe black."

Mr Kendall's character and conduct was put to one side as the chaplain dealt with the more immediate issue.

"Allow me to complete *your* understanding, Mr Hall," he returned. "Mr Kendall was ordained in England, not Australia and you seem to have me confused with the Bishop of Ely. To simplify the matter for you *(you simpleton)*, it was not I who ordained Mr Kendall and I am surprised to hear you say so."

"You have the right," answered William. "Obviously I have overestimated your influence with the Society. I would not have thought that they would have proceeded without your approval."

Well they damn well did.

It was a bitter rebuke that Samuel could not answer.

"To continue," William was enjoying the edge of his triumph, "besides the matter of trading muskets with which you are well acquainted, his wife's adultery and the bastard child that was its fruit –"

"Bastard child? You are the first to say so. What evidence do you have?"

"The evidence of my eyes, sir. The child is quite unlike the others."

"Ah," there was a riposte here for Samuel. "You have intimate acquaintance with the child and the others to make such a judgment?"

"I have seen them about the settlement."

"As have many others and perhaps more closely. Yet you are the only one to say so. The weight of evidence is against you, sir."

William glowered.

The list went on. Samuel had long been concerned by reports of incapacitation through alcohol and laudanum, but to hear William's report he might have gathered that Kendall was in a state of continuous inebriation.

"And it feeds his predilection for violence, sir. He has attempted to stir up the natives against us and it is only through their refusal to be drawn into our quarrels that our lives are not in peril.

"But a week before I left for Australia, on one of his brief visits to Rangihoua – he is hardly ever there, preferring the company of the natives – he reproached me for declining to assist him in building a church at Kaihiki; and when I explained that I would neither assist nor associate ith one so steeped in sin he flew into such a violent rage as to place him beyond all reason. I retreated to my house in fear of my life but he tore the door from its hinges and came at me with a chisel. It took myself and two natives to restrain and disarm him. Had things turned out otherwise, sir," and he pointed an accusing finger, "your priest might well be standing before you arraigned for murder."

The tone, the finger and 'your priest' dissolved any personal sympathy Samuel might have felt but he could not deny that matters were in a grievous state.

But all of Kendall's sins paled beside his latest transgression. It was not news, for Kendall's departure for Kaihiki with his strumpet had signalled a spate of letters to him and, he assumed, to the CMS.

With all the civility he could muster he nodded his appreciation. "I will take heed," he said, "of the information you have brought me. I will advise the Society, but it will take some time before they receive my letter and more time while they make their decision and more time again before that decision reaches me."

William clicked his tongue. "So," he said, "I suppose we can expect matters to continue as they are."

Samuel's level of civility shrank a little further but he answered as evenly as he could. "No, Mr Hall. You may also assure the settlements that I will take immediate action regarding Mr Kendall. I will write to him – do you know where he is staying at present?"

"He left Rangihoua on the eleventh of May - two days after he had returned from Whangaroa – and sailed upon the *Providence* to the Hokianga where I believe he is assisting the captain with his trading. Doubtlessly he will be arming the local natives."

"Doubtlessly. I shall write to Mr Kendall advising him that he is suspended from all further duties pending the decision of the Committee." William advised Samuel of his satisfaction with the outcome and Samuel wondered why he would consider his satisfaction of interest to anyone besides himself.

Then Samuel advised William that he would retire upon the instant to begin the letter and wished him good night and a safe journey back to his lodgings. And William wondered by what stretch of the imagination anyone could consider this night to be a good one.

Then the two brothers in Christ shook hands and each went about his own particular duty.

Samuel's mood lightened as he heard the door close but as he settled at his desk his anger returned and he ground his teeth as he wrote: *I would ask you – What can you want a Church for? Can a Minister living in Fornication want a Church? What do you intend to teach? Who will come to hear you Preach? Is not your Crime a Public Disgrace to the sacred Ministry to which you have been set apart?* Rolling thunder seemed to underline the questions and he pushed the paper irritably away, rising to cross the room and open the curtains. The storm had taken them by surprise and the shutters were not closed; suddenly the farm, the mountains beyond, the sky, everything was exposed in shuddering light.

I would not be out on such a night, he thought, then remembered Hall. But at least he would be warm and dry within the carriage; it was the coachman who would be bearing the brunt of the elements.

It is always the little people who suffer.

He clapped his hands in a burst of exasperation and then again as Richard Stockwell flashed into his mind and his exasperation redoubled and became something else.

He counted off mental points.

Kendall is a mature, educated man; Stockwell is a simple, illiterate boy. Kendall is an ordained priest and a married man; Stockwell is a single convict. Kendall has taken a Maori girl half his age; Stockwell was – probably – seduced by an older Englishwoman. Kendall is defiant in his sin; Stockwell is abject in his repentance. Kendall will probably be dismissed from his post but his life will continue and it may well be a more profitable one; Stockwell sleeps in a stone cell and breaks rocks in rain and the mid-day sun.

Had anyone else pointed out his part in this injustice, he would have flared up in denial and justification. But he could not answer himself that way and his exasperation became disquiet and then something like shame.

He returned to his desk and took up a fresh sheet. Swiftly he wrote, *Sir, would you kindly advise whether the Sentence of the convict Richard Stockwell has yet Expired? If so, would you advise whether you have any Information regarding his present Whereabouts?* He folded the letter, then slipped it into an evelope, addressing it to the Superintendant of Prisons.

He took up the letter to Kendall and his anger was more intense than ever; his pen scored into the page as he wrote: *I know not what to say to you. The deed is done; you have ruin'd yourself in this Life, and lost your honourable and sacred Rank in Society, which you never can regain to the Day of Death.*

CHAPTER 46

Rangihoua July 1822

I wonder if opium is like this.

To inhabit a space which cannot be real yet for the moment is all that there is; and which suggests that the reality which preceded it was only a possibility and a wizened, shrunken one at that.

It was not as though the laws of time or space or physics had been altered or suspended – there were no dragons flying past the window and the table was as inanimate as it had ever been. In fact the scene was quite familiar, utterly ordinary but it said impossible.

The wood range warmed the room and he leaned back in his chair, a cushion against his back, stockinged feet crossed upon an old ottoman, a glass of wine in his hand. His sense of comfort was intensified by the cold, grey winter's day on the other side of the window.

He sat with two of the people he liked most in this world and that was impossible too, for one was a pale, drawn Englishwoman, aged beyond her years and the other was a vibrant, Maori girl who was the mistress of the Englishwoman's husband. They sat together at their ease and the aroha that permeated the room was quite tangible. And that was the most impossible thing of all.

Francis had seen more than he would have believed possible of others and of himself. He had watched a slaughter of the innocents and within twenty four hours he had embraced Herod. He had heard stories that had horrified and disgusted him and within the horror and the disgust had found something heroic. He had found kindness and wisdom in savages and much to be ashamed of in his bretheren.

But for all the absurdity and contradiction he had never lost his sense of proportion. Even when hope had faded, he had known it would return; as he had seen temptation and known that he was tempted, he had also known that he would rise above it. Through it all he had known there was a plan and a purpose and if he could not always see the means he had never doubted the ends. There was a sense and a logic to his faith that kept him strong.

But in this warm and peaceful room, he sensed the beginning of an unravelling. A random thought, *there is a goddess here.* He shook his head and drained his glass.

There came a peeping cry from the next room; Jane made to rise but Tungaroa forestalled her. "I'll get him," she said and Jane nodded her thanks.

Francis watched the sway of her hips as she left the room and for once he did not look away.

If I find beauty there, where is the sin in it?

I am unravelling indeed.

Tungaroa returned with a small bundle. "He is hungry," she said and passed the child to Jane.

And now a dragon flying past the window might have been easier to deal with as Jane unbuttoned her smock and laid the child to her breast. It was done carefully, discreetly, nothing was visible but still ... Tungaroa saw the look of consternation on his face and laughed. "She is feeding her child," she said. "Would you have him go hungry? It is a lovely thing."

And Francis thought, yes, I suppose it is.

Where did my consternation go? Where is my outrage?

He sat and watched the child feed and was touched by the tenderness of the occasion; Jane glows, he thought, she is serene, there is a very old peace here. Then Tungaroa cleaned and dried the little boy and he smiled without knowing.

Smiling without knowing, speaking without thinking, he asked Tungaroa, "How do you come to be here?"

She settled the baby into a makeshift crib as she answered, "I serve here."

"Yes, I see that, but ..." he hesitated.

Jane interceded for him. "What Mr Hall means," she said, "is why are you not with Mr Kendall?"

"Ah," Tungaroa nodded. "Keni is in the Hokianga now. He went there from Whangaroa."

"Whangaroa?"

"He left me at Kaihiki to go to Whangaroa. He said he was a sinner and he needed to be alone to pray for guidance and forgiveness. So I came back here."

"And it was as well you did, dear," Jane smiled affectionately. "With the new baby I needed all the help I could get."

"Ae," Tungaroa nodded again. "I was very pleased to be able to come back to help with the mokopuna and to be closer to my father." She broke off at a burst of congested coughing from the boys' room. "Is the mixture in his room?"

"It is by the bed."

He watched the sway of her hips without knowing as she left the room.

"She has been a godsend," said Jane. "I do not think I could have managed without her."

"Your own daughters are not available?"

"The girls are in Kerikeri. Susannah will be leaving shortly for Port Jackson where the Reverend Marsden has found her a place. She will be happier there."

Francis stared, wondering and gestured vaguely towards Samuel's room. "How can this be?"

"Do you mean, how can I share a space with a girl who has lain with my husband and may do so again? How can I not hate her?"

"Yes," said Francis, "that is what I mean."

Jane closed her eyes while considering her answer. "It is difficult to explain," she murmured at last. "I don't even know that I know."

"Please try," Francis was earnest, "it is very important to me."

"Yes," Jane nodded, "I can see that. Let me see," she paused again.

"Take your time."

"Very well. You see … I am a simple woman, not educated in the mysteries as you and my husband and Mr Marsden and all the men are educated. I have always been taught what to think and thought it my duty to think so. It has been mostly easy. It does not require much thought to be a dutiful daughter and wife and mother."

"If I may say so," said Francis, "that strikes me as a thoughtful position."

"Well yes. When I say I am simple, I don't mean that I am stupid or incapable of an opinion."

"Please," Francis was embarrassed, "I didn't mean to imply –"

"Of course," she waved the protestation away. "Now, where was I?"

"Being taught what to think."

"Yes, thank you. When I fell into sin, my only thought was that everyone thought, or rather knew that I was a sinner. And certainly I thought so, too. I still do. But I had no thought as to what I could do about it. There could be no muru raid, no reparation to right the situation, and so I was a sinful woman beyond all forgiveness."

Francis recalled the remarks of Marsden and Hall, all of them, and nodded his understanding. "We come to preach forgiveness," he said, "but there was none for you."

"I might have stayed like that forever. But when Tho-, Mr Kendall fell into sin, it all changed."

She had waited for the surge of anger towards Thomas, the hypocrite and Tungaroa, the slut, but it had stayed away. But the calmness remained and the door to new thought had remained open. She had struggled with the idea – which still seemed absurd – that there was nothing personal in the affair. Thomas, she knew, with all his impulsiveness would not have given her a thought and she believed that Tungaroa had behaved without malevolence, but rather kindness in the same way Richard had.

But these were only thoughts and they did not account for it.

She knew from everything she had ever heard and been taught – and certainly from her own experience – that Fornication was a terrible sin, an offence to God and man alike. To not condemn it was almost an offence in itself; to hate it, and those who practised it was a sign of virtue. But at bottom she simply did not hate Thomas and Tungaroa for what they had done and, worse, she did not really care that much.

She did not know why she did not hate it. In the early days she had wondered whether this was further evidence of her own sinfulness or perhaps she was just numbed to vice.

Certainly she was upset and the thought of it brought a kind of shudder; but even that eased.

"Do you think," asked Francis, "that because you … understood the situation, um, more thoroughly you forgave them?"

Jane smiled. "See how much cleverer you are," she said. "It took weeks of thinking before I had that idea. But then I became confused again because the more I thought about it, the more I started to see that I didn't even know what forgiveness means."

Francis shook his head. "I cannot understand that," he said. "You, a Christian woman, the wife of a missionary, you don't know what forgiveness means?"

"So," Jane cocked her head quizzically, "what does it mean?"

"Well, obviously, it means the putting away of resentment at another's sin."

"And how do you put it away? And what is the difference between forgiveness and just not caring?"

"You put it away by …" Francis flapped his hands in circles, "by …"

"How do you put away your resentment towards Hongi? How does Mr Kendall put away his resentment towards me?"

And all of the Christian settlement.

"You … pray," said Francis feebly.

"And then one day you notice your resentment has gone away and you tell yourself you have forgiven the sinner. But how do you know that with the passage of time it hasn't just stopped mattering? You might have even forgotten."

"You sound like Rakau," said Francis thoughtlessly, then, "please, I'm sorry, I didn't mean …"

"That's alright; I take it as a compliment. Anyway, it seems to me that if you can't discover the reason for a feeling or a change of feeling, you can't really give it a moral dimension."

Francis was astounded. "You are a philosopher," he said.

"Not really," said Jane. "All I did was discover that I was not angry and I didn't know why. And another thing," she pointed at Francis, "I suppose I was angry with Mr Kendall for a while, but it wasn't long. And I was never angry with Tungaroa. So forgiveness had nothing to do with it."

Francis shook his head again. "I am at a loss," he said.

"So was I. So I thought I would take counsel with the wisest person I knew. I talked with Rakau."

With two settlements of Christian missionaries available, two priests, one of them your husband, you took yourself to an illiterate cannibal. And the awful truth is that it was a wise decision.

There would be some difficulty with communication, but with the Maori she had inevitably learned, the English Rakau had picked up and a measure of mime they would manage.

She had walked with the old man from his whare, slowly, her arm around his waist, supporting the little there was of him. Past the small whare, enclosures, storehouses, the whare nui, a rough manuka picket fence before the open area of the marae and there, impaled upon the pointed stakes a row of trophies from the southern wars. Long experience had tempered her revulsion and now Jane only sighed and shook her head in sorrow. "Their families," she said, "the children."

They sat upon the knoll where James Butler had once taken his ease before fleeing from the careless girl and looked out across the glittering bay and the shining islands.

"E pehea ana koe, how are you?" asked Rakau.

"Pai ana, I am well," she answered, then nodded and repeated more to herself than to her friend, "I am well. I feel more at peace with myself than I have since ... E Rakau," she leaned across and patted an emaciated thigh, "I think I am happy."

"And that surprises you?"

"Yes, I had thought I didn't deserve to be happy. But," she pulled a face, "I feel happy anyway. But I don't know why."

"Does it matter?"

"I suppose it must do or I wouldn't be thinking about it."

"Ah, you pakeha," Rakau smiled. "When you're not happy, you wish you were and when you are you think you don't deserve to be or you worry that it might go away."

"So humour a foolish pakeha. Why am I feeling happy now – when everything would suggest that I ought to be feeling utterly miserable?"

"I think," said Rakau, "that perhaps utu has been taken upon you. I think you have been plundered."

"By whom?"

The old man's eyes were alight with interest and curiosity as he probed the problem. "Yourself to begin with," he mused. "You have been plundering yourself for years now but that only made you weaker. Then Keni took utu upon you, he did unto you what you had done unto him. And that redressed the balance."

"Go on."

"For all my time with Keni," said Rakau, "I still don't understand this notion of forgiveness. And considering the way he and all his bretheren have behaved towards you and each other I don't think they understand it either. The blood debt of your Jesus makes a little more sense, but as for the rest of it," he shrugged. "But I do understand the payment of debt and the restoration of balance. So when Keni lay with Tungaoa, he settled your debt for lying with Richard."

"Two wrongs don't make a right."

"Why not?"

"I don't know. They just don't."

Rakau tutted. "Now you're sounding like all the others and you've stopped thinking again."

"Sorry," said Jane. "So you don't think this has to do with forgiveness?"

"If it has," answered Rakau, "it probably has more to do with your forgiving yourself."

And then she remembered walking in a park in London with Thomas and reproving him for his persistence in his guilt.

I believe that true repentance leads to forgiveness and a new beginning. It seems almost a kind of perverseness or pride to believe that one's sin is so great that even God cannot forgive it.

"Perhaps God has forgiven me."

"I wouldn't know."

"No," said Jane, "and neither would I."

And, thought Francis, neither do I.

"I think," he said, "that I may need to leave this place very soon."

Jane made to answer but looked up as Tungaroa came back into the room. "Samuel is sleeping now," she said, "and his breathing is steady."

Jane nodded. "Thank you." Then to Francis she said, You might be wise to do so. This country changes people. It changes our feelings and it takes away our understanding. And mostly we don't seem to know it."

"But you do."

"Well," she said, "I know that I don't know. And I don't know what will happen next. I am always being surprised. Rakau says that's a good thing. He says the question is often more interesting and 'I don't know' is often the best answer. Do you know," suddenly digressing, "that Mr Kendall travelled all the way from Hokianga to baptise his new son. He travelled continuously, I believe, he was a wreck when he got here. He baptised him, slept for twelve hours, then turned around and went straight back. He drove himself past all endurance to be there for his son. Perhaps when he got back to Whiria he forgot all about it. And I doubt that he gave a thought to Lawrence's birth. Yet he is a loving father. Things do not make sense the way that we were taught."

"It worries me to hear you talk like this. Perhaps you may need to leave, too."

"I don't have that choice. Although," she paused at the disloyalty, "if Mr Kendall continues as he is, the choice may be removed from us."

"Perhaps that would be the best thing."

"I wouldn't know."

As they spoke Tungaroa had been busying herself in the kitchen. Now she came back into the living area with a lighted taper. She bent over the small table that sat between them and her unbound breasts fell soft and heavy against her shift. The room lit in a yellow, flickering glow and Francis registered with some surprise that much of the day had passed. And now the quiet of the afternoon passed too as the three boys trooped in from their room.

"You will dine with us."

"Thank you."

An hour later, replete and comfortable, he was sitting on a tattered sofa, a little boy on either knee in the midst of a meandering tale. In the domestic calm he had been initially charmed when the boys had asked him to tell them a story. Of course, he thought, I know a thousand stories. But as he had turned the pages of his storehouse – the Bible, Greek myths, the brothers Grimm, Shakespeare – he had become alarmed at the litany of oppression and suffering, sin, temptation and untimely death.

I cannot think of a single gentle tale for children.

"Then make one up," said Samuel.

And that was threatening, too.

"Very well," he said at last, "but if I get stuck, you will have to help me."

And away they went with the story of John and Samuel. And now, as they rode across the sea on the back of Maui, the talking dolphin, he found himself becoming as entranced as they were.

Then Maui delivered them safely home and Tungaroa took them off to bed and he leaned back in the cushioned chair with a glass of wine in his hand while Jane nursed the child. Outside the rain pattered on the tin roof.

He sat up with a start, catching himself away from sleep.

"I must be going," he said.

"Why?" Jane looked up, puzzled. "It is a wretched night, it wouldn't be safe to try to sail back to Kerikeri."

"No," Francis agreed. "I won't try that. There's no light and the wind's all wrong."

"Then where will you go?" Tungaroa had come back into the room and was looking at him curiously.

"To the pa, I suppose." He could not imagine imposing on any of the settlers for the night.

"It will be an unpleasant climb in the dark and the rain. And the gates may be closed."

"Then," said Francis more casually than he felt, "I'll just doss down in the schoolhouse. I've got my coat and I've slept in worse."

"Is this worse?" asked Tungaroa. "We've plenty of mats and blankets. You can have the sofa if you like and I'll take a mat. I'm quite used to them, you know."

"Of course Mr Hall knows," said Jane. "He has other considerations."

"Like what?" She looked almost accusingly at Francis. "What considerations?"

Francis discovered that he was squirming. "I wouldn't be, um comfortable with the arrangements."

"You wouldn't be comfortable?" Tungaroa was incredulous. "You'd be more comfortable on the bare boards of a freezing, leaking old shed?"

Francis looked to Jane for help but found only a wry smile.

"I can't explain," he said wretchedly.

"Can't or won't?"

"It's rather complicated."

"No, it's not. You are being offered manaakitia and you are refusing it. I think that's rude."

At last Jane came to his rescue.

"I think, Tungaroa," she said, "Mr Hall feels trapped by the appearance of things, not how they may appear to you or to me, but how they may appear to his fellows. I also think," and she cocked an eyebrow, "that he may really be at a loss to explain."

"I am."

Francis got to his feet. "Please don't be offended," he said. "I am truly grateful for the hospitality you have extended and I am also truly confused." He looked over at Jane. The baby had long ceased feeding and now lay placidly on her breast. "He is a beautiful child," he said, for want of anything else to say.

"Thank you." She looked down at the sleeping child, then said softly, "He will be our last."

"Yes," Francis nodded as though she had said the baby had blue eyes. "What is his name?"

Jane stroked the soft brown hair on the tiny head. "His name is Edward," she said.

CHAPTER 47

Hokianga, August 1822

Thomas sneezed copiously into a sodden kerchief – the aftermath of a tumble into the tide, from which he had been plucked by the crew of the ship's longboat. Later he would see his rescue as further evidence of God's hand and of his call to continuing service. But for the moment he felt more wretched than blessed and the letter lying on the rough table of the pokey cabin told why.

The deed is done: you have ruin'd yourself in this Life, and lost your honourable and sacred Rank in Society, which you never can regain to the Day of Death. May God be merciful unto you, and put away your sin, that you may not die! I shall mourn for you, as Samuel did for Saul.

He knew he had sinned, of course he knew. At the beginning of the month in a letter to Marsden he had owned his weakness and failure to resist the Maori demand for arms. *I was irresolute,* he wrote, *greatly in arrears.* But that offence paled into insignificance next to his most recent transgression. Fornicator, Marsden called him, and how could he deny it, a public disgrace, a ruined man. Judgment was made and sentence passed.

Suspended from all further duties until the will of the Church Missionary Society is known.

Through a grimy porthole he could make out shreds of cloud flying past a pallid moon, carried on the remorseless westerly, carrying the sand across the harbour, over the *Providence*, through the scattered whare that dotted the coastline. *Sand instead of ashes in my mouth.* And himself, shivering in his greatcoat in this cramped cage of a cabin, tossing, wallowing. Alone at the ends of the earth, at the ends of hope.

How could it have come to this?

Eli, Eli, lama sabachthani?

Within the despair and abandonment he could see betrayal, too: the settlements meeting secretly in his absence, keeping their judgments from him but clearly not from Marsden nor the CMS. Depriving him of his opportunity to speak for himself when there was none to speak for him.

He snatched up pen and paper and scrawled furiously.

To Mr Francis Hall, Dear Sir, I am writing to Enquire about your Failure, as Secretary, to Advise me of the Judgments passed against me. It is your Duty, Sir, to forward all Minutes …

Captain Herd's time at Opononi had come to an end, to the satisfaction of all concerned. The *Providence* was laden with the finest spars, which would fetch a tidy profit, and the people of Whiria had an excellent collection of the finest muskets kauri could buy. Even Thomas, in all his anger and despair, had his pockets nicely lined.

He returned to Rangihoua in September and the same tired old round picked up seamlessly from where it had left off.

In early October the settlements' committee met to discuss Thomas' behaviour and consider his letters, pleading for reinstatement. No decision was reached; hardly surprising seeing that they did not have the authority to make one. But battle lines were drawn. Francis Hall urged that Thomas remain, so long as he could find the resolution to stay away from the musket trade and the native women. James Kemp and, surprisingly, John Butler endorsed this view. But William Hall and John King were past all thought of further reprieve.

A month later they met again, this time to hear Thomas in person. His confession, repentance and excuses brought the same result and a week later he fled, despairing and alone to Kaihiki.

And the battle lines hardened.

John Butler took his stand where it had always been and withdrew his support for Francis Hall.

Rakau asserted his stand where it had always been and threatened John King. And John pleased and frightened himself by standing up to it.

Samuel Marsden received word of the CMS's final decision: Thomas Kendall was dismissed and Samuel was to oversee his removal from New Zealand.

"It is all too much for me. I've got to go."

Jane nodded. "I will be sorry to see you go," she said, "but I am pleased to hear it."

"You don't think that I am weak?"

"You are asking me for judgment?"

"Please."

"Probably all my life, particularly since I have been here I have listened to men talking about strength and weakness. And it's just like forgiveness – I really don't understand what they are talking about. They equate strength with persistence, but I wonder whether they're talking about obstinacy or perhaps it's a fear of letting go of what they know – however awful what they know may be."

"Yes. May I?" Francis filled their glasses.

Jane drank her wine and studied the young man. He had aged in his two years here. The sun had darkened and coarsened his skin but there were lines there that had another source. And there was a restlessness to him that was new, the tapping foot, the darting eye.

He was the last of the men who had been kind to her.

Everyone I know goes away in the end.

"Mrs Kendall?"

She started from her reverie.

"You were speaking of weakness."

"O yes. I was saying I don't know what it means."

"I think I am weak," said Francis. "I don't think I can withstand this life. I think it will overcome me. I cannot hold out the way you and all the others have."

"And what do you imagine it is that we are holding out for?"

"Conversion of the heathen."

"Yet in the best part of ten years not one has converted."

"But still you persevere. You do not despair."

Jane smiled and almost laughed. "But we are despairing all the time," she said. "All we have done is survive."

Still Francis would not be deterred. "I do not think I would manage even that."

"You think that you would die?"

Francis shook his head, puzzled. "Well, no," he said, "I suppose I would continue to live. But I might lose my soul."

Jane made no reply but raised her eyebrows in question and Francis nodded slowly and closed his eyes.

And there they were in all their piety, the meanness and spite, surviving. Then a random thought.

Why did you not forward the minutes to Kendall?

I forgot.

Really?

Jane watched the nod become a shaking of the head, heard the drumming of his fingers.

"You are accusing yourself of something," she said.

"I am," Francis stared at her. "How did you know?"

"I didn't," Jane answered, "I guessed. But Mr Kendall looks like that when he is accusing himself."

There is so much accusation and counter-accusation, blame and excuse.

Jane leaned across the table and patted the drumming fingers into stillness. "I don't know whether you are weak or strong," she said, "but I think you are wise to go."

And now there was nothing left to say and he took his leave. She rose with him and saw him to the door.

"Before you go," she said, "I would like to ask a favour."

"Please."

"You may not find it agreeable. I would like to know what has become of Richard Stockwell. I would like to believe that he is at peace." She paused. "I was told some years back that he was well; but it was a brief note and I never heard more. I wondered …, "she sighed and the thought trailed off. "Anyway, I would appreciate some confirmation."

Francis took her hand. "You have my word," he said, "the least that I can do."

Jane watched him begin down the path, the bowed head, young shoulders carrying the weight of the world. "Mr Hall," she said/

Francis stopped but did not turn.

"I shall miss you."

CHAPTER 48

Matauwhi March 1823

"It's your move, Thomas."

"What?" He looked up in brief shock.

"Sorry. Did I drag you away from somewhere more agreeable?"

"You did." Thomas studied the board. "Which is not to say that this is at all disagreeable."

"It could become so if you're not careful. You'd better give thought to your next move."

William Brind chuckled as he tapped out his pipe and reloaded it. To his mind, this was about as good as it got. Looking down from the porch of his comfortable little whare on to shining sands and glistening waters, bush and birdsong, a loaded pipe of the finest shag, a glass of rum, a winning position ... Who could ask for more?

His opponent, he thought, would be a good deal happier if he could take a similar view. Ah well, he shrugged mentally, that was not his concern. He had been pleased to be of assistance to Thomas on his latest flight, using his new vessel to transport the materials he had needed to build a makeshift house here. And it was good to have a neighbour over for a glass or five and a game of chess on such a glorious afternoon. But beyond that ...

Still he seemed to be in a much happier space today, intent upon the pieces and William reminded himself to take care. Thomas' game was invariably a reflection of his mood: when depressed he was hurried and careless, adding to his woes, but when cheerful he was a doughty opponent.

They sat in easy silence while Thomas considered his move. Then he looked up, grinned, "you nearly had me there," and moved his knight to block William's attack.

"Ah well," William sighed amiably and refilled their glasses. "What agreeable place did I take you from?" The question was more designed to fill the space and give him time to think.

Thomas smiled. "I baptised Mihi's mokopuna this morning," he said.

"Did you indeed?" William looked up, surprised. "That's a first, isn't it?"

"The first baptism ever," Thomas replied. "It was wonderful, William. To hold a little Maori baby, to administer the sacraments and see the first tiny steps towards a life with Christ."

"I can see why you're so pleased." William considered, then said, "you remember young Tapsell?"

"Of course." Phillip Tapsell was lieutenant on the *Asp,* a pious young man, Thomas thought, not a common attribute amongst whalers. "Why do you ask?"

"He has formed an attachment to Maria Ringa."

Thomas' mouth turned down. "He would not be the first."

"So I have told him. But he will not be deterred. He wants to marry the wench. Make an honest woman of her and all that."

"Has he asked her?"

"Yes. Evidently she agreed."

"Why?"

"God knows. Anyway, top up? there you go, why don't you marry 'em? It would make young Phil really happy; and it would be another first."

"I don't know." Thomas was dubious. "I would need to talk to them."

"Of course. I'll let young Phil know. He'll be delighted."

Thomas' moods swing more than they ever did. Last night he returned home to announce that he has decided to marry a young Danish sailor to a rather notorious Maori girl. More inroads, he told me, and fell asleep in his chair.

I can imagine how the news will be received at Kerikeri but in truth, dear Emmeline, I am past caring.

Jane laid down her pen and gazed out the window, or rather the frame where one day the window would be. It would need to be soon; autumn was drawing in and the succession of golden days would not last.

The house was a smaller version of the one at Rangihoua but without visitors or servants there was an impression of greater space. Although flung together at some speed, it was nonetheless sturdy and serviceable and when completed – whenever that might be – would be a comfortable home. But it was like most things that Thomas had undertaken: conceived on the moment and begun with enormous enthusiasm, only to be put to one side as a new passion arose. His boat, the *Bulrush* was another case in point, built over a couple of years in bursts of energy, then finished in a great rush. Like the house, like everything, it could have been so much better.

She sipped her wine and waited for the next thought. There was no hurry. She had been a faithful enough correspondent to her sister over the years but since her fall, her loss of self, her letters had become bland recountings of anecdotes – *I have nothing to complain of.* Since Thomas' fall she had begun to find her voice again and had learned that the best thoughts came with patience.

She thought of Thomas at more of a distance now, there was less clutter that way and with dispassion there was more room for kindness.

He has achieved far more than he knows. He understands Maori and is more accepted by them than any other man. He is always in demand as an interpreter, is well-liked by the captains and has accumulated a measure of wealth from trading. We could be entirely independent of the CMS if he chose.

He was a competent builder. When William Hall and Marsden had declined his requests for assistance in erecting a church at Kaihiki – *what can a minister living in fornication want a church for* – he had gone ahead and built one on his own.

It was no mean feat to build a trading vessel but he had done that, too. And learned how to sail her.

And one way or another he had produced and supported a large family.

But he cannot be content with that.

He must fight with Marsden and the CMS and the settlements, defy their edicts and flaunt his defiance.

And yearn for their approval.

Dispassion and patience had also taught her to avoid fruitless lines of thought. She dipped her pen and took a different direction.

Susannah is settled in Port Jackson and writes that she is happy there. Mr Marsden has evidently taken some trouble to place her in useful employment and she is comfortable in her station. But she misses her family, particularly her sister.

Thomas Surfleet is seldom here now; he is away taking employment where he can find it. He is presently serving on a trading vessel. He seems to share his father's capacity for discontent and I – She stopped and left the thought alone.

Elizabeth is lonely and, like her brother, somewhat resentful.

And who could blame her?

She may well have been living in Paradise but she was the only white girl there. She was fluent in te reo now and might have formed friendships among Maori girls of her age, but they were women now and their interests were not for her. And since the rumours of her sister's defloration at the hands of John Butler, unsubstantiated and probably more of another indication of the spite that pervaded the settlements, her separateness had become more assured. But now there was something for her.

For as her mother's blinding, crushing sense of sin had lifted and the doors to new thought had continued to open, she had recognised Elizabeth's loneliness. And she had laid grief and prayer aside and looked for something more useful.

The two began to talk more and Jane discovered in the child, the woman, wells of curiosity and a will to learn.

Together with a flax kete Tungaroa had made they had wandered along the beaches of Rangihoua and further afield, picking up shells, probing into crevices and pools for a crab's shield, carefully prising a starfish free. Elizabeth would take them home and sit for hours, moving them here then there on a polished board; then, tongue between lips she would glue them to their appointed place. The interest expanded when Francis Hall had brought her a book on natural science and she began a book of her own, tracing the creatures' outlines and setting out below in careful print their Latin names, habitat and life patterns.

At Matauwhi they began a garden together and Elizabeth started a book on plants.

She may not be happy but she is not despairing, neither.

She looked anew at Basil and Joseph, now eleven and thirteen and was alarmed by what she saw. Like all the missionaries, like all their children much of their time had been taken up in daily chores, maintaining the physical necessities of life but beyond that, particularly once the school had failed, they had been left to run free. As brown as the boys with whom they played, sturdy, as confident on a rock face as in the water or up a tree, all their interest was enveloped within the physical world of Maori. She watched them speaking to one another in te reo, practising with lengths of manuka and showing an unnerving mastery and she thought, I could lose them altogether.

So she took them in hand. Their lessons at school and particularly at home had come in bursts of intermittent enthusiasm and she worried at how little they had learned or, giving Thomas the benefit of the doubt, how much they had forgotten. And, she owned, she had made little contribution. She would make up for that now.

Every day I take the boys for lessons in reading and number. Basil and Joseph are reluctant pupils but are making satisfactory progress. (Heavens, I sound just like a schoolmistress.) By contrast, Samuel, who is still poorly and spends much of his time at home is showing all the signs of a scholar. Elizabeth is spending time with John and Lawrence. She has a great way with them and they are enjoying their lessons with her and are picking up the rudiments.

Life was much calmer now. Jane's sense of peace had remained with her and it transmitted to the children. So Thomas would return home from his day's labours, preaching or trading to find a convivial family unit gathered about the family hearth. Industriously, usefully employed. It brought back memories of Thoresby.

But for one thing.

Thomas had been quite correct when he told Francis Hall that he and Jane had not discussed his fall. As he had with Francis – indeed as he had done at various times with anyone who would care to listen, including his children – he had confessed and berated himself for a worthless creature. He had apologised for the grief his actions had occasioned and the shame it had brought upon his family. But true repentance and forgiveness had fallen upon the same old thorn.

Say that you hate what you did.

And an even more impossible promise.

Say that you will never do it again.

So any meaningful conversation was impossible and they lived around the edges of his sin. And the only intelligent way the family, particularly the children could manage was to pretend that it wasn't happening. With their father being away so often and their mother becoming accessible again, it was not as bad as it could have been and their lives attained a measure of peace and normality.

But it brought at least one permanent change.

Thomas had returned to Rangihoua to one rejection after another. There was no one in the settlement who would talk to him; his suspension meant that he was a man without standing and there was no friendship to call upon. Even Francis Hall with whom he had maintained a regular correspondence would not meet with him. 'I see no need of it,' he wrote, 'for as you did not take my advice at some time since, I have no reason to think that you will take it this time.'

He had no church to preach in, it was taken over and now John Butler read the lessons.

He had stood before the Quarterly Committee, made his confession and pleaded for reinstatement. And of course it was not forthcoming.

Although he had been welcomed home by the Maori, yet they stood apart from him. When he railed against the settlers and urged Ngapuhi to rise up against them, they turned away. 'You do not interfere in our wars,' they said. 'We will not interfere in yours.'

He spoke with Rakau and found no affirmation.

"You have done what you said you would do, e Keni. And the consequences are as you knew they would be."

"I could not help myself."

"And you cannot help the consequences. And yet they are yours."

And still he would not put the girl away.

And none could see that it was the will of God who had brought him here to succumb to the temptations of the Adversary, that even in his sin, in his continuing sin he remained God's instrument. Everything had happened in God's service.

I embarked in the Church Missionary Society's service at their command, I have laboured in their service, I have sinned in their service, I have repented in their service and I am still desirous to serve them.

How could they put him away?

And then, at last, God came back to him and brought him the strength to send Tungaroa away.

And nothing changed.

On his return from the Hokianga he had laid a mat upon the floor of their bedroom where he slept alone and chaste. And then one night, buoyed up on God's intervention and the removal of temptation as well as the contents of a bottle of Spanish port, he made to return to the marriage bed.

And was rejected again.

Her voice was low, this was not a conversation she would choose to share with the household, but it was firm.

"No, Thomas."

"But I have sent the girl away."

"Keep your voice down." He could hear a scratching in the darkness and then a pool of light shimmered on the bedside table. Her face was calm, her tone even.

"This has not to do with that."

"Then why?" He tried to keep soft but his voice rose and broke on the last word in something like a sob.

"We have borne nine children, eight living, from a grown woman to a babe in arms."

Thomas nodded. "The Lord has blessed our union."

"He certainly has." Did he detect a trace of irony there? "But there can be no more."

"How can you say that?" A sudden lancing thought. "You are not ill?"

"No, thank you for asking. I am not ill. But I am forty three years old –"

"Women well past that age have –"

"Bred. Yes, I know. But I will not be one of them."

"It is not for you to say. The will of God –"

"You are raising your voice again." She waited for the silence to settle and Thomas thought, she is determined and he remembered back fifteen years to when Jane had refused to visit with his mother. She had been implacable then and all his commands, threats, entreaties and tears, nothing had served to move her.

"It's not fair," he whimpered.

A smile tugged at the corners of her mouth as she shook her head. Fairness, justice, she thought, there are another couple to join forgiveness and strength.

"It may not be," she agreed, "but ..." She shrugged and let the thought lie.

Thomas collapsed on to his mat, shaking his head in disbelief. "I cannot believe this. You are punishing me."

"No." Jane was firm. "I'm not. Tungaroa is not a consideration."

"Then what is?"

"The children. I have neglected them, Thomas. I have not given thought to the effects our," she opened a palm, reaching for the word, "our tribulations have had upon them. Susannah is gone some months now, Elizabeth needs company, the boys are running wild, Samuel is sickly and I fear for his health. Edward is a baby. We live amidst hostility and judgment, never knowing where you will be from one moment to the next.

Thomas," she held up her hands appealing, "it is too much. I can take no more."

He had made no answer and she heard the movements of blankets, a pillow being punched into shape and later as she lay awake staring into the darkness, listening to the fragments of a slurred prayer.

Lord give me the strength to endure Thy trials and the burdens Thou hast laid upon me.

Two weeks later he was gone again, back to Kaihiki. For the next two months he itinerated between there and Rangihoua, back to bid Thomas Surfleet farewell, back for Christmas but never long enough in one place to say he was really anywhere.

Hongi's wishes kept him entrapped within the region and it was only when he was at war, as during Thomas' stay in the Hokianga, that Thomas was free to move further afield. Then Hongi was gone again, off to the Waikato where his reputation for slaughter would become even more enhanced, and Thomas fled again to Pomare's pa at Matauwhi. But this time he took his family with him, building a new home there, looking for a new beginning.

Jane did not resist him. Her one act of defiance was established now and she had no wish to add to it. Besides, she was glad to be away from the unforgiving rancour of the settlement.

Do not worry about me, Emmeline. I am as content as I have been in a long time. There is a purpose to my days, watching my children grow, enjoying them. I am at peace.

But, she thought to herself, this is not the place for the children to grow to adulthood. We need to be gone, and soon.

CHAPTER 49

Kororareka May 1823

Kororareka was less than two miles as the crow flies from Matauwhi, a half-hour's walk overland, a little longer around the coast or a twenty minute paddle, depending on the tide. The hell-hole of the South Pacific, some called it, others thought it little different from any English port and perhaps they all were right. But no English port had ever looked less like hell. The sea-loving sailors emptied their crap over the sides as they had always done, but here there were infinitely fewer craft in an infinitely greater space and the waters ran pure. The air was crystal clear, there were not a million smoke-stacks to rain ash and soot into the mud, no fouled cobblestones or running sewers.

But they were working on it. The settlement had grown with the trade and for the moment it was swollen. Later, when the ships had beaten away to sea and other ports it would shrink again, leaving a population that largely had nowhere else to go: deserters, pressed men and disillusioned sailors who fled to hide in Paradise, perhaps holding to a vision of their knowledge and technology making them as gods among the simple savages. It proved to be a strikingly naïve vision; occasionally the Maori killed them but more often they ignored them and the men who would be gods were reduced to the life of scavenging dogs, creeping back starving to the settlement to be ignored and despised again, eking out whatever kind of an existence they could manage. There were permanent traders, negotiating whatever might turn a profit – muskets, alcohol, preserved heads ... But mostly it was a nomadic population for sealers and whalers and general traders, taking a brief respite while they restocked before returning to the sea.

The crew of the *Asp* were more fortunate than most for their captain had built himself a home at Matauwhi where he lived from time to time with the Maori woman he called his wife. Profit was not his only drive and his men were glad of the extended shore leaves.

Now he sat in his well-appointed cabin, a glass before him, a pipe in one hand and a smile behind the other.

The conversation was not going well. Lieutenant Tapsell had enough English for managing a ship or running down a whale but theology called for an altogether different vocabulary. He said he was a 'Christian man' but Thomas was not entirely satisfied; papists had been known to say no less. But he supposed it would have to do. There was no doubt that he was smitten with the girl. "Ahau aroha koe," he said haltingly to her and she laid her hand on his and patted it like a fond mother.

Thomas turned to Maori when speaking to the girl but this became fraught, too. "You follow the way of our ariki, Iehu Karaiti?" he asked and received a blank stare. He repeated himself slowly as one might for a retarded child. "Iehu Karaiti?"

"Jesus Christ," said William helpfully.

And her eyes lit up.

Ae, he knew Jesus Christ, well not personally but she knew of him. He was often in Kelly's drinking shed.

"I think," she said, "he is a heavy drinking man. Or," she amended charitably, "perhaps he is just a clumsy bugger."

Thomas stared aghast and William leaned forward in his chair.

"K, k, je," she struggled with the difficult consonants. "I've often heard his name. 'Jesus Christ, watch where you're going, Jesus, you nearly knocked my glass over.'"

Phillip Tapsell smiled indulgently; William was less restrained as he knocked over his own glass in a burst of laughter.

Thomas shook his head sadly and persevered. And established that she was very fond of the good lieutenant, who had been very kind to her, and if it would make him happy to wed, then she was willing to oblige. Yes, she understood that it was a lifetime commitment and that, as his wife, she would be expected to return to England with him on the *Asp*. She nodded vigorously at that condition; her whanau had been very mean to her lately, complaining that she had not provided them with enough gifts and calling her rude names. They would be sorry when she was gone.

"This is not a strong foundation for a marriage," Thomas said.

But Tapsell was adamant. "She will learn," he said and William from behind his hand lent more support. "Can you withhold legitimacy?" he asked. "They will only persevere with their sin if you don't."

And so, not without reservation, Thomas was persuaded. He was, he thought humbly, the last person to let suspicion inform judgment.

In the event he should have done so. The bans were published, to the outrage of the Kerikeri and Rangihoua settlements, and Phillip and Maria were joined in holy wedlock. Unhappily the union lasted only a couple of weeks. The night before the *Asp* was due to sail Maria reconsidered, or perhaps considered her position and fled. She emerged some weeks later to form another union, this time without the benefit of clergy. This relationship was to last until her death.

Chapter 50

Even if, according to the Book of Regan, the first impulse of woman was 'I'm not going down alone' and the first of man was 'I lust', the urge to know best must be right up there.

It is a perverse urge and one that usually does not make a great deal of sense. Perhaps that is why Rakau equated pride with stupidity. For while the first two impulses may contribute to the survival of the individual or the species, the urge to know best has a peculiarly destructive quality. It is one thing to believe you are right when you are; it is quite another and generally rather dangerous to believe you are when you are not. Yet the need to be right – and then have your way with it – even when all the evidence points the other way seems irresistible. Like Huxley's Savage, demanding the right to be miserable. Or Milton's Satan, preferring to rule in hell rather than serve in heaven.

Perhaps it is aligned to faith and its claim to a nobler sensibility, deriding the man who required proof of a miracle; the kind of belief that is so complete that without the slightest compunction and singing its own praises it can take a life, a hundred lives, a thousand lives.

For Saul has killed in his thousands but David in his tens of thousands.

A man of faith is by definition a man of knowledge. And men whose faith is so strong that it would take them and their families to the ends of the earth are necessarily men of the most profound knowledge. As they knew that their redeemer lived, so they knew the heathen lived in ignorance of the truth. In the same way Hongi, a tohunga and a man of deep faith, knew that what they thought was nonsense.

Perhaps this is simplistic.

Perhaps knowledge of one's rightness is vital to survival. How else can you live in a society when your beliefs are mocked or ignored, where no one takes you seriously, where you and your family struggle to survive in discomfort and danger and deprivation? To think for a moment that you might be in error would be the beginning of utter loss. Commitment to one's faith, the determination to keep believing when there seems no remotely good reason for doing so then becomes the highest of ideals.

If the fool would persist in his folly he would become wise.

And the more that is invested, the greater the faith needs to be. Having sent a thousand men to their death in battle, who could reconsider, whoops, perhaps we were wrong to go to war. What else can you do but send a thousand more?

Like all the missionaries, John Butler was deeply conversant with the will of God. Perhaps his faith and knowledge were not as demonstrably complete as a suicide bomber's but they were what had brought him here and they were the fabric of his life. And as for all intents and purposes mind and soul amount to the same thing, so did John's intellect and sensibility. His drive to lead, like his drive to bring the heathen to salvation was not the result of mere intellectual decision; it was who he was so it was, of course, the will of God.

Like Thomas, his faith in himself faltered from time to time. As when he wrote to Pratt: 'we know nothing of humility ... every one is jealous lest another should have anything more than himself, or that another should have a leaf more in the wreath that adorns his brow.'

There is perhaps some irony in his selection of such a pagan image and it would be interesting to know what victories he perceived that he and his fellows had won that they should have been so adorned in the first place. Probably he did not consider the metaphor and related it only to the amount of credit or reputation that they were shoring up. In any event it shows a capacity for self-doubt; perhaps the same process was briefly in action when he sided with Francis Hall in determining Thomas' future.

But on a fine May Saturday morning as he strode down to the Kerikeri inlet to meet with the captain of the *Active,* such weak uncertainty was far from his mind. His step was purposeful and he nodded at passers-by with the cordial reserve fitting for the Superintendant of New Zealand.

With so many of the men at war and much of the remaining population taking advantage of the weather to attend to the winter planting, the inlet was quiet, almost serene and John took a moment to pause, to breathe in the beauty and to give thanks.

The beauty of this place is overwhelming. This perfect light, the quiet waters by, who could not see the hand of creation here? And a large portion of that beauty lies in the peacefulness. Which will not last. Hongi will be back and there will be new horrors. But for the moment, for the moment he is gone. Tomorrow I will sail to Rangihoua and I will take divine service there. For Kendall is gone, too.

He removed his hat and bowed his head.

The stone store that would become an icon of the new land stood close to the bank and looked down on the placid waters. Within, the *Active's* shipment had been unloaded and crates and boxes were stacked up to the ceiling; the management of the store had picked up a good couple of notches since Mr Wishy-washy had fled back to New South Wales – showing the lack of resilience that he and Mary had espied from the very beginning.

He saw the captain in conversation with James Kemp and made his way across the store to join them.

"Well done, Mr Kemp," gesturing about the store, "a tidy job. Good day, Captain Thompson, I trust you had a comfortable voyage, is there any mail for the mission?"

Thompson grunted an affirmation and pointed to a satchel lying on the counter. "Just arrived," he said, "not sorted yet."

"Very well then," John took up the satchel and hefted it in his hand. "A heavy load," he observed, "I will sort out the private correspondence from official matters and distribute it at evensong tomorrow evening."

"You could sort it here before you go," said Thompson.

"Yes," John agreed, slipping the satchel over his shoulder, "but I think it best to do it at home. No time to waste. Well then," he nodded cordially and left.

"Prick," said Thompson to the retreating back.

"Now, Patrick," said James Kemp, "there is no point in dwelling on such things."

He walked briskly back to the small house he occupied with his wife and son. His good mood was further enhanced by the smell of baking bread and the sight of Mary and Peter at the kitchen table; the boy was reading aloud to his mother from the Gospel of Mark and John was pleased by his fluency and clear articulation. He opened the satchel and tipped the contents on to the table and the bible was put to one side as the three of them sorted through the letters. Hall, Wm, put to one side, Hall, F, return to Marsden, King, Kendall. He held the last up and peered at it. The return address was to Thos Hassell, Marsden's son-in-law. What, he wondered, would Hassell have to say to Kendall; surely it was his proper business to know of all matters pertaining to the mission. But the letter was sealed with Hassell's signet imprinted into the wax. It would be impossible to open without leaving evidence and he did not care to think what Kendall's reaction would be.

Even Kendall is entitled to his privacy. And Hassell even more so.

He placed the letter to one side.

A thick letter caught his eye. It was addressed to 'the missionaries' and he recognised Marsden's hand; he took a thin knife, slit the letter open and laid the contents on to the table. Mary and Peter continued to sort the letters, then, when finished, Peter returned to his bible while Mary opened a letter from her mother.

Marsden had wasted little time in getting to his first point.

"Mary, listen, the committee has sacked Kendall."

She looked up, her eyes alight.

"It's true. At last. Suspension's over. They're getting rid of him."

"When?"

"Doesn't say. It won't be immediately, unfortunately. Marsden's coming over in September to do the job himself."

"O John, I am so pleased for you. At last you will be able to to assert your rightful place and bring the settlements into one righteous Christian whole."

"Yes, I will, won't I? God! Marsden hasn't held back. Listen to this, 'the sword will never depart from his house.' He's damning him And this: 'as a Christian I mourn for him, as a minister of the Gospel I cannot know him.'"

He continued silently with the letter and Mary returned to her own. There was little change from the last anxious missive; how many words, she thought, mother takes to say so little. But it was comforting to feel the contact and she ran a finger tenderly over the spidery script.

Then she jumped in shock as John's hand slammed down upon the table.

"God damn!" he roared. "That conniving piece of shit! That pious whoreson!"

"What is it? What's the matter?"

"What's the matter? Marsden's the damned matter!" His rage was overwhelming and he struggled to speak. "Here," a boney finger jabbed at the letter, "last paragraph. Slips it in at the end. Damn him to hell. I need a drink." He stormed from the room and Mary snatched the letter up. And read:

Mr Henry Williams, newly arrived from England, will be accompanying me to take up his position as the new Superintendant.

CHAPTER 51

A young man sat in a darkened corner and tried to take stock. He had met at taverns with friends and colleagues back in the old country but none of them had been like this. It was not just the physical outlay, rough-hewn planks where he had known polished tables and sawdust instead of carpet, guttering candles that dripped and shivered in the air that moved through the chinks in the walls and windows or extinguished entirely in a sudden blast – *shut the fucking door*; the reason for the tavern's being was something else. In England they met to be together and alcohol enhanced and enlivened that communion. It lubricated the tongue, furthered opinion and added an element of merriment to what might otherwise have been merely bland. Beer and wine and spirits were a means to an end. Here they were an end in themselves.

Certainly there was a quality of conviviality; there, around a keg serving as a table a group of men broke into laughter and close by the corner a pale-faced young man told his sorrows to a nodding ancient. But it would take little for the laughter to turn to acrimony and the tears to anger.

The young man could see the underlying danger in the eyes of a burly, bearded man who drank alone, could hear it in the over-emphatic tones of a pair of disputants but most of all he knew it was there because he could feel it in himself.

There come times in the lives of the most mild-mannered of men where failure and reversal eventually call out for a physical response. And Francis Hall was not a great deal removed from such a time.

Marsden had greeted him on his return with patronising at best, contempt at worst. "We are not all of us equipped to withstand discomfort," he said. And this, delivered from an easy chair by the fire in a well-appointed lounge had brought Francis a good deal closer to understanding the resentment of his namesake on the night when Marsden had turned him out into the storm.

"I am much occupied with weighty matters at the present," the great man continued. Francis understood that he would not be accounted amidst such concerns and the resentment flared a little more. "So what can we do with you?" Francis made no answer for he had no idea himself what he should be doing. That was why he was here. He also understood that no idea was required.

In the event he was engaged as a supernumerary to the Port Jackson chapel, a post that amounted to no more than handyman with some book-keeping. And Francis enjoyed it: he found that climbing up on to the roof, for example, to replace worn shingles carried a point to it; the purpose was clear and when completed he could stand back from the church and contemplate his work.

They are fixed securely and will stand up to the fiercest of winds.
This will last.

He was ambivalent about his immediate employer. The Reverend Winchester was an amiable young man of liberal, even democratic tendencies that saw him invite Francis to table as a colleague rather than an underling.

He and his pretty young wife were fascinated by his sojourn in New Zealand and it was in their questions that Francis learned how much the country had changed him.

"To live in such danger," said Mrs Winchester, "were you not continuously afraid?"

"No," Francis shook his head, "there was a time when things were," he reached for the word, "intense and we were all occasionally frightened but no, there was no continuous fear."

But Mrs Winchester would not settle for that. "How brave you must have been," she said.

But we were not afraid. So how can there be space for bravery?

"I suppose," observed Frederick, pointing with his pipe, "that the companionship of one's fellows in Christ must be a great support."

"Mm," Francis busied himself with rolling a cigarette while considering his answer. The habit had not brought him the solace it appeared to afford James Kemp but he persevered.

Marsden is hardly given to mincing words or guarding sensibilities. Surely Winchester must know something of the cicumstances of my leaving New Zealand or of the state of the settlements.

"Brotherhood is a wonderful thing," he mumbled.

Jesuit.

And the bitterness in him grew a little stronger.

His glass was empty and he picked his way across the shifting floor to lay his money down upon a greasy counter.

"Evening, squire, spare a poor man a penny for a drink, squire?"

Francis turned to face an unctuous smile in a weasel's face.

"No," he said to the weasel, to all of them, to all of it.

The conversation he could not have with Marsden and the Winchesters had extended to polite society.

Whom the Lord calleth he also justifieth.

And Francis found that he was without justification. He found that when, after Sunday service, he was introduced to Frederick's parishioners he had nothing to say to them. It was like his non-conversation with Wharepoaka all over again but much worse because these were his bretheren.

All he could offer about the mission were platitudes and clichés and they felt like lies. And what could he say about himself?

Good day, my name is Francis Hall and I am a failed missionary.

He could not ask for sympathy or understanding because at bottom he had none for himself.

This is what it must have been like for Jane Kendall. God, I miss her, and James, too. I think they may be the only people I know; or rather, the only people who know me.

He had not forgotten his promise to Jane. Indeed, along with mending roofs, finding Richard Stockwell was the only justification he could find for his days. His only mission.

"Odd that you should ask," said the prison superintendent. "I had a letter not that long ago from your chaplain about the same fellow."

"Marsden?" Francis was astonished. "What would he want with Stockwell?"

"No idea. Just wanted to know where he might be. I wrote back he'd been released near a year before and had no idea where he might be. Said I could make enquiries but never heard back from him." He shrugged. "Glass of port?"

"Thank you." Francis considered. "So you made no enquiries?"

"No point."

"But if you had, where would you have begun?"

"Well'" bushy eyebrows furrowed in concentration. "First thing would have been to see if he had claimed his allotment. Emancipists are entitled to a thirty acre block."

"And if he hadn't?"

"Wouldn't have been surprised. A lot don't. Straight to the taverns and whores and damnation."

"And then? To church?"

"Unlikely. If a man's got a religious bent, he's more likely to pick up his allotment."

"Where else?" Francis found he was enjoying the man's economy of words and was slipping into a similar style.

"Might have found a passage back or joined a ship. The odd one," he tapped his forehead, "just starts walking west. Probably ends up as dingo tucker."

Francis sipped his port and tugged at his chin. "Anything seems possible," he said. "Any other ideas?"

"Might have checked amongst the other items –"

"Items?"

"Inmates. See if he had any pals, someone he might have talked to."

"And if that failed?"

"Then I would have given up. Another port?"

This mission proved to be even more impossible than the last one and led to direct lies.

How could the truth have stood?

Thank you kindly, Mrs Winchester, but I must decline your offer of dinner. I'm off to the prison.

O indeed, and why is that?

I'm looking for a former inmate, Richard Stockwell; he was a servant of Thomas Kendall, you will have heard of him, the man who defied the mission and took the chiefs to England, the drunkard and fornicator who helped arm Ngapuhi so they could slaughter and enslave and cannibalise other Maori in great numbers. Anyway, his wife committed adultery with Stockwell and he was sent back in chains to Port Jackson to serve out his sentence. Mrs K asked me to check up on him and let her know that he was happy and getting on with his life.

So he would fabricate some story or another and skulk away into the night.

He passed his evenings making his way to the prison, a lengthy walk, interviewing suspicious felons – what would this fellow want with Stockwell? – who knew little and cared less and then returning to the little room he called home.

He recalled the superintendant's remark about taverns and whores and damnation and added dropping into taverns as another line of inquiry. And more lies.

He would sooner have been alone – *if I've got to be by myself I'd rather be by myself by myself* – but, like the Maori the Winchesters took the view that they would be poor hosts to leave him in seclusion. And as the winter had drawn in, outdoors became less of an option.

He returned to his seat with the glare of the weasel hot upon his back. He settled into his corner and set his glass down upon an upturned crate that the management pleased to call a table and reached into his coat pocket to withdraw a crumpled sheaf of papers. Then he rolled a cigarette and gazed idly about the bar.

The room was warming now and there was a comfortable quality from the fire in the corner. Francis was surprised to note the number of men, there was only one woman here and she was serving behind the counter, who were sitting quietly, staring into the flames.

What do they see there?

The question stayed and he straightened out the sheets and wrote in pencil: what do men see in fire?

After a lapse he had begun a journal again; but it was of a very different kind and he was beginning to find it absorbing. Rather than a series of anecdotes, statements and observations on the behaviour of others, he had started asking questions of himself. The questions mounted, almost invariably to no answers and he was surprised at his curiosity and ignorance. After a time he became comfortable with it.

What are the grounds of my failure as a missionary?

What are the grounds of the others' claim to success?

Why do we say 'discretion is the better part of valour' and yet there is not an Englishman who believes it? Which makes me a weak coward. The Maori chief leads his men to battle, the English general directs his men from behind; the Maori chief will run with his men from a losing cause, the English general will shoot his men for doing so.

How can I be wise to flee New Zealand and be a cowardly deserter at the same time? Where is the merit in persisting with folly? What am I supposed to be doing?

Which brought him back to his mission. There were guards and inmates who remembered Stockwell but none who knew him.

Never said much of anything to anyone ... not the full quid ... you wouldn't want to cross him though, powerful sod ... religious bugger, knew all the hymns ...

Francis had followd up the last hint but found the prison chaplain equally vague. Nor were the churches of much help. He was not free to check for himself – being obliged to the Winchesters every Sunday – and inquiries brought the same impossible question.

Mm, I might have seen him, can't recall. What is your interest, may I ask?

So he sat in dark cubicles and smoked and drank and wondered what he was doing.

Then he was brought abruptly back to the moment.

"Wotcher doin?"

Francis looked up with a start to find a lean, almost scrawny man staring down at him. Freckles stood out against an English pallor, pale blue eyes, narrowed and hostile.

His gloomy mood and the shock did not dispose him towards civility.

"Attending to my own business," he snapped. "May I suggest you do the same?"

The man was not deterred and craned his neck, trying to make out the writing on the crumpled page.

"And what business is that? I seen you round the other pubs, staring and writing stuff down. You some kind of spy?"

Incredulity held the anger back and Francis stared at him. "Spy? What do you mean? Who would I be spying on? Who for?"

"That's what I'm askin you, innit? Gimme a look at them papers." A hand whipped down and the papers were snatched away. Then Francis was on his feet and the crate and glass went flying, heads turned and the tavern sighed in anticipation.

The man bounced back, holding the papers before him; then, in the instant before his anger took over, Francis had a thought and he paused. He watched the man peering at the papers and he could see the imcomprehension.

"Go on then," he said, "help yourself."

The man continued to stare and Francis laughed; at some distance he registered that it was an ugly sound.

"Would you like me to read them to you?"

The man grunted, then thrust the sheets back wordlessly.

"Very well. Let's see, ah yes, my latest entry. 'I am standing in a wretched little dive being confronted by a wretched little man, an illiterate, stupid, ugly, ill-mannered piece of work who –"

"You takin the piss? That's not what you wrote."

"I am anticipating. Would you like to hear more?"

"Fuck you." The man was now as angry as Francis had nearly been but not to the extent that it had entirely deprived him of reason. Francis stood a full head higher and would have outweighed him by several stones. He stared furiously around at the watching, hungry faces.

"He's a spy, boys, a fuckin gummint spy."

The tavern sighed again and Francis registered that all humour had suddenly left the situation.

"That right?" The bearded man was on his feet, advancing and Francis could see the need on him.

"No." The answer began with indignation and ended in fear. "I'm a missionary and these are –"

"Missionary! One of Marsden's men, one of the flogging parson's boys." The ginger man bounced upon the spot. "The cunt what put stripes upon your back, Rufus."

"Look!" Francis put up his arms, placating, then dropped them again and his fists balled. The conversation was clearly over.

Then the bearded man stopped in his tracks and winced as his upraised arm was taken in a vice-like grip.

"No," said a voice. "You must not fight. It is wrong to fight."

Chapter 52

They dressed in the colours of mourning and authority and their faces reflected their garb, drawn and sombre. These were the men God had chosen to bring light to the heathen darkness and the weight of his mighty purpose was heavy upon them. Although they sat in a spacious room in the perfect light of late winter, the mood was dark.

At the head of a polished kauri table Samuel Marsden studied the six apostles and was not well pleased by what he saw. William Hall's sight was fading but his gaze was direct and uncompromising as he held the great man's eye. There was more strength in John King now but it was not the strength of humility and his gaze too was not kind. John Butler, he could see, was holding himself under a tight rein but his resentment was close at hand. The face of Samuel Leigh, the Weslyan, was pale and he looked away towards the shining waters and the chaplain knew he longed to be away from this place. James Kemp, the storekeeper, was of a more placid demeanour, yet his features were as grim as the others', befitting the purpose of this meeting.

There were two empty places, one for Francis Hall who had fled from his mission and the other for Thomas Kendall who would soon be sent after him.

Which left the new man Williams who would shortly take Butler's post from him.

"Brothers," said Samuel Marsden, and the words near stuck in his throat, "this is a painful meeting but our duty is clear and we will not shirk from it."

Was that the royal plural?

"I am referring of course to the dismissal of Mr Kendall. The information you gentlemen have provided me and the Society – along with his own reluctant confession – has made it obvious that he can no longer be associated with this mission. I will sail to his home when convenient and advise him so."

"And if he does not heed your …advice?"

There was insolence in the tone, particularly in the pause before the last word and the chaplain fixed his questioner with a cold stare.

"Perhaps I have chosen the wrong word, Mr Hall," he said, "or perhaps you do not understand it. I am not here to ask Mr Kendall to leave. I am here to tell him."

"And if he declines?"

Henry Williams watched the debate thoughtfully. He knew of the rancour in the community; Marsden had spoken of it and almost immediately, but he was still surprised and a little shocked by the overt antagonism.

The chaplain was irritated. "How can he decline?" he asked. "I have his papers of dismissal from the Society. It is not a matter for negotiation."

John King interposed. He had joined in alliance with Hall against Kendall and it had made him bolder. "Certainly," he said, "Kendall cannot maintain his employment but he might choose to keep his place."

"Then he can starve in it." Marsden's irritation had passed to anger. "All wages and allowances will cease with his dismissal." He could see they were not persuaded but was not prepared any longer to pander to their obduracy. "To pass to other matters, as I adverted in my letter, the Society has decided, in the interests of conciliation with the natives, to appoint a new superintendent. Mr Williams here will take up that position."

John Butler looked at his hands. He could not maintain that his relationship with Ngapuhi was a comfortable one. He could argue that it came from Kendall's poisoning Hongi against him and deny all he liked that he had made his own contribution. But he knew that it would be pointless.

Of course it is hugely unfair, John. But the decision has been made and it is not one that Marsden can undo. We have our security to consider. Please, do not make a bad situation worse.

So he looked at his hands and tried not to hate Williams and not to let his hatred for Marsden show.

The chaplain moved from a bitter but compliant spirit to one of resistance.

"Where is your Christian forgiveness, Matene?"

The question was couched almost naively but Marsden could see the avarice behind it. A long association with Kendall had served Rakau's whanau well and they had taken their profit in the pre-eminent currency.

So he let the question slide and made much of the presents he had brought.

Rakau nodded his appreciation and asked again, "Where is your Christian forgiveness?"

Marsden sighed. He was conscious of the influence Rakau held with Ngapuhi; he was, after all, a tohunga of great mana. And in this society his age was not seen as an impediment to reason but rather as enhancing it. He could not dismiss the question as he would with one of his own congregation. Still, it rankled that his judgment was being queried and that he need justify it.

"Mr Kendall," he said levelly, "has broken the commandments he was brought here to teach. His position requires that he set an example of righteous behaviour and he has failed to do so."

He waited while his response was translated, conscious of the old man's eyes on him. He had known that gaze for many years now and while he would not own it to be unsettling, yet he was reluctant to return it. He looked instead about the whare, taking in the evidence of Kendall's trade, three polished muskets leaning against the wall.

Then there was a further pause as Rakau spoke again and he waited for the English words.

"You have not answered my question," said Wharepoaka and Marsden's fists balled. "You have told Ngapuhi that your god is a god of forgiveness and that if we repent of our evil ways and turn to him we will be forgiven."

Marsden waited but that was the extent of the response and he answered a trifle uncertainly, "that is true."

"Then why will he not forgive Keni?"

"I cannot speak for God - *of course you can; that's why you're here –* "perhaps He will."

"Then why won't you?"

"It is not a matter of forgiveness."

"Then what is it a matter of?"

It is a matter of Kendall's defiance of all authority, of his poisoning you against us, of his arming you, of his drinking and debauchery. Of his lying with a woman who was not his wife, who is your daughter, for God's sake!

But of course he could not say that and as he sat in angry silence as Rakau moved to another tack.

"Hongi will be angry if you take Keni away. The settlers may feel the weight of his anger."

Marsden was more comfortable with threats.

"I don't think so," he said. "Ngapuhi have benefited from pakeha trade. Would Hongi wish the trade to go to other iwi? I don't think he would place his cause at such a disadvantage."

"Ah," said Rakau through Wharepoaka, "would you have turned the guns of the *Active* on Rangihoua as you threatened when you were kept from Ruatara?"

Marsden stared. "Why do you ask?" he said at last. "What has this to do with that?"

"If you had done so, would you not have been placing your cause at a disadvantage?"

Marsden nodded, remembering. "I suppose so," he said uncomfortably, "perhaps I was not," the words stuck, "thinking that far ahead at the time."

"So you might have acted in haste to repent at leisure?"

How does he get to talk like this?

"How do you know that Hongi might not do the same thing? Is he so much a wiser man than you?"

At which point the chaplain rose to his feet and bowed to the old Maori. "I think," he said, "that we will have to agree to disagree."

And turned on his heel and left.

To move from bitter compliance to resistance and threats to madness.

CHAPTER 53

10 August 1823 Kororareka

He stood upon the poop of the *Raven* and gazed down over his congregation. They were a motley crew and not all would have wished to be here. But neither would they wish to disappoint their captain and so here they were: men of varying ages and nationalities in their pigtails and tattoos, joined together in worship. A few were joined by the wahine they pleased to call their wives, at least for the duration of the visit. Some were dressed like their men in canvas trousers and shirts, here a floral dress, there an old seaman's jacket over a flax skirt, a sailor's cap, one woman stood in a full feathered cloak for it was a cool morning. There were babes in arms and toddlers, the products of these brief unions but for the moment they stood together as whanau.

The captain was a dour Scot of strict Presbyterian ethics. There were some who would say he was a hard man, but they would say he was a fair man, too. For this occasion he was a reluctant realist. If he was less equable than his fellow captain, William Brind, about the social habits of his men, he also accepted that denunciation and denial would have little effect and if they wanted their whores and bastards on board for service, what would be the point of denying them? It rankled a good deal more that the Englishman who led them in prayer was himself a confessed fornicator. But he had been welcomed on to the other ships and in the village, too; to deny him a place on the *Raven* would not make for a wider harmonious relationship. A flawed service, he decided, was better than no service at all.

The minister could not have been unaware of the captain's sentiments but for the moment he was satisfied just to be here. And as he led the congregation in the closing hymn he let his eyes wander past them over the shining bay of this glorious world of which he had won a part.

And his heart stopped.

For there, edging her way down the centre of the channel was the *Brampton*, the Society's new vessel. On the line she was tacking she would overshoot Kororareka; she must be making for Matauwhi. Her sails were grey in the morning sun but for the meaning her presence signified they might as well have been black.

His voice failed on the hymn and he mumbled his way through the closing prayer, received the captain's grunted thanks and made his way to the longboat.

As he walked along the shoreline, he tried to gather his tangled thoughts and compose himself for the meeting to come.

This is so like Marsden. No warning, it would have been an instant decision –' ah, the wind is favourable, Captain Thompson, if you would be so kind, drop whatever you are doing, assemble a crew and take me at once to Matauwhi.' And he will expect me to be at home, waiting for him.

He bent suddenly to pick up a pebble and hurl it into the sea. Others followed but there was no relief in the exercise, only a tired arm.

Marsden's letter to the missionaries had not been treated in confidence. To the contrary, its contents had been widely published. John Butler in particular had taken the only comfort he could find in it to advise any who cared to listen that Kendall's days were numbered. Inevitably the information had crossed the bay to Kororareka.

And Thomas had no idea what to do with it.

There was denial. *It can't be true. Surely Marsden would have the decency to advise me along with everyone else.*

Then anger. *It is true. This is exactly what he would do.*

Bargaining. *I have repented, God knows I have repented. This is a test of the strength of my repentance. If I stay in a penitent state and continue to serve Him, surely He will not abandon me.*

Depression. *I am a worthless creature.*

Frequently the moods would overlap and Jane never knew what to expect. And there was no one he could talk to for there was none who understood, none who knew how to sympathise properly.

"Fuck 'em," said William Brind, "yes, that's right, I said 'fuck 'em.' Don't look so shocked. You don't need them. You can manage without them. Tell them to go to hell."

Jane's response was even worse and Thomas could not help but feel that she was secretly pleased. "I suppose we must accept it. And it will be better for the children if we were to leave this place."

The Maori shook their heads, uncomprehending. The offence was over, Thomas had repented.

Where is your Christian forgiveness, Matene?

There were times when his focus was elsewhere and times when he simply forgot. But always the memory would come flowing back and he had no idea what to do with it.

The mid-day sun was suddenly cold and he crossed his arms, hugging himself.

Now he was picking his way around the last headland and there, grounded in the shallows of the little bay lay the *Brampton's* longboat. Four sailors sat in the sand a little further up the beach.

"Pardon, zurr," the broad Yorkshire vowels brought a sudden pang, "Mr Marsden be waiting for thee up in house." Thomas nodded vaguely. "And missus asked me to tell thee that she's taken the young 'uns for a walk along beach." He gestured with his pipe and Thomas could make out a small group of figures disappearing southward.

Abandoned, he thought, then, no that's not it, ah God, I don't know.

The chaplain looked up from a table littered with papers. He patted his wig into place and motioned Thomas to enter.

Inviting me into my own home. But I will be calm, I will be civil, I will be dignified. But his nerves were frayed and a nervous giggle escaped him as he sat. Then, remembering himself, he swiftly pushed himself erect and the chair fell behind him. He thrust his arm out towards the seated man and Marsden flinched. Then, understanding the gesture, he took the outstretched hand; but there was no response in his grip beyond a slight wince as Thomas clutched it tightly.

"Well met, sir, it is a pleasure to –"

"Indeed, Mr Kendall. You may let my hand go now."

Thomas jerked his hand away and stepped back, nearly tripping over the fallen chair. He clutched at the table to steady himself and Marsden watched him closely.

There is a kind of wildness here.

Thomas lifted the chair and sat. For a moment or two they sat in silence, then Thomas remembered himself again. "There should be karakia," he said and in the same breath, folding his hands and bowing his head, "e te ariki, whakarongo mai –"

"Indeed, Mr Kendall, but I think, being two Englishmen in a heathen land our prayer should be in our own tongue. It is also more fitting that the senior man should lead."

It was less a prayer than a denunciation and Thomas squirmed in his seat as the charges were read.

"Teach us humility, Lord, that we may know our place and defer to higher authority … let us always remember that pride is the greatest of the seven deadly sins … lead us not into temptation … let us turn away from the sin of lust … thou shalt not commit adultery …"

He could feel the protest welling within him and he fought to keep the voices down. Looking through narrowed eyes he could see that his knuckles had whitened and his hands were shaking.

Dear God, I could do with a drink. And perhaps a touch of laudanum to settle my nerves.

"… Save us from the vices of intoxication and debauchery …"

I am cold to my bones.

"… Help us flee from self-indulgence and the gratification of the flesh and personal comfort … it is in industry and useful toil that we shall find salvation …"

At last the diatribe was done, amens mumbled and silence filled the room. Thomas looked up to see Marsden's eyes hard upon him. He pushed his chair back and rose. "I am a poor host," he said. "Please, allow me to refresh you with a glass of wine." Without waiting for an answer he hurried across the room to a polished cabinet, talking all the while. "Had I known you were coming I would have but never mind never mind you're here that's the important thing I hope you had a pleasant trip over I know you suffer from sea-sickness as I do but ah here we are may I propose a toast to the successful outcome of your visit?"

The remainder of the visit ran along similar lines. Thomas could simply not hold his tongue and although Marsden was ever the man to rein him in – "Mr Kendall, you are interrupting me, now I believe I was talking about correspondence from the Committee – " Thomas could no sooner be checked than he was away again – "Indeed sir I apologise pray continue I hope the gentlemen are all in good health I have been preparing a series of theses on Maori religious belief fascinating material that I hope will be of interest to them they're right here in my desk let me show you."

And he was scurrying away to return with an armful of crumpled papers, scrawl and sketches, blotches and maps of spilt wine.

A lesser man than Marsden might have become alarmed at the cascade of irrelevance and presumption, for it was clear that Kendall still believed himself to be a servant of the Society and of singular value to them. He sipped carefully from his glass and watched as the renegade emptied his own to refill it immediately.

Does he believe the nonsense he is spouting, can he not know why I am here, does he hope to continuously pre-empt me with the idea that if the words are not spoken the reality will not exist?

Whichever was the answer, whether Kendall knew what he was doing or not, it was becoming clear to the chaplain that here was a man utterly ensnared.

Then there was a knock upon the door, "excuse me, zurr, but Cap'n Thompson wishes to advise that tide be turning," and Marsden was on his feet, packing his papers and brushing away the outstretched hand and the babbling farewell.

The note of dismissal stayed in his pocket.

Two days later his resolve had returned and the letter lay on the table. And this time he would not allow himself to be distracted from his purpose.

"The Committee's decision is clear, Mr Kendall. You are dismissed and required to leave this place."

Thomas nodded slowly. He was calmer this time; knowing the time and place, he was not been caught off-guard and was prepared. A tincture of laudanum had been particularly helpful.

Still he must needs plead his case.

"I have been living an unblemished life for near a year," he said, "and I am penitent. I believe I still have the skills to promote the objects of the Society and I am desirous to do so."

"Your desires are of no relevance, sir." Marsden kindly held back the retort – *your desires are what got you into this mess in the first place.* "The Committee's decision is final. It is not within my power to countermand it even if I wished to do so – and I do not – and there is no point to your arguing against it."

Thomas was not done. "I understand," he replied, "but I cannot believe that were the gentlemen of the Society to be apprised of the changes in circumstance – and the decision is near a year old – they would not reconsider. I can see from their letter that they fear I am in a state of rebellion against God and perhaps when I was ensnared that was true. But now that I am away from the unkindness of the settlements I have found peace and stability and I –"

"Enough, Mr Kendall. If you wish to write to the Committee to appeal their decision, that is your right. But as I said less than a minute ago, there is no point in arguing it with me."

"If they knew –"

"Then tell them but don't," and a heavy fist thumped on each word, "argue the point with me."

Thomas was silent.

"Now we need to attend to the details. You will return with me upon the *Brampton* to New South Wales."

"Why?"

"Because that is the wish of the Society." A stubby finger pointed to the letter. "You have just read it yourself."

The tone and manner were making inroads into Thomas' calm and he struggled to keep his voice even.

"I mean, why go to New South Wales? What happens then?"

Marsden was briefly silent. His brief had been to oversee the dismissal and removal. The Committee seemed to have no concern beyond that point and neither did he. So he said so.

"That is not my concern."

"How are we to live? I have a large family, how am I to support them?"

Marsden shrugged. "That is your concern."

"My wife and children will have no means of support."

"So you have said."

"So we are to be abandoned, perhaps to starve," his voice was rising now, "and you and the Society will stand by, unconcerned, and wash your hands of us?"

And now Marsden's own resolve for calm was threatened by the tone and the implied criticism.

"If you would tax me with scripture, Mr Kendall," he snarled, "you might take heed of the text where it is written that the sins of the fathers will be visited upon the heads of the children."

"So you would punish my children, too!"

Both men were on their feet now.

"I am punishing no one," again a thump accompanied each word. "It is your own foul behaviour that has brought them to this sorry pass."

"And they will have no support from you?"

"They will get what you deserve."

And now Thomas' fist came crashing down on the table. "Then tell me this," he roared. "Why would I take my family away from their home to travel to Australia to be homeless and starve?"

"You will do as you are ordered!"

Perhaps the laudanum had taken a second hold or perhaps even through the red mist Thomas was able to perceive the helplessness of Marsden's position. He nodded and smiled slightly, then turned on his heel to cross to the cabinet where he poured himself a generous glass. He raised it in mock salute to the glaring parson.

"And what will you do if I refuse?" he asked. "Dismiss me?"

"O God, Thomas, then what did he say?" Jane stared at him and for the first time in a long time she was deeply afraid. She had over the last decade considered a variety of dire scenarios but being stranded here with no support and no prospects had not been amongst them.

"He didn't say anything." His tone was dull and the words slurred. "Just snatched up his bag and marched off. Didn't even look at me."

"O Thomas, what," she stopped and lowered her head over clenched fists – *I will not cry* – "what are we to do? The children ... what will become of them?"

Thomas' face was haggard and he too was close to tears.

"I don't know. I just don't know."

Over the next week, because they had to, they learned to talk to each other again. Thomas was still caught in disbelief at the nature of the threat and fell to repeating himself – "'the sins of the father,' he said, how could he?" – but Jane was more pragmatic.

"Well, he has and whether it is out of spite or self-righteousness is really beside the point."

"I will tell him –"

"When have you, or anyone else for that matter, ever been able to tell Marsden anything?"

"I will write to Pratt. He will listen."

"And even if he does, how long will it be before he hears your plea? And how long again before we hear his reply?"

"I just can't believe it."

"We must."

"I shall pray."

"Certainly," she tried to hold the asperity down, "but we need to act, too. The Lord helps those who help themselves."

"Yes," said Thomas, remembering. "Basil talked about that the first time we met."

And I wish he had confined himself to that observation, thought Jane, but she said, "So what do we need to do to help ourselves?"

While Thomas lamented, cursed and digressed, Jane held a steady line and they clarified their position and began to develop a response.

Item: the issue at hand was not Thomas' being able to continue to serve the Lord through the mission, nor his justification. It was the physical survival of his family.

Item: the issue was not Thomas' dismissal, nor the unfairness of it all. It was how they would deal with it.

Item: Marsden could not countermand the dismissal but he could continue to provide support or he could withhold it.

Item: he could not be coerced into support. Any attempt to do so would produce only greater resistance.

Item: appealing to his compassion would in all likelihood produce a similar result.

So where, Jane wondered, was Marsden vulnerable? To whom might he defer? None willingly, but there must be those who could enforce it.

"What would the Society make of Marsden's abandoning us?" she asked.

"Why would they care? It was their decision."

"No." She tapped her fingers on the table, considering. She was finding a new focus in their dilemma and while it was frightening there was also a measure of stimulation, even excitement. "It was their decision that you be dismissed and removed from New Zealand. I wonder if they thought much beyond that. And I doubt that they would be much impressed at your wife and family being turned out homeless to starve."

Thomas filled his glass. "What does it matter what they think?" he said sourly. "Anyway, like you said, it will be months before they even hear about it."

"Yes, yes," Jane was becoming impatient, "but what would Marsden make of the knowledge that such a letter was on its way?"

Thomas put down his glass and stared. "You are speaking of blackmail," he said.

"No," Jane pointed her finger at him. "I am speaking of the survival of my children."

"Yes," Thomas nodded, "and that is the issue."

"Item one."

"And you are on to something." He was becoming caught up in the idea. "Marsden was incensed at the letter I wrote to the Committee."

"Yes, yes. And this would be a more difficult matter for him; if he goes ahead with his plan, he can hardly deny it."

"He cannot bear to be questioned." He clapped his hands suddenly. "Brisbane! The new governor in New South Wales. If I wrote to Brisbane pleading our case and begging for assistance –"

"In the face of Marsden's unchristian lack of compassion and charity –"

"Brisbane would love it. By all accounts he detests Marsden and would seize on any opportunity to humiliate him." Thomas jumped to his feet. "I will begin the letter immediately."

They retired an hour later, leaving the draft lying between two empty bottles of port. And as they settled beneath the covers – for Thomas had been readmitted to the family bed, although on strictly chaste terms – he felt a kind of ease he had not known for a long time. He leaned over and patted Jane briefly on the shoulder. "My clever wife," he said, "my clever, sensible wife."

Within minutes both were asleep.

'… so I would ask you, sir, to reconsider your lack of concern for the fate of my wife and children. I recall that you instructed me not to quote scripture, yet the example of the Good Samaritan stands high in Christian values. And did not our Saviour say, 'suffer the little children to come unto Me'? How can any Christian man, let alone the ignorant Maori, understand how a religion that preaches charity and forgiveness could cast out small children to suffer and starve?'

Marsden's lips curled.

The whining dog; he hides behind his wife and children to argue his own cause. And he is a liar, pleading poverty while I warrant he has accumulated more than enough to attend to their needs. No one is going to starve.

The rest of the letter followed in a similar vein: humble, penitent, pleading but Marsden was not moved.

Then his eyes narrowed.

'… I am also writing to the Church Missionary Society to beg for compassion. Of course by the time they receive my letter it may be too late …'

For God's sake!

'… I am confident they will not stand to one side while one of their servants, however far he may have fallen, is cast into the wilderness …'

And now clenched fists joined the curling lips and narrowed eyes.

'… As a father I must seek every avenue of succour for my family and to that end I fear I will be compelled to write to Governor Brisbane …'

And came crashing down upon the table.

At the far end of the room Henry Williams started.

"Mr Marsden, what can be the matter?"

"Kendall!" roared the chaplain. "Kendall is the matter. The scoundrel is going to – " He bit back the words and chewed his lip.

This is not a quarrel for publication, Samuel.

He twisted his face into an awful smile and his fist turned into a dismissive wave of the hand. "It is nothing, Mr Williams, just a touch of indigestion, I shall walk it off." He crammed his hat upon his head and marched out of the room, leaving the new superintendent gazing wonderingly after him.

He stormed along the beach front, looking neither right nor left and passers-by scurried from his path; then he found a spot where there were none in sight and he let his rage explode. Like Kendall before him, pebbles and maledictions went skimming together across the placid waters. Gradually his breathing eased and his face lost its purple hue, but his mood was none the less black as it dawned upon him that Kendall had him at a serious disadvantage.

Brisbane will question me.

Damn Kendall, he thought, how satisfied he must be with this dark day's work.

It probably would have been of little consolation but Thomas was in fact very far from being satisfied. After the elation of the riposte and the brief alliance with Jane he sat alone, head bowed, absorbing the knowledge that his service was coming to an end.

He moved into a state of perpetual brooding, simmering with anger at Marsden, the Society, the settlers who had betrayed him and even Tungaroa who occasionally became the woman who had ensnared him. But, like Eve, she was only an agent. It was the Adversary who had placed her in his way, who had drawn him into the web of temptation. And the Adversary was an agent, too, for it was God who had suffered him to fall. Perhaps to fall, as he had fallen to Evelyn the Whore, that the scales might be lifted from his eyes and he would rise, a wiser and better man, a truer Instrument of the Lord. But there would be no rising this time: if the plea/threat to Marsden was successful, his family would be saved; if not, they would be destitute. He seemed not to see the option of cutting himself free from the Society, of staying and trading on his own account and building up his own congregation, with or without Marsden's blessing.

Jane saw the option clearly but she was pleased that Thomas did not. For her part, the elation remained.

We will be out of this god-forsaken place, Emmeline, away from the horror and the cruelty and the loneliness. We can realise our assets and with aid from Marsden and our, or rather my savings we will be able to establish ourselves in Australia. We still have our holding there. There will be a wider, kinder, English society, opportunities for the children ... Dear God, we may even manage to return home.

So she managed the negotiations that flowed between Kerikeri and Matauwhi, dictating correspondence to her miserable, despairing husband.

Within a week they had reached an agreement. Marsden would absolutely not assist in any way a passage to England; Jane could understand why and did not press the issue. But he would assist with their resettling in Port Jackson, hoping that it would be a brief stay, Kendall was the last neighbour on earth he would have chosen, and he undertook to maintain support until they were independently established. In return there would be no letter of complaint to the Society and no contact at all with Brisbane. It was, of course, an entirely unenforceable contract, dependent upon probity on both sides. With neither having any confidence in the other, nobody was happy. But it was the best that they could do.

Departure date was set for the sixth of September.

September 6

Opiates held the pain of his despair at a distance. He knew he was suffering, knew that this was the worst day of his life and that he wished his life was over, but he knew it only vaguely from within a grey and woolly cocoon.

When Jane had finalised the agreement with Marsden, he had nodded his understanding and obediently penned their acceptance. She had also helped him with his letter to the committee of missionaries. 'I am in an unfit state of mind,' he wrote. 'My head is often in a distracted condition and my spirits broken down.'

This was no exaggeration. Jane feared for him but had no time for comfort. There was a great amount of organising to be done, endless packing and transporting their belongings to Kerikeri to be laden on to the *Brampton*. Thomas moved in a haze, carrying when directed, sitting at the helm of the *Bulrush*, bearing his world away.

And now all was done and he stood alone in the bow of the *Brampton*, gazing into eternity. Jane and Elizabeth were below with the children, securing their property – 'it may be a rough journey,' said Captain Thompson – settling the young ones into their cabins. Marsden and Leigh would also be in their cabins; he had had no conversation with either man.

It was a fitting day for the final journey. Black, swollen clouds, a bitter wind that cut across the heaving sea and flung sudden flurries of dark rain into his upturned face. Beyond the inlet the conditions would be worse and beyond the bay they would be worse again. He heard the sailors grumbling as they prepared the ship.

"This is going to be a bastard of a trip ... Captain tried to tell Marsden but the whoreson can't be told ... in all kinds of a hurry ... hope he empties his fat fucking guts all over himself ..."

Neither the language nor the sentiments bothered him.

Above the eastern hills the sky was darkening further, to be suddenly lit in streaks of lightning; a glowing portal seemed torn into the sky and he fancied he saw written above it in letters of fire, 'abandon hope all ye who enter here.' He watched his fear as he had watched his suffering.

Then there was the grinding of chains as the anchor was weighed and the *Brampton* groaned as she turned into the wind. Her bow rose and Thomas clutched at a stay to keep from falling backwards. Then she was plunging down and he staggered forward. As she found her line, her movement steadied and he was able to maintain his place, watching the waters break against the bows and shatter on the sides. The sea churned and he thought of the maelstrom, of faces in the water but any song was lost to the wind and the sea and the groaning ship.

The *Brampton* bucked her way out of the inlet and into the wider reaches of the bay and the sea and the wind rose together; buffeted by the wind above and the tide below, maintaining a single line became an impossibility as she slid and reared and plunged and keeping her clear of the islands and crags became the only task at hand. Although it was not yet midday, the world was becoming dark, then light in sudden, great sheets of thunder.

There is a godhead here.

All the opiates in the world could not have dulled him now as adrenalin poured through him, but still he was not afraid.

And then the wind was suddenly a northern gale that near flung the *Brampton* on to her side and she was turning to run before it. Beyond the bay they would have cast out sea anchors to slow her flight but here with shallows and crags to catch at them they did not dare. The sails were not yet fully unfurled but even so she flew at a speed she was not built to bear.

Snatches of voices cut across the howling of the gale that was becoming a storm – "draw up the sails, cap'n says that … can barely hold on … slash 'em, let 'em shred … bastard'll be the death of us …"

Jane and the children, I must be below.

But all his effort was in clutching at the stay, just to remain where he was. Then all the sounds of chaos were overwhelmed in the rending crashing of wood meeting rock and the *Brampton* shuddered to a halt. The force of the stop ripped Thomas' hands free of the stay and he hurtled forward for his head to crash against the railing.

When he opened his eyes the fury of the storm had passed, lashing the shores of Waitangi to the west and Kororareka and Matauwhi to the east on its southern rush. The wind persisted and the sea heaved, yet the *Brampton* sat as still as if anchored in a pond. Then there were light fingers brushing back the few lank strands that stood between him and baldness, probing gently at the gash that stretched across his forehead and a sigh of relief.

"Thank God."

She helped him sit and supported him as he held his throbbing head.

"What has happened?"

"See for yourself. Can you stand?"

He climbed to his feet and staggered to the railing. And looking down into the turbulent sea he could make out the rocks that held the *Brampton* secure.

"We are safe, Thomas. The ship is holed on both sides and below but she cannot sink. The rocks are holding us safe."

He held up his hands in thankful prayer, then turned his palms towards him, staring at the bloody striations left by the stay.

He stood steadily upon a heaving ocean and saw the miracle of their rescue.

"See," he pointed, "how God has reached up through the depths and cupped us in His palm."

The miracles kept mounting up. The sea settled with uncommon haste and longboats were lowered from the stricken vessel. Marsden was amongst the first to leave, finding safety and comparative comfort at Waitangi and then back to Kerikeri. But Thomas and his family remained on board. Their cabins had suffered no damage from the grounding – further evidence of a divine intervention – and they were cramped and uncomfortable but as the weather continued to lift they were able to spend most of their time on deck. Across the channel he could see their home at Matauwhi, waiting for them.

They remained on board for three days, and Thomas was not insensible of this further significance, while he communicated via letters with the chaplain. There were unconscionable delays and he understood the spite and strategy behind them. But he was beyond such petty concerns now; his downcast spirit had been raised on high by his Saviour and nothing could diminish him. There was no call for Jane's aid and she watched gloomily as he presented his demands and waited with him.

Support would be maintained, Marsden wrote, until further arrangements could be made, but only on the condition that the Kendalls return to Matauwhi.

The return was a triumphant one.

Who can remember what he was thinking at fifteen? We can recall the beliefs of earlier childhood, indeed, there are probably many of us who still hold to them, but the adolescent years seem to be a blur of thought and sensation. They must be the most frightening of times, when we start to know things we would sooner not know: death exists, it waits for me, I am unique which means that no one will ever truly understand me, I am alone. And these betrayals of innocence are added to by other betrayals: my parents are less than I had considered, my body grows and reacts to its own plan, I am too short, I am too tall, I am not not clever enough, I am too clever.

We grieve for these losses as we grieve for all loss, initially in denial and anger and for many of us this is as far as we get, for by the time we are resigned the time is gone.

Bursts of awareness come, if they come at all, after the event and we long for things to be simple and normal and behave as though they were.

So a fifteen year old might write in his journal, 'the last of the native females quitted the house by the desire of the Revd. Thos. Kendall.' He would not think it might have been, 'the bitch who had been as a sister to me, as a mother to my young brothers, as a friend to my mother, who became the whore of the man who calls himself my father was finally thrown out.'

For an adolescent, the refuge from uniqueness and separation is to join with other adolescents, to behave and appear like them and find being within a group. But the young men with whom Thomas Surfleet might have joined were not available to him. They were either preparing for war or were away, actively engaging in it. And it was not for him to be a warrior. Nor was there a sense of being or belonging within his family, for betrayal there had been complete.

When he was eight, the man who had been his friend and often his father had become his mother's lover and then had been bound in chains and sent away.

In her shame and disgrace his mother had gone away, too.

His father had been at war with all who might have been his friend; then he had gone away and he, too, had found shame and disgrace.

And the sins of the father (and the mother) shall be visited upon the heads of the children.

Thomas Surfleet did not know that he, more than anyone, more than Marsden and Butler and Hall and King and all the rest of them, had just cause for anger with his father. Anymore than his father had known that he had had just cause for anger with his mother.

But the anger was there and it was a turbulent, growing thing and he had no idea what to do with it. He had no idea that there was any alternative to being a dutiful son. So he honoured his parents and cuffed his brothers and ground his teeth in his sleep.

He wrote in his journal as a dutiful son, 'the Revd. Kendall and Mrs Kendall have recovered their belongings from the *Brampton* and are settled again in Matauwhi. At the behest of the Revd. Marsden, the Revd. Kendall is revising his work upon the Maori language.' He did not write, 'my father is in a continuous rage at being required to undo his work. Since her return to Matauwhi, my mother has become still and silent again. I hear her crying in the night.'

He wrote, 'Captain Brind has engaged me to make extensions to his house. To save time, I am staying there.' He did not write, 'Captain Brind's house is less than two miles away. I am staying there because I cannot bear to be at home.'

October 4

After driving the *Brampton* into the cup of his mighty hand, the Lord had fallen silent and the elation Thomas had known began to sour. He could not doubt that he had been redeemed, but it was a lonely redemption and it seemed that he was the only celebrant. Particularly galling was Jane's obvious disappointment and he had taxed her with it. She looked up, red-rimmed eyes in a drawn, pallid face and he had known before she spoke what she would say.

"I have nothing to complain of."

And when Marsden had set him the task of revising his work as a means of settling his ongoing debt, he had set his teeth and complied.

I am undoing what I have achieved. Altering te reo to accord with English pronunciation, anglicising and censoring the vocabulary to make it more chaste, less offensive to Marsden's tender sensibilities. It is stupid and spiteful and utterly wrong.

Now he cast down a handful of sheets on to the table and stood, like an errant schoolboy before an unforgiving headmaster.

Marsden ran his eyes down the first sheet. "It is a beginning," he said. "It is good that you have something useful to do while we await our passage back."

I will be calm, I will be civil, I will be dignified.

"As to that," he said, and Marsden's eyes narrowed, "it seems to me that if I am not to remain in New Zealand – and I cannot but think that there was a clear sign in the foundering of the *Brampton* …"

Marsden could not help himself. "Have a mind to pride, Mr Kendall," he warned. "To think that God destroyed a ship exclusively for your benefit …"

I don't think that. Yes, I do.

"… is of an order of pride that borders on blasphemy."

Thomas swallowed. "Thank you," he said, "now, as I was saying *(before I was so rudely interrupted)*, it seems to me that if I am not to remain in New Zealand, then it is the Society's duty and responsibility," Marsden's face blackened and he continued quickly, "to return me and my family to England."

"And yet," growled Marsden, "we have agreed otherwise. Your word –"

"My word was to board the *Brampton*. I did so. And," he intoned solemnly, "the Lord did cast the *Brampton* on to the rocks."

"The Lord did cast?" Marsden was incredulous. "Do you think you are a prophet now? I fear for your reason, Mr Kendall, I truly do."

"And I fear the Lord, I truly do."

The pride and the piety and the irrelevance of the last retort caught the chaplain short and the two men glared at one another in silence.

"Kia ora, nga mihinari."

They jumped in shock and turned and there at the door stood Hongi, gravely regarding them.

"E Hongi." Thomas hurried to him and they stood, hands on one another's shoulders, breaths intermingling. Marsden watched with a frustration that grew to anger as they broke into conversation. He made out 'Matene' several times and had no doubt that Kendall was already well into complaint. His own greeting was awkward, restrained and formal.

Damn Kendall. Once again he has me at a disadvantage.

His fears were well founded for over the next few weeks Thomas' demands expanded dramatically. Of course there was nothing miraculous in Hongi's return, he had in fact been back for over a week, but the timing of his arrival became a part of a grand pattern.

The elation he had known with the grounding of the *Brampton* returned, along with the depression of knowing there were none to share it with him. Marsden and the settlers were appalled, his family disappointed and the ships' officers and traders uninterested. Once again, his only support lay with the heathen.

But he was not deterred. In solitude he prayed and meditated and in solitude the message of the Lord became clear.

'I would be failing in my mission,' he wrote, 'were I to abandon the responsibilities the Lord has laid upon me ... to abide by your terms and leave New Zealand would be to defy the edicts of a Higher Authority ... I am called to Kerikeri to take up my Rightful Place among the missionaries and the Maori ...'

"Well, well," Henry Williams scratched his forehead, "he certainly seems to have the bit between his teeth."

"An apt metaphor." And a frivolous one, too, thought Marsden, but held his tongue. "The man has bolted beyond all reason."

"Well," the new Superintendant hesitated, "I suppose his position is understandable."

"What?" Marsden stared, "you think there is some sense in this?"

"No," Henry replied, "I didn't say that ..."

Are you correcting me?

"I said it was understandable. Flawed but understandable. It's like chess," he explained, "if you can't understand the logic behind your opponent's moves, whether they be flawed or not –"

"You'll lose the game," Marsden finished the sentence for him. "But this is not a game. It is a very serious business."

"Of course it is, which makes it all the more important to understand. And the first question is, is he serious?"

"I don't doubt it."

"Can he enforce his demands? If not directly, can he do it through Hongi?"

It was the same dilemma that Pratt and Woodd and Lee had faced in London three years before and the answer was much the same.

For another fortnight the same correspondence ran between Matauwhi and Kerikeri, the same demands, the same refusals. Then Thomas raised the stakes.

"Matene will have no satisfaction. He will expel me from my home and my friends and my mission."

Hongi patted his arm sympathetically. "He is wrong to do so," he said. "The offence is over, you have repented –"

"– And God knows I have been punished. Ah, it is good to speak with someone who can understand.

"And Butler will keep me from Kerikeri and my rightful place. He judges and mocks and he is no friend to Ngapuhi."

"Kendall has been to Hongi." James Kemp's tone was grave.

"He is poisoning Hongi against me," John Butler began furiously. "He will –"

"Please, Mr Butler," the chaplain raised a hand. "There are wider issues here. It is not just about you. Let us keep our personal feelings out of this."

"As it happens," said James, "Mr Butler has cause to be concerned. Hongi's message was that he is a bad man and that he should leave –"

"See! I told you!" Butler smacked the table in a sudden excess of rage and his glass jumped and toppled; wine poured across the minutes of their last meeting.

"Damn it!" Marsden forgot his most recent advice. "Kendall hardly needs to defame you; your own lack of control speaks for itself."

James took out a grubby handkerchief and mopped up the wine in silence while Marsden and Butler glared at one another and Henry Williams shook his head in disbelief.

"And that was it! That was the extent of his reaction. To revile me for being upset by Kendall's poison. Kendall defies him on all counts – the whoreson is now speaking of moving here – and all Marsden can do is tell me to control myself." Butler raised his glass to the officers gathered in the *Dragon's* mess. "Curse him and all like him."

He drank alone.

Pater Noster Valley
Matauwhi
New Zealand
22.11.1823

Dear Susannah,

I am so upset I think I may be going Mad. Which would not be surprising because everyone else is. Father is becoming quite Strange and Wild, he mumbles to himself and says he is talking to God because no one else will listen. He has become determined to move us all to Kerikeri to live at the mission there. But they don't want him there, Susannah, they Hate Father and all of us, too. But he says it is the Will of God and the Will of Hongi, too. And he says that if they won't give us provisions, then he will set us down outside the store at Kerikeri and we will all Starve together! He wrote this in a letter to the Reverend Marsden, I know he wrote it because he read it aloud to Mother and she cried and he shouted and then Thomas Surfleet became angry, too.

It is too much for me, Susannah. When we planning to move to Australia I was so happy, we would be together again and away from all this, back with our own kind. I would have you, I thought and other friends and perhaps. Anyway now we must stay and it will be worse than before. At least when we moved here it was more peaceful and Mother got better. But now she is like she was before but worse because she us starting to get angry, too.

And Father gets angry and unhappy and then he becomes happy but it is the wrong kind of happy. When Mr Marsden returned to Sydney, he took Mr Butler with him. Father watched them sail out through his eyeglass and he danced and sang and then he became drunk, too.

He said it was the will of God and that Hongi would come for us and take us all to live in Mr Butler's house even though Mr Williams, he's the new Superintendant and all the other settlers said we may not. He said he didn't care what they thought, they were only cooks and then Mother got angry and said we would starve and he said no, we wouldn't because he had gone to Kerikeri after Mr Marsden had left to get us provisions and when he got there Mr Kemp refused him but Father insisted and then Mr Kemp offered to sell him provisions and Father got angry and then Mr Kemp said he could have whatever he liked. He said that proved God was looking after us and mother said no it didn't, it only proved the settlers were afraid of what Hongi might do. And Father said that proved Hongi was an agent of God and Mother said that it only proved the settlers thought he was a bloodthirsty, unpredictable savage and then Father became really angry and I thought he might strike Mother. Then Thomas Surfleet jumped up and said if he laid a hand on Mother he would strike him down and Father yelled and Thomas Surfleet yelled and

The remaining words on the page were lost in a blur where tears and ink had run together.

CHAPTER 54

December 9

"E Hongi, tell me of the taking of Mokoia."

"E Rakau, I have already told you."

"I know, and it is a fine tale. Tell me again."

"We paddled down the east coast past Motiti Island to Waihi where we entered the Pongakawa Stream. It is a narrow, twisting thing and often we had to lift and carry our great waka across shallows and around bends. Then we came to Lake Rotoehu, across that and into bush; now there was work for our axes, widening the path, and then the way was clear, from Lake Rotoiti to Lake Rotorua.

"And there was Mokoia, sitting in the middle of the lake and there was Te Arawa, waiting for us.

"We camped on the shore that night and planned our attack. We would paddle in as a flying wedge; I would take the front, Te Wera Hauraki and Pomare would lead the middle and the rest would bring up the rear.

Our cause was just and strong for two of Te Arawa tribes, Tuhourangi and Ngati Whakaue had treacherously taken the life of Paeoterangi, a Ngapuhi rangatira."

"I knew Paeoterangi. Tell me about Aokapurangi."

"Ah yes, Aokapurangi, wife to Te Wera. Her blood is from the Tapuika hapu of Te Arawa and her kinsman, Hikairo, was on Mokoia with her people.

"She spoke to the chiefs, saying that her kin had taken no part in the killing of Paeoterangi and asked that we spare them. Te Koki and

Tawaewae who were most closely related to Paeoterangi assented to her plea and Te Wera said that she should go to Mokoia to advise Hikairo to stay away from the fighting."

"Did he agree?"

"You know he did not. Hikairo is a man of honour, a warrior. He would not stand by and leave his kin alone. It was no less than we would have expected but we did not know it then, for Aokapurangi stayed on Mokoia.

"We took our rest and rose with Ra. Ah, it was a good day for battle, e Rakau; you could feel the wildness in it, the spirits were strong and as we crossed the lake Turikatuku, my first wife, my warrior wife called out to them to calm the waters. But Te Arawa called, too, to their spirits, to the taniwha of their lake and they stirred the waters and grew it into waves. And they called upon the winds of Tawhiri to blow upon the waters and make them wilder. And the spirits of the wind and the taniwha of the lake hearkened to them and our waka were in danger of being overturned. But above it all, across the winds and the waves you could hear Turikatuku and her voice was high and keen and wild and I raised up the jawbone of Mahia, our ancestor, and Te Kemara and Taonui joined their voices to Turikatuku. And we prevailed and the waters stilled and we flew on.

"We flew in a great wedge and my waka was in the forefront. I stood to look back at those following to make sure they had kept their line when Te Arawa fired their only musket. There was a great blow to my head and I was flung into the waka. But you know, because I have shown you the dent in the helmet, how the king of England saved my life.

"We drew our waka up to the shore and there they were, Te Arawa, lined up and waiting for us. We beached our waka and climbed out while they waited. We took our position and primed our muskets and still they waited."

"They were most considerate."

"Challenges were thrown down and accepted, all with due tika and then they charged and fell before our muskets. Three times they charged and three times they fell in great numbers. Some survived the fire and broke into our lines and then Ngapuhi fell, too.

"But our victory was never in doubt.

"They fled from us, running back to their village and we pursued them. And when we reached the village, ah, what a sight awaited us."

"Tell me what you saw."

"There stood Tamatekapua, their whare nui and there, standing upon the backbone, holding to the ancestor was Aokapurangi. Over the shouting and the roaring of the guns we could hear her calling to her hapu.

"'Haere mai, come within and you will be saved.'

"Her people poured in three hundred of them and they were saved."

"It is an astonishing thing."

"Ae, that Ngapuhi warriors, men whose blood was up, caught in the rage of warfare, should have hearkened to a single woman's voice and not pursued their foe. But so it was.

"We sat down to determine how we would finish the business and the four chiefs who were most closely related to Paeoterangi presented their opinions. Te Wera Hauraki, husband to Aokapurangi, spoke for peace and the three others, Pomare, Te Koki and Tawaewae concurred. Then we sent for Hikairo to confirm the agreement.

"Hikairo spoke to Ngapuhi, saying, 'Your cause for utu was just, for Te Arawa slew Paeoterangi and although it was not my hapu that took his life we are kin to those who did. And when, through my sister Aokapurangi, you offered to spare us I declined; I could not have stood to one side and watched my bretheren battle.'"

"Noble sentiments."

"Ae, he went on to say, 'And so, Ngapuhi, I acknowledge that the fault lay with us. And it has cost us dearly in lives and mana. Now I ask, have you had satisfaction enough?'

"We agreed that we had utu and peace was established. We stayed with Te Arawa for two and a half weeks before returning home."

"It is a fine story," said Rakau, "and one that will be long remembered, for there is much mana in it." Then he said, "Turning to matters of much less mana, have the missionaries resolved their differences?"

Hongi smiled. "How would it be," he asked, "if, instead of squabbling like children and making threats they cannot keep, they settled the matter like men?" His smile grew broader. "I would love to see that," he said, "Pata and Keni with taiaha or swords or whatever they chose – their bare hands – facing up to one another."

"It would be a fine sight."

"But that is not the way they do it. So I instructed Matene to take Pata away and he has done my bidding. Now Keni wants to move into his home but the others will not have it and the new rangatira, Wiremu, has said they will resist his return and if it is forced upon them they will leave."

"What will you do?"

"Although Keni is my friend, I see no point in antagonising the others. I also can't understand why he would wish to live among people who hate him."

"He wants them to love him."

"I can't understand that, either."

"Neither can I, but I believe that it is so."

"Anyway, I would not wish to see them leave and I particularly would not wish to see them take their trade and skills to another iwi."

"Te Wera Hauraki would love to have them. And Pomare, too."

"Well, they're not going to get them. So Keni can stay at Matauwhi, I do not want him leaving, either, and the others will stay at Kerikeri under my protection."

And so the question Rakau had put to Marsden – 'is Hongi that much a wiser man than you are?' – was answered.

Life settled back into a regular routine and remained that way after Hongi left for war two months later.

CHAPTER 55

April 1824

A year has gone by and at last the house is being enlarged. The family will benefit from the new space but it is not being done for them. It is done for the men who spend their lives at sea away from a properly mediated communion with their god. Here they may worship, knowing that the Word is brought to them by a consecrated priest. Here they may look to the salvation of their souls.

The priest's wife sat at a western window and looked down upon the bay, upon a small canoe that bobbed gently on the placid waters. Through an eyeglass she could see the boys clearly, Joseph in the stern, Lawrence and John ahead, each holding to his line. It was a game and a lesson that Joseph took seriously and a glint of silver scales told that he was teaching his brothers well. It was ironic, she mused, that here, in a savage country at the ends of the earth, unsupervised in a home-made canoe and half a mile from shore, they were probably a good deal safer than they would have been playing in the streets of London. Sitting at the kitchen table, Samuel was engrossed in his art. With the care and precision of a tohunga tapping in the spirals of a moko, he drew the swirls of a giant whirlpool. A carved stern that might have belonged to Hongi's waka or to the ship of a Grecian hero was being drawn into the whirling depths. An encyclopaedia lay open beside him; it was his source for the maelstrom of Charybodis as it was his father's for the theories of Pythagoras that he twisted and knotted through the beliefs of the Christians and the Maori. The last child, Edward, now two, slept on a flax mat. For all that his father had gone to great lengths to baptise him, he would not disclose for whom the boy was named. Jane wondered whether he knew.

These were now the last of her children living here: Elizabeth was staying with the Weslyan missionary Nathaniel Turner in Whangaroa, Basil was away at sea, serving as a cabin hand, Susannah was still in New South Wales and now Thomas Surfleet was gone far away, to London to serve as apprentice to a carpenter. She missed him and was glad that he was gone.

Children start by loving their parents.

After a time they come to judge them.

Rarely, if ever, do they forgive them.

Flippant perhaps, but true enough of Thomas Surfleet. Jane had watched his resentment grow and neither had known what to do with it. Like his father, like all of them, he was held within a web of belief that kept him mute. He competed furiously, silently with Thomas. When building the chapel at Bethel, he had driven himself to outlast and outperform his father. On one occasion they had carried a heavy beam between them and the boy had thought that his muscles might burst under the strain. But he had said nothing and had kept his face still and when at last his father had lowered his end, he had silently exulted. And then been afraid.

At last he had found a choice he could believe in and when Thomas and Jane had clashed over the move to Kerikeri he had found his part. And for all her own anger, Jane had seen the culmination in him and had stepped between and held him safe from himself. Soon after he had left for England. Jane had wept to see him go and had felt a final wall come down. She had not closed down as she had before but some of the old habits had returned.

Well done, Jane, you have made it through another day.

She rose and stretched and crossed the room to look over Samuel's shoulder, along a thin, pale arm to delicate fingers. The outline of the drowning ship was clear but she knew he would spend hours more upon it, completing every last detail. A little further off stood his father's desk, laden with papers in the same cramped hand. She had taken them up once, perhaps hoping to find a meaning there that might give a reason for the suffering. But there was none, or at least none that she could find.

These are the First Principles from which man derives his Origin; namely the Breath of Life or fishing line, Likeness or the fishhook, and the Knowledge or the bait... man is dead as to past time and only lives in present time ... the First and Last only eats or more properly preserves his own dung. He is the Keeper of his own Existence ... the First State is literally a state of Death or an Universe a field of skulls ... the ngarara is the Keeper or Coverer of the Eternal Word in the First State ... he exists upon his own tail ... the vowel 'a' signifies Universal Existence ... the vowel 'i' is the vital part of the body ... it is remarkable indeed that the sound of the vowel 'o' from whence originates the idea of the Wisdom of the First and Last exactly agrees with the revolving of the Tongue or the act of Speaking ...

Years before this lack of meaning would have been further evidence of her own lack of understanding – *I am a simple woman, Mr Hall, not educated like you and my husband, like all you men* – but it had since become clear that no one else, even the brilliant Professor Lee, could make sense of it, either; and she had begun to wonder whether Thomas might be mad. Not that such a diagnosis would make any difference to her life. They survived quite comfortably, even more than comfortably. In a foolish moment Thomas had bragged to Henry Williams that he took a considerably better income from the ships' captains than he had ever taken from the CMS. Since then he had been obliged to purchase his provisions. So she lived as the wife of a successful businessman who thought he was a priest. Ah, well ...

She was taken from her reverie by a knock at the door and turned to see Tungaroa standing there; flax skirt, bare feet and a rough, unwashed calico shirt that served warmth rather than modesty, a flax basket hanging over her shoulder. Jane felt a flush of pleasure that was followed by a sudden anxiety.

"Your father, he is..?"

"Rakau is well," replied Tungaroa. She shrugged. "That is, he lives."

"He is in pain?"

"Sometimes there is pain, but Keni's medicine mostly keeps the atua still." She smiled. "He is happy enough, e Heini, but he will be pleased to be gone. It is his time." She crossed to the table where Samuel remained engrossed and ruffled the towelled locks. "Kia ora, Hamuera," she said, "e pehea ana koe?"

The boy looked up with a wide smile. "Tungaroa," he exclaimed, "pai ana ahau. Titiro," he pointed to his drawing and began an elaborate explanation. Jane smiled and went into the kitchen.

Later Samuel was back into the realm of Charybodis while Jane and Tungaroa sat by the window and drank tea.

"I have something for you." She reached into her basket and took out a letter.

Jane took it and turned it over in her hand. "Thank you," she said, "but you needn't have taken the trouble. Thomas could have collected it with the rest of the mail."

"It was sent to me," said Tungaroa, "to bring to you. It is not for Keni." She cocked her head quizzically. "It is for you. It is from Francis Hall."

Jane set her cup down on the window sill and her hand was shaking. "I see," she said.

"Are you going to open it?"

Jane shook her head and swallowed. "I don't know," she began.

"Here," Tungaroa took the letter and broke the seal. "Take it outside and read it," she said. "I will sit with Hamuera and watch him draw."

Port Jackson
March 24 1824
Dear Mrs Kendall,

I recall that when you asked me to discover the whereabouts and welfare of your former servant, Richard Stockwell you said that I might not find it an Agreeable Task. I gave that no thought and I gave you my word. And when I arrived in Port Jackson, lost and dispirited, it became something of a mission to distract me from my sorry Circumstances. Soon I found that my search brought with it Deceit and Evasion and I quickly saw that I would have been Wiser to have declined. It became so obvious that my only Concern was how I had become Embroiled in the first place. I can only think that there is an Insidious Element at work in that land that seduces men from their Apprehension of God's Will.

I have gained the information that you require and I have learned a lot more besides along the way. And while my Misgivings remain – this is not a Proper Curiosity for you to entertain nor for me to gratify – yet some Good may come of it. For my own part, the Lord has vouchsafed me a greater understanding of my Weaknesses and Failings. He has taken the Scales from my eyes that I may see my way clear to being His Instrument. Not my Will but Thine, O Lord, be done.

I am very conscious that this is not an Appropriate Correspondence and I will own that I am fearful of the Consequences of its Discovery. But I gave my word and 'though it was given in Wilfulness and Ignorance I will stand by it. I have taken extracts from my Journal pertaining to Stockwell along with other matters relevant to my new Understanding. It is my Prayer that you may learn from this as I have done and put the matter behind you once and for all.

This will be my Final Corresespondence.

Your Brother in Christ
Francis Hall.

Jane's lip curled. Poor Francis, she thought, another good man seduced by this wicked land. Pompous ass. Then she started as Tungaroa spoke in her ear. "Hamuera and I are going down to the beach to wait for the boys. He is warmly dressed and the exercise will do him good." Jane nodded absently and watched them head down the hill. Then she gathered up the pages and walked back into the house. She went to the wine cabinet and poured herself a generous port, then settled at the kitchen table to return to the revelation of St Francis.

17 May 1823

I found Richard Stockwell in a tavern. Or rather, he found me. I had quite needlessly provoked one man and was about to be attacked by another, a big man who was clearly intent upon doing me damage. At first I was quite afraid, although I did not think to run, but as he drew closer and I knew that I would have to fight I felt a sudden fury pour through me, a cleansing thing, an utter purity of intention and I was elated, exulted and I

Anyway Richard forestalled the attack, laying a hand upon his shoulder, you must not fight, it is wrong to fight, but the fellow leaped forward, breaking Richard's grip, flying towards me. I suppose I could have avoided him but I needed to hit him and so I did. It was a lucky blow, catching him flush upon the point of his chin and he fell unconscious. And that was when Richard saved my Life. For I was not content with the damage I had done and I stepped over to where the man lay. I believe I would have stamped upon his head but Richard caught me and bustled me outside.

He led me away from the tavern, saying it would be dangerous to return. I had just enough sense to ask him his name although of course I already knew it. I began to tell him of my Mission but he politely interrupted me, he is a most courteous man, to say that he needed to be back about his business. He told me his place of employment and we agreed to meet later in the week. Then I went home where my landlady exclaimed at my bruised hand and I told more Lies.

May 23

Richard works at a bakery, helping at the ovens and delivering the bread in a handcart for the closer calls and in a pony trap for those further away. I told him of my mission and he nodded politely but said nothing. I asked him if he had any messages for Mrs Kendall or any other members of the family and he shook his head. I asked him if he held any Resentment and he said no. I believe him. He seems to be a man entirely without Guile or Malice. I don't know if this reflects a pure soul or whether he just can't be bothered to care.

Richard has a second job: at the tavern where we met, keeping the peace. Evidently he is very good at it and is respected by the proprietor and patrons. It is also very dangerous work. I told him, 'sooner or later, you will come across someone who will not respond to your strength or your gentleness. There will be a man who envies your reputation or knows how to fight or will use a weapon or will take you unawares.' He nodded his agreement – I am sure he has heard the argument a score of times – and said he thought it was probable. He does not seem to be much interested in the Future.

May 26

At luncheon today the Reverend Winchester invited me to take a more Active Part in Church matters. I was, he said kindly, being wasted in my more menial occupation. Would he have been so generous in his assessment had he known of my Shameful Behaviour at the tavern? But I could not decline and that very afternoon I called upon Mrs Dunning, a most pious lady. Any Apprehensions I had were quickly dispelled: the good lady was in no need of advice or Spiritual

Counsel. Quite to the contrary, she had a good deal of both to offer me along with much information pertaining to her Life and Opinions. At the close of the visit, she thanked me for coming and assured me that her Spirits had been quite Uplifted.

I cannot stop thinking about Richard Stockwell and how close I could have come to Murder. It is a conundrum. Had I not been seeking him out I would not have been in that place and could have saved myself much Anxiety and Reproach. Had I not been there I might never have known how close I am to Cain. It seems to me that I am bound to do something with that Knowledge.

May 29

I met with Richard this afternoon after he had completed his rounds. Perhaps he is getting used to me for I was able to coax him into longer conversation.

He is, he assures me, quite content in his present occupations. Evidently his father was a Baker and perhaps the work brings back memories of a more Agreeable Time. He shrugged at that and said that he liked the smell of fresh bread. And he likes the delivery, counting out the loaves til all are gone.

I painted the prospect of taking up his allotment in the rosiest of terms and he agreed that it would be very fine to have his own house and land. But, he said, I have a very nice room and a comfortable bed at Mrs Johnson's and she is very pleased with the garden I am making.

I made the same Argument about the dangers of his work at the tavern and he made the same response. I asked him if he was so Reconciled to his own Death and he said that he supposed he was.

I could now send back this information and have the business over and done with. But I delay.

June 3

A surprising visit from the Reverend Marsden. I must own that when I saw him last – some months ago now – I did not feel kindly Disposed towards him. Nor did he seem to entertain much regard for my Person or Position. However on this occasion he seemed in a much kinder frame of mind. He had recently met *with Mrs Dunning who had evidently been generous in her opinion of me and in her assistance to his Orphanage. He urged me to 'put myself about more'.*

He spoke at length about the mission in New Zealand. It would seem that relationships continue to deteriorate on all sides and he asked me if I would put together my Impressions of the settlements for the CMS. "A more Level and Dispassionate view,' he said, 'could be invaluable.' He asked, asked, mind you, if I would run these impressions by him before forwarding them.

I am not so naïve as I was not to see the Benefits in both tasks for Mr Marsden, but I am grateful, too. I feel the stirring of a sense of Purpose and Usefulness.

He also advised that he had received word from the CMS, dismissing Mr Kendall from its Service. He had so advised the missionaries but would be sailing to New Zealand himself, when he had the time and opportunity, to deliver the decision personally. 'If I want the matter properly settled,' he said, 'I can see that I will have to do it myself.'

June 12

Hard upon the heels, it seems, of Mr Marsden's visit, I have received a letter from Mr Kendall – a most Disjointed Affair. I think it must have been written over a period of days, if not longer, for the mood shifts from Doubt and Self-reproach, he does not say that he knows of his dismissal but the mood suggests he does, to a positive view in which he sees himself as a Trusted and Valuable Servant of the Society. Much of the letter is given to explaining the Spiritual Beliefs of the Maori and even after several readings I can make little sense of it.

The visit and the letter have exacerbated my Reluctance to write to Mrs Kendall. More and more I perceive that it was, at best, a Foolish Undertaking. And how am I to communicate with her? Her husband would be rightfully entitled to enquire after a letter's contents and I do not care to guess at his Reaction.

Perhaps it would be wiser to wait. Mr Marsden has said that the family will be returning to New South Wales; then I could quite properly call upon her and briefly advise her of what she wishes to know without committing myself to paper.

There is an Ugly Feel to the whole wretched business.

June 24

I don't know why I continue to keep in contact with Richard Stockwell. He has no Insights, no useful Perspectives of life in New Zealand, he is illiterate and uneducated and for his own part prefers silence. He answers my questions only because he is polite.

I asked him of his Liaison with Mrs Kendall and he called it sin. I asked him if he had repented and he said, "I know I have done wrong. Is that Repentance?" I asked him if Hated what he had done and he said he had Enjoyed it at the time. I asked him whether he ever wished to repeat the act or whether he was ever Tempted and he said "no." I asked whether he might take a wife that he could enjoy the act with the Blessing of God and he said, "no." I asked whether he would ever wish to have children and he smiled and said, "yes." I asked whether he believed himself Forgiven, whether he had forgiven himself and he said that he did not know what Forgiveness meant. Then I remembered Mrs Kendall saying the same thing and my mind went Blank.

He has owned his sin and has been punished. He says his prayers and goes to Church and does no man harm. Why am I so Unsettled by him?

July 16

I have, following Mr Marsden's Advice, been putting myself about. The Circumstances of my return from New Zealand seem to be less of a Consideration now – perhaps I was making too much of it in the first place - and I am pleased to find new and different ways in which I may serve. I have been much Engaged in Correspondence.

I am advised that Mr Marsden will shortly be leaving for Kerikeri to finalise Matters there. I shall hold all Communication in abeyance until the outcome.

November 22

I ran into Richard Stockwell in the High Street today and we paused for the briefest of Conversations. His life has in no wise changed since last I saw him and there is no Expectation that it will. Therer seems little point in maintaining Contact.

Messrs Marsden, Butler and Leigh returned from New Zealand with a sorrowful tale of Mr Kendall's Decline and Defiance. At the same time I received a letter from Mr Kendall which also makes for sorrowful reading. I must own that I am Hard Pressed to maintain the Christian Charity which I know I owe him. The man speaks of Temptation as though he were the only one ever to have Endured it. There is Pride at work here – the idea that he has been singled out by the Adversary for Particular Attention. He has sunk again into the Antinomian Heresy that his fall was a part of a Divine Plan that he might Rise the higher for it. And so, to use a common metaphor, he will have his cake and eat it, too.

I fled from a loss of Hope, yes, and from Temptation, too, and I was ashamed. And he is not nor ever will be.

We pray to God to lead us not into temptation and I cannot help but think that Kendall went looking for it.

I have written back, urging reflection, moderation and obedience; casting words into a Tempest.

March 21 1824

And now the matter is Done. There is no more to be written and the only question is, how do I communicate?

Tungaroa. There is something Awful here – using the husband's mistress to carry word to the wife of her lover. But there is no one else. No one else who can understand the original kindness of my Intention and not be outraged by the Wronfulness of it.

Tungaroa. She lit a part of me I would sooner have remained in Darkness. He lives with the Murderer and I will put them both away. I have learned more than I was Supposed to know and I will put that Knowledge away. I will not be Curious.

Richard Stockwell was killed last Saturday night in a tavern brawl by a single knife thrust through the Heart. In all the Confusion it has not been ascertained who did the Deed or why he did it. It might even have been an Accident – taking a blow intended for someone else.

A Service was held at the Port Jackson Chapel with the Reverend Winchester officiating. A modest gathering attended: His Employer and fellow-workers from the Bakery and their Families, the Proprietor from the tavern and his Family and a number of patrons. No mention was made of his Past – that he was a Thief and a Fornicator and a man who had Betrayed his Master. The Reverend

Winchester, acting upon the information that he had, spoke of one who loved God and served Man.

May God forgive him his sins and let him rest in Peace.

I will not speak of him again.

Tungaroa and the boys found her holding to the last page and staring out the western window. Her eyes were dry but her face was set and distant and Tungaroa hurried the boys away to clean and prepare the fish. Later she sat with Jane.

"He's dead," said Jane briefly, then, before Tungaroa could respond, she asked, "Will you be writing back to Mr Hall?"

"Ae," Tungaroa nodded. "He made some strange remarks. He said –"

"No," Jane held up a hand. "I already know more than enough. But when you reply, would you convey a message for me?"

"Of course. What is it?"

"Tell him," said Jane, "that it is finished."

CHAPTER 56

Autumn fades almost imperceptibly into winter here and it is only as you hug your shoulders and slip into your coat for the first time that you recognise that something has gone and something else has come along. As people do when they see that age is here or that love is gone. And then it is hard to remember when it was otherwise.

So they lived through the winter as they had lived through spring and nothing was changed.

The businessman who thought he was a priest plied his trade and prospered and preached and baptised and read the banns and said the last rites and it was all a part of the same enduring whole. The distance between him and his wife was a palpable thing now. She had publically defied his intention to move to Kerikeri, 'he must not take a step,' she had said to Hongi and his eldest son had sided with her. 'I have nothing to complain of' was sullen where it had been resigned and now it carried a regular qualification. *This is not the place to raise our children. We need to be away.*

With Butler gone, he reached out to the new man at Kerikeri. On more than one occasion Henry Williams would look up from his pulpit to see the renegade amongst his congregation. His heart went out to Kendall, 'he has been greatly tried and greatly punished,' he wrote but he could not trust him. And when Kendall complained of his straitened circumstances and then boasted of the income he was taking from the ships, he knew that he was wise to do so. So when Kendall invited him to Matauwhi to join in service, he refused. He could sympathise with him and see the good that Marsden could not see, but he would not offer him access to the settlement.

Throughout the winter Thomas' loneliness had grown. He wrote at length to the CMS, pleading his changed circumstances but they would not hear him. Letters to Hassell and Hall and others brought answers but they all said the same thing and none was encouraging. And William Brind was gone to sea.

Rakau was leaving him, too. He visited Rangihoua rarely for he was reluctant to take the chance of running into William Hall or John King; the school house stood as a mute reproach and often not so mute because now King was taking lessons there. There were new people in his house.

Rakau was still there but was old and frail and his life was turning more and more inwards. Like Susanna in her last days, he seemed to have no time for Thomas; they no longer shared a space.

And then spring had become summer and he was in flight again, sailing to Whangaroa in his new vessel to meet with the Reverend William White and take him to Thames. She was named *The Industry* but *The Spiteful* might have been a more apt title. For when Thomas was not approaching the missionaries, contritely, seeking admission to their circle, he was reacting to their rejection with reproach and competition. Such was the birth of *The Industry*. Thomas had viewed the building of the new settlement vessel, had mocked it and encouraged Ngapuhi to join him in his mockery and then, in customary haste, had laid the keel for his own, larger vessel.

Like everything else, she could have been so much better, but she sailed well enough and for the moment, as she rode at anchor in the shelter of a kindly bay, she was all that he needed.

The two apostles took their ease upon a broad deck, drinking their rum and telling their stories.

"It is difficult to conceive," said the Reverend White, "as we sit here in peace and solitude in the midst of such beauty," he gestured towards the shore where the breaking of the little waves spread silver lace along the sand, "that savagery and ignorance are so close at home."

"And yet," answered the Reverend Kendall, "it is so. In fact," he emptied his glass and held up a portentous finger, "they are closer than that. In this Eden there are no serpents. The Adversary has found more subtle forms."

"Indeed. There is a, what?" William paused, then continued slowly, "a pervasive allure? Am I being absurd?"

"You are not," said Thomas solemnly. "There is such a richness and bounty in the land and the sea that there is no particular call to industry or thrift. And the climate is so benign that warm and modest clothing and sturdy housing are almost a luxury. It is a world that whispers pleasure."

"Aye," William took his mood, "it has whispered to me."

"And to me. And I hearkened to it."

They filled their glasses and hearkened a little further. Then William said, "I think I can understand."

"Indeed? Then you would be the first to do so."

"Will you tell me how it was?"

Thomas considered. He was, he knew, already drunk and therefore bolder than he ought to be. But it also dawned upon him that he had never spoken directly of the deed, of how it had begun. "It was a night such as this," he said, "at," suddenly he was reluctant to say, "at a spot such as this. I sat in the shadows there," he pointed, "and she came out of the shadows there. She walked into the moonlight and she shed her clothes upon the sand and she walked into the sea."

"Like Bathsheeba upon the roof."

"Precisely like Bathsheeba. She swam out to about where we are anchored, then she swam back. She stood in the shallows in the moonlight and she cast back her hair –"

"And she possessed you."

"Yes." Thomas stared. "There was a kind of possession. I rose without thought or will and I walked to her."

"She was not alarmed? She did not cry out?"

"Not at all. She spoke my name and smiled at me."

"Did she cover herself?"

"Nor that neither. Her hands were by her sides."

"I can picture it," said William and Thomas felt a flush of resentment. "You did not go seeking her, she came to you and in that way and in that setting," he shook his head, "I cannot see how a saint could have remained unmoved."

The resentment passed and Thomas nodded. "Thank you," he said. "It is a comfort to speak with one who can understand."

"They are not men," said William White, "who would condemn you for your part." He bowed his head. "I, too, have been called to sin and was hard put to withstand it."

Long into the evening they discussed the ways in which the Adversary laid snares for righteous men, such snares as had taken Thomas and would soon take William. They were weak men, they owned it, they could not stand without support; only in God's hands could they be safe from themselves.

And later, as his friend lay snoring where he had sat, Thomas continued the train of thought.

All my earthly supports are gone; yet this world is too much with me… Beneath my feet the waters are inviting and Tangaroa whispers, 'shed your clothes and come into me.' Then Tangaroa becomes Tungaroa and the message is the same. And were Hongi to say, 'shed your clothes and come to war with me,' I would of course deny him. But …

The serpent is become a fish, te ika a Maui, the leviathan that a god drew from the ocean. It never died; even after Maui's brothers tried to divide it, it writhed beneath their blows and grew mountains and valleys. It is still a living thing and it is always whispering to me. And there are times, many times, when the whispers have muffled the word of my God and the wisdom of my fellows.

If I lose myself again, I may lose myself forever.

Speak to me, O Lord; teach me how to serve Thee and how to save myself.

Two nights later it seemed to Thomas that God had heard his prayer and was giving His reply.

He chose an unlikely mouthpiece. Captain James Florance was a plain-spoken, no-nonsense Protestant Irishman, the kind of fellow inclined to call a spade a bloody shovel. But he was a pious Christian, too, and Thomas had had no qualms when Basil had signed on as cabin boy for a journey along the east coast. The *Industry* had caught up with the *St Patrick* in the Firth of Thames and had moored alongside her. Now the two captains were relaxing together in the *St Patrick's* spacious quarters.

"He's a good lad, your boy," said Captain Florance, gesturing at a blushing Basil, hovering in attendance. "Don't have too much to say for himself and that's a fine quality in a sailor, or in any man for that matter. I'd recommend him for any service."

"Thank you," Thomas smiled at his son's bowed head. "I have always sought to instruct him in the ways of piety and industry."

"Well, you've made a good job of it. Off you go now, lad. Your father and I can manage the bottle." He nodded after the closing door. "What are your plans for him?"

Thomas was obliged to own that he had none.

"Indeed," tutted Captain Florance as he filled their glasses. "That's no good. Boy needs a career or a trade. Can't just fritter about. Have you thought he might follow you into the clergy?"

Again Thomas was obliged to own that none of his sons had shown any particular leaning towards the cloth. He did not add that his own history was unlikely to gain them any preferment, should they have been so inclined.

This was Jane's theme – *what kind of a future are we preparing for them?* – and Thomas was beginning to yield to it.

Several glasses later he was more candid. "I know," he said sadly, "that I have become something of an outsider here, *I am a fallen man,* and I fear that my children will carry that stain."

"Well then," said Florance simply, "take 'em somewhere else."

It was not a new thought but still Thomas shrank from it.

"It is not such a simple matter," he began.

"Why not? You're not tied here." He jabbed a finger. "You said yourself you're not wanted."

I never said that.

"So what's to stop you just selling up and leaving?"

"Ngapuhi might not let me."

"How will they stop you? By force?"

"Perhaps."

"Then you'll need to sneak away when they're not looking."

"Hongi will be offended."

Captain Florance set down his glass with a thump. "Listen to yourself, man," he growled. "You would set the well-being of your family beneath the sensibilities of a savage? Tell me straight, why do you hesitate?"

Thomas shook his head. "I must serve God," he whispered.

"There are other ways to serve. Do you think the clergy have a monopoly?"

"No," Thomas was very quiet, "no, I don't think that. But it is the only way I know. I was born for it."

Captain Florance scratched his head. "I see," he said, then correcting himself, "no, I don't see. But I believe that is what you think."

"Thank you."

They spoke of other things then, of the captain's son, Thomas, who was presently serving with his father on the *St Patrick*, of his wife and other children, of his mother and ailing father who would be dead before he saw him again, of his love for his home and his love for the sea. And Thomas heard the tenderness in his voice and he thought of the cold distance that stood between himself and his wife, of his son in England and his daughter in Australia and of the uncertain future he was mapping for them all.

This is not the place to raise our children. We need to be away.

Captain Florance's voice was at a remove now, blending with creaking of his ship and he stared into his glass and whispered to it, "we must be away."

Florance broke off his speech and watched him carefully. Then he said, "Are you partial to where you you may serve? Because," continuing before Thomas could answer, "I know of a settlement, an English one, that is looking for a priest

"Valparaiso," said Thomas. "It is Spanish for Paradise Valley, it's in Chile on the west coast of South America at the same latitude as New Zealand so the climates are similar." He spoke dully like a schoolboy reciting a lesson. "It is a very popular harbour with a growing English population. Not many, but enough for a consulate, not enough for a priest to minister to them."

"And they will appoint you?" Jane was torn between hope and incredulity.

"I don't know. Captain Florance said he thought they would. There is also a call for a school teacher. But nothing is certain."

"So we just pack up everything, the children and sail to South America on the chance that there may be a post for you?"

"I don't know. I suppose I could write, inquiring –"

"It would be months before we'd get a reply." Jane pushed back her chair and started circling the living room while Thomas stared ahead. "And what happens if we go and there is no position there?"

"I don't know."

Thoughts crowded in and she held her hands to her temples as though to keep them still. Another sprang out.

"You would be engaged to preach to the English, to teach their children? There is no call for missions to the natives?"

"The position would be for the English only."

She gave up on sleep some time after midnight, pulled on her robe and headed down to the beach. There she sat and with a twig scored points into the sand.

Item: the wretched suddenness of it all. Like every other opportunity, every other move it had come out of the blue, it was huge and there was little time to weigh the consequences. Very well, this is not a matter for consideration, there are no pros or cons here, move on.

Item: it was clear that Thomas was sinking into the same hopeless lethargy that had consumed him prior to the sailing of the *Brampton*. Score that as a good thing, but bear in mind that any little thing, some new sign from the Lord might spin him into sabotage.

Item: consider the worst scenario. They sail to Valparaiso and there is nothing for them. All alone, with no support and seven children to care for. No, strike that. Elizabeth is a woman now and can do a woman's work and Basil had impressed Captain Florance with his capacity and industry. So: four adults and five children, albeit one a toddler and one an invalid. Not such an intimidating equation. And they would not be stranded there. There was sufficient funding to move again, to England, unlikely, or Australia where there were plenty of prospects. And Susannah.

Item: item three is not the worst scenario. The worst scenario would be to stay here.

The next morning Thomas trudged off miserably to Kororareka to do whatever it was he would find to do there. Elizabeth, back from Whangaroa and away from William White, was in the kitchen, clearing the breakfast dishes. Jane settled the boys to their lessons, then motioned to her daughter. On the porch, overlooking the glittering bay, she shared the news.

"Elizabeth, we may be moving soon."

"To Australia?" Her face lit up. "We will be with –"

"No." Elizabeth's disappointment was tangible and Jane patted her hand sadly. "No, we may be moving to a place called Valparaiso."

She watched Elizabeth's face as she spoke, registering the movement from disappointment to curiosity to the beginnings of excitement.

"We will be living in a town?"

"Not a large town, dear."

But a town, nonetheless.

"And there will be other English families there?"

"Not many, dear. There may only be about a dozen or two families."

She might equally have said a million.

"There will be English girls of my age?"

"I would expect so."

"And young men, too?" She stopped to blush.

"Them, too." Poor Elizabeth, she thought, never a chance to dream or hope.

And the decision was final.

Had Jane been one to look for omens, she might have been struck by a similar time line to their last desparture. For the *St Patrick* would be stopping at Kororareka towards the end of the month before embarking for Chile. After a decade here they, or rather, she would have barely three weeks to complete preparations for a final departure.

And of course Thomas prevaricated. As before, he trudged through the motions. And at the same time he prepared the way for sabotage.

He knew it was because he would be leaving it soon and forever that the world was so much brighter. Pohutukawa red, kowhai yellow and every shade of green shone beneath a perfect sky, sand glittered white and sea green and blue, the chiming tui … God was in His heaven but all was not well with the world.

He carried his sadness like death, it kept others away from him and he was more than ever a man apart.

So he sat alone in Kelly's drinking house, nursed his rum and brooded. Through the stagnant brew of helplessness and self-pity a small thought bubbled to the surface, *if I remain like this I will drink myself into insensibility.* The idea was not unattractive, but something got him to his feet and he headed for the foreshore. The *Industry* rode at anchor and without will or purpose he pushed her dinghy into the sea and rowed out to her. Slowly, methodically, numbly he raised the sail, drew in the anchor and turned out into the bay. Past the headland she gathered speed under a steady easterly and he turned west, opened the sails and ran before it, past the *Brampton*, stripped and empty but still secure in the rocky hand of God, mute testimony to something that entirely escaped him, past Rangihoua and on to Kerikeri. There he lowered the sail, dropped anchor and sat for a while, wondering what would happen next. And then he was in the cabin and taking up a new musket, still wrapped in oilskin, into the dinghy and rowing, not towards the settlement and the stone store on the western bank but to the eastern where Hongi's kainga stood. Now he was beaching the dinghy, taking up the musket and climbing the gentle slope.

And Hongi was stepping back from the greeting with a smile – "e Keni, if I breathe your breath much longer, I will be as drunk as you are" – and exclaiming over the fine gift that Thomas had brought for his son.

Thomas pushed away the purpose to which the gift would be put and drank in the appreciation. He still had no words and Hongi was touched by the sadness on him. But his gentle enquiry brought only shrugs and then "I have no cause for complaint,' followed by a hiccup that was partly a laugh but mostly a sob.

"You have been away from us for too long, my friend. We would be happier and I think you would be, too, if you were closer at hand."

Thomas nodded mutely.

"Then that is what we shall do. There is an excellent piece of land at Wairoa, not half a mile from here, fresh water, rich soil, a perfect place for you and your whanau. I will bring you there and then I shall see you smile again."

And Thomas agreed.

"You have done *what*?"

"I could not refuse him. It was an act of great kindness."

"Had you told him we were leaving?"

"No, I was too downcast to speak of it."

"But not too downcast to provide him with a gun and purchase land!" Thomas' head ached. At any other time such a challenge and such tone of voice might have moved him to anger, but now he lacked the energy for it. And he was bewildered, too. In all their years together, through disagreement, conflict, betrayal and all of it, he had never seen Jane like this. Her cheeks were flushed, her eyes glittered and she stabbed an accusing forefinger like a dagger. And her words were daggers, too.

"Have you told anyone?"

"Not yet?"

"So you haven't made any arrangements for the sale of the *Industry*, some consideration from Te Wera for the use of the house? For God's sake!" She clutched her temples. "The *St Patrick* is due here within a week. What were you thinking?"

"I told you, I have been much downcast, I have not been thinking." And the inevitable chestnut, beloved of those without excuse. "I have been doing my best."

"Your best!" The words were near a scream. "And what has been your best? Drink and self-pity! And running to Hongi for sympathy."

Thomas rallied then as his own temper began to stir and carried him into further inevitability. "Perhaps I would not need to go there if there were some sympathy closer to home."

"Jesus Christ!" Her fist came crashing down on to the table to cries of alarm from the children, Lawrence bursting into tears and Edward joining him. In their passion the children had been forgotten and now both Thomas and Jane fell silent.

"Please!" Elizabeth was stroking a howling Edward. "Mother! Father! Please!"

Truce was declared as the children were settled. But it was short-lived.

"Now hear this, Thomas Kendall. There was a very clear agreement here. There was the opportunity for you to persist with," she paused to draw a slow breath, "your clerical work and more importantly, yes, I said more importantly, for it is their turn now, there was an opportunity for your children to enjoy a civilised life and build the skills and experience for a future of their own. You gave your word that they would have this chance and this time you will keep it. We will board the *St Patrick* as we boarded the *Brampton* and if God chooses to scuttle her, then so be it. But it is not for you to do so."

In the intervening time, Thomas had retreated from his anger. And the worthless creature reappeared. He nodded. "I have not played the part I promised," he said, "and I hope you do not believe it was wilful." He waited for an agreement that did not come, then continued. "I will put those things in place, for you and the children, if not for myself." He saw her mouth turn down and his voice became a little harsher. "If it is God's will that we go, then we shall go. If He shows us otherwise …" He shrugged.

Jane eyed him narrowly. "Very well," she said at last, "but," she held up a warning finger, "if we stay, it will be because of God's clear will and through His workings. Not through yours."

He returned after four days. "It is all done," he said. "Te Wera has provided a fair trade for the house and Henry Williams has agreed to purchase the *Industry*." He gave a short laugh. "It was a much better price than I had anticipated. I can guess why.

"I have bade farewell to the people of Rangihoua and Kerikeri. But you need to know, Hongi was not at all pleased."

They settled into an uneasy peace for now all there was to do was to wait. After the flurry and rush of the last days the time crept by, punctuated by an incessant "is the boat here yet?"

And then she was and the final packing began. Departure was less than a week away.

It was a late afternoon and Thomas and Jane were sitting in their living room in a silence that had become habitual. It sat well with the surroundings for they were living out of boxes now and the house whispered abandoned. Edward lay sleeping on a rush mat while Samuel was sprawled over his latest creation. John and Joseph were somewhere about. Elizabeth had taken Lawrence for a walk along the beach. Jane did not doubt that her steps would lead her to Kororareka where the *St Patrick* lay at anchor. The family had already been down to be shown their quarters by the captain and his son. "Excellent," said Jane, "I am sure we will all be very comfortable here." A good deal more comfortable, she had thought, than we had been on the *Earl Spencer.* Thomas said nothing. The tour had been a short one and at its closure Master Florance, blushing had diffidently inquired whether Miss Kendall might be interested, if she could find the time and inclination, in a more complete tour. Miss Kendall, blushing had diffidently replied that a tour would be agreeable. Jane, thinking back to her conversation with her daughter, had smiled to herself.

Then the peace of the afternoon was broken by hurried footsteps and the boys shouting, "Father, mother, there are Maori coming up to the house. They look angry."

Without bidding her mind flashed back to Rangihoua and the night when Towhi had called for utu from Thomas for his use of Tungaroa.

It is a muru raid and we are ripe for the picking.

"What is this? Why are they here?"

"I don't know. Wait here with the boys and I'll go and find out."

"No." The word was close to a snarl. "I'm going with you. Boys, stay inside, your father and I will be back directly, there is nothing to worry about."

They stood on the porch and watched the visitors approach, a few dozen, mainly youths although there were several older men and a small number of girls and young women. Their faces were hard and there was no response to her smile of welcome.

Thomas raised his arms in welcome but his words were lost beneath the shouting. Then a thick-set man stepped forward.

"You are leaving us," he yelled and it was an accusation.

Again Thomas tried to speak, apologising, explaining and again his words were lost.

"You are a friend to Hongi, you are a man of Ngapuhi, you must not go."

A young man in the crowd was unable to contain his feelings at the thought of Thomas' leaving and a rock shattered the front window. And then another and now the boys' cries within were added to the tumult.

"Stop it," Jane screamed and then to Thomas, "tell them to stop," and she turned and rushed into the house.

And now Thomas found his voice as he roared above the noise, "This house is promised to Te Wera Hauraki. Will you destroy his property?" There were no further rocks then but the korero was no less agitated.

For all her fear and anger, new emotions plucked distantly at her as she found her boys, huddled behind the sofa, Samuel and John both trying to calm the wailing Edward, Joseph kneeling beside them, his face white but his hands steady as he primed his father's musket, *ah God, are these the skills that they are learning?* A shard of jagged glass lay close by where Edward had been sleeping and her rage soared. But she was calm, too, as she hurried to her bedroom and back and time slowed as she kneeled beside the boys, priming her own gun with a steady hand. And all the while at the back of her mind she heard again and again, *you must not go.*

Her body was aching for action but she kept it still and for what seemed an age she crouched beside her sons, musket in hand and the scene was as a metaphor for her life.

Finally the voices diminished and then were stilled and Thomas was at the door, face drawn and she heard the words before he uttered them.

"It is as I feared. Hongi will not release me and I have had to promise that we will stay."

This is what you wanted, Thomas, admit it, here is the voice of God telling you where your duty lies.

But it is not the voice of God, it is the voice of Hongi, claiming me and if I cannot distinguish them, then I am lost forever.

He sat in silence with his children. Jane was long gone – *there is an energy that consumes me and I am fearful it will lead me into doing or saying things I will later regret, I must take it away.* For once, any thoughts or feelings of his own were submerged beneath the sorrow of his family. He dreaded Elizabeth's return.

She arrived, hurrying, with Lawrence in her arms, her eyes wide. He had no words for her, nor did he need them, for the boys together pre-empted him – "Hongi said …

smashed windows … can't go … have to stay." Then her hands were at her mouth and he feared that she would scream but all that came out was a strangled "where is my mother?" and she was running away towards the beach, for the comfort that he could not give.

And then it seemed that God did act, for the next day taua poured in from the Hokianga, preparing their waka for an assault on Whangaroa. They gathered at Rangihoua and Ngapuhi flocked to join them. At the same time, the people from Kerikeri moved away towards the interior to begin the winter's planting. Suddenly the bay was empty.

Five days later Thomas was standing at the bow of the *St Patrick*, without hope or expectation, simply waiting to see what would happen.

And what happened was a clear sky, a quiet sea and a kind wind that filled the *St Patrick's* sails and moved her smoothly, safely out of the bay, into the Pacific and on her way to Chile.

Ending

The 'Brisbane' drove up the New South Wales coast, sails open to the following wind, harsh and salty and cold. The sea slid in wave and current, yet she held an even line.

She was a good vessel, thought the man at the wheel, sturdy and strong she would make a swift trip in these conditions. True, she was sailing with a full cargo, but she would manage. This was the fourth time he had brought her up to Sydney and on each occasion she had behaved well. A quick trip would also go down well with the owner; there might even be a bonus in it.

With the thought his attention moved to the still figure by the bow. Clad in grey leather, a broad-brimmed hat over a full coat, he was the colour of the sky and the sea. There had been a time when he had taken the wheel of the 'Brisbane' and of other ships, too, but now he left her to younger, stronger hands. He occupied his place at the bow and sometimes in his cabin, but in either place he stood apart and silent. And, thought the master, judging from the sorrowful cast of his countenance, that silence was probably for the best.

He stood as he had always stood, feet planted thus, hands just so. It was force of habit mainly, for the trip would be a short one, over before his guts would begin to rebel.

He was a wealthy man now; besides the 'Brisbane', he stood possessed of several extensive estates where he had profited in lumber and cattle. He had built them up with a determination and industry that would have earned a salute from William Hall. But he drove himself in a vacuum; in the intensity of his labour, he drove away other, darker distractions.

He had arrived in Australia from Valparaiso, where he had served as a minister and teacher for the English community. It was a peaceful and undemanding time and he had begun to find himself.

But the sirens still sang and he had begun work on a Maori grammar. His reformed life and a testimonial from the British Consul to his 'unimpeachable moral character' softened the Church Missionary Society and they encouraged his efforts. But they would not help with funding. That would be left to Marsden.

True to his word – 'as a minister of the Gospel I cannot know him' – Marsden refused Thomas. Nor would he offer him any kind of employment. The Anglican bishop was kinder with the offer to conduct services, but only if there were no one else in the vicinity able to do so.

His family was reunited now and had united further abroad. Thomas officiated at the weddings of Thomas Surfleet and Elizabeth and he read the burial service for his son, Samuel. And that was largely the extent of his pastoral work.

Now he stared through the darkening air and sifted through the same, sad questions.

What does it mean to be lonely? How can I be lonely? I live in the bosom of a large and largely loving family (he smiled at the conceit) and there are many that I might account as friends.

What do friends do? I trade with some, I drink with some and I ... can talk with Samuel Leigh. He has seen me at my worst and yet consents to talk with me. I believe he understands me.

Leigh had heard his confession.

"You know that I am miserable," the words were slightly slurred. "In my rush-covered hut where you used to visit me, I was happy. The pleasure I experienced in the service of God, the joy of a good conscience and the approbation of Christian friends at home and abroad mitigated risk and made me indifferent to poverty and danger."

What answer could Leigh have made to that?

"How can you say that? How can you believe that?

"I cannot understand," he might have said, "why you deny your life."

And Thomas might have answered, "Consider this. There were many times when I considered myself as an instrument of the Lord (and many times when I did not). When I argued against the evils of warfare with Hongi and beseeched him to change his ways, I knew that I acted in good conscience (for all that I knew my words would fall upon deaf ears). When

I kneeled before the Bishop of Ely and received ordination, I knew the approbation of Christian friends (for all that, on reflection, I have feared that they acted out of fear).

And there the conversation would have ended, leaving Thomas to whisper to himself, 'I was where I was supposed to be; doing what I was supposed to do."

The rain was driving harder now and he clutched at the railing as a sudden gust caused the *Brisbane* to heel. And the wind was howling a wild song from somewhere and he knew that song, he knew that voice and then the other sound broke through and he understood that it was sea crashing into rocks.

Christ! In his quest for a fast trip, perhaps a record trip, the idiot helmsman had let her run too close to the coast and now the wind and the tide were joining to sweep her closer in. He dragged himself along the rail and the sails swung over his head as the crew released them. The *Brisbane* steadied from the immediate risk of capsizing but now her speed was gone and she was sliding towards the coast. He could see it through the rain, cliffs rising darkly from the foaming sea, and hear the booming of the surf. He strained desperately to see if he could make out any opening in the massive wall, any gap that they might turn to, a bay where they might find shelter or run the *Brisbane* aground or capsize in the shallows or abandon ship with a shore in sight. But there was nothing. And they were rolling in the waves and sliding ever closer.

"Point!" he screamed, "point," and his words were blown away. Not that there was any need for them for now he could see the man wrestling with the wheel that turned the rudder that was held by an imperious sea. He scrabbled across the deck to join with him and together they found some success as the *Brisbane* gained a point or two. But even as she began to turn away from the coast she continued to slide towards it. And the swell was turning to waves.

There was no time for fear yet; they were caught in the extremity of the moment and blood surged through muscle as they grunted and strained to save their lives. Then above the sirens in the wind and the percussion of the deep there came another sound. Thomas had resumed his ministry.

"Dear God," he roared, "look down upon Thy servants in their hour of need. Thou Who created the mighty depths and Who can calm them with a thought, pray, make them still and bring Thy servants to safety. But if that be not Thy will, O Lord, then judge us for the good that we have tried to do and take our souls unto Thee. We ask this in –"

The last words were lost as a mountain of grey and green and foam reared over the staggering vessel and crashed down upon her, turning her on her side and over. The mast splintered on impact and the sails were torn and ripped away.

Along with the others, Thomas was torn from his place, flying over the rail and clear of the wreck.

Now there was time for fear that became panic and terror as he was driven down, spinning in the maelstrom. He could not fight towards the surface, he did not know where it was, he could not loosen his coat and boots, he was blown like a leaf in a liquid gale, he could see nothing and could hear only the roaring of his pounding blood. He could not fight the horror yet he tried to and in the end all he could do was breathe water.

As his lungs filled, a peacefulness descended upon him and in all the wild tumult of the ocean there was a place of stillness. His eyes were still closed against the salt but he could see and feel a golden, reddish blur that was enveloping him. The currents stripped his clothes from him and now he was naked and swimming freely. There was more light ahead and he flowed towards it. And there it was: the folded opening between smooth, glowing boulders. Seaweed grew like hair about it and as he drew closer he could see that it was lined with sharp stone and rock and pointed shells. But he did not slow and as he neared the opening the stone and shell shifted and turned their points away.

And now he was flowing into the opening and the rock lining softened and became as flesh and the ocean was warm and red and viscous. The wall contracted and held him safe, then contracted again behind him and squeezed him forward. Unresisting he went with the movement, understanding that nothing was required now beyond acceptance.

Ahead he could see glowing white and he knew, beyond all certitude, that he was welcome. And the peace went past serenity as he was borne into the perfect light.

END

GLOSSARY

A

ahau   I, me
aniwa   rainbow
ariki   chief, priest, God
atua   God, ghost, supernatural being

E

e pehea ana koe   how are you
e haere atu   goodbye

H

haere mai   come here, welcome
haka   (war) dance
hapu   sub-tribe
he   a
hine   girl
hoa   friend
hoihoi   horse
homai   give
huruhuru   caterpillar

I

ia   he, she, it
ika   fish
ingoa   name
iti   small
iwi   tribe

K

kahore   no
kai   food
kaiako   teacher
kakariki   green
ka mutu   it is finished
karaka   a tree (and its fruit)
kei hea koe   where are you from
kereru   wood pigeon
kete   basket
ki   to
kia ora be well
kina   sea urchin
kino   bad
ko   placed before name
koe   you (singular)
koha   gift, donation
korero   speech, conversation
koro   old man, father
korua   you (two)
koura   crayfish
koutou   you (all)
kowhai   a tree, yellow
kumara   sweet potato
kuri   dog

M

mana   authority, standing
manaakitia   hospitality
manawa   mangrove, heart
manu   bird
manuhiri   visitors
manuka   a shrub, bush
marama   light, understanding
matua   father
mate   dead
mauri   life principle
mere   club
mimi   urinate
minihari   missionary
miromiro   a tree
moana   sea
moi   sleep
moko   tattooing
mokopuna   child
muru   wipe, rub off

N

ngaio   a tree
ngarara   reptile, monster
noa   free from tapu
nui   large

O

oma   run
ora   wellness

P

pa   fort
pai ana   I'm fine
piro   putrid
pitoitoi   robin
piwakawaka   fantail
poi   light ball
poroporoaki   farewell
poti   pot

pohutukawa   a tree
pu   gun
puka   a tree
pukana   pull a face
puriri   a tree

R

rangatira   chief
rata   a tree
reo   (Maori) language
riri   angry
roa   broad

T

taiaha   spear
take   cause
taku   my
tama   boy
tamariki   child
tangata   people
tangi   weep, mourn
taniwha   monster
taonga   treasure
tapu   sacred, forbidden
tataeko   a bird
taua   war party
te   the
teina   younger brother
tena   that
tena koe   greeting
terakihi   a fish
tika   correct
tino   very
titiro   look
ti whanake   flax
toku   my
tuakana   elder brother
tuatua   cockle
tui   a bird
tuna   eel
tupuna   ancestor

turangawaewae home territory
turi turi be quiet

W

wahine woman
wai water
wairua spirit
whakapapa lineage

whakarongo mai listen
whaea mother
whanau family
whenua land

U

umu oven
utu balance, revenge

CPSIA information can be obtained
at www.ICGtesting.com
Printed in the USA
BVHW031205270221
601119BV00033B/1001/J